David A. West
University of Missouri

Glenn L. Wood
California State College at Bakersfield

PERSONAL FINANCIAL MANAGEMENT

Houghton Mifflin Company **Boston**
New York Atlanta Geneva, Illinois Dallas Palo Alto

Printed in the U.S.A.

Library of Congress Catalog Card Number: 75–172124

ISBN: 0–395–12428–X

PREFACE

This book emerged from the authors' strong conviction that a text on this subject should focus upon important personal financial problems from a decision-making viewpoint. Our basic objective has been to use the fundamental concepts of financial management to build a framework for personal financial decisions. This has led us to omit descriptive material that is not directly relevant to solving personal financial problems.

Although we have attempted to omit as many technical details as possible, the balance between excessive detail and oversimplification is a difficult goal. How can a person consider the effects of income taxes on his financial decisions without knowing the basic income tax laws and regulations—which always seem to have exceptions to the exceptions without end? Or how can a person plan his financial security without some knowledge of the complex and ever-changing provisions of the Social Security Act? The amount of detail in a book is always a result of the judgment of the authors. We hope—and believe—that we have struck a desirable balance. Still, we are well aware that many students and some teachers will undoubtedly think we could have simplified more of the material.

Because we believe a textbook—as well as a teacher—has an obligation to the students to make the material as interesting as possible, we have tried to capture the interests of the students by writing as much as possible from the perspective of the students. We owe much to our own students for challenging our efforts in this regard. Most of the examples pertain to young people, and material that is relevant only to older people is either covered briefly or omitted altogether.

Many friends and colleagues have contributed ideas, criticisms, suggestions, and encouragement for this book. We are indebted to Professor Albert Auxier, University of Missouri; Mr. John Bachmann, Partner, Edward D. Jones and Co.; Mr. Lloyd Baylord, Marketing Representative, International Business Machines Corporation; Professor Randolph H. Bobbitt, Jr., The Ohio State University; Professor Robert E. Bray, University of Missouri; Professor Charles Crain, Miami University (Ohio); Professor Norman Gysbers, University of Missouri; Professor Don Marshall, University of Missouri; Mr. Ralph E. Joynes, Regional Director, Participating Annuity Life Insurance Company; Mr. Walter Poylner, Director, CUNA International; Mr. George Peters, Registered Representative, Merrill Lynch, Pierce, Fenner & Smith, Inc.; Professor Jerry S. Rosenbloom, Temple University; Professor Dick L. Rottman, University of Nevada; Professor Michael Scanlan, University of

Missouri; Professor Lloyd Seaton, California State College, Bakersfield; Mr. Edward S. Tichacek, Property Manager, R. T. Crow Development Corp.; and Mr. Russell Thompson, Senior Analyst, National Bank of Detroit.

A special note should be made of the contribution of Professor Duke Nordlinger Stern. Without his authorship, our treatment of estate planning in Chapter Eighteen would have been much less effective, and we certainly wish to acknowledge our appreciation of his efforts.

Our gratitude is particularly strong for the following persons who reviewed the entire manuscript with far greater care and diligence than normal: Dr. Robert Dolphin, Jr., Chairman, Department of Finance, Wright State University; Dr. Robert A. Lynn, Dean, College of Commerce, Kansas State University; and Dr. Robert B. Pierce, Dean, School of Business and Economics, Central Missouri State College.

For providing considerable research assistance, we express our appreciation to Mr. Roy Beck, Mr. Gene Hendrix, Mr. Robert Hurst, and Mr. Charles Schmitz.

For handling the fantastic amount of secretarial work that is always required for a textbook, we must thank Mrs. Connie Groh, Mrs. Jerry Haner, Mrs. Mary Hays, Miss Kathy Pickett, and Miss Rhonda Roberts.

The contribution of our editors, also, must be recognized; without the efforts of Mr. John Baack, Mr. Hugh Joyce, and Mrs. Loren Stephens, all other efforts could not have been as successful or satisfying.

And now we know the true meaning of those who acknowledge their wives. Without the complete cooperation and personal sacrifices of our wives, Jane and Pat, this book would still be nothing more than an unfulfilled ambition.

David A. West
Glenn L. Wood

CONTENTS

CHAPTER ONE
THE IMPORTANCE OF FINANCIAL PLANNING   1

Financial Management / Some Personal Qualities
to Watch For / Summary

CHAPTER TWO
FINANCIAL PROBLEM SOLVING   14

Education / Establishing an Emergency Fund /
Establishing an Insurance Program / Starting an
Investment Program / Summary

CHAPTER THREE
MANAGING CASH INCOME   37

Income Planning / Borrowing Cash Income /
Sources of Loans / Types of Loans / Cost
of Borrowing / Saving Cash Income / Summary

CHAPTER FOUR
CONTROLLING EXPENDITURES   75

Expenditure Planning / Using Financial Records /
Components of a Budget / Summary

CHAPTER FIVE
HOME OWNERSHIP   101

Reasons for Owning a Home / Costs of Home
Ownership / The Decision to Buy or Rent / Deter-
mining How Much You Should Pay for a House /
Other Types of Housing / Financial and Legal Prob-
lems / The Importance of Professional Help /
Summary

CHAPTER SIX
THE IMPORTANCE OF TAXES   147

Fundamental Income Tax Concepts / Special
Problems / Minimizing Taxes / Seeking Income Tax
Advice and Assistance / Summary

CHAPTER SEVEN

CHOOSING A CAREER   183

      Recognizing Needs for Working / Finding Your
      Occupational Needs / Tomorrow's Occupations /
      Investigating Specific Occupations / Incomes in the
      Various Occupations / Education and Occupations /
      Summary

CHAPTER EIGHT

LEARNING TO INVEST   218

      Buying Stocks / Understanding the Securities
      Markets / Buying Real Estate / Summary

CHAPTER NINE

BUILDING AN INVESTMENT PORTFOLIO   267

      Constructing an Investment Portfolio / Managing an
      Investment Portfolio / Summary

CHAPTER TEN

SELECTING YOUR INVESTMENTS   306

      Qualitative Factors / Quantitative Factors /
      Selecting Specific Stocks / Summary /
      Appendix: Publications on Stock Information

CHAPTER ELEVEN

USING PROFESSIONAL PORTFOLIO MANAGEMENT   355

      Buying Mutual Funds / Special Mutual Fund
      Features / Selecting Specific Mutual Funds /
      Summary

CHAPTER TWELVE

OWNING A BUSINESS   409

      Deciding to Own a Business / Choosing the Right
      Business / The Problem of Raising Capital /
      Choosing the Legal Form of Organization / Acquiring
      Your Own Business / Managing Your Company /
      The Small Business Administration / Summary

CHAPTER THIRTEEN

SAVING FOR FINANCIAL EMERGENCIES   462

      Effective Savings Plans / Savings Media / Saving
      Through Life Insurance / Summary

CHAPTER FOURTEEN

PROTECTING YOUR ASSETS   497

> Homeowner's Policies / Automobile Insurance /
> Other Property and Liability Policies / Choosing an
> Insurance Company and an Agent / Summary

CHAPTER FIFTEEN

PROTECTION AGAINST PREMATURE DEATH   532

> Reasons for Buying Life Insurance / Determining the
> Amount of Life Insurance to Buy / Types of Life
> Insurance Policies / Choosing the Appropriate Type
> of Coverage / Understanding Policy Provisions and
> Using Policy Options Effectively / Choosing Life
> Insurance Riders / Comparing Contracts and
> Costs / Selecting the Company and the Agent /
> Summary

CHAPTER SIXTEEN

PROTECTION AGAINST DISABILITY   582

> The Cost of Disability / Methods of Financing
> Disability Losses / Types of Health Insurance
> Coverages / Important Purchase Decisions /
> Summary

CHAPTER SEVENTEEN

PROVIDING RETIREMENT INCOME   614

> The Importance of Planning Retirement Income /
> Sources of Income During Retirement / Employment
> During Retirement / Retirement Benefits Under Social
> Security / Pensions / Providing Retirement Income
> Through Real Estate / Investments in Securities /
> Annuities / Summary

CHAPTER EIGHTEEN

THE IMPORTANCE OF ESTATE PLANNING   653

> Wills / The Use of Co-Ownership / Estate, Gift,
> and Inheritance Taxes / Trusts / Summary

INDEX   693

CHAPTER ONE

THE IMPORTANCE OF FINANCIAL PLANNING

Few problems plague more people, take more time, cause more pain, and deserve more serious thought than the problems of personal finance. A glance at the number of personal bankruptcies, mortgage foreclosures, or repossessions of automobiles indicates that financial problems are acute for large numbers of people. Recent studies show that half the families in this country would have less than $2,000 in assets after subtracting their debts. And a single month without income or help in the form of loans, charity, or the sale of personal assets would bring many families to the verge of starvation.

Since financial problems are real if not acute for all of us, they are worth serious consideration by anyone who wants a genuinely satisfying way of life. This book deals with some of the most pressing financial problems, and each chapter takes direct aim at one of them. For example:

How can you go about increasing your income?
When is it wise to borrow money, and what are the best sources for various kinds of loans?
What is a suitable insurance program?
Is it better to buy a home or to rent one?
How can you control expenses, and how can you tell when they are too high?
How can you begin an investment program—and what are stocks and bonds anyway?
Is it really possible to set up a long-range financial plan that will work?

Many people ask such questions, and there are answers that will help all of them. This book gives many of the most important answers.

FINANCIAL MANAGEMENT

We begin with a broad view. There are four aspects to financial management, whether personal, corporate, or public. First of all, financial management must be based on sound overall financial planning. Second, it must provide enough income to sustain the plan. Third, it must control expenditures. And fourth, it must solve specific problems. Since all these functions are concerned with solving problems, it is fair to say that all financial management is, in a sense, problem solving. These functions differ from each other, however. Financial planning is the analysis of problems, alternative solutions, and the means of achieving them. Making a plan is the first step of all. Providing income is both an initial and a continuing function, and increasing income is a problem with alternative solutions. Controlling expenditures is one problem until a satisfactory budget has been worked out, and living within the budget then presents another problem. Once these initial stages are completed and the plan is in operation, specific problems continually arise which must be faced and solved.

It is a sad fact that while most financial problems are neither new, unique, nor insoluble, few people really solve them. Many consider them, and would like to solve them, but literally do not know how. They would like to plan, but they do not know where to begin. They do not like insecurity, but they do not know how to shake free of it. This chapter and the next describe personal financial planning for just those people who want to help themselves but until now have not known how. Later chapters take up the three other aspects of financial management, and stress alternative solutions to problems. Every chapter attacks a problem you have already pondered, though some you may not have pondered very deeply. Certainly every chapter takes up a problem worth your attention and can make a real difference in your personal well-being.

PLANNING, THE FIRST STEP

Wise planning is the first step toward success, but planning wisely is neither easy nor simple. To some extent the quality of your planning, and the firmness of your decisions, will be affected by your personal security. If you enjoy considerable security, for example, your planning and decision making will probably be fairly realistic and dependable. One's financial security is greatly influenced by his or her income. If you have a relatively small income, a great many minor crises can thoroughly frustrate your most conscientious financial planning. Financial planning requires three things: (1) dissatisfaction with the existing situation; (2) selection of a desirable goal; and (3) a course of action that overcomes all obstacles and reaches the goal.

Dissatisfaction, or The Painful Present.   A given situation—say financial dependence—may be galling to one person and quite comfortable to his next door neighbor, depending on their backgrounds, temperaments, ambitions, values, and goals. But enough people find dissatisfaction in their financial situation so that the painful present is a common predicament. Its main symptoms are not enough income, financial insecurity, lack of capital, immobility through dependence on a job. These aggravations bring on fear, shame, discontent and boredom. Becoming discouraged or lacking in vision, some people bow under these discouragements and plod on unmurmuring throughout their working lives. For many older people despair, discouragement, and disillusionment are the main seasoning of a dreary life. They look back upon years of hard work, years of their best contribution to a wealthy society, and still depend as much as they ever did on a regular paycheck. They have no more independence, no more security, no more capital than they had 30 or 40 years before. For some people an existence on the bare edge of solvency is acceptable. For many it is bitter but unavoidable. For still others it is neither, and fortunately more and more young people are both able and interested in doing something to improve their condition before it is too late. Acutely aware of the painful present, and the danger of its stretching into an endless future, they take steps to achieve ultimate financial security and independence.

Setting a Goal. Being dissatisfied, they plan, and if they plan wisely, they first set a goal. There are a world of goals to choose from. We are not mainly concerned in this book with listing all the worthwhile goals that one can project as some of them need to be implemented by financial resources. Certain of these goals are worth mentioning, not only in their own right, but because it is important for you to see the kind of thinking and planning you must do if you are to plan wisely. Setting realistic goals that can be reached through clear and workable courses of action demands serious effort.

Warning: some nongoals. What if you have no really specific goal, but just want to be farther ahead in 30 years than you are now? Maybe you cannot say anything more specific than "I want to make a million," or "I want to be completely secure." Such goals are so vague that they offer no specific guidance direction, and if you cannot do any better, perhaps you had better think hard about what you want to do with your life as well as with your financial future. True, for some people money is an ultimate goal, but these are fewer than you might think. Most young people today do not put making money very high on their priority list. Most modern college students expect adequate incomes from whatever they choose to do, and look to other interests for much of their personal satisfaction. Actually when people say they want to make a lot of money they usually mean they want to provide for their children more amply than their parents were able to provide for them, or to do things they have never been able to afford.

Education. One important goal which in the long run may be only a step toward other goals is education. But whether viewed as an end or an intermediate stop, education is expensive, has to be financed somehow, and should be planned with great care. For many students education is only a means to a better job. But all students must eat, buy books, pay fees, and keep a roof of some sort over their heads. And funds for such expenditures must come from somewhere. For many students, the cost of education is borne by parents. Even for those, the cost of education should be carefully balanced against the financial as well as other costs and benefits, and not gone into blindly.

Career. Since long and expensive financial training is necessary for many professions, often the career should be thought of as the ultimate goal and education as intermediate. In many careers financial management is essential to professional success. Not only must education often be financed ahead of time, but in many professions the financial rewards in the earlier years are sharply below the average for the profession, and the initial costs of starting out are high. Moreover, most professional people have to maintain financial records, prepare some sort of budget, and make regular financial reports. Hence even if one's major goal is a career of service, he must have some understanding of financial management in order to be even moderately successful.

At the end of a long career most professional people want to retire. For those who have been self-employed, the quality and satisfaction of the retirement years may depend more on success as financial managers than on success in a profession. A lawyer or a doctor who did not collect his accounts receivable may be in distress almost as soon as he stops working. And one who made a fortune but allowed it to slip away with no provision for the future may face starvation overnight. Some professional people focus on their careers and ignore finances; others are so concerned with money that they can hardly be called professional. Between these extremes lies a better way, and a very modest amount of attention to financial management can make it happen.

Service. Increasing numbers of young people want to be of service to others. Those who can be socially fulfilled through their careers are especially fortunate. But most people in this country cannot get this kind of satisfaction from the jobs they take to earn their living; they find it only through civic, social, or political activities for which they are not paid. For them the need for careful planning is great, both during their active years, and to provide properly for their retirement.

Family. Probably more people achieve their greatest personal satisfaction through their families than in any other way. Most people will make greater personal sacrifice, and expend greater effort, for their families than for any other purpose. Nor is this goal necessarily antithetical to many other goals. In fact, it often goes hand in hand with career and service, but it often raises conflicts, too. Most parents find it hard to refuse a daughter's plea for a new party dress, even when it clashes with a long-range commitment such as an insurance premium that may fall due in the same week.

On the other hand, financial planning can be less irksome when one realizes that firm management is important to the happiness of all members of the family. In many families, such management aims solely at increasing total happiness through less uncertainty, more security, and more desired consumption than would be possible otherwise. Financial uncertainty, unpaid bills, and unnecessary spending brings much unpleasantness to many families. Few people want such unpleasantness, but many live with it because they do not know how to avoid it. If your goal is simply to have a family, join the majority. But if you want a family that is happier and more secure than the average, you must give serious thought to the financial problems every family faces but few families solve.

Consumption.   We live in a consumption-oriented society, in which few people save or accumulate much, many live most of their lives in debt, and few make a sustained effort to increase income or control expenditures except for still-increased consumption. Americans are widely criticized as materialistic, envious, jealous, and petty for this, and there is justice in the criticism. Yet some of our most vocal critics would defend a life of personal freedom and leisure as one of the higher goods, often without realizing that leisure and freedom are consumer items just as truly as cereal and soap. One must buy leisure in our society by giving up other goods which could have been bought with the income one chooses to forego. The point, then, is not so much that consumption as a goal is good or bad per se, but that those who choose it should do so with clear minds and open eyes. The real unfortunate ones in our society are the people who choose to live for material things but are so greedy for things today that they fail to provide for tomorrow. And they are legion.

Progress.   Many people, less consumption-oriented, find that the idea of progress—of simple unspecified improvement—is a satisfying goal and a sufficient motivation for financial planning. For them it can be a deep source of satisfaction to be able to say, at the end of the year, that they have $100 or $500 more in the savings account than they had the year before. Indeed, many such people are better off without a specific goal than they would be if they were shooting for, say, $250,000 at age 65, for then the $500 might fall short of expectations and give them vague anxieties and sleepless nights. Just how much progress is necessary in order to feel pleased and comfortable? Nobody can answer for anyone else. Some need a clear view and a carefully charted course. Others find such a course more of a burden than a help. Think for yourself, but *think*. Until you can identify a desirable goal, whether a Ph.D. in chemistry, the ability to spend $100,000 a year, freedom to work in a nonpaying job, or merely to be better off this year than last—you can really pursue no course of action because you simply do not know which way you want to move.

Financial security. Financial security involves much more than the establishment of a specific dollar figure as an ultimate goal. Only as one can feel a sense of personal satisfaction with his present position and achievement, can he feel any significant degree of security. Such a sense of security does not necessarily depend upon personal financial independence. Many people who are quite dependent upon a regular salary from a specific employer do feel a real sense of personal financial security. Such a feeling derives-more from a sense of self-confidence, personal mobility, personal productivity, and value than upon any achievement of an ultimate objective. But they are not the same. Some people who do feel self-confident and productive also face serious financial uncertainty and insecurity. Sometimes this is because they do not know where they are going, or whether or not they are getting anywhere. Sometimes they know where they want to go, but cannot seem to get there. Such feelings may be complicated for many by short-term scarcity of cash due to excessive or uncontrolled expenditures, or by little if any provision to handle emergencies. Actually, financial security in a sense summarizes a number of the goals previously discussed. Indeed, one may feel great financial security when he is providing for his family the consumption pattern that he considers necessary, financed through a career of real service for which he is well prepared, in accordance with a financial plan that permits reasonable and sustained progress toward some ultimate financial objective. Such a financial program can be immeasurably satisfying to the whole family.

It might be surprising to all of us to know how many people have had no serious thoughts about the need for a financial goal. Some people never become concerned about financial planning, and even for those who do, it may be a long time coming. Sometimes this awareness is stimulated by a conversation with a friend or a newspaper article. Sometimes it occurs because someone asks you about his financial problem. Sometimes it occurs to a finance teacher because a judge asks him to help solve the personal financial problems of some fine upstanding family in the community that has found itself in the most unbelievable financial mess that he has ever seen in his life. Whatever the stimulant, however, a little time and imagination may permit anyone to identify a financial goal that is acceptable to him. It is indeed possible to determine a specific quality of life that is acceptable, and to estimate the amount of financial resources that would be necessary to sustain such a quality of life. For example, you can estimate the standard of living you consider necessary both now and in the future; you can estimate the present and future income required to permit such a standard of living; and you can estimate the investment program necessary to provide that future income.

Then you can compute the amount of current income needed to provide such necessities. Providing that income, maintaining that standard of living, and progressing toward that future investment objective can mean a quality of life sufficient for many.

Financial security has different meanings for different people; it should be defined by each individual to fit his own personal philosophy of life. Each has his own goal. Each finds some things tolerable and some unbearable. The important point to note is this—until you can identify some desirable goal, no courses of action can be considered because you simply do not know in which direction you want to move. With the acknowledgment of an unacceptable painful present, however, and perhaps the resulting identification of a desirable and attainable personal goal, you can then consider courses of action that will enable you to reach your chosen goal. When you have determined your goal, then and only then can you take definitive action toward reaching it; and only when you are persistently progressing toward what you perceive as a better way of life, can you enjoy your life to the fullest. You can define financial security this way if you will, and in fact there are indeed worse ways to express your personal goal. As a way to summarize many personal desires, we will use financial security as the ultimate financial goal toward which all financial management efforts are directed in order to reach whatever personal goal you have chosen.

Courses of Action.   Several courses of action may provide financial security. First on the list might be inherited wealth. Many would recommend this course of action, but unfortunately it is difficult to choose your own great uncle. A second course of action might be to marry the boss's daughter. A third course of action is to get a good job and keep it until you get a better job. This particular course of action is highly recommended, particularly if you include in this course of action the provision for adequate formal education and training to enable you to get a job that you really want and one that will provide sufficient income and future job mobility. Unfortunately, a job does not guarantee financial security, although it certainly can go a long way toward reaching the goals of a great many people. Consider how many hard working job holders there are in this world who are daily sinking into an ever more painful present.

A fourth course of action is to build a personal financial plan designed to (1) increase income, (2) control outgo, (3) provide savings, (4) construct a sustainable investment program, (5) protect against risks, and thus give you a fighting chance of reaching your goal of financial security. Such a personal financial plan is the very essence of this book. We recognize that there are all kinds of goals, many of them nonfinancial; fewer, but still some, utterly unrelated to financial security. But we believe that a personal financial program designed to achieve financial security is a worthy course of action leading to a worthy goal. If you are really concerned about your financial future, you might well construct a realistic, workable, and liveable financial plan. If you set your sights too high with respect to expected income, for example, you may belatedly learn your spending plans have exceeded proper proportion with all the additional problems that unexpected debts entail. Or if your budget requires such tight control over expenditures that your desired scale of living is prohibited, you will find your financial program unsustainable. Furthermore, if you have failed to recognize certain obstacles in your path, extended illness or inflation, for example, your best efforts can be undone over the years or even in a very short time. If there were no obstacles, we would have no problem. We would all immediately jump from our painful presents to the most desirable goals we could imagine. Unfortunately, certain obstacles do exist in the way of any course of action designed to reach any goal, and these obstacles must be identified before they can be isolated and subdued. On the other hand, without a plan, you are lost anyway. With even a poor plan, you have some chance of success. With a good plan, you have an even better chance; not a guarantee, but a better chance.

No one course of action can possibly fit the financial objectives of everyone or even a majority of people. Just as each person must select his own personal goal, so each one must select his own means of achieving that goal. However, the process by which you determine the sufficiency and acceptability of your alternative courses of action is indeed similar to the process we all must use. Furthermore, the obstacles likely to hinder the success of your course of action are the same uncertainties that most people must face. This process and these obstacles must be considered at some length if your financial program is to be successful. This book is directed toward facilitating your efforts to construct a personal financial plan that will enable you to overcome all the obstacles that might interfere with your effort to achieve your goal. Although you must tailor these proposals and suggestions to your own needs, if you make the effort, you really can have a plan that will permit you to reach your own concept of financial security.

PROVIDING INCOME

Providing income is the second step in financial management. Income is relative, and what seems a great deal to one person may be pitifully inadequate for another. A person's attitude toward income can change dramatically over the years, so that what once seemed princely may come to look like a pittance. Moreover, if you expect to earn much more later than you do now, your plans for education, for other expenses, and for borrowing should be very different than if you expect your income to stay about the same. Income is a highly personal thing, closely related to your self-image. So whether your plan is realistic and likely to succeed depends not only on your prospects and abilities, but on your idea of yourself. Most people are financially motivated to the extent that they will seek the best income alternatives available to them, all other things being equal. Given two equally satisfying jobs, they will take the one with the higher salary. Or given two houses otherwise equally attractive, they will buy the cheaper one because it leaves them more income for other uses.

An important aspect of planning income involves recognizing the need for more education, acquisition of capital, alternative income sources. Increased future income usually results from increased productivity. Deciding whether to provide more income now or later is a necessary part of financial management. Managing cash income in the light of your life pattern can greatly increase total satisfaction. Chapters Three and Seven consider these and other problems of income in detail.

CONTROLLING EXPENDITURES

This third phase of financial management is essential to reaching any reasonable financial goal. However large your income, expenditures can always exceed it, and all your life long your expenses will have to be controlled. Disposable income is what you have left after necessary expenses, and if you define "necessary" broadly enough, you may never have any disposable income. Getting some is largely a matter of discipline and self-sacrifice. Nobody—or almost nobody—can ever buy everything or even almost everything he wants. To have any savings at all, expenditures have to be planned and controlled. In order to acquire enough savings to yield you earned income in the future, controlling expenditures is crucial.

Nationally, saving is a function of income, and the larger the national income the larger the total savings. For the individual, however, saving is more a function of personality and temperament than of income. If you cannot save at one level of income, you probably cannot at another.

Some people can never control their expenses, but almost all of us find it hard to control them without some motive. And to get any satisfaction out of it, most of us have to keep a purpose of great personal importance firmly in mind. Usually a negative purpose is not enough: to avoid bankruptcy, for instance. Most people need something a good deal more positive. In Chapter Four we propose a simple set of controls that can help greatly to hold expenses down. But without real concern, and without a specific objective, no such general advice can help you very much.

SOLVING SPECIFIC PROBLEMS

This fourth aspect of financial management can be thought of as the fine tuning that can make a plan succeed. Many problems, of course, can be anticipated in a general way from the beginning stages of any plan: choices among alternative ways of saving money, choices among investments, as between real estate or stocks and bonds, and provision for various kinds of insurance. Many of these problems can be solved easily enough if they are foreseen and properly prepared for. Most of this book is designed to give you that kind of preparation, and you should expect to modify your plan as need be when emergencies arise. If properly anticipated, few such problems are big enough or important enough to cause a major wrench in your overall plan.

To show you how true all we have said can be, we devote the next chapter to an extended case study of one man's financial plan. Meanwhile we conclude this chapter with a warning about some common personal qualities which have brought the financial planning of countless men to naught.

SOME PERSONAL QUALITIES TO WATCH FOR

UNAWARENESS

Unawareness, the inability to see problems and to sense danger, takes many forms. Some people are dissatisfied with their present financial situation, and can formulate a reasonable financial goal, but have not the least idea how to reach it. Such people are numerous. Have you ever known somebody who would like to be successful financially but cannot ever take any positive action? Such people simply cannot visualize what steps to take, and so can make no financial progress. Unfortunately, people who have no financial success all too often lose all enthusiasm and ambition.

But unawareness is an obstacle that can be overcome. You can learn how to increase your income, or how to construct a budget. Millions have done these things, and you can too. If your basic problem is not knowing how to construct a financial program, or how to overcome the various other financial problems you face, these things can be learned. Simply discovering that there are solutions to problems, that there is a better situation, and that there are alternative ways of reaching it, may be all you need.

EMOTION

Every successful businessman has learned how to live with his emotions. Not everyone can control his feelings as completely as he would like, but it is almost impossible to become a financial success without achieving a reasonable degree of control over emotion. Financial decisions made on the basis of feeling rather than sound practical considerations can lead to ruin.

In administering a financial program that requires saving and the control of expenditures, no one has a chance unless his psychological make-up gives him the steadiness of purpose to resist the urge to spend.

There is good evidence to support the belief that saving for the individual is less a function of income than of temperament. You may think of a number of people with low incomes who have yet been able to buy their homes, build pension programs, and invest additional savings besides. And you may think of other people with sizable estates or large incomes who could not control their expenditures and have lost everything they had. The amount a person saves is often a function of income. But whether he saves at all is more likely to be a function of emotional make-up or temperament.

Part of this emotional difficulty may result from inexperience. If so, one may be able to profit by the experiences of others and avoid the traps that caught them. At the very least, as one gains experience he may learn what his own emotional problems are. Some people are cursed with such emotional complexities that they can never achieve the degree of financial security they long for. But even they will be the better for recognizing their problem. Indeed, some such people may even be able to direct their emotions away from spending to saving, and come to get almost the same satisfaction out of putting money in the bank that they once got from buying a color television.

For spendthrifts with low income there may be little or no hope. But for most of us there is hope. While emotion is an obstacle to orderly financial behavior, few are so helpless that they cannot control themselves at all. If you are more emotional than most, then you must settle for less financial security or you must try a little harder. Recognizing the problem can take you a long step down the road toward solving it.

DISCIPLINE

One personal characteristic absolutely essential to financial success is financial discipline. There are probably many characteristic differences between the financial success and the financial failure, but the one which distinguishes the two types most clearly is the ability to save. A successful person almost always has a margin between his total expenditures and his income. This margin enables him to earn an income on his savings, and to plan his expenditures more effectively. The person who never saves, or who finds it hard to save even when his income increases, may never have any financial success at all. You almost always have to save before you can invest. Just a little self-control, just a little financial discipline is all you need. But that little bit is absolutely crucial to the achievement of your ultimate goal: financial security.

SUMMARY

To achieve a genuinely satisfying way of life and to reach the goal of financial security, no one exercise is more important than that of financial management. Financial management consists of: 1) making an overall financial plan which reflects your personal goals; 2) providing income; 3) controlling expenditures and 4) solving specific problems—the fine tuning that can make a financial plan succeed. Successful management requires three personal qualities: awareness of problems and alternative solutions, the ability to control your emotions and financial discipline. If you can recognize the need for these qualities and the need for beginning a financial plan early you have already gone a long way toward achieving your goals.

Case Problems

1. Sally Welch, a sophomore at a large midwestern university sat daydreaming in personal finance class. The professor asked her a question about what was being discussed. Sally stuttered for a few seconds and finally admitted that she had not been listening. The professor then informed her that the discussion was about planning. He then suggested that in the future Sally should get more sleep, and also that she prepare a 1,000 word paper on planning due the next class period. You will probably agree that Sally now has a problem. But so do you. Do the same thing.

2. Roger is a college graduate and will soon be married. He and his prospective bride, like most young people, have many dreams. One of their dreams is early retirement, perhaps at age 50. They realize that to accomplish this dream they must manage their finances. What problems of financial management must they consider?

3. Larry Debts is employed as a car salesman. His income is about $12,000 a year, which for most young married men with two children seems adequate. But Larry cannot get above water financially. His money seems to disappear. At present he does not make a measurable effort to manage his finances. Needless to say, Larry and his wife are unhappy because the Joneses seem to have more, even though Mr. Jones makes less. The Debts have a financial problem to solve. At this point has Larry started to solve it? What steps must Mr. and Mrs. Debts take before their problem will be solved? What are some courses of action available to solve financial problems?

4. Your best friend who is in the same financial situation as you are comes to you for advice about his financial difficulties. How would you help him or her?

Selected Readings

Basic Principles in Family Money and Credit Management. Washington, D.C.: National Consumer Finance Association.
Clark, D. R. "Planning for Personal Progress." *Office,* January 1969.

Cohn, J. B. and Hanson, Arthur W. *Personal Finance*. 3rd edition. Homewood, Illinois: Richard D. Irwin, Inc., 1964. Chapters 1 and 2.

College Placement Annual and Annual Salary Survey of Offerings to College Graduates. Bethlehem, Pa.: College Placement Council, Inc.

Donaldson, E. F. and Pfahl, J. K. *Personal Finance*. 3rd edition. New York: Ronald Press Company, 1961.

The Family Financial Planner. The Prudential Insurance Company of America, 1964. A free copy is available by writing to Prudential Plaza, Newark, New Jersey.

How to Plan Your Spending. Connecticut Mutual Life Insurance Company. Free copies available on request.

"Income of Families and Persons in the United States." In *Current Population Reports, Consumer Income*. Washington, D.C.: U.S. Department of Commerce. Latest year.

Lasser, J. K. *Managing Your Family Income*. New York: Doubleday and Company, 1968.

Personal Money Management. American Bankers Association. Latest edition. Copies are available from your local bank.

"Persons Financial Asset Accumulation and Debt Operations." *1963–67 Survey of Current Business*, May 1968.

"Planning a Family Budget." *Supervisory Management*, June 1970.

Unger, Maurice and Wolf, Harold A. *Personal Finance*. 2nd edition. Boston: Allyn and Bacon, Inc., 1969.

United States Bureau of Labor Statistics. *Three Standards of Living for an Urban Family of Four Persons*. Bulletin No. 1570–5, Spring 1967.

CHAPTER TWO

FINANCIAL PROBLEM SOLVING

To illustrate the process of financial planning and problem solving described in general terms in Chapter One, this chapter details the financial plan of a young college student, Seymour Green, who is anticipating a middle-income professional career. As we shall observe, Seymour goes through all the steps in planning which we have read about, and a good deal more. At the moment we meet him he has decided on his goals and has gone a long way toward knowing how he will reach them. He wants to accumulate $250,000 in assets by the time he is 65. He knows what he needs by way of further education, and what it will be worth to him financially. We shall see in detail how he has reached this latter determination. We shall see how he provides for emergencies. We shall see how he builds safeguards into his plan by insurance against risks of many kinds. We shall see how he expects to extend his income by an investment program. And we shall see all these things in some detail.

This plan is presented neither as an ideal course of action, nor as a typical one. But the specific details of it can be modified and adapted to suit the personal needs of many young people today.

The personal financial plan of Seymour Green, then, consists of four parts:

1. Education
2. Emergency fund
3. Insurance program
4. Investment program

Built into the plan are ways in which particular risks may be minimized or overcome. These risks are applicable to most financial plans and goals. They include:

14

1. Insurable risks: unemployment, mortality, excessive longevity, morbidity, property and liability
2. Investment risks: financial, market, inflation and interest-rate

Even though a person makes careful plans and manages his financial problems well by providing protection against these risks, he still cannot be guaranteed financial success. But if he does not plan carefully and does not develop methods of handling problems before they occur, he will be extremely fortunate if he has any success at all.

EDUCATION

The first step in the plan, then, is to complete a formal education. This is a primary means of increasing income. How extensive the education should be depends upon interests and abilities. It is a historical fact that people with a higher education on the average earn higher incomes than those without. Education is perhaps the single most important asset that can be acquired. A high school graduate may earn an average annual income of $6,000, whereas the same person might earn $10,000 if he completed college. We can compute the value of that education. Any asset that provides a $4,000 annual income can be valued by determining the appropriate rate of return that such an asset should pay. Perhaps it should earn a 10 percent rate of return. In this case the education would be worth $40,000, that is, a $40,000 asset earning 10 percent would provide an income flow of $4,000 a year ($4,000 ÷ .10 = $40,000).

There are two ways to look at this method of valuation. First, consider the process in terms of income flow:

$10,000-income for a typical college graduate
−6,000-income for a typical high school graduate
_____

$ 4,000-additional income
÷ .10-rate of return
_____

$40,000-asset value

Second, consider the process from the view of the asset:

$40,000-asset value
× .10-rate of return
_____

$ 4,000-annual income from the asset

This valuation process applies to any flow of income and any asset, although certain modifications must often be made to reflect length of life, depreciation or appreciation of the asset, and risk factors.

When you expect a 10 percent rate of return on an asset, it is generally an asset that involves considerable risk. In this instance there is not much risk, either that you would lose your college education—although it does depreciate over time—or that it would not be of considerable value to you in getting a better job. So you might judge this asset so low a risk that it would require only a 5 percent rate of return. If so, you would value the education at $80,000, that is, an $80,000 asset earning 5 percent a year would provide a $4,000 annual income ($80,000 × .05 = $4,000). Whether an education is worth $40,000 or $80,000 is indeed significant, and it must be determined whether this asset is worth more than the cost involved in acquiring it.

Most people believe that a college education worth $40,000—or $80,000—and acquired at a relatively low cost is worth buying. Although they may not make all these calculations, many people go to college for this reason alone. Nor should such a reason be ignored. A significant part of your financial planning should be directed to increasing your income to the desired level. If you have enough investment capital, that alone will take care of your income requirements. If not, as is true for almost everyone, you will want to gain capital in some form. The best kind of capital to acquire first is human capital, i.e., the skills and abilities a person accumulates in his head or hands which enable him to earn income. Education—whether college or post graduate—may be the most important form of insurance against unemployment. No one who is formulating a lifetime financial plan should overlook the possibility of unemployment at some time or other.

EDUCATION AND THE RISK OF UNEMPLOYMENT

It was once commonly held that only those without the will to work could be threatened by unemployment. The dangers of becoming unemployed are much greater than is commonly believed. In the 1930's almost one fourth of the labor force was unemployed; in recent years the rates have generally ranged from 3 to 6 percent. But these rates are misleading when you consider the chances for any given person. The publicized rates indicate unemployment for a particular week; the percentage of workers unemployed during a substantial part of a year, or even for a few weeks, would be much higher. One source indicates that, although the unemployment rate was 6.8 percent in 1958, unemployment struck at least 18 percent of all families in that year![1]

While the danger of unemployment is lower for professional people than for unskilled and semiskilled workers, it is far from nonexistent. In 1970 investment firms released many well-educated employees, and large

---

[1] *Report of the Special Committee on Unemployment Problems,* Eugene McCarthy, Chairman, 86th Congress (Washington, D.C.: U.S. Government Printing Office, March 30, 1960), p. 3.

numbers of engineers were the targets of industry cutbacks. Even when professionals find other jobs they may not be paid for all their work because of economy measures within an industry, and their incomes may not be high since so many similar professionals are looking for jobs at the same time. Still, the employment problems of unskilled and semi-skilled workers are very different. Many of them are employed by companies that shut down factories, stop production, and fire employees in large numbers.

Particularly for young people, the best protection against the risk of unemployment due to economic factors is a good education and employment experience. Education provides a foundation for further education and for other jobs. With others as with Seymour Green, the best protection against unemployment is acquired abilities and skills, and the will to serve a profession well.

ESTABLISHING AN EMERGENCY FUND

A second step in the creation of a personal financial plan is to establish an emergency fund. Such a fund can do a number of good things for you. Perhaps the most important of these is that it can be a way for you to start regular saving. And as we saw in Chapter One, it is a rare individual who càn begin to increase his usable income through investment without first being able to save. For those who find saving difficult, there are many ways to make it easier. Some people join a bond-a-month club, in which they authorize their employer or bank to withhold $18.75 a month, $37.50 a month, or some other figure, for the purchase of U.S. savings bonds. Some people have their banks deposit a fixed amount in a savings account each month. Some employers are willing to withhold a regular amount for deposit in a credit union, which pays interest. At least one man we know of, after vainly trying to save for many years, finally thought up the idea of borrowing $600 at the beginning of each year and paying it back $50 a month! The interest he paid on his loan was a little more than he got on the money he put in his savings account, but to him this cost was nothing compared to the satisfaction he got from being able to save at last.

Having an emergency fund does other good things for you. For example, it can let you carry a cheaper automobile policy, say one with a $100 deductible clause instead of $50, because you could, if you had to, pay the other $50 out of your emergency fund. An emergency fund could also let you assume a greater portion of your medical expenses, and enable you to pay the first $1,000 hospitalization, rather than carry a more expensive policy which pays all expenses over $500. An emergency fund could help you to avoid the forced sale of some asset—such as a stock or a valuable painting—in a financial crisis. And an emergency fund can always provide cash for some unusual financial opportunity.

Essentially, an emergency fund provides a cash cushion that lets you maintain your financial plan regardless of unforeseen circumstances. Without an emergency fund, financial planning becomes difficult if not impossible, because emergencies do arise, and money that has been allocated for other purposes is forced into some other use.

It may be hard to protect your emergency fund from nonemergency consumption spending. Some people find it very difficult not to spend whatever money they have in their savings accounts. If you are like that, perhaps you should plan to keep your emergency funds in some other form than readily available cash. Perhaps you should use loan funds, such as a line of credit at your bank. Or you might use the loan value of your life insurance policy in an emergency.

ESTABLISHING AN INSURANCE PROGRAM

A third step in building a personal financial plan is setting up an adequate insurance program. Various types of insurance risks must be recognized and overcome if you are to reach your goal of financial security. We will consider first the insurable risks: (1) the mortality risk, (2) the risk of excessive longevity, (3) the morbidity risk, (4) the property risk, and (5) the liability risk.

THE MORTALITY RISK

The mortality risk is the possibility of premature death. In the case of Seymour Green, were death to occur late in life when he had no more dependents, there would be no financial loss. But if he were to die young his death would cause very great financial loss. Because every part of his plan assumes a regular income, his death would end all hope of further income from his labors, and his dependents would suffer.

What are the chances of dying at an early age? Table 2–1 shows the probability of death within a year at certain ages, and the probability of death before age 65. A young person is correct in believing that his chances of dying soon are not great. According to Table 2–1, a person 20 years old has only a .0012 probability of dying within a year. This means that only 12 out of 10,000 persons aged 20 die within a year. But almost one-third of the people aged 20 will die before they reach 65. Table 2–1 indicates that a young person who assumes that premature death will not happen to him is taking a considerable risk. It is a mistake, therefore, to make your financial plans as though you will certainly live to 65—or to any particular age, for that matter.

How can a person protect himself against financial losses caused by premature death? Ordinarily, with life insurance. If a person insures his life and dies prematurely, the life insurance proceeds can be used to meet his financial objectives just as though he were still alive. His family's financial security, their home, and college education for his children can

Table 2–1 Probabilities of Death

Age	Within a Year	Before Age 65
0	.0259	.34
5	.0006	.31
10	.0004	.31
15	.0008	.30
20	.0012	.30
25	.0013	.29
30	.0014	.29
35	.0020	.28
40	.0030	.27
45	.0046	.25
50	.0078	.22
55	.0108	.17
60	.0177	.10

Source: The data used to compute these probabilities are taken from the mortality tables of the United States total population (1959 — 1961) published in the *1970 Life Insurance Fact Book*, Institute of Life Insurance, pp. 118-119.

all be provided despite his death. Only when you realize how dependent financial planning is on continued income can you appreciate the importance of covering mortality risk.

Perhaps you have already given some thought to your need for adequate life insurance. If so you have probably wondered just what "adequate" means and what types of policies are desirable and under what circumstances. It may not therefore be necessary to convince you that you should have life insurance. But for many young people the whole area of insurance is something of a mystery, and few people of any age understand the fundamentals of insurance and how it operates. This kind of information can help any insurance buyer to get the protection he most needs at the least cost.

The only sensible way to assess the adequacy of life insurance coverage is to consider the value of a person's income and what he hopes to do with his future income. Does he have a family he is responsible for? Does he have a mortgage on his home that he plans to pay off out of future income? Does he have children he wants to send to college? Is he trying to provide all of these things whether or not he is around to go on earning the income that would buy them?

Once more consider the case of Seymour Green. He is now a recent college graduate, age 25, father of two, and an aspiring professional man. He wants to know just how much life insurance he needs and what it will cost. A rough rule of thumb is that one's life insurance coverage should be three to four times his income. Since Seymour has an annual income of $12,000, we may figure that he should carry from $30,000 to $40,000 worth of life insurance. Since he is 25 years of age, he could decide to buy $40,000 worth of permanent insurance with an annual premium of about $600. But what if he feels that he cannot afford a $600 annual premium? Can he get along with less? In all probability, his income will rise in the future, so that if anything, he needs more than $40,000 coverage rather than less. He might wish to carry $10,000 of one type of insurance (permanent), costing him an annual premium of $150, and $60,000 of another type of insurance (temporary), costing him an annual premium of $120. His total yearly insurance bill would then be $270 for $70,000 worth of coverage.

There are many alternatives he should consider and these are discussed thoroughly in Chapter Thirteen. Regardless of the specific amounts of life insurance needed and finally purchased, it is important to recognize that life insurance must be considered early in the construction of a personal financial program because financial security for a family is simply not possible without a continuous flow of income.

THE RISK OF EXCESSIVE LONGEVITY

It may seem strange to speak of excessive longevity as a "risk." How can one live too long? Good health and long life are usually regarded as desirable goals, not risks. Yet it is easy to outlive one's financial resources. And when a person can no longer maintain himself and his dependents, he faces serious financial problems. The chances of living past retirement age are good for a young person. If about one-third of the people aged 20 will die before reaching age 65, as shown in Table 2–1, then obviously about two-thirds will live beyond that age. Furthermore, those who do live to 65 can expect to live quite a few years longer, and the life expectancy for persons 65 is increasing, as is shown in Table 2–2. In 1940, a man could expect to live about 12 years after reaching 65, but by the year 2000, a man can expect to live more than 16 years (under the low mortality assumption). Table 2–2 also shows that women have a greater life expectancy than men.

Table 2–2 Life Expectancy at Age 65

Year		Number of Additional Years That Can Be Expected	
		Male	Female
1939–41		12.07	13.57
1949–51		12.74	19.95
2000	Low mortality	16.11	18.39
	High mortality	13.80	16.69

Source: *Illustrative United States Population Projections,* United States Department of Health, Education, and Welfare, Social Security Administration (Actuarial Study No. 46), May 1957, p. 15.

If Seymour Green were earning $20,000 a year when he retired at age 65, he would suffer a loss of $20,000 a year thereafter. This loss, of course, might be partially offset by social security benefits, income from a pension plan, or income from other sources such as life insurance and investments. Still, there is no way around the conclusion that excessive longevity will cause major financial problems for many people. One of the main problems in planning adequate retirement income is that no one ever knows how long he will live. The figures given in Table 2–2 are averages, and they are not reliable for an individual. The only safe course is to plan for the possibility of death at any age. Some of the risk of excessive longevity can be overcome through modification of life insurance policies still in force at age 65, so that to some extent this risk and mortality risk can be partially managed through the same vehicle. Nevertheless, the provision of adequate income during retirement will mainly depend on other investments acquired during one's working years.

THE MORBIDITY RISK

Morbidity risk is the possibility that a person will become disabled, either by illness or accident. This risk is greater than the risk of early death. Many disabilities are very brief. You might miss work a day or so with a cold or for a week or ten days with mumps or flu. Such disabilities are very common and usually present no serious problems. But serious disabilities can ruin financial plans since they may continue for a long time—even a lifetime. They cause major financial problems because they create medical expenses at a time when income has been stopped. Most people cannot continue to meet their financial and family obligations when their income is stopped for a very long period, and they certainly cannot afford to pay medical expenses.

Table 2–3 Probabilities of a Serious Disability (1,000 exposed lives)

Age	Probability of Disability of 90 Days or More in Year Indicated	Probability of Death in Year Indicated	Ratio of Disability Probability to Probability of Death
22	6.64	1.27	5.23
27	6.57	1.26	5.21
32	7.78	1.60	4.86
37	9.81	2.28	4.30
42	12.57	3.62	3.47
47	16.76	5.73	2.92
52	22.39	9.29	2.41
57	31.10	13.52	2.30
62	44.27	20.82	2.13

Sources: The data used to compute these probabilities are among those published by the Health Insurance Association of America, *1964 Commissioner's Disability Table,* Vol. 3, p. 13 and by the Institute of Life Insurance, *1970 Life Insurance Fact Book,* pp. 118–119.

Table 2–3 indicates that the chances of serious disability increase with age. Even so, the chance of serious disability is greater at every age than the chance of death. At age 22, the chances are about five times greater that a person will be disabled for more than 90 days than the chance that he will die.

The usual protection against loss from the morbidity risk is health insurance. There are health policies that pay an income when the insured is unable to work, or that pay some or all medical expenses. A person with no health insurance is taking a great risk because it is always possible that disability will destroy all his financial plans. Some people try to pay disability losses from emergency funds. Although minor disabilities may wisely be paid for by savings, this is not a good way to manage serious disabilities. When you consider that a continuous flow of income is a major determinant of any financial program, the risk that you may someday be unable to work can be truly frightening. The probability is not great, but its impact is staggering to contemplate. Because the probability is low, the premium on disability insurance is also low. For about $100 annual premium, Mr. Green could buy insurance with a four-week deductible clause, that would guarantee his family an income of $5,000 a year for five years should he become ill, and for life should he be disabled by accident. This would supplement any coverage provided by his employer and social security. For a healthy young man, a $100 annual premium on a policy that would pay disability claims of $400 to $500 a month is a relatively small price to cover a potentially devastating risk.

THE PROPERTY RISK

The property risk is the possibility that property will be destroyed, lost, stolen, or damaged. All types of property are subject to this risk. If you own real estate, your building may burn to the ground. If it does, you will suffer a financial loss. Young people often underestimate the importance of property risk. One reason is that they overlook the fact that this risk applies to personal property as well as to real estate. Personal property subject to property risk are clothes, furniture, and automobiles. If you own any of these assets, you are subject to the property risk. Virtually everyone, then, has a property risk of some type.

Sometimes a person can suffer a financial loss even when he does not own the property that is damaged. Consider the college student whose lease is cancelled because of a fire in his apartment building. Even if the fire does not damage his property, the cancellation of his lease could cause a loss in the form of moving expenses and perhaps higher rent in a new apartment.

Fire, windstorms, and lightning can also damage property. Many people realize that property can be damaged or stolen, but they consider only the well-known perils. A complete list of all possible perils would have to include fire, windstorm, riot, lightning, hail, civil commotion, smoke, falling aircraft, freezing water, electrical disturbances, explosion, vehicle vandalism, landslide, earthquake, flood, termite damage, and war. Indeed, such a list would probably never be complete because new perils are constantly developing. The peaceful use of nuclear energy, for example, may be a boon to society, but it also poses the possibility of fantastic property destruction.

The property risk includes indirect as well as direct losses to property. When a fire destroys a home, the owner is likely to incur additional living expenses while the home is being repaired. A small business damaged by fire can earn no income while the property is being restored. Consider the cost of demolition. If you own a building 60 percent destroyed by fire, it may be necessary to demolish the rest of it in order to start a new building. The cost of demolition is a loss in addition to the direct damage caused by the fire. The possible indirect losses are almost endless, and these are overlooked by most property owners, sometimes with serious effect, because indirect losses may be larger than the direct loss.

Although property risk is serious, it can become manageable if moderate attention is given to needed protection. Consider the person who has worked long and hard to acquire a home, a house full of furniture, an automobile, or even a business, but has failed to protect his assets against property risk. In one fell swoop, years of successful effort can be cancelled out. Whenever a person is in a position to lose if property is damaged or stolen, he is said to have an insurable interest in the property. When insurable interest exists, an intelligent person has no choice but to insure the property. Not all property risks are covered in a standard home owner's or renter's policy, or even a standard business policy; but a great many are, and additional ones can be added, and all for a small annual premium.

LIABILITY RISK

The liability risk is the possibility of becoming legally obligated to make payment for personal injury or property damage. If your actions cause injury, the law gives the injured person the right to sue. If a judgment is rendered by a court of law against you, you are obligated to pay the amount of the judgment to the injured person. Most families do not give liability insurance the consideration it deserves. Yet it is especially important because liability claims can be made against future income as well as present wealth, and as a man becomes more successful financially, there could be more frequent and larger liability claims against him. Consider the following illustration.

A few years ago a construction contractor employed a high school student to do odd jobs after school. One day the contractor sent him to pick up a sack of nails. The young man jumped in his car and started downtown. On the way he saw a pretty young girl walking along, and accidentally plowed into the back of a car occupied by three women, all of whom developed instant back trouble. They sued the contractor since the boy was his agent on a business errand, and through the suit they appropriated the contractor's corporation. An adequate insurance program would have protected him against the risk of such a loss.

Do not assume that you cannot be liable because you have no money. Most people think they can lose no more than their present surplus of wealth. This is not so. You have a significant asset in your earning power, and that can be attached with resulting loss of future income. Consider this:

A minister had an automobile accident in which a husband and wife were injured. Their lawyer, a member of the minister's church, came to see him to ask if he had any liability insurance on his car. He said of course he did. He had $10,000–$20,000–$5,000, which means that he had $10,000 worth of coverage for any one person injured in any one accident, $20,000 worth of coverage for all persons in any one accident and $5,000 worth of coverage for property liability in any one accident. The husband and wife, with their lawyer, decided to have a "friendly little lawsuit" to make the insurance company pay off. The judgment turned out to be $40,000. The minister protested, "But, Judge, you don't understand. I only have $20,000 worth of insurance coverage!" And the judge said, "Well, then you will have to pay the other $20,000 out of your own pocket." The minister answered, "I don't have $20,000. I don't have my car or furniture paid for; I have four children to support; I live in a house owned by the church; I don't have any money or any assets. Where would I get $20,000?" And the judge said, "Then you must pay $90 a month for the next 20 years."

It is simply not true that anyone who can earn an income has no assets. The most important asset any young person has, and the one he first acquires, is his ability to earn. Your education has provided you with this ability, and it is an asset against which claims can be made. Without liability protection, you can spend years paying off such claims.

What happens if your mailman slips on your steps, falls and injures his back, and incurs substantial medical and hospital bills? Are you responsible? Suppose your child accidentally shoots a toy arrow into the face of a neighbor? If your German shepherd dog attacks and injures someone trespassing on your property, can you be held liable? The answers to these questions depend on liability law.

Legal liability can rest on one of three bases:

1. Intentional invasions of the interests of others, such as assault, battery, false imprisonment, and seduction
2. Negligence
3. Absolute or strict liability

Most personal liability judgments arise from negligence. The usual definition of negligence is the failure to act as an ordinary, reasonable, and prudent person.

Suppose you are driving your car, and because you are watching some students on the corner, you drift into the wrong lane and hit a parked car. The law would say you have been negligent because a reasonable, prudent person would have driven more carefully. To determine negligence all you must do is ask yourself how a reasonable, prudent person would have acted in the same circumstances. One who acts differently is guilty of negligence. The law considers the circumstances of each case. A bystander would not be expected to risk his life by swimming to rescue a drowning person. But the law might declare him negligent if he did not throw a nearby rope.

You can be guilty of negligence and not be legally liable. Negligence alone does not create liability. A person is held responsible only when his negligence causes injury or damage to someone else. Furthermore, negligence must be the proximate cause of the loss. This means there must be an unbroken chain of events leading from the negligent act to the damage or injury. Consider this case. You are driving your car into the garage and you knock over a large trash can that rolls up against a ladder on which a painter is standing. The painter falls from the ladder and breaks his leg. Are you responsible? Yes, because there is a direct, unbroken chain of events from your negligent act to his injury. On the other hand, what happens if you damage someone else's car? If you have been negligent, you are responsible for the damage. But suppose the owner of the damaged car is then late for a business appointment and loses a valuable sale. Are you responsible for the lost sale? Probably not, because many factors besides the accident could have been responsible for the lost sale. The court would require proof that the accident was the main cause of the loss, and that there was an unbroken chain of events from one to the other.

In addition to recent changes in the legal causes of liability, the courts have also been changing the concept of damage. In the past, a person who negligently injured another would be responsible for the medical and hospital bills of the injured person. In addition, if it could be shown that the injury caused loss of income, the judgment might also include some compensation for that loss. Now courts routinely make awards for pain, suffering, and mental anguish. In addition, punitive damages, designed to punish the guilty, are also becoming more common. In recent years, husbands and wives have collected judgments for loss of conjugal relations. Furthermore, such damage awards have become larger and larger.

Now that liability suits have become so frequent and judgments so high, the only logical protection is liability insurance. Many types of liability policies are available, e.g., automobile, home owner's, business and professional. The person who does not protect himself adequately is taking the chance of an expensive suit for negligence. Since liability judgments can now be so large, an uninsured loss could easily destroy a person's financial plans and prevent him from ever reaching his goal. Therefore, Mr. Green's insurance program will include life, disability, property, and liability insurance to provide protection against various risks. These coverages are treated in greater detail in later chapters. Suffice it to say that no intelligent planner will overlook the necessity of an insurance program.

STARTING AN INVESTMENT PROGRAM

The fourth step in the construction of a personal financial plan is the creation of an investment portfolio. An investment "portfolio" is merely a list of one's investments. The term generally refers to securities, but it need not. Some people prefer to invest in real estate and others find enjoyment in owning paintings, antiques, stamps, and other collectable items. A personal business may be considered part of an investment portfolio, although it may also be seen as a fifth step in a financial plan. In some cases, the establishment of a personal business precedes the development of an investment program.

Mr. Seymour Green, however, does want to begin investing in securities. He has no inherited wealth. As a matter of fact, he has incurred debts in completing his education and putting together his household. He must now pay off these debts and further furnish his home. Since he is married, now has two children, and may wish to have more, his family expenses are of primary importance to him. In short, his investment portfolio begins with zero cash and zero securities. Although he does have an interest in beginning an investment program as a part of his long-range financial plan, he has many other financial demands. He does not want to strain his financial position, nor does he expect to get rich quick. He merely wishes to initiate a relatively modest savings-investment program that will be adequate, and that he can sustain. Following is the investment program he adopted. It is a modest program, not a typical case, nor an ideal one; just one example.

Figure 2-1   Mr. Seymour Green's Investment Plan

Age 25 through 29	$25 per month ($300 per year)
Age 30 through 39	$50 per month ($600 per year)
Age 40 through 65	$100 per month ($1,200 per year)
	X 9 percent annual rate of return on investments
	=$250,000 Investment portfolio (at age 65)

As can be seen in Figure 2–1, this is a three-stage program beginning at age 25 and going to age 65. From age 25 through age 29, Mr. Green will invest $25 a month; from age 30 through age 39, he will invest $50 a month; from age 40 through age 65, he will double the investment again to $100 a month. With an annual return of 9 percent, the investment portfolio would be $250,000 at age 65.

This investment plan is not so ambitious that it cannot be sustained. The $25 a month should be possible for Mr. Green or for almost anyone who has any kind of a middle-income position. By the age of 30, some of his early debts should be paid. When a new $25 salary raise comes along, simply holding the line on consumption will permit doubling the investment rate. By age 40, most people are approaching peak incomes and the third stage should be possible without undue strain. In some cases a Christmas or vacation bonus alone can serve as investment funds. This phase of Mr. Green's personal financial plan should indeed be workable, livable, and sustainable.

Such an investment program can be readily modified. For instance, if at age 25 you have $2,000 that you inherited, were given, or already saved, and you have a reasonably good income and a genuine interest in investments, you might be able to skip the first stage of the program and begin with a $50 monthly investment which would permit you to retire with $250,000 at age 60. Or if you are interested in an earlier retirement age, but have nothing to begin with, you may be able to save a little more than $25 a month to start with, and to double and redouble at higher figures. Furthermore, it may be possible, though difficult, to earn a little more than a 9 percent rate of return. The rate of return makes a great deal of difference. For example, if $1,000 earns a 9 percent annual rate of return with no additional saving, it will be worth $45,000 after 40 years. But if that $1,000 can earn a 14 percent annual rate of return, it will be worth $180,000. And compounded at 15 percent per year, it would be worth $267,000. A 1 percent additional rate of return over a sufficient number of years makes a very considerable difference in the end value. However, if there is one all-encompassing financial principle, it is this: potential return varies directly with risk; i.e., if you try for a larger percentage return on your portfolio, you must assume greater risk. If you add more risk without adding better portfolio management, any increase in risk could very well result in a loss.

The key to any investment program is consistency. It is essential to start saving and to begin an investment program early, perhaps by the age of 25 or 30, even though the program may be a very modest one. If a saving habit is established early, even if the saving is a relatively small percentage of income, the probability of a persistent, consistent, successful investment program is greatly increased. Similarly, since 9 percent is a relatively modest rate of return, it is considerably easier to sustain than a higher rate. Thus 15 percent will be much harder to sustain because it is about double the average return on investments after taxes. Whatever modifications you make in the above example to create your own personal investment program, even if the modifications are so great that you can see no resemblance, the very fact that you have considered the need for such a program and have initiated one yourself can be a source of great satisfaction and financial achievement.

There are, however, some major risks in investment that must be considered: (1) financial risk, (2) market risk, (3) inflation risk, and (4) interest-rate risk. As in the case of insurable risks, each one of these can keep you from reaching your financial objective. Although there is no way to insure against these risks, there are ways to overcome them. They must be well understood and carefully considered if you are to reach your goal. At the very least each of these risks can mean loss and delay. At the worst, they can reduce your hope of security to frustration and failure.

FINANCIAL RISK

The first investment risk to consider is the financial risk, the chance that the earning power of an asset may decline. Since this risk is assumed by almost every owner of an earning asset, and since owning such assets is a major component of a solid financial program, this risk is indeed important. Every business, corporate or otherwise, and every piece of property, for that matter, faces some possibility that its earning power may decline. For example, if an asset such as a common stock is earning $2 a share and selling for $40, it may be said that investors believe that the risk of owning that stock requires a 5 percent return on their money ($40 × .05 = $2). If the earnings of the company declined to $1 and investors still required the same rate of return, the price of the stock would probably decline to $20 ($20 × .05 = $1). It is possible that investors could view such a decline in earning power as temporary and still be willing to pay $30 or so. On the other hand, if the decline were the result of a major shift in consumer demand or input costs, or of a major managerial blunder, still lower earnings might be anticipated, bondholders could become concerned, creditor actions could develop, bond prices could decline drastically, and the price of the stock could decline to $5 or even lower. Even a relatively minor decline in the financial strength of a company can mean a serious loss for the investor. The owner of any earning asset must be prepared to suffer such financial loss when he assumes ownership of the assets, and unless he protects himself from it in some way, this obstacle could seriously hinder progress toward his goal.

There is no safe way of eliminating financial risk. But there are several ways an investor can protect himself and minimize the problems it causes. Some investments entail more financial risk than others. In fact, it is possible to rank general types of investments according to degree of financial risk. For example, U.S. Treasury bonds, including savings bonds, have the very lowest financial risk; they are the closest thing to money in terms of this factor. Next are corporate bonds, securities issued by corporations promising to pay regularly whatever interest the bond coupon requires. Not all corporations are equally sound, but the bonds of some are close to being as free of financial risk as bonds issued by the government. Then in order of increasing risk are preferred stocks, conservative common stocks, growth stocks, and speculative stocks. With both growth and speculative stocks, the investor may assume considerable financial risk. He can reduce it somewhat by buying a variety of assets. That is, he may diversify his portfolio by buying low-risk bonds, preferred stocks, and conservative stocks along with growth and speculative stocks. Through diversification, an investor hopes that any unusual adversity among his high risk assets will be offset by holding low risk assets. The purchase of a portfolio of high risk common stocks is a risky business. More will be said about defensive investment techniques and the reduction of financial risk in later chapters.

THE MARKET RISK

The second investment hazard is market risk, the possibility that the market price of an asset may decline when there is no decline in its earning power. In discussing financial risk, we suggested that a common stock might fall in price from $40 to $20 because its earnings fell from $2 to $1 per share. The price can also decline from $40 to $20 or even less even if the $2 earnings remains unchanged, if investors decide that a 5 percent return on their money is not enough. For example, if they decide they want a 10 percent return, this would mean that a $20 stock would earn $2 ($20 × .10 = $2).

The concept of market risk may be clearer if we use a price-earnings multiple rather than a percentage return. A price-earnings multiple is simply the number of times by which a stock's price is greater than its earnings. If a stock is earning $2 a share and selling at $40, it has a price-earnings multiple of 20 (20 × $2 = $40). A stock selling for $20 and earning $2 has a price-earnings multiple of 10 (10 × $2 = $20). The price-earnings multiple is merely the reciprocal of the percentage return. It tells how much investors are willing to pay for a dollar's worth of earnings, or to put it the other way around, how big a return they want on an investment. Such a multiple is determined by many things, but especially by risk.

There are numerous causes of market declines even when earning power does not change. Some of these result from economic forces and some simply from changes in public opinion. As an example of a change in economic conditions, consider the 1966 and 1969 restrictions on bank credit. Tight money caused businessmen and investors to sell securities in the various securities markets to raise money they would have borrowed from the banks if there were no credit restrictions. In such instances, the supply of securities flooding the market tends to exceed the demand, with a resulting decline in prices regardless of earnings. Such broad economic conditions tend to affect the market price of all securities.

Only those investments that are very nearly cash, such as savings accounts, life insurance reserves, or short-term notes are subject to little or no market risk. Some such assets should be included in all investment programs simply to provide liquidity for emergency conditions. If one builds a source of ready cash into his investment program, he should be able to weather any temporary storm. Simply being aware that market risk exists may enable the investor to avoid hasty or ill-timed actions, and limit any serious impact this obstacle might have upon him. But if an investor builds his program around a rather large proportion of growth stocks, to say nothing of speculative stocks, he must recognize that he has assumed considerable market risk, and that market fluctuations will occasionally cause significant, if only temporary, declines in portfolio values. Furthermore, the more speculative the stocks, or the larger the proportion of such stocks in your portfolio, the greater the fluctuations you must expect.

INFLATION RISK

A third investment risk that must be considered is inflation risk, sometimes called purchasing power risk. This risk is the uncertainty of the purchasing power of money received in the future, or the risk that an increase in the price level will reduce the purchasing power of the dollar. When a person invests or saves, he expects to receive something in return. Usually an investment return is received periodically (in the form of interest or dividends) and a principal amount is returned when the investment is sold, redeemed, or matured. The dollars the investor or saver receives are current dollars, that is, the value of the dollars is determined by prices at the time the investment return is received. The dollars received may or may not purchase as much as at some other time —they may be worth more or less than when the investment was made. If prices have not changed, they will be worth the same. If prices have increased, they will be worth less, and vice versa.

The important consideration for the individual is his real income. This is the amount of goods and services his money will buy. In order to know what has happened to real income over time, it is necessary to convert current dollars into constant dollars. This conversion removes the effect of changes in price level. Figure 2–2 will help explain these concepts. Part A of Figure 2–2 shows that an individual's real income (in constant dollars) decreases when the price level increases, but the amount he receives does not increase. For example, if Mr. Green places $1,000 in a savings account, later withdraws his savings, and prices have

Figure 2–2   Illustration of the Purchasing Power Risk

A. When Price Level Rises and Amount of Income is Constant

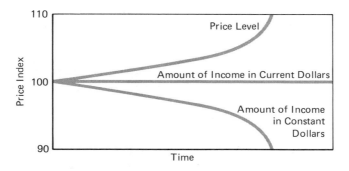

B. When Price Level Rises and Amount of Income Rises Proportionately

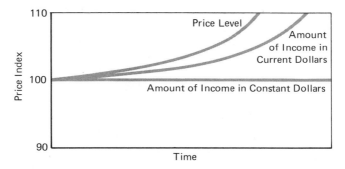

Source: Harry Sauvain, *Investment Management,* 3rd edition (Englewood Cliffs, N. J.: Prentice-Hall, Inc., 1967), p. 191.

increased in the meantime, the purchasing power of his dollars will have decreased. Part B of Figure 2–2 shows that a person can maintain real income during inflation only if the amount he receives increases enough to offset the rise in prices.

Much attention has been drawn in recent years to the fact that inflation has been a serious problem in our economy, and that it has been more serious at some times than at others. But just how serious has it been? Table 2–4 can be useful in determining the magnitude of losses that have occurred in the past as a result of the inflation risk. For example, Table 2–4 shows that consumer prices have increased in every year covered by the table, and the increases for the past few years have been sizable. To use this index to measure the impact of inflation risk on owning a $1,000 bond, all you do is divide the amount invested by the index of prices when the investor purchased a bond for $1,000, and received this amount when he sold it. The value of his investment can be found by dividing $1,000 by say 120 (the index of prices at the time of sale): $1,000 divided by 120 equals $833. This means the investor lost $167 or about 20 percent in constant dollars.

As long as inflation occurs at the rate of no more than 1 percent or 1.5 percent per year, it is not sharply painful, although it is still serious over an extended period of time. At a 1 percent rate of inflation, $1,000 would be worth $500 in purchasing power after 40 years. At a 2 percent rate of inflation, $1,000 would be worth $500 in purchasing power after only 20 years. When inflation reaches an annual rate of 4 percent, the value of $1,000 is cut in half in 10 years! An even higher rate of inflation, or a 3 or 4 percent rate over a 30- or 40-year period, can have a disastrous impact on the value of fixed-dollar investments.

A person trying to provide his family with a flow of dollars in case of his death or retirement must consider inflation as the most serious investment risk he faces. It is a substantial obstacle standing in the way of his reaching financial security. Consider the loss from 4 percent inflation over only ten years to someone who only has that long to prepare. A man at the age of 55 would be giving serious consideration to his retirement years and might by trying to put the finishing touches on his plan to provide financial security for himself and his wife after retirement, now only ten years off. Furthermore, he might well be more concerned than earlier with investments that have greater dollar guarantees—government bonds, life insurance, savings deposits, mortgages, and so on. All these without exception are fixed-dollar investments, exactly the ones that have the most inflation risk. You might hope that at 55 you could see fairly accurately only 10 years into the future just how many dollars you might

Table 2–4   Consumer Price Index (1957–59 = 100)

Period	Index
1958	100.7
1959	101.5
1960	103.1
1961	104.2
1962	105.4
1963	106.7
1964	108.1
1965	109.9
1966	113.1
1967	116.3
1968	121.2
1969	127.7
1970	136.0 (est.)

Source: *Federal Reserve Bulletin* (Washington, D.C.: Board of Governors, Federal Reserve System), April 1970.

require to maintain a desired scale of living. Yet with a 4 percent annual rate of inflation, you would find that upon retirement, you would have exactly half the purchasing power you anticipated. That is a significant obstacle.

INTEREST-RATE RISK

A fourth investment risk is interest-rate risk, i.e., the possibility that the market price of a fixed-income investment (such as a bond, a mortgage, or a preferred stock) will decline to equalize its yield with the yields on new securities with higher current interest rates. Consider an outstanding corporate bond paying an annual interest rate of 5 percent due to mature 20 years from now. If the current market interest rate is 5 percent, this $1,000 bond with its annual coupon of 5 percent would be paying the investor exactly the current market price, $50 interest per year. But if the bond is competing against a new 20-year bond paying a current market interest rate of 6 percent or $60 a year, the yield is too low. If the yield on the old bond is not equal to the yield on the new bond nobody will buy it. No one would pay $1,000 for a bond paying $50 per year when he can buy a comparable bond paying $60 a year for the same price. In order to equalize the yield of the old bond with the yield of the new bond, the market price of the old bond must fall to $880. The old bond is then said to be selling at a discount but it will yield 6 percent if held to maturity. But notice that the investor who bought the bond at par value or face value of $1,000 when it was originally issued several years ago now has lost $120 of his principal.

In recent years, with interest rates rising so dramatically, interest-rate risk has indeed been significant to the conservative investor. Every investment portfolio, whether it be an individual's portfolio or that of an insurance company, a bank, a trust, or a mutual fund, has been hurt in recent years to the extent that its portfolio has included fixed-income securities. Although this risk may not be as significant in the future as it has been in the recent past, there is no guarantee either way. Some bond authorities are now predicting interest rates between 6 and 12 percent for the next 20 years. If these forecasts are valid, interest rates will rise considerably, and fixed-income instruments will be selling for still larger discounts, resulting in a loss to the seller.

One way an investor can avoid loss of principal due to the interest rate risk is to hold his securities to maturity. If he does not have to sell a security earlier—when it may be selling at a discount—he can wait until maturity and collect the full par or face value at that time. The market price of bonds and other investments that have a maturity date always moves toward face value as maturity approaches. But to avoid loss of principal, the investor incurs loss of income, because while he is holding a discounted bond to maturity to collect par value, the market interest rate on other new and old bonds is higher than the coupon on his investment. Either way, the portfolio suffers a loss due to a decline in the rate of interest.

The only way an investor can really avoid problems caused by the interest-rate risk is to purchase securities that are not subject to this risk. The interest-rate risk applies to most bonds, mortgages, and preferred stocks because these are all fixed-income investments. The interest or dividend they pay each year is fixed by contract and cannot be changed. Therefore, their market price must change to account for changes in interest rates.

Common stocks and real estate investments are also somewhat affected by changing interest rates, but the impact is usually minor. This is because other factors (such as financial risk and market risk) are so much more important in determining the price of common stocks and real estate. Through buying investments less subject to this risk, as in the case of the other investment risks, the portfolio is protected against interest-rate fluctuations.

For some protection against all the investment risks, a portfolio should include all types of investments. However, when you try to reduce the impact of one risk, you necessarily increase the impact of another. There is no way to eliminate all risks. For example, you may buy high-grade bonds to avoid financial and market risk, but in buying them you assume great inflation risk and interest-rate risk. Only by maintaining a balanced portfolio including both bonds and growth stocks, can you protect yourself somewhat against all risks. If you are especially concerned about one particular risk, you may do much to reduce it, but only by assuming more of the others. If financial or market risk concerns you, you may buy high-grade bonds, but by doing so you would suffer heavy losses from inflation. If inflation concerns you, you may negate it by buying growth stocks, but only at the cost of fluctuations in price. There is no way to eliminate all risks, and it is because there are risks that there is financial return. The investor must decide which risks he wants to assume and which he wishes to avoid.

An investment program is the final step toward the goal of financial security. It should be designed in such a way that you can advance it consistently, without feeling undue pressure to remove funds for consumption purposes. For similar reasons you need an emergency fund and an insurance program. Once your investment program is well under way it is extremely important that your savings program continue and that your portfolio be protected from unnecessary spending. If your investment program is to succeed, it must be built to overcome investment risks as well as other obstacles that stand between you and your ultimate goals. Although not all obstacles can be overcome through any one course of action, any one obstacle can be sufficiently overcome, and with careful planning, you can go a long way toward reaching your financial goal.

SUMMARY

The path to financial success is strewn with obstacles. To accumulate assets one must first learn the various courses of action available to him, and he must develop the financial discipline that will enable him to progress. He must then make sure that his assets are protected against the insurable risks. One automobile accident, one fire, or any one of many, many perils can easily destroy all the financial progress a person has made through years of effort. As an individual begins a savings and investment program, he encounters investment risks that are also troublesome. To make matters worse, investment risks cannot be transferred to an insurance company, and every investment program involves some type of risk. A person who attempts to minimize financial risk and market risk can buy fixed-income investments such as savings accounts and bonds, but these involve the risks of inflation and the interest rate. And a person concerned with inflation and the interest-rate risk may buy common stocks or real estate, but these investments are plagued by financial and market risk. There is no simple solution to the investment risk dilemma.

While there is no guaranteed formula for achieving financial security, there is no substitute for carefully developed plans and a meaningful course of action. Logical financial decisions can only be made in the context of an individual's present situation, his goals, and the course of action he has chosen.

Case Problems

1. Johnny Benchrider is a high school senior with college potential. At present he is trying to decide whether to go to college. He has been approached by a scout from the St. Louis Cardinals who feels that Johnny is a great fielding shortstop but a modest hitter. The scout feels that Johnny could make it in the majors as a utility infielder, and command a salary of about $15,000 a year. To get Johnny to sign, the scout has offered him a $25,000 bonus. On the other hand Johnny feels that his college education should earn a 10 percent rate of return, and that he will make $16,000 upon graduation. Is he financially better off to go to college? Assume $17,500 salary in the business world, now what? Assume $20,000, now what?

2. Mike Smith is 21 years old and has just returned home after serving four years in the Navy. He completed high school before joining the Navy but has not been to college. Mike is considering two alternatives. First, he has a job offer with a local department store that will pay him $400 a month after four years. The second alternative is to go on to the university for a degree in business administration. This would take four years, and even with his V.A. benefits he will probably have to go into debt. Mike is seriously considering taking the job especially since he would

lose over $20,000 in income if he went to the university. What other factors would you mention if you were helping Mike with his decision?

3. Suppose Mike decides to go to the university for a business degree and after graduation is hired by a local bank for an annual salary of $9,000. Compare this to his annual salary of approximately $5,000 had he taken the job with the department store. What would be the asset value of his college education assuming a 6 percent rate of return? What is the annual income from this asset?

4. Joe Risktaker is 30 years old, married, and the father of four children. Joe has a good income, and feels that buying insurance is giving money away. However, Joe's wife feels that he does need insurance although she can't seem to convince Joe. What arguments would you offer to Mrs. Risktaker to help convince Joe?

Selected Readings

Bracket, J. C. "Now BLG Budgets Provide Yardsticks for Measuring Family Living Costs." *Monthly Labor Review,* April 1969.

Facts You Should Know About Life Insurance. Educational Division, National Better Business Bureau, Chrysler Building, New York, New York.

How Much and What Kind of Life Insurance Should I Own? Hartford: The Connecticut Mutual Life Insurance Company. Free copies are available on request.

Insurance Facts. (Property and Liability related.) Insurance Information Institute, 110 Williams Street, New York, New York.

Mathews, H. Lee. *Causes of Personal Bankruptcies.* Bureau of Business Research, Ohio State University, 1968.

New York Life Budget Book. New York Life Insurance Company. Free copies available at 51 Madison Avenue, New York, New York.

Polner, Walter. "The Family That Does Not Save." *Business and Economic Dimensions,* July 1969, pp. 6–11.

Task Force on Economic Growth and Opportunity. *Poverty: The Sick, Disabled and Aged.* Washington, D.C.: U.S. Chamber of Commerce, 1965.

CHAPTER **THREE**

MANAGING CASH INCOME

As a result of your efforts to apply the comments in Chapters One and Two, you may have already done some long-range planning. Such planning must have included some consideration of your future income needs, but income is so vital a topic that considerable attention should be given to it. In this chapter, specific attention is given to providing and managing income—the second function of financial management. Although one can never consider all topics simultaneously, it is difficult to discuss income planning and expenditure planning separately. Income is indeed distinct from expenditures, but these two topics are so closely related that each must be partially considered in relation to the other. In this chapter, income is the main focus, but it is closely related to expenditures. In the next chapter, controlling expenditures is treated in detail, but income is necessarily considered as one of the truly significant constraints upon expenditures. Actually, income and expenditures are so completely dependent upon each other, and their relationship to overall financial security is so vital, that this chapter and the next could be likened to two sides of the same coin.

There are many definitions of income. Two in particular will be used in this chapter. First, income means earnings, e.g., wages, salaries, dividends, interest, and rental income. More broadly, income means any cash received, from earnings and from other sources such as bank loans or the sale of assets such as securities, real estate, etc. Defined in this broader sense, income can be related to outgo, which is any outflow of funds whether for current consumption, the payment of debts, or the purchase of assets, including investments. Income and outgo together make up a cash planning system, a cash budget, and a cash accounting system, regardless of the source or use of funds.

In any effort to manage cash income, income planning must consider not only current financial resources and requirements, but long-term resources and needs as well. With an understanding of the typical life income pattern, you can better plan your current cash needs because you have a better awareness of your long-term cash income. If you can see that early in your life income pattern your earned income will be inadequate to cover necessary expenditures, but that later your earned income will exceed expenditure requirements, you can then see that borrowing additional cash income in the present against earned income in the future is a solution to the problem of inadequate finances.

Borrowing is simply the process of shifting future earned income into the present to provide the cash income for consumption goods when the need for them is greatest. However, income planning is a primary restraint upon the life expenditure pattern, and it is a primary requirement for appropriately directing your income flow toward those consumption goods and investment objectives to which you attach highest priorities. Furthermore, income planning is a long-range function, because without such planning, borrowing additional cash income for immediate consumption could create long-range problems more significant than the current ones it solves. If you do plan your income over your lifetime, borrowing may be seen as only the first step toward stabilizing your lifetime income, one that will be followed in later years by a second stabilization effort, namely, storing your income in the form of savings invested in various financial assets.

The first problem in managing cash income that most young people must face is the inadequacy of current earned income. This chapter places primary emphasis upon borrowing as a solution to that problem. However, any discussion of borrowing must include some warnings about the problems that borrowers may experience. Therefore, considerable attention is given to such topics as who should borrow, how much should be borrowed, the sources of loans, and the types of loans. Most young people do need to borrow, but they do not need to borrow to their credit limits. Nor should they borrow from every potential source using every type of loan available. They should borrow only to the extent that borrowing enables them to increase their total satisfaction by managing cash income more effectively. Nor should they fail to recognize that borrowing is only the first step in their income stabilization effort. Borrowing is important, but so is saving. In a very real sense, the second step in an income stabilization effort, namely, saving cash income, is even more important in terms of achieving one's long-range objective of financial security. Such saving is not likely to occur without adequate planning, and cannot occur without sufficient control over expenditures.

Income planning, borrowing, expenditure planning, and saving are all essential to financial success, and through appropriate income and expenditure planning, financial security is a realistic objective.

INCOME PLANNING

Although almost everyone has some type of financial plan, not everyone does what could really be called financial managing. Even when there is a plan, disappointment is frequently a problem because many plans are poorly structured and fail to be of any real benefit to the user. As a result, a whole series of problems may arise simply because one does not know where he is, where he has been, or where he is going. Planning is essential to every phase of the financial program, and that includes providing income. In order to make an effective plan, it is necessary to know the flow of income—how much it is, where it is coming from, and where it is going. It is not necessary to collect large amounts of data about your financial resources in order to apply the various managerial techniques in an effort to attain previously identified goals. But it is necessary to have enough information to know how much income will be needed, both in the immediate present and in the future, in order to attain your economic and personal goals. By planning an income, directing the income flow, and saving income according to a predetermined schedule that accomplishes an effective stabilization of your income for maximum financial satisfaction, you will have accomplished a monumental task.

THE LIFE INCOME PATTERN

If you are anything like the typical individual, your life income will go through three stages, depicted in Figure 3–1. In the first stage your primary source of income is your parents; this stage lasts until you are about 20 years of age. The second stage is one of increasing income as you increase your productivity; this stage lasts until you are about 50

Figure 3–1 The Life Income Pattern

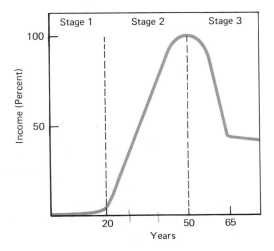

years of age. The last stage is one of declining income; your productivity will probably begin to decline somewhat prior to your retirement years, gradually at first and then drastically at retirement; this stage lasts until death.

Within the second stage, there are various levels of productivity and income. At the beginning of this stage, income is relatively low, although it may seem very high, comparatively speaking. It will increase at an increasing rate for the first 15 to 20 years. At about 40 or 45 years of age your productivity may reach its peak or begin to increase less rapidly. Consequently, your income will increase at a less rapid rate. Beginning at about age 50, income begins to decline, and for most people it declines dramatically with the beginning of the retirement years. In many instances, real income, that is, purchasing power, continues to decline each year during retirement as inflationary forces in the economy cause consumer prices to rise faster than retirement income adjustments occur.

There are many variations of this basic pattern. Persons who do not attend college begin receiving incomes sooner than those who do. On the other hand, noncollege graduates experience a decline in earnings earlier than college graduates, perhaps at age 45, whereas college graduates may continue to receive peak earnings until perhaps age 60. Furthermore, there are times when an individual is in need of more income temporarily, and he may take on a part-time job in addition to his regular employment in order to satisfy his income requirements. In many instances both the husband and the wife choose to work before they have children. Thereafter, the wife may not work for several years until the children are in school or even until they finish.

There may well be jumps, humps, and drops in your own life income pattern that will require major readjustments. It is the purpose of income planning to eliminate as many surprises as possible. If you can reduce the probability of an unexpected drop, your chances of reaching your goal are that much greater. If you fail to plan your income accurately, you must expect more uncertainty which, by its very nature, reduces your financial security.

DIRECTING THE INCOME FLOW

Directing the income flow is accomplished by making a budget. To many people, budget is a dirty word. One problem with a family budget (or a business budget or a government budget for that matter) is that it will not do what is expected of it. Many families have tried to use a budget, but unsuccessfully; and consequently, they have given up on the idea. Nevertheless, in most cases a family would benefit from knowing how much of its income was spent in various ways and what its expenditures will be in the future. It might be of particular benefit to know that your actual spending is much lower or much higher than your anticipated spending. If you plan a monthly budget for next year and find that you are exceeding that budget, you might be able to control a little better those expenditures that are exceeding your plan; if you should decide against controlling that part of your spending pattern, you could adjust your budget in some other area. If it is used correctly, a budget can be an effective means of controlling expenses and attaining objectives. What is the reason for all the unpleasantness over budgets? It may well be caused by an expectation that a budget can actually control the income flow. Since it will not, no wonder people are disappointed when their budgets fail to perform as expected. A budget will identify where the money has gone; it can also picture where you want your money to go. A budget can help you direct your income toward those expenditures you want to make by telling you where your money has gone; but only you can control your outgo.

For many people, perhaps most people, the budget is only a means of controlling expenses and nothing more. A complete budget, however, should place an equal emphasis on controlling income. This is particularly true when you make a two-, three-, or even five-year budget. A one-year budget is necessary, but not sufficient. For many people, during every year they remain in school, their expenses exceed their earned incomes. No one considers this at all unacceptable; as a matter of fact, most counselors recommend continuing your education and training as long as possible because doing so is a means of increasing the income flow over your lifetime through the acquisition of assets and skills. During the time that you are acquiring these earning assets, however, you may have a relatively low income. It may be so low that your consumption level exceeds your earned income each year, and you must provide additional cash income through bank loans. Similarly, for many families, the early years of marriage are years in which debts increase as consumption needs exceed earned income. At some point in the second stage of your life income pattern, however, preferably while you are still on the upward slope of your life income curve, net borrowing should cease, and repayment should commence. Beyond this point, earned income will exceed your consumption requirements, and you should begin to store income for future use.

STORING THE INCOME FLOW

If you can plan your income, direct your income, and supplement your earned income with borrowed income, at some time in your life surely you can expect to store some of your income in the form of tangible and financial assets. However, this is by no means as easy as it sounds. If you are a typical high school graduate, or even college graduate, you will have almost no assets; perhaps a stereo, a fairly weathered vehicle, and a reasonably good graduation watch. As for financial assets, you may have a small sum of cash, perhaps a few savings bonds, and maybe some insurance. Your only real asset of significant value, however, is your ability to earn an income. Thus, in the early stages of your productive life, you must be content with less quantity and quality of consumer goods, for example, a low priced or even a used car. As income increases, however, you might expect to satisfy both the quantity and quality of your desires and still have income left over. After reaching your desired standard of living, you might expect to have an adequate saving and investment program without difficulty.

What actually happens may be another matter. As your income increases, your desire for much more may also increase, and your consumption goals, once set, may be reset and again reset on an ever higher standard of living. For example, you may want a new Oldsmobile 98 or even a Cadillac every year. If you are consumption oriented but still want to direct some of your income into a savings-investment program, you must consciously choose to direct it. By so doing, you actually include savings as one of your consumer products, that is, you budget a certain amount of income for saving. It is important, though, that you establish a pattern of saving early. For many people, saving is contrary to their pattern of life. Perhaps for most families, limited income is the only reason for restricting consumption. These families are entirely consumption oriented, and as long as there is any income available, consumption will continue to expand. Indeed, this pattern might even be encouraged by observing that some savings is built into the purchase of any consumer good that is partially durable in nature, such as an automobile. When you buy a car you cannot possibly consume it totally in one year (at least most people cannot). When you buy appliances and furniture, or a home, you do not consume it in one year. On the other hand, you may not pay for an automobile, appliances, furniture, or a home in one year. If you pay for an asset faster than you consume it, you are saving (not consuming) the difference. On the other hand, it is possible for you to pay for a durable consumer product less rapidly than you consume it. In such a case you are not only not saving; you are not even breaking even; you are dissaving. Nevertheless, to the extent that you do not consume as much as you pay over the period of payment, you are indeed saving. For example, say you decide to buy a $4,000 car, use $1,000 of your savings as a down payment, and pay for the car in a two-year period. If the car is worth $2,000 at the end of that two-year period, you have saved $1,000. Instead of having $1,000 in cash, you have $2,000 in the form of a car. You have purchased a $4,000 asset, and consumed half of it in the two-year period. The purchase of any other durable good can be your first saving effort.

Necessary consumption is one reason why initiating a large savings-investment program in the early years of your productive life is neither wise nor necessary. There are simply too many consumption goods that must be acquired in order to equip the average home with the essentials of a desired scale of living. The danger, however, is that once a consumption pattern is established, particularly if it includes only consumption goods, you may find it very difficult not to consume all your income continuously. The personal satisfaction, or the "psychic value," of having a fancy new automobile every year or so, as well as the amounts of money that go into home improvement projects, can indeed consume all the income that you are able to earn. For some people, this is perfectly acceptable, while for others it is not. If you are unhappy about a lack of stored and invested funds you should begin a savings-investment program early in your financial planning. This is very important. In the financial plan presented in Chapter Two, an investment program was initiated at age 25. With only $25 a month, however, a savings-investment program does not add up very rapidly; how can it be all that important? The primary purpose of beginning at age 25 is to firmly establish in your financial planning some income storage in financial assets as part of your consumption pattern.

Looking into your own future, do you see a savings-investment plan? Do you see some specific point toward which you can strive? Remember, without a plan, chance takes over. With such a plan, and specifically with a crucial point built in to your plan, the fact that you are not making especially rapid progress in the earlier years, need not cause you undue alarm because you will know that your long-range plan calls for better progress later. If you should find in those earlier years that you have excessive difficulty in storing a very small portion of your income, this should be a sufficient clue that more serious difficulties might arise later. If you see the clue, you can decide to solve the problem before you have reached the crucial point in your long range financial plan. Unless you can find a solution to such a problem, if it should arise—and it has happened to almost everyone—you can never reach your goal of financial security. Actually very few people do; less than 2 percent of the families in this country have as much as $30,000 in debt free assets. If you should select anything approaching the $250,000 investment goal of Seymour Green, it will require considerably more financial management than most people have been able to provide. There is an old saying that might be helpful at this point: "Life is hard by the yard, but by the inch it's a cinch." Persistence generally pays off in most things, but in financial management, it pays off with even greater dividends than most.

INCOME STABILIZATION

As you are reading these words, you may still be in Stage One of your life income pattern. If you are, your income will increase shortly. Very likely, you now anticipate that your earned income will soon be more than adequate to finance your consumption pattern. Unfortunately, this may not be so. Very likely in the years immediately ahead, your desired consumption pattern will force you to supplement your earned income with borrowed funds.

There are two problems that arise in borrowing, however. First, there is the necessity of repayment. Your debts need not be paid off immediately; ultimate repayment can be postponed by borrowing the money to pay off loans as they come due. Your debts may even increase steadily during the early years of Stage Two without undue difficulties if your income also increases at a steady pace. But at some time, debts must be repaid. Repayment of debts can only occur as you save some of your income, i.e., as you use some of your income for a nonconsumption purpose. Consequently, in subsequent years, you cannot use all of the income you might wish for consumption purposes.

A second problem may also arise. It is possible that as your income continues to increase and your borrowing power continues to increase, you will continue to borrow all that you can in order that you may consume all that you can. Thereby, you continue to consume more than you earn. In such an instance, you do indeed have a very real problem— if you want financial security—because continuing to borrow to finance an ever-expanding scale of consumption will eliminate the possibility of a savings-investment program. In such an instance, your whole life is consumption oriented. The only limitation on your consumption is your income, and any increase in income is simply the means to more consumption. Furthermore, your immediate consumption could increase by more than any increase in your immediate income because your larger income could support more debt. You will not be able to invest for the simple reason that you have all your money tied up in debt.

On the other hand, if you view your life income pattern as an entirety with a view toward realistic financial management, you may see your primary borrowing years as the first third or half of Stage Two, and your primary saving years as the last third or half of Stage Two plus Stage Three. With such a long-range viewpoint, you may find your earlier years nonetheless debt-ridden, although considerably less guilt-ridden, simply because you have an overall financial plan. Making the plan work will still require some control of your own emotion and recognition of the potential problems involved, but simply being aware of a breakdown in your saving program in its early stages of your plan may be sufficient to encourage you to find solutions to such a problem if it should arise.

There are still a number of people who are quite opposed to personal debt. Some feel that debt is dangerous, almost cancerous, in that once anyone borrows his first dollar, he is hooked on a habit that he can never break. Indeed, for some people this may be true. Still other people feel that debt in itself is bad. For those who hold this viewpoint, borrowing is unlikely to add very much net satisfaction. Although some additional satisfaction could be gained by transferring excess future income into a painful present with inadequate income, it would be offset by the dissatisfaction of achieving a desired goal through an unacceptable course of action. If you consider borrowing either dangerous or wrong, you may have relatively little choice but to operate on a cash only basis, unless, of course, your feelings toward debt have been based upon a short-range viewpoint or have failed to recognize the true function of borrowing, and can be changed through better perspective. If you are able to acquire a long-range income viewpoint, if you can appreciate the need for adequately directing your income flow over your lifetime, and if you understand borrowing as one function of an overall financial plan that places just as much importance upon a savings program as a borrowing program but at different stages of your income pattern, then you may be better able to see borrowing in its proper perspective, namely, as one means of increasing your total satisfaction through greater stabilization of your income flow.

The plain fact is that for most families, initial incomes are simply inadequate to finance all the consumer goods they need to establish an acceptable scale of living. Similarly, when the necessities of a home are provided, it need not take all the family's current earned income to maintain the given scale of living. If such is the case, more total satisfaction can be achieved through more consumption earlier than through more unincumbered income later. It is possible, of course, to buy only for cash, never on credit; it is also possible to be forever extended. But both of these are extremes, and both are undesirable and unnecessary. They are both ditches on either side of the road. Each ditch has its potential pain period. But there is a road between them that can be driven, a road of stabilized income over time, a road of planned borrowing and planned saving, a road of personal financial management that can lead to personal financial security. This being the case, consider the sources of borrowed funds from which you may choose.

BORROWING CASH INCOME

Debt, like other four-letter words, is not passive. It is as active as a bill collector and as colorful as an irate letter from a pride-injured housewife who has received a bill from an unpaid magazine company. Although certainly a financial term, debt has moral as well as financial implications. For centuries lending was practiced by people held in very low esteem; debtors were jailed, not billed. "Neither a borrower nor a lender be," Shakespeare wrote in *Hamlet,* and for centuries most people agreed that this was good advice.

Although many carry-overs exist from that heritage, borrowing is now more often recognized for what it is and no more. It is the current use of future earnings. Involving more than 70 percent of U.S. families, only a few consider borrowing unethical or immoral. Nearly every kind of business uses and offers some sort of credit; the government recognizes, reinforces, and regulates it; about half of all families think it is a good idea, and no more than a third view consumer debt unfavorably.

The odds overwhelmingly indicate that virtually every young person will borrow shortly after marriage if he has not done so already at that time. With such blessed assurance, assuming you are a young person, you are well advised to familiarize yourself with the vast sea of credit buying before taking the plunge. Although a recent college graduate's credit is good—much better than he probably thinks—he quite likely is not aware of the number of lenders who would be glad to help him when he wishes to borrow. Unfortunately, he may not investigate all these various possibilities until he really needs a loan. If he does not familiarize himself with borrowing and credit plans, he will probably be more emotional and less thoughtful about borrowing, and have considerably more pressure on his decision as a result. This increases the chances that he will be embarrassed or harmed by having to seek a loan because he must do so under financial pressure, or because he is not aware of alternative sources of loan funds, or because he borrows too much or pays too much for the loan. In short, unawareness impairs the good judgment he might normally exercise in other business transactions. A better approach is to learn about and understand the system of borrowing before you are faced with an immediate decision. By establishing your credit and making your contacts before they are needed, you are in a much better position to choose among alternative sources of borrowed funds when you do need them. If you better understand the attitudes of loan officers, the process of borrowing money, the various sources of loans, services offered, requirements and different rates charged, you can apply for a loan calmly, without apology, fear or guilt.

WHY BORROW?

People use credit for many purposes, one of which is to aid their consumption process. They buy goods or services on credit for personal and family consumption on a promise of payment in the future. This can be done because in the future, they expect to earn more and consume less than they earn. When this expectation is valid, it may make very good sense to transfer some of that future earned income into a present consumption pattern through borrowing. For example, your salary upon graduation will not be sufficient to pay for a car, television set, refrigerator, and washing machine the first month or even the first year. Because you probably can expect a fairly rapid improvement in your financial position after college, you can reasonably buy more than current earned income would allow if you borrow from expected future prosperity. If a television set costs $300 and it takes you a year to accumulate that amount of savings, you may either wait a year and pay cash or buy on a one-year installment plan. In this latter case, you can enjoy the set an extra year while you are saving the money. The additional cost of the set for the extra year is the finance charge you pay; it may or may not be quite modest.

Another reason for using credit is convenience. A person doesn't have to wait until he has an available supply of cash. In many stores, a credit purchase is purposefully made easier than a cash purchase because it is to the store's advantage to have credit customers. Not only does the store make a profit on the interest charged on credit accounts, it also avoids many of the problems of bad checks. Consequently, charging is made easy and payment by check is made more difficult. Perhaps some case can also be made for the convenience of writing only one check a month to cover all the purchases charged at a store, as compared to writing many checks for each purchase. And if the bank charges a nickel or dime per check, it may actually be somewhat cheaper not to write so many checks. These reasons are, however, supplementary; the primary reason for borrowing is to shift future earned income into the present to enable one to buy consumption goods now. And borrowing for this reason has greatly increased in popularity and profitability; thus, its growth in the billions of dollars.

WHO NEEDS TO BORROW?

Personal debt has increased more than 600 percent since the end of World War II. Total consumer credit now exceeds $120 billion. Additionally, mortgage debt outstanding on residential property is more than $300 billion. (See Tables 3–1 and 3–2.) Of the $120 billion in total consumer credit, approximately $100 billion consists of installment debt. A great portion of this installment debt is owed by young families who are more prone to incur installment debts than older, more well-established families. Over 60 percent of all spending units whose head is 35 years of age or under have installment debts. These families may owe up to 40 percent of their annual disposable income in installment payments alone. Add to this mortgage or rental payments, and a very significant portion of disposable income is obligated. On the other hand, this should not be too astounding considering the initial cost of setting up a household.

Consider for a moment the merchandise that is purchased through the use of credit. About 50 percent of all families own furniture that is being paid for on installment plans. Furniture stores conduct only about 20 percent of their sales on a cash basis and another 20 percent of their sales on charge accounts. Therefore, about 60 percent of their sales are made on some installment basis. The same thing is true for appliances. Although couples may use coin laundries for a while, many soon buy washing machines for convenience purposes and it may well be cheaper in the long run. Such expenditures for furniture and appliances, however, will often exceed the earned income of the average new family. Only through borrowing can the furniture, the washing machine, the dryer, and perhaps even a dish washer be purchased immediately. When you add a few million automobiles, you have a still larger consumer debt

Table 3-1 Total Consumer Credit (in millions of dollars)

End of Period	Total	Installment					Noninstallment			
		Total	Automobile paper	Other consumer goods paper	Repair and modernization loans[1]	Personal loans	Total	Single payment loans	Charge accounts	Service credit
1939	7,222	4,503	1,497	1,620	298	1,088	2,719	787	1,414	518
1941	9,172	6,085	2,458	1,929	376	1,322	3,087	845	1,645	597
1945	5,665	2,462	455	816	182	1,009	3,203	746	1,612	845
1950	21,471	14,703	6,074	4,799	1,016	2,814	6,768	1,821	3,367	1,580
1955	38,830	28,906	13,460	7,641	1,693	6,112	9,924	3,002	4,795	2,127
1960	56,141	42,968	17,658	11,545	3,148	10,617	13,173	4,507	5,329	3,337
1964	80,268	62,692	24,934	16,333	3,577	17,848	17,576	6,874	6,195	4,507
1965	990,314	71,324	28,619	18,565	3,728	20,412	18,990	7,671	6,430	4,889
1966	97,543	77,539	30,556	20,978	3,818	22,187	20,004	7,972	6,686	5,346
1967	102,132	80,926	30,724	22,395	3,789	24,018	21,206	8,428	6,968	5,810
1968	113,191	89,890	34,130	24,899	3,925	26,936	23,301	9,138	7,755	6,408
1969	122,469	98,169	36,602	27,609	4,040	29,918	24,300	9,096	8,234	6,970
1969—Mar.	111,950	89,672	34,262	24,306	3,874	27,230	22,278	9,139	6,340	6,799
Apr.	113,231	90,663	34,733	24,399	3,903	27,628	22,568	9,216	6,557	6,795
May	114,750	91,813	35,230	24,636	3,964	27,983	22,937	9,218	6,971	6,748
June	115,995	93,087	35,804	24,956	4,022	28,305	22,908	9,227	7,002	6,679
July	116,597	93,833	36,081	25,172	4,039	28,541	22,764	9,120	7,039	6,605
Aug.	117,380	94,732	36,245	25,467	4,063	28,957	22,648	9,073	6,988	6,587
Sept.	118,008	95,356	36,321	25,732	4,096	29,207	22,652	9,075	7,005	6,572
Oct.	118,515	95,850	36,599	25,855	4,084	29,312	22,665	9,025	7,085	6,555
Nov.	119,378	96,478	36,650	26,223	4,076	29,529	22,900	9,000	7,238	6,662
Dec.	122,469	98,169	36,602	27,609	4,040	29,918	24,300	9,096	8,234	6,970
1970—Jan.	121,074	97,402	36,291	27,346	3,991	29,774	23,672	9,092	7,539	7,041
Feb.	120,077	96,892	36,119	26,987	3,970	29,816	23,185	9,074	6,789	7,322
Mar.	119,698	96,662	36,088	26,814	3,951	29,809	23,036	9,054	6,645	7,337

[1]Holdings of financial institutions; holdings of retail outlets are included in "other consumer goods paper."

Note: Consumer credit estimates cover loans to individuals for household, family, and other personal expenditures, except real estate mortgage loans. For back figures and description of the data, see "Consumer Credit," Section 16 (New) of *Supplement to Banking and Monetary Statistics*, 1965, and Dec. 1968 *Bulletin*, pp. 983-1003.

Source: *Federal Reserve Bulletin* (Washington, D.C.: Board of Governors, Federal Reserve System) May 1970, p. A-54.

Table 3-2 Installment Credit (in millions of dollars)

End of Period	Total	Financial Institutions						Retail Outlets		
		Total	Commercial banks	Sales finance cos.	Credit unions	Consumer finance[1]	Other[1]	Total	Automobile dealers[2]	Other retail outlets
1939	4,503	3,065	1,079	1,197	132		657	1,438	123	1,315
1941	6,085	4,480	1,726	1,797	198		759	1,605	188	1,417
1945	2,462	1,776	745	300	102		629	686	28	658
1950	14,703	11,805	5,798	3,711	590	1,286	420	2,898	287	2,611
1955	28,906	24,398	10,601	8,447	1,678	2,623	1,049	4,508	487	4,021
1960	42,968	36,673	16,672	10,763	3,923	3,781	1,534	6,295	359	5,936
1964	62,692	53,898	25,094	13,605	6,340	6,492	2,367	8,794	329	8,465
1965	71,324	61,533	28,962	15,279	7,324	7,329	2,639	9,791	315	9,476
1966	77,539	66,724	31,319	16,697	8,255	7,663	2,790	10,815	277	10,538
1967	80,926	69,490	32,700	16,838	8,972	8,103	2,877	11,436	285	11,151
1968	89,890	77,457	36,952	18,219	10,178	8,913	3,195	12,433	320	12,113
1969	98,169	84,982	40,305	19,798	11,594	9,740	3,545	13,187	336	12,851
1969—Mar.	89,672	78,006	37,257	18,253	10,294	8,927	3,275	11,666	320	11,346
Apr.	90,663	79,062	37,854	18,418	10,508	9,008	3,274	11,601	325	11,276
May	91,813	80,155	38,347	18,636	10,699	9,080	3,393	11,658	329	11,329
June	93,087	81,388	38,916	18,961	10,939	9,146	3,426	11,699	333	11,366
July	93,833	82,130	39,248	19,127	11,054	9,293	3,408	11,703	335	11,368
Aug	94,732	82,910	39,532	19,265	11,220	9,436	3,457	11,822	336	11,486
Sept.	95,356	83,440	39,793	19,360	11,347	9,450	3,490	11,916	336	11,580
Oct.	95,850	83,949	40,006	19,569	11,438	9,436	3,500	11,901	338	11,563
Nov.	96,478	84,301	40,047	19,668	11,491	9,532	3,563	12,177	337	11,840
Dec.	98,169	84,982	40,305	19,798	11,594	9,740	3,545	13,187	336	12,851
1970—Jan.	97,402	84,531	40,144	19,703	11,468	9,683	3,533	12,871	333	12,538
Feb.	96,892	84,393	39,990	19,652	11,459	9,691	3,601	12,499	331	12,168
Mar.	96,662	84,308	39,956	19,586	11,533	9,650	3,583	12,354	331	12,023

[1] Consumer finance companies included with "other" financial institutions until 1950.

[2] Automobile paper only; other installment credit held by automobile dealers is included with "other retail outlets."

Source: *Federal Reserve Bulletin*, May 1970, p. A-54.

figure. Actually, between 30 percent and 40 percent of all consumer debt is assumed for the purpose of buying automobiles. In the last few years about 60 percent of all cars sold has been sold on credit. Not all of it is readily identifiable since some automobiles are purchased with borrowed funds but are not specifically pledged as collateral for the loans. This may well be the case if the loan is from a bank, a savings and loan association, or a credit union. On the other hand, if an automobile is financed through a consumer finance company or sales finance company, the automobile usually serves as collateral. Loans from relatives may not even show up in the total dollar figures.

The point of all this is that a very great many people need to borrow. Consequently, any problem common to so many individuals should command some careful attention. What is an appropriate amount of debt? What are the various sources of the debt, and which are better under what circumstances? What are the various types of the debt? One can borrow money from a disreputable "loan shark" either because he has no other alternative or because he does not know what he is doing. Either one of these is to be avoided if at all possible, and a little preparation, a little investigation, before the funds are needed may be all that is necessary to avoid a considerable pain in the clavicle. Certainly, if as you make your long-range financial plans, you decide to utilize borrowed funds to stabilize your lifetime income flow, you should also decide to learn enough about when and how to borrow those funds to enable you to make intelligent and rational decisions.

HOW MUCH BORROWING IS PLENTY?

Some observers feel that the recent and rapid increase in consumer debt is an irresponsible trend, especially for those in the younger age brackets. As a matter of fact, some young people apparently are willing to incur debt regardless of their incomes and find themselves in serious financial trouble. Consequently, there is rather widespread criticism of the young for their misuse of credit. To some observers, these criticisms are validated further by the fact that installment debt declines with increasing age. Many feel that young people run their financial affairs atrociously, that they are so wrapped up in the rhythm of monthly payments, that they hardly think about the cost of money at all. Yet most of these young people are patriotic, sober members of suburbia, go to church, are salaried members of large organizations, own homes, and nearly one-half have gone to college.

Why do these individuals often find themselves financially overextended? Many consumers cannot resist the temptation of buying when it is so easy to obtain goods through charge accounts or installment contracts. Elaborate displays and extensive advertising do stimulate emotions, and emotional decisions can easily draw people into an overextended credit position. From the merchant's standpoint, this credit ties his customers to the store and helps bring them back, thereby increasing sales volume. When you have accounts in several stores, though, the question must be asked, "Could I pay off all this debt in a relatively short time if I had to?" Or a companion question may be asked, "Do I have a sufficiently large guaranteed income to support all this debt?" If the answer to both these questions is no, perhaps some serious re-evaluation of your financial position and practice is indeed in order.

In most cases personal debt does get out of hand because there has been no real planning to precede it; no guidelines to indicate how much is plenty or too much. There are many yardsticks or variables by which to measure adequate, appropriate, or excessive debt, for example, size of family, assets, income, expenses, age, health, employment. All these different factors have a bearing on the appropriate amount of debt to carry. There are also differences in the type of debt held. Owing $100 a month for two years must be handled differently than a $2,400 single payment loan. For families in the low income groups, it may be inadvisable to accumulate noninstallment debt greater than one week's wages. In middle income brackets, in which college graduates probably fall, much more debt is possible and supportable.

Several plans for measuring appropriate debt may be considered. First, consider, a very simple rule: keep your total personal debt down to 20 percent of your annual take-home salary. For example, assuming a salary of $10,000, the maximum debt should be no more than $2,000. As some debt is repaid or as income increases, new and additional borrowing can occur, but even then only within the prescribed percentage limit. Limiting personal debt in such an arbitrary way has the advantage of establishing a firm rule that could be used in deciding to postpone a purchase that would strain your budget, but it has the disadvantage of substituting a general rule for serious, rational consideration of later problems. If you believe that rules are made to be broken but not too often, or if you have trouble controlling your emotions, then such a percentage limitation might be of some value to you.

Another plan is to calculate the amount you would be able to pay off within one to two years. If your take-home pay is $600 a month, and you could use $60 of that to make payments on what is owed, you could borrow $700 to $1,400 depending on whether you give yourself one year or two years to pay off the loans. A modification of this plan might be an even better one; specifically, you can use "discretionary" income as a basis for measuring maximum appropriate debt. Discretionary income is what is left after spending for food, shelter, and clothing. Perhaps an appropriate debt limit would be to owe no more than half of your discretionary income. If your take-home pay is $7,000, and your spending for the three basic needs is $4,600, you would have $2,400 left for discretionary spending. In such cases, perhaps $1,200 is an appropriate personal debt figure.

Another plan is to relate current debt to future income. In the case of many young people, current earnings are far below any reasonable expectation of future income. In calculating an appropriate debt figure on the basis of future earnings, however, this is no time to be blindly optimistic. Nevertheless, if your present income is $5,000 but your income in the immediate future (next year, for instance) will be $10,000, a 20 percent rule would support a $2,000 debt level without undue difficulty. Furthermore, if the debt can be stretched over a three-, five-, or ten-year repayment period, one of the other plans could permit a considerably larger debt limit than would be supportable on the basis of a low current income figure.

If you have property or financial assets that could be sold if necessary, your debt level can be calculated to take these assets into account. But in most cases, the only asset a young person has is his ability to earn income. Although your financial assets may be sold for cash at almost any time, your ability to earn an income can only be converted into earned income as you continue to work except when you borrow. Then you have transformed some of your future earned income into current cash income in return for a promise to limit your possible consumption level at some future period.

Any or all of these methods of measuring appropriate debt may be applicable, but it may be helpful to consider all of them before determining your attitude toward borrowing. As your debt policy is being determined, it is well to remember that you cannot borrow yourself out of debt, although you can postpone repayment for a time by refinancing. Debts must be repaid sometime. If you have a plan, if you know what you are doing, and if what you are doing is controlled and working well, then you have a satisfactory and satisfying borrowing policy. If you are uncomfortable and dissatisfied with your debt level, your efforts to increase your total satisfaction by transferring some of your future income into the present for current consumption is obviously a failure. In such a case, reduce your debt, widen your smile, and sleep at night.

SOURCES OF LOANS

When you consider how many Americans borrow, it must be obvious that there are many sources of loans. Some sources are so significant that they should be given rather close attention. The four sources that are discussed in this section are: (1) commercial banks, (2) consumer credit companies, (3) savings and loan associations, and (4) credit unions. These institutions are the primary ones to which individuals look for loans, and together they make up the great bulk of personal loans.

COMMERCIAL BANKS

Almost every city or town has a First National Bank or its equivalent. Commercial banks play a very important role in financing our economic activity; in fact, they are the heart of our financial system. These banks accept the deposits of millions of people, governments, and businesses, and make funds available to millions of others through lending and investing. For example, they loan department stores money to finance charge accounts; in addition, banks provide a wide variety of services, perhaps the most important being that of a checking account. Probably the first financial institution of which many people are aware is their local bank.

As of 1970, commercial banks had outstanding loans and investments of well over $400 billion, $300 billion in loans alone. These loans and investments are possible because the banks hold over $400 billion in deposits, of which over $200 billion are demand deposits or checking accounts, and almost $200 billion are time deposits or savings accounts. A demand deposit, or a checking account, is a deposit account held in a commercial bank against which withdrawals can be made upon demand by written statement, or check, to the bank. Money can be withdrawn by means of a check at any time, or on demand, and thus they are called demand deposit. These checking accounts are revolving in nature. There are billions of checks written every year aggregating trillions of dollars in total value.

In addition to checking accounts, most commercial banks accept time deposits or savings accounts. This type of account is considered a long-term account that supposedly will not be used very often. The funds from a savings account cannot be withdrawn by check; and in some such accounts, the depositor is required to carry on his business in person at the bank. Whereas checking accounts pay no interest on the balance, savings accounts are interest-paying accounts, paying perhaps 4 percent, 5 percent, or even more on the balance of the account.

Checking accounts and savings accounts are the primary sources of loan funds for banks. Although there is tremendous banking activity in deposits, checks, and withdrawals, there are also very large balances left with the bank. These deposits are the basis for loans and it is only as bank customers borrow money from the banks that they can earn a profit. In years past, some banks were exceedingly stringent in their credit requirements. In some cases, it almost seemed that only wealthy individuals could borrow money—just those individuals who did not need money. In more recent years, however, commercial banks have been very aggressive in offering loans.

New kinds of loans have been instituted. In particular, considerable emphasis has recently been placed on consumer loans of all kinds. Installment loans are among the more profitable ones that commercial banks make. Since the interest charge is computed on the original amount of the loan, for the entire length of the loan, and yet the loan is actually repaid in installments over a period of months, the real interest rate is about twice the stated rate. For example, a $1,200 loan for a year at 6 percent would cost $72 ($1,200 × .06 = $72). Since an installment loan would be repaid at the rate of $100 per month, after 6 months only $600 is due; after 11 months only $100 is due. Since the interest paid is $72, and the average balance of the loan is about $600, the real interest charge is closer to 12 percent than it is to 6 percent ($600 × .12 = $72). The bank has bookkeeping expenses to cover, of course, and may experience certain other costs as well, but nevertheless, installment loans are a very profitable business for commercial banks. As a result they are very pleased to make them.

CONSUMER CREDIT COMPANIES

The second most important source of consumer loans is the consumer credit companies, that is, the sales finance companies and consumer finance companies. Such firms are especially important as a source of installment credit. Consider the data on Tables 3–2 through 3–5. For

Table 3–3   Installment Credit Held by Commercial Banks (in millions of dollars)

| End of Period | Total | Automobile Paper | | Other Con- sumer Goods Paper | Repair and Mod- erniza- tion Loans | Per- sonal Loans |
		Pur- chased	*Direct*			
1939	1,079	237	178	166	135	363
1941	1,726	447	338	309	161	471
1945	745	66	143	114	110	312
1950	5,798	1,177	1,294	1,456	834	1,037
1955	10,601	3,243	2,062	2,042	1,338	1,916
1960	16,672	5,316	2,820	2,759	2,200	3,577
1964	25,094	8,691	4,734	3,670	2,457	5,542
1965	28,962	10,209	5,659	4,166	2,571	6,357
1966	31,319	11,024	5,956	4,681	2,647	7,011
1967	32,700	10,927	6,267	5,126	2,629	7,751
1968	36,952	12,213	7,105	6,060	2,719	8,855
1969	40,305	12,784	7,620	7,415	2,751	9,735
1969—Mar.	37,257	12,224	7,168	6,188	2,670	9,007
Apr.	37,854	12,388	7,273	6,299	2,690	9,204
May	38,347	12,541	7,367	6,406	2,721	9,312
June	38,916	12,727	7,457	6,557	2,763	9,412
July	39,248	12,814	7,501	6,709	2,780	9,444
Aug.	39,532	12,859	7,513	6,818	2,787	9,555
Sept.	39,793	12,864	7,543	6,929	2,808	9,649
Oct.	40,006	12,914	7,597	7,023	2,798	9,674
Nov.	40,047	12,883	7,618	7,100	2,779	9,667
Dec.	40,305	12,784	7,620	7,415	2,751	9,735
1970—Jan.	40,144	12,664	7,569	7,472	2,714	9,725
Feb.	39,990	12,585	7,533	7,474	2,691	9,707
Mar.	39,956	12,552	7,538	7,476	2,678	9,712

Source:*Federal Reserve Bulletin,* May 1970, p.A-55.

example, commercial banks had total installment loans outstanding of about $40 billion, whereas sales finance companies and consumer finance companies had total installment loans outstanding of about $29 billion. A great many installment plan purchases, those for automobiles and furniture in particular, are sold by a dealer but financed through some consumer credit company. Sometimes the consumer knows about the financing arrangement and sometimes he does not. Some credit companies are subsidiaries of major, national manufacturing and distributing firms, such as General Motors Acceptance Corporation and Sears Roebuck Acceptance Corporation. Other companies, though national in nature, finance sales for dealers and purchases for consumers directly, such as Commercial Credit Corporation and Household Finance Corporation. In addition, there are hundreds of smaller, local finance com-

Table 3–4 Installment Credit Held by Sales Finance Companies (in millions of dollars)

End of Period	Total	Automobile Paper	Other Consumer Goods Paper	Repair and Modernization Loans	Personal Loans
1939	1,197	878	115	148	56
1941	1,797	1,363	167	201	66
1945	300	164	24	58	54
1950	3,711	2,956	532	61	162
1955	8,447	6,905	1,048	28	466
1960	10,763	7,488	2,059	146	1,070
1964	13,605	8,285	3,022	207	2,091
1965	15,279	9,068	3,556	185	2,470
1966	16,697	9,572	4,256	151	2,718
1967	16,838	9,252	4,518	114	2,954
1968	18,219	9,986	4,849	74	3,310
1969	19,798	10,743	5,306	65	3,684
1969—Mar.	18,253	9,988	4,868	70	3,327
Apr.	18,418	10,095	4,896	70	3,357
May	18,636	10,246	4,945	69	3,376
June	18,961	10,440	5,039	70	3,412
July	19,127	10,538	5,088	70	3,431
Aug.	19,265	10,570	5,139	69	3,487
Sept.	19,360	10,557	5,191	69	3,543
Oct.	19,569	10,693	5,227	67	3,582
Nov.	19,668	10,727	5,247	66	3,628
Dec.	19,798	10,743	5,306	65	3,684
1970—Jan.	19,703	10,660	5,310	65	3,668
Feb.	19,652	10,604	5,324	64	3,660
Mar.	19,586	10,575	5,297	64	3,650

Source: *Federal Reserve Bulletin,* May 1970, p. A-55.

panies. Nor are all these installment loans granted for the purpose of making new purchases. Consumers may merely wish a small loan to finance a summer vacation trip, or refinance earlier purchases.

For most people, purchases of automobiles and large furniture items do require financing. Although commercial banks lend money for such purchases, consumer credit companies also provide funding. Commercial bank interest charges on such loans tend to be lower than those of consumer credit companies. The risk to the finance company that such loans will not be repaid on time is greater than the risk to a commercial bank because consumers who can arrange commercial bank loans will usually choose to do so because bank interest rates are less. Since consumer credit companies will grant loans to consumers unable to obtain

Table 3–5   Installment Credit Held by Other Financial Institutions (in millions of dollars)

End of Period	Total	Auto-mobile paper	Other Con-sumer Goods Paper	Repair and Modern-ization loans	Per-sonal Loans
1939	789	81	24	15	669
1941	957	122	36	14	785
1945	731	54	20	14	643
1950	2,296	360	200	121	1,615
1955	5,350	763	530	327	3,730
1960	9,238	1,675	791	802	5,970
1964	15,199	2,895	1,176	913	10,215
1965	17,292	3,368	1,367	972	11,585
1966	18,708	3,727	1,503	1,020	12,458
1967	19,952	3,993	1,600	1,046	13,313
1968	22,286	4,506	1,877	1,132	14,771
1969	24,879	5,119	2,037	1,224	16,499
1969—Mar.	22,496	4,562	1,904	1,134	14,896
Apr.	22,790	4,652	1,928	1,143	15,067
May	23,172	4,747	1,956	1,174	15,295
June	23,511	4,847	1,994	1,189	15,481
July	23,755	4,893	2,007	1,189	15,666
Aug.	24,113	4,967	2,024	1,207	15,915
Sept.	24,287	5,021	2,032	1,219	16,015
Oct.	24,374	5,057	2,042	1,219	16,056
Nov.	24,586	5,085	2,036	1,231	16,234
Dec.	24,879	5,119	2,037	1,224	16,499
1970—Jan.	24,684	5,065	2,026	1,212	16,381
Feb.	24,751	5,066	2,021	1,215	16,449
Mar.	24,766	5,092	2,018	1,209	16,447

Note: Institutions represented are consumer finance companies, credit unions, industrial loan companies, mutual savings banks, savings and loan assns., and other lending institutions holding consumer installment credit.
Source: *Federal Reserve Bulletin*, May 1970, p. A-55.

loans at commercial banks, the likelihood of tardiness and repossession will, of course, be greater. Because of such additional risk and trouble, interest rates must be higher than would be necessary if such losses and troubles could be avoided.

Nevertheless, consumer credit companies should not be confused with such illegal lenders of money as loan sharks. Whereas the consumer credit companies are licensed, regulated lenders, loan sharks are not licensed or regulated. They operate without legal sanction and extort illegal interest rates from borrowers, in many cases through schemes specifically designed to bilk unsuspecting borrowers. State laws vary on legal interest rate maximums, and many consumer credit companies will approach the maximums, whatever they are, even in excess of 25 percent. In some cases, however, loan sharks have been discovered charging several hundred percent per year.

SAVINGS AND LOAN ASSOCIATIONS

Savings and loan associations are the most important single source of home mortgage loans. Of the almost $300 billion in nonfarm residential mortgage loans, savings and loan associations hold about half that total, about three times as much as commercial bank mortgage loans outstanding. As such, savings and loan associations are indeed a significant source of home loan funds.

A savings and loan association is a locally owned and privately managed financial institution that exists to accept deposits or savings accounts from its members, and make long-term loans to them. These associations are one of the most popular types of savings outlets in the United States, and because of their popularity they may be one of the principal sources of home-financing loans. They only accept savings from their depositors; they do not accept checking account funds. They make only long-term loans to purchasers of homes, or to home owners who want to make home improvements, for the purpose of house construction, repair, purchase, or certain other purposes. A primary feature of their loans is the fact that they are amortized over time, i.e., the principal of the loan is reduced regularly, usually monthly, as regular payments are made according to the contract. Consequently, each month a borrower returns a portion of his loan which permits the granting of additional mortgage loans. Only about 7 percent of the savings and loan associations in this country are stock companies. The remaining 93 percent are owned by their depositors, and they distribute their earnings to those who save with them. All those people who save in mutual savings and loan associations are considered shareholders and the board of directors is elected from their ranks. In those states that permit branches, these associations have become very large financial organizations with a large number of depositors. Consequently, they have become a major source of loan funds for home owners.

Savings and loan associations in most cases are not limited by law to any maximum dollar amount they can accept or loan. As in the case of commercial banks, savings and loan associations may require advance notice before a withdrawal request is paid, but this requirement is not normally effective and is not likely to be unless there is some kind of disaster. They pay an insurance premium to the Federal Savings and Loan Insurance Corporation to insure depositors' accounts up to $20,000 against loss. They pay slightly higher interest rates to savers than commercial banks are permitted to pay. Their losses have been extremely small. Consequently savers have deposited almost $50 billion of their savings in such associations to the benefit of potential home owners who could only buy their own homes through the use of borrowed funds.

CREDIT UNIONS

Although commercial banks, consumer credit companies, and savings and loan associations grant the bulk of the formal consumer loans (that is, excluding charge accounts), there are several other sources of loan funds as well. One of the more attractive of these that is available to some borrowers is a credit union. As you may note on Table 3–2, credit unions grant over $11 billion in installment loans alone, not an astronomical figure, but surely a significant one. Not everyone can borrow from a credit union, of course, since all such borrowers must be credit union members in order to save or borrow through them, and not all companies offer such credit union membership. In those instances, however, in which a credit union is available to employees, it often proves to be the most desirable financial institution through which to borrow, since such loans tend to have the lowest available interest rates, even lower than those of commercial banks in many cases. Not all types of loans can be made through the credit union, and in many instances there are maximum loan limitations. But because of the services provided by the credit union, and because of the relatively low interest rate charges, credit union loans are highly recommended in many cases and should not be overlooked in any case in which a borrower can become a member.

TYPES OF LOANS

Regardless of where you borrow money, or what particular type of loan you make, all lenders and all borrowers (hopefully) are concerned that those loans can and will be repaid. It is to the advantage of the lender that loans be repaid since without successful completion of that part of his business he would shortly be out of work. It is also to the advantage of the borrower that his loans and the loans of others be repaid since if they are not and to the extent they are not, future loans will be more difficult to get and interest rates will have to be higher in order to cover those losses. Since denial of a loan is a very serious matter, it is important that you apply for the type of loan that most nearly suits your needs, that you have the financial resources and income to support the loan, and that your residence and employment records will justify the loan. But the most important single factor in borrowing is personal integrity or character, that is, the willingness to meet your financial obligations as they come due or at least as soon as possible. Even if you have a good job, a sumptuous home, and fat wallet, if you are notoriously slow in paying your bills, borrowing will be very difficult. By knowing what types of loans are available, and making certain that you use the types of loans that are most applicable to your needs and repayment abilities, you can go a long way toward assuring yourself of a large and ready supply of credit when you need it. If you use the wrong type of loan for the wrong purpose, or use too many types at any one time, or abuse your creditors, you can find yourself unable to borrow a dime at perhaps a most inconvenient time.

CHARGE ACCOUNTS

A major type of loan that is sometimes not recognized as a loan at all is the charge account. Until recent years, the charge account unlike other debt was a sign of prestige. It was a privilege that was extended only to the world's best customers. Today, charge accounts are at least the option, if not the opiate, of the masses. Over 70 percent of American families have charge accounts. Our whole marketing system revolves around a complex array of charge accounts. Consumers charge purchases to a retail charge account; retailers buy from wholesalers on charge accounts; and wholesalers in turn acquire their merchandise on credit from the manufacturers. Charge accounts exist in the office of every professional man, doctor, dentist, plumber, accountant, and veterinarian alike.

The most common type of charge account is the 30-day account. With such an account, the customer promises to pay for the goods he purchases by the end of the month or at the end of the next month. There is no interest charge on such an account; the cost to the retailer of providing this financial service is included in the purchase price of the merchandise. This is an extremely easy type of credit line to acquire. The store is delighted to open such an account since it often encourages customer loyalty and stimulates per customer sales. By simply asking for such an account, and perhaps filling out a simple application form, you can have a line of credit of several hundred dollars.

Revolving Charge Accounts.   Many stores have attempted to modify the charge account to include a semi-installment plan feature. This has been done to aid those customers who cannot pay their total bills at the end of the normal charge period and to encourage customers to buy more at certain times than their cash or charge account privileges would permit. These revolving charge accounts have still further advantages to the store; since the customer must continue to pay a given amount over a 3-, 6-, or 12-month period, regardless of subsequent purchases, he may be strongly tempted, indeed compelled, to continue to purchase from that store on a charge basis to whatever the extent of his monthly payments. Thus, he is said to have "customer loyalty." He must use some of each month's income to make his monthly payments, but he needs to buy additional items continually: however, he cannot since he is using his cash to make payments. Since he automatically re-acquires more credit as he makes his monthly payments, he does his buying where he can, namely at the store where he has his revolving charge account.

Since these revolving charge accounts have carrying charges or finance charges on the unpaid balances, stores encourage not only increased purchases and continuing purchases, but also make a profit on the financing of those purchases. In most cases, the monthly payment on a revolving charge account is a fraction of the balance, so a customer can pay for almost half of his purchase over a five- or six-month period, and if he has not made additional purchases on the account his payment will be half what it was the first month after his initial purchase. In this way, as the monthly payment continues to decline, the customer could actually pay for a purchase over a several year period rather than in the 10 or 12 months required by the contract. The interest charge is usually 1½ percent per month or more, which is high enough to make this type of financing very attractive to the store. From the customer's point of view, since he finds it much easier to charge items to a revolving account than to have cash to pay for whatever he cares to buy, he is happier with his account than without and therefore willing to pay the additional charges.

CREDIT CARDS

Credit cards are another variation of a charge account, but they are such a large source of credit, they are often considered a type of credit in themselves. In most instances they offer a straight charge account, but recently credit card accounts have been offered with a revolving charge option by commercial banks and other financial institutions. By using a bank charge card, a customer is not bound to any one particular store but may buy at many retail stores using the same credit card and receive only one bill from the bank at the end of the month.

Most special purpose credit cards require no fee so one is able to buy commodities at the same price as with cash and get the advantages of convenience and later billing free. These special purpose cards are distributed in large numbers and with great liberality. The credit investigation required before issuing a general purpose credit card, however, is another matter; it is usually extensive and quite expensive to the company. Consequently, many companies are making it harder to get a credit card with them; they are increasing their rejection rates and requiring higher income levels. This includes such organizations as American Express, Carte Blanche, and Diners Club who also charge yearly membership fees. However, obtaining a special purpose card, such as with a petroleum company, is often easier than opening a charge account or some general purpose card such as bank cards which are also readily available.

Most national credit cards are relatively new. Some charge a membership fee, and also charge the retailer a certain percentage of each sale made with the credit card. These cards, covering a wide range of products and services, are particularly convenient if one is a frequent traveler, but home-bodies also are using them increasingly. Ultimately, the number of credit cards could decline to a few major national, general purpose cards, but in the immediate future the number could multiply.

INSTALLMENT PLANS

Installment plans generally involve higher cost, more durable goods. For a long time only such goods as automobiles, washing machines, television sets, and furniture were purchased on the installment plan. But now soft goods such as clothes are being bought more and more on the installment plan. Twenty percent of all retail sales are made through installment plans. Over 70 percent of the households with heads between the ages of 18 and 34 have installment debt. The use of installment plan buying has greatly facilitated the wide ownership of durable consumer goods. Many consumers who would otherwise be unable to save enough to buy such goods with cash can do so under an installment plan.

There are many important advantages to buying in installments. For instance, you might be unable to buy an automobile that you really need for your work. If you buy the car on an installment plan, you might be able to improve your earning capacity. You also can obtain immediate use of the car with only a minimum down payment. By purchasing the car immediately rather than waiting until you save the cash, you can save the bus fares you would have to pay during the time you would have been saving. It may be more convenient for you to pay over a period of months than in a lump sum. Installment payments may often discipline people in their budgeting. Some people might otherwise waste their money on less durable goods, and the installment payments often force them to develop thrifty habits. If an individual is paying for an item by installments, he may sometimes find the seller more willing to replace or repair defective parts than he would be otherwise. Moreover, an individual has a much longer time to repay the loan with the installment loan than with the charge account. Table 3–6 may be helpful to you in comparing the various features of charge accounts and installment loans.

There are two basic types of installment loans, chattel mortgages and conditional sales. Chattel mortgages are much like regular mortgages.

Table 3–6 Comparison of Charge Accounts and Installment Plans

	Charge Accounts	Installment Plans
Period of payment	Usually paid off within a month.	Paid in monthly payments over a period which may cover several years.
Interest	Interest is seldom charged except on delinquent accounts.	Interest can be quite high and is explained in a contract which the consumer must sign.
Ease of credit	Credit references must be fairly solid. The seller is not charging directly for this service.	Credit is somewhat easier since interest is being charged and because contracts legally bind the buyer.
Continuity	Once the buyer opens the account, he may make as many purchases on it as he wishes.	The buyer must sign a new contract for every item purchased.
Types of accounts	Revolving or 30-day.	Chattel mortgages and conditional sales.

The buyer usually signs a note which is a contract for the amount to be paid. In some states, the seller keeps the legal title to the goods until the last payment is made. If the buyer is unable to make a payment, the seller can repossess the item, even if it is nearly paid for, and sell it to make up the difference in payments owed. In most states, however, the chattel mortgage does not give the item back to the seller in case of default, but the seller is given an equitable interest in the good. This means he can ask the court to sell the goods to make up the difference in payment. For complete protection, a buyer should always be sure he receives all paid notes, that a discharge of a mortgage is recorded at the county courthouse, and that he understands the particular statutes governing chattel mortgages in his state. As a practical matter, very few consumers do any such thing. The primary protection against difficulties of any similar nature is to deal only with reputable dealers.

In some cases, a bailment lease can be used in almost the same way as a chattel mortgage. The seller keeps the title to the good until the final payment is made. The buyer then has to purchase the title for a small price which is usually waived by the seller. Under this arrangement, the payments made on a good until the final payment is made are regarded as a rental charge. If the buyer cannot meet a payment, the seller can legally repossess the good and keep all previous payments. Legally, payments are made for the use of the goods for the period. The bailment lease is seldom used outside of Pennsylvania.

The most common arrangement used by installment buyers is the conditional sales contract. It resembles the terms of the bailment lease but is less harsh on defaulters. Like the bailment lease, the title is kept by the seller and payments are regarded as rent. The defaulter, if he has paid a substantial sum on a good, is entitled to the return of that sum (less the depreciation). The depreciation of the good is usually determined by the cost less the amount obtained from an auction resale.

For example, Mr. Green buys a television for $250. He pays $50 down and is to pay ten installments of $20 each. He pays five installments totalling $100 but then loses his job and misses the sixth payment. The seller repossesses the television and sells it for $175. He then owes Mr. Green $75 out of the $150 he has paid because the down payment, five installment payments, and the resale value add up to $325 or $75 over the original cost. It can be important that Green learn exactly the price at which the television was auctioned since some sharp sellers may "rig" the auction to get a low price for the good in order to keep more of his money. If the television had sold for only $90 at the auction, a judgment could be secured against Green through court action requiring that he pay the $10 difference. In case of any loss, theft, or damage to goods when Green starts paying his installments, the loss falls on him.

Many of the disadvantages and sad stories of installment buying would be done away with if the buyer would take time to understand fully his contract before he signs it. Often he feels embarrassed to take the time to read it all, especially the fine print. If the print is fine, there may be even more reason for the buyer to read it. You can be sure that the seller was not too embarrassed to hire a qualified lawyer to carefully write out the contract. Many contracts contain hidden clauses and waivers of certain legal rights. One's signature should never fall on the dotted line until every blank is filled in. With honest dealers, the worry is removed, but a dishonest dealer can put the buyer into a helpless position so the buyer should not gamble on his character judgment. The courts will back the dishonest dealer.

There are several clauses about which one should be fully aware when signing a contract. The acceleration clause is one such clause. It states that the seller has the right to demand the total amount owed if the buyer misses one payment. For example, Mr. Green buys a car for $1,800 with a down payment of $100 and $50 per month. He is a month late in paying his seventh installment. The seller can then demand the remaining $1,400 on the next installment. If Mr. Green can't pay it, the seller repossesses the car and keeps the $400 already collected. This clause is a tool of unethical sellers who are able to get several owners to pay for the merchandise and still keep it by continual repossession. In many states the seller has the right simply to pick up the merchandise without even notifying the buyer. If the buyer is dishonest, the harsh acceleration clause is necessary, but its terms can be near-tragic for many persons.

The add-on clause is another such clause. These are also called open-end contracts. As with a charge account, these contracts can have a series of purchases added to them. The seller, however, retains the title to all the goods until the final payment is made. For example, Green may buy his $250 television under an open-end contract. If while he is paying this, he buys an $1,800 car, a $75 chair, $35 worth of clothes, his payments could stretch over a four-year period. Then when he has one $25 payment left on the chair and a $35 payment left on the clothes, he might lose his job and miss his last payment. Although he has paid $3,100 and completely paid for the car and television, the seller could repossess everything. Since depreciation of these goods is tremendous in the first years, Green would probably get very little of his $3,100 back.

One other problem clause is the balloon contract. This contract is often looked upon as a technique to make it possible to repossess often or to make exorbitant profits on a good. Mr. Green may be required to make a down payment of only $100 on his car and then pay only $25 a month for 48 months with a $500 payment due on the 49th month. The $25 a month may look quite easy to Mr. Green and it is possible, though hardly likely, that he may not even notice the huge sum due on the final payment. More likely, he may choose not to think about it, but the final payment may force him to refinance two or three times. It is quite possible under this arrangement for Mr. Green to find that after six years he has paid nearly $3,000 on an $1,800 car and still owes from $100 to $200. The balloon contract can mislead the buyer into thinking he can afford something which he really cannot.

The role of the finance company is one that is not usually fully realized. They are highly important financial institutions. One often finds that the installment agreement he signs is not with the automobile dealer at all but with a sales finance company. Sometimes he is told of this arrangement immediately and in other cases he is not. The arrangement is nothing to be alarmed about. In order to have sufficient capital to finance his business, a car dealer may not be, and usually is not, able to wait for installment payments. He simply gains the sales brought by offering credit and is paid by the finance company which takes over collection and receives the interest profit. Finance companies hold over 25 percent of all consumer installment paper outstanding. They hold over half of the automobile paper. Most finance companies offer fair deals and reasonable rates. It is often safer to deal with a finance company than to take a chance on having an unscrupulous dealer.

Finance companies do have problems with installment loans. One of the real problems is that of handling faulty merchandise. It is difficult and inadvisable for a buyer to hold back payments from a finance company when the purchased goods are defective. Many contracts now call for the buyer to settle his claims directly with the seller rather than going through the finance company. This is a definite disadvantage to the installment debtor. Without the threat of nonpayment, he loses much of his bargaining power. More recently, however, some courts have held that finance companies are legitimate places for airing grievances. The most important point is that the installment debtor know who the creditor is and that he know the arrangement of the contract.

SINGLE PAYMENT LOANS   *One Payment at end*

All the previous types of loans have required monthly payments of one kind or another. In addition to such loans, there is also the possibility that sometime you might take a single payment loan of six to 12 months or even longer. Essentially, a loan contract with monthly installments, but with a large balloon installment on the end is a combination installment loan and single payment loan, although monthly payments are being made over the life of the loan. A single payment loan, then, is really a balloon payment installment type loan without the installments. Only one payment for the entire amount of the loan is made at the time the loan is due. Banks are not inclined to make this type of loan to consumers because there is the ever-present problem of repayment on due date, and because real interest rates are higher for installment loans than they are for single payment loans. Nevertheless, commercial banks still make this type of loan occasionally and other financial institutions do so as well. Credit unions, perhaps more frequently than many others, will make this type of loan available to their members. In addition, life insurance companies make this type of loan to policyholders. As a matter of fact, life insurance companies are an especially good source of single payment loans, usually at a quite reasonable interest rate. Although there are some problems involved, particularly problems of urgency, some people use the loan values on their permanent life insurance policies as a primary source of emergency funds.

For individuals with regular incomes who plan to repay their loans out of regular income receipts, a single payment loan can cause a very serious problem upon due date. Just how does one squeeze an extra $1,000 out of a paycheck? On the other hand, there are any number of circumstances in which a single payment loan is highly desirable; and under those circumstances, any number of such loans may be far preferable to the installment types discussed earlier.

COST OF BORROWING

The real cost of borrowing, of course, is the forced reduction in future purchases of consumption goods and investments. However, when most people refer to the cost of borrowing, they usually mean the interest charges and other explicit costs of financing. These costs are indeed significant and worth considering, but one should not forget that the primary purpose of borrowing is to permit the present use of future earning power. This is a two-edged sword. You gain more consumption goods immediately than your current earned income can buy. But you also obligate some of your future earned income to repay your debts, thereby restricting your future freedom of choice. Those loans must be repaid. Consequently, not all of the future income will be available for future discretionary use. The purchases which you cannot make for lack of discretionary income are the real costs of borrowing.

On the other hand, there are also costs involved in not using credit. Since there is no extra cost for buying on a charge account, for example, the buyer is actually saving money when he does not buy with cash. He has the use of that money for the extra time that he is allowed to pay, or—to put it another way—he has the use of the goods for that period of time that would be necessary for him to save enough money to pay for it. The convenience of making a purchase which would be impossible immediately without the advantage of credit is more than worth the cost for many people. Because a person does not have to keep cash constantly available he does not have to anticipate as accurately all his consumption needs. In particular, the convenience and low cost of charge accounts are perhaps their most distinct advantages in their use. In many cases, the retailer finds that his increased volume more than makes up for the cost of selling on credit, and the losses incurred through unpaid charge accounts are quite small indeed.

Credit can also create savings. For example, Mr. Green may need some furniture. The department store at which he regularly trades could be changing its stock and offering its present furniture at a 33 percent discount. But if Mr. Green will not have enough money for the purchase until some two months into the future, he will not be able to buy, even at a discount unless he has a charge account with that store, or a line of credit at his bank, or some other source of credit. By borrowing the money now he might be able to buy $1,200 worth of furniture for only $800, thus saving $400. The interest costs and other charges associated with borrowing for this purchase might very well be considerably less than $400. Even if he extends his repayment program several years into the future, he would save the difference.

For all the convenience of having consumer goods earlier than would be possible on a strictly cash payment basis, there are, of course, some disadvantages and problems involved in credit buying. Some customers are led into buying more than they can afford, and exercise less planning and judgment in the purchases that they make simply because credit buying is so easy. Since they cannot say no to themselves, they need to have some credit manager who will say no for them. It may also be assumed that if all stores offering charge accounts were to cease doing so, overall prices of consumer goods might fall to some extent, since all stores that have charge accounts and accept credit cards do pass those costs on to the consumer. As was indicated earlier, if you go to a restaurant that does accept credit cards, that restaurant is required by the credit card organization to pay 5 percent of the bill; therefore, in a sense, you are paying more for your steak dinner if you pay cash than you would if you use a credit card. But the disadvantages of charge accounts are much like the disadvantages of automobile ownership. Automobiles have a number of problems and dangers, not only in the ownership but also in the operation of the vehicle, but very few people are willing to forego the tremendous opportunities offered by automobiles. Similarly, most people fully recognize that there are costs and dangers involved in credit buying; nevertheless, they decide that the advantages sufficiently overcome the disadvantages to warrant the use of charge accounts, credit cards, installment loans, and what have you. And they are perfectly willing to pay the costs required.

INTEREST RATES

An important provision in any loan contract and one that is seldom fully understood is the interest rate or finance charge. Because of various ways of charging interest, the actual meaning of a carrying charge or an interest rate is not clear. There are several common methods of stating credit charges. One of the most common is by use of the term "6 percent." For many years, 6 percent has implied fairness and reasonableness. Unfortunately, its meaning has been twisted and may be used in any number of situations which range from actual interest rates of 6 to 30 percent. For example, Mr. Green buys a guitar priced at $120. He is to pay 10 percent down or $12 and then pay off the remaining $108 in six monthly payments plus a 6 percent carrying charge of $7.20. When Mr. Green actually examines the terms, however, he finds that he is paying much more than 6 percent. First he is paying 6 percent interest on only a half year loan when interest rates are actually computed on an annual basis. This raises his interest rate charge to 12 percent immediately. Next, although Mr. Green pays $12 right away, he still has to pay the 12 percent on his down payment. Finally, he will owe the $108 only the first month. Each month thereafter he will be paying interest on successively smaller monthly balances. Altogether he finds that instead of paying 6 percent, he is actually paying almost 24 percent.

On such short-term installment plans, one may use the following formula to compute the actual interest rate:

$$A = \frac{2Ni}{L(n + 1)}$$

where A = actual interest rate (in decimal form); N = number of payments which the contract requires in one year; i = interest charged in dollars; L = net amount of the loan; and n = total number of payments to be made. Mr. Green would compute his guitar interest costs as follows:

$$A = \frac{2\ (12)\ (\$7.20)}{\$108\ (6+1)} = \frac{\$172.80}{\$756.00} = 0.2285$$

A equals 0.2285, or an actual interest rate of almost 23 percent.

The same formula can be used when no specific rate is charged for credit. This means the price of credit has already been included in the price of the good. In order to find what the installment plan costs, one would ask how much the good costs on a cash purchase. Then the same formula can be used to compute interest.

For example, Mr. Green buys $79 worth of sporting goods for $9 down and $10 a month for seven months. He finds that he can buy his goods for $7 less with cash.

$$A = \frac{2\ (12)\ (\$7)}{\$63\ (7+1)} = \frac{\$168}{\$504} = .3333$$

A equals .3333, or an actual interest rate of 33⅓ percent.

Still other loans are made by adding a flat dollar charge as a carrying charge. For example, Mr. Green buys a stereo console for $250. He pays $50 down and agrees to pay installments of $10 a month for 20 months and a $21 service charge for the privilege of taking 20 months to pay.

$$A = \frac{2\ (12)\ (\$21)}{\$200\ (20+1)} = \frac{\$504}{\$4200} = .12$$

A equals .12, or an actual interest rate of 12 percent.

It is important to understand what the cover charge actually covers when considering the interest rate. It pays for more than mere use of money; it also pays for collection costs, bookkeeping expenses, reconditioning, the expense of making a credit investigation, the possibility of the cost of repossession. Also, the losses resulting from bad debts which occur on installment accounts must be covered in this charge. The seller often passes on still other costs to the consumer, for example, fire and theft insurance premiums. Some of the costs such as bookkeeping are just as high on a seven dollar shirt as on a $300 washing machine. Therefore, the interest rate may be higher on less expensive goods. The ease of buying a $120 article for 10 percent down and $19.08 per month may be well worth the cover charge of $7.20 to many persons; in other cases, alternative and cheaper sources of loans should be investigated.

The 1968 truth-in-lending laws require sellers to list the actual interest charge per year on all loan contracts which have carrying charges or interest. Consumers can be fairly sure that these will always be listed. The above methods of computing interest can be used if the interest is not listed or to check the accuracy of the interest figure listed and the actual cost of a purchase. Since the advantages of installment buying are so great, most people do borrow for such purposes. The important thing is to understand what one is paying for these advantages and whether it is worth the money. If interest costs are too great from one loan source, simply check out the alternative sources available.

OTHER COSTS

In addition to the interest or finance charges, there also may be legal fees, investigation fees, and insurance charges that are required when buying certain goods on credit. In some instances, these costs are quite heavy; in others, they may be waived for qualified borrowers. In the case of some loans, these costs are quite necessary for the lender to be able to loan funds at the particular interest rate he is charging, and they can be a sizable percentage of the funds borrowed. For example, at least one young man in this country tried to borrow $100 in order to enable him to buy a $200 car. But the lender would have required him to buy additional automobile insurance costing $100 annually. Although he was indeed getting additional insurance coverage, the point is that the insurance premium was a necessary additional cost of borrowing and was indeed a significant percentage of the loan. Although these other costs can be very large in the case of some loans, they usually are not. For the sake of those few instances in which they are large and avoidable, the borrower is well advised to check on such other costs, ask that they be waived when such a request is appropriate, and investigate alternative sources of loan funds when he feels that such costs are exorbitant.

SAVING CASH INCOME - not consuming

As has already been stressed throughout this chapter, borrowed funds must be repaid. What has not been emphasized quite as much is the fact that repayment in itself is saving; that is, saving is income that is not consumed. If you have $10,000 in a given year available for consumption expenditures and use $3,000 of that income to pay off previously incurred debts, in a sense, you are saving $3,000 in that year. This is simply the other side of borrowing. When you have a $10,000 income and you buy $13,000 worth of goods, you must borrow the extra $3,000 in order to finance your consumption expenditures. You make no progress in saving, however, if in a given year you have a $10,000 income, make $3,000 worth of payments, and still consume $10,000 worth of goods because you are merely increasing your debts as fast as you are paying them off. In effect, your debt position remains unchanged as the result of the year's financial activities.

At some time in Stage Two of your life income pattern, you should reach the point where consumer needs are not quite as pressing as they were. At this point your debt would be increasing less rapidly; as you continue through Stage Two, you finally come to the point where you are not increasing your consumer debt at all. Following that point, you should be reducing your net debt position as your savings increase faster than your borrowing, if indeed your borrowing is increasing at all. This does not mean that your total debt will be eliminated, but serious consideration should be given to eliminating the more expensive types of loans that you have had. If you can earn 6 percent on your money in a savings account but some of your debts are costing you 20 percent in interest charges, you might well prefer to use those savings to pay off those particular debts. In the case of other types of loans that you have primarily for convenience purposes, such as credit cards and charge accounts, they may have no separate interest costs and you may well continue to borrow for a few weeks at a time indefinitely.

There are some advantages to establishing savings accounts of various kinds for emergency fund purposes even before you repay your more expensive loans completely. There are also some advantages in initiating a savings-investment program before you repay all your installment consumer loans. As you proceed through Stage Two of your life income pattern, however, your objective should be to maintain sufficient control of your consumption expenditures to permit you to improve your net financial position to the break-even point, that is, that point where you have as much savings as debts. Thereafter, your objective would be to increase your net savings and investments in accordance with your financial plan. Several of the methods of handling savings are discussed at length in Chapter Thirteen. In Chapter Four, the problem of controlling expenditures is treated.

SUMMARY

In this chapter, primary emphasis was placed upon managing cash income over a lifetime. Considerable attention was given to the life income pattern, and the need for directing, storing, and stabilizing income. Since early in an individual's career, his consumer needs considerably exceed his ability to earn income, he must supplement his earned income with borrowed funds. Various sources of loans and types of loans are available, and attached to these loans are various direct and indirect costs and benefits. Reference was made throughout the chapter to the necessity of debt repayment. Placed in perspective, borrowing can be a most salutary measure; but without such perspective, unplanned or excessive borrowing can lead straight to the morass of personal bankruptcy. Responsible personal financial management requires such perspective, and the comments made in the next chapters should help to provide that perspective.

Case Problems

1. Waldo and Mary Lou Rogers have a major financial decision to make. They have spent several weeks shopping for a new car and have finally decided on Brand X, which will cost them $2,500. They can afford to pay $500 down, and must finance the balance. Mary Lou is urging Waldo to finance the car through a local finance company since it would be easier and require less time; thus they could get the car more quickly. However, Waldo insists that consideration should be given to all possible loan sources. List three or four other loan sources, and discuss their advantages and drawbacks.

2. Joe Martin has been out of school for several years. Just after he married, he accumulated quite a few debts. Because of poor planning he had several items repossessed. His credit rating, of course, was low when he finally went to a finance company for help. Now, after five years of paying the finance company, he is out of debt. Joe has learned a lesson, he feels, and is now going to be a better planner. Joe realizes he must have an itemized list of his flow of income to plan effectively. He now makes $8,000 per year so he assumes he will make $8,000 a year indefinitely. Do you agree with Joe's reasoning? Why or why not?

3. Gene and Cathy are newlyweds. They are very happy, at least most of the time. It seems that every time Cathy wants to buy some furniture or talks about buying a house, Gene says that they can't afford it. Cathy is upset because she can't understand why. She knows that Gene makes a good salary, at least as much as her friends' husbands make, yet they are able to buy the things that she wants. The problem is that Gene refuses to borrow money or use any form of credit. He believes that one shouldn't buy anything unless he can pay for all of it. Analyze Gene's thinking.

4. Joe Fish is an avid hunter, and he has decided to buy a new rifle. The model he wants, a 30–40 calibre Kraig, is available at two gun shops. Shop A will sell the rifle for $200 on credit terms. He must pay $50 down and the balance in 10 monthly payments of $15, plus an 8 percent service charge of $16. Shop B offers the same gun for $190 with credit terms of $40 down and monthly payments of $30 for 5 months, plus a 6 percent service charge of $12. Which shop would you recommend and why?

5. Last June, Farmbelt University graduated 3,000 people. Among them was George Nelson, a young accountant. Because he is bright and has a good personality he was able to land a $1,000 a month job with a large CPA firm. Presently George spends about $50 a week for food and entertainment. His rent is about $200 per month. George also spends about $600 a year for clothes. What is an appropriate personal debt figure for Mr. Nelson?

6. Seymour Green has just bought a beautiful new stereo entertainment center. Seymour purchased the center on an installment basis. Seymour, being rather impulsive, signed the contract not realizing the cost or the actual interest rate. After he got home, he decided to look at the contract

to find out these items, but he couldn't find the contract. All he remembered was that the salesman told him that the stated interest rate was 6 percent, and that the total interest would be $120. Can you figure out the cost and the actual interest rate? If you can and you should be able to, what are they?

7. John Booth earns $800 a month selling cars. He has the following expenses: $20 a week for food, $150 a month for rent, and about $50 a month for clothes and miscellaneous. In addition John pays a car payment of $75 a month, and $50 a month for a home entertainment system. He owes a balance of $2,000 on his car and $250 for the entertainment system. Evaluate John's personal debt and financial situation.

8. Mr. White bought a stereo for $350 on a conditional sales contract. He paid $50 down and agreed to make payments of $25 a month for one year. However, Mr. White ran into trouble. While on a skiing trip in Colorado, he broke his leg and wasn't able to work. As a result he defaulted on the stereo after six payments. The seller, We Take Em Back, Inc., repossessed the stereo and resold it for $300. Mr. White felt that he should have received some money back, so he decided to go to a lawyer for advice. If you were the lawyer, what would you tell Mr. White? If you feel he is entitled to some payment, how much?

9. We Take Em Back, Inc. has sold a number of items to Joe Jobless over a three-year period. The list of items sold includes a stereo for $350, an automobile for $2,000, and $650 worth of clothes. The sales were made under an open-end installment contract. After paying in $2,700, poor Joe lost his job because the factory where he worked closed and moved south. Needless to say, Joe defaulted on the contract and the goods were repossessed and sold. The stereo sold for $200, the car for $900 and the clothes for $75. How much money, if any, is Mr. Jobless entitled to? What did it cost him for the use of the car, stereo, and clothes over the three years?

10. Dr. Stone teaches a personal finance course at Goodwater University. He has been very busy this semester. He is writing a textbook along with all his other duties. Professors are only human, and like students, they too relax occasionally. During the last week of the semester Dr. Stone had to write a final exam for his class. About this time he was tired of writing questions. So he gave his students the following answer for their final and asked them to write a question to fit the answer. The answer is below:

$$A = \frac{2(12) \; (\$50)}{800 \; (9 + 1)}$$

Write a problem that this formula answers.

11. Greg Newman has just been hired by a large department store as a salesman. He will sell furniture and appliances. Greg knows quite a bit about the merchandise, and he is quite confident that he will be a knowledgeable salesman. Whenever a customer has a question, he wants to be able to answer it. After his first two days on the job, however, Greg is disappointed. Many customers have been asking him questions about dif-

ferent methods of financing, and Greg doesn't know very much about it. So he decides to ask some questions about different financing methods. Greg is particularly interested in the difference between charge accounts and installment plans. What are the differences?

Selected Readings

Basic Principles in Family Money and Credit Management. Washington D.C.: National Consumer Finance Association.

Bowman, N. H. "Meeting Truth in Lending Head-On." *Burroughs Clearing House,* October 1969.

Cohen, Jerome B., and Hanson, Arthur W. *Personal Finance.* 3rd edition. Homewood, Illinois: Richard D. Irwin, 1964, Chapter 2.

Curran, B. A., and Fand, D. I. *An Analysis of the Uniform Consumer Credit Code.* Research contribution of the American Bar Foundation, 1970.

Dolphin, R. J. Jr. *Self-Correcting Problems in Personal Finance.* Boston, Mass.: Allyn & Bacon, 1970, Chapter 4.

Donaldson, E. F., and Pfahl, J. W. *Personal Finance.* 3rd edition. New York: Ronald Press Company, 1966. Chapter 2.

Federal Reserve Bank of San Francisco. "Credit and Credit Cards." Free copy available by writing to the Bank, 400 Sansome Street, San Francisco.

Growth in Importance of the Credit Function. Dun and Bradstreet, Inc. A free copy is available by writing to Dun and Bradstreet, 99 Church Street, N.Y., N.Y.

"How Families Fight Inflation." *U.S. News and World Report,* February 16, 1969.

"Income of Families and Persons in the United States." *Current Population Reports.* Washington, D.C.: U.S. Department of Commerce. Latest year.

Kirk, J. "Some Bankers Get a Charge Out of Giving All the Credit." *Banking,* December 1969.

Lindberg, P. "Ten Most Misunderstood Points About Borrowing Money." *Better Homes and Gardens,* August 1969.

Making the Most of Your Money. New York: Educational Division, Institute of Life Insurance.

Margolius, Sidney. *Family Money Problems.* Public Affairs Pamphlet #412. New York: Public Affairs Committee, 481 Park Avenue, N.Y., N.Y.

Mathews, H. Lee. *Causes of Personal Bankruptcies.* Columbus: Bureau of Business Research, University of Ohio.

Nadler, P. S. "Bank Credit Cards in the 1970's." *Banking,* September 1969.

"Need Money." *Credit Union Magazine,* October 1969.

"The Family That Does Not Save." *Business and Economic Dimensions,* July 1969.

"Truth in Lending Changes Coming for Debtors, Creditors." *U.S. News and World Report,* May 27, 1968.

Unger, Maurice A., and Wolf, Harold A. *Personal Finance,* 2nd edition. Boston, Mass.: Allyn and Bacon, Inc., 1970. Chapters 2, 3, 4 and 5.

U.S. Chamber of Commerce. *Money and Finance,* Washington, D.C.: U.S. Government Printing Office. Free copies available.

Wilcox, M. C. "Installment Finance and the Banks." *Banker,* August 1969.

"Your Bank: How to Choose It, How to Use It." *Changing Times, The Kiplinger Magazine,* April 1965.

Your Driving Costs. American Automobile Association, 1712 G Street, N.W., Washington, D.C.

CHAPTER FOUR

CONTROLLING EXPENDITURES

After planning and providing income, the third step in any successful financial management effort is the controlling of expenditures. Every individual and every organization has difficulty with this particular financial function. Controlling expenditures may be an especially serious problem for individuals who have relatively high income expectations and material aspirations but have only modest earned incomes in the present. They rub elbows rather continuously with friends and neighbors who may be just slightly ahead of them in their consumption patterns; they know that a more satisfying scale of living exists than the one they now have, and they have every reason to believe that they will have sufficient incomes in the future to support that higher scale of living. Furthermore, for a great many middle-income families in this country, their entire orientation has been toward consumption. As a matter of fact, lack of income has probably been the only limitation on their consumption patterns in the past. For such individuals, loans are readily available. With the expectation of greater incomes in the future, and with many sources of loans available to them, families may find their spending habits out of hand. More than in any other phase of personal financial management, controlling expenditures may be the source of greatest stress and pain. For all the above reasons and perhaps many others as well, some considerable attention should be spent on the techniques and methods of controlling expenses.

EXPENDITURE PLANNING

For some strange reason, a great many people feel hesitant about planning their expenditures although they feel little or no such hesitancy about planning their incomes. In fact most people give considerable thought to salary increases, alternative job opportunities, and other ways of increasing their incomes. Although union members are somewhat more visible aspirants of higher salaries, they are not the only ones who try to increase their incomes through bargaining; a good many employees and professional people belong to organizations and professional groups that exist for the purpose of increasing their members' income. Although income is rather personal, most people are quite curious about the incomes of other people, and make rather extensive effort to determine and compare the relative incomes of friends and associates. In part, of course, this effort can be explained on the basis of idle curiosity; it may also be explained as a further indication of our competitive natures; it may also be an indication of the degree to which we judge our success on the basis of income. To some extent, one's income does indicate the value that society places on his contribution to the total national product. On the other hand, just because other people judge our worth to them on the basis of our contribution or service to them, this is no reason for using this single determinant as the basis of evaluating ourselves. Income is indeed worth planning; but expenditures should be planned, too. Very often, they are not.

Just exactly why expenditures are not planned is very difficult to explain. Especially in a society composed of people who are so oriented toward consumption, one would expect some serious and careful thought about expenditure planning. Of course, it is possible to explain people's disinclination toward saving on the basis of their consumption orientation; they do not save because they want to spend all their income. However, this does not explain why people are so disinclined to plan and control any of their expenditures. It would seem logical that a highly consumption-oriented people would be especially inclined toward consuming specific items on some sort of priority scale and would therefore try to exercise considerable control over their expenditures for low priority items. However, most people seem relatively unconcerned about controlling their expenditures. Although they can have so much more control over their expenditures than they can their incomes, their attentions are still far more directed toward income planning than expenditure planning. Occasionally, income planning can be especially beneficial in improving one's financial position, but a great deal of income planning, if you want to call it that, results in merely a large expenditure of time and energy with relatively little hope of changing income at all. On the other hand, with a relatively small amount of time and energy expended in an effort to control expenditures, considerable impact can be made upon one's expenditure pattern.

Through an understanding of one's probable life expenditure pattern, the need for expenditure controls, and the methods of controlling expenditures, anyone can considerably improve his chances of achieving long-run financial security. Considering how much we are all inclined toward consumption, and yet at the same time assuming that we are all vitally concerned with achieving financial security, your serious efforts to control your expenditures must be viewed as an absolute necessity. Without sufficient control over your expenditures, your life will be characterized by financial uncertainty. With sufficient control over your expenditures, you can make regular and sustained progress toward your predetermined financial goals and can experience considerable pride and satisfaction throughout your efforts. Such control is by no means easy; it is a real challenge. If it were easy, everyone would be doing it. Relatively few people, if any, would purposefully choose uncertainty over certainty, or crisis over financial security. Yet a great many people do live lives of uncertainty and crisis. You do not have to be one of them. Controlling your expenditures can make all the difference. With even excessive income but with inadequate controls, financial security is impossible. But with only modest income and sufficient controls, financial certainty can be greatly facilitated, and the chances of achieving financial security can be greatly enhanced. For most effective results, income planning and expenditure planning must go hand in hand. Either one without the other may be of some help, of course, but since each one depends upon the other, each one can be more effective if both are used together.

THE LIFE EXPENDITURE PATTERN

Just as there is a life income pattern, so also there is a life expenditure pattern. As you may note in Figure 4–1, the life expenditure pattern can be divided into three stages, somewhat comparable to the three stages of the life income pattern introduced in Chapter Three. Stage One, which

Figure 4–1   The Life Expenditure Pattern

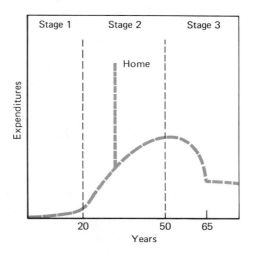

lasts to around age 20, is a period in which relatively little consumption spending occurs at the discretion of the individual. During this period, a great deal of consumption spending may occur for him by his parents, but most of his consumption is not at his sole discretion for about the first 15 years of his life. Then there is a general increase in the expenditure level, with a dramatic rise when he establishes a home of his own, marking the beginning of Stage Two. At some time around 20 years of age, he usually does establish a family and home of his own, and expenditures in the early years of Stage Two will exceed income markedly. At somewhere around age 30, he usually will buy a home which, in that one year, doubles, triples, or perhaps even quadruples his average annual expenditures. Expenditures generally rise through Stage Two, but at a decreasing rate. In Stage Three expenditures begin to decline, and after age 65 the decline may be very serious indeed if retirement income is significantly less than the income received during Stage Two.

To relate the life expenditure pattern to the life income pattern, consider Figure 4–2. Note particularly the light area which indicates net borrowing and the dark area which indicates net saving. Through such a comparison, it is evident that there is no way to finance the desired consumption pattern through earned income, but neither is there any particular need to do so. Since the total savings area at the last half of Stages Two and Three exceeds the total borrowing area in Stage Two, there will be more than enough earned income over the entire lifetime pattern to finance all expenditures. A definite problem does exist, however, because the need for extra expenditures precedes the availability of the extra earned income. This problem is solved through borrowing as was discussed in Chapter Three. If one begins to borrow out of habit

Figure 4–2   Comparison of Life Expenditure and Income Patterns

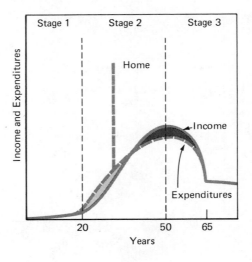

to finance ever-expanding consumer wants, financial security is impossible. If you really want financial security, you must recognize consumer borrowing as no more than a means of solving a temporary shortage of earned income. Borrowing must not be used continually as a means to supplement earned income to finance an ever-increasing consumption pattern. Only by planning your life expenditure pattern in the light of your life income pattern can you plan for financial security. And only by controlling your expenditures can you be sure of paying for what you buy, either when you buy it or through debt repayment, and at the same time be sure of a savings-investment program that can provide an income and expenditure pattern in your later years.

NEED TO CONTROL EXPENDITURES

Perhaps the ultimate need to control expenditures lies in the fact that a great deal of emotional stress and strain must be tolerated when there is no control over spending. Although some authors place a good deal of emphasis upon personal bankruptcy at this juncture, perhaps a million times more emotional pain is experienced by those families that do not undergo personal bankruptcy than by those who do. Furthermore, some families seem to excuse their lack of expenditure controls in the midst of all their emotional stress and strain with the explanation that they are a long, long way from personal bankruptcy, as indeed they are.

For many more people, the need to control expenditures stems from a desire to attain certain financial priorities and objectives. If indeed your personal financial objective is to avoid personal bankruptcy, then controlling your personal expenditures only to the extent that you avoid such personal bankruptcy is indeed sufficient to permit you to reach your objective. For the great majority of people, however, other financial priorities and objectives are far more significant. They want to buy a house, or a better house; they want to buy a new automobile or more clothing; they want to go to school or to Europe; they want to get out of debt or simply have a decent meal at the end of the month; some families want to begin an investment program, or to own a large number of investments.

It is possible, even probable, that all of these objectives cannot be accomplished within any limited time period, if at all. Consequently, there is a real need to establish priorities. For many families, consumer goods are so high on a priority scale that the establishment of a savings-investment program has never reached the top of their priority list, nor will it, nor should it, if present consumption spending is of primary importance to them. In such cases controlling expenditures is only of importance in order to facilitate the consumption spending pattern desired. On the other hand, if your primary long-range financial objective is financial security, then controlling consumption expenditures for the purpose of establishing a vital, meaningful, sustainable financial program is essential. Saving does depend upon income in the sense that no one with an $800 income per month can save $1,000 per month. In a far more significant way, however, saving depends upon temperament and attitude, that is, upon a willingness to save. Saving a great deal may well depend upon a great deal of income; but saving anything at all is far more dependent upon a willingness and a decision to save.

Rather than being so very concerned about exposing and emphasizing the dire consequences of personal bankruptcy, a short look at four of the primary causes of uncontrolled spending may be more valuable. First, there is a very real possibility that the consumer does not control his expenditures because he does not know how. He may not have adequate financial information; he may not know how to use a budget effectively; he may not have a simple, quick, and accessible accounting procedure for providing the kind of information that is necessary to exercise the very control over his expenditures that he would like to have. In many cases when a consumer becomes concerned about providing for himself adequate financial information, he is already in such serious financial trouble that he is likely to establish such an extensive accounting and budgetary system that he could not maintain it for very long. Consequently, he tries it for a month or two, thereafter gives it "a lick and a promise," and concludes that he cannot live within a budget. This is, of course, not true. Everyone lives within a budget, although it may not be a planned budget or a rigid budget, but a budget should not be so planned and so rigid that it does not provide for changing consumer desires. With a very simple cash accounting system that utilizes the checkbook as a primary tool, and a very simple cash budget, considerable information about expenditures can be maintained with perhaps no more than an hour a month. With such a system one can determine exactly how his money is being spent. Assuming he is pleased with his consumption pattern, his record of expenditures will be his budget. On the other hand, if he is displeased with his consumption pattern before or after he sees how his money is being spent, then he may be able to adjust his consumption pattern by limiting certain expenditures.

Since very few people have more money than they can spend, almost any expenditure restricts the decisions to make certain other decisions —that is, if you buy this, you cannot buy that. If you never know exactly how much you are spending, you may for many years have a general sense of dissatisfaction with your consumption pattern without really knowing why you feel the way you do. A little information, or more adequate information, may provide you with exactly what you need to significantly improve the efficiency with which you spend your money.

A second reason for uncontrolled spending is emergencies. All our best laid plans occasionally break down; sometimes only minor emergencies are at fault, but occasionally major emergencies are the cause. Since there is no way to determine when an emergency is about to strike, the only way you can help avoid the financial impact of such emergencies is to assume that they will occur on an irregular basis, and prepare for them by allocating a small portion of your income to an emergency fund. Very often this regular allocation can be in the form of an insurance premium. For example, through the use of insurance policies, hundreds of families that face the possibility of some dire medical emergency can contribute small amounts to one big pool of funds that will be used to cover the financial losses of those few insured families that actually suffer the emergencies. Through insurance, you guarantee yourself a small regular loss as a means of avoiding a large possible loss. Not all emergencies can be handled in this way. However, the same general idea is applied by the individual when he contributes a small regular amount to his own emergency fund not knowing just exactly which one of hundreds of possible emergencies might afflict him but knowing very well that one or another will, given enough time. Although an emergency fund may not be adequate to cover very serious emergencies, the impact of many minor ones can be controlled through such a device. By their very nature, emergencies do not happen very often. If a very serious emergency does occur, there is not really very much you can do to prevent it or to prepare for it. Most people, in fact, handle serious financial difficulties by maintaining a sufficiently flexible consumption pattern to permit some control of expenditures after a disaster.

A third cause of financial difficulties is emotion. Perhaps more than any one other cause, emotional or compulsive buying frustrates any effort to control expenditures. For many people, this is the only way they can enjoy their incomes; their consumption patterns seem to be left completely to whim. And, in fact, there is often a great deal of satisfaction to be gained in spending money for entirely emotional purposes, for doing something you just feel like doing because you feel like doing it. Nor is there anything particularly wrong with such a spending spree if it does not create financial havoc in the process. In some cases, however, it does. Some people just seem to spend their lives staggering from one financial crisis to another, and although they seem at certain times to be enjoying themselves immensely, at other times they seem to be thoroughly miserable. There may be some reason to believe that pleasure is indeed heightened by pain. To the extent that this is true, emotional spending may be the most satisfying way of life. In such case, controlling expenditures is purely and simply a mechanism for reducing satisfaction, and this may explain why some people react to budgets negatively. For other people, although emotional spending does indeed cause more pain after the fact than satisfaction during the spree, they can nevertheless no more control themselves than they can fly. For such people there is no apparent hope.

For still other people the insecurity that accompanies such emotional buying is unsatisfactory. For them financial security is a serious matter, a goal worth pursuing. For such people, there may be considerable emotional satisfaction in the successful pursuit of their goal. They may receive satisfaction not merely by having the goal, they may also receive considerable satisfaction in the pursuit of that goal. Their goal, of course, is financial security. For such families, there are just as many obstacles, and just as many problems, just as many temptations, and just as many unsatisfied consumer wants. Since financial security is fairly high on their priority list, and since they are receiving some satisfaction from gradual but persistent movement toward their goal, their emotional involvement with this part of their consumption pattern may be sufficient to overcome the immediate crying need to buy a new stereo, automobile, sailboat, or nine-foot grand piano.

Complicating one's emotional inclinations to spend beyond his income is the excellent sales performance of the retailers in this country. Their very lives depend upon their abilities to discover latent consumer desires which they can pamper and prod into fully matured needs. Only when the salesman has been able to convince his potential customer that this particular product can provide greater and more lasting personal satisfaction than any other competing product in the world, can he feel the ultimate satisfaction in his work. It is gratifying to watch an effective salesman at work, but it is almost a foregone conclusion when you put an unprepared consumer in the same room with a trained salesman. There is an unverified rumor that one salesman upon the successful completion of his training program was sent to northern Wisconsin to pass his final exam, which consisted of selling two milking machines to a farmer with only one cow and to take the cow as a down payment. (Still less verified is the rumor that he did so successfully.) Although some consumers seem to be rather antagonistic toward the salesman, such a consumer may be implicitly admitting that he is vulnerable.

For those people who respond to the urgings of a salesman, such intangibles as potential emergencies and financial security probably have relatively little hope of achieving a high place on a priority scale. Furthermore, in such cases, adequate financial information will probably provide no more than frustration and guilt, and the consumer might be better off without it. Essentially, the need for control over one's expenditures exists for only those who wish to make sure they are allocating their available funds among all alternative uses in the most appropriate way. Although those families who have no control over their financial affairs do need some help, in another very real sense, they do not really want any help; and for them, considering the various methods of controlling expenditures is probably a waste of time.

METHODS OF CONTROL

There are several ways of controlling expenditures, some of them planned and some unplanned. For some people, the only method of controlling their expenditures is to spend all the money they have available. For some people this means spending all their earned incomes; for still other people it means spending all their earned incomes plus all the money they can borrow. Although neither of these methods can lead to financial security, both methods do in fact control expenditures up to some limit. Everyone has a limit of some kind. The difference is that some people impose a limit on themselves, whereas for others it is imposed by their employers or by their employers and their creditors. With this method of control, however, one can never have a successful savings-investment program.

A slight modification of the above method is to consume to the limit after a previously selected portion of your income has been deposited in a savings account. By deciding that you want to deposit 1 percent, 2 percent, 5 percent, or 10 percent of your income, in a savings account, you actually build your savings-investment contribution into your consumption pattern at the very top of your priority scale. Thereafter, you can buy whatever you care to, without any reservation, to the limit of the remaining funds in your checking account. This method may contribute little or nothing toward greater satisfaction through more appropriate use of consumer expenditures, but it does have the advantage of building a savings program into the consumption pattern.

Still other families have decided that they want to consume a given amount of goods expressed in dollars. By using this limited consumption approach to controlling expenditures, the consumer would presumably buy various necessities with part of that limited consumption fund, and then spend the remainder emotionally on an unplanned basis. With this method, the emphasis is upon limiting consumption, and the satisfaction received is apparently derived through the successful limitation of consumer expenditures no matter which particular consumer goods are purchased. However, limited consumption for its own sake is only marginally attractive at best to a great many people. Far more people are interested in maximizing their consumption rather than limiting it unnecessarily.

Expenditures should be controlled according to planned priorities for the express purpose of maximizing total financial satisfaction. This means the construction of some kind of priority scale, perhaps written, perhaps mental. On that priority scale might be educational expenditures, consumption expenditures for durable and nondurable goods and services, and investment expenditures. Perhaps clothing is the most important expenditure item in your life. If so, all other expenditures than clothing should be controlled as closely as possible in order that all available extra funds can be spent on additional clothing. For some people, an automobile is the most important expenditure item; for others it is a backyard or a cottage on the lake. For a few people, it is an investment program. For whatever purpose, however, expenditures can be controlled. A little financial data may be of considerable help in determining just where the appropriate control is needed, but only by serious effort can a habitual consumption pattern be changed.

USING FINANCIAL RECORDS

Although corporate and government budgets are truly mammoth volumes, financial records do not have to compose some great ominous tome requiring hours or days of compilation and computation. Financial records can be very simple, and many very simple record-keeping systems are very helpful. In this section, four simple financial recording techniques are suggested:

1. A checkbook
2. A monthly detailed budget
3. A monthly summary budget
4. An annual balance sheet

The monthly detailed budget and the monthly summary budget depend upon check stubs to a considerable extent as a source of data. The balance sheet is less dependent upon check stubs but quite dependent upon budgets. Preparation of these financial records should take no more than an hour or so a month, and a few extra hours once a year, assuming that you already have a checking account and use checks to pay some of your bills. You have no guarantees that by using these financial records you will have fewer financial problems, but having some plans and records will aid you in your problem-solving effort. The simple fact that you spend some time dealing with your financial records will make you more aware of when and how much your future expenses will be. It is also important to remember that the purpose of controlling expenses is not to reduce total satisfaction but to increase it as you realize real progress toward your goal of financial security.

As a rather homely analogy, consider the need to consult a road map occasionally during an automobile trip to some place you are going for the first time. Most of the time, you only need to consult the signs along the highway, but occasionally a road map can be of some value. Similarly, a budget is a device designed to help you arrive at your chosen destination. Neither the road map nor the budget will guarantee that you will wind up at your destination. You might ignore or lose your map but you might also decide somewhere along the way that you didn't really want to go there after all. Perhaps you are so emotionally attached to all your old friends back home that you just have to turn around and return to your old stomping grounds. Some people simply would not be happy with financial security if they ever achieved it. Their pain at the end of the month seems to enhance their pleasure at the first of the month. The tension and excitement associated with living at the ragged edge of solvency seem essential to their happiness and self image. Nonetheless, there are many people who would gladly trade their financial uncertainty for some security. If you are such a person, the four record-keeping techniques are worth your careful attention. They could make all the difference between financial uncertainty and success.

CHECK STUBS

A checking account is of great importance to anyone trying to control his expenditures because check stubs provide a primary source of financial information. Without check stubs it is considerably more inconvenient to determine just what expenditures have been made. It can be done, of course, by keeping a pocket diary on spending, but since checks are often used for other reasons they can also serve as a primary record-keeping mechanism. Without some technique for obtaining information on what expenditures have been made, it is almost impossible to estimate a realistic budget. Even the laziest people have a technique for obtaining information on expenditures—their memories (faulty though they may be). However, the point is that with just a little sophistication and effort in record-keeping, a budget can be more realistic and effective. Without a realistic budget, the whole process of keeping records becomes an academic exercise totally unrelated to real problems. On the other hand, with a record of expenditures, it is possible to determine from month to month whether or not budget estimates are too high or low and need appropriate adjustments. Such monthly evaluations provide a guide to how much progress is actually being made.

There is by no means any reason to write a check for everything, any more than there is reason for keeping a record of all expenditures. For many purchases, however, records are already being kept for tax purposes. The simplest record system is a monthly deposit of all income, and a check drawn for that entire amount. For example, one deposit for $800, and one check for $800. This is the simplest but by no means the most helpful record. You could construct the world's simplest budget, as depicted in Table 4–1, with only a total income figure and total outgo figure. Although this is a very simple budget, it is not very helpful either. If a budget is to be of some value, it must be neither too simple nor too complicated. With too few check

Table 4–1 World's Simplest Budget

Income	$800
Outgo	$800
Balance	0

stubs, your system will be insufficient. If the number of check stubs is too large, you simply waste your time with arithmetic puzzles that provide very little useful direction, and your system will be impossible or impractical to maintain.

Whatever you use initially, however, will probably require some adjustment, and it is perhaps better to begin with a system that is too simple but can be readily sustained, rather than one that is too complicated and might be discontinued. Perhaps only a few summary figures would be enough for some people. For others, more detailed information would be more helpful. In either instance, the important point is that your check stubs can provide a useful record of expenditures.

MONTHLY DETAILED BUDGET

By grouping your estimated expenditures into broad categories, you have prepared a budget. To be realistic, the estimates should be based on some experience, and to be helpful, they should provide some detail. Nevertheless, any estimate of income and expenditures is a budget. For example, consider the budget in Table 4–2. This is the first budget of Seymour Green. Through this budget, Mr. Green indicates that he is

Table 4–2   Mr. Seymour Green's First Budget

Food and Sundries	**$200**
Home	200
Clothing	100
Car	100
Other	200
TOTAL	**$800**

willing to spend a total of $800 a month. He further indicates that food and related items are of sufficient importance to him to warrant $200 a month. He is willing to spend $200 a month on his home. He wants to spend $100 on clothing, and $100 on his car each month. The remaining $200 will go for other items, and hopefully this includes a savings figure.

This is not a very precise budget, but in his own mind, Mr. Green knows the breakdown. He knows, for example, that his house rent costs him $120, utilities cost him about $50, with telephone and water about $10 each, and gas and electricity about $15 each. He knows his furniture costs him $30 each month. Under clothing, he knows that he does not spend exactly $100 each month on clothing, but he does pay $50 on his

Sears Revolving Charge Account each month, and about $50 on a Penney's Charge Account, so that his cash outlay is about $100 each month. He knows that his car payment to the First National Bank is $80, and that his gas costs him about $20 a month. Furthermore he has some idea of what his other expenditures include. He has insurance premiums to pay; he makes regular charitable contributions; he has periodic visits to a local dentist; he is saving a little money for his summer vacation; he plays an occasional round of golf, buys lunch each day, and pays for those perpetual piano lessons. Once in a while he even puts a few dollars in a savings and loan account. It is important to point out the relationship between Mr. Green's budget and the source of his financial data. He knows how much his expenses are because he has some technique for obtaining financial information, either his memory or hopefully his check stubs.

Another way to set up the same budget is presented in Table 4–3. With this budget, Mr. Green indicates more precisely how much of his total monthly expenditures are fixed in nature, and how much flexibility he has after his fixed payments are made. For many families, there is remarkably little flexibility in their consumption patterns. Month after month, about the same amounts are spent for the same items. Some

Table 4–3   Mr. Seymour Green's Second Budget

Food and Sundries		$200
Rent		120
Utilities:		
Telephone	$ 10	
Electricity	15	
Gas	15	
Water and Garbage	10	
	——	50
Gasoline		20
Payments:		
Sears	50	
Penney's	50	
Discount Furniture	30	
First National Bank	80	
	——	210
Other:		
Savings	25	
Insurance Premiums	50	
Piano Lessons	15	
Miscellaneous	110	200
	——	——
TOTAL		$800

items, of course, are bunched into one month more than another, such as school clothes, insurance premiums or taxes. But many are quite predictable, monthly or yearly. For this reason, the most realistic way to estimate your future expenditures is to use an average of what you actually spent for the last six or 12 months as indicated by your check stubs. By forecasting six or 12 months into the future what you expect to spend, you have a series of measures or benchmarks against which you may compare your actual expenditures as the months go by; that is, at the end of each month, you can transfer from your check stubs to your budget exactly how much you spent during that month and see how close it is to your estimated or budgeted expenditure figure.

For example, consider Table 4–4. Mr. Green's actual expenditures in January might have been as follows: food, $200; rent, $120; utilities, $46; gas, $19; payments, $210; and other, $190; for a total of $785. As he writes his checks at the beginning of each month, he can enter his actual expenditures in the appropriate monthly column beside the appropriate budget estimate. Thereby, he can compare the amounts to see

Table 4–4   Mr. Seymour Green's Monthly Detailed Budget

	Budget		Actual			
			January		February	
Food and Sundries		$200		$200		$200
Rent		120		120		120
Utilities:						
Telephone	10		12		18	
Electricity	15		5		5	
Gas	15		21		25	
Water and Garbage	10	50	8	46	8	56
Gasoline		20		19		22
Payments:						
Sears	50		50		50	
Penney's	50		50		69	
Discount Furniture	30		30		30	
First National Bank	80	210	80	210	80	229
Other:						
Savings	25		0		25	
Insurance Premiums	50		42		30	
Piano Lessons	15		15		15	
Miscellaneous	110	200	133	190	142	212
TOTAL		$800		$785		$839

whether his budget estimate is accurate, too large, or too small. He can also use his monthly detailed budget sheet to make sure he has written all the checks he should, thereby avoid any unintentional error. As he sees certain actual expenditures exceeding his budget estimates repeatedly, he can make appropriate changes in his budget. And when certain expenditures show up regularly in his "other" category, he may wish to identify them specifically in his budget. If he finds his total expenditures exceed his total budget estimate several months in a row, he may need to reduce some part of his consumption pattern or increase his cash income. For example, Mr. Green's February estimate did not include those unpaid Christmas bills he piled up a couple of months ago. As a result, he ends February with a much reduced balance causing him to exceed his budget estimate considerably.

Several adjustments can be made if he knows what he wants to happen, what is actually happening, and what alternatives are available. Without such information, however, he could find himself in rather serious financial difficulty before he even suspected trouble. For example, if Mr. Green found himself short of funds, he might be unable to make his car payment. His car would, of course, be taken away and his past payments lost. But if he adds a monthly summary budget to his records, he can better anticipate needed changes in the total budget before those changes reach the critical stage.

MONTHLY SUMMARY BUDGET

The summary budget also provides estimates for several months into the future, but it does not provide detailed information for particular months. Consider the example in Table 4–5. Although most of the monthly estimates of both income and expenditures are the same, the May income estimate is $200 above normal due to an anticipated income tax refund, and the August expenditures estimate is $200 above normal due to an anticipated canoe trip down the Colorado River. In January, Mr. Green started the month with $300 in the bank, and he anticipated an income of $800 which meant a total available cash of $1,100. His estimated outgo was $800 which left him an estimated balance of $300 at the end of the month. Comparing his actual expenditures with his estimated expenditures, Mr. Green may note that he spent $15 less in January than he had anticipated. This $15 is thus added to his balance available for February which, in addition to his February income provides the cash available for his total February expenditures. But with all his Christmas bills yet to be paid, Mr. Green finds February a very tough month. His Penney's bill hit him especially hard, but his other expenditures were up too. Not only did his February expenditures exceed his January expenditures; they also exceeded his February estimate. Consequently, his balance at the beginning of March was reduced to $276. If he should find over the months that his balances are progressively less than he had anticipated,

Table 4-5 Monthly Summary Budget

Budget	Jan.	Feb.	Mar.	April	May	June	July	Aug.	Sept.	Oct.	Nov.	Dec.
Balance	$ 300	$ 300	$ 300	$ 300	$ 300	$ 500	$ 500	$ 500	$ 300	$ 300	$ 300	$ 300
Income	800	800	800	800	*1,000	800	800	800	800	800	800	800
Total Available	1,000	1,000	1,000	1,000	1,300	1,300	1,300	1,300	1,100	1,100	1,100	1,100
Outgo	800	800	800	800	800	800	800	**1,000	800	800	800	800
Balance	300	300	300	300	500	500	500	300	300	300	300	300
Actual Data												
Balance	300	315	276									
Income	800	800										
Total Available	1,100	1,115										
Outgo	785	839										
Balance	315	276										

*Additional $200 of budgeted income due to an expected income tax refund.
**Additional $200 of budgeted outgo due to an expected vacation expense.

as those months go by he may need to arrange for some additional borrowed funds or make other adjustments. If he should find that he is spending more for one category than he had anticipated, he may decide to adjust his budget accordingly. In order to avoid a financial crisis, it is very important to know in advance that one's income and expenditure estimates are not accurate because such advance notice provides adequate time to consider alternative adjustments. Without advance notice, a crisis can be upon you before you know it, and in such crises, there may be no alternatives readily available and no choice to make. Almost invariably, the only escape is one that would not have been the first choice in less hectic circumstances.

Because of the need to compare actual balances to estimated balances, a budget must include not only estimated expenditures but also estimated income. A budget is usually related to a particular standard of living. This standard incorporates a set of objectives that a particular family considers necessary, but income is a primary constraint that cannot be ignored. The budget is actually a very useful tool when it is used correctly; it can be an effective aid in controlling expenditures and meeting objectives. However, no budgets are really accurate, whether they are business, government, or family budgets. Nor can budgets be expected to increase income or work other miracles. However, businesses and governments use them in their financial planning as necessary aids to carrying out their operations. They do not use budgets as fixed time tables, but rather as estimates. Similarly, a budget can be of aid to any individual or family that must live within a certain income. In order to be effective, it must not be too rigid or inflexible; nor can it be too restricting or complicated. But without some financial plan, or budget, there is the very real possibility that a family can find itself in serious financial trouble, with excessive debts, unable to buy those items that are really important, and perhaps unable to pay for those things purchased on installment plans.

A budget does not guarantee financial security, but it can indicate future financial problems before they reach the crisis stage. It can indicate how much money a family thinks should be spent for various items, and how much is actually being spent. Therefore, it can indicate where expenditures are inadequate or excessive. A budget cannot decide, control, or force desired changes in a consumption pattern. Those people who expect the impossible from a budget are the very ones who say they cannot live within a budget. As mentioned before, all of us do live within a budget. But not all of us live within a planned budget, and not all of us are satisfied with our present spending habits. By using a monthly detailed budget to make sure that bills are actually paid, and to determine exactly how much was actually paid, you have a detailed record of monthly expenditures. By using a monthly summary budget, you can determine whether or not your actual expenditures are what you expected them to be, and when they are exceeding the total that you expected. With these two budget forms, you may see the need for providing additional cash income or controlling specific or total expenditures well in advance of any serious financial difficulty. Any techniques that can provide so much must surely be worth your serious consideration.

BALANCE SHEET

The balance sheet is the fourth financial tool that may be of value to any financial manager, corporate or personal. A very simple example is presented in Table 4–6. The assets listed are the resources or property of the family, although the most important asset is traditionally not listed on the balance sheet, namely, the income-earning capacity derived from education, skills and abilities. All financial debts are listed, and the difference between assets and debts is the net worth. As the net worth increases over the years, progress is made toward financial security.

There is no need for great detail or complexity. A relatively simple breakdown of assets and debts once each year can indicate just how

Table 4–6   Balance Sheet

Assets		
Cash	$ 300	
Savings Account	500	
Life Insurance Cash Value	1,000	
Investments	1,000	
Home	20,000	
Other Assets	4,000	
Total Assets		$26,800
Debts		
Bills Payable	1,000	
Notes Payable	2,500	
Mortgage	15,000	
		$18,500
Net Worth		8,300
Total Debts and Net Worth		$26,800

much progress the family is making toward its goal, and this is the purpose of the balance sheet. There is some value perhaps in considering all physical assets, although they should be realistically valued. Of greatest importance, however, is the accumulation of financial assets such as savings, life insurance cash values, stocks, and bonds. Your home, household furnishings, and automobiles are very important to your total welfare. But from the standpoint of your objective or goal of financial security, the gradual accumulation of financial assets to the point where they equal your debts, and then proceed to exceed them, is of utmost importance. As you will recall earlier in this chapter, the purpose of controlling expenses is not to reduce total satisfaction but to increase it as you recognize real progress toward your goal of financial security. The annual balance sheet can provide you with a real sense of satisfaction, as you are made aware from year to year that you are indeed on schedule. On the other hand, if you are not making the progress you want to make, you should know that too, and the annual balance sheet will tell you so. In either case, the balance sheet can indeed be a helpful financial record, one that can be used to determine your progress along the way. As with monthly budgets, the balance sheet indicates where you are going and how long it will take to get there. Such a device can be extremely valuable to you in your personal financial management efforts.

Now that we have discussed these four financial recording techniques individually, they should be considered as one unit. Although each one may be helpful individually in solving specific problems, used together they provide a simple yet effective control of expenditures. They provide adequate financial data to prepare a monthly check list of bills paid; they identify over expenditures through item-by-item analysis all on one page; they provide monthly totals of all expenditures that can be compared against earlier estimates to permit month-by-month evaluations of financial progress, and the potential need for future adjustments in either income or expenditures; and they provide the data necessary to enable you to annually evaluate your financial progress toward your ultimate objective. It is important to remember that all these techniques actually complement each other. Your check stubs are of some help to you even if you make no real use of them, but they are of far greater value to you if you use them to make a realistic detailed monthly budget. Such a budget can be useful to you if that is the only one you use; but since a detailed monthly budget only does part of the job, a monthly summary budget added to it and built upon it can be of still more help, assuming that it is designed to estimate your future transactions and check on the validity of your estimates. An occasional balance sheet can always be of some help in several ways; for example, a current balance sheet is usually required for a bank loan application, but if the annual balance sheet can serve as a summation of the events recorded on the check stubs and in the budgets, it can provide a regular measure of your financial progress over time. You must use all four of these techniques in order to maximize their value to you; if you leave out any one, the value of all three of the others is reduced as well.

COMPONENTS OF A BUDGET

Perhaps some time can be well spent considering more specifically some of the components of a budget. Whether or not all these components are specifically listed in any monthly detailed budget, all of them must be a part of the thought process of any individual who is trying to plan and control his financial affairs. It is all well and good to try to construct and maintain a simple, uncomplicated, sustainable budget, and for most purposes such a budget is all that is necessary. Nevertheless, somewhat more than intelligent guesses about appropriate income and expenditure figures are desirable for more thorough understanding and awareness. A simple budget, using only the broad general categories in the monthly detailed budget previously considered, is usually sufficient for the required and desired planning and evaluation, but an awareness of what lies behind those broad categories may be helpful, too. It is not necessary to consider all of these specific items on a daily basis, but it is necessary that all of them be considered sometime. Furthermore, if only as a protective measure, it is absolutely crucial that one be aware of these various items in order to make appropriate allowance for them in the budget.

In a very real sense budgeting is a process of listing priorities. What is more important is allocated more money as an indication of its relative weight in the budget maker's mind. In some cases, the expenditures that are very important for one person and thus have a very high priority, are of little or no importance to another and would have a low priority of one or zero. Just because an item is listed at zero estimated expenditures, however, does not mean that the financial manager is unaware of that component of a consumption pattern. It does exist; it is just not important to him. For the great majority of people, however, there are some items that are always present in their consumption patterns even though some families do weight them more highly than others.

INCOME

Cash income is essential to each and every budget. Income is received from a great variety of sources, e.g., salary, wages, bonuses, commissions, interest, dividends, and rent from property owned. All these are examples of earned income. In addition, income can be received in the form of gifts or borrowed funds. We have already discussed at length the importance of providing the necessary income for a desired consumption pattern. Not only are there various sources of income, there are also various ways of increasing income, and these methods are discussed at some length in Chapters Eight through Eleven. It may be highly desirable that a person increase income by improving his educational or technical skills in order to support the standard of living and the investment program that he wants. Any budget that indicates a great disparity between estimated earned income and estimated total expenditures must clearly indicate the need to improve that budget maker's income-producing capacity. Income is the primary constraint upon most total expenditure figures, but it is certainly not the only constraint and may not even be the most significant one; however, it is the point from which all budgets start.

SAVINGS

Many family budgets will include a regular savings feature. It is not necessary, of course, that this be a monthly matter. Some families have found it more convenient to save out of the Christmas bonus, or out of the summer vacation bonus, or by using some other method. But for many people monthly saving is the most satisfactory method, despite the fact that occasionally, or even regularly, some months are so crowded with necessary expenses that saving during those months is virtually impossible. Actually, some families find Christmas and summer vacation months the very ones in which they find saving least possible.

Regardless of exactly when or how, any hope of financial security is closely tied to this saving component. It really matters very little whether an individual saves $25 each month during the year or $50 in only six months of the year. The end result is the same; either way, he succeeds in saving his selected goal of $300 per year. The important point is to actually succeed in reaching his goal, not only at the end of his financial plan but also along the way.

Essentially, this savings-investment component may be the most important one in the budget. Regardless of the income figure, and regardless of the weights placed upon various expenditure items, the savings component can be included in the budget. If it is included, and if it is protected against the pressures that tend to erode any estimated saving figure, then financial security may indeed be a realistic goal. If saving is not included, or if it is not protected, achieving financial security is probably impossible.

FOOD AND SUNDRIES

The various expenditure items in the budget are by no means unimportant, of course. For most families food represents a very important consumer expenditure, often about 25 percent of the total expenditure budget. These food and sundry items include not only groceries *per se,* but also items normally bought in grocery stores including hundreds of household items. In addition, this item frequently includes restaurant dining and lunches purchased at work.

Generally, as the family income increases, the dollar amount spent on food increases, but the percentage of total income spent on food declines.

Some families spend much more on food than others, sometimes because they feed more children, but often because this item in their consumption patterns provides a significant source of personal gratification. For other families, less expensive foods are perfectly acceptable alternatives, and actually preferable, because they choose to spend more of their money for housing, transportation, clothing, or entertainment. However, since food is usually a very significant portion of the total expenditure budget, careful grocery shopping with an eye toward bargains and quantity purchases can often mean a considerable difference in the total food and sundry budget figure.

HOUSING

This component of the family budget is also a very significant one. Often, this item includes not only the rental or mortgage payments, but also the utility payments including telephone, electricity, gas, water, and garbage collection, as well as some repairs, home furnishing, garden supplies, and many other items. The amount of money that can be spent on a home is truly astounding. Not only could you spend $100,000 on a house if you so chose, the amount you could spend on improvements is also unlimited. The choice to spend a very large percentage of a total expenditure budget on housing is directly related to the personal satisfaction one receives from his home, and this is entirely an individual matter. For you, the care and feeding of your weeping willow may be the one most important thing in your life. If this is true, no one can rightly fault you for spending any amount you decide to spend in making that tree feel welcome, comfortable, happy, and content. For others, housing is simply shelter from the wind and cold, not a source of personal fulfillment. Suffice it to say that this item is likely to be a fairly large proportion of the budget, and control of so large an item is quite necessary.

TRANSPORTATION

Today automobiles are a great deal more than mere transportation. Furthermore, they are a major part of many budgets. Many families make installment payments on cars for years. Before the car is free of debt, a family buys another. The need for a new car is actually compulsive for some people. Apparently, such people are almost unconcerned about the price of a car or its total cost. The important thing is the monthly payment, regardless of alternative values, interest rates, total debt, or number of payments. Whether or not they can make the payments is the prime determinant of a purchase. Consequently, they buy from dealers and finance through companies that offer the lowest possible monthly installments, which of course are the ones that must charge the most to cover their greater risks. For other people, such behavior seems strange at best because they feel no such compulsions. Transportation must include not only installment payments on the car, but also gasoline, repairs, insurance, etc. Using the second budget approach proposed in this chapter, the installment payment would actually go into a payments category, and repairs and services would go in another category. Nevertheless, as viewed from an overall transportation expense, all of these may be seen as a part of total transportation expenses. Some effort to control transportation expenses may be justified in these supplemental areas, but the greatest success will be achieved when the effort is directed at the major item, the car itself. Sometimes some money can be saved by changing insurance companies, garages, or gas stations, but any really large saving on transportation expenditures can only be accomplished by keeping a car a year or so longer than planned, or buying a significantly less expensive car.

CLOTHING

Some families include in this budget category not only clothing purchases, but also storage and maintenance of clothing. For some people, clothing is an extremely important category; for others it is relatively unimportant. For some professional people, clothing is a much more important expenditure item than it is for others. It may not be at all wise to economize on clothing if you are judged somewhat on your appearance. Such efforts to economize on clothing may be very shortsighted if, as your appearance suffers, your income suffers as a result. For other people clothing is simply a source of satisfaction, and any efforts to economize can only result in a serious reduction in personal satisfaction. In either situation, clothing is too significant a part of the consumption pattern to be severely controlled. For other people, clothing may be somewhat important, but not crucial. For them, clothing expenditures could well be reduced with a little more awareness of just how much they are spending on clothes and how many other things they are unable to buy as a consequence.

OTHER EXPENDITURES

This category includes a multitude of expenditures such as medical and personal care. Recreation and entertainment, magazines, hobbies, sporting events, travel, vacations, and so on may also be included as well as charitable contributions and education expenses. In many instances, "other" expenses are the very ones that ruin budget estimates. Some wit once said that the only way to make a budget work was to list every conceivable expenditure and then add $200 for miscellaneous items. This may not be quite accurate, but it is true that you can absolutely other-expenditure yourself to death. Some control here is indeed important if control of overall expenditures is to be achieved.

SUMMARY

Controlling expenditures is just as essential to personal financial management as planning and providing income, if indeed not more so. All the planning in the world is useless unless expenditures are controlled. This does not mean that spending should never exceed earned income; at times it should. What it does mean is that outgo should be less than earned income over one's lifetime. An awareness of the life expenditure pattern as it relates to the life income pattern can provide an understanding of the need for financial records and controls. By using a monthly detailed budget and a monthly summary budget, any specific expenditure excesses can be identified, and the need for appropriate adjustments can be recognized before any serious damage to the total financial plan has been suffered. These two budgets and an annual balance sheet can provide regular measures of spending. Because people differ so much in their attitudes and desires, any of many components of a consumption pattern can be the crucial expenditure item in a budget. With excessive controls, total satisfaction will be reduced; therefore, this is not the purpose of controls. But without sufficient control, it is impossible to achieve financial security. With appropriate control over expenditures, regular saving and investing can proceed according to plan, and much personal satisfaction can be gained throughout the effort. Ultimately, the prize of financial security can be won along with all the personal and financial satisfaction that that prize entails.

Case Problems

1. Greg is a high school senior. He is presently working 20 hours per week at a local filling station to save as much money as he can in anticipation of college expenses. Greg is planning to go to a state college, he will live in a dorm his first year, and will not have a car. Greg feels that he'll be able to work part time while in college. His parents will help him to some extent financially. At present he is trying to draw up a budget for his first year in college. Since he's never been to college, he isn't aware of the expenditures involved. What should he consider?

2. Gene and Mary are both seniors in college. They are planning on getting married this June. Neither Gene nor Mary's parents approve, so they know they will receive no financial help from their parents after they are married. With this in mind they are beginning to worry about their finances. Gene is planning on going to graduate school, and Mary will work. Gene hopes he can get a part-time job that pays about $30 a week. Mary feels she can make about $100 a week as a secretary. However, at present they don't have a realistic anticipation of their expenditures. Draw up a budget for them.

3. A few days ago, a friend of Joe Smith was looking through one of Joe's textbooks, one on personal finance. Tom, Joe's friend, was looking

specifically at a couple of graphs in Chapter Four. Tom, being an engaged man with personal finances predominant in his mind, found the graphs quite interesting. However, he didn't quite understand what they showed. Specifically the shaded areas on the second graph were a mystery to him; he thought the two areas should be equal. He knew Joe had read the chapter, so he asked him to explain. I know you're not Joe Smith, but I'm sure you've read the chapter so, please explain the significance of the two graphs.

4. Rog and Al are a couple of college students with average mentality. They are very good friends, but the relationship is such that Rog is always making suggestions to Al on how to run his life. An example may illustrate what I'm talking about. Just a few days ago, Al was talking about what he would do with his money when he got a job. All Al talked about was buying clothes, cars, and taking trips. Rog said that his priorities were all wrong. Rog said that a savings plan should be the first priority with everyone. Is Rog right? If he isn't, what should everyone's priority be?

5. As everyone probably realizes, fathers and sons occasionally have disagreements. For example, Seymour Adams and his father recently had one such disagreement. One night while eating dinner, Seymour's dad made a remark that anyone who couldn't control his expenditures was stupid and lazy. Seymour immediately took issue with the remark. After making many philosophical points, however, Seymour couldn't convince his father that his remark was incorrect. What are some arguments you can offer Seymour in helping to change his father's ideas?

6. Bertrand Bellow has been concerned, lately, about his son, Truman. Bertrand felt that his son should control his expenditures in an attempt to gain financial security. After several conversations with Truman, he finally convinced him that he should control his expenditures. Bertrand is now more at ease. However, now Truman is worried. He controls his expenditures, but has trouble remembering all his payments. He realizes that he needs some record-keeping system. Can you suggest a record-keeping system for him. I'm sure you can, so please do.

7. Vernon Stelzer is generally a very bright fellow. He feels that he is doing an adequate job of controlling his expenditures. Vernon makes a good salary, and is very thrifty. Vernon realizes, however, this isn't enough. He knows he needs a financial record-keeping system. He read about a system that included check stubs, a monthly detailed budget, a monthly summary budget, and a balance sheet. Vernon felt this system is good, but didn't think he needed to use all four of the tools. "After all," he thought, "if I use two of them I will get 50 percent of the benefits of the system." Do you agree with Vernon? Why or why not?

8. A lovely freshman coed at Midwestern State University needs some help. Her name is Helen Hetter. Helen is in home economics and is always dreaming of when she will marry. She realizes that when she is married a budget could be a great help in gaining financial security. But right now she doesn't know exactly what should be considered in a budget. She comes to you for help. What should she consider in a budget?

Selected Readings

Basic Principles in Family Money and Credit Management. Washington, D.C.: National Consumer Finance Association.

Bracket, J. C., "New BLG Budgets Provide Yardsticks for Measuring Family Living Costs." *Monthly Labor Review,* April 1969, pp. 3–16.

Cohen, Jerome B., and Hanson, Arthur W., *Personal Finance.* 3rd edition. Homewood, Illinois: Richard D. Irwin, 1964, Chapter 2.

Connecticut Mutual Life Insurance Company. *How to Plan Your Spending.* Free copies available by writing to 140 Garden Street, Hartford, Connecticut.

Donaldson, E. F., and Pfahl, J. W., *Personal Finance,* 3rd edition. New York: Ronald Press Company, 1966, Chapter 2.

"How to Buy a New Car." *Consumer Report,* December 1969.

"Inflation and Family Budgets." *America,* January 17, 1970.

"Is Your Family's Spending Out of Line?" *Changing Times, The Kiplinger Magazine,* April 1970

Lasser, J. K., *Managing Your Family Income.* New York: Doubleday and Company, 1968.

Money Management—Your Budget. Chicago: Household Finance Corporation. Latest issue.

"Need Money?" *Credit Union Magazine,* October 1969.

New York Life Budget Book. New York: New York Life Insurance Company. Free copies available at 51 Madison Avenue, N.Y., N.Y.

Personal Money Management. New York: The American Bankers Association, 1967.

"Planning a Family Budget." *Supervisory Management,* June 1970.

"Planning Effective Personal Records." *Industry Week,* June 29, 1970, pp. 34–38.

"Rush to Apartments." *U.S. News and World Report,* December 8, 1969.

"Spring 1969 Cost Estimates for Urban Family Budgets." *Monthly Labor Review,* April 1970.

"What a Young Family Should Do With Its Money." *Changing Times, The Kiplinger Magazine,* December 1967.

"What's the Best Way to Get Money for Remodeling." *Better Homes and Gardens,* May 1969.

"Where You Should Keep Your Rainy-Day Money." *Changing Times, The Kiplinger Magazine,* September 1969.

"You Can Save in Spite of Yourself." *Changing Times, The Kiplinger Magazine,* October 1970.

CHAPTER **FIVE**

HOME OWNERSHIP

From the time the earliest cave man moved into a cave, shelter has been recognized as a basic necessity of life. Housing—of some type—is a problem everyone faces. Whether you live in a mansion in the suburbs of New York or in a tent on the Southern California beach, you are faced with the problem of providing housing for yourself (and possibly for a family).

This chapter is concerned with the basic, important problems a person faces when he deals with housing decisions. Should you buy or rent? If you do buy a home, how do you determine how much you should pay? How should you finance the purchase of a home? What are the legal problems that arise from home ownership? What are the tax implications of owning a home? What are the advantages and problems of building a house? You cannot become a real estate expert by reading this chapter, but if you study this material carefully you will be able to deal effectively with the important problems that arise from home ownership.

REASONS FOR OWNING A HOME

A person who owned his home was in the minority until about 1947. But now, well over 60 percent of all families own their home. This is shown in Figure 5–1. While less than 10 percent of families in which the head of the household is under 24 owns a home, it is obvious from Table 5–1 that a majority of all families own a home at some time. And it is becoming increasingly common for young families to own their homes. Apparently many people have sound reasons for buying a house.

A young person may have some trouble in recognizing many reasons why home ownership might be desirable. But there are a number of social, historical, demographic, and economic forces that help explain

Figure 5–1   Percentage of Families Owning Their Homes, 1890–1969

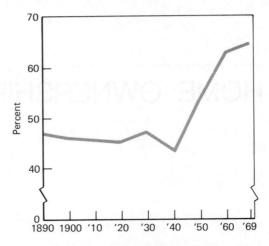

Source: Bureau of the Census, depicted in the *Savings and Loan Fact Book*, United States Savings and Loan League, 1970, p. 45.

Table 5–1   Home Ownership, by Age

Age of Head of Household	Percent
18-24 years	8
25-34 years	46
35-44 years	67
45-54 years	75
55-64 years	71
65 years or older	68
All nonfarm families	61

Source: Survey Research Center, Institute for Social Research, University of Michigan, shown in the *Savings and Loan Fact Book,* United States Savings and Loan League, 1970, p. 46.

the attractions of home ownership. The most important reasons given in one real estate text are:[1]

---

[1] Alfred A. Ring and Nelson L. North, *Real Estate: Principles and Practices,* 6th edition, p. 445 © 1967. By permission of Prentice-Hall, Inc., Englewood Cliffs, N.J.

1. Adventure. Home ownership, as well as the selection of a home, is one of the most interesting adventures in family life. It involves, in most instances, the largest single financial transaction that a family undertakes. It is indeed adventurous not only to invest one's life savings, but also to roam around the community or countryside to find the best location, to choose a plot, and to select the design and layout of a home if one is to be built, or to look at the innumerable buildings already constructed in anticipation of the home purchaser's demands.

2. Education. With home ownership, an entirely new world is opened to the buyer. He learns about value and prices, contracts and building materials. As he considers his tax bill and governmental action that directly or indirectly touch upon his home, he is led to inquire into civic affairs—how government is run and its local problems—and sooner than he realizes the home owner develops a feeling of "belonging" which induces him to take active part in community affairs.

3. Credit. Home ownership improves one's credit standing. It makes for stability, better employment relations and discourages the restless, wasteful practice of frequent moving about. As a home owner reduces his mortgage, he comes to be known as a "property owner." His patronage is solicited and his credit rating may be counted as a financial asset.

4. Thrift and savings. Home ownership encourages saving, unwittingly as a rule, for the mortgage amortization provisions are specifically designed to increase the owner's equity or property at a rate faster than the counteracting losses incurred through wear and tear, depletions, or other forces contributing to depreciation, i.e., loss in the value of the home. The home owner, too, must set aside sums to meet his various payments, and true thrift habit becomes ingrained.

5. Security. The renter is always insecure. His rent may be raised, or the landlord may want possession. The home owner is "set." Conditions may change, the economic cycle may go up or down, but he has his roof over his head and if he meets his payments regularly no one can disturb him; he will be subject to no eviction notice.

6. Citizenship. The ownership of a home brings with it an entirely different attitude toward social, economic, and political problems. Home ownership as a rule contributes to better citizenship by promoting civic pride. Home owners tend to be politically conservative and prove more resistant to the introduction of "isms" or measures that may lead to a totalitarian state.

7. Purpose. Many people are drifters. They have no definite goal or purpose. Buying a home supplies the stimulant they need. It gives them something to work for. They must meet the payments, and each one met stiffens their confidence.

8. Independence. It is a wonderful feeling indeed for a home owner to stand on a segment of mother earth and call it his own; to be king of his castle no matter how modest the realm. To a large extent the owner can do as he wishes. There is no landlord to restrict him.

9. Peace of mind. As soon as the initial payment on the home is made, the owner commences building up an equity, and this gives him peace of mind. To be sure, he has payments to make, but the renter also has his obligations each month. The great difference is that the renter is building up nothing for himself. The home owner, by making equal or slightly higher payments, is slowly paying off his debts, and after a while the home is paid for and becomes a real refuge.

10. Character development. A community where homes are largely owner-occupied reflects better care of properties, better landscaping, cleaner thoroughfares, and stability of home and property investments. As a rule, a home owner wants a nice home. Therefore he must save and can ill afford to be shiftless.

11. Fun. It is a delight to own one's home; to have a place in which to entertain and do the things that a tenant may be prohibited from doing. The children can play about as they please without any complaint from landlords.

12. Creative instinct. The ownership of a home gives the owner an opportunity to play with his ideas. People do not design or build their rented quarters—they take them as they find them—and very often simply because they are the best they can get for the price or most conveniently located. Home owners are people who satisfy their instinctive desire to develop their own background. If building, the architectural design and layout may be what the home owner wishes. Even if he is purchasing an old house, he may bring into play his ideas of alteration and remodeling. He gets an opportunity to work in his garden. He landscapes his grounds. He may have, even without a large expenditure, a delightfully balanced home, set in most attractive surroundings.

All the reasons in the above list may not apply to you. But there are, undoubtedly, some important psychological and sociological reasons for home ownership as well as financial reasons. Almost everyone who has owned a home appreciates these intangible factors.

Despite the advantages of home ownership, a person cannot make a rational decision until he has analyzed, in some detail, the costs of owning a home.

COSTS OF HOME OWNERSHIP

Every person who considers buying a home should analyze the true costs of home ownership. This is a much bigger job than it might seem! The first step is to distinguish between *costs* and *expenses* of home ownership. Expenses are made up of charges the home owner actually pays. Sometimes these are called "out-of-pocket" expenses to emphasize that these are actual payments. Costs include expenses, but in addition, costs include the dollar value of all *direct sacrifices* made by a home owner. Many people make the mistake of considering expenses only.

EXPENSES

Down Payment.   Unless you pay cash for a home (the wisdom of doing this is considered later) you will be required to make a down payment and monthly payments after the home is purchased.[2] The first expense of home ownership, then, is the down payment. Lenders usually require a down payment of at least 10 percent of the appraised value of the property. In some cases a buyer may be able to pay a smaller down payment, but more often, a larger down payment is required. Twenty percent or even 25 percent is not an uncommon down-payment requirement. The size of the down payment depends on several factors, but the important factor is the supply and demand for mortgage funds. When lenders are about "loaned up" they can afford to make loans only to those who represent better credit risks. And these, in general, are people who can afford to make large down payments.

Closing Costs.   Many home buyers, particularly young people, are surprised when they learn that they must pay—in addition to their down payment—several hundred dollars when they buy a house. This cost is really a miscellaneous set of expenses that arises when a home is purchased. And since practices differ across the country, closing costs vary somewhat. Table 5–2 shows the average closing costs on mortgage loans.

Table 5–2 shows that closing costs are comprised of a number of charges, but the three important costs are for title insurance, attorney fees, and service charges. If you purchase real estate, there is always the possibility that the title to the property is defective in some way. A paper could have been forged in the past, a wife could have failed to sign when her signature was required, or numerous other defects in the title could exist. Title insurance protects a policyholder for any losses that he incurs if the title to his real estate proves to be defective. The policy does not guarantee that a person has a sound title, and it does not assure a policyholder that he can retain possession of the property. It simply guarantees to defend him and reimburse him for losses that he suffers because of a

---

[2] Practically all modern home mortgages require monthly payments. In the past, a person could buy a home and not make any payments until the end of the loan period. At that time the loan became payable and the home owner either had to pay off the loan, arrange a new loan, or default on the mortgage. Since many home owners defaulted, these "straight mortgages" are very rarely used now on homes.

Table 5-2 Average Closing Costs

Items	Chicago	Indianapolis	Newark	Metropolitan Area St. Louis	St. Paul	San Antonio
Title insurance	$ 54	$ 45	$ 80	$ 29	$ 25	$ 26
Other title related costs	0	8	22	28	5	1
Attorney fees	6	10	206	0	5	15
Property survey	2	12	20	8	3	17
Service charge	104	71	21	103	103	52
Other lender services	19	13	22	19	6	5
Recording fees	2	7	11	12	4	7
State and local taxes	0	2	0	0	11	0
All other costs	7	4	2	14	10	2
Total Costs	$194	$172	$384	$213	$172	$125

Source: United States Savings and Loan League, *Savings and Loan Fact Book*, 1966, p. 41.

defective title.[3] A person who has a defective title may be required to give up the property to some one with a prior claim. An unusual characteristic of title insurance is that the premium is paid only once—at the beginning of the coverage. Normally, title insurance is purchased each time the property changes ownership.

The fees paid as "service charges" are intended to pay the lender for his costs in making a loan. The costs might include clerical expenses, appraisal fees, survey charges, and other miscellaneous expenses.

Moving-In Expenses. A person who buys a house normally incurs expenses for curtains, carpeting, and other items. New homes usually involve higher expenses for these items than older homes. New homes often need landscaping (which can be expensive) and miscellaneous items that are already provided with a home that has been occupied.

Mortgage Interest and Principal. The greatest expense, in almost all cases, after a person buys a house is the monthly payment of principal and interest. It is important, therefore, to understand how a home mortgage loan is amortized.

Each time a payment is made, part of the payment is applied to interest on the loan and the remainder is applied to reduce the principal amount of the loan.[4] In the early years of the loan, most of the payment is applied as interest. But as time passes, a greater and greater portion of the payment is applied to reduce the principal.

Table 5–3 deserves your close attention. It shows that a person pays $96.67 each year for each $1,000 borrowed on a 20-year, 7.5 percent real estate loan. The $96.67 is obtained by adding the principal and interest in any one year, e.g., $22.43 and $74.24 in the first year. But in the first year of the loan, even though $96.67 is paid, the amount of the balance is reduced only $22.43. Most of the payments during the year are allocated to interest. Each year more and more is allocated to reduce the principal, and the amount necessary to pay interest decreases.

---

[3] In some states (or counties in some states) the Torrens system is used. Under this system, a hearing is held to discover defects in titles. If no defects are found, the title is registered and the owner is assured of a clear title. If a person later can show that he has some rights in the property, he can be reimbursed for losses from the insurance plan—but the present owner of the property cannot be required to give up the property. The Torrens system is preferable to normal title insurance in some ways, but it is slow and expensive.

[4] This chapter considers only the level mortgage payment plan. With this plan, the monthly payment remains at the same amount but a greater and greater portion of the payment is used to reduce the principal. Another plan, which is not popular, requires the borrower to reduce the principal each month, but because the interest is payable on a smaller and smaller debt, the total monthly payment declines with each payment.

Table 5–3 Annual Summary of Monthly Amortization (per $1,000 at 7.50% interest up to 20 years)

Year	Principal	Interest	Balance
1	$22.43	$74.24	$977.57
2	24.17	72.50	953.39
3	26.05	70.62	927.34
4	28.07	68.60	899.27
5	30.25	66.42	869.02
6	32.60	64.07	836.42
7	35.13	61.54	801.29
8	37.86	58.81	763.43
9	40.80	55.87	722.63
10	43.96	52.71	678.67
11	47.38	49.29	631.29
12	51.06	45.61	580.24
13	55.02	41.65	525.22
14	59.29	37.38	465.93
15	63.89	32.78	402.03
16	68.85	27.82	333.18
17	74.20	22.47	258.98
18	79.96	16.71	179.02
19	86.17	10.50	92.86
20	92.86	3.81	0.00

Source: Paul F. Wendt and Alan R. Cerf, *Tables for Investment Analysis* (Berkeley, California: The Center for Real Estate and Urban Economics, 1966), p.250. Used with permission.

A significant fact derived from the table is that a person actually pays $1,933.40 (20 × $96.67) for each $1,000 he borrows for a 20-year period. This is simply a reflection of the effect of interest over a long period of time.

Since Table 5–3 is in terms of $1,000, it is easy to apply to other amounts. Suppose, for example, that you borrow $22,000 to finance a house. If the loan carries an interest rate of 7.5 percent over 20 years, at the end of the first year you will owe $21,506.54 (22 × $977.57), even though you have paid $2,126.74 (22 × $96.67) during the first year. It is a little discouraging for a home owner to realize that his first payments reduce his balance so little, but this is one of the costs of owning a home.

Insurance Premiums. In addition to title insurance, a person may pay insurance premiums for property insurance, mortgage redemption life insurance, and possibly F.H.A. insurance. Usually, but not always, premiums for these coverages will be built into the monthly house payment the home owner makes.

The subject of property insurance is covered in Chapter Fourteen, so little will be said here. As a general rule, though, the annual premium is usually estimated at one-half of 1 percent of the value of the house. Lenders will insist upon property insurance.

Mortgage redemption life insurance is optional. It is designed to provide funds to pay off the outstanding mortgage debt if the head of the household dies before the home is completely paid for. Since the balance due on a mortgage decreases each time a payment is made, the face amount of the life insurance policy decreases accordingly. All the leading life insurance companies offer some type of mortgage redemption policy, and these policies are a wise purchase for a person who does not want to take the chance of leaving an unpaid mortgage to his family.

If you obtain an F.H.A. mortgage you will pay one-half of 1 percent on the outstanding amount of the principal with each monthly payment. This is an insurance charge that is used to build up a fund to pay losses lenders would incur when home owners default on their mortgages. The insurance protects the lender, not the home owner, but an F.H.A. loan provides advantages to a home owner. (These are described later in this chapter.)

Taxes. State and local governments derive most of their revenue from property taxes. These taxes may or may not be built into a home owner's monthly house payment, but in any event, they are a true expense of home ownership. This is not to say that renters escape the property tax. If you rent a home, the landlord undoubtedly includes the property tax as part of the total rent payment.

Because property taxes are levied by state and local governments, they vary widely across the country. And since state and local governments have been requiring more money for their operations, property taxes have been rising rapidly.

The property tax is frequently misunderstood by home owners. Suppose a governmental unit has a budget of $50,000,000, and that $400,000 must be obtained from the property tax. Tax assessors may place a value on all the property in their jurisdiction and arrive at a total value of $16,000,000. The tax rate, then, would be determined by dividing the needed $400,000 by the assessed valuation of $16,000,000. This would give a tax rate of $.025 per $1 or $2.50 per $100 of assessed valuation. (The tax rate is usually expressed in terms of $100 of assessed valuation.)

Tax assessors usually attempt to determine the fair market price of each piece of property in order to determine its property tax, but in some areas assessors use only a percentage of fair market value to determine the tax. Your home, for example, may have a fair market value of $20,000, but the assessed value may be only $10,000 because the assessors tax only 50 percent of the value of the property. This is no bargain for the home owner, however. The practice of using fractional valuation has developed primarily because of laws that limit the rate at which the government can tax. The law, for example, may limit the tax to, say, $3.00 per $100 of valuation. By using fractional valuation, a state or local government can increase its revenue, not by raising the tax rate but by raising the percentage of assessed valuation. Rather than taxing at only 50 percent, the assessors can base the tax on 60 percent of the fair market value.

Maintenance.   An expense that is often overlooked or underestimated by home owners is the cost of maintaining a home. These expenses, of course, vary considerably from one home to another. An old home is apt to involve considerable expense to maintain, while a new house should have few maintenance costs. The type of construction also makes a big difference. A brick home, for example, should cost less to maintain than a normal frame house. With all these factors bearing on maintenance costs, it is hard to provide a general rule of average maintenance cost, but real estate experts usually believe that annual maintenance costs should range between 1 percent and 3 percent of the value of most homes.

OTHER COSTS

In addition to the out-of-pocket expenses described above, there are two other important costs of home ownership. These costs do not involve a cash outlay, and as a result, are frequently overlooked by home owners.

Loss of Income.   When you buy a home, a down payment must be made. This expense has already been described. *Another* cost (which should be distinguished from the down payment itself) is the loss of income that could have been earned on the money used for the down payment. Suppose you save $3,000 and use it as a down payment on a home. If you could have earned 6 percent on your money in the year following the purchase (if you had not bought the house) you must account for the $180 (6 percent of $3,000) you have lost. The loss of income, in fact, should be accounted for each year you own the house.

Depreciation.   If your house declines in value as a result of wear and tear, obsolescence, or neighborhood deterioration, you must consider the decline in value as a cost of home ownership. Not all homes depreciate, however. Some houses have not changed much in value while others have appreciated.

INCOME TAX CONSIDERATIONS

The cost of owning a home is actually less than the total of all the expenses and other costs described above. This is because our federal income tax laws give preferential treatment to home owners. Since the next chapter deals with income taxes we will not elaborate here on the tax implications of home ownership. But it is important to see exactly how homeowners receive an income tax advantage.

In computing your federal income taxes, you are allowed to deduct certain items from your income. A person may deduct mortgage interest and property taxes, and since these are usually sizable amounts, there is a large reduction in taxable income. Consider this example: Fred pays $960 a year in mortgage interest and $340 each year in property taxes. He is in the 20 percent income tax bracket. Because of these two deductions, his income for tax purposes will be reduced $1,300 ($960 plus $340) and he will save the amount of taxes he would have paid on $1,300. Fred, therefore, saves $260 each year (20 percent of $1,300). This $260 must be regarded as a direct reduction in Fred's housing cost. As a person earns a higher income and gets into higher income tax brackets, the income tax advantage becomes greater.

THE DECISION TO BUY OR RENT

Now that we have examined the costs of home ownership, we can deal with the very practical problem of whether it is better to rent or buy. The decision should be based on four interrelated factors: cost, flexibility, convenience, and other factors, such as the need for space and pride of ownership.

COST

Is it cheaper to rent or buy? You know now that the answer depends on the true costs of owning a home, the individual's income tax bracket, and the cost of renting.

It would be convenient if you could develop a reasonable set of assumptions for all the items that enter into the cost of renting or buying, and ask a computer to give you some answers. This has been done, and the answers are shown in Figure 5–2. If the assumptions embodied in Figure 5–2 are reasonable, we can draw several conclusions. The break-even line near the bottom of the figure makes it clear that renting is less expensive than owning a $20,000 home for short periods of time. A home is normally a poor investment for a short period of time because of the down payment, loss of income on funds used for a down payment, closing costs, and costs that are incurred when the house is sold. But, as a general rule, owning a home is much less expensive than renting for long periods. This is because a home owner pays off his mortgage debt, gets income tax advantages, and may benefit if his house appreciates in

Figure 5–2   The Buy or Rent Decision

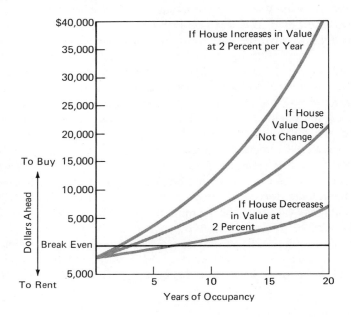

Assumptions for Buying:

Purchase price for house	$20,000
Down payment	$2,000
Term of mortgage	20 years
Mortgage interest rate	7.5 percent
Property taxes	3 percent of the value of the house annually
Insurance costs	½ percent of the value of the house annually
Maintenance costs	1 percent of the value of the house annually
Income tax deduction	20 percent of the amount paid for real estate taxes and interest annually
Value of money (loss of income on down payment)	5 percent each year
Closing costs	$300
Moving-in costs	$1,000
Selling costs	10 percent of the value of the house at the time of the sale (includes renovation prior to sale)

Assumptions for Renting:

Moving-in costs	$1,000
Rental rate	13 percent of the value of the house annually

Source: "Is a Home Still a Good Investment?" *Better Homes and Gardens,* Vol. 47, No. 9 (Special Building Issue, September, 1969), p. 46. © Meredith Corporation, 1969. All rights reserved.

value. According to the figure if a house appreciates in value 2 percent each year, it is financially advantageous to buy if you expect to live in the house two years or longer. After 20 years you would be approximately $40,000 better off if you had purchased the house.

If the value of the house remains unchanged, you are better off financially to buy if you expect to live in the house about three and one-half years or longer. This advantage results from building up equity in the house and the income tax deductions. Even if the house depreciates 2 percent each year, you can benefit by buying if you remain in the house seven and one-half years. In other words, with a depreciating house, you would be better off financially to rent unless you remain in the house for a fairly long period.

Figure 5–2 can be extremely helpful to you even if you cannot directly apply it to your own case. Suppose, for example, that you are in the 25 percent income tax bracket rather than the 20 percent bracket. This would mean that the advantages of buying would be greater than those shown in the figure, and you would break even earlier. Although you cannot make precise adjustments in the figure, you can determine whether a different assumption would be an advantage or a disadvantage of buying, and the figure can give you a helpful reference.

FLEXIBILITY

Renting provides more flexibility than home ownership. A person who rents can move more easily than a person who owns his home. This is an important advantage to many young families.

It is also easier for a renter to make adjustments in his housing costs than it is for a home owner. If a renter has a decrease in income or an increase in expenses he can usually find a house or apartment that rents for a smaller payment. But a home owner does not have this degree of flexibility. He cannot move easily to a less expensive home if he experiences financial difficulties.

CONVENIENCE

An apartment often provides convenience that is not available with a house. Consider for a moment a husband and wife who both work. They may need to live near public transportation and this may require living in an apartment. Apartments may also have services that are provided with a house. Many apartments, for example, offer laundry facilities, swimming pools, lawn work and other services.

OTHER FACTORS

There are other factors that might influence the decision to rent or buy. The reasons for home ownership described at the beginning of this chapter might be important to some people. These reasons will not be repeated here, but it is important to realize that many of these reasons are subjective. Their importance cannot be measured. How do you, for example, put a dollar value on pride of ownership? The fact that these subjective factors enter into the decision means that the decision to rent or buy can never be completely answered by a simple formula or rule.

IMPORTANT PROVISIONS IN A LEASE

A person who decides to rent an apartment or house has not necessarily solved all his housing problems. A contract of some type must be arranged with a landlord. The contract may be an oral agreement, but usually it is better to sign a lease.

Most people believe that a lease is strictly for the benefit of the landlord. This is not true. A lease can give rights to a tenant as well. The most important right a lease can give to a tenant is the right to occupy the premises for a certain period of time. In a written lease a tenant is reasonably assured that he can live in the apartment or house until his lease expires. Furthermore, a lease can stipulate the amount of rent that is payable during the rental period, and therefore the tenant can have assurance that his cost of housing will not be increased during the period of the lease.[5] But not all the provisions in a lease give rights or benefits to a tenant. In fact, since most written leases are prepared by the landlord (or his attorney) it is safe to assume that most of the provisions in a lease are designed to protect the landlord. This means a tenant should exercise care before he signs a lease. The following provisions should be checked carefully:

1. Period of the lease. Obviously a lease should make the beginning and ending dates for the lease quite clear. But the lease should also spell out the obligations, if any, of both parties when the lease expires. Some leases continue on a month-to-month basis when the original lease period expires. Others give the tenant an option to renew the lease. An especially dangerous provision provides an automatic extension of the lease. This type of clause can obligate the tenant to another full term of the lease unless the landlord is notified in advance (usually thirty or sixty days) before the original term expires.
2. Destruction of property. What happens if fire destroys or damages an apartment you have leased? Some leases terminate if a certain portion of an apartment is damaged, but others continue if the landlord restores the property within a certain period. Another important provision deals with the problem of destruction or damage caused by the tenant. If a deposit for damage is required, a tenant should know exactly how and when his deposit will be returned.

---

[5] In some leases the landlord has the right to increase the monthly rent under certain circumstances. For example, the lease may give the landlord the right to pass property tax increases to the tenant.

3. Utilities. A lease should specify who is responsible for paying heat, light, and water bills, and other services such as lawn care. As a tenant, you should know if you will be responsible for these payments.

4. Repairs. Problems sometimes arise when a lease does not spell out the responsibility for repairs. Generally, landlords are responsible for major repairs, but tenants may be expected to pay for minor repairs.

5. Military service. Some leases give a tenant the right to terminate his lease if he is required to go into military service. Some leases go even further—they let a tenant cancel his lease if he is transferred by the U.S. government (or in some cases by any employer). In some cases, the lease gives the landlord the right to occupy the premises if he (the landlord) is released from military service. This could mean an expensive and inconvenient move for the tenant.

6. Landlord's relief. Although a tenant may have no intention of missing his rent payments, every tenant should know the rights of the landlord when rents are not paid. Eviction, of course, is always a possibility, but some leases give the landlord the right to charge the tenant for attorney's fees and other legal actions. A "landlord's lien" is found in some leases. This gives the landlord a claim on the tenants' personal property if rent payments are missed.

7. Other provisions. It is impossible to describe all the possible provisions in a lease.[6] Some leases prohibit pets, loud music, and subleasing. Some give the landlord the right to sell the property if a buyer is found. Other leases require a tenant to make his apartment available for display anytime the landlord wants to show the apartment to prospective renters. Some of the clauses can create serious problems for a tenant. The solution is clear: a tenant should always study his lease carefully before he signs it. If the lease is complex, it is probably wise to have the lease checked by an attorney.

DETERMINING HOW MUCH YOU SHOULD PAY FOR A HOUSE

If you are typical you will be buying a home within a few years. If you do, one of the first problems is locating a house that appeals to you and deciding how much you should pay. You may need professional help (using professional people is discussed at the end of this chapter). Every home buyer should have a good understanding of how much he should pay for a house. The problem can be divided into two parts: obtaining adequate value in your purchase and determining the amount you can afford to spend for a house.

---

[6] The major provisions that should be checked by a tenant are described in "Renting? Make Sure the Lease is Fair," *Changing Times, The Kiplinger Magazine,* September 1968, p. 13.

REAL ESTATE APPRAISAL

Some type of appraisal is always necessary before you buy a house. You would not want to spend $18,000 for a house—even if you could afford it—if the house were worth only $15,000. The appraisal process is an attempt to determine the value of a house. The value of a house might be considerably different from its selling price. For example, suppose you see a house that can be bought for $25,000. You might determine that the value of the house is only $22,000. If so, the house is overpriced. Value is a standard or measure of worth, and it is independent of price.

The ultimate purpose of appraising a home is to protect yourself against losses if the house must be sold. If you purchase a house that is *underpriced,* there is a good chance that you can sell it at a profit or at least not suffer a financial loss. But if you buy an *overpriced* house, you can lose—and sometimes you can lose a substantial amount of money. Determining the value of a house, then, is important to anyone who might be interested in selling the house later.

But how do you determine the value of a house? There is no simple formula that always gives an easy answer. In fact, even professional real estate appraisers will give different answers on the same property. When one real estate broker was asked what determines the value of a home,

Table 5–4   A Guide to Effective Evaluation of Home Location

Item	Relative Weight
Proximity to place of work	15
Quality of available schools	10
Distance to school	5
Nearness to church of own choice	5
Neighborhood—reputation and characteristics	10
Degree of owner occupancy and owner's pride in area	5
Quality and proximity of shopping area	5
Transportation (public) facilities and cost	5
City tax structure	10
Zoning stability	5
Availability of necessary utilities	5
Recreation opportunities	5
Extent of neighborhood development	5
Nature of terrain—drainage and topography	5
Absence of noise, traffic, smoke and dust	10
Effective fire and police protection	10

Source: Alfred A. Ring and Nelson L. North, *Real Estate: Principles and Practices,* 6th edition, p. 452 © 1967. Reprinted by permission of Prentice-Hall, Inc., Englewood Cliffs, N.J.

Figure 5–3 Average Price Per Square Foot of Homes*

Region

Region	Price
Entire U.S.	$15.35
North-east	$16.60
North Central	$17.15
South	$13.80
West	$15.80

*Based on exterior dimensions.

Source: Bureau of the Census and Department of Housing and
Urban Development, shown in the *Savings and Loan Fact Book*,
United States Savings and Loan League, 1970, p. 30.

he said, "Three things—(1) location, (2) location, and (3) location."
Of course, location is not the only factor that gives value to a home, but
it is hard to overemphasize the importance of location.

Table 5–4 can be very helpful in evaluating the location of a home.
This table gives the factors that determine the desirability of a location
and some suggested weights for each factor. The weights in the table, it
should be emphasized, are only the opinion of one real estate authority
and they may not apply to you.

After considering location, a home buyer should attempt to determine
the value of the house itself. The usual method is based primarily on the
floor space in the house. To use this approach, you must first find out
what is the cost per square foot to build a new house in the neighborhood
(or similar neighborhood) that is practically identical or similar to the
house you are considering.

Figure 5–3 can be helpful in getting some general ideas about the price
per square foot of homes in different parts of the country. Notice that the
average price per square foot is $15.35 for the entire country, but the
price varies among regions. Consider a house with 2,000 square feet. In
north central United States, the price of a house this size is likely to be
near $32,000 ($16 times 2,000). But a house of the same size in the
South would probably cost only about $26,300 ($13.15 times 2,000).

You can refine your estimate of the price per square foot of homes in a
neighborhood by asking bankers (or others) in the area who make mortgage loans. You may also consult builders and real estate agents or
simply estimate the price yourself by comparing a number of homes. After

estimating the average price per square foot, measure the house under consideration to determine the number of square feet in the house. Then, multiply the average cost per square foot by the number of square feet in the house. This gives you the value of a "standard" house in that neighborhood. You must make additions for property improvements (such as fireplaces, patios, and other improvements) that are *not* included in similar houses and make deductions for depreciation and needed repairs. Finally, you must estimate the value of the land and add this value to get the total value of the property.

As an example, suppose you find a house you like, but you want to make sure it is not overpriced. You ask a building contractor and a banker what the average cost per square foot is for a house in that neighborhood. Suppose they tell you it is $15. By measuring the house, you find it has 1,500 square feet. This would indicate a value of $22,500. But the house has a fireplace, which most other houses in the neighborhood do not have, and you estimate the value of the fireplace at $750. The house also has a patio (worth $250). Therefore, the house is now worth $23,500. But, after careful inspection, you find that the roof must be replaced and the outside repainted. For these expenses you deduct $1,000 (your estimate of the cost). This produces a final value for the house of $22,500.

The next step is to place a value on the lot. Suppose you believe the lot is about average in value for the neighborhood, and after asking several knowledgeable people you find an average lot is worth $3,000. This amount, then, would have to be added to your figure of $22,500. This would indicate a total value for the property of $25,500.

But now the problem is this: the owners are asking $28,000 for the house. This is not uncommon. As a matter of fact, many sellers purposely overprice their houses 10 percent or so to have room when they are bargaining with the buyer.[7] In this situation, you should realize that if you pay more than $25,500 for the house, you probably would not be able to sell the house and recover your cost if you sold it in the near future.

HOW MUCH CAN YOU AFFORD TO PAY FOR A HOUSE?

The amount you *should* spend for a house is determined not only by the value of the house, but your financial ability. In other words, you should not buy a $40,000 house—even if it is a bargain—if you cannot afford the financial obligations that go along with a $40,000 house.

The amount you can afford to spend on a home depends on four important factors: the size of your down payment, the duration of the mortgage, the interest rate on the mortgage and your monthly income

---

[7] The practice of adding 10 percent or so for bargaining apparently is rather widespread. This is the recommendation in the May 16, 1970 issue of *Business Week*, p. 122.

and expenses. Rules of thumb that are intended to indicate how much you can afford to spend for housing are not very helpful because they do not consider all these factors.

Amount of the Down Payment.   For many young people, the amount they can afford to spend for a house is determined by the amount of money they have for a down payment. Normally, lenders will require a down payment of at least 10 percent of the appraised value of the property. In some cases, a buyer may have to put up a larger (or possibly a smaller) down payment. If the required down payment is 10 percent, and you want to buy a $20,000 house, you must be prepared to make a down payment of $2,000. This is a sizable amount of cash for a young family.[8] And you need at least $5,000 if the down payment is 15 percent and you want to buy a $25,000 house! Many young families, therefore, find that the amount they pay for a house is limited by the amount they have saved for a down payment.

Sometimes, however, a person has more money than is needed for a minimum down payment. This situation raises the question of whether the buyer should make a larger down payment. A larger down payment will enable the buyer to either pay off his loan earlier or reduce his monthly payments. In either case, the total cost of the loan will be less than it would be with a smaller down payment since he is borrowing less money. Another possible advantage of a larger down payment is the possibility of a lower interest rate. For example, sometimes lenders charge a certain rate, say 8 percent, if the down payment is 20 percent of the value of the property and they may charge 8¼ percent if a smaller down payment is made. As we will learn, the extra one-fourth of one percent adds up to a surprisingly large amount over a long period of time.

Tying up funds is a major disadvantage of a larger down payment. When you make a larger than necessary down payment, you are losing the use of the additional money. This additional money could be earning interest in a bank or some other investment outlet. Another possible disadvantage is that it may be easier to sell a home that has been purchased with a small down payment.

Consider this example: Mr. A and Mr. B each bought identical houses, and they each paid $20,000 for their home. Mr. A, however, made a down payment of $2,000 and Mr. B made a down payment of $8,000. If each decided to sell his home, a buyer could pay Mr. A $2,000 and possibly assume his mortgage obligation. But a buyer would have to pay Mr. B $8,000 to purchase the equity in his house. Of course it will be harder to find a buyer with $8,000 than one with $2,000. For this reason, some real estate authorities recommend that young families who are apt

---

[8] In addition, closing costs and moving-in expenses would have to be paid.

to move should make only the minimum down payment when they buy a house, even if they could actually afford a larger down payment.

A third disadvantage of a larger down payment is that the buyer receives a smaller income tax deduction. As explained previously, the interest paid on a mortgage is deductible for federal income tax purposes. A small down payment requires larger monthly payments because the interest is higher, but the interest is deductible. A person who makes a larger down payment gets a smaller income tax deduction.

Length of the Mortgage.   Not long ago, mortgages on homes ran for only five or ten years. But the practice of providing mortgages over longer and longer periods developed, and mortgages may now run as long as 30 or even 35 years. The average duration is now approximately 25 years.

The reason for the trend toward longer term mortgages is the effect of the mortgage duration on monthly payments. The longer the duration of a mortgage, the smaller the monthly payments that are necessary to pay off the loan. This is shown in Table 5–5.

Table 5–5 is expressed in terms of $1,000, so it is easy to use. Consider the problem of a person who must borrow $20,000 and repay the loan over ten years. Using Table 5–5, we know that such a person would have a monthly payment of $242.60 ($12.13 × 20). This covers interest and principal only—real estate taxes and other expenses are not included. But how much would a person have to pay each month if the $20,000 were borrowed over 30 years? The answer is $146.80, or almost $100 a month less. Spreading payments over a long period, then, provides one way to bring down the monthly cost of a house so that more people can afford to make the payments.

Table 5–5   The Effect of the Mortgage Duration on Monthly Payments and Total Interest Cost (per $1,000 at 8% interest)

Duration of the Mortgage (in years)	Monthly Payment (covering interest and principal)	Total Interest Cost
10	$12.13	$ 455.60
15	9.56	720.80
20	8.36	1,006.40
25	7.72	1,316.00
30	7.34	1,642.40
35	7.10	1,982.00

Source: Computed from Paul F. Wendt and Alan R. Cerf, *Tables for Investment Analysis,* Special Report No. 3 (Center for Real Estate and Urban Economics, University of California, Berkeley, 1966), pp. 256-257. Used with permission.

But there is a danger in stretching out the mortgage payments over too long a period. Notice that in Table 5–5 the monthly payment decreases a lot when the duration of the mortgage is extended from 10 to 15 years. But the reduction in the monthly payment gets smaller and smaller as the duration is extended for additional five-year periods. When the duration is changed from 30 to 35 years, the monthly payment is not substantially reduced. The reason for this is that longer mortgages require smaller monthly payments, but they eventually require the borrower to pay more in interest. This is only natural since the borrower who borrows for a long time should pay more interest than one who borrows for a short period. Look at the total interest cost in Table 5–5. Suppose you want to borrow $20,000 and you have a choice between a 20-year mortgage and a 30-year mortgage. On the shorter term mortgage you would pay $20,128 in interest (20 × $1,006.40), but the total interest cost on the 30-year mortgage would be $32,848 (20 × $1,642.40). You would have to weigh the advantages of the lower monthly payment against the additional interest cost.

The Interest Rate on the Mortgage. The interest rate on home mortgages fluctuates—depending on the supply and demand for funds. And they vary from one part of the country to another. If there is a heavy demand for loans in the Midwest, interest rates will be high. At the same time, demand may not be so great in the South, therefore, interest rates are then lower.

Mortgage interest rates also change from time to time. They have been increasing rather steadily in recent years as shown in Figure 5–4. Not shown in the figure, however is the sharp drop in interest rates that started in 1971.

High interest rates can cause home buyers to pay much more for their homes. Though almost everyone knows that higher interest rates require higher monthly house payments, most people do not have a very good idea of *how much* a higher rate costs. This information is provided in Table 5–6.

It is easy to use Table 5–6 to determine the effect of higher interest rates. A loan of $20,000 at 5 percent would require a payment for principal and interest of $117 (20 × $5.85). And a loan of the same amount at 9 percent would require a payment of $167.80 (20 × $8.39). As a general rule, an interest rate increase of one-half percent adds about 30 or 31 cents to the payment for each $1,000 borrowed. When interest rates go up several points, the difference in the monthly payment is sizable. Furthermore, the increase in the total interest cost over the life of the mortgage can easily amount to several thousand dollars.

To make matters worse, home owners frequently run into the problem of "points." At certain times the stated interest rate is really not as high as the lender would like to charge. For example, the maximum rate

Figure 5–4   Average Interest Rates on Mortgage Loans

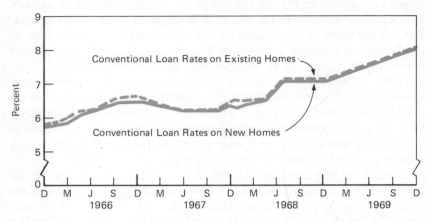

Note: Conventional loan rates are the combined average charged by savings associations, savings banks, commercial banks and insurance companies.

Source: United States Savings and Loan League, *Savings and Loan Fact Book*, 1970, p. 43.

Table 5–6   Monthly Payments Per $1,000 of Mortgage Debt at Various Rates of Interest (25-year mortgage)

Interest Rate	Monthly Payment
4 %	$5.28
4½	5.56
5	5.85
5½	6.14
6	6.44
6½	6.75
7	7.07
7½	7.39
8	7.72
9	8.39
10	9.09

Source: Computed from Paul F. Wendt and Alan R. Cerf, *Tables for Investment Analysis*, Special Report No. 3 (Center for Real Estate and Urban Economics, University of California, Berkeley, 1966) pp. 208, 214, 220, 226, 232, 238, 244, 250, 256, 260, 263. Used with permission.

permitted by law on certain types of mortgages might be lower than the rate available on other investments, and therefore lenders may discount the face value of the mortgage by charging points. A point is 1 percent of the face amount of the mortgage. Therefore, if you are charged three points on a $20,000 loan, $600 will be deducted and you will actually receive only $19,400. But you are still obligated to pay the full $20,000. Points are more often charged to a buyer, but they can be assessed against a seller, or both. ∪ A + FHA seller pays.

The effect of charging points is to raise the true rate of interest on the loan. This is shown clearly in Table 5–7. Notice that the true rate of interest is higher when the mortgage is paid off sooner. This is because the charge is spread over a shorter period.

When mortgage interest rates are high, some people argue that a home buyer should postpone his purchase in order to wait until interest rates come down. There may be some merit in this view, but this strategy runs into two problems. One, interest rates are difficult to forecast. No one knows for sure when they will decline. Even when interest rates are at historic peaks, there is no assurance that they will not go even higher or possibly remain fairly level for a long period. A second problem of waiting for lower interest rates is that the cost of housing may increase substantially while you are waiting for the interest rates to come down. In the two-year period from 1966 to the end of 1968, for example, the cost of houses increased more than 10 percent and the cost of building lots rose more than 15 percent.[9]

Another way to avoid high mortgage interest rates is to buy a home on which there is a low interest rate mortgage. If you find a seller who bought his home when interest rates were low and you are willing to assume his mortgage, you can take over the payments that are based on a favorable interest rate. In this type of situation, the seller should receive a "premium" for his house because of the inexpensive mortgage, but most sellers probably underestimate the value of this benefit. One possible disadvantage of this approach from the point of view of the buyer is that a larger down payment will normally be required. This is because the seller probably will want to recover his down payment, appreciation (if any), and the equity he has built up in his home.

A home buyer can minimize the problem of high mortgage interest rates by shopping around carefully for a mortgage loan. While it is true that most lenders in one area will charge about the same rate, some lenders may be more anxious to make loans than others, and they might lend their funds at a lower rate. Remember, a reduction of one-fourth or one-half percent in the interest rate can make an important difference in cost over a long period of time.

---

[9] United States Savings and Loan League, *Savings and Loan Fact Book, 1969,* pp. 28–29.

Table 5-7 Actual Interest Rate on a 20-Year Mortgage If Paid Off in 10 or 20 Years

No. of Points Paid	6% Paid Off In 10 yrs.	20 yrs.	6½% Paid Off In 10 yrs.	20 yrs.	7% Paid Off In 10 yrs.	20 yrs.	7½% Paid Off In 10 yrs.	20 yrs.	8% Paid Off In 10 yrs.	20 yrs.	8½% Paid Off In 10 yrs.	20 yrs.	9% Paid Off In 10 yrs.	20 yrs.	9½% Paid Off In 10 yrs.	20 yrs.	10% Paid Off In 10 yrs.	20 yrs.
1	6.156	6.125	6.658	6.627	7.160	7.130	7.662	7.632	8.165	8.135	8.667	8.638	9.170	9.141	9.672	9.643	10.175	10.146
2	6.314	6.252	6.818	6.757	7.323	7.262	7.828	7.767	8.333	8.273	8.837	8.778	9.343	9.284	9.848	9.790	10.353	10.296
3	6.474	6.381	6.981	6.888	7.488	7.396	7.995	7.904	8.502	8.412	9.010	8.921	9.518	9.429	10.026	9.938	10.534	10.447
4	6.637	6.512	7.146	7.022	7.655	7.532	8.165	8.043	8.675	8.554	9.185	9.066	9.695	9.577	10.206	10.089	10.717	10.601
5	6.801	6.645	7.313	7.158	7.825	7.671	8.337	8.185	8.850	8.699	9.362	9.213	9.876	9.728	10.389	10.243	10.903	10.758
6	6.968	6.780	7.482	7.295	7.997	7.812	8.512	8.328	9.027	8.845	9.542	9.363	10.058	9.881	10.575	10.399	11.092	10.918
7	7.138	6.917	7.654	7.436	8.171	7.955	8.689	8.474	9.207	8.994	9.725	9.515	10.244	10.036	10.763	10.558	11.283	11.080
8	7.309	7.057	7.829	7.578	8.348	8.100	8.869	8.623	9.389	9.146	9.911	9.670	10.432	10.194	10.955	10.719	11.477	11.245
9	7.484	7.198	8.005	7.723	8.528	8.248	9.051	8.774	9.575	9.300	10.099	9.827	10.624	10.355	11.149	10.884	11.675	11.413
10	7.660	7.343	8.185	7.870	8.710	8.399	9.236	8.928	9.763	9.457	10.290	9.988	10.818	10.519	11.346	11.051	11.875	11.584

Source: Reprinted by permission from *Changing Times, The Kiplinger Magazine* (June 1970 issue). Copyright 1970 by The Kiplinger Editors, Inc., 1729 H. Street, N. W., Washington, D. C. 20006.

Another possible way a home buyer can minimize the cost of mortgage interest is to refinance his home. If you buy a home when interest rates are high and later they decline, it may pay you to obtain a new loan (at the lower interest rates) and pay off the old loan that carries a high rate. The advantages of obtaining a new mortgage with a lower interest rate might be worthwhile, but refinancing to get a lower interest rate can sometimes be problematical since the reduction in interest rates must be large enough to compensate you for all costs you incur in getting the new mortgage. Most of the closing costs will be incurred again, and in addition, the old mortgage may have a penalty charge. A penalty clause in a mortgage contract simply states that a fee (usually 1 percent of the balance on the mortgagee) will be charged if payments are made ahead of schedule. Lenders impose this clause primarily because of the loss in investment income they experience when high interest rate mortgages are exchanged for low interest rate mortgages. In many mortgages the penalty clause becomes ineffective after payments have been made for a certain period, which is usually about five years.

YOUR INCOME AND EXPENSES

The amount you can afford to spend for a house depends—to a great extent—on your income. But many people do not understand the relationship between income and the maximum price you should pay for a home.

A popular rule of thumb is that you should not spend more than two or two and one-half times your annual income for a house. Applying this general rule, if you make $10,000 a year, you can afford to spend $25,000 for a house. But this rule is filled with pitfalls. It completely ignores your other financial obligations, the size of your down payment, the mortgage interest rate, and the duration of the mortgage. And we have seen that all these factors have an important bearing on the expenses of home ownership. The truth is that one family that earns $10,000 a year might be able to afford only a $15,000 house while another family with the same income might be able to spend $40,000 for a house. (The second family, for example, might be able to make a $25,000 down payment). This rule of thumb, therefore, can be misleading and dangerous.

The best way to determine the maximum amount you should spend for a house is to apply the procedure lenders use. Their basic rule is that a person should not spend more than 20–25 percent of his total income for housing expenses. Some lenders will make a loan to a person who plans to allocate 25 percent of his income to housing, but other lenders limit the percentage to a lower figure—some as low as 20 percent.

The percentage limit applies to a person's gross income. That is, his total income before any deductions for taxes, social security, pension benefits, and other expenses. But in figuring the person's outlay for housing, some lenders include not only mortgage interest and principal, but real estate taxes, property insurance, home maintenance, and utilities. Some lenders will not include a wife's income—particularly if she is under a certain age—or maybe only a portion of a wife's income will be counted.

Many real estate authorities believe that a person should not necessarily follow the rules used by lenders, but instead, calculate how much can be spent on housing by working with the family budget. This basic approach is shown in Figure 5–5.

If a person follows the approach used in Figure 5–5, he should be able to get a good idea of how much he should spend for housing. One of the problems of this approach though, is that some expenses are difficult to estimate, and a person can be overly optimistic and therefore underestimate his expenses.

Sometimes it is helpful to have some idea of what others spend on housing. This type of information should never be relied upon too heavily, but a person should be aware of his extreme expenditures if he is

Figure 5–5 An Example of a Housing Budget

A. Family Income

Husband's salary _____
Wife's salary _____
Commissions and bonuses _____
Interest and dividends _____
Other income _____
Total deductions _____
Net income _____

B. Nonhousing Expenses

Food _____
Transportation _____
Clothing _____
Education _____
Furniture _____
Insurance _____
Donations _____
Entertainment _____
Medical _____
Other _____

Housing Budget

Net income (from A above) _____
Nonhousing expenses (from B above) _____
Available for housing and savings _____
Desired savings _____
Housing allowance _____

Table 5–8 Housing Expenditures, by Income Categories[1]

Monthly Income (After Taxes)	Monthly Housing Expense[2]	Percentage of After-Tax Income
$355	$125	35.2
455	155	34.1
545	185	33.9
645	210	32.6
890	260	29.2

1 The figures in the table apply only to V.A. guaranteed home loans, but the average monthly housing cost for new homes with F.H.A. insured mortgages was exactly the same in 1969. See U.S. Department of Commerce, *Statistical Abstract of the United States, 1970* (Washington, D.C.: U.S. Government Printing Office, 1970) pp. 688-689.

2 Payments for mortgage principal and interest with an additional allowance for taxes, insurance, heat, utilities and maintenance.

Source: Veterans Administration, unpublished data, 1970.

spending much more or less than other people in the same income category. Table 5–8 shows this type of information.

OTHER TYPES OF HOUSING

CONDOMINIUMS

Suppose you like the idea of owning your own home and you want to deduct mortgage interest and taxes from your income for income tax purposes, but you would actually prefer to live in an apartment. If so, a condominium may be for you. Condominiums were permitted in only six states prior to 1963, but now nearly all states have laws that permit condominiums, and their popularity is spreading rapidly.

In a condominium a person has individual ownership of a one-family unit in a multifamily building *plus* joint ownership with other apartment owners in the land, halls, heating equipment, and other common property. In other words, a person owns his own apartment and shares in the ownership of the other facilities and property.

Since a condominium owner has his own mortgage, he pays mortgage interest and property taxes—which are tax deductible. In addition, he pays a small monthly fee for maintenance of the common property. This is considered a big advantage by many people. A condominium owner has the responsibility for the upkeep on the apartment he owns, but he does not have to worry about yard work or other work around the apartment building.[10] However, a person who is interested in a condominium

---

10 If an apartment owner fails to pay his share of common expenses, the apartment owner's association (which is operated by a board of managers elected by the owners) places a lien upon the owner of the apartment.

should check the provisions for managing the property and the maintenance fee carefully. If and when a condominium owner decides to sell his apartment, he can sell it just as he would an individual house. He can sell it to anyone he chooses and at any price he can obtain.

Condominiums have few disadvantages for people who want to live in an apartment but also want the advantages that go along with ownership. One possible disadvantage, however, is that the interest rate on the mortgage may be higher than it would be on regular home loans.

COOPERATIVE APARTMENTS

Many people make no distinction between a condominium and a cooperative apartment. But there are some important differences between the two. In the usual cooperative apartment, a person does not actually buy the apartment. Instead, he buys shares of stock in a corporation that owns an apartment building and the corporation leases apartments to stockholders.[11] The tenants, as stockholders, elect a board of directors that manages the apartment building. Expenses of operating and maintaining the building are met by assessments on each tenant.

There may be several advantages of living in a cooperative apartment rather than renting. Potential advantages include:[12]

1. Rent cannot be raised at the whim of a landlord
2. Living quarters can be redecorated by the people who live in the apartments
3. Greater security, since the apartment dweller can remain in the apartment as long as he wishes (if he meets his obligations to the corporation)
4. Lower operating expenses
5. Prestige of ownership
6. Income tax advantages (even though each apartment dweller does not own his apartment and therefore actually has no mortgage or real estate taxes, he can deduct *his share* of mortgage interest and taxes paid to the corporation).

While cooperative apartments may have some advantages over renting, it may be more beneficial to compare cooperatives to condominiums. In this comparison, cooperatives have two major disadvantages. In a cooperative apartment, each individual is dependent upon the solvency of the whole project. If the corporation that owns the building fails to meet its debts, an apartment dweller can lose his apartment. In a condominium, each individual is responsible only for his own mortgage debt

---

11 In some cases, the apartments will be owned by a trustee or by the apartment dwellers as tenants in common.

12 These are the advantages given in *Real Estate Finance* by Hoagland and Stone, loc. cit.

and taxes (and his share of the costs of operating the common property). There are no responsibilities or liabilities arising from other apartments.

Another major advantage of a condominium over a cooperative is that it is easier to sell a condominium. If you own a condominium, you can sell it to anyone at any price a buyer will pay. But in a cooperative, a purchaser must be approved by the board of directors and the buyer must pay cash to assume the seller's share of the unpaid mortgage debt of the corporation.

MOBILE HOMES

The popularity of mobile homes has been booming in recent years. One out of every six new single-family homes is a mobile unit, and mobile homes account for one-third of all housing priced under $10,000. Furthermore, this type of housing is especially important for young families. Many college students are living in mobile homes while they are attending college.

A distinction should be made between travel trailers that are intended primarily for recreation and "vacation" homes and large mobile homes that may be up to 12 feet in width and up to 70 feet in length. These large mobile units meet the same needs as apartments and houses.

There are many possible advantages of living in a mobile home. First, a mobile home might provide the most inexpensive housing. Some new models are available for as little as $3,500. This is, of course, a great reduction in the cost of housing. Other models are priced as high as $17,000, but these are rather luxurious mobile homes. Even the largest mobile units are not expensive on the basis of floor space. A mobile home usually costs about ten dollars a square foot of floor space, but traditional houses normally cost between $15 and $20 per square foot. The basic reason mobile homes are inexpensive (on the basis of floor space) is that they are mass produced.

A careful buyer can save considerably by buying a used mobile home. Depreciation is much greater in the first year or two than it is in later years, and as a result, the price of a mobile home that is three or more years old will be much less than the cost of a new trailer.

In estimating the cost of living in a mobile room, you should keep in mind that it is necessary (in most cases) to rent a space for the trailer. Most trailer parks charge $25–$50 a month to rent a space. The charge depends greatly on the services provided by the park. Some trailer parks have laundry facilities, food, and recreational facilities, in addition to normal utility service. In locations near lakes, beaches, and golf courses, monthly rentals may be as high as $100 or more.

It is extremely difficult to make a valid comparison between the cost of owning a mobile home and a conventional home. The comparison is similar, in many respects, to the comparison between owning and renting. Much depends on financing arrangements, depreciation or appreciation, estimated monthly expenses, and the length of time over which the comparison is made. Still, it is helpful to make some type of comparison to see if one generally has a cost advantage over the other. Table 5–9 provides such a comparison.

Table 5–9 should be interpreted with caution. It does not prove that a mobile home is always less expensive than a conventional home. The table does imply that the monthly expenses for taxes, maintenance, heating and utilities, and insurance should be less for a mobile home. However, the income tax savings generally will be smaller. The table covers only the first five years, but it is obvious that the cost of a mobile home will be extremely low after the loan is completely paid off (seven years in the example in the table). The cost of a conventional home after seven years will tend to be higher, but this might be offset by appreciation in the value of the home.

Young families often find advantages in buying a mobile home because there is less need to buy furniture and appliances. Many mobile homes come equipped with stoves, refrigerators, washing machines, built-in beds, mirrors, and many other extra features. A young family that does not live in a mobile home usually has a drain on income for several years to finance the purchase of furniture and appliances.

Table 5–9   The Cost of a Mobile Home Versus a Conventional Home After Five Years

Financing Terms	$6,000 Mobile Home		$24,000 House	
type of loan	consumer installment loan		FHA mortgage	conventional mortgage
maturity	7 years		30 years	30 years
interest rate	12%		8½%	8%
down payment	$1,200		$2,400	$6,000
Monthly Costs				
loan repayment and interest	$ 84.74	$120.74	$165.32	$132.08
park rent*	36.00		- - - - -	- - - - -
taxes*	9.20		50.00	50.00
maintenance	3.00		15.00	15.00
heating and utilities*	30.00		50.00	50.00
insurance*	5.00		10.00	10.00
	$167.94		$290.32	$257.08
income tax savings (20% marginal tax rate)	− 8.79		− 42.20	− 35.73
net cost	$159.15		$248.12	$221.35

*Estimated.

Source: *New England Economic Review*, May-June 1970, published by Federal Reserve Bank of Boston. Reprinted with permission of the Federal Reserve Bank of Boston.

As strange as it sounds, mobile homes may or may not offer mobility. The smaller units, of course, can be moved by a car, but the larger mobile homes can be moved only by a large truck. And the cost of trucking a large mobile home is high. This means, for all practical purposes, that the large mobile homes are not very mobile.

The most obvious possible disadvantage of mobile home living is compactness of the home. Although some units are surprisingly large, most mobile homes do not offer the space that can be found in an apartment or a conventional house. The rooms are normally small in comparison to the rooms in apartments and houses.

There is another possible disadvantage if the buyer of a mobile home cannot afford to pay cash for his trailer. The financing of mobile homes is more similar to the financing of cars than it is to financing conventional homes. If you buy a mobile home from a dealer, the dealer will arrange the financing (if you do not want to arrange it yourself). The dealer usually places the loan with a bank or finance company. Normally, the lender will require a down payment of at least 20 or 25 percent of the price of the mobile home and make the loan for a maximum of six or seven years. More importantly, the interest rate is likely to be high. In many cases the true annual rate of interest will be 16 or 17 percent, which is considerably more than the interest rate payable by a home owner.

Another possible disadvantage of mobile home living is the fact that many trailer parks are run down, unattractive, and generally dirty. But this is becoming less of a problem as many trailer parks are recognizing the problem and keeping their places neater and cleaner.

FINANCIAL AND LEGAL PROBLEMS

THE PURCHASE CONTRACT

After selecting the type of housing you want and deciding how much you can afford, the next step normally is to make a deposit and sign a purchase contract. The laws in all states require that contracts to purchase real estate must be in writing and signed by the parties to the contract. Naturally it is extremely important for a home buyer to know what he is signing and to insist upon certain terms in the contract.[13]

The basic purpose of the purchase contract is to provide assurance that both parties will complete the transaction, subject to certain conditions. A buyer usually needs time to arrange financing, and during this period the seller should agree not to sell the house to someone else. In return for holding the house off the market while financing is being arranged, the seller normally requires the buyer to make a deposit.

---

[13] It is desirable for both parties to the contract to have their attorneys study the agreement and provide advice. The use of professional people in real estate transactions is discussed later in this chapter.

There are a number of important clauses in a purchase contract, and a buyer should understand these provisions well. Perhaps the most important clause is the one that specifies what will happen to the deposit made by the buyer in the event the buyer does not purchase the house. This occurs fairly often because a buyer can decide he prefers another house, or it may be impossible to obtain adequate financing. A buyer should make sure that he has the right to have his deposit returned to him with no penalty if he is unable to obtain appropriate financing. Therefore, the contract should spell out exactly how much time the buyer has to arrange financing, and it should also define what is meant by "appropriate financing." In other words, what happens if a buyer can finance the house, but only with a larger down payment and higher interest rate than he anticipated? In this situation, the buyer may feel that he has been unable to obtain "appropriate financing," but the seller may not agree. The purchase contract, therefore, should spell out precisely the type of financing that will require the parties to complete the transaction.

The purchase contract should specify the exact sales price of the home. Sometimes a seller will want to have the right to increase the price of the home under certain conditions. As an example, a builder may want to increase the sales price of the house if his costs increase before the home is actually purchased. A buyer, of course, should not give this right to the seller, but if the seller insists upon this privilege, the buyer should understand the conditions under which the price of the home may be increased, and a maximum increase should be stated in the contract.

Another important provision in a purchase contract is the clause that sets forth the responsibilities the seller may have after the buyer takes possession of the house. For example, suppose you move in and two days later you find out that the heating system does not work. Or, what happens if the seller has not completely finished the house when you move in? The contract should require the seller to correct any substantial defects in the house that you discover within a certain period of time after you take possession, and of course, the contract should require the seller to deliver a completely finished house. This means that if you take possession before the house is completely finished, you should make a list of all the unfinished items and the seller should agree, in writing, to finish each item.

It is vitally important to make sure that you are protected against mechanics' liens. When a person buys a house, he usually assumes the responsibility for all unpaid claims of people who have provided the labor and materials for the house. If a builder, for example, has not paid the house painters and you buy the house, it is very possible that you may be legally obligated to pay the painter.

The purchase contract should also set forth a date when the property will actually be transferred. In addition, the contract should spell out the responsibilities of the seller to deliver a valid title to the property and to provide other necessary legal documents.

DEEDS

A deed is the written instrument that transfers ownership of property from one person to another. But there are numerous types of deeds, and some transfer more rights than others.

The simplest type of deed is called a *quitclaim* deed. With this type, a seller transfers whatever rights he has, but he guarantees nothing. With another type of deed, a warranty deed, the seller guarantees that the deed transfers a good, marketable title to the property. If you purchase property and receive a warranty deed and later someone claims they own the land you bought, a warranty deed will enable you to sue the person who sold you the property. And if you have suffered a financial loss there is a good chance that you will collect a judgment.

A warranty deed is the most desirable type of deed for a buyer, and a quitclaim deed is least desirable. In between these two types are all kinds of deeds. From a buyer's point of view, a warranty deed should be required. Any other type of deed will give the buyer fewer guarantees.

SELECTING A LENDER

Does it make any difference where a person goes to obtain his home loan? Most of the time, mortgage loans will be quite similar in any one geographical area at any one time. But a person should "shop around" for a mortgage because there may be important differences among lenders in the amount of the down payment, the mortgage interest rate, and the terms of the contract.

Loans for houses are made by savings and loan associations, commercial banks, life insurance companies, and individuals.[14] Savings and loan associations are much more important sources of loans than other financial institutions, as shown in Figure 5–6.

The lending practices of various financial institutions differ, and these differences can create advantages or disadvantages for borrowers. Life insurance companies, for example, tend to finance homes when the buyer can afford to make a large down payment. On this type of loan there is a smaller chance of default, and so the insurance company can charge a lower interest rate on the mortgage. Life insurance companies, therefore, are said to be desirable sources of funds for people who have enough money to make large down payments. Commercial banks also have tended to prefer large down payments, and as a result, their mortgage interest rates might be low. Savings and loan associations and mutual savings banks have made all types of loans, but they have a tendency to

---

[14] These types of organizations are described in detail in Chapters Three, Thirteen, and Fifteen.

Figure 5–6   Mortgage Loans Outstanding on One- to Four-Family Non-farm Homes, by Type of Lender, Year-End 1969

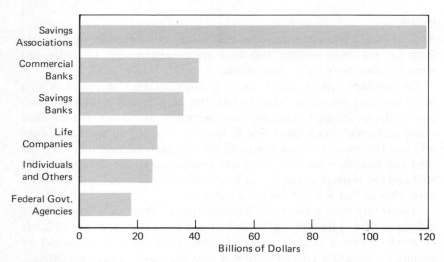

Source: Federal Home Loan Bank Board, depicted in the *Savings and Loan Fact Book*, United States Savings and Loan League, 1970, p. 37.

prefer longer term mortgages and smaller down payments. To the extent this is true, they have had to charge slightly higher interest rates.

It is a mistake for a home buyer to place too much emphasis on the differences among the types of lenders. Life insurance companies and commercial banks do not always require larger down payments, and savings and loan associations will not always provide long-term, small down payment loans. It is much more important for a home buyer to compare the loans offered by one lender versus the loans of another lender—without excessive regard to the type of company. The best loan for a borrower might be obtained from a life insurance company, a commercial bank, a savings and loan association or from some other source.

TYPES OF LOANS

Housing loans can be classified in several ways, but from the point of view of a home buyer there are three important types of loans: Federal Housing Administration (F.H.A.) loans, Veterans Administration (V.A.) loans, and conventional loans.

F.H.A. Loans.   Regardless of whether you obtain your loan from a bank, insurance company, savings and loan association or some other type of lender, you may want to (or may be forced to) use an F.H.A. loan. These loans are *not made* by the Federal Housing Administration.

The F.H.A. does not make direct loans, nor does it build or plan homes. It simply insures loans that meet its regulations.

An F.H.A. loan works this way: you obtain your loan from a lender and then the F.H.A. insures the lender if you default on the loan. Notice that it is the lender who is insured—not the borrower. Why then, you might ask, would a person ever want an F.H.A. loan?

There are three primary advantages of F.H.A. loans. First, you may be able to borrow more if the loan is insured. Normally, a lender will require a down payment of at least 10 percent, and in many cases, he will require more. But if the loan is insured, the risk to the lender is smaller and they may make a larger loan. In some cases a loan of 97 percent of the appraised value of the house may be provided.[15] For example, a family could purchase a $15,000 home with only a $450 down payment. Young families who do not have enough money to make a large down payment, therefore, may be particularly interested in F.H.A. loans.

Another advantage of F.H.A. loans is that the Federal Housing Administration sets up strict requirements for the construction and location of the homes it insures. Before a house is eligible for an F.H.A. loan, it must have met a lengthy, detailed list of minimum requirements. As one example, an F.H.A. insured house must have a minimum number of electrical outlets and the electrical wiring must be a certain minimum size. The third possible advantage of an F.H.A. loan is the appraisal. Before the government will insure a loan, a careful inspection and appraisal of the house will be made.

The mortgage interest rate on F.H.A. loans is regulated by the Federal Housing Administration. The maximum rate a lender can charge on an F.H.A. loan is changed periodically to reflect changes in money conditions. In general, the government tries to keep the interest rate at competitive levels, but there are times when the maximum rate is lower than the rate on other loans. In this situation lenders are reluctant to use F.H.A. loans. The duration of an F.H.A. loan is also subject to regulation and is changed periodically. In 1970 F.H.A. loans could not exceed 30 years or three-fourths of the remaining economic lifetime of the property, whichever was less.

V.A. Loans.   Since the end of World War II the federal government has helped veterans purchase homes. Accordingly, the Veterans Administration makes loans directly to home buyers, but more commonly the government *guarantees* loans made by other lenders.

---

[15] The amount that can be financed on an F.H.A. loan is subject to change and the amount differs under various circumstances. But the formula that is most often used is: 97 percent of the first $15,000 of appraised value, 90 percent of the next $5,000 and 80 percent of the excess over $20,000. The maximum mortgage loan is now $30,000.

To be eligible for a G.I. loan, a person must have served 180 days or more in active military service and have been released from the service without a dishonorable discharge. Korean War veterans are eligible for G.I. loans until January 31, 1975 and more recent veterans are eligible for loans up to 20 years after they are discharged.

Although the purpose of the G.I. home loan program is to enable veterans to buy homes with a minimum down payment, the size of the down payment is negotiated between the borrower and the lender. However, many lenders have been willing to make loans to veterans with no down payment at all or only a small down payment. This is because the Veterans Administration guarantees each loan up to 60 percent of the amount of the loan. If a borrower defaults, the Veterans Administration becomes liable to the lender and the borrower remains responsible for repaying the full amount of the loan. From the point of view of the lender, then, the loan is well protected. In the past, the Veterans Administration limited the amount that would be guaranteed but now there is no maximum. The Veterans Administration, however, must give its prior approval before loans exceeding $25,000 will be guaranteed.

The maximum interest rate permitted on V.A. loans has been changed periodically. In 1970 the maximum rate that could be charged was 7.5 percent. The maximum term at that time was 30 years.

Conventional Loans.   A conventional loan is one that is not insured by the F.H.A. or guaranteed by the V.A. A lending institution (such as a bank, savings and loan association, or insurance company) simply lends its own money and takes the chance that the borrower may default. Because conventional loans provide less protection to lenders than F.H.A. or V.A. loans, lenders normally require a larger down payment. They like for a borrower to make down payments of 25 or 30 percent, but sometimes they will require only 10 or 20 percent. As a general rule, conventional mortgages are not made for a period exceeding 25 years.

SECOND MORTGAGES

Although second mortgages are not as popular as they were at one time, they are still used occasionally. They may be particularly useful for some young people because they offer one method of dealing with the problem of insufficient funds for a down payment.

Suppose you find a house that you would like to buy but it costs $20,000 and the largest loan you can obtain is 80 percent. This means you would have to pay $4,000 as a down payment. (Eighty percent of $20,000 is only $16,000 and the difference between $20,000 and $16,000 usually must be paid as a down payment.) Therefore, if you have only $2,000, you need an additional $2,000. You may be able to raise the additional $2,000 if you are willing to use a second mortgage.

A second mortgage is simply a lien on property that has a lower priority than a first mortgage. That is, in the event of default by a borrower, the claims of a person or organization that has a first mortgage will be satisfied in full before the claim of a person or organization with a second mortgage is honored. A lender who has a second mortgage, therefore, has weaker security than the lender who holds the first mortgage.

The advantage of a second mortgage to a home buyer is that he obtains the property with a smaller down payment. But there are several disadvantages of second mortgages. Second mortgages are usually available only for a fairly short period of time. Often a second mortgage runs for only five or ten years. As a result, the payments on the second mortgage may be substantial. When a buyer has to meet the payments on the second mortgage and all the other expenses of home ownership, he may be asking for financial trouble.

To make matters worse, the interest rate on a second mortgage is invariably higher than the interest rate on a first mortgage. This is only natural since the lender who has only a second mortgage is assuming more risk. But, from the point of view of the buyer, the higher interest rate means additional cost—just when the monthly cost could be a serious problem. Second mortgages may be justified in some cases, but as a general rule, they should be avoided. A person who cannot afford an adequate down payment usually should postpone his purchase.

IMPORTANT MORTGAGE PROVISIONS

It is impossible for most people to understand completely all the legal technicalities that are involved in buying a house. Each transaction involves a number of laws and legal documents, and the laws are not the same in all the states. But still, there are a few provisions in real estate contracts that are so important that every home owner should understand them.

Acceleration Clause. Most mortgages have an acceleration clause. This clause gives the lender the right to declare the full amount of the obligation due and payable when the borrower defaults. In other words, the acceleration clause permits a lender to demand complete payment of the debt as soon as the borrower fails to meet a stipulated number of payments. This number of payments, obviously, is extremely important to a home owner. Some clauses let the lender foreclose 60 days after a payment is missed; in others the period is 90 days. A home buyer should always carefully inspect the terms of the acceleration clause and insist upon at least 60 days of grace for his house payments.

Prepayment Privileges. Home owners, more often than you might think, have a reason for paying off a large portion or all of their mortgage debt. Sometimes, for example, it is necessary to pay off the debt before the property can be transferred to a new owner. Money may not be a problem because the seller usually receives enough money from the house to pay off the indebtedness, but the terms of the mortgage might cause some difficulties.

Most mortgages in recent years have contained some type of pre-payment clause. Some are unqualified. That is, a home owner can pay off his debt at any time without penalty. V.A. loans *must* give a borrower the right to repay his debt without penalty.[16] But many mortgages contain some type of penalty. The penalty can be a certain percentage of the amount of the loan, a stated number of months' interest, or a flat amount. In some cases a penalty is invoked only if the mortgage is repaid within the first few years of the loan.

A home buyer, even one who believes there is no chance of prepaying his loan, should attempt to avoid any type of prepayment clause that restricts or penalizes his right to prepay the loan. If the lender insists upon some type of prepayment penalty, the borrower should make sure the penalty is not unreasonable.

Open-End Mortgages.   Suppose a home owner needs money for major repairs, remodeling, or additions to his home but does not have enough cash to pay the full cost. How should he arrange financing? He can bor-row money for a short period or possibly refinance his house, but both approaches are usually costly.[17] An open-end mortgage, however, would solve the problem.

An open-end mortgage gives the owner the right to borrow additional money from the lender up to the original amount of the mortgage. In other words, a person can make house payments, reduce the mortgage debt, and later increase the debt back to its original amount. This is a valuable privilege, but the exact terms of this clause should be looked into before the original loan is obtained. A borrower should know if a fee is charged when additional funds are obtained and if there is any effect on the interest rate.

Escalator Clause.   Another important clause, commonly called the "escalator clause" allows a lender to raise the interest rate on the loan after a specified date. If the lender is given this right, it usually cannot be used until the loan has been in effect one or two years. This clause is not as popular now as it was in the past, but it is still used.

Lenders justify escalator clauses by arguing that they have an obliga-tion to those who save and invest money with them. If interest rates go

---

[16] F.H.A. contracts provide that early payments will be accepted but they decrease the number of payments from the final payment working backwards so the home owner does not save much in interest. The early payments, however, reduce the number of years on the principal to be paid.

[17] Home improvement loans are available from the F.H.A. These loans are made by banks, insurance companies, savings and loan associations and others, but they are insured. While the quoted rate is about 5 percent, the true annual rate of interest is approximately twice this rate.

up and the lender is forced by competition to raise the rates it pays to savers and investors, lenders should (they argue) have the right to raise the interest rates they charge those who have borrowed from them. This argument makes more sense when the escalator clause is tied to the interest rates paid to investors. Some escalator clauses do this. They give the lender the right to raise mortgage interest rates only when there is a corresponding increase in the rates paid to investors.

An escalator clause is undesirable and should be avoided by all borrowers. This is not hard to do. If you discuss a home loan with a lender and the lender insists on an escalator clause, you should go to lenders that do not use the clause.

An "interest equalization" clause is similar to an escalator clause. But an "interest equalization" clause raises *and lowers* the interest rate on *outstanding* mortgages automatically according to changes in the cost of money to lenders.[18] In other words, with this clause you can obtain a mortgage at a certain rate, say 8 percent, and when interest rates go up, your mortgage interest rate increases. When interest rates go down, however, the interest rate on your mortgage is reduced. This is the big difference between an escalator clause and an "interest equalization" clause. With the latter, your interest rate fluctuates up or down. This seems fair to both the borrower and the lender.

Package Mortgages. Many families, especially young families, find it difficult to save enough money for a down payment, pay closing costs, and buy household equipment. The cost of refrigerators, cooking ranges, dishwashers, washing machines and dryers, and garbage disposals often puts a financial strain on a family. This problem is alleviated by a package mortgage. This type of mortgage includes household equipment in the mortgage, and the equipment is paid off over the life of the loan. By spreading the cost of household equipment over a long period the home buyer reduces his household expenses during the first few years.

Although package mortgages provide a convenient way to finance household equipment, these mortgages (simply because they require a larger loan) involve a higher interest cost. This disadvantage should be considered before a package mortgage is used.

THE IMPORTANCE OF PROFESSIONAL HELP

You should believe, after studying the previous material in this chapter, that you do not know everything about home ownership. Purchasing a home involves many detailed, technical legal and financial problems. Fortunately, it is usually easy to obtain the services of professionals who can help with your problems.

---

[18] The type of clause is described in "Outlook for Home Buyers," *U.S. News and World Report,* No. 12, March 23, 1970, p. 72.

THE REAL ESTATE BROKER

Does a home buyer need a broker? This question arises often because a broker's commission, which usually amounts to 5 or 6 percent of the purchase price, can involve a substantial amount of money. On a $20,000 house, the commission (at 5 percent) is $1,000. Although the commission is legally paid by the seller, it is sometimes difficult to know who *actually* pays the fee. This is because a home owner can decide that he must receive a certain amount, say $20,000, for his house. He can then either sell the house himself for $20,000 or let a real estate broker sell it for $21,050 and the seller can receive approximately $20,000. In other words, if the seller simply marks up the price of the house enough to cover the real estate broker's commission, the buyer has actually paid the commission. If the price of the house is marked up, but not enough to cover the full real estate commission, the commission is actually paid by both the buyer and the seller. In deciding whether a real estate broker is needed, therefore, it is necessary to understand the advantages a broker can offer to both buyers and sellers.

The primary service a real estate broker provides to a home buyer is help in selecting prospective homes. A buyer can tell a broker exactly the type of house he wants and how much he wants to pay. The real estate broker, then, can quickly narrow down the list of prospective homes to those that meet the buyer's needs. Brokers are typically well informed about city growth, price ranges, quality of schools, real estate taxes, neighborhood patterns, and many other factors that are important in purchasing a home. By concentrating only on the houses that seem to meet the buyer's needs, a great deal of time and effort is saved in looking for a house.

One of the valuable services provided by real estate brokers to a home seller is advice about an appropriate price for the property. In many cases a home owner has made improvements to his house and neighborhood values have changed since the time he bought the house. As a result, a home owner may not have a very good idea about the price at which he should sell. A broker, since he is in constant contact with the prices of homes, can offer valuable suggestions. Incidentally, advice on this matter can also indirectly benefit a home buyer. Although a broker is obligated to obtain the highest price for the seller, most brokers will not tie up their time and money with an overpriced home. If a seller is attempting to sell his house for a great deal more than it is worth, a broker probably will not try to sell the house unless he can persuade the seller to reduce his price. Thus, a home buyer is protected to some extent against overpayment when the transaction is handled by a real estate broker.

Perhaps the most important service of brokers to home sellers is reaching a wider market of prospects. Real estate brokers have contacts with other brokers and they know how to advertise a home effectively. Brokers can also separate genuine prospects from those who do not actually intend to buy, and brokers can arrange to visit the house only at convenient times. Brokers also attend to negotiations, contract preparations, and other details in the transaction.

THE LAWYER

Even though most real estate brokers are very familiar with some of the legal problems involved in transferring ownership of a house, it is wise for a home buyer (and seller) to employ the services of an attorney. This chapter has not attempted to describe all the legal problems that can arise in a real estate transaction. But there are many different types of deeds and titles, and numerous other legal questions usually arise. Most of these questions can be handled properly only by a person with legal education and experience.

OTHER PROFESSIONAL PEOPLE

If you are planning to build a house rather than buy an existing home, you must be extremely careful. The basic problem most people encounter when they build their own house is that they have a tendency to continually revise their plans and add refinements before the house is finished. Often, the house ends up costing much more than was anticipated. This problem can be minimized if a person selects his architect and building contractor carefully and works with them throughout the entire building process. Before hiring an architect or building contractor you should check into their past experience and reputation. It is generally a good idea to talk with people who have employed them on previous projects. Also, it is important to deal only with architects and building contractors who have a sound financial position. As pointed out previously, mechanics' liens can be a problem if you are working with architects and building contractors who get into financial trouble. The advantages of having a custom-built home can only be achieved if your architect and builder both perform well.

In some situations it is wise to employ a professional appraiser. The fees charged by appraisers differ, but usually the cost is only a small fraction of the value of a house. In many cases the fee is around $50. This is a small price to pay to assure yourself that the price you intend to pay is reasonable. The services of an appraiser, of course, are needed more if you are not too familiar with real estate values.

SUMMARY

Before a person buys a home, he should investigate several important questions and problems. One of the first logical questions that arises is why a person should own a home. Some people have important reasons that are nonfinancial. Others own a home in order to obtain financial advantages. The financial advantages of home ownership cannot be studied unless a person first analyzes the costs of home ownership. These costs are not always easy to identify, but even if they are recognized they are sometimes hard to estimate.

After the costs of home ownership are estimated, a person can face the decision of whether he should rent or buy. In some cases, it is less expensive to rent, but in other cases it is cheaper to buy. From a decision-making point of view, the best a person can do is make reasonable assumptions and then compare the costs under the assumptions he has made. Again, financial results may not be the only considerations.

If a person decides to buy a home, he must decide how much he should pay. This decision should be viewed as two separate problems: how much is the house worth, and how much can you afford? The amount a buyer can afford is determined primarily by the size of the down payment, the duration of the mortgage, the interest rate on the mortgage, the buyer's monthly income, and his other financial needs.

Many young people should consider the types of housing other than traditional homes. Condominiums, cooperative apartments, and mobile homes are becoming more and more popular.

A home buyer is also faced with a number of financial and legal problems. He should understand the nature and importance of the purchase contract, which lender should be used, the pros and cons of the different types of loans, and the important provisions in his mortgage agreement. Since these problems are often technical, the home buyer should consider another question—is professional help needed?

Case Problems

1. Bill and Joan have rented an apartment for the past several years. But now Joan is anxious to buy a home. She tells Bill that their savings account is large enough to make a down payment and their combined income is enough to meet the mortgage payment. Bill, on the other hand, argues that they cannot afford to buy a house right now. Furthermore, since Bill is expecting his company to ask him to move to another city in a few years, he believes a home would be a poor purchase.
   (a) What are the costs, other than the mortgage payment, that Bill and Joan might incur if they buy a home?
   (b) What are the possible financial advantages of owning a home rather than renting?
   (c) Joan believes that some benefits cannot be stated in dollar amounts. What are the possible nonfinancial benefits of owning a home?

2. Although Bob does not have much money, he has saved for several years and has a well-paying job. His wife, Kathy, is a legal secretary and also earns a nice income. They have decided that they will buy a house rather than rent, but they believe they should not spend as much for housing as

they could actually afford. Bob thinks they should live in a modest home for several years and invest several hundred dollars each month in the stock market. If they do this, they believe they will be able to afford a much nicer home later.

Bob has found a house for sale by the owner (no real estate broker is involved) but he wonders if the house is worth the asking price of $18,000. The house is only six months old and similar homes in the neighborhood sell for about $20,000. Because Bob is concerned that the house may not be worth the asking price, he has talked with two home owners in the neighborhood, and they have both told him that they think the house would be a bargain at $18,000. However, they admit that they have not been inside the house and they think it may be a little smaller than most other houses in the area.

(a) If you were Bob, what would you do to decide whether or not the house is worth $18,000?

(b) Why should Bob be so concerned about the purchase price if he likes the house and he can easily afford it?

3. Dave Seaton and his wife, Dorothy, have been looking for a house to buy. Because they have some savings and they made a profit on the previous house they owned, they have $8,000 they might use for a down payment on a new house. However, Dave believes a person should always try to make the smallest down payment possible. He has been thinking that he might buy a house (in the $24,000–$26,000 range) and make a 10 percent down payment. Then, he will still have several thousand dollars that he can keep in savings and investments. The Seaton's thought their house hunting was finished when they found a house they both liked at $25,000 which could be purchased with a 10 percent down payment. But Dorothy complicated matters (as wives often do) when she found a house for sale that they liked just as well, also for $25,000. To solve the problem Dave and Dorothy decided to select the house that provided the best financial arrangement.

The banker has indicated that the first house would have a mortgage with an interest rate of 9 percent and that monthly expenses in addition to the mortgage payment (which covers only principal and interest) would amount to $40. The second house carries a mortgage with an interest rate of only 6 percent (since the mortgage was obtained several years ago when interest rates were low). To assume the existing mortgage Dave would have to make a down payment of $6,000. In addition to the mortgage payment, monthly expenses on this house would be $45.

(a) If Dave and Dorothy decide that $170 is the maximum monthly payment they can afford, can they buy either house? (Use Table 5–6 to help you calculate the monthly mortgage payment)

(b) What are the advantages and disadvantages to making a large down payment?

4. Although the wedding is several months away, John and Sue are starting to think about where they will live after they are married. John still has two years of college remaining and he has no substantial savings, so they have decided they will rent. But several of John's married friends are

living in rented house trailers, and they have been telling John that it is better than renting an apartment.
   (a) What are the advantages and disadvantages of renting a house trailer rather than an apartment?
   (b) In either case, John should check the provisions in the lease. Make a list of the important factors John should check in his lease.

5. Jenny has been arguing with Fred about the merits of using a real estate broker. Jenny believes a broker is always desirable for both the buyer and the seller. Fred, on the other hand, thinks a broker is helpful in selling a house, but the benefits do not accrue to the buyer. What do you believe? Why?

6. After a long and careful search, John has found a house to buy. But John believes he should check with several lenders to get the best possible mortgage terms and rates. John found that he could obtain a loan from "Bank A" at 8 percent and no points would be charged. He learned that he could get the same type of mortgage from "Bank B" at 7½ percent, but this bank wanted to charge John four points. Which bank offers John the lowest true interest charge? (You should use Table 5-7 to arrive at your answer.)

7. Al and Betty Hoff have been anxious to buy a home. It appears that they will live in the same city for a long time and they have been saving money for a down payment for the past several years. Betty has found a house she likes but Al is concerned about the mortgage interest rate. Al's concern is this: interest rates are high and the lender wants to charge 9 percent for the loan. Al thinks he would be wise to wait until interest rates fall so that he will be able to get a mortgage at a lower cost. Do you agree with Al? Give specific reasons for your answer.

8. Ted and Alice have been trying to figure out whether they should continue to rent an apartment or buy a house. They have discussed the pros and cons several times, but Alice cannot understand Ted's point when he talks about income taxes. Alice says that the apartment rent is $150 a month and the house payment would be $170 a month. Therefore, she says a house would cost $20 more each month. Ted says the house would actually be less expensive because the house payment includes about $100 a month for interest and real estate taxes of about $30 a month. He argues that $130 of each monthly payment, therefore, could be deducted from his income tax. Ted believes this is important because they both work and they are in the 30 percent tax bracket. Would you agree with Ted or Alice? Can you be more specific and calculate an *after-tax* monthly cost for the house?

Selected Readings

Babcock, Henry A. *Appraisal Principles and Procedures.* Homewood, Illinois: Richard D. Irwin, Inc., 1968.
Bowman, Arthur G. *Real Estate Law in California.* 3rd edition. Englewood Cliffs, N.J.: Prentice-Hall, Inc., 1970.

Changing Times, The Kiplinger Magazine:
>"A Brand-New Home for $6,000," April 1968, pp. 39–42.
>"At Last, a Guide to Home Fire Alarms," October 1967, pp. 13–14.
>"Buy a House—or Wait Awhile?" April 1966, pp. 29–32.
>"Buy a Lot and Build a House?" May 1969, pp. 25–28.
>"Buying a House: The Nine Most Common Questions," February 1966, pp. 13–15.
>"Can We Ever Build Cheaper Houses?" October 1970, pp. 15–19.
>"Coming Flexible, Inflatable Mortgages?" December 1970, pp. 21–24.
>"Coping With the Mortgage Squeeze," August 1969, pp. 13–14.
>"Deeds: A Guide for Home Buyers," December 1967, pp. 33–35.
>"Don't Fall for Home-Repair Gyps," May 1967, pp. 43–46.
>"For House Hunters: Sizing Up the Neighborhood," July 1970, pp. 45–47.
>"Home Building Is Ripe for a Boom," August 1970, p. 6.
>"Home-Loan Rates and Terms, City by City," July 1970, p. 6.
>"How Much Your Mortgage *Really* Cost," June 1967, pp. 51–53.
>"How POINTS Hike the Interest Rate on Your Mortgage," June 1970, p. 12.
>"How to Collect on House or Auto Insurance," December 1970, pp. 7–10.
>"Is That Lot Safe to Build On?" August 1967, pp. 22–24.
>"It Costs to *Sell* a House Too," October 1968, pp. 17–18.
>"Learn to Spot What's Wrong With a House," February 1970, pp. 3–5.
>"Let Your House Cut Your Tax Bill," October 1967, pp. 39–41.
>"Second Mortgages: How and When to Use 'Em," January 1967, pp. 15–17.
>"Setting Up Housekeeping? Here's What It Costs," March 1969, pp. 24–28.
>"Should You Own a Home—or Rent?" November 1967, pp. 15–18.
>"The How and Why of Taking Over a Mortgage," January 1970, pp. 21–23.
>"The Months Ahead: A Guide for Your Work and Personal Living," January 1967, pp. 3–5.
>"The Months Ahead: A Guide for Your Work and Personal Living," February 1967, pp. 3–6.
>"The Months Ahead: News and Ideas to Help You Plan Ahead, Stay Ahead," December 1967, pp. 3–6; March 1968, pp. 3–6; April 1968, pp. 3–6; September 1968, pp. 3–6; February 1969, pp. 3–6, March 1969, pp. 3–5; June 1969, pp. 3–6; September 1969, pp. 3–5; February 1970, pp. 3–5; September 1970, pp. 3–5, November 1970, pp. 3–6; December 1970, pp. 3–6.
>"The Science of Sizing Up a House," April 1967, pp. 43–46.
>"Thinking of Remodeling the House?" September 1970, pp. 24–28.
>"Tips on Selling a House Today," March 1967, pp. 31–33.
>"What Can You Afford to Pay for a House?" June 1968, pp. 43–46.
>"What Living in a Mobile Home Is Like," October 1968, pp. 7–11.
>"Why Not Mortgages With Variable Payments?" July 1967, pp. 51–53.

Griffin, Al. *So You Want to Buy a House.* Chicago: Rignery Co. 1970.

Hoagland, Henry and Stone Leo. *Real Estate Finance,* 4th edition. Homewood, Illinois: Richard D. Irwin, Inc., 1969.

Knowles, Jerome. *Single Family Residential Appraisal Manual.* Chicago: American Institute of Real Estate Appraisers, 1967.

Kratovil, Robert, *Real Estate Law,* Englewood Cliffs, N.J.: Prentice Hall, Inc., 1969.

Maisel, Sherman J., *Financing Real Estate.* New York: McGraw-Hill Book Company, 1965.

Moger, Byron and Burke, Martin. *How To Buy a House.* New York: L. Stuart, 1969.

Ring, Alfred A. and North, Nelson L. *Real Estate: Principles and Practices.* 6th edition. Englewood Cliffs, N.J.: Prentice-Hall, Inc., 1967.

Shelton, John P. "The Cost of Renting vs. Owning a Home." *Land Economics,* February 1968.

Unger, Maurice Albert. *Real Estate.* 4th edition. Cincinnati: South Western Publishing Co., 1969.

Watkins, Arthur Martin. *How to Avoid the Ten Biggest Home Buying Traps.* New York: Meredith Press, 1968.

Wendt, Paul F. and Cerf, Alan R. *Real Estate Investment Analysis and Taxation.* New York: McGraw-Hill Book Company, 1969.

Winstead, Robert W. *Real Estate Appraisal Desk Book.* Englewood Cliffs, N.J.: Prentice-Hall, Inc., 1968.

CHAPTER **SIX**

THE IMPORTANCE OF TAXES

The April 9, 1970 edition of the *Wall Street Journal* reported that many taxpayers included some strange items with their federal income tax return. One taxpayer sent a shirt—which had been soaked in blood. Another income tax form was reproduced on a shirt that presumably was the shirt off the taxpayer's back, and one form was reported on a piece of butcher's paper. One man sent a comb with his return, explaining that he "didn't need it anymore because he pulled all his hair while figuring his taxes."

Perhaps you have never felt so exasperated or confused as those taxpayers. If not, you probably have never filled out an income tax form, or you have a remarkably even temper.

Most people handle income tax problems very poorly, particularly young people. When you are young, it is easy to tell yourself that income taxes are not important because your income is small. The result, of course, is that many young people fail to appreciate the importance of income taxes. As your income begins to rise, it will become obvious that taxes are important. And they are important not only because taxes must be paid each year but also because the effect of taxes should be considered in many financial decisions. For example, what are the tax effects of changing jobs? If the effects are significant, they should be considered in your decisions to change jobs. Income taxes have effects that should be considered in buying or selling a home, buying or selling securities, making contributions to churches, and many other financial decisions.

Some people overemphasize the importance of taxes. They make financial decisions almost entirely on the basis of the tax effect. Others completely ignore the impact of taxes. A person who is financially wise does not go to either extreme—he lets taxes *influence* his financial decisions. A person should manage his financial affairs so that his objectives

147

are reached with a minimum payment of taxes. It is not unpatriotic or unethical to legally minimize taxes. In fact, the United States Supreme Court has stated that a taxpayer has a right to decrease the amount of his taxes (or avoid them entirely) by means which the law permits.

But a person cannot minimize his taxes unless he has some knowledge of income tax rules and regulations. Although a young person might prefer to postpone the problems involved in learning about taxes, it is better to prepare yourself with some knowledge of the tax laws rather than pay heavily through ignorance later.

This chapter does not attempt to set forth a complete description of the income tax laws and regulations. These laws and regulations are extremely complex and constantly changing. Therefore, you will not be a tax expert after reading this chapter. Almost every income tax rule has exceptions, and usually these are exceptions to the exceptions. But if you study this chapter carefully, you will be in a position to handle some common income tax problems without much difficulty. More importantly, this material provides a brief tax background so that you will be able to recognize the importance of various tax problems. The chapter is organized and treated according to the major problems that arise in connection with tax questions. It emphasizes problems that are particularly important to young taxpayers.

FUNDAMENTAL INCOME TAX CONCEPTS

When a person first glances at an income tax form, he is confronted with a maze of lines, blocks, boxes, and instructions. It is not surprising, then, for a person to be confused. Actually, however, income tax problems are not so complicated if a person understands a few basic concepts.

Every taxpayer starts with a basic, one-page form which is Form 1040. This form is reproduced as Figure 6–1 so that you can refer to it in our discussion. Many taxpayers are required to file only this form; others, however, will be required to file special schedules with their Form 1040 to supply additional information.

The basic formula for Form 1040 is:

$$
\begin{aligned}
&\quad\text{Gross Income} \\
&- \text{ Adjustments to Gross Income} \\
\hline
&= \text{ Adjusted Gross Income} \\
&- \text{ Exemptions} \\
&- \text{ Deductions} \\
\hline
&= \text{ Taxable Income} \\
&\times \text{ Tax rate} \\
&= \text{ Tax}
\end{aligned}
$$

Figure 6–1   Form 1040

Form **1040**   U S   Department of the Treasury / Internal Revenue Service
Individual Income Tax Return   **1970**

For the year January 1–December 31, 1970, or other taxable year beginning .... 1970, ending .... 19 ......

Please print or type

First name and initial (if joint return, use first names and middle initials of both) | Last name | Your social security number

Present home address (Number and street or rural route) | Spouse's social security number

City, town or post office, State and ZIP code | Occupation | Yours | Spouse's

Filing Status—check only one:

1 ☐ Single;   2 ☐ Married filing jointly (even if only one had income)
3 ☐ Married filing separately and spouse is also filing. If this item checked give spouse's social security number in space above and enter first name here ▶
4 ☐ Unmarried Head of Household
5 ☐ Surviving widow(er) with dependent child
6 ☐ Married filing separately and spouse is not filing

Exemptions   Regular / 65 or over / Blind

7 Yourself . . . . . . ☐   ☐   ☐   Enter number of boxes checked ▶
8 Spouse (applies only if item 2 or 6 is checked) ☐   ☐   ☐
9 First names of your dependent children who lived with you _____   Enter number ▶
10 Number of other dependents (from line 34) . . . ▶
11 Total exemptions claimed . . . . ▶

Income

12 Wages, salaries, tips, etc. (Attach Forms W–2 to back. If unavailable, attach explanation) . | 12
13a Dividends (see page 5 and 9 of instr.) $ .... 13b Less exclusion $ .... Balance . ▶ | 13c
(Also list in Part I of Schedule B, if gross dividends and other distributions are over $100)
14 Interest. Enter total here (also list in Part II of Schedule B, if total is over $100) . . . | 14
15 Income other than wages, dividends, and interest (from line 40) . . . . | 15
16 Total (add lines 12, 13c, 14 and 15) . . . . | 16
17 Adjustments to income (such as "sick pay," moving expense, etc. from line 45) . . . | 17
18 Adjusted gross income (subtract line 17 from line 16) . . . . | 18

● See page 2 of instructions for rules under which the IRS will figure your tax and surcharge.
● If you do not itemize deductions and line 18 is under $10,000, find tax in Tables. Enter tax on line 19.
● If you itemize deductions or line 18 is $10,000 or more, go to line 46 to figure tax.

Tax and Surcharge

19 Tax (Check if from: Tax Tables 1–15 ☐, Tax Rate Schedule X, Y, or Z ☐, Schedule D ☐, or Schedule G ☐) | 19
20 Tax surcharge. See Tax Surcharge Tables A, B and C in instructions. (If you claim retirement income credit, use Schedule R to figure surcharge.) . . . . . . | 20
21 Total (add lines 19 and 20) . . . . | 21

Payments and Credits

22 Total credits (from line 55) . . . . | 22
23 Income tax (subtract line 22 from line 21) . . . . | 23
24 Other taxes (from line 61) . . . . | 24
25 Total (add lines 23 and 24) . . . . | 25
26 Total Federal income tax withheld (attach Forms W–2 to back) . | 26
27 1970 Estimated tax payments (include 1969 overpayment allowed as a credit) | 27
28 Other payments (from line 65) . . . . | 28

Make check or money order payable to Internal Revenue Service.

29 Total (add lines 26, 27, and 28) . . . . | 29

Bal. Due or Refund

30 If line 25 is larger than line 29, enter BALANCE DUE. Pay in full with return . . . ▶ | 30
31 If line 29 is larger than line 25, enter OVERPAYMENT . . . . ▶ | 31
32 Line 31 to be: (a) Credited on 1971 estimated tax ▶ $ .... ; (b) Refunded ▶ $

Under penalties of perjury, I declare that I have examined this return, including accompanying schedules and statements, and to the best of my knowledge and belief it is true, correct, and complete.

Sign here

Your signature | Date | Signature of preparer other than taxpayer, based on all information of which he has any knowledge. | Date

Spouse's signature (if filing jointly, BOTH must sign even if only one had income) | Address | 16—81160-1

This formula can be very helpful in understanding income tax problems. It shows that a person's income is adjusted and deductions and exemptions are subtracted before a person can determine his taxable income. After a person calculates his taxable income, it is a simple matter to look at the appropriate table and find the amount of income tax that is payable. Then a person compares the amount of the tax payable to the amount that has been withheld from his paychecks during the year. If too much has been withheld, the taxpayer will be entitled to a tax refund. If, on the other hand, the taxpayer has not had enough withheld from his paychecks, he will be required to pay an additional tax.[1]

DETERMINING GROSS INCOME

You might think that it is always easy to know how much you earned during the year. After all, your employer is required to furnish you with a withholding statement (Form W-2) that shows how much you earned and how much tax has been withheld.

The problem is not quite that easy, however. The law states that all types of income are subject to income taxes—with certain exceptions. Examples of income that must be reported are:

> Wages, salaries, bonuses, and commissions
> Interest from bank deposits, bonds, and notes
> Pensions, annuities, and endowments
> Rents and royalties
> Military pay
> Business profits
> Income from a hobby

In addition to the examples in the above list, there are certain other types of income that sometimes cause problems. Many students work as waiters, waitresses, or in some other job that provides income in the form of tips. This income is fully taxable. There is some confusion about this, but the confusion arises from the rules for withholding. If you received less than $20 a month in tips, the tips do not need to be reported to your employer. But you will be required by law to report this income on your federal income tax return and you may be required to pay a tax on it. If you receive more than $20 a month in tips, the income should be reported to your employer and he will withhold income taxes for your tips. Legally, tips are considered compensation for services and therefore they are taxable. Contrary to what many people believe, true gifts and inheritances are *not* subject to federal income taxes.[2]

---

[1] Some people are required to file a Declaration of Estimated Tax. Basically, this form is intended for those who receive income without sufficient withholding for taxes. The general rule is that you must estimate your taxes (and pay them during the year) if you receive more than $200 in taxable income not subject to withholding *and* you estimate that your total tax for the year will exceed your withholding by $40 or more. But the rules regarding the Declaration of Estimated Tax are complicated. If you expect to receive taxable income and no tax (or insufficient tax) will be withheld, you should check the rules carefully. See *Your Federal Income Tax* (current edition), Department of the Treasury, Internal Revenue Service.

[2] *Income* from a gift or inheritance is taxable, and a gift or inheritance may result in a gift or inheritance tax but not an income tax.

If you win a contest and receive a prize, is this taxable income? Yes, if you win a prize in a contest, you must report the prize as income. If the prize is in the form of merchandise, the merchandise is taxed at its fair market value. However, you do not pay taxes on awards you receive in recognition of past accomplishments, such as educational awards for which you were selected without action on your part and for which you are not expected to render any future services. This is the reason scholarships and fellowship grants are not included in your income for tax purposes.[3]

Usually, dividends are taxable income. However, every taxpayer may exclude up to $100 in dividend income. When filing jointly, a husband and wife may deduct $200 if each spouse had a dividend income of at least $100.[4] Interest earnings on deposits in banks, savings and loan associations, credit unions and similar financial institutions are regarded as interest and not "dividends." Even if they are called dividends they must be reported as income and they are not eligible on the dividend exclusion.

It is often said that a husband and wife can exclude $200 of their dividend income. But suppose a husband receives $130 in dividends and his wife receives $70 in dividends. The husband can exclude $100 and his wife can exclude $70, for a total of $170—not $200.[5] The wife cannot exclude the $30 her husband was unable to exclude, even though they filed a joint return.

Some types of corporate distributions may be completely, or partially, exempt from income taxation. When a corporation pays a "dividend" that represents earnings of the company and a partial return of capital, the return of capital is not taxed. When this type of distribution is made, the check from the company will indicate the portion that represents taxable income. Life insurance dividends paid to policyholders (not stockholders) are not taxable. They represent a partial return of a premium, and they are not considered to be earnings on an investment. Also, a *stock* dividend (which is a dividend from a corporation in the form of the corporation's stock) does not increase a stockholder's proportionate interest in a corporation is not taxed.

The sale or exchange of property, such as profit from the sale of a house or profit from the sale of an asset such as stock, can increase your taxable income. Because special rules apply to these transactions and a

---

[3] Income from scholarships and fellowships *is* taxable if the income is paid to compensate you for past, present, or future services, or if the income allows you to study or perform research primarily for the benefit of the person or organization that pays the scholarship.

[4] The dividend exclusion does not apply to alien corporations, tax exempt farmers' cooperatives, and real estate investment trusts.

[5] This is not the rule in some community property states.

separate schedule (Schedule D) must be completed, capital gains and losses are treated later.

Subject only to rare exceptions, the following items are *not* to be included in your income for tax purposes:

Life insurance death proceeds
Life insurance dividends paid to policyholders (but dividends paid to stockholders and earnings on policyholder dividends are reportable)
Benefits for servicemen for subsistence, uniform, and living quarters
Dividends on veteran's government insurance
Gifts and inheritances
Social security benefits
Unemployment compensation
Workmen's compensation
Interest on state and municipal bonds
Railroad Retirement Act benefits

It is important to realize that employers are required to report your *gross* income to the government. Even though the employer may make deductions from your paycheck for union dues, savings bonds, social security taxes and other things, the total income is reported to the government. Also, if you receive room and board, merchandise, and other valuable items as part of your compensation, you must include these items in your income at their fair market value.

ADJUSTMENTS TO GROSS INCOME

A person does not pay a tax on his total gross income. After a person determines his total gross income, the next step is to make adjustments and arrive at a figure that represents "adjusted gross income." This is a very important figure because a person's adjusted gross income may have an important effect on the amount of exemptions and deductions he may claim.

Adjusted gross income is determined by deducting from gross income the following:

Sick pay[6] (Form 2440 must be attached)

---

[6] A brief explanation of the sick pay adjustment might be helpful. The other adjustments are discussed later in the chapter. If you are absent from work because of injury or sickness and continue to receive wages or salary, this income will be partially or fully excluded from your gross income if: (1) you receive 75 percent or less of your regular wages during the first 30 days of your disability, (2) you exclude up to $100 a week after 30 days of disability (regardless of the percentage of wages received). If your rate of pay is 75 percent or less, you can exclude sick pay (up to $75 a week) starting with the first day you are hospitalized or starting on the eighth day if you are not hospitalized.

Moving expenses (Form 3903 must be attached)

Employee business expenses (Form 2106 must be attached)

Payments to a self-employment retirement plan (Form 2950SE must be attached)

EXEMPTIONS

Your taxable income is decreased for each exemption you claim. In other words, an exemption is an amount of income that will not be taxed. For many years prior to 1970, this amount was $600. Now, the amount for each exemption has been scheduled as follows:

1970	$625
1971	$650
1972	$700
1973	$750

It is important to claim all the exemptions for which you are legally entitled. In 1972, if you miss one exemption it will cost you the amount of tax paid on $700.

Every individual who files an income tax return is permitted to claim at least one exemption. A person can count himself as an exemption. In fact, you may be entitled to take yourself as an exemption even if you have been claimed as a dependent on another person's tax return. Therefore, if you are a student and file a return, you might be able to claim yourself as an exemption even though you have also been claimed on your parents' return as their dependent. You are also allowed an exemption for your spouse if you file a joint return. In addition, you are allowed an additional exemption for each person who qualifies as your dependent.[7]

There are five requirements that must be met to claim an exemption for a dependent. The first requirement is called the "gross income test." Under this requirement, a dependent must have had a total income of less than the amount of one exemption. However, there is an exception to this requirement that is especially important to young people. A person may be able to claim his child, stepchild, or adopted child regardless of his income if the child is under 19 years of age, or is a full-time student. This is interpreted to mean a student at a regular school during some part of five different months in the year.

The second requirement is that you must provide more than one-half of the dependent's support. To do this, you must determine the dependent's total living expenses and what proportion of his support is provided by someone else.

---

[7] A spouse may qualify as a dependent if you file separate returns. Also, a person is given an additional exemption if he (or she) is over age 65 or blind.

The third requirement that must be met before you can claim someone as a dependent is the "relationship test." A dependent must be related to you or be a member of your household for the entire year except for temporary absences. You can meet the relationship test if the dependent does not live with you provided he is related in one of the following ways:[8]

Your child, grandchild, or great grandchild
Your stepchild
Your brother, sister, halfbrother, halfsister, stepbrother, or step-sister
Your parent, grandparent (but not foster parent)
Your stepfather or stepmother
A brother or sister of your father or mother
A son or daughter of your brother or sister
Your father-in-law, mother-in-law, son-in-law, daughter-in-law, brother-in-law, sister-in-law

The fourth test is the citizenship or residence test. A dependent must be a citizen or resident of the United States, Canada, Canal Zone, or Mexico during some part of the year.

The last requirement for a dependent is the joint return test. A tax-payer cannot claim a deduction for any person who files a joint return with someone other than the taxpayer. Therefore, a married student whose wife is working would not be eligible to be claimed by his father if the student and his wife file a joint return. If his father is providing more than 50 percent of his support he may choose *not* to file a joint return with his wife.

DEDUCTIONS

Following the basic formula for Form 1040, a person deducts certain items from his adjusted gross income to arrive at his taxable income. You can do this either by taking one of the standard deductions or itemizing your deductions. Since this is an important decision, it is treated later in the chapter.

IMPORTANT DECISIONS

SHOULD YOU FILE A FEDERAL INCOME TAX RETURN?

One of the first decisions a person encounters with federal income taxes is the question of whether or not he should file a tax return. Because the United States Treasury Department naturally emphasizes the question of who *must* file a return, some problems arise.

---

[8] If you file a joint return, you do not need to show that the dependent is related to both of you.

If you are a citizen of the United States (or resident) you *must* file a federal income tax return if your gross income is more than the amounts shown in Table 6–1.

Table 6–1   Incomes and Filing Requirements

| | Under Age 65 | | Over Age 65 (Both Spouses) | |
	1972	After 1972	1972	After 1972
Single	$1,700	$1,750	$2,300	$2,500
Married	$2,300	$2,500	$3,500	$4,000

Table 6–1 shows that a single person who has an income in 1972 of $1,700 or more must file a federal income tax return. Also, every individual with net self-employment income over a certain amount ($400 in 1970), and every corporation and partnership must file a return. A partnership must file an information return even though a partnership itself pays no federal income taxes.

You are not excused from federal income taxes if you are a minor (under the age of 21). Furthermore, a minor's earnings are subject to tax even if under local law his parents have the legal right to the earnings. But suppose you worked for a part of the summer and earned only $550. *Should* you file a return? The answer is yes, if you had any income tax withheld from your income when you worked. If you file a return and claim your personal exemption, you will get a refund of the tax you have had withheld from your income. The tax is refundable even if some other taxpayer (your father, for example) claimed you as a dependent in his own tax calculations.[9]

Actually, the best procedure for a person who earns a low income is to file Form W-4E. This form provides an exemption from withholding. In other words, if you qualify for the exemption your employer will not deduct anything for federal income taxes from your pay.

To qualify, an employee must file a statement showing that he owed no federal income taxes for the preceding year and he does not expect to owe any taxes for the current year. But how does a person know that he probably will not owe any taxes for the current year? The easiest way to know this is to look at Table 6–1. If your annual income is less than the amounts shown in the table, you will incur no federal income tax liability. Later, if your income increases (enough so that you will be required to file a return) you will have to notify your employer and he will start withholding tax from your paycheck. (Some states also follow the federal procedure and will let an employee skip withholding *state* income taxes

---

[9] A minor's income is *not* included in his parents' federal income tax return.

on the basis of the federal exemption.) Form W-4E is particularly important for young college students. If you work only during the summer and earn less than $1,750 (after 1972) you will not need to file a return and federal income taxes will not be deducted from your pay.

WHEN TO FILE

It is important to file your return on time because you may incur penalties for a late payment. The deadline, for most taxpayers, is the fifteenth of April each year.[10] If April 15 is not a business day (a business day is any day other than a Saturday, Sunday, or legal holiday) you can file your return on the next business day.

Under some unusual circumstances you can be given an extension of time. But extensions are not given without very sound and persuasive reasons. In order to get an extension, you must file a form or write a letter and explain reasons for requesting an extension, indicate whether you filed your tax returns on time in the three preceding years, and state whether you were required to file an estimated tax return. If you are a serviceman (or the wife of a serviceman) and you need additional time to prepare your tax return, you should check into the rules that give additional time for taxpayers in the military service.

Even though April 15 is the normal deadline, it may be advantageous to file as soon as possible after the end of the calendar year. If the amount withheld from your paychecks exceeds the tax payable, you will be entitled to a refund. It is beneficial, of course, to file the return and receive the refund as soon as possible.

SELECTING THE APPROPRIATE TAX RATE

It would be simpler and easier (but perhaps less equitable) if our federal tax system used only one tax rate for all individuals. But the fact is that there are several rates, and a person must choose which rate is appropriate for him. The decision may be important because the tax rates are substantially different. For example, a person whose taxable income is $10,000 pays $3,200 under one tax rate schedule and only $2,200 under another. This is a difference of more than 45 percent. The choice of the tax rate schedule, therefore, should be made carefully.

Table 6–2 contains some important information. It shows the rates that make up the four different rate schedules. Table 6–2 shows very clearly an important feature of the federal income tax system. All the tax tables (not just those for single taxpayers) are progressive. That is, a person with a higher taxable income pays a higher percentage of his income for taxes than a person who earns a lower taxable income. According to Table 6–2, a single person who has a taxable income of

---

[10] You should check with the Internal Revenue Service if you file for any period other than the calendar year.

Table 6–2 Tax Rates

Taxable Income	Single Taxpayers	Head of Households	Married Filing Joint Return and Surviving Spouse	Married Filing Separate Returns and Estates and Trusts
Up to $ 500	14%	14%	14%	14%
Over 500	15	14	14	15
1,000	16	16	15	16
1,500	17	16	15	17
2,000	19	18	16	19
3,000	19	18	17	19
4,000	21	19	19	22
6,000	24	22	19	25
8,000	25	23	22	28
10,000	27	25	22	32
12,000	29	27	25	36
14,000	31	28	25	39
16,000	34	31	28	42
18,000	36	32	28	45
20,000	38	35	32	48
22,000	40	36	32	50
24,000	40	38	36	50
26,000	45	41	36	53
28,000	45	42	39	53
32,000	50	45	42	55
36,000	50	48	45	55
38,000	55	51	45	58
40,000	55	52	48	58
44,000	60	55	50	60
50,000	62	56	50	62
52,000	62	58	53	62
60,000	64	58	53	64
64,000	64	59	55	64
70,000	66	61	55	66
76,000	66	62	58	66
80,000	68	63	58	68
88,000	68	64	60	68
90,000	69	64	60	69
100,000	70	66	62	70
120,000	70	67	64	70
140,000	70	68	66	70
160,000	70	69	68	70
180,000	70	70	69	70
200,000	70	70	70	70

$4,000 pays a tax of 21 percent or $840. But a single person who has a taxable income of $10,000 pays a tax of 27 percent or $2,700. Our tax system is progressive at every income level (until the maximum rate is reached); the more taxable income you have, the higher your tax rate will be. The tax rates start at 14 percent and increase to 70 percent. Notice the tax rate schedule that applies to single taxpayers provides higher taxes than the other schedules. You can question the fairness of these higher rates, but the fact that they are substantially higher cannot be disputed.

To determine if you are required to use the single taxpayers rates, you must answer two questions. First, you must be ineligible for the table that applies to the head of a household or surviving spouse (described later). And second, you must be unmarried on December 31 of the taxable year. Your marital status during the year makes no difference, the important factor is your marital status on the last day of the year.

Eight states (Arizona, California, Idaho, Louisiana, Nevada, New Mexico, Texas, and Washington) are "community property" states. In these states, the state laws provide that the earnings of a married couple belong to each spouse equally—no matter who earns the income. Prior to 1948 this created a problem. A married couple who lived in a community property state had an income tax advantage over married couples in other states.

Consider this example. The Smiths lived in California (a community property state) and Mr. Smith had a taxable income of $10,000. Even though his wife had no job and actually earned no income, the law required the Smiths to divide the income equally. They each paid an income tax on $5,000. The Jones lived in Pennsylvania (not a community property state) and Mr. Jones also had a taxable income of $10,000. Consequently, Mr. Jones had to pay a tax that was more than the total tax paid by Mr. and Mrs. Smith. This resulted because of the progressive nature of the federal income tax law.

The income tax is still progressive, but to be more fair to people who do not live in community property states, the federal income tax law was changed in 1948. The purpose of the change is to provide equivalent tax treatment to residents in all the states. Now, a married couple in any state can file a joint return and this type of return has the effect of "splitting" the income of a married couple. This usually results in a lower tax than would be paid if separate returns were filed.

Not everyone can, or should, file a joint return however. Only a husband and wife can file a joint return. Again, the test is whether or not you were married on the last day of the tax year. If you are married on December 31, you can file a joint return for all the income earned during the year. If you are divorced or legally separated before the last day of the year, you cannot file a joint return for that year. You can also file a joint return if your spouse died during the year (if you do not remarry during the year).

A married couple can file a joint return even if one spouse has no income. If a joint return is used, all the income, exemptions, and deductions of both the husband and wife are combined on the same form.

As a general rule, it is advantageous for a married couple to file a joint return because the tax is usually lower than it would be if they filed separate returns. A married couple, however, can elect to file separate returns, and in some cases, it will be to their advantage to do so. Therefore, a person should estimate his tax on the joint return and compare it to an estimate of the tax he would have to pay if he and his wife filed separate returns.

A person may be unmarried or legally separated and still have the expense of maintaining a household. For such persons, tax schedules can be used that provide a lower tax than the tax for single taxpayers. (As shown in Table 6–2 these generally are between those paid under joint and separate returns.)

To be eligible to file as the head of a household, a person must meet certain requirements. A person must be unmarried or legally separated on the last day of the year and must have furnished over 50 percent of the yearly cost of maintaining a household for a relative. This includes:

1. An unmarried child or grandchild (not necessarily your dependent)
2. Your father or mother if they are one of your dependents (they do not necessarily have to live in your home)
3. Any other relative who is your dependent and lives in your home

In determining whether you have provided at least one-half of the cost of maintaining the household, you may include the cost of rent, mortgage interest, property taxes, insurance on the home, repairs, utilities, domestic help, and food. You cannot include the cost of such items as clothing, education, medical treatment, vacations, transportation, life insurance, services provided by you or a member of your household, and the rental value of a home you own.

SHOULD DEDUCTIONS BE ITEMIZED?

Do you know what can be deducted from your income when you are calculating your federal income tax? You probably are not aware of all the possible deductions you may take. This is because the tax laws concerning deductions are extremely confusing, detailed, and complex. And, as a result, it is easy to miss legitimate deductions and pay a higher tax than you should.

There is a good chance that your income will increase rapidly over the next several years and income taxes will become more important to you. As your income grows, you will realize that one of the easiest ways to cut down substantially on your income tax is to become more familiar with the items that can be deducted from your income.

Choosing the Method of Calculating Your Deductions. You have a choice of three methods that can be used to determine your deductions: (1) you can itemize your deductions, (2) you can take the percentage standard deduction, or (3) you can use the low income allowance. In making the choice, it is wise to make a preliminary estimate of all three ways (unless you know from experience which method will give you the largest deduction). If estimates are made, it is wise to keep in mind that married people who file separate returns must take the same type of deduction. If one spouse uses the percentage standard deduction, the other must also use it. If a spouse itemizes deductions, the other must also itemize.

In 1972 the percentage standard deduction is 14 percent of adjusted gross income with a limit of $2,000. In the years after 1972 the percentage standard deduction will be raised to 15 percent of adjusted gross income, but the maximum deduction will remain at $2,000. The low income allowance is easy to understand. It is simply a flat $1,000. The amount of income a person earns is not a factor.

Suppose that in 1973 you are married and have one child. If you have an adjusted gross income of $8,000 and you estimate that your itemized deductions would amount to $900, which type of deduction should you use? The percentage standard deduction would provide a deduction of $1,200 (15 percent of $8,000). This would be the best choice because the low income allowance is only $1,000 and your itemized deductions would amount to only $900. But the other types of deductions can give important advantages under other circumstances.

Itemizing Your Deductions. Many people will be able to obtain larger deductions by itemizing their deductions. To do this, however, a person must be aware of the items that are deductible.

(1) Medical and dental expenses. Medical and dental expenses you pay during the year are deductible, but only under certain conditions, and the deduction is subject to several limitations. The expenses must have been incurred by you, your spouse, or your dependents. If you pay medical expenses for one of your parents, for example, and your parent does not qualify as one of your dependents, you cannot deduct the medical expenses. To deduct medical and dental expenses for your spouse you must have been married at the time the expenses were incurred or when the bills were paid. Notice that the usual rule of being married on the last day of the year does not apply.[11]

Medical and dental expenses that are reimbursed by insurance are *not* deductible. However, you can deduct one-half of the premiums you have paid for medical insurance. This deduction is limited to $150. These premiums must be for insurance that covers you (or your dependents) for hospital, surgical, and other medical expenses. You are not allowed to include the premiums for policies that reimburse you for loss of limb or sight, or for policies that reimburse for lost income when the policyholder is disabled. You cannot deduct life insurance premiums.

---

[11] The same type of rule applies to dependents. To deduct medical and dental expenses paid for a dependent, the person must have been a dependent at the time the expenses were incurred or paid.

Very often tax problems arise with group health insurance plans. Consider this case. Fred works for the Ace Manufacturing Company and the company has a health insurance plan. The plan covers hospital, surgical, and medical expenses and also covers loss of limbs and provides disability income. The cost of the plan is split equally by the Ace Manufacturing Company and its employees. Fred's monthly contribution for the insurance is $13.40. How much can he deduct on his federal income tax return? Fred will have to find out what portion of his monthly premium goes to the part of the coverage that can be deducted (that is, the hospital, surgical, and medical expense protection). Suppose this is $7.20 a month. Fred, therefore, can deduct $43.20 ($7.20 × 12 = $86.40 and one-half of $86.40 is $43.20). The easiest way to determine which portion of the premium is deductible is to ask the employer or to ask the insurance company.

Medical and dental expenses can be deducted only to the extent that they exceed 3 percent of your adjusted gross income. Expenditures for medicines and drugs may be included in medical and dental expenses only to the extent they exceed 1 percent of your adjusted gross income. Both of these types of expenses must be reduced by the amount of any reimbursement (such as insurance benefits).

An example can help you understand how medical expenses are deducted. Assume that your medical expenses (doctor and hospital bills) amount to $700, and medicines and drugs cost you an additional $180. During the year you paid $200 for health insurance but were reimbursed $300 for doctor and hospital bills and $50 for medicines and drugs. If your adjusted gross income was $9,000, how much can you deduct? You should be able to determine the deduction from the rules described above.

Your deduction would be calculated as follows:

One-half of the medical insurance premium			$100
Net cost of medicines and drugs			
($180 − $50 reimbursement)		$130	
Less: 1 percent of $9,000		$ 90	
Balance considered as medical expenses		$ 40	
Other medical expenses	$700		
Balance of insurance premiums	$100		
Less reimbursement	$800		
	−$300		
		$500	
Total medical expenses			
Less: 3 percent of $9,000		$270	
			$270
Total deduction			$370

Prior to 1966 there were maximum limitations that applied to medical and dental expense deductions. Since that time there is no dollar maximum limitation on deductions.

One of the major problems a person encounters when he actually tries to calculate his medical and dental expense deduction is the question of which expenses may be legally included. Many people believe that only medicines and drugs purchased by prescription may be deducted. This is not true. You may deduct any expenditures for items legally obtained and generally recognized as medicines and drugs, even if they are purchased without a prescription. You cannot deduct expenditures for toothpaste, toiletries, and cosmetics. A special food or beverage is deductible if it is prescribed by a physician solely for the treatment of an illness or medical problem. For example, if your doctor prescribes two ounces of bourbon twice a day, the cost of the whiskey is deductible. (If you use this deduction, make sure you have a doctor's prescription.)

Transportation expenses may be deducted if the transportation costs are primarily for and essential to your medical care. Expenses for meals and lodging are not deductible unless they are incurred in a hospital, nursing home, or similar institution and the expenses were paid as a result of the patient's poor health. It is practically impossible to know all the expenses that might be deductible, but by glancing over the checklist in Table 6–3, a person can obtain a better general knowledge of the types of expenses that may be deductible. (The list does not cover every possible deductible expense.)

(2) *Contributions.*   You can deduct contributions you make to religious, charitable, educational, and other qualified organizations. The well-known organizations that qualify are churches, nonprofit hospitals and schools, United Fund, Community Chest, Red Cross, Boy Scouts, Girl Scouts, CARE, and the Salvation Army. You cannot deduct contributions to social clubs, civic leagues, chambers of commerce, political organizations, propaganda organizations and labor unions. If you are in doubt as to whether an organization is qualified, you can inquire with the organization or check with an Internal Revenue Office. It is well to keep in mind, however, that contributions made to individuals are never deductible. (Direct gifts to a needy family, for example, would not be deductible.)

Most contributions are made in the form of cash, but other types of gifts are deductible. You can deduct gifts such as clothing, food, equipment, securities, real estate, furniture and books. It is important to realize that a taxpayer who gives property to qualified organizations should be careful to keep complete records of all such gifts. If you make a gift of property for which you claim a deduction of more than $200, you must provide a statement that shows the name and address of the organization, the date of the gift, a description of the property, an explanation of how you acquired the property, the method you used to determine the fair

Table 6–3   Check List for Medical and Dental Expenses

Deductible	
Abdominal supports	Gum treatment
Ambulance hire	Hearing aids
Arch supports	Infections
Artificial teeth	Insulin treatments
Back supports	Invalid chair
Blood tests	Iron lung
Braces	Metabolism tests
Chiropodist	Nursing
Chiropractor	Optician
Cleaning teeth (by dentist)	Optometrist
Contraceptive devices (by prescription)	Oral contraceptives (if prescribed by physician)
Convalescent home (for medical treatment only)	Oral surgery
Crutches	Osteopath
Dental X-Rays	Pediatrician
Drugs	Physician
Electric shock treatments	Podiatrist
Eyeglasses	Prescriptions
Filling teeth	Psychiatrist
Psychoanalyst	Sickroom supplies
Splints	Surgeon
Use of operating room	Vaccines
Vitamins, tonics, etc., prescribed by a doctor (but not taken as a food supplement or to preserve general health)	Wheelchairs
Whirlpool baths	X-Rays

Nondeductible	
Antiseptic diaper service	Dance lessons advised by a doctor
Athletic club expenses to keep fit	Illegally procured drugs
Bottled water bought to avoid drinking fluoridated water	Illegal operations or treatment
Cemetery plot or monument	Specially designed car for a polio victim
Costs of trips for a change of environment to boost morale or an ailing person, even though prescribed by a physician	Swimming pool
	Cost of fallout shelter

market price of the property, and your cost (if you owned the property less than five years). Of course, you may be required to provide supporting evidence for gifts of less than $200.

You are not allowed to deduct the value of your personal services. Suppose you donate paint and help paint your church. You can deduct the paint, but you cannot deduct anything for your labor. You may deduct out-of-pocket expenses (such as postage, phone calls, food, the cost of uniforms you wear while performing services, and the cost of using your car for charitable work) but you cannot claim a deduction for personal services.

If a person gives cash to a qualified charity, he can deduct the amount given (subject to the limitations below). But if the property is donated, the amount of the deduction that can be claimed is sometimes difficult to determine. To determine the amount of the deduction, a contributor must first ask himself how he would have been taxed if he had sold the property instead of giving it away.

If selling the property would have produced ordinary income or a short-term capital gain, the amount of the deduction is usually the property's fair market value less the amount of appreciation. For example, Jerry bought some common stock and paid $3,000 for it. Three months later he donated it to a charity when it had a value of $5,000. Therefore, his deduction would be $3,000 and not the full market value of the property at the time of the gift. If selling the property would have produced a long-term capital gain, the amount of the deduction for an individual is the property's fair market value at the time of the gift.[12]

As a general rule, deductions for contributions cannot exceed 50 percent of your adjusted gross income. But if a person is thinking about a sizable contribution to a private foundation, he should check the tax rules carefully because deductions to certain types of organizations are limited to 20 percent of your adjusted gross income. In some cases a person may deduct the maximum amount in one year and carry forward the deduction in future years.

(3) *Taxes.*   As a general rule, state, county, and other local taxes are deductible for federal income tax purposes. Federal taxes are not deductible.

State income taxes, which might be sizable, are deductible. Property taxes are also deductible except those that increase the value of your property (such as assessments for improvements in streets, water mains, and sewers). Another important deduction is state and local general sales taxes (and some cities have an additional sales tax). Because it would be so difficult to show the amount paid in sales taxes, the Treasury has

---

[12] This rule is subject to some important exceptions. The amount of the deduction may be reduced by one-half of the appreciation if tangible personal property is given to a charity and the property is unrelated to the charity's function or if the gift is made to certain private nonoperating foundations.

authorized the use of optional tables to compute your sales tax deduction. Three of these tables are illustrated in Table 6–4.

State taxes on gasoline are also deductible. Tables are available that show the amount of the tax per gallon of gas. With these tables a person only has to estimate the number of miles he has driven and the number of gallons of gas used to compute his deduction for state gasoline taxes.

Personal property taxes are deductible if they are based on the value of the property. For example, if you buy a new car and incur a state property tax, the tax is deductible.

You are *not* allowed to deduct the following taxes in calculating your federal income taxes:

Admission tax	Federal gift tax
Alcoholic beverage tax	Federal income tax
Assessments for local benefits	Social security taxes
Automobile license fees (not	Federal or state excise taxes
qualifying as a personal	Federal gasoline taxes
property tax)	Poll taxes
Cigarette tax	State gift taxes

(4) *Interest and finance charges.* The interest you pay on personal debts and finance charges on installment purchases are deductible. Of course, the most important interest cost for many people is the portion of their monthly house payment that represents mortgage interest.

It is usually easy to determine how much interest you have paid through your monthly house payment. In most cases the bank, savings and loan association, insurance company or other mortgagee that holds your mortgage will indicate the amount of interest on your monthly receipt or it will be shown on a separate statement at the end of the year. A person who owns a share of a cooperative apartment house can also deduct his share of the mortgage interest paid by the apartment unit.

The amount of interest paid on installment purchases is not so easy to determine. In some cases, the amount of the interest is specifically stated, but often it is difficult or impossible to know how much you have actually paid. Consequently, the Internal Revenue Service will permit you to deduct the amount of interest paid up to a maximum amount equal to 6 percent of the average monthly unpaid balance on the indebtedness.[13]

(5) *Casualty and theft losses.* A casualty is the partial or complete destruction of property that results from an identifiable event of a sudden, unexpected, or unusual nature. Examples of casualties are hurricanes, storms, sonic booms, vandalism, and car accidents. Losses that are *not* deductible as casualties include the breakage of china or glassware, diseases to trees and shrubs, and termite damage. An individual can

---

[13] Actually, a taxpayer is permitted to use the 6 percent rule or deduct the actual carrying charges for the year, whichever is less.

Table 6-4 Optional State Sales Tax Tables

Income	Florida Family size (persons)				Georgia Family size (persons)					Minnesota Family size (persons)		
	1&2	3&4	5	Over 5	1	2	3&4	5	Over 5	1&2	3,4&5	Over 5
Under $3,000	$ 39	$ 48	$ 51	$ 51	$ 40	$ 49	$ 59	$ 65	$ 65	$21	$ 23	$ 23
$3,000-$3,999	51	61	65	65	50	61	72	80	80	27	30	30
$4,000-$4,999	62	73	78	78	58	72	85	94	94	33	36	37
$5,000-$5,999	72	84	90	90	65	82	96	106	107	38	42	44
$6,000-$6,999	82	94	101	101	72	91	106	118	120	43	48	50
$7,000-$7,999	91	104	112	112	79	100	116	129	133	48	53	56
$8,000-$8,999	100	114	123	124	85	109	125	140	145	53	58	62
$9,000-$9,999	109	123	133	135	91	117	134	150	157	57	63	67
$10,000-$10,999	118	132	143	146	96	125	143	159	168	61	68	73
$11,000-$11,999	126	141	153	157	102	133	151	169	179	65	73	78
$12,000-$12,999	134	150	162	167	107	140	159	178	190	69	78	83
$13,000-$13,999	142	158	171	177	112	147	167	187	200	73	82	89
$14,000-$14,999	150	166	180	187	117	154	174	196	210	77	87	94
$15,000-$15,999	158	174	189	197	122	161	181	204	220	81	91	99
$16,000-$16,999	166	182	198	207	127	168	188	212	230	85	96	104
$17,000-$17,999	174	190	206	217	132	174	195	220	240	89	100	109
$18,000-$18,999	182	197	214	226	136	180	202	228	250	93	104	114
$19,000-$19,999	189	204	222	235	140	186	208	235	259	96	108	119

Note: If you itemize your deductions, you may use these tables to determine the general sales tax to be entered on Schedule A. However, if you are able to establish that you paid an amount larger than that shown you are entitled to deduct the larger amount. The sales tax paid on the purchase of an automobile may be added to the table amount except in Vermont. If your income was more than $19,999, but less than $100,000, compute your deduction as follows:

Step 1 – For the first $19,999, find the amount for your family size in the table for your State.

Step 2 – For each $1,000 of income (or fraction thereof) over $19,999, but less than $50,000, add 2 percent of the amount you determined in Step 1.

Step 3 – For each $1,000 of income (or fraction thereof) over $49,999, but less than $100,000, add 1 percent of the amount you determined in Step 1.

If your income was $100,000 or more, simply deduct 210 percent of the amount determined in Step 1, above.

deduct for casualty and theft losses to the extent they exceed $100 per occurrence. However, you cannot claim a deduction for losses to the extent that they are reimbursed by insurance or by a person who was legally responsible for the loss. Consider Mike's case. Because of his negligence,[14] he had a car wreck, and his car cost $180 to repair. Because he had a $50 deductible collision policy, his automobile insurance company paid him $130. Mike could not deduct anything as a casualty loss on his income tax return because his net loss was less than $100. The $100 limitation applies to each separate casualty.

Money or other property that is stolen is deductible, but property that is simply lost or misplaced is not considered a theft and therefore is not deductible. Neither is a loss that results from the misrepresentation of a buyer or seller.

If you have a casualty or theft loss in excess of $100 that is not covered by insurance, you should include it among your deductions if you itemize your deductions. But be careful to support your claim carefully. Since it is easy to pretend that losses have occurred, the Internal Revenue Service is likely to check all claims for casualty and theft losses. The amount of the loss is limited to the fair market value of the property at the time of the loss (or cost less depreciation, if smaller), and the Internal Revenue Service is likely to demand reasonable proof of the amount of the loss.

(6) *Employee business expenses.*   An employee is permitted to deduct certain expenses that are incurred as a result of his employment. To be deductible, however, expenses must be associated with employment (personal expenses are not deductible), and they are not deductible if they are reimbursed by your employer.

Examples of deductible business expenses include uniforms (that are not generally wearable off the job), the repair and cleaning of uniforms, instruments, technical books and journals, supplies, business travel expenses, business entertainment expenses, business gifts (generally limited to $25 per recipient), fees paid to an employment agency to get a job, premiums for professional malpractice insurance, and the cost of a bond if required for employment. You can also deduct the expenses of an office in your home if your employment requires it. You *cannot* deduct the expenses of traveling to and from work or the cost of entertaining personal friends.

SPECIAL PROBLEMS

In working with income tax decisions, a person very often runs into special problems. Of course, it is impossible to provide answers to every

---

[14] When an accident is a result of gross or willful negligence, nothing can be deducted. Losses caused by ordinary negligence, however, are deductible.

conceivable problem that might arise, but it is helpful to have some knowledge of the problems that are fairly common. In the following pages, we will analyze these problems, and emphasis will be placed on problems that are particularly important to young people.

MOVING EXPENSES

If you are a typical young person, the chances are great that you will change jobs several times in the early stages of your career. Even if you work for one company, there is a good chance that you will be required to move from one location to another. If you are transferred to a new job or change employers, you may be able to deduct the cost of moving to your new location. To claim a moving expense adjustment, you must file a special form (Form 3903) but it is important to realize that moving expenses are subtracted from gross income and can be taken even though you do not itemize your deductions.

There are two basic requirements that must be met before you can benefit from the moving expense adjustment. First, the new job location must be at least 50 miles farther from your old residence than the distance from your old residence to your old job site. Notice that the distance requirement does not apply to the location of your new residence. In other words, the test is whether or not you would have been required to travel more than 50 miles farther to work if you had not moved. The second requirement is that you must be a full-time employee (not self-employed) in the general location of the area you move to for at least 39 weeks immediately following the move. However, you can deduct expenses if the 39 weeks are not completed when your income tax form is filed, but you *expect* to live in the new general area for at least 39 weeks.[15]

The expenses that can be deducted include any reasonable expenses incurred in moving your household goods and personal property. Meals, lodging, car expenses, and mover's fees are deductible. You can also deduct (within certain limits) the cost of trips made to find a new house, meals and lodging in temporary quarters for up to 30 days in your new location, and certain expenses in selling an old house and buying a new one. Losses on the sale of your home and other expenses that result from the move but are not moving expenses are not deductible.

What happens if your employer reimburses you for part or all of the expenses you incur in moving? If the moving expenses are greater than the amount you receive as reimbursement, the *excess* expenses are de-

---

[15] You do not have to be employed by one employer for 39 weeks, and the weeks of employment need not be consecutive. If you expect to meet the requirement, claim the expenses, and later fail to meet the requirement, the expenses must be reported as "income" the following year. This requirement is waived if death, disability, or discharge (except for willful misconduct) prevents a person from living at his new location for 39 weeks.

ductible. If, however, the employer's reimbursement is more than your actual moving expenses, the difference is taxable income.

EXCESS F.I.C.A. TAX

As explained previously, the social security tax (F.I.C.A. tax) is *not* deductible in figuring your federal income tax. But what happens when you change jobs during the year? If you work for two or more employers and more than the maximum tax is deducted from your paychecks, you should claim the excess social security tax withheld as a credit against your income tax.

Consider this simple example: Bob earned $800 each month during 1970. But he worked for one company for one-half the year and another company for six months. His first employer deducted 4.8 percent from each check and his second employer did the same. This meant Bob paid a total tax of $460.80 ($38.40 was deducted from twelve checks. The $38.40 is 4.8 percent of $800.) But the F.I.C.A. tax was payable only on the first $7,800 in 1970. Therefore, the maximum tax was only $374.00. As a result, he should receive a credit against his income tax of $86.40. In many cases, the credit can be much higher. If a person makes considerably more than the maximum taxable wage base for social security and works for several employers, the credit can be several hundred dollars. Unfortunately, many people are unaware of the fact that excessive social security taxes should provide a direct credit to federal income taxes.

EDUCATIONAL EXPENSES

Since our society is putting increasing emphasis upon training and education, many people find it necessary to take "refresher" courses and periodically engage in other educational activities. In certain cases, the ordinary and necessary expenses you incur as an employee for education are deductible.

You are *not* allowed to deduct educational expenses that are incurred to meet your own general educational ambitions or education needed to fulfill the minimum requirements to qualify for a position or profession. Suppose you are studying general business now, and you plan to become a lawyer. The expenses you incur in this type of education are *not* deductible. But the tax laws permit you to deduct the cost of education if the expenses are incurred to enable you to get a promotion or advance in your business, trade, or profession. For example, Sam is an auto mechanic. He is taking a course in the study of automobile air conditioners. The cost he incurs is deductible, because he is attempting to improve or maintain skills in his work. Or, consider Mary's case. She is a high school Spanish teacher. During the summer she visited Spain and visited Spanish families and schools, attended plays and lectures. Mary can deduct the travel expenses she incurs on her trip. If Mary had simply taken a vacation to France, her expense would not have been deductible.

CHILD CARE

Working mothers may be entitled to special income tax benefits. Since more and more women are employed, this provision of the tax law should be of interest to many young families.

Basically, deductions can be taken for the expenses of caring for dependent children under the age of 13 or any dependent who is unable to care for himself. To take these deductions, you must file a special form (Form 2441) and you must itemize your deductions. It is important to realize that baby-sitting fees are not deductible; only those expenses that are incurred while you are employed (or actively seeking employment) are deductible.

Many people believe these expenses are deductible only if you are a widow, legally separated, or divorced. This is not true. The expenses for child care are also deductible for working wives. However, the limitations on the deductions may be lower for married women who are working. For women who are widowed, legally separated, deserted, or divorced, the maximum deduction is $600 a year for the care of one dependent, and $900 for the care of two or more children. For working wives, the deduction is reduced one dollar for each dollar of income over $6,000. Therefore, with one child, there is no deduction if the adjusted gross income is over $6,600 and with two or more children there is no deduction if the income is over $6,900.

ALIMONY AND SEPARATION PAYMENTS

Alimony payments are deductible by the husband and includible in the gross income of the recipient. A husband can take the deduction, however, only if he itemizes his deductions. If he takes either the percentage standard deduction or the low income allowance, he cannot deduct alimony payments. Notice that this may have some important tax implications. For example, John and Mary never had a large income because John was in school. Because their income was small they rented an apartment. They always used a standard deduction. (John was happy about this because he didn't want to bother with itemized deductions anyway.) But after the unfortunate divorce, John realized that his alimony payments were large enough to enable him to itemize his deductions rather than use one of the standard deductions.

Child support payments are *not* deductible by the husband or taxable to the wife.[16] However, in determining whether the husband or wife is

---

[16] Very often a husband will actually pay less than the amount called for in the divorce decree. If this is the case, the payments are considered as child support (and therefore not deductible) before any amount will be considered as alimony.

entitled to take dependency exemptions for the children, the child support payments are counted as support by the father.

CAPITAL GAINS AND LOSSES

When you sell or exchange property, you may have gains or losses to account for in your income tax. These transactions sometimes raise difficult problems, but there are only three basic, important questions that must be resolved in most transactions.[17]

The first major problem is to calculate how much your gain or loss is from the transaction. The basic rule is that the gain or loss is generally the difference between the cost and the net sale price. In determining the cost, you can include the cost of additions, improvements, purchase expenses (such as commissions and fees), and other legitimate costs. When you sell the property, your net sale price is the price you receive, less any expenses of selling the property (such as commissions, taxes, and fees).

The second major problem is determining whether the gain or loss is subject to treatment as a capital gain or loss or as an ordinary gain or loss. As a general rule, capital assets are everything you own and depreciable business property. But inventory held for resale to customers is *not* a capital asset. This is a most important distinction because the tax rules sometimes differ for capital assets and noncapital assets.

The third basic question with regard to capital gains and losses is whether it is long term or short term. If you hold property for more than six months, it is a long-term gain or loss when it is sold. If you hold the property six months or less, the gain or loss will be short term.

The distinction between long-term and short-term capital gains and losses is important because they are treated differently for tax purposes. To understand how long-term capital gains are given preferential treatment, you must understand the basic rules of taxing capital gains and losses.

The first step is to combine all short-term gains and losses to arrive at a *net* short-term gain or loss, and combine all long-term gains and losses to determine the *net* long-term capital gain or loss. Then, if you have an overall gain, it must occur in one of the following ways:

1. Both a long-term and short-term gain
2. The short-term gain exceeds the long-term loss
3. The long-term gain exceeds the short-term loss

---

[17] A factor obviously considered is whether or not the gain or loss will be recognized as taxable. Some exchanges of property are called "tax free exchanges" and they do not produce a gain or loss as far as income taxes are concerned. These are fairly unusual, however. Most of the time gains or losses will be recognized when ownership changes.

If you have both a long-term and short-term gain, the short-term gain is fully taxable but only one-half of the long term gain is taxable. If the short-term gain is greater than the long-term loss, 100 percent of the excess must be included in your income. If the long-term gain exceeded the short-term loss, only one-half of the excess is included in your income. In other words, only one-half of long-term gains are taxed, but short-term gains are fully taxable.

In the event that you have a loss, you may deduct net capital losses from ordinary income. However, deductions for losses are limited to $1,000 a year, and only one-half of long-term capital losses can be deducted. (It takes $2.00 of long-term capital losses to offset $1.00 of ordinary income, or $2,000 in long-term losses to obtain the maximum deduction of $1,000). Losses greater than these amounts can be carried forward to future years and deducted.[18]

Actually, a person can calculate his capital gains taxes in one of two ways. You can either pay the tax, at ordinary income rates on one-half of your net long-term capital gains or pay a tax of 25 percent of your full net long-term capital gains.[19] Since you can use either method, obviously you should choose the method that extracts the lowest tax. Unless your income is very high, it will always be to your advantage to pay on the basis of one-half of your gains. This will result in a tax of less than 25 percent.

SELLING YOUR HOME

There are special income tax rules that apply when a person sells his home. Since many young people will own several homes during their lifetime, these rules are important.

If you sell your home for less than you paid for it (to be more accurate—if your cost basis is higher than your net selling price) you are *not* allowed to deduct the loss. If you make a profit on the sale of your home, however, all or part of the gain might be taxable.

If a person sells his home at a profit and buys and occupies a new residence within one year, and the purchase price of the new home is as much or more than the net sales price of the old home, the gain is *not* taxed in the year of the sale.[20] You will be required to pay a tax on the

---

[18] Limitations on these deductions should be checked carefully.

[19] Gains in excess of $50,000 are taxed without the benefit of the alternative tax. Therefore, since one-half of long-term capital gains is taxed and the maximum tax rate is 70 percent, the maximum capital gains tax rate is 35 percent for gains in excess of $50,000.

[20] You will be given 18 months to occupy a new home if you desire to *build* a new house rather than buy an existing residence. Also, if you are on active duty in the armed services, the running of the one year (or 18 months) will be suspended up to four years while you are in the service.

gain if you do not buy a new home within one year or if you pay less for the new house.

You actually do not avoid paying a capital gains tax when you sell your house at a profit—you only postpone paying the tax. This is because the gain you make on the house reduces the cost basis of your new home. Consider this example: Jerry bought a house for $10,000 when he was a student. Later he sold the house for $12,000, but he bought a new house one month later and paid $14,000 for it. Jerry did not have a taxable gain when he sold his first house because he bought a new one within a year and paid more than he received from his old home. Later Jerry sold his second home for $18,000 and did not buy a new one. He will have to pay a tax, but on what amount? Ignoring commissions and other expenses to adjust the selling and buying price, Jerry received $18,000 for the house and his cost basis was only $12,000. He will pay a tax, then, on the $6,000 gain. Make sure you understand why he has a taxable gain of $6,000. He paid $14,000 for his second house, but the $2,000 gain on his first house reduced his cost basis to $12,000 ($14,000 − $2,000 = $12,000). When his cost basis was $12,000 and he received $18,000 for the sale, the taxable gain must equal $6,000.

You can understand that a person normally never has a taxable gain if he buys a house that is at least as expensive as his previous home and he does so within a year. But what happens if a person finally sells and makes a profit without buying a new house? He will either pay a tax on the gain (as in Jerry's case above) or he will be eligible for the special rules that apply to persons over age 65.[21]

TAX AUDITS

One of the most serious and certainly most frightening problems a tax-payer can encounter is an income tax audit. In the past, the Internal Revenue Service was not prepared to carefully check all the income tax forms that were filed. Returns were checked for abnormalities and a sample of forms was checked thoroughly. Since 1966, however, the Internal Revenue Service has computerized its operations and now every income tax return that is filed is scrutinized and tested for completeness and accuracy. This does not mean every return is audited. In 1970, it was estimated that less than 3 percent of all returns were audited.

Although the Internal Revenue Service is understandably leery about explaining which returns will be audited, there are several features that

---

[21] If a person over age 65 sells his home, there will be no tax at all if the home is sold for $20,000 or less. If the house is sold for more than $20,000, only a portion of the gain is taxed. To determine the tax free portion of the gain, a ratio is set up with $20,000 as the numerator and the selling price of the home as the denominator. This ratio is then multiplied by the taxable gain and the result is the tax free portion of the gain.

increase the chances of being audited. An unusually large claim for a refund may result in a close examination of your return. It is said that large casualty losses receive special attention. And employees who claim business travel and entertainment deductions may also be subject to such audits. Perhaps the most frequent and troublesome area for audits is the size of your deductions. If you claim unusually high deductions, the Internal Revenue Service might examine your return more closely. While it is hard to know how much can be deducted for the various items, it is helpful to have some idea of the average amount of some of the important deductions. Table 6–5 gives this information by income categories.

If you are notified by the Internal Revenue Service that your return is being audited, you should realize that the governmental representatives are completely within their rights to request complete information concerning your financial affairs. After the examining officer completes his study of your return, he will indicate the adjustment he plans to make. If additional tax is payable, you may incur penalties. There is an interest charge of 6 percent per year that starts when the tax is due. In addition, a penalty of 5 percent of the deficiency may be levied. If, however, there is a fraudulent intent to evade taxes, the penalty is 50 percent of the deficiency,[22] and criminal penalties may be enforced.

As a general rule, the Internal Revenue Service may examine a return and assess additional taxes any time within a three-year period after a return is filed. This three-year period does not apply to a fraudulent return or cases where a person fails to file a return. In these situations, the tax can be assessed at any time, without limitation.[23]

If you cannot reach an agreement with the examining officer, you have the right to request a district conference or Appellate Division hearing. Beyond this, you can appeal to the United States Tax Court.[24] These audits, of course, are costly and time-consuming affairs. They are only worthwhile when a large amount of money is involved.

The best solution to many of these problems is to keep accurate and complete records. In fact, the law requires you to keep records that will enable you to file a complete and accurate income tax return. Although the law does not specify any special form of records, a person should maintain all receipts, cancelled checks, and any other evidence that might be used to support his claims. Records that are used to support claims for income and deductions should be kept at least three years, since the government normally can request information any time within the three-year period. As far as property transactions are concerned,

---

[22] If a person fails to file a return, the penalty is 5 percent for each month, but the total penalty cannot exceed 25 percent of the original tax due on the return.

[23] The Internal Revenue Service is given six years to proceed against a person who omits more than 25 percent of his gross income.

[24] Or you can carry the suit to the United States District Court or the Court of Claims.

Table 6–5   Average Deductions Claimed

Type of Deduction	Adjusted Gross Income		
	$10,000-$15,000	*$15,000-$20,000*	*$20,000-$25,000*
Contributions	$312	$ 434	$ 586
Interest	736	914	1,111
Taxes	792	1,093	1,453
Medical	294	316	372

Source: *Wall Street Journal,* February 24, 1971. Used with permission.

records should be kept for as long as necessary to determine the cost basis of the property. This means records may need to be kept for 30, 40, 50 years or even longer.

CORRECTION OF ERRORS

If you have studied the previous material in this chapter carefully, it is easy to understand how errors can creep into your tax return. You should know how to handle errors in your return because handling mistakes properly might allow you to recover a previous overpayment or help you avoid penalties for underpayment of taxes.

If you discover an error after your return has been filed but before the regular due date of the return, you can remedy the mistake by filing a proper return and labeling it as a corrected copy. The word "corrected" should be in large printed letters on the face of the return.

If you discover an error after the date the return is due, you can file another return and indicate that it is an "amended" return. Again this type of return should be clearly labeled. The deadline for filing an amended return is three years after the due date of the original return.

MINIMIZING TAXES

There is a difference between tax avoidance and tax evasion. And as a practical matter, the difference is important. A person who denies or fails to report a tax liability is guilty of tax evasion and can be penalized (even sent to jail). Tax avoidance, on the other hand, prevents (or minimizes) a person's tax liability through legal means. A wise person never uses tax evasion, but he should use tax avoidance plans to legally minimize his taxes.

There are many ways a person can legally minimize the amount he pays in income taxes. In fact, there are so many ways to decrease taxes that it is impossible to describe all of them. It is important, however, to be aware of some of the methods that are commonly used by people of moderate income.

INCOME AVERAGING

Because the federal income tax is progressive, a person whose income fluctuates from year to year pays a higher tax than a person who has a stable income—even if their average incomes are the same. This means a person who has an unusually large income in one year (compared to his average income), will have a disproportionate tax bill. To provide help for taxpayers who have a large jump in income in one year, the tax laws provide a substitute method of calculating tax. Young persons who are changing jobs or working part time often have a sizable increase in their income. If a person qualifies for the income averaging approach, he can usually decrease his taxes—and sometimes the decrease will be large.

Income averaging is *not* what most people think it is—you do not pay a tax on your average income. It works this way: a person first computes his "averageable income." This is done by determining your average base period income (the average of your income for the four immediately preceding tax years); then, your "averageable income" is the amount by which your adjusted taxable income for the current year exceeds 120 percent of your average base period income. To qualify, a person must have an "averageable income" of at least $3,000.

Look at this example: Frank Smith's income was as follows:

1968	1969	1970	1971	1972
$4,000	$6,000	$8,000	$10,000	$20,000

If Frank decides to use income averaging in 1972, how much is his averageable income? His average base period income is $7,000. Multiplying this figure by 120 percent produces a figure of $8,400. How much is Frank's "averageable income?" This amounts to $11,600 ($20,000 − $8,400).

Remember that a person can use income averaging only if his "averageable income" is more than $3,000. It is obvious from the above explanation and example that a person whose income is $3,000 higher than his normal income will *not* have $3,000 in "averageable income" because his average income is multiplied by 120 percent.

If you qualify for income averaging, you must use a special income averaging form (Schedule G). Using this form will enable a person to reduce his income tax liability—sometimes by a substantial amount.

To use income averaging, a person must have been a citizen or resident of the United States throughout the computation year and all the base period years. In addition, the support test requires a person to have furnished (or if married, you and your spouse must have furnished) at least 50 percent of your support during each of your base period years.[25]

---

[25] The support test is subject to three important exceptions. These should be checked carefully if you believe you are eligible for income averaging.

BUNCHING DEDUCTIONS

It is sometimes advantageous for a person to use a standard deduction in one year and itemize deductions the next. Suppose you estimate that your standard deduction will be more than your itemized deductions. If so, perhaps you should use a standard deduction and postpone payment of deductible obligations until the next year when you will itemize your deductions. It is usually easy to postpone contributions and it is sometimes easy to postpone medical and dental expenses. By taking a standard deduction one year and itemizing deductions the next, you might be able to increase your total deductions and thereby reduce your total tax bill.

Even for a person who itemizes deductions every year, the bunching of deductions might save taxes. You can only deduct the part of your medical expenses that exceeds 3 percent of your income. Therefore, if your medical expenses are approaching 3 percent near the end of the year, it decreases your tax bill to pay outstanding medical bills before the end of the year and include them with your medical deduction.

CAPITAL GAINS

Since long-term capital gains are taxed at a lower rate than ordinary income, it is often wise to seek long-term capital gains. Often a person has the option to sell an asset after he has held it for several months. For tax reasons, it might be desirable to hold the asset until it has been held longer than six months and then sell it. Another common method of seeking long-term capital gains is to choose investments that pay low dividends (or no dividend at all) rather than investments that provide high dividends. When a person receives a dividend, he is taxed (after the dividend exclusion) on the dividend he receives. But if a person buys a stock and the company retains the earnings to help future growth, the common stock should appreciate in price over the long run. If it does, the appreciation will be taxed at long-term capital gains rates.

SPREADING INCOME

Since our income tax structure is progressive, it saves taxes to shift income to as many persons as possible.[26] For example, a father can shift a savings account, mutual fund shares, or other investments to a child and normally decrease his tax bill. Consider Fred's situation. His father is not wealthy, but he is well-to-do and not worried about his level of income. He is worried, however, about providing Fred with money while he is going to school. Why, then, can't he give Fred some income-producing property and let Fred pay an income tax on it rather than himself? If Fred's income is low enough he will not have to pay any tax (because of his own personal exemption and standard deduction).

[26] A person can often lower his tax payments by making gifts, either outright or in trust. These methods are discussed at length in the final chapter of this book.

EMPLOYEE BENEFIT PLANS

Most "fringe benefit" plans involve a tax advantage for employees. Many plans are elective and, from an income tax point-of-view, a person should participate in employee benefit plans as much as possible. For example, consider group life insurance (which is discussed in a later chapter). A person can either earn an income, pay taxes, and then pay his life insurance premiums with his after-tax income or participate in his company's group life insurance plan. If he does the latter, his company will pay the premium (or at least a portion of it) and no income tax is normally payable by the employee. Group life insurance, of course, is only one example of a "tax sheltered" program. The same tax benefits are available with many other employee fringe benefits.

MAINTAINING ADEQUATE RECORDS

If a person fails to keep records of his legitimate deductible expenses, he has no alternative except to estimate these expenses at the end of the year. This can result in losses in two ways. If the Internal Revenue Service conducts an audit and decides you owe additional taxes, you will probably have to pay the additional tax because you have not kept adequate records. Secondly, if you are forced to estimate your deductions, you must keep in mind the problems that might arise if your estimates are too high. As a result, a person has a good reason to make conservative estimates. To the extent that your estimates are less than your actual deductions, you have simply increased the amount of taxes you owe.

SEEKING INCOME TAX ADVICE AND ASSISTANCE

Many people are not aware of all the possible ways they can legally minimize their income taxes. And many people understand income tax matters fairly well but do not work out their own income tax problems because they are too busy or for some other reason would like to avoid the required work. For these people, it is often desirable to seek income tax advice and assistance from a qualified individual or organization.

Many accountants provide income tax services. Of course they charge a fee—usually based on the amount of time they spend. The quality of their work depends on their desire to do a good job and their professional competence. However, most accountants who provide income tax services are extremely knowledgeable and can handle most income tax problems very well.

Companies are also actively providing income tax services. The largest of these companies has offices in many cities. Their fees depend primarily upon the amount of work required for each case.

It would be a grave mistake to assume that you do not need to bother studying income tax problems because you intend to let another individual or organization work out your tax problems. A person who is familiar with the fundamentals of income tax is able to make better financial decisions and work with others who actually solve income tax problems.

SUMMARY

Federal income taxes are important not only because they may involve a substantial amount of money but because the influence of taxes should be recognized in many different types of financial decisions. In most cases, income taxes should not be the only factor in a financial decision, but it is usually wise to consider the income tax consequences of certain actions.

While it is quite easy to determine whether or not you should file a federal tax return, and the rules for selecting the appropriate tax rate schedule are fairly easy to follow, a taxpayer is often confused in determining the types of income that should be included in his return, and the method of calculating deductions. If deductions are itemized, a person should be sure to claim all the legitimate deductions to which he is entitled. This is a major problem for most taxpayers, but a basic understanding of the common deductions is not too difficult.

Special problems often cause difficulty. If a person has incurred moving expenses, has had a sizable change in income, has paid excess F.I.C.A. tax, has incurred educational expenses, has been separated or divorced, has sold a home or other assets, he should be aware that special income tax rules may be involved.

After becoming familiar with the normal types of problems and decisions, a person should be able to recognize his personal financial problems and opportunities for minimizing his federal income taxes.

Case Problems

1. Martin is just starting to calculate his federal income tax for the year. His first step is to determine the gross income for both his wife and him. Martin realizes that wages are taxable, but he is uncertain about the following items. If you were Martin, how would you treat each of the items in the following list?

> Income received from the National Guard
> Interest earned on savings account
> Money given to Martin by his father
> Dividends on a life insurance policy
> Tips for Larry's wife in restaurant

2. Bill and Carol have only been married a few years and they have never worried much about income taxes. Bill is still in college and works only

20 hours a week. Carol is a full-time secretary, but together their adjusted gross income is $8,600. They have one child. Bill has always used the percentage standard deduction because it is simple. He once thought about itemizing his deductions but because he does not own a home, he could not deduct mortgage interest and real estate taxes and therefore his itemized deductions would have been less than the percentage standard deduction. In 1973 Bill estimated that he could claim itemized deductions of $1,120. Which method do you believe Bill should use to determine his deductions? Your answer should include actual calculations under three different methods.

3. Dean Carpenter has calculated his adjusted gross income and he believes, from past experience, that he will itemize his deductions. Although he is still in college, he owns a home and two small cars. He had to move during the year because he was promoted by his company. In the past, Dean has itemized deductions and later remembered deductions he had overlooked. This always made Dean mad because he hated to lose deductions because of his own negligence. This year Dean decided to handle the problem a little differently. His first step was to prepare a list of possible deductions and then determine which items he could claim. If you were asked to prepare such a list, what items would you include?

4. Larry has always been bothered by the confusing rules that apply to deductions for medical expenses. Since he has never had unusually large medical bills, he has simply skipped over the medical expense deductions and not claimed any of the deductions. This year, however, Larry's young son was sick for several months and the medical bills were staggering. Larry was covered under a group health insurance policy, but he neglected to have his dependents covered. As a result, none of the medical bills for Larry's son were covered by insurance, but most of his other family medical expenses were covered. Larry has decided that he will make a hard effort to understand the medical deduction this year. Larry's first step was to gather information. His medical expenses amounted to $1,200 and medicines and drugs came to $290. During the year Larry paid $180 for health insurance premiums but he collected only $300 for doctor and hospital bills and $100 for medicines and drugs. Larry's adjusted gross income for the year was $8,800. How would you calculate his deduction?

5. Dave Ward sold his home during the year. He had bought the house three years ago for $16,000, but he sold it for $20,000. Of course he was happy about the profit, but when he started to calculate his income taxes, he realized he didn't understand how to treat the gain on the house. How would you explain the income tax rules to Dave in his situation?

6. Denny and Nancy are still in college. They had saved a little money before they were married and they are both anxious to graduate as soon as possible. Therefore, they are both carrying the maximum number of courses and they both go to summer school. Denny works part time but will only earn about $180 a month (for 12 months) this year. Nancy didn't work during the year, but she received $800 for a scholarship. She won the scholarship for her grades in the previous year and she is not obligated

in any way to the company who established the scholarship. How should Denny and Nancy handle their income tax problems? Explain.

7. Bart has decided to itemize his deductions this year for the first time. However, he is uncertain about the items in the following list. Are they deductible?

(a) Fee paid to an employment agency for Bart's wife to get a job
(b) $80 in cash stolen from Bart
(c) Tuition and fees Bart pays to attend his state college
(d) Social security taxes
(e) Personal services donated to Little League baseball team
(f) Child support payments awarded in a divorce agreement

8. Frank and Rhonda have never worried about income tax problems before, but now they realize that they must file a return. They have been told that they should file a joint return, but Frank has several questions in his mind. First, he did not marry Rhonda until December 20, so can he still file a joint return even if he were married for only 11 days of the year? Secondly, Rhonda earned no taxable income during the year. Does this mean Frank cannot file a joint return? Third, can he file a joint return if he does not itemize deductions? How would you advise Frank on each of these questions?

Selected Readings

Changing Times, The Kiplinger Magazine:
   "Best Bets for Cutting Your Tax Bill," February 1969, pp. 43–47.
   "If They Challenge Your Tax Return," April 1969, pp. 29–30.
   "People Who Do Tax Returns for You," January 1969, pp. 17–20.
   "Sure, You Can Save on Taxes . . . But Start Now," November 1970, pp. 11–12.
   "Tax Mistakes *Anybody* Might Make," February 1970, pp. 7–9.
   "13 Chances to Cut Your Taxes," December 1969, pp. 13–14.
   "What the New Tax Law Does to *You*," June 1970, pp. 41–44.
   "What the Tax People Don't Tell You," March 1970, pp. 17–20.
   "What's *Your* Tax Problem?" February 1971, pp. 41–42.
   "Yes, Taxes Are Unfair to Single People," November 1967, pp. 31–33.
Dickerson, William E. and Stone, Leo D. *Federal Income Tax Fundamentals.* 3rd edition. San Francisco: Wadsworth Publishing Co., 1968.
Explanation of Tax Reform Act of 1969. Chicago, Illinois: Commerce Clearing House.
Federal Income Tax Regulations. Englewood Cliffs, N.J.: Prentice-Hall, Inc. Published regularly.
Federal Tax Course. Englewood Cliffs, N.J.: Prentice-Hall, Inc. Published annually.
Federal Tax Handbook. Englewood Cliffs, N.J.: Prentice-Hall, Inc. Published annually.

Instructions for Preparing Your Federal Income Tax Return. Washington, D.C.: U. S. Treasury Department, Internal Revenue Service. Published annually.

Lasser, J. K. *Your Income Tax.* New York: Simon and Schuster, Inc. Published regularly.

Sommerfeld, Ray M., Anderson, Hershel M., and Brock, Horace R. *An Introduction to Taxation.* New York: Harcourt, Brace, and World, Inc., 1969.

Tax Ideas. Englewood Cliffs, N.J.: Prentice-Hall, Inc. Published regularly.

U.S. Master Tax Guide. Chicago, Illinois: Commerce Clearing House, Inc. Published annually.

Your Personal Tax Return. Englewood Cliffs, N.J.: Prentice-Hall, Inc. Published annually.

CHAPTER SEVEN

CHOOSING A CAREER

You are probably facing one of the most important decisions of your life—the choice of an occupation. Your occupational choice will have an important, long-lasting effect upon your life.

Many people like to postpone their occupational decision as long as possible, but eventually a decision must be made. When a person refuses to make a definite choice, *fate* will influence his life, and sometimes the results are most unfortunate.

Would you like to be a bookkeeper? or a carpenter? These are respectable occupations, and many people are happy they are involved in these jobs. The real problem arises when a person finds himself unhappy in his occupation. Consider John Stubbs' case. John attended college for almost two years, but did not graduate. He was somewhat concerned about the type of work he would choose, but he never investigated different career opportunities and he never forced himself to make a definite decision to pursue a career. John spent two years in the Air Force and got married. He needed an income to support his family. He found a job in a department store and in a few years was promoted to office manager for the store. For a while he was quite pleased with his progress. But soon John realized that his life was miserable because he received very little satisfaction from his job, and he belived he was not earning enough money. John considered changing jobs, but being realistic he realized that his financial obligations prevented him from changing jobs. John could do nothing but look forward to a lifetime of unhappy work.

The tragedy of John's case (which is a common situation) was *not* the fact that he was an office manager. The real problem was that John realized that he would much prefer to do some other type of work. Looking back, John realized that he might have avoided his problem if he had taken the trouble to examine his objectives and to study different career opportunities.

The occupation you choose (or find yourself in) will have a substantial impact on your personal financial accomplishments. Workers in some occupations earn a great deal more and have greater financial security than those employed in other occupations. Therefore, if a person wants to improve his financial position, one approach is to change occupations. Or, from the point of view of a student, an approach to a higher income is to select a financially rewarding occupation.

But it would be a great mistake to base your occupational choice entirely on the amount of money you can earn in a certain occupation. The occupation you choose has an important effect on your income, but it also has a strong influence on your personality, social role, family life, and the image you hold of yourself. It is not an exaggeration, in fact, to state that your occupation will play an important role in the total satisfaction you receive from life. Viewed in this light, you can appreciate the importance of your occupational choice. And it is clear that selecting an occupation is a decision that is filled with many important, practical problems.

If you have considered the problem of choosing a career, you probably have asked yourself what you would like to find in a certain job, how you should go about finding the types of work that would interest you, how you should find the occupations in which you could perform well, how many opportunities certain occupations provide, how much money income you would earn, and how you should prepare yourself for certain types of occupations. These are the fundamental questions that are involved in selecting a career. This chapter cannot solve all the problems you will face in the choice of an occupation. But it deals with the above questions, and more importantly, the material attempts to provide a *logical approach* that a person may use to select a vocation.

RECOGNIZING NEEDS FOR WORKING

Have you ever asked yourself why you plan to work? This may seem like a meaningless (or even silly) question at first glance, but it is actually a rather complicated and important question. If a person worked for only one purpose, it would be easy to choose an occupation. Consider the imaginary situation of a person who works only for money. His choice of an occupation could be made when he found the profession with the highest income. Or, a person who wants only prestige could set his sights on the most prestigious occupation. But the truth is that most people work to meet a *number of needs* rather than for one specific purpose. In other words, most occupations provide more than one type of reward. Moreover, each occupation not only provides a number of rewards, but provides rewards in various amounts. An occupation, for example, can be very rewarding in certain respects and not very rewarding in others. Each occupation, then, provides a *combination* of rewards. The essential problem in choosing an occupation, therefore, is to find a career that provides the rewards (in the proper proportions) to meet your own needs.

The first step, in selecting an occupation is to become aware of the various types of rewards people receive from their jobs. It is a mistake to assume that all people work primarily for money. In fact, in order of importance, money is down several notches on the list of reasons most people give for working. Table 7–1 shows, in order of importance, some of the important rewards people want from their jobs.

You should not accept the reasons given in Table 7–1 as the only explanations of why people work. Undoubtedly some people work because they believe work is "good." In other words, a person might satisfy his need to feel moral or worthy by working. Others may work in order to help others. Social welfare and service to others have been important to an increasing number of young people in recent years. Part of the reason some people work is to satisfy their need to feel dominant. A supervisor, for example, may enjoy his work because his job lets him direct others. For those who have high positions in companies and the government, the drive to dominate may develop into a strong desire for power.

Although you should recognize that there are many motives for working, almost all the important motives reduce to four general reasons. These are: (1) security, (2) satisfaction, (3) advancement, and (4) recognition.

SECURITY

A number of studies have shown that people place a heavy emphasis on security in their occupation. As a matter of fact, when people have been asked what they want in a job, security is mentioned first and with more frequency than anything else. Of course, a person could argue that the

Table 7–1   Important Occupational Motivators

1. Security	7. Supervision
2. Interesting work	8. Social aspects of the job
3. Opportunity for advancement	9. Opportunity to learn or use ideas
4. Recognition	10. Hours
5. Working conditions	11. Ease of job
6. Wages	12. Fringe benefits

desire for security is a part of the desire for money, but the important point is that many people place heavy weight on the *continuity* of their income, as well as the size of their paycheck.

SATISFACTION

Most people also believe it is important to have interesting work. When a person is interested in his work, it is easier to succeed and do a job well. This, in turn, results in satisfaction, and satisfaction tends to produce new interest. This is why a successful person seems to have so much interest and enthusiasm in his work. But it is often difficult to discover what types of activities are interesting to you. Some people find their work interesting if they feel they are contributing something worthwhile. Perhaps nothing is more dissatisfying than work that seems to have no significance. Other people find interest in their occupation if they have an outlet for self-expression. An artist, for example, is usually highly motivated by work that lets him express his ideas and emotions. Others find that their work is more interesting to them when they have a variety of activities. Many people are bored by dull, repetitive tasks.

ADVANCEMENT

The need to advance is another important reason why people work. To many people, a promotion to a higher job title is more important than a pay increase. It seems that Americans have a strong urge for upward occupational mobility. In a sense, a part of the "American Dream" is to "get ahead."

According to Table 7–2, students who have a father in an unskilled occupation generally do not plan to follow their fathers' career. But 50 percent of the students in four-year colleges have fathers in managerial and professional occupations, and 89 percent of these students have professional or managerial ambitions.

RECOGNITION

Another important need that can be fulfilled by occupation is the need for recognition. The status or prestige attached to an occupation is an important need to many people. Some occupations, of course, offer a great deal of prestige; others are not highly respected. Table 7–3 (on pages 188–189) shows how much prestige is associated with a number of occupations. Since the scores in the table represent the average grade given (by a large number of people) to the standing of each occupation, those with higher scores are more respected than those with lower scores.

FINDING YOUR OCCUPATIONAL NEEDS

We have seen that various occupations meet different needs. And an occupation that does not meet your needs (or meets needs that are

Table 7–2 Student's Occupational Aspiration Compared with Father's Occupational Status (in percent)

Occupational Level	Noncollege	Junior College	Four-Year College
Unskilled occupations			
Father's status	42	23	17
Student's aspiration	14	6	1
Skilled and semiprofessional occupations			
Father's status	36	45	33
Student's aspiration	49	30	10
Managerial and professional occupations			
Father's status	23	32	50
Student's aspiration	36	64	89

From *The Junior College Student: A Research Description,* p. 26, by K. Patricia Cross. Copyright © 1968 by Educational Testing Service. All rights reserved. Reprinted by permission.

unimportant to you) can lead to frustration and unhappiness. The key, therefore, to a satisfying career is to find an occupation that satisfies your own personal needs and ambitions. So now the question becomes, "How do I determine what occupations will satisfy my personal needs and ambitions?"

There is no simple answer, but experts in vocational guidance approach the problem by analyzing five important criteria. These are: (1) expressed interests, (2) manifest interests, (3) inventoried interests, (4) personality, and (5) aptitude.

EXPRESSED INTERESTS

What kind of occupation do you believe you would like? Your answer is your expressed interest for an occupation. In other words, your expressed interest is simply the recognition and acknowledgment that you are interested in an occupation.

A person's expressed interests are useful because a person normally expresses an interest in an occupation only when he finds something attractive about that occupation. But an individual's verbal statements of his interests cannot always be accepted as a reliable indication of his real or basic interests. A person's expressed interest may be based on a small sample of experience and may be almost completely subjective. Advice or pressure from relatives and friends, for example, can have an excessive influence on a person's expressed interests. While there may be

Table 7–3 Occupational Prestige Ratings

Occupation	Score
U.S. Supreme Court Justice	94
Physician	93
Nuclear physicist	92
Scientist	92
Government scientist	91
State governor	91
Cabinet member in the federal government	90
College professor	90
U.S. representative in Congress	90
Chemist	89
Lawyer	89
Diplomat in the U.S. foreign service	89
Dentist	88
Architect	88
County judge	88
Psychologist	87
Minister	87
Member of the board of directors of a large corporation	87
Mayor of a large city	87
Priest	86
Head of a department in a state government	86
Civil engineer	86
Airline pilot	86
Banker	85
Biologist	85
Sociologist	83
Instructor in public schools	82
Captain in the regular army	82
Accountant for a large business	81
Public school teacher	81
Owner of a factory that employs about 100 people	80
Building contractor	80
Artist who paints pictures that are exhibited in galleries	78
Musician in a symphony orchestra	78
Author of novels	78
Economist	78
Official of an international labor union	77
Railroad engineer	76
Electrician	76
County agricultural agent	76
Owner-operator of a printing shop	75
Trained machinist	75
Farm owner and operator	74
Undertaker	74
Welfare worker for a city government	74
Newspaper columnist	73
Policeman	72
Reporter on a daily newspaper	71
Radio announcer	70
Bookkeeper	70
Tenant farmer	69
Insurance agent	69

Table 7–3 (continued)

Occupation	Score
Carpenter	68
Manager of a small store in a city	67
A local official of a labor union	67
Mail carrier	66
Railroad conductor	66
Traveling salesman for a wholesale concern	66
Plumber	65
Automobile repairman	64
Playground director	63
Barber	63
Machine operator in a factory	63
Owner-operator of a lunch stand	63
Corporal in a regular army	62
Garage mechanic	62
Truck driver	59
Fisherman who owns his own boat	58
Clerk in a store	56
Milk route man	56
Streetcar motorman	56
Lumberjack	55
Restaurant cook	55
Singer in a nightclub	54
Filling station attendant	51
Dockworker	50
Railroad section hand	50
Night watchman	50
Coal miner	50
Restaurant waiter	49
Taxi driver	49
Farm hand	48
Janitor	48
Bartender	48
Clothes presser in a laundry	45
Soda fountain clerk	44
Sharecropper	42
Garbage collector	39
Street sweeper	36
Shoe shiner	34

Source: R.W. Hodge *et. al.* "Occupational Prestige in the United States," *American Journal of Sociology,* The University of Chicago Press, Vol. LXX (November 1964), pp. 290-292. Used with permission.

some validity in an individual's expressed interests, he should always take other criteria into account.

MANIFEST INTERESTS

A person's demonstrated interests are known as his manifest interests. These are indicated primarily by the activities a person has been involved in during recent years. A student, for instance, can ask himself what he has been doing in addition to going to school. He may occupy his time with sports, church functions, music, literature, cars, or many other activities. The main reason a person's manifest interests are important in choosing an occupation is that normally a person tends to gravitate to the activities he enjoys. And a person naturally shys away from activities that he finds unpleasant. Although manifest interests can be helpful, a person should not normally rely too heavily on them. These interests are always limited by a person's past experiences, and most people want to expand their career opportunities beyond their previous activities.

INVENTORIED INTERESTS

Any individual who is trying to select an occupation should arrange to have his interests tested. Although there are several interest tests, the Strong Vocational Interest Blank (S.V.I.B.) is the most widely used. This test and similar tests are administered regularly by counseling services at most colleges and universities.

The S.V.I.B. is designed to measure how a person's interests compare to the interests of others who have been successful in particular occupations. The principle is that if an individual shares interests with successful people in a particular occupation, there is a good chance that the individual would be satisfied in that occupation. Interest tests are *not* designed to indicate a person's intelligence or ability; they are intended only to show a person's interests. The test scores are related more to what a person would *like* to do rather than what he can do.

The primary advantage of an interest test is that it provides objective measures of a person's interests. And the measures are relatively free from personal biases and limited experiences. Without an interest test, a person may be only able to make an informed guess at his genuine interests. Another valuable aspect of most interest tests is that they give "answers" in terms of specific occupations. Refer to Figure 7–1. This figure shows how the results of the S.V.I.B. are presented. It is beyond the scope of this book to provide a complete explanation of the S.V.I.B. scores (they should be interpreted by a professional counselor), but the important point is that the "answers" are shown in terms of "basic interest scales" (such as public speaking, business management, nature, and adventure) and also in terms of "occupational scales." This kind of information can be extremely helpful in choosing an occupation.

Naturally, the reliability of the test scores on an interest test is often questioned. Many students probably ignore interests tests because they believe the tests are not reliable. But research has shown that most interest tests are highly reliable and extremely accurate. Studies have shown that a person can take the S.V.I.B., for example, at different times and receive about the same scores.[1]

---

[1] Some individuals have been tested 40 years after they took the first test and they received approximately the same scores.

Figure 7–1 Answer Form from the S.V.I.B.

PROFILE – STRONG VOCATIONAL INTEREST BLANK FOR MEN

FOR USE WITH SVIB FORM T399 OR T399R, HAND-SCORED ANSWER SHEET, AND HAND-SCORING STENCILS

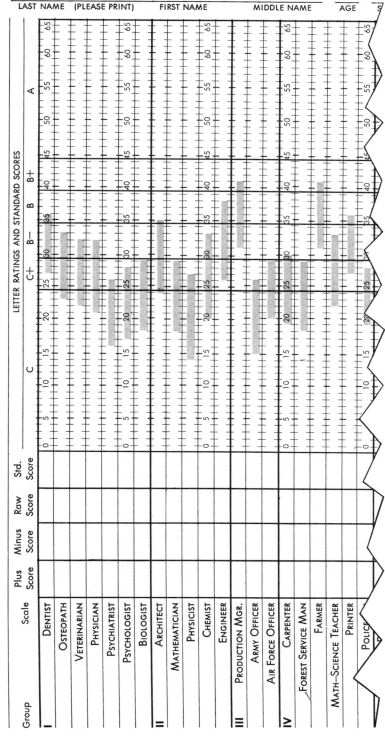

Exerpted with permission of the publisher from *Manual for Strong Vocational Interest Blanks*, by Edward K. Strong, Jr., revised by David P. Campbell (Stanford: Stanford University Press, 1966) Figure 3, p. 6.

PERSONALITY

An individual's personality should be taken into account in his occupational decision because some types of personalities are not well suited to certain occupations. But personality is hard to assess. It is not a simple question of having a "good" or "bad" personality. For purposes of choosing an occupation, a person should try to determine what *type* of personality he has. A fairly objective method of assessing personality is to take a personality inventory test. These tests are usually not directed toward certain occupations. Instead, their basic purpose is to provide a means by which a person can better understand himself. Nevertheless, when the results of a personality test are interpreted in terms of occupational decisions by a professional counselor, they can be extremely useful. With the aid of a personality test, a counselor may be able to see that an individual's personality would be well suited (or entirely inappropriate) for a certain occupation.

APTITUDE

A person can meet all the other criteria for entering an occupation but not have the necessary ability to perform reasonably well in that occupation. If you, for example, simply cannot learn mathematics you probably should not try to be a mathematics teacher. But usually the decision is not so obvious. The ability to perform well in an occupation usually depends on a person's ability to learn, rather than on his physical abilities. And this *ability to learn* is called aptitude. But do you have the necessary aptitude to become a doctor? or a lawyer? or automobile mechanic? In many situations a young person cannot determine very well if he has the aptitude required for a particular occupation.

Rather than make a hasty guess at whether or not you have certain aptitudes for a particular occupation, it is advisable to investigate your aptitudes in a systematic manner. One approach is to look for objective evidence of your abilities. If you make good grades in a certain subject, for example, you have objective evidence of ability in that field. You can also gather evidence from competitive situations or opinions of knowledgeable persons.

Probably the best way to measure your aptitude is to take an aptitude test. Although there are a number of aptitude tests, the Differential Aptitude Tests (D.A.T.) are used often. They measure a person's capacity to learn by evaluating nine different factors. These are: verbal reasoning, numerical ability, scholastic aptitude, abstract reasoning, spatial relations, mechanical reasoning, clerical speed and accuracy, spelling, and language usage (sentences). Aptitude tests such as the D.A.T. will not pinpoint exactly what occupation you should choose. But the answers provided by the tests can be very helpful in showing you the areas in which you have capacities. For example, if you are thinking of becoming an English teacher, but your aptitude scores are low in

Figure 7–2 Perspectives of Vocational Exploration

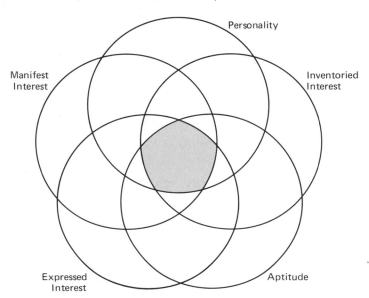

Personality

Manifest
Interest

Inventoried
Interest

Expressed
Interest

Aptitude

language usage and verbal reasoning, you will have a warning that you might not be a good English teacher. High scores, of course, could provide legitimate encouragement.

It is easy to place unwarranted emphasis on any one of the criteria that have been discussed. Some people are concerned only with their expressed interests, others place too much emphasis on personality tests, and some give too much weight to aptitude. Actually, it is important to take *each* of the factors into account. Figure 7–2 can be of value in showing how the criteria interact and overlap.

The area where all the criteria overlap should tell a person about his occupational needs. In other words, a person should take all the criteria into consideration before he makes an occupational decision. If a person considers only one criterion, he has the advantage of keeping a broad spectrum of occupational opportunities open for himself. But such a person is apt to find himself in an unsatisfactory occupation. Consider the case of a person who puts undue emphasis on personality. He may find himself in an occupation for which his personality is suited, but he could discover that he is not really interested in his work.

TOMORROW'S OCCUPATIONS

A person should not make an occupational decision until he has investigated the outlook of specific occupations. It is of little value to decide to become a blacksmith if you cannot get a job in this occupation.

In studying the outlook of specific occupations a person should be concerned with such questions as: (1) what kind of jobs are available? (2) what is the expected income? (3) what are the working conditions like? (4) what are the chances for advancement?, and (5) what are the educational requirements? These questions are crucial in deciding upon an occupation.

But how can a person find out which occupations will offer opportunities in the future? A helpful approach is to start in terms of broad classifications (such as major industry divisions) and then study occupational groups and finally specific occupations.

MAJOR INDUSTRY DIVISIONS

In the early years of our country, we were primarily an agricultural society. Farming was the way of life for most people. But the industrial revolution made the United States the leading industrial country in the world. This transformed our country from a farming economy into a society built on machinery and production. A change of this type has had important effects on jobs and occupations. New, highly technical, industrial jobs were created, and many farmers were driven from the farms into the cities.

There is strong evidence that our economy is just now experiencing *another* "revolution" that will change occupational opportunities greatly. According to many experts, we are starting to shift from an industrial society to a service economy. This means more than half of the employed population will *not* be involved in the production of food, clothing, houses, automobiles, or other tangible goods. Instead, most employees will be working in service industries. These include the following:

1. Government (local, state, and federal governments and public schools)
2. Transportation and public utilities
3. Trade (wholesale and retail)
4. Finance, insurance, and real estate
5. Service and miscellaneous[2]

Now examine Table 7–4 closely. It shows projected employment figures for each of the major industries. The most important feature of the table is the tremendous growth that will take place in the industries that provide services. Notice that all the high growth industries (except contract construction) provide services rather than tangible products. People who will be working in the near future will find the greatest

---

[2] Notice that the word "service" is used in two different ways. Narrowly defined, the service industry includes nonpublic education, medical service, and repair services. Broadly defined, "service" industries refer to all industries that do not produce a tangible product (and they include the five industries in the above list).

Table 7–4 U.S. Employment of Wage and Salary Workers, by Industry, 1964 and Projected 1975 (numbers in thousands)

Industrial Group	1964 Employment		Projected 1975 Employment		Percent Change
	Number	Percent	Number	Percent	1964-1975
Agriculture	4,761	7.6	3,745	4.7%	-21
Mining	633	1.0	620	.8	- 2
Contract construction	3,056	4.9	4,190	5.3	+37
Manufacturing	17,259	27.4	19,740	24.8	+14
Durable goods	9,813	16.0	11,500	14.4	+17
Nondurable goods	7,446	11.4	8,240	10.4	+11
Transportation and public utilities	3,947	6.3	4,425	5.6	+12
Trade, wholesale and retail	12,132	19.3	16,150	20.3	+33
Finance, insurance, and real estate	2,964	4.7	3,725	4.7	+26
Services and miscellaneous	8,569	13.6	12,275	15.4	+43
Total government	9,595	15.3	14,750	18.5	+54
Federal government	2,348	3.8	2,525	3.1	+ 8
State and local govt.	7,248	11.5	12,225	15.4	+69
Total All Industries	62,917	100.0	79,620	100.0	+27

Source: U.S. Department of Labor, Bureau of Labor Statistics, *America's Industrial and Occupational Manpower Requirements, 1964-1975,* January 1, 1966, p. 10.

employment opportunities in government work, services and miscellaneous, contract construction, and trade. Employment opportunities will be scarce in the agricultural and mining industries.

The implications of the "service revolution" are important to persons who are planning their careers. Those industries and occupations—such as physicians, teachers, beauty shop operators, salesmen and others—that provide services will expand tremendously in the future. Another important implication of the "service revolution" is that women will be able to compete on more equal terms with men. Physical strength is more important in an industrial economy than in a service economy. Consequently, as we move toward more services, the physical strength of men will be less of an advantage over women. Part-time employment opportunities will also expand rapidly as a result of the "service revolution." This is because businesses that provide services often need employees who can work at particular hours of the day and particular days of the week.

Sometimes it is helpful to consider the unemployment rates of the various industries. An industry may be expanding rapidly in terms of employment, but still be plagued by seasonal unemployment. Even though the construction industry has been expanding rapidly, it has the highest rate of seasonal unemployment. Above average seasonal unemployment is also a characteristic of agriculture and some types of manufacturing.

MAJOR OCCUPATIONAL GROUPS

Occupations can be grouped in a variety of ways, but it is helpful to look at the difference between white-collar and blue-collar jobs. White-collar workers have been increasing since 1900, and in 1956 they outnumbered blue-collar workers. Furthermore, this important trend is expected to continue as shown in Figure 7–3.

According to this figure, we can expect a more rapid growth of white-collar occupations and a slower growth in blue-collar jobs. By 1975, white-collar occupations will employ almost one-half of all workers. The demand for white-collar workers will grow because of the increased demand for services (service industries employ a high proportion of white-collar workers) but also because there will be a tremendous demand for persons who are able to perform research, teach, and handle the paperwork that is necessary in all kinds of businesses. More specifically, Figure 7–4 shows the major occupational groups and their projected growth in employment.

Figure 7–3   White-Collar Versus Blue-Collar Jobs (1947–1975)

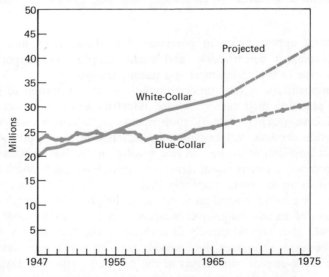

Source: United States Department of Labor, Bureau of Labor Statistics, *Occupational Outlook Handbook*, Bulletin No. 1450, 1966-67 edition; and United States Department of Labor, Bureau of Labor Statistics, "Changing Occupational Structure," *Tomorrow's Manpower Needs*, Bulletin No. 1606, February 1969, p. 4.

Figure 7–4   Projected Employment Growth in Major Occupational Groups

Decline	Major Occupational Group	Projected Growth				
		No Change	Less Than Average	Average	More Than Average
	Professional, Technical				X
	Service				X
	Clerical				X
	Skilled			X	
	Managers and Proprietors			X	
	Sales			X	
	Semiskilled		X		
	Laborers	X			
X	Farm Workers				

Source: United States Department of Labor, Bureau of Labor Statistics, *Occupational Outlook Handbook* Bulletin No. 1450, 1966—67 edition, p. 16.

The occupational group with the fastest rate of growth in the future will be professional, technical, and kindred occupations. People in this category will be in high demand in the 1970's. Such fields as cryogenics, biconics, ultrasonics, and microelectronics were hardly known a few years ago, but they will be growth areas of the future.

Clerical workers will also be highly valued. However, the growth in this field will be for persons who are capable of handling technical data and public contracts. Traditional clerical workers, such as file clerks and calculator operators, will not be in great demand.

The major occupational groups that will have the slowest rate of growth (or actual decrease) are workers who have the least technical skills and the lowest educational attainments. Employment opportunities for farmers, laborers, and semskilled workers will not be in high demand.

THE OUTLOOK OF SPECIFIC OCCUPATIONS

While it is useful to know something about the demands for various occupational groups, the critical factor is the outlook for the specific occupation you are considering. In general, the occupations that will enjoy the greatest growth are the scientific and technical occupations. Figure 7–5 shows that engineers, physicists, mathematicians, chemists, and other scientists generally will be in high demand.

Figure 7–5 Percentage Increase in Employment in Scientific and Technical Fields (1965–1975)

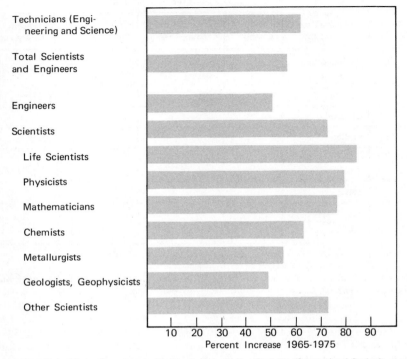

Source: United States Department of Labor, Bureau of Labor Statistics, *Occupational Outlook Handbook,* Bulletin No. 1550, 1968-69 edition, p. 19.

The professions will experience better than average growth, but they will not expand as rapidly as many other occupations. For example, the demand for dentists, physicians, surgeons, lawyers and clergymen will not increase as rapidly as the demand for clerical workers. Although teaching opportunities will expand, most of the increased demand in the near future will be for secondary and college teachers—not elementary teachers. The number of elementary teachers will increase, but a surplus of these teachers already exists, and by 1975 there will be a large surplus.

Table 7–5 does not contain all the possible occupations a person can choose, but it shows the outlook for a large number of occupations and it can be very helpful. Suppose you are considering the possibility of becoming a mining engineer. Table 7–5 shows that all occupations are expected to increase about 33 percent from 1960 to 1975, but the number of mining engineers will probably only increase about 7 percent. In other words, the career opportunities for mining engineers will expand only slightly and will decline compared to other occupations. The information for Table 7–5, therefore, might be extremely useful to you.

Table 7-5 Total National Employment, by Occupation, 1960 and Projected 1975 (expressed in thousands)

Occupation	1960 Employ- ment	Projected 1975 Re- quirements	Percent Change
Industry, total	66,681	88,660	32.96
Professional, technical, and kindred workers	7,475	12,924	72.90
Engineers, technical	810	1,450	79.01
Engineers, aeronautical	46	69	50.00
Engineers, chemical	40	62	55.00
Engineers, civil	146	248	69.86
Engineers, electrical	175	320	82.86
Engineers, industrial	83	170	104.82
Engineers, mechanical	154	255	65.58
Engineers, metallurgical, etc.	20	33	65.00
Engineers, mining	14	15	7.14
Other engineers, technical	133	279	109.77
Natural scientists	236	465	101.27
Chemists	91	175	92.31
Agricultural scientists	30	53	76.67
Biological scientists	30	64	113.33
Geologists and geophysicists	18	29	61.11
Mathematicians	21	51	142.86
Physicists	24	58	141.67
Other natural scientists	22	35	59.09
Technicians, except medical and dental	731	1,418	93.98
Draftsmen	233	375	60.94
Surveyors	44	82	86.36
Air traffic controllers	12	13	8.33
Radio operators	17	27	58.82
Technicians, other	425	920	116.47
Medical and other health workers	1,321	2,240	69.57
Dentists	87	125	43.68
Dietitians and nutritionists	27	37	37.04
Nurses, professional	496	860	73.39
Optometrists	17	20	17.65
Osteopaths	13	16	23.08
Pharmacists	114	126	105.26
Physicians and surgeons	221	374	69.23
Psychologists	17	40	135.29
Technicians, medical and dental	141	393	178.72
Veterinarians	19	26	36.84
Other medical and health workers	171	223	30.41
Teachers	1,945	3,063	57.48
Teachers, elementary	978	1,233	26.07
Teachers, secondary	603	1,100	82.42
Teachers, college	206	455	120.87
Teachers, other	158	275	74.05
Social scientists	46	79	71.74
Economists	17	31	82.35
Statisticians and actuaries	23	36	56.52
Other social scientists	6	12	50.00

Table 7–5 (continued)

Occupation	1960 Employment	Projected 1975 Requirements	Percent Change
Other professional, technical and kindred workers	2,386	4,210	76.45
Accountants and auditors	429	660	53.85
Airplane pilots and navigators	29	55	89.66
Architects	30	45	50.00
Workers in the arts and entertainment	470	774	64.68
Clergymen	200	240	20.00
Designers, except design draftsmen	66	116	75.76
Editors, and reporters	100	128	28.00
Lawyers and judges	225	320	42.22
Librarians	80	130	62.50
Personnel and Labor relations workers	100	191	91.00
Photographers	51	57	11.76
Social and welfare workers	105	218	107.62
Professional, technical and kindred workers, not elsewhere classified	502	1,276	154.18
Managers, officials and proprietors	7,067	9,035	27.85
Conductors, railroad	43	44	2.33
Creditmen	50	89	78.00
Officers, pilots, and engineers, ship	35	36	2.86
Postmasters and assistants	39	34	-12.82
Purchasing agents	115	164	42.42
Managers, officials, and proprietors, not elsewhere classified	6,785	8,667	27.74
Clerical and kindred workers	9,783	14,762	50.89
Stenographers, typists, and secretaries	2,386	3,900	63.45
Office machine operators	375	700	86.67
Other clerical and kindred workers	7,022	10,162	4.47
Accounting clerks	383	470	22.72
Bookkeepers, hand	667	900	34.93
Bank tellers	127	263	107.09
Cashiers	479	973	103.13
Mail carriers	206	290	40.78
Postal clerks	243	340	39.92
Shipping and receiving clerks	325	365	12.31
Telephone operators	355	452	27.32
Clerical and kindred workers, not elsewhere classified	4,238	6,109	44.15
Sales workers	4,401	5,906	34.20
Craftsmen, foremen and kindred workers	8,560	11,357	32.68
Construction craftsmen	2,554	3,102	21.46
Carpenters	832	900	8.17
Brickmasons, stonemasons, and tile setters	186	228	22.58
Cement, concrete finishers	46	75	63.04
Electricians	360	450	25.00
Excavating, grading, and road machinery operators	245	335	36.73
Painters and paperhangers	416	455	9.38

Table 7–5   (continued)

Occupation	1960 Employment	Projected 1975 Requirements	Percent Change
Plasterers	50	61	22.00
Plumbers and pipefitters	304	425	39.80
Roofers and slaters	50	69	38.00
Structural metalworkers	65	105	61.54
Foremen, not elsewhere classified	1,137	1,650	45.12
Metalworking craftsmen, except mechanics	1,081	1,208	11.75
Machinists and related occupations	491	504	2.65
Blacksmiths, foregemen and hammermen	34	24	-29.41
Boilermakers	24	27	12.50
Heat treaters, annealers	20	22	10.00
Millwrights	69	88	27.54
Molders, metal except coremakers	54	56	3.70
Patternmakers, metal and wood	40	49	22.50
Rollers and roll hands	32	34	6.25
Sheet metal workers	137	183	33.58
Toolmakers and diemakers	180	221	22.78
Printing trades craftsmen	302	330	9.27
Compositors and typesetters	183	155	-15.30
Electrotypers and sterotypers	9	5	-44.40
Engravers, except photoengravers	11	15	36.36
Photoengravers and lithographers	24	55	129.17
Pressmen and plate printers	75	100	33.33
Transportation and public utilities craftsmen	374	457	22.19
Linemen and servicemen	286	400	39.86
Locomotive engineers	47	50	6.38
Locomotive firemen	42	7	-83.33
Mechanics and repairmen	2,017	3,174	57.36
Airplane mechanics and repairmen	112	139	24.11
Motor vehicle mechanics	679	940	38.44
Office machine mechanics	51	104	103.92
Radio and television mechanics	103	140	35.92
Railroad and car shop mechanics	39	41	5.13
Other mechanics and repairmen	1,033	1,810	75.22
Other craftsmen and kindred workers	1,096	1,436	31.02
Bakers	103	97	-5.83
Cabinetmakers	66	75	13.64
Cranemen, derrickmen, and hoistmen	124	172	38.71
Glaziers	16	30	87.50
Jewelers and watchmakers	37	39	5.41
Loom fixers	25	24	4.00
Opticians, lens grinders	20	25	25.00
Inspectors, log and lumber	20	25	25.00
Inspectors, other	96	141	46.87
Upholsterers	59	78	32.20
Craftsmen and kindred workers, not elsewhere classified	531	730	37.48
Operatives and kindred workers	11,986	14,806	2,35
Drivers and deliverymen	2,375	3,332	40.29

Table 7–5   (continued)

Occupation	1960 Employment	Projected 1975 Requirements	Percent Change
Drivers, bus truck, and tractor	1,774	2,325	31.00
Deliverymen and routemen	601	845	40.59
Transportation and public utilities operatives	156	162	3.84
Brakemen and switchmen, railroad	103	111	7.76
Power station operators	21	24	14.28
Sailors and deck hands	32	27	-15.62
Semiskilled metalworking occupations	1,453	1,828	25.80
Furnacemen, smeltermen, and pourers	52	56	7.69
Heaters, metal	7	9	28.57
Welders and flame cutters	355	575	61.97
Assemblers, metalworking, class A	101	140	38.61
Assemblers, metalworking, class B	468	545	16.45
Inspectors, metalworking, class B	179	210	17.31
Machine tool operators, class B	259	256	-1.16
Electroplaters	12	15	25.00
Electroplaters helpers	20	22	10.00
Semiskilled textile occupations	780	939	20.38
Knitters, loopers and toppers	44	44	--------
Spinners, textile	50	31	-38.00
Weavers, textile	61	41	-32.78
Sewers and stitchers, manufacturing	625	824	31.84
Other operatives and kindred workers	7,222	8,707	20.56
Asbestos and insulation workers	20	29	45.00
Attendants, automobile service and parking	380	520	36.84
Blasters and powdermen	5	6	20.00
Laundry and dry cleaning operators	392	450	14.80
Meat cutters, except meat packing	190	223	17.37
Mine operatives and laborers, not elsewhere classified	281	200	28.83
Operatives and kindred workers, not elsewhere classified	5,954	7,280	22.28
Service workers	8,349	12,740	52.59
Private household workers	2,216	2,700	21.84
Protective service workers	766	1,183	54.44
Firemen	148	250	68.92
Guards, watchmen, and doorkeepers	331	415	25.38
Policemen and other law enforcement officials	287	518	80.49
Food service workers	1,737	2,638	51.87
Bartenders	172	233	35.47
Cooks, except private households	557	860	54.40
Counter and Fountain workers	158	320	102.53
Waiters and waitresses	850	1,225	44.12
Other service workers	3,630	6,219	71.32
Airline stewards and stewardresses	13	32	146.15
Attendants, hospital and other institutions	450	1,083	140.67
Charwomen and cleaners	200	372	86.00

Table 7–5 (continued)

Occupation	1960 Employ- ment	Projected 1975 Re- quirement	Percent Change
Janitors and sectons	625	980	56.80
Nurses, practical	225	465	106.67
Service workers, not elsewhere classified	2,117	3,287	55.27
Laborers, except farm and mine	3,665	3,778	3.08
Farmers and farm workers	5,395	3,352	-37.87

Note: Because of rounding, sums of individual items may not equal totals.
Source: United States Department of Labor, Bureau of Labor Statistics, "Total National Employment by Occupation, 1960, and Projected 1975," *Tomorrow's Manpower Needs*, Vol. IV, Bulletin No. 1606, February 1969, pp. 27-31.

According to Table 7–5, the specific occupations that are expected to have the most rapid growth are industrial engineers, biological scientists, mathematicians, physicists, pharmacists, medical and dental technicians, college teachers, social and welfare workers, bank tellers, cashiers, airline stewardesses and hospital attendants. But a number of occupations will have only a minimal increase. This will be true for carpenters, painters, machinists, automobile mechanics, jewelers, and laborers. Some occupations (such as farmers, typesetters, bakers and sailors) will actually employ fewer workers in the future. People who are looking for jobs in these occupations will often be disappointed.

You should not decide upon a career simply by looking at the demand for that occupation. It is very possible that you can find an occupation that meets your needs but is not expected to grow rapidly. However, every person who is planning to enter an occupation should have some idea about how fast his chosen field is growing.

CAREER OPPORTUNITIES FOR WOMEN

In addition to the employment "revolution" of the service industries, there is a similar "revolution" underway in the employment of women. Not long ago, few women worked outside their homes. But the proportion of women who work has been rising for several years and it is expected to continue.

As shown in Figure 7–6, the percentage of women who work is increasing in every age category. In 1975, approximately 58 percent of all women in the 45–54 age group will be employed outside their homes. And a majority of young women (aged 20–24) will be employed.

It is a mistake to believe that only single women or married women without children work. Of the married women under age 35, about 60 percent are employed if they have no children under 18; about 40 percent

Figure 7–6   Labor Force Participation of Women (proportion of women who work)

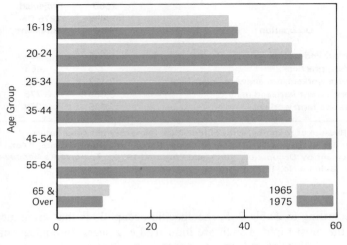

Labor Force Participation Rate (Percent)

Source: United States Department of Labor, Bureau of Labor Statistics, *Occupational Outlook Handbook*, Bulletin No. 1550, 1968-69 edition.

are employed if *all* children are of school age, and 20 percent are employed if the children are infants. Many women, therefore, not only have a career while they are single, but also when they are married and have children.

While women make up over one-third of the total labor force, it is evident from Table 7–6 that employment opportunities are concentrated in certain industries. Women account for one-half or more of the labor force in two of the major industries shown in the table, but in two other industries there are practically no women employees.

It is also helpful to study the major occupational groups of women. As Table 7–7 indicates, women comprise nearly 70 percent of all workers employed in various clerical positions, and women are "gaining" on men in almost every occupational group. The proportion of women has increased in every group except professional and technical workers. This does not mean that women are not demanded in the professional and technical occupations. To the contrary, they are in tremendous demand in these fields. They have not, however, kept pace with men in the professional and technical occupations.

But what are the specific fields that offer jobs for women? The answer is that a young woman can now look for a job in almost any occupation that does not require physical strength. Many companies do not regularly recruit college women through campus interviews but they will employ

Table 7–6 Employed Women

Industry Division	Number (in thousands)	Percentage of Employees in Each Industry Division
Total	22,854	35
Mining	34	5
Contract construction	154	4
Manufacturing	5,437	28
Transportation and public utilities	800	19
Trade	5,185	39
Finance, real estate, and insurance	1,563	50
Services	5,072	52
Government	4,609	41

Source: United States Department of Labor, Bureau of Labor Statistics, *Employment and Earnings and Monthly Report of the Labor Force,* Vol. 13, No. 8, February 1967, p. 85.

Table 7–7 Major Occupational Groups of Employed Women, 1950 and 1965*

Major Occupational Group	Number (in thousands)		% Distribution of All Women Employed		Women as % of Total Employment**	
	1965	1950	1965	1950	1965	1950
Professional and technical workers	3,323	1,862	14%	11%	37%	42%
Managers, officials, and owners (except farm)	1,106	941	5	6	15	15
Clerical workers	7,756	4,539	32	26	70	59
Sales workers	1,881	1,516	8	9	41	39
Craftsmen and foreman	281	181	1	1	3	2
Operatives	3,656	3,215	15	19	28	27
Laborers (except farm and mine)	116	68	1	1	3	2
Private-household workers	2,025	1,771	8	10	98	92
Service workers (except private-household)	3,829	2,168	15	13	55	45
Farmers and farm managers	140	253	1	2	6	6
Farm laborers and foremen	534	663	2	4	30	27
TOTAL, ALL GROUPS	24,648	17,176	100%	100%	35%	29%

*Women 14 years of age and over.
**Both men and women.
Totals may not equal 100 percent because of rounding.
Source: United States Department of Labor, Women's Bureau, *1965 Handbook of Women Workers,* p. 89.

them upon application. The occupations for women that have been expanding most rapidly are shown in Table 7–8.

Until recently there may have been a social stigma attached to working wives. But we must conclude, from the evidence in the preceding figures and tables, that our society has given its approval to the employment of women. Employment opportunities for women have expanded so that women have realistic employment choices.

INVESTIGATING SPECIFIC OCCUPATIONS

After deciding what your occupational needs are and learning something about various employment opportunities, you may find that several occupations interest you. The next step, then, is to find out about these occupations. And this is an important step. You may learn that you are well suited for a certain occupation and the employment opportunities seem attractive, but you may still be left with the important question, "Just what do the people *do* who work in these occupations?" In other words, if you believe you might want to be a building contractor, for example, how do you find out what the day-to-day life of a building contractor is like?

Table 7–8 Rapidly Expanding Fields for Women

Profession	Increase 1950-1960
Recreation workers	132%
Personnel/labor relations workers	105
Medical and dental technicians	104
Other technicians (electrical, etc.)	56
Elementary school teachers	51
Professional nurses	47
Librarians	46
Accountants and auditors	43
Editors and reporters	42
Musicians and music teachers	42
College professors	36
Physicians	33
Secondary school teachers	25
Artists and art teachers	22
Religious workers	22
Lawyers and judges	19
Social workers	17
Dietitians	15
Natural scientists	10

Source: Mildred S. Springer, "Special Outlook: Special Challenge," *College Placement Annual, 1969* (Bethlehem, Pa.: College Placement Council, Inc., 1970), p. 31. Reprinted with permission.

The *obvious* source of information about particular jobs is the original source. Original sources include the worker that actually does the job you are interested in, but they also include employers and government agencies that issue licenses and regulate employment. However, original sources are not always the most *reliable* source. Knowledgeable people may be hard to find or difficult to communicate with, and they may give you a biased opinion. A teacher, for instance, may love his work and try to convince you that his work is more rewarding than any other. But you must remember that his opinion is based primarily on his own experiences.

Perhaps the most widely used source of information about specific occupations is the *Occupational Outlook Handbook* published biennially by the United States Bureau of Labor Statistics. The Handbook describes several hundred occupations. The *Handbook* describes for each occupation the nature of the work, where workers are employed, training, other qualifications, advancement, employment outlook, earnings, working conditions, and where to go for more information. The *Handbook* can usually be found in public libraries, school libraries, college libraries, and counseling bureaus such as a college counseling bureau or a local employment agency.

Other sources about specific occupations include: the *Dictionary of Occupational Titles* (D.O.T.) where more than 25,000 separate occupations are listed alphabetically. Each occupation is defined in a short paragraph that describes what work gets done, how, and why, and the functions performed by the worker in relation to people, data and things. A second volume is also available that describes the various requirements necessary for each worker engaged in a specific occupation. The D.O.T. can also be found in most libraries. The *Job Guide for Young Workers* (which is published by the United States Employment Service) can prove to be an invaluable source of information for a young or beginning worker. Under each occupation discussed you will find information about the duties performed, the characteristics of the job, employment prospects, qualifications necessary, chances for advancement, and where the various jobs can be found. Another source, although used mainly by professional counselors, is the *Counselor's Guide to Occupational and Other Manpower Information,* published by the U.S. Government Printing Office. The *Guide* is an annotated bibliography of federal and state government publications, including sections on job descriptions, careers in government, summer jobs, apprentices, minority groups, handicapped, older workers, labor standards and part-time employment.

There are many other sources of information. These include: the *Career Index,* published periodically by Chronicle Guidance Publications, Inc. (Moravia, New York). The *Index* tells you how to locate books, pamphlets, and magazine articles describing different occupations. Other sources include the *Career Guidance Index,* published by Careers

(Largo, Florida), *Counselor's Information Service,* published by B'nai B'rith Vocational Service (Washington, D.C.), *Occupational Index,* published periodically by Personnel Services, Inc. (Jaffrey, New Hampshire).

A person who is interested in learning more about a specific occupation should also consult his state employment agency, the U.S. Bureau of Employment Security, Washington, D.C., or the U.S. Civil Service Commission. These sources are useful for many types of occupations but they are particularly helpful in finding summer jobs (and summer employment is an excellent means of getting first-hand information about an occupation).

There are literally thousands of sources of information about various jobs. In most cases a prospective job seeker should browse through the local library, make a trip to an employment agency, see a professional counselor, and write letters to various agencies requesting information. When you consider that the job you choose or the career you choose could conceivably last a lifetime, it makes good sense to seek out the necessary information about particular occupations so you will make the best decision possible.

INCOMES IN THE VARIOUS OCCUPATIONS

How much income would you like to earn? Although we have seen that people have several reasons for working and income is not necessarily the most important consideration, the amount of money you receive is important.

Starting salaries differ greatly among occupations. If you had received a masters degree (in a technical field) in 1971, your starting salary probably would have been more than $1,000 a month. But if you had been starting as a draftsman, your income probably would have been less than $500 a month or less than half as much.

Of course, a person should not put too much weight on starting salaries. In some occupations, beginners start at a rather low salary but they progress quickly. The law profession is a good example. Starting salaries of attorneys are relatively low, but experienced attorneys are often able to increase their income substantially. Table 7–9 shows some interesting facts. It compares the salaries of four major occupations for workers who have been out of school five years and ten years. Engineers usually have a good starting salary and they typically do very well for a few years. But engineers have not (as a group) increased their earnings as much as accountants, salesmen, and general business graduates. According to Table 7–9, the group that has the greatest increase in income in the first ten years after graduation is the group of general business graduates. In the sample taken, salaries of general business graduates increased by almost 25 percent.

Table 7-9 Comparison of Salaries of Four Major Occupations

			Average Monthly Earnings of College Men Employed 5 Years Ago (Class of 1965)								
Field	No. of Companies	No. of Men	$900 or Less	$901 to $1000	$1001 to $1100	$1101 to $1200	$1201 to $1300	$1301 to $1400	$1401 to $1500	Over $1500	Average Salary*
Engineering	77	4103	2	10	33	20	8	3	1		$1107
Accounting	45	777	6	15	9	4	3	5	1	2	$1091
Sales	40	572	5	11	10	8	3	1	1	1	$1080
General Business	71	2808	9	22	17	7	11	3	2		$1088

			Average Monthly Earnings of College Men Employed 10 Years Ago (Class of 1960)								
Field	No. of Companies	No. of Men	$1000 or Less	$1001 to $1100	$1101 to $1200	$1201 to $1300	$1301 to $1400	$1401 to $1500	$1501 to $1600	Over $1600	Average Salary*
Engineering	66	3120		7	10	21	12	11	1	4	$1354
Accounting	33	369	1	5	6	8	2	3	2	6	$1352
Sales	32	295	2	7	3	5	7	3	1	4	$1310
General Business	56	1716	2	9	6	9	9	6	5	10	$1358

*Salary figures are the average of company responses to the question which follows: "Please estimate, as accurately as you can, the average monthly earnings now (November, 1970) for men whom you hired from the graduating classes of 1965 and 1960 and who *started with you* in the fields indicated."
Source: Frank S. Endicott, "Trends in Employment of College and University Graduates in Business and Industry" (Evanston, Illinois: Northwestern University, 1971). Used with permission.

EDUCATION AND OCCUPATIONS

Just a few years ago, most high school graduates did not go on to college. But look at Figure 7–7. It shows that well over half of all high school graduates continue their education. It is no longer a status symbol to attend college because those who do not go to college or receive some form of advanced training are actually in the minority.

Figure 7–7   Number of High School Graduates Who Go to College

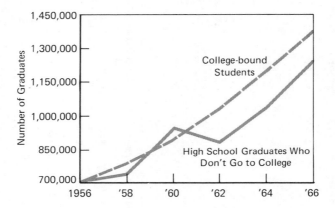

Reprinted with permission from *Changing Times, The Kiplinger Magazine* (January, 1969 issue). Copyright 1969 by the Kiplinger Washington Editors, Inc., 1729 H Street, N.W., Washington, D.C. 20006.

Why do the majority of all high school graduates decide to go to college or receive some kind of after-high-school advanced training? Undoubtedly, there are many reasons; some reasons are social, some are economic. There are several major financial reasons why it makes good sense to get a college degree or at least some advanced or specialized training.

First, a college education is necessary to enter some occupations. Many occupations have no formal requirement of a college degree, but as a practical matter, a person must have a degree to work in the occupation.

The United States Department of Labor regularly publishes a list of jobs for which a college education is *usually* required. Although this list does not include every occupation that might require a college education, it includes many occupations and can be quite informative. One of the recent publications listed the following:

accountant   advertising worker
actuary   airline dispatcher

anthropologist
architect
astronomer
bank officer
biochemist
biological scientist
chemist
chiropractor
college placement officer
cooperative extension-service worker
counselor, rehabilitation
counselor, school
counselor, vocational
dentist
dietitian
economist
engineer
F.B.I. special agent
forester
geographer
geologist
geophysicist
historian
home economist
hospital administrator
industrial designer
landscape architect
lawyer
librarian
manufacturer's salesman
marketing-research worker
mathematician
medical record librarian
medical technologist

meteorologist
newspaper reporter
oceanographer
optometrist
osteopathic physician
personnel worker
pharmacist
physician
physicist
pediatrist
political scientist
protestant clergyman
public relations worker
psychologist
purchasing agent
rabbi
range manager
recreation worker
Roman Catholic priest
sanitarian
securities salesman
social worker
sociologist
speech pathologist
statistician
systems analyst
teacher, college or university
teacher, elementary or secondary
technical writer
therapist, occupational
therapist, physical
urban planner
veterinarian

Another major reason why young people decide to attend college is the fact that college graduates earn much more than those who do not graduate from college. In fact, the higher the educational level of a person, the greater his income—as shown in Figure 7–8. This figure shows a direct correlation between education and income. As indicated in the figure, the better educated groups have a higher income.

Not only do well-educated people earn more income, their jobs are much more secure. Unemployment is a major problem for people who have little education, but it is not nearly so serious for the well educated.

Figure 7–8 Education and Income

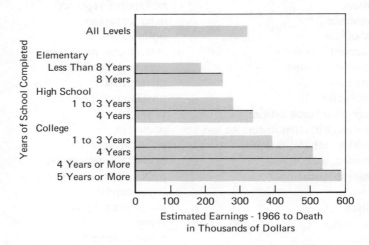

Source: United States Department of Labor, Bureau of Labor Statistics, *Occupational Outlook Handbook,* 1970-71 edition, p. 19.

Figure 7–9 shows the unemployment rates by educational level. Education also allows an individual more career choices and the ability to move from one profession to another. Another major reason why education is important is that people with good educations will have greater job opportunities in the future. Examine Table 7–10 closely. It shows some important relationships. The table shows a very strong correlation between columns 2 and 3, which is evidence that the occupational groups

Figure 7–9 Education and Unemployment

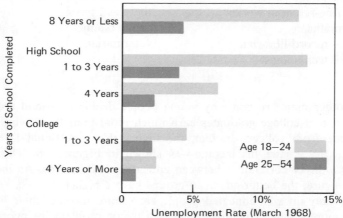

Source: United States Department of Labor, Bureau of Labor Statistics, *Occupational Outlook Handbook,* 1970-71 edition.

Table 7–10 Years of Schooling and Anticipated Growth in Employment

Occupational Group	(1) Average Number of Years of Schooling Completed in 1965*	(2) Rank by Number of Years of Schooling Completed	(3) Rank by Percentage Increase in Projected Employment 1965-1975
Professional and technical	16.3	1	1
Managers, officials, and owners	12.6	2	4
Clerical workers	12.5	3-4	3
Sales workers	12.5	3-4	6
Craftsmen and foremen (skilled)	11.7	5	5
Operatives (semiskilled)	10.6	6	7
Service workers	10.1	7	
Laborers (unskilled)	9.5	8	8
Farmers and farm workers	8.6	9	9

*Average here is the median, which is the middle number in a distribution of numbers ranging from the highest to the lowest. Half the people have more than the median number of years of schooling and half the people have less.

Source: D. Johnston and H. Hamel, "Educational Attainment of Workers in March 1965." Special Labor Force Report No. 65, U.S. Department of Labor, Bureau of Labor Statistics, pp. 4-13; U.S. President and U.S. Department of Labor, *Manpower Report of the President, 1967,* p. 274.

that will be in the greatest demand in the future are those that require the most education. Professional and technical workers are expected to increase more rapidly than any other group, and they are the most highly educated. The group with the least education (farmers and farm workers) will grow less than any other group. Service workers are the only group that will grow rapidly which does not require advanced education.

We may conclude that education enables a person to substantially improve his financial position. Education permits people to enter certain occupations, earn a greater income, and reduce their unemployment problems.

SUMMARY

Most young people probably choose an occupation in a rather haphazard way. But since the decision is of such great importance, a person should try to use a careful, logical approach.

As a first step, it is important to understand that people derive many different things from their jobs. And the key to a satisfying career is to find an occupation that meets your own personal needs and aspirations.

This can best be approached by studying your expressed interests, manifest interest, inventoried interests, personality, and aptitude. But even after finding an occupation that is apparently suitable, a wise person will investigate the future outlook of that occupation. Some fundamental changes are taking place in our society and these changes are making some occupations obsolete while others are becoming much more important. In general, occupations that require a good education will be in the greatest demand in the future. Furthermore, the highest paid occupations generally require a good education. Most people find that education, financial success, and occupational satisfaction are all interrelated. The approach suggested in this chapter for choosing an occupation should be a great improvement over a haphazard approach.

Case Problems

1. Mark Johnson is in his second year of college. While he has not selected a career yet, he has been thinking about the problem a lot in the last few months. He would like to start preparing for a career, but at the same time he doesn't want to hurry his decision. Mark is not naive, but he believes he can measure all the important factors in terms of money. In other words, the jobs that pay the highest incomes also, according to Mark, have the best working conditions and the most prestige. To what extent do you agree with Mark? Your answer should provide specific reasons.

2. Terry has decided to become a salesman. He reached this decision over a long period of time, but basically his method was quite simple. His father is a successful salesman and Terry has many characteristics that are similar to his father's. Terry is fairly extroverted, and he believes this is desirable for a salesman. Terry also thinks his decision is sound because he once took an aptitude test and the test tended to confirm his decision to be a salesman. Terry has used some logic but still his approach could be improved. How would you criticize Terry's approach to making a career decision?

3. Although Barry Gold is interested in working in the field of medical science, he has decided that he does not want to become a physician or a dentist. Barry's tentative study has indicated that he might want to become an optometrist. He thinks he would be well suited for this profession and he has developed a strong interest in this possibility. However, Barry is acutely aware of practical considerations because his father is educated in a field that has been declining in importance and his father has had difficulty finding employment. Use Table 7–5 to get some information that could be helpful to Barry. How would your answer be different if Barry was thinking of becoming a medical technician?

4. Joe Lame has had a lot of trouble in college. It's not that Joe does not have the ability; on the contrary, Joe is convinced that he could get good grades if he wanted to make the effort. Nevertheless, Joe is considering

dropping out of college and starting to work. Joe has worked around construction projects every summer for the past six years and he has decided to become a carpenter and eventually a building contractor. One of Joe's reasons for wanting to drop out of college is that he believes a building contractor does not really need a college degree. Do you agree with Joe? Why or why not?

5. Frank has finally decided to become serious about planning his career. He has worried about the problem through his first two years of college, and now he is going to actually do something. He took several types of tests. He then talked with a professional counselor and some of his father's friends. He is starting to shape some tentative ideas, but he still believes he needs additional information. His next step is to spend a day in the college library. If you were to make a list of the published sources Frank could turn to for information, what would you include in your list?

6. Most people recognize that income is not the only factor that should be considered when a career is selected. Mike Johns has been offered a job as a traveling salesman, and the salary alone is substantial. In addition, if Mike does well at all his income will be supplemented by commissions and bonuses. Mike figures that he could earn at least twice as much as his other friends who are graduating from college. Although Mike knows factors other than income are important, he has never thought about them much. He has, therefore, decided to sit down and make a list of occupational motivators (reasons for working) before he decides how important each factor is to him. If you were asked to make such a list, what would you include?

7. Fred and his wife, Betty, have been talking about their problems in choosing careers. They are both juniors in college now and Betty plans to work at least five or six years before they will start their family. As a result, Betty is somewhat more interested in a career than many young women. They have heard about the "service revolution" that is taking place, and they are discussing the effects this might have on their careers.
   (a) What is meant by the "service revolution"?
   (b) What are the implications of the "service revolution" for someone like Fred and Betty?

8. Dave has tried to select a career by using a fairly scientific approach. He has taken all the important types of tests, he has talked with professional counselors, and he has tentatively decided to become a geologist. He is satisfied with the projected employment outlook for geologists and he believes he should start preparing himself. Still, Dave is a little worried because he simply does not have a very good idea of what a geologist does. How should he approach the problem of finding out what the day-to-day work of a geologist is like.

Selected Readings

Baer, M. F., and Roeber, E. C. *Occupational Information.* 3rd edition. Chicago: Science Research Associates, Inc., 1964.

Borow, Henry (ed.). *Man in a World of Work.* Boston: Houghton Mifflin Company, 1964.

Byrn, D. K. *How to Express Yourself Vocationally.* Washington, D.C.: National Vocational Guidance Association, 1961.

Calvert, R., Jr. and Steele, J. E. *Planning Your Career.* New York: McGraw-Hill Book Company, 1963.

Career Guide for Demand Occupations. Washington, D.C.: U.S. Government Printing Office. See latest edition.

Chiselli, E. E. *The Validity of Occupational Aptitude Tests.* New York: Wiley and Sons, 1966.

Cross, Patricia K. *The Junior College Student: A Research Description.* Princeton, N.J.: Educational Testing Service, 1968.

De Grazia, S. *Of Time, Work and Leisure.* New York: Twentieth Century Fund, 1962.

Dubin, R. *The World of Work: Industrial Society and Human Relations.* Englewood Cliffs, N.J.: Prentice-Hall, 1958.

"Education for Jobs." *Changing Times, The Kiplinger Magazine,* June 1966, p. 32.

Education Is the Key to a Good Job. Detroit, Michigan: Burroughs Corporation.

Endicott, Frank S. "What Are You Worth?" *Careers In Business/70.* New York: Career Publications, 1969.

Form, W. H. and Miller, D. C. *Industry, Labor, and Community.* New York: Harper & Row, 1960.

Gardiner, G. L. *How You Can Get the Job You Want.* New York: Harper & Row, 1962.

Ginzberg, E. *et al. Occupational Choice: An Approach to a General Theory.* New York: Columbia University Press, 1951.

Guide to College Majors. Moravia, N.Y.: Chronicle Guidance Publications. See latest edition.

Handbook for Young Workers. Washington, D.C.: U.S. Government Printing Office, 1965.

Hatt, P. "Occupation and Social Stratification." *American Journal of Sociology,* Vol. 55, 1950, pp. 538–43.

Herzberg, F. *Work and the Nature of Man.* Cleveland: World Publishing, 1966.

Herzberg, F., Mausner, B., and Snyderman, Barbara B. *The Motivation to Work.* New York: Wiley and Sons. See most recent edition.

Larison, R. H. *How to Get and Hold the Job You Want.* New York: David McKay Company, Inc., 1950. Includes directions for starting a job-finding forum.

Levinson, H. *Emotional Health in the World of Work.* New York: Harper & Row, 1964.

Magoun, F. A. *Successfully Finding Yourself and Your Job.* New York: Harper & Row, 1959.

Manpower Implications of Automation. Washington, D.C.: U.S. Department of Labor, 1965.

Manpower Report to the President. Washington, D.C.: U.S. Department of Labor, Bureau of Labor Statistics. See latest edition.

McLean, A. (ed.). *To Work Is Human: Mental Health and the Business Community.* New York: Macmillan and Co., 1967.

Miller, J. N. "Seven Steps Toward Getting a Job." *Reader's Digest,* March 1963, p. 72.

Mueller, Kate H. *Educating Women for a Changing World.* Minneapolis: University of Minnesota Press, 1954.

Occupational Outlook Quarterly. Washington, D.C.: U.S. Department of Labor, Bureau of Labor Statistics. See latest edition.

President's Commission on the Status of Women. *American Women.* Washington, D.C.: U.S. Government Printing Office, 1963.

Roe, Anne. *The Psychology of Occupations.* New York: Wiley and Sons, 1956.

Seligman, B. B. *Most Notorious Victory: Man in an Age of Automation.* New York: The Free Press, 1966.

Sinick, D. *Your Personality and Your Job.* Chicago: Science Research Associates, Inc., 1960.

Smuts, Robert W. *Women and Work in America.* New York: Columbia University Press, 1959.

Sociological Studies of Occupations, A Bibliography. Washington, D.C.: Manpower Administration, U.S. Department of Labor, 1965.

Springer, Mildred S. "Special Outlook: Special Challenge." *College Placement Annual, 1969.* Bethlehem, Pa.: College Placement Council, Inc., 1970.

Strong, E. K., Jr. *Vocational Interests 18 Years After College.* Minneapolis: University of Minnesota Press, 1955.

Summer Vacation Jobs in Federal Agencies. Washington, D.C.: U.S. Civil Service Commission. See latest edition.

U.S. Department of Labor, Bureau of Labor Statistics. *America's Industrial and Occupational Manpower Requirements, 1964–1975,* January 1, 1966.

U.S. Department of Labor. *Dictionary of Occupational Titles.* Washington, D.C.: U.S. Employment Service. See latest edition.

U.S. Department of Labor, Bureau of Labor Statistics. *Employment and Earnings and Monthly Report of the Labor Force.* See latest edition.

U.S. Department of Labor, Bureau of Labor Statistics. *The Occupational Outlook Handbook.* Washington, D.C.: U.S. Government Printing Office, See latest edition.

U.S. Department of Labor, Bureau of Labor Statistics. *Tomorrow's Manpower Needs,* Vol. III, Bulletin No. 1606, February 1969.

U.S. Department of Labor, Women's Bureau. *Handbook of Women Workers.* See latest edition.

Vroom, Victor H. *Work and Motivation.* New York: Wiley and Sons, 1964.

Wolfbein, S. L. *Employment and Unemployment in the United States.* Chicago: Science Research Associates, 1964.

Wolfbein, S. L., and Goldstein, H. *Our World of Work.* Chicago: Science Research Associates, Inc., 1961.

CHAPTER EIGHT

LEARNING TO INVEST

econ - invest for increased produ

Although getting a better job and acquiring additional educational and technical skills are rightfully uppermost in the minds of most young people who are trying to improve their financial positions, there are other ways. Your ability to earn an income is an asset, probably the least expensive asset you can acquire. However, there are other assets which you can acquire that will produce an income and improve your financial position. This process of acquiring assets to produce income is called *investing*. Actually, all your efforts to improve your educational and technical skills fall within this broad definition of investing. In addition, investing includes buying physical assets (such as real estate), financial assets (such as stocks), or intangible assets (such as a franchise).

Although investing in your own income-producing ability is probably the wisest investment early in your life, other investments are also appropriate, particularly for those who wish to improve their financial positions at the same time they wish to pursue other nonfinancial goals, such as more leisure or freedom. Actually, the quickest way to improve one's financial position is to reduce leisure; that is, instead of working a 40-hour week, work an 80-hour week. Indeed, some bright young professional people do exactly that as a means of improving their financial positions, either in the present or in the future. Many others hold second jobs, usually part time, either on weekends or daily, which can quickly improve one's financial position. Most people who give up that much leisure and work that hard are trying to achieve a particular objective, and they usually consider their extra efforts temporary. After all, there are many more important aspects of life than financial ones.

When you consider the possibility that you could continue to work very hard for many years, and still have no financial security, the need to improve your financial position through investing becomes apparent. When you depend only upon your own personal abilities to provide income, you must continue to work as long as you expect to receive income. But when you can depend upon your investments for income, either wholly or partially, you may continue to receive an income from those investments as long as you hold them, regardless of how you spend your time and energy. Your investments work for you, and their income is your income. If you continue to work as you acquire productive investments, you contribute to the sum total of goods and services both through your work and through your investments, and you receive income from both sources. Although investing occurs through several media, most investors do so through corporate ownership. Since corporations need tremendous amounts of capital to make their employees more productive, a great many owners are needed to provide investment funds. In exchange for funds, corporations issue shares of ownership called *stocks* which are considered investments by those who own them.

You may recall from Chapter One that the fourth part of the illustrative financial plan leading to financial security is a three-step savings-investment program. From age 25 to 29, $300 per year is to be invested; from age 30 to 39, the rate is doubled to $600 per year; and from age 40 to 65, redoubled to $1,200 per year. Assuming this rate of investing and a 9 percent rate of return, an investment portfolio worth about $250,000 could be acquired by age 65. However, it was stressed that there are many risks which often make the attainment of a financial goal difficult, if not impossible.

In this chapter, you may learn still more reasons why success is improbable, but you may also become convinced that you should join the investing minority. Although this minority is a fairly sizable one of perhaps 30 million people, it is still a minority. Furthermore, the proportion of the population reaching retirement with $250,000 is minuscule indeed. Unawareness is certainly one obstacle that may be partially overcome by what you will read in this chapter and the following three. The various investment risks are also obstacles you should at least better understand after digesting the following pages. Emotion must be recognized as the crucial obstacle that it always is, and must be overcome in any way possible. However, as in the case of other experiences, if you know where you are going, how to get there, and the problems you may encounter along the road, learning to invest can be a stimulating, challenging, and satisfying experience.

An investment, by definition, is an asset purchased or held with the expectation of earning a financial return. Usually implicit in such a definition is the assumption of reasonable risk. Financial return may be received in the form of rental income in the case of a real estate investment, interest income in the case of bonds or savings accounts, or dividends in the case of stocks. Furthermore, a financial return can occur if you sell an asset for more than you pay for it, either in the case of stocks, bonds, real estate, or other commodities. Thus, there are two parts to an expected financial return, namely, regular income payments of one kind or another, and increases in the market value of the investment itself.

Although real estate investments are discussed later in the chapter, attention is focused primarily upon stocks—and, more specifically, upon common stocks—as the primary investment medium. This approach is taken because it is assumed that the typical investor—planning his savings-investment program early in his career—starts with zero savings and investments. Granting this assumption, the investor must begin his investment program a bit at a time, perhaps with only $300 per year. Only after he has acquired sizable assets can he consider investments which require substantial cash outlays, such as real estate. Real estate has a whole series of special features, some of which make it extremely attractive (such as tax advantages) and some features which make it highly unattractive (fixed location, maintenance, and resale problems, for example). Bonds are almost exclusively owned by large banks and insurance companies, and with the exception of U.S. savings bonds, they are in $1,000 minimum denominations which make them unattractive for the new investor. Furthermore, bonds are fixed-income securities which do not respond to growth during prosperous economic periods; thus they have the serious problem of inflation risk, plus interest-rate risk. Paintings, jewelry, coins, stamps, antiques, cattle, Chihuahuas, and other extraordinary investment avenues are special cases, and are not considered specifically.

Although real estate has some very real advantages to certain investors and many of the comments made in the following pages apply to real estate to some extent, most of our attention will be focused on stocks. They are readily available and salable in small quantities; they are readily movable from city to city or state to state; they are readily expandable as additional saving occurs, and they appreciate in value over time. Through a well-planned and well-managed savings-investment program, you should be able to improve your financial position substantially over time.

BUYING STOCKS

Stock is a means of investing. Stock represents ownership of property; it is risk assumption; it is a claim on the earnings of a corporation; it is a means of improving your financial position; it is a way of protecting yourself against inflation; it is one way of contributing to the nation's production process without endangering your total asset position. Stock ownership is not gambling, although some people use the stock market to gamble. Nor is it necessarily speculation, although some people speculate in the stock market. There are different kinds of stocks and different kinds of stock buyers, fortunately and, in some cases, unfortunately. You can find many kinds of satisfaction from buying stocks. If you simply want to play around with an exhilarating hobby, you can do so by buying stocks; just do not expect it to cost you any less than golf. If you are interested in improving your financial position, you can do that too through a serious effort to acquire a group of investments called a portfolio.

WHAT IS A STOCK?

Stock Is Ownership.   A stock is a piece of paper that represents part ownership or a share in all the assets of a corporation; not specific property like a brick or a notebook, but a share, or a part, of all the property owned by the company. When you buy a stock, you own a share of that company; you are an investor in that company. Corporations need huge amounts of money to acquire extremely expensive facilities; costly machines and trained manpower are needed to produce consumer products for all of us, and industrial products for other corporations. To obtain these funds, corporations sell stock. In a large company, you are in effect joining with perhaps 300 or 3,000,000 other people in buying a large stamping machine or a whole factory. As the machine is used to produce a salable product, the profit generated from its sale is either reinvested in the corporation or paid to the stockholders (shareholders) as a return on investment, called a dividend. As the company shows ability to consistently use its machines profitably, the value of your investment increases through such reinvestment and additional expected dividends. Consequently, you have dividend income and you may expect your stock to rise in price.

As an example, suppose you buy ten shares of Miscellaneous Shoe Corp. Further, suppose that these ten shares are part of a block of new stock that Miscellaneous Shoe is offering to the public. Say 10,000 shares are being issued, and they are valued at $30 per share. Your aggregate investment is $300 (10 shares × $30). Since Miscellaneous Shoe is a new company, $30 is also the book value, i.e. the value of total net assets divided by the number of shares outstanding ($300,000 ÷ 10,000 shares = $30). As soon as a company begins buying plant and equipment, the market value and the book value will no longer be the same. The book value will still be equal to total net assets (total assets less debts) divided by the number of shares owning those net assets. On the other hand, market value will be whatever the highest bidder is willing to pay for your shares in the market, and his willingness to pay will depend upon his expectations of profit potential. If Miscellaneous Shoe were an old, well-established company, we might assume that $30 is the market value of the existing shares of Miscellaneous Shoe, the market value being the price you can get for them if you decide to sell them.

Claim on Earnings.   Owning stock also means having a claim on some of the earnings as profits of a corporation. Carrying our hypothetical example further, suppose that this company loses money the first two years, breaks even in the third, and then starts to show a profit; say it earns $100,000 profit in its fourth year of operation. Assuming the company does not wish to reinvest all its earnings, it will pay out some of its earnings as dividends to its stockholders, and retains some for expansion. If the company should adopt a 50 percent dividend pay out policy, for example, it will pay total dividends of $50,000 or $5 per share (10,000 shares × $5 = $50,000). The other $50,000 is retained for expansion of the business. With $100,000 earnings or $10 per share, the market value of the stock would undoubtedly rise, perhaps to $100 per share or more. A $100 price on a stock earning $10 is quite reasonable; it is only ten times earnings. Many stocks have much higher multiples, or ratios, between price and earnings. In fact, many investors are most interested in a stock's price-earnings ratio since it indicates how much they will have to pay for their claim on the corporation's earnings. Since ten times is actually fairly low, Miscellaneous Shoe's price might be expected to rise considerably above $100 per share if it can continue with this earnings rate.

Earnings mean success. Any company that is successful in satisfying consumer demand will grow. As the company grows, its need for funds will increase to a point that cannot be satisfied with retained earnings alone, so more stock will be issued. If Miscellaneous Shoe at the beginning of its fifth year wants to raise an additional $300,000, it will have to issue only 3,000 shares since the market value is now $100 per share. After selling the additional 3,000 shares, a total of 13,000 shares will be outstanding (10,000 shares originally issued and 3,000 additionally issued). If the company can double its profits with twice as much plant and equipment, total earnings would be $200,000, but the earnings per share would be about $15 per share ($200,000 ÷ 13,000 shares), up from $10 per share ($100,000 ÷ 10,000 shares). Obviously, a share of stock earning $15 per share with expectations of still greater earnings will rise in market price because investors will want shares in such a rapid growth company. Furthermore, dividends may increase. The price could now go to $150 or $200 per share, quite a price appreciation from that original $30 per share. Therefore, stock is an investment, that is, an asset acquired or held with the expectation of a financial return. If a corporation does well, the stockholders do well. If not, they do not. Corporate losses, or even frustrated expectations, can mean falling stock prices.

Limited Liability. Stock ownership also means limited liability. You are liable to any or all creditors of the corporation in which you hold stock only to the extent of the money you have already invested. In the case of default, insolvency, or bankruptcy, the creditors of the corporation may take the entire corporation, but they cannot claim any other assets that you or any other stockholder may own. Of all the reasons why corporations in this country have been able to aggregate the billions of dollars necessary to finance their productivity, one of the most significant is the limited liability now associated with common stock ownership. Limited liability has not always been associated with common stocks, but now it is an integral part of the corporation statutes of all states.

For example, consider the man who has worked all his life in a drugstore, first as an employee, then as a partner, then as sole owner. The drugstore has continued to do well, and from the profits in the drugstore, he has expanded into a stationery store on one side and a malt shop on the other. In addition, he has been able to acquire commercial property, residential property, stocks, bonds, and part ownership in a local funeral parlor. If after all these years of strenuous and successful effort, some man should drink one too many malted milks while sitting on a bar stool in the malt shop some afternoon, fall off the stool, and hit his head on the corner of a counter, he or his parents can sue the owner for not only the malt shop, but also for the drugstore, stationery shop, commercial and residential property, stocks, bonds, and his part ownership in the funeral parlor. If the malt shop were incorporated, however, as a separate business entity, a lawsuit such as the one described could result in no more loss than the loss of the malt shop. All the other assets of the malt shop owner could not be touched. This is called limited liability, that is, the stockholder's liability is limited to the amount of money he has invested in that specific corporation.

When you buy a common stock, you have bought an investment that does not endanger any of your other assets. Therefore, it is possible to invest in a number of different corporations, that is to diversify, in order to reduce further the risk of loss in any one company due to any management mistakes, shift in consumer demand, international competition, labor union strikes, tornadoes, earthquakes, or what have you. In each and every case of stock ownership, you can lose no more than the total amount of money you have invested in that specific corporation alone. You can lose that much, but your liability is limited by the amount you have decided to invest, rather than by the amount someone else decides to claim.

WHY BUY A STOCK?

Assuming you decide to save and invest, why buy stock? There are indeed numerous reasons why investors buy stock in general, and a given stock in particular. The evaluation of individual securities is treated in detail in Chapter Ten, but a few comments about the purpose behind stock purchases in general should be considered now. Specifically, consider these four reasons for buying stocks: (1) dividends, (2) price appreciation, (3) protection against inflation, and (4) portfolio adjustments.

Dividends. Although dividends may not be your primary concern in the early stages of an investment program, they are a significant reason for buying stock. Although there are growth companies that do not pay dividends and many more that do not pay substantial dividends, and for very good reasons, these growth companies will presumably one day reach a more mature corporate status when regular dividends will be paid. Dividends are an immediate cash flow to the investor, and the dividend/price ratio, or yield, is a very significant figure especially for more mature companies. Investors do expect a return on their investments. Although dividends need not necessarily be as large as a guaranteed interest payment on a savings account or a bond, assuming that the stock has some possibility of appreciation, present and future dividends are very important since investors have only a limited amount of money and have many alternative savings outlets.

Dividends are especially important to those investors who want to supplement their other incomes. People with limited or stabilized incomes, such as those living on pensions or social security payments, often find that dividends make a welcome contribution to their incomes. In most cases perhaps, dividends are important because they are presently tangible; they indicate today that the corporation is making a profit and is distributing a portion of that profit to its owners. Although most corporations retain larger portions of their earnings for reinvestment, there is always the possibility that those funds can be lost if the corporation's investment in a new factory, or what have you, results in a loss. When dividends are received, however, there is no danger that they may be lost, at least in that company. Furthermore, present dividends may be an indication of larger future dividends, assuming that the corporation continues to prosper. Then too, the present value of cash income received today is greater than the value of future cash income even though guaranteed. In the case of Miscellaneous Shoe, we assumed that $5 per share would be paid to the stockholders as dividends.

The primary disadvantage of dividends is income taxes. Since dividends are considered ordinary income for income tax purposes, all dividends received are subject to that income tax rate applicable to additional income. If a corporation does not pay dividends, on the other hand, and can put those profits to use in a way that makes even more profits, the stock should become more valuable through the capitalization of higher earnings with no additional tax obligation unless and until the investor decides to sell his stock.

Price Appreciation.   Perhaps the reason most often present in the mind of an investor when he buys a stock is the hope that the stock's price will appreciate in the years ahead, that is, he hopes that his capital will appreciate, in other words, that he will have capital gains. Capital gains occur as the stocks in a portfolio rise in price over a period of years. In the case of a conservative company, the capital appreciation or the rise in the price of the stock, may parallel the growth of the company and the economy in general. For a relatively young or rapidly growing corporation, there may be negative earnings initially, i.e., losses. Then, an increase in earnings to the breakeven point is a sign of financial success.

young person
growth stk

As a corporation continues to prove itself, increases its earnings, and initiates a dividend policy, investors will be more and more willing to pay higher prices for the stock. As the corporation continues to reinvest part of its earnings, it will have more funds with which to buy more plant and equipment. If it is successful in producing desired consumer goods efficiently, its growth should continue.

Stock prices have generally appreciated in the market about 6 percent a year, in addition to dividends, with great variation from one company to another. For example, a stock selling at $100 per share in 1970 might sell at $106 in 1971. A large conservative company will tend to perform about as well as the general economy performs, perhaps with an 8 percent rate of return, 4 percent in dividends and 4 percent in price appreciation. Growth companies may pay no dividends but may appreciate in price by 15, 20, or 40 percent for several years consecutively, after which they too become large conservative companies. Sometimes, growth stocks appreciate much more rapidly than is warranted by the actual financial success of the corporation, and when this occurs, their stock prices tend to fall dramatically if investors discover that they have been excessively optimistic. Speculative stocks fluctuate still more widely, sometimes tripling in price or more in only one or two years. Sometimes, they all but eliminate the market value of the company in the case of severe corporate losses. For example, a speculative stock like Plastic Shoe Inc. could triple in price from $3 a share to $9 a share in one year, and following a very unfavorable financial report fall to 12½ cents a share. This type of price fluctuation is not uncommon for speculative stocks.

If Mr. Seymour Green is interested in owning a variety of stocks as part of his savings-investment program to reach his goal of $250,000 at age 65, he might invest 50 percent of his portfolio's funds in Tried and True Shoe selling at $50 a share with a fairly certain expectation that he will receive a $1 dividend this year, and that next year his stock will be selling at $51 a share. For growth purposes, he might put 40 percent of his portfolio's funds in Miscellaneous Shoe selling at $100 a share with the expectation of receiving a $3 or $5 dividend, and the possibility that the stock could be selling at $140 next year. Then 10 percent of his portfolio could be devoted to the speculative Plastic Shoe selling at $3 a share with the possibility that he could really make phenomenal profits if the company did very well, but not lose too much of the portfolio even if he lost all of the money he had invested in plastic shoes.

Since most young investors have sufficient incomes to finance their consumption patterns and certainly desire to pay no more income taxes than is absolutely necessary, they may favor stock in corporations that pay relatively small dividends but have fairly good capital appreciation possibilities. Since the income tax rate on capital gains is only one-half the rate that it is on ordinary income for most young investors, and even then only payable if the stock is actually sold, growth stocks with rising prices are a very real attraction. Since the investor is trying to build a portfolio and plans to reinvest his dividends in the portfolio anyway, dividends are less attractive than price appreciation as long as the stocks he owns are appreciating. He does not plan to sell his stocks. So long as he does not, he will have zero income taxes to pay on those paper profits.

Price appreciation, although fairly dependable over a considerable number of years, does not occur in a straight line. There are considerable fluctuations in stock prices. Sometimes the entire stock market falls 15 or 20 percent in one year; sometimes the entire market rises 50 percent in one year. This is an especially unnerving experience for a new investor. He has purchased stock with the expectation of price appreciation only to see his stock prices falling. For every investor, the first bear market (a market of generally falling prices) is a considerable psychological and emotional strain. And bear markets are an integral part of market fluctuations. Nevertheless, over longer periods (hopefully), even a stock like Plastic Shoe would recover its financial equilibrium and appreciate in value. Whether or not any one specific stock does so, however, the stock market in general has done so and may be expected to continue to do so.

Protection Against Inflation.   In Chapter Two, you may recall, inflation risk was presented as one of the most significant obstacles en route to financial security through a planned financial program. As long as inflation occurs at no more than one to 1.5 percent per year, loss of real value is not too significant in any one year or even in a decade. When inflation begins to occur at 2, 4, or 6 percent per year, however, inflation risk is a very significant factor indeed. At a 1 percent annual rate of inflation, the value of an asset will be cut in half in 40 years; at a 2 percent annual rate of inflation, that asset will lose half its value in 20 years; but with a 4 percent annual rate of inflation, an asset loses half its value in only ten years. This means that when a couple begins planning for retirement, considerably more funds may be necessary to finance their desired consumption pattern than they anticipated at the time of their planning.

Take an example of a couple at age 50 planning for retirement only 15 years hence. If they decide they need $8,000 to meet their current expenses, including maintenance on their home, automobile, food, clothing, medical expenses, travel, gifts to the grandchildren, and an occasional movie, they can construct a 15-year plan to provide for themselves an annual income flow of $8,000. If they have not accounted for inflation, however, when they actually reach those years, they might find that instead of having the cash income necessary to finance an $8,000 consumption pattern, they are woefully in need. If there has been an annual inflation of 3 percent over 15 years, they will only have a cash income necessary to finance a $4,000 consumption pattern. Since pension incomes and social security payments often are not adjusted to the general rate of inflation, their only alternative is less consumption. And a 3 percent rate of inflation is not an unrealistic probability. They simply must build into their investment program some investment instruments that will appreciate in value over time as inflation occurs.

Common stocks are such instruments; they are considered a protection against inflation risk, or an inflation hedge, because they do tend to rise in price over time as other consumer prices tend to rise. Consider the case of a 3 percent annual rate of inflation in which clothing, groceries, and other prices in general are rising 3 percent each year. The grocer is selling his groceries for 3 percent more this year than last, but then he is also paying his employees 3 percent more, his wholesale prices are 3 percent higher and his various other costs of operation are also 3 percent higher than they were last year. Since he will certainly want his total profits to be enough to keep pace, he will price his grocery items to provide a total profit to his firm 3 percent higher than it would have been had there been no inflation. Since his total profits are somewhat higher than they would have been without inflation, the price of the common stock in that company may also be somewhat higher than it would have been had there been no inflation. It does not always work this way, of course, but generally speaking, over time, stock prices do tend to rise as corporate profits tend to rise, and corporate profits for established firms do tend to be somewhat higher in periods of inflation.

With the exception of a well-diversified real estate investment program, it is indeed difficult to protect yourself against inflation risk through any investment medium other than common stocks. Although common stocks are by no means a perfect inflation hedge, they are not fixed in terms of dollars. Although fluctuating values cause problems, when all other consumer prices are rising, ownership of an investment that can rise in value can be some protection against that inflation risk. When you put $1,000 into a savings account or buy a bond which is held until maturity, you know that you will get back that $1,000 and no more; but when you put $1,000 into a stock, there is some possibility at least that your investment can rise in price as other prices rise. If you put $1,000 into a bank account that pays 5 percent interest over a year, an annual rate of inflation of 4 percent will mean that your real or actual return is only 1 percent on your money. On the other hand, if you buy a successful stock that would ordinarily earn 10 percent, but because prices in general are rising, the corporation is able to raise the prices of its own products and to increase its profits by more than had been anticipated, the return on your stock could actually be 14 percent, 10 percent real or actual return plus 4 percent inflation.

Portfolio Adjustments. Thus far when answering the question, why buy stock, the three reasons presented—dividends, price appreciation, and protection against inflation—have all been reasons for buying stock in general. But why buy a particular stock as compared to another stock? Much more will be said on this subject in the following chapters but, in short, one stock is preferred to another because of one or more of the above three reasons. As you build your investment portfolio, you will find that you can own only a few stocks at any one time since you do not have a limitless supply of investment capital. You may continue to buy more shares of the stock you own, or you may decide that some other stocks are preferable to the ones you already own in satisfying your investment requirements. Furthermore, it is possible that as you continue your investment program your investment objectives or constraints may change somewhat. For example, you may decide that you want less dividends and more price appreciation, or visa versa. In one case you may decide that since Miscellaneous Shoe and Collapsable Chair are both paying the same dividends, earning the same profits, and have the same financial prospects, you would sell Miscellaneous Shoe for $100 and buy Miscellaneous Chair for $80. By so doing you have strengthened your portfolio by adding more shares, more dividends, more earnings, for the same amount of money. In another case you might decide that you want more price appreciation from your portfolio and less dividends. In this case, you might decide to sell your shares of Tried and True Shoe, and with the proceeds of the sale buy still more shares of Miscellaneous Shoe, Collapsable Chair, or some other growth company. With all stock purchases of this type, the purpose is really to improve the return on the portfolio, or to reduce the risk of a loss.

Stock purchases for the purpose of adjusting a portfolio can be of two different kinds. They may be exchanges of one stock for another when both stocks are of the same risk category—that is, conservative, growth, or speculative. In such a case, the portfolio adjustment is merely an effort to reduce the risk or increase the return without any major change in the relative proportions of conservative, growth, and speculative stocks. Still other adjustments in the portfolio can be modifications of the relative proportions of stock types. If an investor decides that too much of his portfolio is in high dividend-paying stocks, he may well wish to exchange some of his conservative stocks for more aggressive securities. If, on the other hand, he feels that he has been trying for too much price appreciation, he may decide that he should exchange some of his growth stock for more conservative securities with higher dividend yields. Either one of these portfolio adjustments may be worth considering at any time. It is highly questionable, however, that a very large portion of any portfolio should be invested in speculative stocks. It is certainly most inadvisable for an amateur investor, who suddenly learns of some highly speculative security with unbelievable potential for immediate profits, to decide on the spur of the moment to sell some of his more conservative stocks in order to purchase a highly speculative stock.

Stock ownership does tend to be profitable but stock trading—that is, rapidly exchanging one stock for another—tends to be costly, and stock trading in speculative issues can be extremely costly. Buying good stocks, representing strong companies with able management, producing quality products, making reasonable profits, paying adequate dividends, is indeed somewhat less exciting than the exhilaration of constant speculation. If what you want is real excitement, however, nothing has yet managed to beat Russian roulette. If what you want is real financial security, a portfolio approach to the purchase of common stocks has a much higher probability of success. This does not mean that you cannot have one or two speculative issues in your portfolio; but it does mean that if you decide to buy another speculative issue, you should exchange it for one of the two or three speculative stocks you presently own. Occasionally, it may be helpful to remember that whenever you buy a stock, someone somewhere has just sold that stock to you, and he is chuckling to himself that he has the great good fortune to get rid of it at the price you paid. In many cases, your judgment may be better than his, but you are a most unusual person if your judgment is always correct, and this is especially true in the case of more speculative securities whose entire present value is based upon potential future earnings that are hazy at best. If you are really serious about investing, not gambling, not playing games, not using stocks as a hobby, but really serious about investing as a means of achieving financial security, you will have a much greater probability of success. If you buy stocks that are already paying dividends, you can have much greater confidence in that corporation's future dividends. If you buy stocks that have been experiencing earnings growth rates that are sustainable, you can have much greater confidence in that corporation's future earnings growth. If you buy stocks using a portfolio approach, you greatly improve the probability of achieving your investment objectives.

USING A PORTFOLIO APPROACH

Throughout this discussion, frequent reference has been made to your investment portfolio, the stocks in your portfolio, and to a portfolio approach to investing. A portfolio approach requires a plan to achieve certain investment objectives, and a portfolio should include stocks selected because they will facilitate that plan. All stocks should be bought with such a plan in mind. Rather than buying some stock because you have a few extra dollars available, or because it happens to attract your fancy, or because some broker or friend recommended it, a stock should be bought because it fits into your portfolio. Actually, a portfolio is any list of investments regardless of whether or not that list has been acquired according to some plan. But a better portfolio is a list of investments that have been acquired because each one relates to the ultimate objectives that the investor has in mind, and because each relates to the other investments held in the portfolio.

Some investors have very conservative portfolios composed almost exclusively of very high-grade stocks and bonds. They place primary emphasis upon security and stability; they want to avoid price fluctuations and risk and they place more emphasis upon dividends than they do upon price appreciation. Such conservative portfolios will produce very steady income flows with relatively minor fluctuations in value. Ownership of such portfolios requires very little risk assumption, and very little portfolio management or supervision, but the return on such a portfolio may not be as large as some investors want. Furthermore, dividends are largely subject to income taxes. Consequently, investors trying to accumulate a portfolio might prefer larger total returns including capital gains despite larger temporary fluctuations in value, and less current dividend or interest income to avoid larger income tax payments, and might therefore want to include less conservative stocks and more growth or speculative stocks in their portfolios.

On the other hand, some investors have very speculative portfolios composed of stocks that pay no dividends and may not even be earning any profits. They may have ten such stocks, each representing relatively new companies, perhaps all trying to produce new products. The risks associated with such stocks are extremely high; the probability that each company will go bankrupt and each stock become worthless may be very real. Of course, the investor (or speculator) has bought the stocks hoping that if only one of those ten companies can actually produce a new product that millions of consumers are eagerly awaiting, ownership of a relatively modest number of shares in that one company could make the investor a very wealthy man. However, ownership of such a speculative portfolio can hardly be considered investing. Although each stock is an asset purchased or held with the expectation of earning a financial return, and therefore meets our definition of an investment, owning speculative stocks, exclusively, exceeds the assumption of reasonable risk. Although speculative securities may have a place in any investor's portfolio, placing all of one's savings in such high-risk instruments is hardly prudent.

Assuming the investment needs of a young professional man such as Seymour Green, an appropriate portfolio might be one composed of a balanced list of securities, each selected because it fulfills some part of the portfolio's function. Such a balanced portfolio would include some conservative securities, some growth securities, and perhaps some speculative securities. The proportion of each type would depend upon the investment objectives of the particular investor. For example, Mr. Green is just initiating an investment program and he is relatively growth oriented. Consequently, for many years, he may wish to have perhaps 60 percent of his portfolio invested in growth stocks. The remaining 40 percent of his portfolio may be invested in conservative stock exclusively, but he might wish to place 10 percent of his portfolio funds in speculative stock. As his first purchase, he might decide to buy growth

Bull *price increase* Bear *down*

stocks. After buying two or three growth stocks, he might decide to buy one or two conservative stocks, and thereafter perhaps one speculative stock. Subsequent purchases would then be made to strengthen whichever portion of the portfolio needed strengthening; some would be made to replace stocks sold; others would be made as additional investment funds became available. If a conservative stock is sold from the portfolio, it would be replaced with the purchase of another conservative stock. Similarly, if a growth stock is sold, it would be replaced with a growth stock. At no time should a growth stock or a speculative stock be bought just because such a stock appears attractive about the same time that a conservative stock appears overpriced and is sold. By so doing, the investor would be changing his portfolio policy to a more aggressive one. Only by replacing a conservative stock with another conservative stock can the portfolio policy continue unchanged. By using a portfolio approach, each specific investment can be related to all the others held in the portfolio. No single stock exists as an entity in and of itself; it exists as part of the overall portfolio investment plan.

There are times when the portfolio policy should be changed, that is, when you should take a more conservative approach or a more aggressive approach. When the whole market appears overpriced, a more conservative portfolio policy should be followed; and when the whole market appears to be underpriced, a more aggressive portfolio policy should be followed. Furthermore, as you continue to build your portfolio over time, you may become more interested in conserving the value of your portfolio as you have more to lose and less time to recover any losses. Certainly, any older investor wholly or partially dependent upon income from the portfolio to pay his grocery bills should have a much more conservative portfolio policy than he had during his younger years of portfolio accumulation. At all times, however, some portfolio approach should be selected and used, rather than buying stocks on a first come first served basis, unrelated to each other and unrelated to any portfolio objective.

Even the investor who is about to buy his first stock can use a portfolio approach. Although he probably cannot buy all types of stocks at once, he can buy a stock that would most nearly represent his overall objective. If he is basically conservative, he should buy a conservative stock first; if he is basically growth oriented, he should buy a growth stock first. Without such a portfolio approach, however, you may buy a stock that does not represent your general attitude toward investing, and you may continue to buy stocks that do not fit your present holdings very well, or your long-range objectives, simply because some stock happens to attract your attention. You may also be sold a stock simply because someone is trying very hard to get rid of it. Such a stock might very well fit into your portfolio if you would first sell some other stock that is similar to it, but without first selling something that you now hold, that one additional purchase could substantially alter the total composition of your holdings. By using a portfolio approach, you may categorize all your stocks by their conservative, growth, or speculative characteristics to determine whether each is performing the function you had in mind when you bought it. Furthermore, with a portfolio approach, you can see how each potential purchase might fit into your present holding pattern. Buying stocks because they improve your portfolio can implement your existing policy or any desired change in your approach, and can provide an additional sense of security with each new purchase.

UNDERSTANDING THE SECURITIES MARKETS

Although you can buy stocks without any real understanding of how the securities markets work, and as a matter of fact a great many investors do, more awareness of the various markets and how they work can be helpful to you in your decision-making process. By becoming more aware of those markets in which different kinds of securities are traded, and by knowing something of the requirements and regulations of those markets, you may be in a somewhat better position to determine the characteristics of any specific security that you are considering.

Basically, there are two securities markets—the market for listed securities, which is the organized exchanges, and the market for unlisted securities, which is the over-the-counter market. There are subdivisions of each of these markets, of course, but after all, a security is either listed or unlisted. Most people, perhaps even most investors, think of markets in general, and securities markets in particular, as being at one particular place. Investors might say that the securities market is on Wall Street, or the securities market is the New York Stock Exchange. In a sense, that is true; the New York Stock Exchange is the most visible and widely recognized of all the securities markets, and it is on Wall Street. Nevertheless, only 3,000 securities are traded on the New York Stock Exchange whereas almost 50,000 securities are traded in other markets. The New York Stock Exchange is a specific place, and there are other exchanges that exist at specific places, such as the American Stock Exchange and various regional exchanges, but actually most securities are not traded on any exchange. Rather, they are traded in the over-the-counter market, which is certainly a market, but does not exist at any specific place. Furthermore, as long as buyers and sellers of securities have a means of communicating their desires to each other, no specific place is necessary. A market exists when there are buyers and sellers for any item, and since there are investors who wish to buy and sell securities, the securities market will continue to exist. There are advantages in buying securities listed on an organized exchange, but there are also advantages in trading in securities that are not listed on an organized exchange. Likewise, there are disadvantages to each. Both are healthy markets, both serve very real economic functions, and both should be understood for maximum flexibility in managing your portfolio.

There are two primary purposes of any securities market, namely, to raise capital and to provide investor liquidity. It may come as a shock to you, but the securities market does not exist primarily so investors can make money. If that were the primary function of the securities markets, many investors might well blow the whistle on them because not all investors do make money. But as a means of raising capital for industry and providing liquidity for investors, the securities markets perform their function very well. A great deal of capital is raised to increase our economic productivity, and most investors can sell their securities very quickly without price discounts. Overall, the securities markets in the United States have been highly effective in serving both corporations and investors alike.

ORGANIZED EXCHANGES

An organized exchange is a formal meeting place where members buy and sell from each other a limited list of securities according to the regulations of the exchange for their customers all over the world. The New York Stock Exchange is the best known such organized exchange, and it is indeed on Wall Street, but there are several other organized exchanges as well. These exchanges provide the very best markets for securities since they have many active members who in turn have many active customers. Through these exchanges, many offers to buy and sell are focused on just one spot in the world, thus enabling any investor who wants to sell a stock to sell it to the one investor who is willing to pay the highest price for it at that time, and any investor who wants to buy a stock to buy from the one investor who most wants to sell it at that time. Consequently, there is a great deal of activity in stocks that are listed on organized exchanges, and the probability of buying and selling at the best possible price at any given time is very real. There is, therefore, more interest in listed than in unlisted stocks.

As a consequence, corporations whose stocks are listed on organized exchanges tend to have more stockholders, and more potential stockholders. As more investors are aware of a company's stock and its financial characteristics, more investors tend to buy that stock. Thus, an organized exchange facilitates the efforts of its listed corporations to sell additional stock, and facilitates the efforts of existing stockholders to sell their shares whenever they decide to do so. By so doing, the organized exchange accomplishes the two functions of a securities market, raising capital and providing liquidity, and does so better than most people could have imagined possible.

New York Stock Exchange.   The first official agreement creating what is now the New York Stock Exchange was signed by 24 brokers in 1792.

intra-State no fed Reg.

For several years before that date, trading in securities had occurred on an informal basis on Wall Street. The rules and regulations of the exchange and even the name of the exchange have changed over the years, some in order to better facilitate the work of the brokers, and some in response to various congressional investigations. The New York Stock Exchange (N. Y. S. E.) has had a long and illustrious career, and has long been the center of American business finance. As an organization, it is neither a corporation nor a partnership, but an unincorporated association. There are 1,366 members of the exchange, some of them individuals, some partnerships and an increasing number of corporations. The memberships can be bought and sold, but only members of the exchange can trade on the exchange. It exists as a voluntary association primarily to provide an orderly and convenient place for members to trade securities. Because only members can trade, but members can trade for clients who pay commissions of 1 to 2 percent of the value of the stock traded, a membership is a valuable asset, and such a membership, or seat, may cost half a million dollars.

Under the regulations of the Securities Exchange Act of 1934, the N. Y. S. E. is registered with the Securities and Exchange Commission (S. E. C.) as are all other exchanges. Under this registration, the exchange agrees to comply with any and all of the regulations of the S. E. C. It must file rules, procedures, organizational data, membership data, constitutions, and by-laws with the S. E. C., and must discipline any of its members who violate any such regulations. The exchange is governed by a board of governors composed of 33 governors representing 29-member firms, three representatives of the public, a chairman, and the president of the exchange. The board's composition is designed to represent adequately brokers doing business with the public, whether they work on the exchange floor or not, regular and allied members in the New York metropolitan area, and those in outlying areas, their investing clients, and the general public. The board makes and administers policy for the exchange; it disciplines members, approves new members, accepts new securities for listing on the exchange, assigns the post on the floor at which a new security will be traded, and designates a member of the exchange to act as a specialist who is charged with the responsibility of maintaining an orderly market for each stock.

The members of the exchange execute buy and sell orders for their customers on the floor of the exchange for which they receive commissions. In most instances members represent brokerage firms that receive orders from the public. The orders are transmitted to them on the floor of the exchange where the actual trading occurs at auction where the highest bid and the lowest offer complete a transaction. The exchange itself neither buys nor sells stock. Although the members of the exchange may buy and sell for themselves, most of the millions of shares traded daily are bought and sold for brokers' customers, for which service those customers pay a commission.

One of the most important floor members is the specialist. He acts both as a broker and as a dealer. If no buyer for a stock is available when the seller wants to sell, the specialist will buy that stock himself; similarly, he will sell as a dealer, risking his own capital, in order to maintain a market for the stock in which he specializes. When investors place buy and sell limit orders that cannot be executed at market prices because some specific price is attached to the order, the specialist places those buy and sell orders in his book, to be executed if, as, and when the price of the stock ever reaches the investors' price limitations. When such orders are executed by the specialist, he is acting as a broker for his customers for which he is paid a commission. By keeping the book and executing those limit orders as they can be executed, and by buying and selling for his own account, the specialist attempts to maintain an orderly market for his stocks.

All these orders are executed on the N. Y. S. E. floor in round lots, that is, 100 shares (in most cases). All are executed on the floor of the exchange at the assigned post in round lots. But by no means all of the orders investors send in are in 100 share lots. What happens then?

When orders for less than 100 shares, called odd lots, are placed with brokers, the orders go to special brokers called odd lot brokers, who buy and sell from their own inventories. If they have insufficient inventory in that stock, they will buy a round lot on the floor of the exchange, and sell whatever shares the investor has ordered and keep the remainder as inventory. For this service the odd lot brokers receive a special commission in the form of a price differential, ⅛ of a point for stock selling at above $40 a share and ¼ point for stocks selling at or below $40 a share. All transactions that take place on the N. Y. S. E. and the prices of those transactions are indicated by a symbol on the stock ticker tape. Subsequently, that afternoon or the following day, the aggregate of those transactions, the price ranges, and the opening and closing prices for each stock are published in a host of daily newspapers.

Most companies that can meet the N. Y. S. E. listing requirements choose to be listed on that exchange. Since a more continuous market and more publicity tend to attract investors, and since supplemental stock issues are more marketable as more investors learn more about the company and create a better market for the stock, most corporations want to be listed on the N. Y. S. E., or some exchange, to facilitate their own efforts to raise more capital and to make their stockholders happier. Corporations seeking N. Y. S. E. listing must earn $2.5 million before taxes, must have $14 million in net tangible assets, $14 million common stock market value, 1,000,000 shares of common stock outstanding, 800,000 of which held publicly, 2,000 shareholders, of which 1,800 must own round lots. These listing requirements are increased occasionally, and currently listed stocks have somewhat less restrictive requirements. Listing also requires regular disclosure of financial data and other information that may affect security prices or influence investment deci-

sions. Compliance with such requirements is enforced primarily by the
N. Y. S. E.

The New York Stock Exchange thus consists of some 1,366 brokers,
regulated and supervised, buying from and selling to each other some
1,500 stocks, as well as some 1,400 bonds, on a trading floor in a
building on Wall Street. However, they are not the market. Nor do they
make the market. The market consists of thousands of other brokers
around the country, and millions of investors. The N. Y. S. E. exists
because having a specific place on Wall Street, or somewhere, provides
investors a better way to buy the stock they want and to sell the stock
they want to sell. When investors want to buy and sell securities other
than those listed on the N. Y. S. E., other markets arise. And when the
N. Y. S. E. fails to perform its functions in accordance with investors'
desires, those investors tend to find alternative ways of buying and selling
their securities. All in all, however, the N. Y. S. E. is a very fine securities
market; it performs vital functions very well; millions of investors have
paid and continue to pay their commissions in order to buy and sell the
stocks listed on that exchange, and almost every corporation in the
country wants its stock listed on that exchange. The N. Y. S. E. has some
weaknesses and problems, to be sure, and will surely continue to improve
its effectiveness; but despite its need for some additional corrective
measures, in many ways the N. Y. S. E. is the very best securities market
there is. Consequently, investors who are seeking the very best stocks
find them more often than not listed and traded on the New York Stock
Exchange.

American Stock Exchange.   The American Stock Exchange (Amex) is
the second largest organized exchange in the United States. When compared to the New York Stock Exchange, the Amex is quite small, yet it
is larger in share volume than all other U.S. exchanges combined. In
many ways, it is similar to the N. Y. S. E. in that it has members, it has a
board, it accepts stocks for listing, it has rules and regulations, it has a
floor in a building close to Wall Street, it has a ticker tape, specialists,
floor traders, round lots, odd lots, and commissions. Nevertheless, in
many other significant ways, the Amex is quite different from the
N. Y. S. E.

Particularly, the Amex is different in the type of corporations it tends
to list. Whereas the N. Y. S. E. has rather rigorous requirements for
listing thus restricting its list to larger and more well established companies, the Amex will list companies with much less financial stature.
Although stocks listed on the Amex must still represent fairly sizable
corporations, the requirements are not nearly so rigorous as those for
listing on the N. Y. S. E. The requirements on total market value, number
of shares outstanding, number of stockholders, net assets, and net income
are all significantly less for listing on the Amex than they are for listing
on the N. Y. S. E. Therefore, smaller companies, newer companies, and

less well-established companies are listed on the Amex. Viewed another way, more speculative companies and those with greater growth potential may more often be found on the Amex. Furthermore, corporations whose stocks are listed on the Amex tend to keep their stocks priced much lower by issuing many more shares for any given total market value. Traditionally, companies whose stocks could not meet the listing requirements of the N. Y. S. E. have traded on the Amex, and to a considerable extent, this continues to be true. Consequently, investors seeking growth stocks and especially more speculative stocks, may find many from which to choose on the American Stock Exchange.

Other Exchanges.   In addition to the New York Stock Exchange and the American Stock Exchange, there are a number of other exchanges in the country. The National Stock Exchange, the newest exchange, was created in 1962 to provide a third national market. Although its growth has been fairly rapid, it is still very small in comparison with the other two national exchanges. In addition, there are a number of regional exchanges. The Midwest Exchange in Chicago, the Pacific Coast Stock Exchange in Los Angeles and San Francisco, the Philadelphia-Baltimore-Washington Stock Exchange, as well as several other regional exchanges have been expanding in recent years, but their total volume is still relatively small. Many of the stocks traded on the regional exchanges are also traded on the national exchanges, but some smaller, regional corporations do have their stocks listed on the regional exchanges. In recent years, when they could, brokers have tended to use the regional exchanges more for larger blocks of stock ordered or offered by large institutional investors (such as universities, insurance companies, etc.) because the regional exchanges have offered reduced commissions to encourage such business. All in all, however, the regional exchanges do not trade a significant volume of securities when compared to the national exchanges. If the trend toward using the regionals for institutional business continues, the regionals could become a much more significant aspect of the industry in future years. If competition should develop, investors could benefit from a greater awareness of the regional exchanges. To date, however, although these other exchanges do exist, they are of little significance to most investors. Another possibility is that all markets could be so interconnected as to create one large market.

OVER-THE-COUNTER MARKET

There are a number of differences between the organized exchanges and the over-the-counter securities market. Primarily, the basic functions of the over-the-counter (O. T. C.) market are different from the main functions of the organized exchanges. Specifically, the two primary functions of the over-the-counter market are to raise new funds for business and government through the distrbution of new issues, and to make markets for those securities that are not listed on an organized exchange. Consequently, investors who buy securities over the counter buy them from dealers who carry them in inventory, make markets in them, and wholesale and retail them to ultimate investors on a negotiated price basis. Rather than providing a continuous market at a specific place on an auction basis, dealers in the over-the-counter markets are located all over the country. However, they are in constant communication with each other by telephone and telegraph trying to locate unlisted securities for their customers and trying to locate customers for the securities they have in their inventories. As in the case of any merchandiser, a securities dealer buys at one price and tries to sell at a higher price. Somewhat different from other merchants, however, a securities dealer who is making a market in a stock stands ready, willing and able to either buy or sell a given stock continuously. The bid price is the price he is willing to pay for that stock if anyone offers it to him, and the asked price is the price he is willing to take for that stock if any investor should want to buy it from him. Prices are negotiated. Different prices for the same security may be quoted by different dealers at any given time, and quotations are certainly different at different times. A broker, by inquiring about a given stock from several dealers before he buys, will try to find the one willing to sell the stock for the price offered, or at least the lowest possible price.

The over-the-counter market is a very large market. It consists of securities of greatly different quality, some issued by the United States Treasury, states, municipalities, banks, insurance companies, some very large industrial corporations, and many very small corporations. All of the marketable United States Treasury bonds are traded in the over-the-counter market, and these are the very best bonds in terms of financial risk. All of the state bonds and municipal bonds are traded over the counter; and some of these are also top quality bonds, although some are relatively low grade. About 80 percent of the corporate bonds of the country are traded over the counter. In all, over 90 percent of the bonds business in this country is transacted in the over-the-counter markets.

In addition to the over-the-counter bond business, many stocks are also traded over the counter. Most of these cannot meet the listing requirements of the organized exchanges, but some simply do not choose to be listed. Bank stocks and insurance company stocks, particularly, have traditionally avoided listing on organized exchanges in order to retain dealer sponsorship and a more stable market. Some have felt that listing on an organized exchange would add some greater fluctuations to their stock prices, and they have feared that such fluctuations might make their depositors or policyholders feel that their banks or insurance companies are risky corporations. Although this may be true to some extent, this hesitancy seems to be breaking down. In most cases, the other stocks traded O. T. C. cannot meet the exchange requirements. This may be because too much of the outstanding stock is closely held by the officers of the corporation, often because such a corporation was started as a family business and most of the stock continues to be held by members of the family. In other cases, the corporations are too small, with too few stockholders, with too little public interest, and with too short a history of financial success to meet exchange qualifications.

Investors who own such securities occasionally want to sell them, and there are investors who may want to buy such securities; consequently, a market for those securities must exist. In many cases, the investment house that handled the original issue of such securities will continue to provide dealer sponsorship in the stock. Although the house is no longer serving as an investment banker, it is still interested in the stock, nevertheless, because it served as the investment banker, and may serve in that capacity again one day if additional shares are offered to the public. Therefore, the investment house will act as dealer, will make a market in the stock, will carry some inventory, and will stand ready, willing and able to buy at a bid price and sell at an asked price upon request. Those bid and asked prices may be quoted for many weeks without any takers. Although a stock may be listed in the paper daily with bid and asked prices quoted beside it, there may have been no trading activity in the stock at all for weeks or months. As a matter of fact, one of the major determinants of the spread between the bid and the asked prices is the amount of the activity in the stock; if the dealer must carry his inventory for a relatively long time without activity, the spread, or mark up, will have to be larger to compensate him for his funds invested. Particularly, if the stock does not pay a dividend, (or a bond is not paying interest), and it is a relatively high risk instrument, the spread, or commission, must be greater in order to compensate the dealer for the additional risk he assumes. The more interest there is in a security, and the more active it is, the smaller the spread necessary to compensate the dealer for making the market. If activity increases, the spread will be reduced; but if activity all but disappears, no dealer will want to make a market in the stock.

Whenever corporations offer their stocks to the public, whether such issues are new or supplemental to original issues, such stocks are offered through the over-the-counter market. Even additional issues of well-established companies whose stocks are listed on organized exchanges are offered through the over-the-counter market. Once those additional shares of listed securities are underwritten, or sold, by the investment banker, however, subsequent trading in those shares will occur on the organized exchanges since all common stock shares issued by any given corporation are alike. In the case of newly issued stock of corporations going public for the first time, (that is, issuing stock for purchase by investors) their stocks continue to trade over the counter. Such stock cannot be listed immediately, and trading in those stocks will continue over the counter for some years, perhaps indefinitely. Many corporations, however, whose stocks are traded O. T. C. for a few years, do gain sufficient financial stature to warrant listing on an organized exchange. In most instances when they meet the qualification, they will seek listing on such an exchange to indicate to their own stockholders, and to investors in general, that they have reached sufficient financial maturity to warrant such listing. With the exception of bonds and bank and insurance company stocks, investors tend to consider the securities traded over the counter as being lower quality securities; as a matter of fact, in many cases, they are lower quality securities. However, some of the risk associated with buying O. T. C. stocks has been reduced since 1964 when the securities acts were amended to regulate many such securities, and to require additional information from companies whose securities were traded over the counter. Consequently, although there are still some serious disadvantages in buying many over-the-counter securities, these disadvantages have diminished somewhat in recent years, and more investors have been attracted to these securities, in particular, with the hope of finding undervalued growth stocks with promising prospects.

REGULATION

There are basically three statutes governing the interstate securities markets, all of which are administered by the Securities and Exchange Commission (S. E. C.). The Securities Act of 1933 regulates the issue of new securities; the Securities Exchange Act of 1934 regulates trading on organized exchanges; and the Securities Act Amendment of 1964 regulates trading in the over-the-counter markets. In addition to these three acts, the Investment Company Act of 1940 and the Investment Advisers Act of 1940 regulate investment companies and investment advisers; and certain other federal laws regulate certain specific securities. Furthermore, each state has a set of securities laws, called blue sky laws, regulating the securities issued and traded within their respective states.

All of these laws are basically designed to prevent fraud and to provide adequate information for investors interested in the securities markets. Neither the S. E. C. nor the state regulatory commissions make any guarantees about the values of any particular securities. All types of stocks can be issued and traded, whether conservative, growth, or speculative. Old, well established, low risk companies with years of earnings and dividends are welcome, but so are new, untried, high risk companies with years of probable loss ahead of them. These commissions do not protect the investor from risk; rather, they protect him from false, misleading, or inadequate information. It might be "convenient" to have some commission guarantee investor profits, but these commissions are charged only with the responsibility of providing adequate information, preventing fraud and stock manipulation, and regulating some types of transactions, such as short sales.

In addition to these commissions, the securities business also polices itself. The exchanges themselves have many regulations protecting investors trading in securities listed on those exchanges. For investors trading in unlisted securities, the over-the-counter brokers and dealers have formed the National Association of Security Dealers (N. A. S. D.) which is a self-regulatory association supervised by the Securities and Exchange Commission. The self-regulating efforts of the exchanges and the N. A. S. D. members have done much to eliminate illegal and unethical practices in the securities markets. Although no one would suggest that all false and misleading conduct has been eliminated from the securities markets, almost everyone would agree that tremendous progress has been made in recent years through government regulation and industry self-regulation to protect the investor. Truly monumental amounts of information are now available about a great many securities, and many securities representatives are highly professional in their attitudes and actions. For most investors today, the regulations upon the securities industry are adequate; the information is available to any investor who cares to use it. However, there are no laws requiring the investor to use his own good sense, and such self regulation may indeed be the most crucial regulation of all. In some cases in years past, the unprofessional attitudes and actions of some brokers and dealers have caused havoc and panic in the securities business. Even today, some of the members of the exchanges as well as some of the professional investment portfolio managers have displayed attitudes and practices that indicate the need for additional regulation. Overall, however, existing regulations provide current investors with considerable protection against the greed and abuse of others; a far greater danger is the investor's own greed, ignorance, stupidity, and irrationality, against which self-regulation is his only protection.

USING THE SECURITIES MARKETS

After learning all these facts about what stocks are, why you might want to buy stocks, and how the securities markets work, you may well want to know how to buy some stocks.

Where to Buy Stock. Your first task is to locate someone through whom you may buy stock. Such a person is known as a stock broker. A stock broker can generally be described as a person who makes his living by buying and selling stock for other people. You will find him in his brokerage office somewhere near 101 Main Street in your own home town right next to the First National Bank; that is, he is right downtown in almost any city. Actually all you have to do is look in the *Yellow Pages* under "Brokerage firms."

Assuming that you find a brokerage firm, what do you look for in a broker? How do you know that he is the man you want to deal with? Since most brokers are regulated by the Securities and Exchange Commission and the various stock exchanges, they are generally reputable people. But there are differences in brokers. A good broker will ask you several questions before he will serve you. He is not prying; rather, he *and* you should both be trying to ascertain whether you should buy stock, and if so, what kind. Usually his questions involve your employment, bank, and financial position. A good broker will usually recommend that you have an adequate emergency fund and an adequate insurance program; for most people, these are essential before beginning an investment program. According to your answers to these questions and others about your investment goals, the broker will then recommend a certain class of stocks and certain specific stocks.

As mentioned earlier, stocks are classified as conservative, growth, or speculative. Essentially, conservative stocks are quite dependable in their earnings patterns; they are not likely to fluctuate. Although serious problems may arise, they will usually fluctuate by no more than 10 percent in any one year. Growth stocks are those experiencing two to three times as rapid an increase in earnings as the rate of national economic expansion; they have fairly sizable price increases in prosperous times, and fairly sizable price declines in more troublesome years. Their prices may fluctuate 20 to 50 percent or more in any one year. Speculative stocks are those in which you may double, triple or quadruple your money in a few years, or lose all or nearly all of it, depending upon whether the company's new and better mousetrap actually works, attracts the public, and costs no more than was expected.

Each broker and each investor acquires an investment approach, i.e., a philosophy about investing. If possible, yours should be close to that of your broker in order to facilitate communication, trust, and satisfaction. Since you pay the same commission for the purchase or sale of a stock, no matter which broker you use, the key difference between brokers is their relative willingness and ability to provide you with the kind of professional service you want. If you can find a broker who wants your business, thinks as you do, is concerned about your financial welfare, understands your situation, and is competent, you have found a winning combination. You should know, however, that a small investor can be a costly nuisance to a broker. For example, a $300 stock purchase may cost you $9 in commission, $3 of which may go to your broker. Although most brokers are interested in encouraging new investors to begin an investment program, investors with only a small amount of capital may not always be given the attention and time that a customer with a million dollar account might receive since potential commissions from the latter will obviously be larger than from the former.

After finding a broker to act for you in a manner acceptable to you, how do you actually go about buying shares of the particular stock? The first thing to do is to set up an account with the brokerage firm; then find the stock that you want to buy, determine how many shares of that stock you want, and place the order with the broker. From there, he will act for you according to your instructions to acquire the stock at the price you have determined.

Opening an Account.   In some ways, opening an account at a brokerage office is similar to opening a checking account at a commercial bank. Once you provide your broker with the information he needs to know about you and sign a card or two, that is about all there is to it. It is important for the broker to know that you are a responsible individual, however, and that you understand your obligations, since almost all of the buying and selling of stocks takes place over the telephone.

When you make your call to the broker and tell him that you want so many shares of Miscellaneous Shoe, he must take you at your word, that is, he must assume that you will pay for the stock four or five days after he manages to execute 'your order. Since there are occasionally individuals who refuse to pay for the stock they have ordered, your broker will be concerned that you understand the responsibilities that he is assuming and those that you have assumed when you place an order. Although it is hard to believe, there are a few naive (or dishonest) investors who feel that they have a right to refuse to pay for stock if it has not performed in the first few days of their ownership in a way they consider acceptable. For example, if they buy a stock at $30 a share that in the next day falls to $29 and the day after to $28, they feel that the stock has let them down because what they had in mind was a rising price. So they may tell the broker that they did not order the stock, or that he misunderstood the order when they placed it, or that they will not pay for such a shoddy piece of merchandise. Although there are guarantees on television sets and automobiles, there are no guarantees that a stock will rise in price as soon as you buy it.

You may use your account in several ways depending upon what you want from it. Many investors want to have the actual pieces of paper, called certificates, representing their shares of corporate ownership; they want them locked in their lock boxes or safe deposit boxes. So they ask their brokers to order the actual stock certificates for them in their own name, and to mail them out. Other investors are not so concerned about handling the actual pieces of paper, so they are willing to let the brokerage firm lock the stock certificates in its vault for them, and they receive a monthly statement from the brokerage house stating what is being held for them. There are reasons for handling your stock ownership both ways. If you want to receive your dividends directly, or want corporate quarterly and annual reports sent to your home directly, then you should obtain the stock certificates. On the other hand, if you are planning to leave the dividends in your brokerage account, and are in no great rush to read your annual reports, perhaps leaving the stock with your broker is preferable.

Much the same can be said for any cash resulting from a sale of securities. If you should decide to sell your 10 shares of Miscellaneous Shoe at $100 per share and buy 100 shares of newly issued Plastic Shoe for $5 a share, you would have $500 in extra cash. You can either ask your broker to transmit that $500 to you, or leave the money in the brokerage account with the expectation that you will buy some other security with it before too long anyway. Again there are advantages to both methods. If you want to spend the cash, then request a check. But if you do not want to spend the cash, and there is some possibility that you might if you put it in your checking account, then leave it in the brokerage account.

If you have stock and cash with your broker, it is possible that, at some time, you can borrow funds from him to enable you to buy some additional stock. Such an account is called a margin account, and buying partly with borrowed money is called buying on the margin. Margin accounts permit you to borrow money from the broker if you do not have enough cash in the account to cover all of the purchase of a stock, but such borrowing is limited, varying somewhere between 20 and 50 percent of the purchase. As you transact business with your broker, either sending additional funds to him or asking for some of your money back, or buying or selling securities, or having certificates mailed to you, these various operations are reflected on your monthly statement that you receive from your broker. Again as in the case of a checking account, if you do not transact any business, or if you have no cash or securities held for you by the brokerage firm in any given month, you would not receive a report of activity in your account because there had been none.

Finding a Stock.   In deciding upon a particular stock, you should be concerned to see that the stock you are buying fits into your portfolio plan. Do you want to buy a conservative stock like industry leader Tried and True Shoe, Inc., or a growth stock like Miscellaneous Shoe, or a speculative stock like Plastic Shoe, Inc.? Any one of these securities can be the one you might choose to buy at any particular time. (If all the stocks in your portfolio already, however, are those representing companies in the shoe industry, it is hardly recommended that you buy any of these three stocks.) Your broker may recommend one or several stocks, you may read an article about some company, or you may buy some new product that you enjoy unusually well, perhaps a new pair of loafers. In short, ideas can come from many sources.

Assume, though, that you are interested in buying stocks of a shoe company, that you have a fairly representative group of conservative stocks in your portfolio already, and that you are not especially interested in a speculative issue at this time. You might therefore be most interested in a growth company like Miscellaneous Shoe Corp. You have investigated the company and found that its earnings pattern has been considerably above average, that it has a dividend policy that you find acceptable, that it has a management that can continue to produce the kind of products and profits that a growth stock must have to continue its price appreciation. Its sales are progressing nicely, its costs seem to be under control, its labor relations have been favorable, and maybe as an extra added attraction, it has recently contracted to provide 500,000 pairs of shoes for the Women's Army Corp. These are the characteristics of the kind of growth stock anyone might want to buy, and these matters are the ones to consider. Although the shoe industry is by no means new or exciting in the sense of oceanography or space investigation, you might do a whole lot worse than to buy stock in a fairly rapidly growing company with above average earnings in a good solid industry. In short, you think you have found the stock you want to buy.

How Many Shares?   Assuming you have a limited number of dollars to invest at any given time, a fairly reasonable assumption for most people, the number of shares you decide to buy will depend upon the price of the stock. You can ask your broker, of course, for a current price quote on Miscellaneous Shoe, but the most common method of determining the price of a stock is to read the financial page in a newspaper. A great many companies, certainly the larger ones and the ones trading on the New York Stock Exchange, have their prices quoted daily in hundreds of newspapers.

Stock prices are quoted in points. Each point is a dollar. Seven fractions of points are used in quoting stock prices, ⅛, ¼, ⅜, ½, ⅝, ¾, and ⅞. Each ⅛ represents 12.5 cents. A stock quoted at 30½ is actually selling at $30.50 per share assuming you buy a round lot, i.e., 100 shares. In addition to this price, you must pay a commission of between 1 and 3 percent which has been determined by the exchange on which you are buying the stock, and that same commission rate will apply no matter which broker buys the stock for you. The size of the commission depends on the size of the purchase and the stock. In the case of a purchase of less than 100 shares, you must also pay a small additional commission because it is an odd lot, i.e. less than 100 shares, and this commission is paid to an odd lot broker for his efforts to sell you less than a round lot.

Consider a typical newspaper stock quotation:

| | | | | | | | | | Net |
High	Low	Stock	Div.	Sales	Open	High	Low	Close	Chg.
120	60	Mis. Sh.	5	24	101	101	99	100	−½

The two columns to the left of the name of the stock, *High* and *Low,* indicate the highest price and the lowest price per share at which a round lot of Miscellaneous Shoe has been bought and sold during the year, that is, the highest price of any transaction has been $120 and the lowest price of any such transaction is $60. To the immediate right of the name of the stock is the amount of dividend the stock is paying, in this case, $5 per year. Next, the *Sales* column indicates how many round lots were traded on the particular day in question, 24 round lots means that 2,400 shares of Miscellaneous Shoe actually changed hands. The *Open* column indicates the price of the first transaction to take place on that given day; $101 per share was the first price agreed upon by buyer and seller when the exchange opened for business. Next, the *High* column indicates the highest price paid during the day was also $101 per share. As trading continued during the day, the price of the stock continued to trade lower with the lowest price for any round lot selling for $99 per share, according to the *Low* column. Then the market rebounded, and the final transaction taking place at the *Close* of the day was for $100 per share. The *Net Change* column indicates the difference between the closing price of this particular day and the closing price of the previous trading day; that is, if you are reading Friday morning's paper, Thursday's close of $100 per share was ½ or .50 per share less than the closing transaction price on Wednesday which was $100.50 per share.

Now you have determined that the price of Miscellaneous Shoe is $100 per share, if you have $300 that you want to invest, you can buy three shares at $100 per share (plus commission) assuming you can still get it at $100 per share today.

Occasionally, you may run into someone who feels that buying 100 shares of a $3 stock is more desirable than buying three shares of a $100 stock. Apparently, he feels that many shares of anything is better than fewer shares of anything else. Occasionally also, you run into someone who feels that if a stock splits two for one, i.e., it now has twice as many shares outstanding with each share selling at half price, this in itself makes the stock more desirable since you now have twice as many shares of stock despite the fact that each share sells for half the price of the previous stock. Any corporation can split its stock into more shares. There is absolutely no problem in splitting a stock two for one; simply issue twice as many shares. By splitting the stock, it also splits company worth, earnings, and dividends as many ways as the stock is split. The most comparable analogy perhaps is taking your apple from you, cutting it in half and giving you back two halves. When you buy stock, you buy a share of a company. If you buy stock worth $300, whether you buy 100 shares of a $3 stock or three shares of $100 stock, you have still bought $300 worth of property and earning capacity in that company. Whatever the fractional relationship between your $300 and the total market value of that company, it will continue to exist regardless of any stock split or reverse split. The $3 stock may be better than the $100 stock, even 100 times better, but it is not better because it is cheaper. When you know the number of dollars you have to invest, and you decide which company you want to own along with all its other stockholders, do not worry about how many or how few shares your money will buy. Determine how many shares to buy by the stock price and your money to be invested; do not determine what stock to buy by the number of shares you can get for your money.

Placing the Order.　When you have an active account with a brokerage firm, you may simply call your broker and tell him you have decided to buy three shares of Miscellaneous Shoe Corp. at the market price, that is, at the best price he can get for you when the order is executed. You may also tell him to buy three shares of Miscellaneous Shoe at a specific price, for example, $100. In the first case, you have placed a market order; in the second case, you have placed a limit order. The broker will take your order over the telephone, noting on his pad the decision to buy, the stock to be bought, the number of shares, whether it is a market or limit order, and if it is a limit order, the price required. The broker will go to the office teletypist who will transmit the order to the New York office where another clerk will take the order off the teletype machine and note the various components of the order on another pad. The order then will be conveyed to a telephone operator who will telephone the order to still another clerk who will take the order to still another broker, either an odd lot broker in the case of an odd lot or a floor broker on the floor of the exchange in the case of a round lot. If it is a market order, it will be executed immediately; if it is a limit order, it will be executed when the conditions of the order are met, that is, when the stock can be bought at $100 per share or less. After the transaction occurs, the communication process will be reversed until your broker telephones you to confirm the transaction. Throughout this process, 30 or more people may handle your order for a commission charge of 3 percent or less, and yet you may receive confirmation within five minutes of the time you place the order. Not all orders are executed as smoothly as this, of course, since there are delays of one kind or another. Sometimes the exchange floor is an extremely busy place, and all orders cannot be transacted instantaneously. In the case of a limit order, of course, the market might never again trade a $100 a share, so the order would simply never be completed.

Who Had It?　Although it is not especially important for you to know exactly where your shares of stock come from when you buy them, it is important that you realize that there are three different sources from which you can buy such securities: straight from the corporation, from a dealer's inventory, or from an investor through an organized exchange.

　(*1*) *The corporation.*　When Miscellaneous Shoe Corp. first came into existence, as you recall, it decided to offer 10,000 shares of common stock to the public. If you were one of the investors who bought those shares, you could well have bought them from the corporation itself. New issues are sold through investment bankers (also called underwriters or syndicates) who either act as agents for the corporation when trying to sell the stock, or buy it outright from the corporation for immediate resale to investors. In both cases, the broker-dealer-investment banker is acting both for the corporation and for you, the stockholder. As an intermediary between you and Miscellaneous Shoe, he fulfills a very real need. Since the corporation needs to find sources of funds and stockholders need to find outlets for their investment funds, the broker or dealer who manages to bring these two needs together is serving a very real economic function. If the security representative who sells you the stock is acting for the corporation, he is acting as a broker. He does not take title to, or own, the stock himself; he is merely acting as an agent for the corporation and for you, the buyer. On the other hand, if the corporation has sold the stock to the broker's firm, then the firm owns the stock; the security representative then is acting for his firm as a dealer. Since the firm has bought the stock, and owns it outright, it has taken title to the stock and stands ready, willing, and able to transfer that title to you if you will meet the asking price. In this case the dealer's commission will be his share of the difference between the price the firm paid for the stock when they bought it from the corporation and the price you pay for the stock when you buy it from the dealer.

In many instances, stock sold this way is extremely speculative. Consequently, most investors who are willing to buy such stock on a new issue basis are willing to devote only a very small portion of their portfolio funds to any such stock purchase. However, since a new corporation will not need to raise a great deal of capital, no *one* stockholder must buy a large amount of stock if a great many security salesmen are in successful contact with a great many potential investors. If the new offering is to be successful in raising the desired amount of money for the corporation, many investors must each be willing to invest small amounts of their funds. With many investors responding to perhaps hundreds of security salesmen, willing to allocate only a few hundred dollars each, millions can be raised for a new corporation. If you buy such stock on a new issue basis, you are buying stock that no other individual has already owned. However, being new does not carry with it any connotation of being unsullied or even better. Nor will you necessarily be selling a second-rate stock if you should decide to sell the stock. Hopefully, the corporation will prosper each year, thus making the stock ever more valuable. In the case of a newly created corporation, you may well have considerably more apprehension about its stock than that of a large, well-established company with more predictable financial prospects.

You may also, occasionally, buy stock directly from a large, successful, expanding corporation that is issuing additional stock to supplement its resources. In most cases, the risk involved in such an issue is much less than the risk associated with buying the stock of a brand new corporation that may or may not succeed. For example, the investors who bought the first 10,000 shares of Miscellaneous Shoe were indeed speculating, but the investors who participated in the 3,000 share additional issue were much more able to determine what they were buying because the corporation had been in existence for a few years at least. If the corporation issuing additional new stock is one that has been successful for 50 years or even longer, it will have well-established earnings and dividend patterns, well-known products, and reliable financial data. An investor can participate in such an offering with relatively little risk indeed if he makes any effort at all to determine what he is buying. Corporations, new and old, do need to raise capital funds through common stock issues, and obviously, some investors must buy them if such funds are to be raised. Relatively few stock purchases are of the new issue variety, although at times they hold great promise of unusual financial returns and brokers like to sell them because of their relatively high commissions. Comparatively speaking, however, new issue stocks are very small in total value simply because the total market value of already outstanding stock is so very large.

(2) *A dealer.* Although it is certainly true that an investor often decides to buy a stock basically because of earnings, dividends, and capital appreciation, those reasons would hardly be sufficient to facilitate the capital accumulation required of our society if an investor were never again able to exchange his stock for cash. But the corporation will not buy back the stock; common stock is issued as perpetual stock, that is, it is issued forever. Since the corporation will live forever, or can at any rate, the ultimate owners must own shares of stock that will last forever. Since the stock will last forever but some investors may want to sell it, there arises the need for a market for second hand stock. Since almost all common stock owners at least want the chance to sell their shares in case they should ever decide to do so, and since almost no corporation will want to buy back its shares from its stockholders, some mechanism for the resale of stock is essential if corporations are to attract investors' funds. Furthermore, new investors want to buy the stocks of corporations already in existence. With such a potential supply of and demand for existing stocks, a market is bound to arise if it does not already exist. Such a market for stocks has existed for many years, and a market for any new stock will arise shortly after it is first offered to the public.

As discussed earlier, a corporation's stock will initially trade in the over-the-counter market. Later, if the corporation prospers, issues more stock to still more stockholders, sells more goods, and earns larger profits, it may be of sufficient public interest to warrant application for listing, or trading, on an organized exchange, such as the New York or American Stock Exchange.

Consider the role of a dealer in the over-the-counter market. Since the market is so informal, potential buyers and sellers would have considerable difficulty in finding each other without a little help from a dealer. He stands ready, willing and able to buy a few or several hundred shares of a stock from anyone who cares to sell it, or to sell shares to anyone wanting to buy them out of the inventory of stock that he carries for just such a purpose. By so doing he actually makes a market for the stock. Usually, there are several firms that make a market for any particular stock, and each firm deals in numerous stocks at one time or another.

When a company goes public, there are usually one or two investment banking firms that aid the corporation in its stock sale or underwriting effort. These investment bankers then function as dealers in the second-hand market. If trading activity in a stock is fairly heavy, other houses will also carry some inventory and make a market in the stock themselves, rather than go to another brokerage house for the stock every time a customer wants to buy some. Then if public interest in the stock should diminish, only a few firms will continue to make a market in the stock. Almost any stock that trades O. T. C. will have the market sponsorship of at least one firm. There are hundreds of dealers, and thousands of stocks held in those dealers' inventories. Sometimes dealers carry only token inventories, but at other times or in other stocks, dealers take very large positions, that is, they own thousands of shares of one stock. At such times, the dealer will want to sell some of that stock to investors in order to make himself a profit. The dealer is not so much an investor in stocks; he is a merchandiser of stocks. He buys at one price and sells at a higher price to make a profit. The difference between the two prices is profit, and sometimes the profit is quite profitable. Occasionally, the dealer acquires a large block of stock, perhaps thousands of shares, at a price substantially below the market price because the seller of the block cannot sell that much stock in the open market without seriously depressing the price. He can negotiate with a dealer in such cases to reach a mutually acceptable price, and then the dealer can offer to his sales people a fairly healthy commission to sell the stock to investors at a price somewhat below the prevailing market price. A considerable sales effort will result and many investors will buy their first shares of that stock from the dealer at a discounted price. Conversely, a buyer may wish to acquire a large block of a given stock and negotiate with a dealer to buy it for him without driving the price too far above the prevailing price. Since the dealer is in the market continually, he is in a position to provide a fairly orderly market for the stock, that is, he can support the stock price at certain times with increased purchase orders for his own inventory, and at other times sell out of his inventory to keep a temporary excess of buy orders from pushing up the price too far too fast. This is what is meant by dealer sponsorship, and it is very helpful to a corporation, to stockholders, and to potential stockholders. The dealer's willingness to buy or sell the stock at any time provides a ready market for the investor.

(3) *Another investor.*   Although some stock is indeed bought on original issue from a corporation, and still other shares are bought from dealers in the over-the-counter market, far and away the majority of stock is bought on the floor of the organized stock exchanges. Regardless

of the particular exchange, stocks are bought through brokers and they come from other investors. For example, if you call your broker to ask him to buy 100 shares of Plastic Shoe, through a series of teletype, telephone, and footrace messages, a broker on the floor of the exchange receives the order and proceeds to the post on the floor of the exchange where trading in that stock occurs.

When he gets to the post, he notes that the price range at that time is 2⅞ to 3⅛, which means that someone is willing to bid $2.875 per share for the stock and someone else is willing to take $3.125 for the stock. He offers $3 by open outcry as a bid. Some other broker, representing another investor, hundreds or thousands of miles away, will cry, "Sold." Neither broker has taken title to the stock; both brokers have merely represented their respective clients. As you ordered, your broker has bought for you 100 shares of Plastic Shoe directly from the other investor. If any other investor had been more anxious to sell his shares, your broker would have been able to get the stock for an even lower price. Since there was none, your broker in an auction market bought your shares at the best price possible at that time from the one investor who was most anxious to sell the stock.

In the off chance that at that exact moment when you have ordered your broker to buy your 100 shares at the market, there is no other investor in the country who has also ordered his broker to sell his 100 shares at the market, the specialist located at the post has the obligation to sell that 100 shares to you within that bid and asked price, at his own risk. He may either sell to you some of the shares that he then owns, or sell some that he does not own that he expects to acquire in the immediate future (this is called selling short, that is, selling something that he does not have that he expects to buy shortly). Since the specialist stands ready and willing at all times to try to maintain orderly price moves, any investor at any time can either buy or sell any stock listed on the exchange without either being forced to pay an exorbitant price or accept a substantial discount. When the specialist acts on his own account, he is acting as a dealer temporarily, but he will shortly match his transaction with a purchase or sale transaction with another investor. In the case of most of your stock purchases, you will buy from other investors utilizing brokers as facilitating agents. By understanding his function and his place in the securities markets, you can use his help effectively in your efforts to build a successful common stock investment program.

BUYING REAL ESTATE

As indicated at the beginning of this chapter, some investors are highly attracted to real estate, and for some very good reasons. Although initiating a real estate investment program from scratch with perhaps only $300 per year to invest is a very real problem, you may be more familiar with real estate and more interested in buying it, and thus, you should do so. Furthermore, if you accumulate a sizable amount of money, you could consider investments which take larger sums of money. Although real estate is somewhat less liquid than stocks (that is, somewhat less readily marketable), and may require more care and maintenance, you may very well feel that the advantages easily overcome these problems.

TYPES OF REAL ESTATE

There are several types of real estate that attract investors. In this discussion, real estate will be broken down into three categories: (1) land, (2) residential property, and (3) commercial property. Each has its own special attractions and problems.

Land. Land is probably the simplest of the three types to define. Land is a part of the earth with no buildings or structures on it. When you own land for investment purposes, you can rent it, develop it, sell it, or leave it idle. Many investors might want to rent, develop, or sell land to make financial gain. But why would anyone just leave land idle? Again, the basic motives are financial although they may be more obscure. Sometimes developers leave land idle in order to create a loss which can be deducted for income tax purposes. Of course, another reason might be to have the land ready and available when greater demand for that particular piece of land arises. Vacant land—especially in densely populated areas—is becoming scarce. Furthermore, the demand for land is rising rapidly.

One of the main ways to use land to your financial advantage is to lease it. Leases generally run for many years with the lessee actually building on the land. In many commercial districts, the outlook for appreciation in land value is so bright that the landowner may wish to keep the land but also receive rent. Through leasing the owner receives rent equal to the land's current value but still retains ownership. If your financial assets are sufficient to enable you to invest in land, it can be a great contribution to your investment program.

Residential Property. The second type of real estate investment is residential property. Residential property is quite simply real property that people reside in or live on, and for which they pay rent. It can take the form of a single-dwelling house or an apartment complex. Basically, the value of any piece of residential property is determined by the rental income now and that expected in the future. Various factors affect rental income, such as size, fixtures, privacy, neighborhood, and vacancy problems. Location may well determine several of these factors. Location near and within a city, and the relevant zoning ordinances, are very important determinants of real estate values. When considering apartment buildings, or even duplexes, the area on which they can be built must be properly zoned. For example, a ten-unit apartment building cannot be built on a lot zoned for houses. A lot that is zoned for multi-dwelling units is usually of more value than a lot in a comparable location that is not, and generally, zoning is directly related to location. Since multi-dwelling investments have the potential to earn more income than most single-dwelling property, the capitalized value of such property is not only greater but tends to rise more rapidly.

Commercial Property.   The third type of real estate is commercial property. Commercial property is rented for commercial purposes, such as retail stores, gas stations, offices and any other type of business enterprise. As with residential property, zoning is an important determinant of land use. If you wish to invest in commercial property, you should check to be sure that the property is zoned for various commercial activities. Generally, commercial property permits higher rents than does residential property, and consequently the value of such property tends to be higher. Again, location is an important factor. Many business establishments must be near high concentrations of people, and are willing, therefore, to pay higher rents in order to obtain locations that they feel will improve their business. Some industrial operations require access to rail connections or other transportation facilities, and therefore, seek locations near such facilities despite higher rental prices. In addition, existing commercial property is usually occupied, and zoning changes to permit the construction of new commercial property are often difficult to obtain. With rising demand on one side and scarce supply on the other, no wonder rental prices and real estate values are rising, and investors are interested in buying such property.

WHY BUY REAL ESTATE?

The reasons for buying real estate can be broken down into three areas: (1) income, (2) price appreciation, and (3) tax advantages. All three reasons usually apply to any piece of investment real estate. In buying property, one may buy for one primary reason, perhaps income, but this does not mean that the property will not appreciate in value or that the tax advantages will disappear.

Income.   Over the long run, the income a property earns is its most important characteristic. Property earns income through rent. The owners of property allow others to use their property because they pay them, and without that rental income, use will cease. However, just because a rent is paid is no guarantee that any net income after expenses will exist; the amount of net rental income is an important factor. For example, assume that you own some real estate that cost $40,000, and you desire to earn a 10 percent return. The net income of the property, thus, should be $4,000 a year after all expenses have been paid. If your rental income less your expenses does not equal $4,000 or more, you will be dissatisfied with your investment, and its value may well decline accordingly. However, if your net rent should exceed $4,000, you will be satisfied at the very least, and perhaps even delighted if your net rental income is considerably in excess of your expectations.

Price Appreciation.   Another reason for buying real estate is the expectation of rising real estate prices. As in the case of common stock, people buy real estate in the hope that it will increase in value. Like stock appreciation, real estate appreciation is one way to counteract the inflation risk. As inflation occurs, rents rise with prices in general, and the price of real estate will increase correspondingly. If inflation occurs at the rate of 3 percent per year, the value of real estate should also increase at that rate in addition to any appreciation resulting from other economic factors. As rent increases and is capitalized at the same rate applied to previous rental income, the value of the property will rise. And if rental income increases more rapidly during a period of greater inflation, property values should increase more rapidly. Furthermore, if the monetary authorities should tighten the money supply to combat inflation thus forcing interest rates higher and restricting construction, the demand for existing rental property could increase still more causing substantially higher rents and property values.

Real estate may also increase in value because of other factors. For example, assume that you own property in Texas, and the federal government decides to build a large air base near your property. Suddenly, the location of your property is extremely important because more people are there to bid for its services. On the other hand, if you own a gas station on a highway that has been used heavily in the past but is about to lose most of its traffic to a new super highway, the value of your property is likely to be worth considerably less now than it was a few years ago. Thus, appreciation can occur because of a general rise in prices, or because your property becomes more desirable, but property can decline in value despite inflation if other economic conditions deteriorate.

6 Mo + 1 day — capital gains

Tax Advantages.   The tax advantages of real estate investment are derived from: (1) capital gains treatment, (2) the depreciation deduction, and (3) the property tax deduction.

(1) Capital gains.   Capital gains are realized when one sells property for more than his tax basis. The tax basis is defined as the cost of the property less any depreciation deduction taken for tax purposes. The taxable amount then is the selling price minus the tax basis. For example, assume you bought property for $20,000 and have deducted depreciation of $5,000. If you sell the property for $25,000 your taxable amount is $10,000. The advantage of capital gains is that the $10,000 could be taxed at one-half the rate of your ordinary income. If you are in a

30 percent tax bracket, any additional ordinary income would be taxed at 30 percent; but your capital gains income of $10,000 would be taxed at only 15 percent. The advantage is obvious; you save $1,500 in taxes ($10,000 × 15% = $1,500). In order to receive capital gains treatment, you must have owned the property at least six months; any sale of property held for less time is eligible for a different and higher tax rate; the profits then would be treated as ordinary income.

(2) *Depreciation deduction.*   The second tax advantage of real estate investment is the depreciation deduction. The Internal Revenue Code allows an annual deduction from income for depreciation of any investment property. This depreciation is merely a means of apportioning the cost of an asset over several years rather than one. For example, if you invest in real estate, you are in effect entering into a business; the business of renting. All business expenses are deductible for tax purposes but not all are deductible in one year. Your biggest expense as a landlord is the cost of your property, and that particular cost can be deducted only over a number of years as depreciation occurs. Thus, this cost can be deducted from income over the expected life of the property. For example, assume you have a building that costs $50,000 and you expect it will stand 50 years. In this case, you might be allowed an annual deduction of $1,000 per year for 50 years ($50,000 ÷ 50 years equals $1,000 per year). This allows a total deduction of $50,000 over the life of the building, which is exactly what the building costs. Since any deduction you can claim reduces your tax bill, if you were in the 30 percent bracket, you would save $300 a year ($1,000 × 30% = $300), or $15,000 over 50 years. Some additional provisions of the Internal Revenue Code allow deductions under a method of accelerated depreciation. For example, you might write off $8,000 the first year, then $6,500 the second, $5,000 the third, $4,000 the fourth, and so on. The deduction would decrease each year over the 50 years, and the total deduction would still be $50,000. But taxes can be reduced more immediately by this method, thus further encouraging investment. One final point on depreciation. The cost of land cannot be depreciated. If you buy a lot with a building on it and together they are worth $50,000—the land is worth $10,000, the building is worth $40,000—you can only deduct for depreciation on the cost of the building.

(3) *Property tax deduction.*   The third tax advantage to a real estate investment program is the property tax. For example, assume your property taxes to local and state governments are $5,000. On your federal income tax return you are allowed a deduction of $5,000. Thus, if you are in the 30 percent bracket, you will save $1,500 ($5,000 × 30% = $1,500) in income taxes. Consequently, your actual taxes on your property will be $3,500 ($5,000 − $1,500 = $3,500). With the depreciation deduction and the tax deduction, plus perhaps an interest deduction, assuming you borrow some money to buy the property, in addition to your other actual out-of-pocket expenses, it is indeed possible that your

total expenses might exceed your rental income. However, you still might want to invest in real estate since the property might be appreciating in value, and the depreciation expense is not an actual out-of-pocket expense. Furthermore, the loss on your real estate investment could reduce your income taxes on your salary income.

VALUATION

Why is real estate worth anything? and how much is it worth? People buy real estate as an investment because they expect a financial return. When you buy real estate, you must place a value on the property by estimating what the future income of the property is worth to you. If property is currently earning a net income of $5,000 a year, in order to determine what that property is worth to you, merely divide the annual earnings by the rate of return you would require from that investment. If you would be satisfied with a 10 percent annual return, then you would be willing to pay $50,000 for the property ($5,000 ÷ 10% = $50,000). If you pay $50,000 for the property and receive $5,000 annually, your return will be 10 percent. You must be careful, however, to calculate your value estimate using a net rental income figure computed after taking at least all out-of-pocket expenses into consideration. Certainly one of the costs you should never ignore is the amount of your own time and energy needed to maintain the property. Then the rate of return applied to that income figure can represent the risk associated with that particular investment compared to the rate of return you could receive on alternative investments.

Once you compute the value you place on the property, you can compare it with the current market price. Sometimes the price will be too high, sometimes too low, but there is a middle ground. Some property is valued above or below according to other investors' desires and their estimates of earnings and risks. But on the whole, there is a generally accepted rate of return. If your desires conform with the rate, then you will be satisfied with market prices in general. If you desire higher rates of return you will have a harder time buying at your prices because other investors will outbid you. Thus, the value of property is a function of expected income and the rate of return; that is, the value is merely the anticipated annual earnings capitalized by an appropriate rate of return. When you find a piece of property priced below its computed value figure, you may very well have found a bargain investment.

SPECIAL PROBLEMS OF REAL ESTATE INVESTMENT

Having a successful real estate investment program is not as easy as it may seem. Just as there are special advantages to investing in real estate, so there are many special problems. Real estate investing involves considerably more than simply calling a broker, sitting back, and waiting to get rich. In fact, real estate investments involve several problems that we have yet to discuss. The returns may be very rewarding, but having any successful financial program is no snap. Real estate investment presents the following special problems: (1) divisibility, (2) resale, (3) loans and closing costs, (4) risk, (5) high leverage and (6) management.

Divisibility.   As mentioned earlier, one can hardly consider buying a real estate investment unless he has significant financial resources. Real estate must be bought in large dollar amounts. Whereas you can buy a share of common stocks for a few hundred dollars, you cannot buy real estate in such convenient quantities. You simply cannot go out and buy real estate every time you save $25 or $100. Real estate is bought in dollar quantities in the thousands. For example, if you think a multimillion dollar corporation is a good investment, you can purchase several shares at a time. On the other hand, if you think a $200,000 apartment building is an equally good investment or better, you cannot buy it unless you can come up with a significant down payment. When investing in common stock, you can adapt the quantity of stock to fit your program. But when investing in real estate, you must be able to buy the whole property, either with your own money, or enough of it to finance a mortgage.

Liquidity.   One of the more significant problems with real estate investing is reselling property, that is, turning it back into cash. When you decide to sell your real estate for whatever reason, perhaps you have found a better investment or are going to retire, it is not a simple matter of calling a broker, placing your order, and waiting ten minutes for a confirmation. If your particular real estate has not been valued recently, there may be no current market value on it. Thus, you have two major problems: first you must find someone who wants your real estate, and second you must find someone willing to pay an acceptable price. It is possible that a real estate agent could sell it for you quite easily, but this is not necessarily true. You might have to wait quite some time before your real estate broker could find another investor who wants your property, and even then he might not be willing to pay the price you had in mind. You probably can sell the property quickly if you reduce the price, but if you wait for the right buyer, it may take time. Time could be an important element, and the sale could take months. Thus, a major problem with real estate investment is lack of liquidity or mobility. Real estate is not a highly liquid asset like stock. If you are likely to want your funds that are invested in real estate, you must know as long as possible before hand, and initiate resale efforts early to give your broker as much time as possible.

Loans and Closing Costs.   When you have found a suitable piece of real estate at the price you want to pay, there is still one major obstacle ahead of you. You have to pay for it. Since most of us are not able to write out five and six figure checks, we must borrow some money in order to invest in real estate. In real estate transactions, this is usually done through mortgage loans. A down payment is required that can run from 10 to 30 percent or more. In any case, the rest must be borrowed. Borrowing mortgage money is just like buying anything else; you look for the "best deal" you can find. Since all money is alike, the main difference in loans is their cost, that is, the interest rate. A 7 percent loan, of course, is cheaper than an 8 percent loan, all other factors being equal. So, you must compare interest rates. However, another item that sometimes adds to the cost of a loan is "points." Points are additional percentages of interest that are paid in advance. For example, if you have a 7 percent loan with two points, this means you must pay 2 percent of the principal in advance, and 7 percent over the life of the loan. Thus, it is possible that an 8 percent loan may be cheaper than a 7 percent loan with points added.

Still other factors to consider when evaluating loans are the life of the loan and the size of the payments. The longer the loan, the smaller the payments, but the greater the interest paid. It is important to have the payments small enough that they can be met, but the faster you can pay off the loan, the smaller the total interest that you have to pay. In addition to the interest rate, points, and the life of the loan, closing costs must also be taken into consideration when financing your real estate purchases. They really create no problem, but one should realize that there are additional fees to be paid when the mortgage loan is arranged. These include abstract fees, legal expenses, insurance payments, and a few other items. In most cases, they are legitimate costs, but some people are unaware of these expenses and may be taken by surprise when they occur. (Mortgages, points, etc. are discussed in detail in Chapter Five.)

Risk.   Real estate, like any other investment, is subject to investment risks. Of the four investment risks discussed in Chapter Two, the financial and market risks are of the greatest importance regarding real estate. Financial risk, as you will remember, is the possibility that the earning power of an asset may decline. Since the value of any asset is a function of its income, this is indeed a very important risk to consider. If you cannot rent your real estate, if you cannot rent it for as much as you expected, or if your expenses should be excessive, your net income for the year will be less than expected. Expenses certainly can exceed expectations, and any number of factors can cause rents to decline. A deteriorating neighborhood, a super highway on your doorstep, a slow-down in the community, even undesirable construction, all can cause rent to decline. This is financial risk; it is always present in real estate investing. If your net rent falls, not only is your income reduced, but the value of your property declines as well.

Market risk is another obstacle with which the real estate investor must contend. Market risk is the possibility that the value of an asset may decline without any such decline in the earning power of the asset. The value of real estate is determined not only by income, but also a desired rate of return. Market risk is the possibility that the desired rate of return will increase, which, if it happens, will cause the value of the real estate to fall. For example, if interest on government bonds should go up, or banks are allowed to pay higher interest rates, investors will demand a higher rate of return on real estate investments because the difference between the rates of return on real estate and those on the bonds or savings accounts will no longer be enough to account for the difference in risks between the two investment alternatives. Furthermore, sometimes some types of investments simply cease to attract investors as they have in the past, and the demand for such investments falls with correspondingly falling values. Sometimes this disinterest is disillusionment following excessive optimism and enthusiasm. Whatever the cause, real estate investors do face the risk that the market value of their property may fall for no apparent financial reason.

High Leverage. Leverage means borrowing, and in real estate investing, leverage is the result of mortgaged property. For example, assume that a building costing $100,000 earns $10,000 annually. If you were to pay $100,000 outright for the building, your rate of return would be 10 percent, that is, you invest $100,000 and receive $10,000 return. However, assume that you only pay $20,000 down, and obtain an 8 percent mortgage for $80,000. Now what is the rate of return? Your net rental income is $10,000, minus your interest charges of $6,400; your net income is $3,600. Since your investment is $20,000, your rate of return is 18 percent instead of 10 percent. This increase in the rate of return is the result of leverage. Leverage exists when you borrow funds at a lower rate of interest than the rate of return your invested funds earn for you. In the above example, funds are borrowed at 8 percent, and there is a 10 percent earnings rate; thus, leverage creates a net 18 percent rate of return. In effect, the extra 2 percent earned on the $80,000 borrowed is equivalent to earning an extra 8 percent on $20,000, which when added to the 10 percent being earned on $20,000, makes an 18 percent total net return on a $20,000 investment.

Obviously, if leverage creates an 18 percent rate of return out of a 10 percent rate of return, leverage is a highly attractive financial technique. However, on a highly mortgaged investment, if income declines at all, you may be in serious trouble. Since risk of declining income is a very real possibility on much real estate, and since many real estate investments are rather highly mortgaged, value could fall below the amount of the mortgage. Furthermore, the larger your mortgage, the larger your payments, and these payments are fixed. As with most property owners, your payments will be paid out of the income the property earns. If the income decreases, the mortgage payments must still be met, or you lose the property. For example, assume that your $100,000 building was rented as a warehouse to a local industrial corporation. The corporation decides that it should move its factory to another state because it would be able to operate cheaper. You now have an empty building, your income is now zero, the value of the building has declined drastically; but your payments are still the same, and you still owe that mortgage.

The point is that highly leveraged real estate can be very risky. Property with greater possibility of fluctuating income should be mortgaged less heavily for the sake of safety, whereas real estate with a more stable income may be mortgaged more heavily. However, if you apply a large amount of leverage in your real estate investment program, you may have unintentionally created more uncertainty than you are aware.

Management.   The last problem of real estate investing is management. No matter how much or how little real estate you acquire, you must manage it properly if you are to have a successful investment program. When you own real estate there are many things about which you, or someone, must be concerned. Someone must decide on all of the following points:

1. How much rent to charge
2. How to rent the building
3. How and when to advertise
4. How to select the tenants
5. How to fill vacancies
6. How to make collections
7. How to handle complaints and maintenance

Depending on how much real estate you own, you may take care of all or most of the above items yourself, or hire someone to manage your property for you. Many banks and realtors offer such services to their clients. Of course, like all services, there is a fee involved. However, if your real estate investment program is to be successful, it must be properly managed by someone. If you are unable or unwilling to manage it, someone else will have to be employed to do so. In some cases, professional management is actually cheaper when account is taken of your own time and energy. In many cases, investors may feel that they can manage their own property until they try it, only to discover that truly inspired management is essential to their success. It should be apparent that some of the return from a real estate investment that you manage yourself is actually a payment for your own management efforts. If you cannot or will not provide proper and necessary supervision over the property, you should seriously consider employing professional management or choosing some other investment alternative.

REAL ESTATE INVESTMENT TRUST

A real estate investment trust is an organization that owns and manages real estate investments for its shareholders. It must have at least 100 shareholders with transferable shares, no five of whom can own more than half the shares. These trusts are created by law to aid real estate investment. If the trust meets certain requirements regarding dividends and sources of income, it will be exempt from corporate income taxes. However, many of the advantages of incorporation are still available. There is limited liability to the shareholders. The problems of divisibility, resale, loans and closing costs, and management are solved with this corporate form. Although risk and high leverage may still be problems, for the investor interested in real estate investment who cannot finance it or manage it himself, the real estate investment trust could be the answer.

Trusts do have some disadvantages that should be considered. First of all, if the trust has a loss it cannot be used by the shareholders for tax purposes to offset their other taxable income, and in some cases cannot be used advantageously by the trust itself. Second, trusts have to meet certain requirements in order to be exempt from the corporation tax. For example, profits from the sale of real estate held less than four years must not exceed 30 percent, thus restricting the trust from selling property freely in order to take advantage of better investment opportunities. A trust must hold more than one piece of property, and if it holds only a few pieces of property, none of them can be sold for four years for fear of failing the 30 percent requirement. Furthermore, a trustee cannot have any relationship with anyone who helps manage the trust, including people who offer management advisory services, real estate brokerage, and insurance services. Consequently, these requirements keep real estate men and other competent people from becoming trustees, so some of the very people who are most qualified to run a trust, are restricted from doing so. However, these disadvantages are not always material. A real estate trust does have the advantages of continuity, centralized management, transferable shares, and limited liability, all of which are definitely worth the investor's consideration. Considering the success of the common stock mutual funds in recent years, and considering how many potential real estate investors are limited by some of the problems involved in real estate investing, the future may be very bright for real estate investment trusts that can offer to investors all the advantages of real estate investing with few of the disadvantages.

HOW TO BUY REAL ESTATE

When anyone wants to buy real estate, the first problem is to find property that meets his desires. He must know what type of property he wants, what price range he is willing to pay, and what income or appreciation prospects he wants. Once such decisions have been made, the property desired must be found. Most often, such property is found with the help of real estate brokers. Once the broker understands what kind of property you want, he will check his listings. The broker will act as mediator between you, the buyer, and his other client, the seller. If price agreement can be reached, then a deal is made. However, suppose the broker does not have a listing of the type property you desire. Many cities have multiple listing services which result from agreement among local brokers that any broker can try to sell the listings of any other firm. In this way, you can deal with just one broker, but in fact have the selection of all available selling clients of all the brokers in the area. Thus, if your broker does not himself have a proper listing to sell, it is likely that he can still find a suitable property.

Real estate brokers like anyone else must be paid for their services. Real estate commissions, generally 5 or 6 percent of the sales price of the property, are paid by the party selling the property. However, the commission is also important to a buyer because it is almost always shifted to the buyer in the form of a higher sales price. It is possible, of course, to find and buy property by yourself without a broker in order to avoid a broker's commission. Sometimes such a saving is well worth the effort, but more often a broker's expertise can add materially to the success of your efforts. Furthermore, if the property you want is already listed by the seller with a broker, the commission will have to be paid anyway. But it is possible for a buyer to find an independent seller with desirable real estate, and in such cases, the price paid may be lower because the seller knows he does not have to pay a broker's commission. However, in today's expanding metropolitan areas, the volume of property exchanged is very large, so large that the use of a broker may be essential to finding and buying a property that fits the buyer's specifications.

SUMMARY

Learning to invest can be an extremely challenging and satisfying experience. Even the investor who must begin his investment program with a relatively small annual savings, can accumulate a sizable investment portfolio given sufficient time and management. By understanding the purpose and process of investing, any investor can begin a sustainable investment program designed to achieve his own personal goals. His initial efforts may be directed toward common stocks; in many instances, he may have little other choice. On the other hand, as his portfolio continues to accumulate, he may find real estate investing more attractive. Whichever investment media are used, he should understand the risks, processes, and problems related to those markets.

Although there seems to be some mystique about investing in stocks, buying stocks is really very simple. Any investor who would like to own a share of a corporation, and participate in the profit of that corporation, may open an account at almost any brokerage office to order however many shares of that stock he can afford. Such stock may be purchased from the corporation itself, occasionally, but usually an investor would buy such stock from another investor who is willing to sell it, or from a dealer in that stock who has been holding it temporarily in his inventory. Such stock is purchased for one or a number of reasons—dividends, price appreciation, protection against inflation, portfolio strengthening. In using a portfolio approach, the investor must keep all his investment objectives in mind, avoid the purchase of unacceptable stocks, see how all of his investments and his potential investments fit into his portfolio plan, and determine those that are performing as they should. If all his conservative stocks, growth stocks, and speculative stocks are performing as anticipated, no portfolio adjustments would be necessary unless the investor decided to make his portfolio more conservative or more growth oriented. If any of the securities held in the portfolio do not perform according to plan, however, regular evaluation of the portfolio will identify such poor performance, and appropriate portfolio adjustments could be made.

Although stocks are a very real attraction to many investors, still other investors find real estate even more attractive. Some investors prefer undeveloped land, others prefer residential or commercial property. Although buying real estate may require considerably more money, even for a down payment than some stock purchases, many of the other comparative advantages and disadvantages involved in buying real estate versus stocks tend to cancel each other out. By using a real estate broker, appropriate real estate investments can often be found that provide the income and price appreciation that the investor desires; there are also several tax advantages to owning real estate. On the other hand, there are some special problems in owning real estate, for example, the indivisibility of real property, the ready resale of such property, the acquisition of loan funds, and the management efforts required of any real estate investor. Although the risk in heavily mortgaged real estate can be considerable, the risk in stocks can also be considerable.

There is no way to eliminate risk, although there are ways to reduce risk. By definition, investing requires the assumption of risk, and it is because of that risk that investors receive financial returns. The conservative investor may build a portfolio composed of investments carrying less risk than one constructed by an aggressive investor, but he will be required to assume some risk. In return for assuming more risk, the aggressive investor anticipates a greater return on his portfolio. In either case, the effort should be a serious one. The frivolous investor may have a great deal of fun despite perhaps mediocre returns on his portfolio, but if he is investing primarily as a hobby, and is having fun at it, he may not want anything more. On the other hand, the serious investor constructs a portfolio designed to achieve given investment objectives and goals to achieve financial security and therefore must have an appropriate rate of return on his portfolio to insure his success. Constructing and managing such a portfolio presume an understanding of the material in this chapter but are a serious matter in and of themselves. In the next chapter, building and managing a successful portfolio are given primary attention.

Case Problems

1. Joe Doaks came to see John the other day. Joe wants to invest in stocks because he heard "they are a good deal." However, he first wants to learn something about stocks. John told Joe that the earnings of a company have a lot to do with the value of its stock. Later on John learned that Joe was buying stocks in companies with high earnings. Is he wise to do so? Explain the relationship between stock value and earnings.

2. One evening, Morton Perry was milling over a bunch of paper on his desk for about two hours. Finally his son, John, who had been watching him, asked him what he was doing. Morton told his son that he was trying to determine which stock he should buy. John being rather naive asked why his father wanted to buy stock. Morton said, "So I can make some money." John then asked how stocks make money. Morton explained how dividends and price appreciation work. John then said, "There must be some other reasons for buying stock." Is he right? If he is, what are some other reasons?

3. Miss Cathy Winter has just inherited $10,000. Cathy realizes the possibilities of investing in the stock market. She has consulted a friend on stock values and other factors. Now, she is all set to invest. But she forgot to ask her friend how you buy a stock. Well, guess who gets to tell her how to buy a stock? That's right, go to it.

4. Miss Ann Polk is a sophomore in college. She is a very avid student always raising her hand to answer or ask questions. The other day the professor asked her friend, Tiny, what a securities market's purpose is. Tiny stuttered around and didn't say anything. Because Ann had a crush on Tiny, she raised her hand to take him off the hook. The professor called on her and she answered that the purpose was to make money for investors. The professor was so displeased that he asked the two of them, and the whole class, to prepare a two-paragraph report on the subject. Join them.

5. If you remember, Morton and John Perry are father and son. Morton is an investor in stocks. His son is a naive boy who asks a lot of questions. Well, John has his dad in the position again where he can't explain something. John asked where stocks are sold. Morton told him that most are sold on several organized exchanges. He then explained where they were. But John wanted to know the similarities and differences between the exchanges. Please help the old man; what are they?

6. Miss Helen Hetter has just inherited $100,000. She is trying to decide how to invest her money. She is presently considering stocks and real estate. Through some research she is aware of the reasons for investing in stocks.

But as of now she doesn't know the advantages of investing in real estate. Please explain to Miss Hetter the reasons for investing in real estate.

7. Eldon has a little money to invest. It seems he has just received an extra $200 and would very much like to invest in real estate. But since he has only a small amount to invest he feels he will have to invest in stocks. However, a friend told Eldon that there was a way he could invest in real estate. The friend informed him that there were such things as real estate investment trusts. Eldon was happy with the idea of being able to invest in real estate, but wanted to know more about these trusts. Give Eldon some information on real estate investment trusts.

8. Construct different portfolio approaches that might be appropriate for a 30-year-old single working girl, a 30-year-old married man with two children, and a retiring couple.

Selected Readings

Amling, Frederick. *Investments: An Introduction to Analysis and Management.* 2nd edition. Englewood Cliffs, N.J.: Prentice-Hall, Inc., 1970.

Clendenin, John C., and Christie, George A. *Introduction to Investments,* 5th edition. New York: McGraw-Hill Book Company, 1969.

Cohen, Jerome B. and Zinbarg, Edward D. *Investment Analysis and Portfolio Management.* Homewood, Illinois: Richard D. Irwin, Inc., 1964. Chapters 1, 2 and 3.

Dougall, Herbert E. *Investments.* Englewood Cliffs, N.J.: Prentice-Hall, Inc., 1968.

Engel, Louis. *How to Buy Stocks.* New York: Bantam Books. A free copy may be obtained by writing to Merrill Lynch, Pierce, Fenner and Smith, at 70 Pine Street, N.Y., N.Y.

Fortney, Ned. *The Successful Practice of Real Estate.* Englewood Cliffs, N.J.: Prentice-Hall, Inc., 1967.

Graham, Benjamin. *The Intelligent Investor.* 3rd edition. New York: Harper and Row Publishers, 1965.

How to Understand Financial Statements. New York: New York Stock Exchange. Published annually.

Leffler, George L. *The Stock Market.* 3rd edition, revised by Loring C. Farwell. New York: Ronald Press Company, 1963.

Let's Look at Stocks and Bonds. Published by the Pacific Coast Stock Exchange, 301 Pine Street, San Francisco, California. Free copy available upon request.

Maisel, Sherman J. *Financing Real Estate: Principles and Practices.* New York: McGraw-Hill Book Company, 1965.

Market for Millions: The Role and Function of a Stock Exchange in the National Economy. Published by the American Stock Exchange, 86 Trinity Plaza, N.Y., N.Y. Free copy available upon request.

Mayer, Martin. *Wall Street: Men and Money.* New York: Collier Books, 1966.

Over-the-Counter Securities. Published by Merrill Lynch, Pierce, Fenner and

Smith, Inc., 70 Pine Street, N.Y., N.Y. Free copy available upon request.

Superior Equipment of the Realtor. Brief history of real estate. Published by the National Association of Real Estate Boards, 155 East Superior Street, Chicago, Ill. Free copy available upon request.

Understanding Preferred Stocks and Bonds. Published by the New York Stock Exchange. Free copy available by writing to N. Y. S. E., 11 Wall Street, N.Y., N.Y.

Understanding the New York Stock Exchange. Published by the New York Stock Exchange. A free copy available upon request.

Understanding the Over-the-Counter Securities Market. Published by the National Association of Securities Dealers, Inc., 888 Seventeenth Street, N.W., Washington, D.C. A free copy available upon request.

Vaughn, Donald E. *Survey of Investments.* New York: Holt, Rinehart and Winston, Inc., 1967.

West, David A. *The Investor in a Changing Economy.* Englewood Cliffs, N.J.: Prentice-Hall, Inc., 1968.

pq 284 end

BUILDING AN INVESTMENT PORTFOLIO

The construction and management of a successful investment portfolio can do much to improve your financial position. Although learning to invest can be an enjoyable academic experience, and even reading the financial section of newspapers and various other financial publications can provide some sense of personal satisfaction, the purpose of learning to invest is not purely academic. Only as your learning is put to use in the form of a well-constructed and well-managed investment portfolio, can you hope to achieve your long-range goal of financial security. It must be apparent that the obstacles involved in achieving financial security through investing are rather difficult to overcome. On the other hand, any relatively young, middle-income, professional man can prepare a financial program that includes the building of an investment portfolio designed to achieve financial security. Such a portfolio can be constructed using a reasonable portfolio approach designed to achieve an appropriate portfolio goal consistent with acceptable investment objectives and constraints. By selecting a portfolio goal that is appropriate to the investor's personal objectives and constraints, and by selecting an appropriate course of action that can overcome all obstacles en route to that goal, the investor can have considerable confidence that he will reach his goal successfully.

The obstacles that must be overcome, however, are indeed serious. As discussed in Chapter Two, unawareness, emotion, and investment risks must all be overcome if you are to achieve your goal. As you begin to construct and manage your portfolio, you will gain additional awareness of the investment process and markets, and of necessity, you will test your own emotional stability. In part, your ability to manage an investment portfolio with sufficient skill to overcome the various investment risks will be determined by your own personal judgment and the time you choose to devote to your portfolio management efforts, but your success at overcoming the various investment risks may be largely determined by the degree of risks you choose to assume. If you decide to construct a relatively conservative portfolio using relatively conservative securities, you may manage your portfolio by using defensive portfolio policies designed to avoid considerable investment risk. However, a defensively managed portfolio may provide a lower rate of return than is desired, and you may choose to construct a slightly aggressive portfolio with the expectation of earning a slightly higher than average rate of return. If you decide to construct a somewhat aggressive portfolio, using somewhat aggressive securities, you may manage your portfolio by using aggressive portfolio policies designed to assume more of the various investment risks for the purpose of earning an above average rate of return. However, any investor who decides to construct an aggressive portfolio must recognize that as he assumes more risk, the obstacles en route to his goal assume larger proportions. In an extremely aggressive portfolio, the obstacles are truly monumental. The more aggressive the portfolio an investor decides to construct, the more managerial time, effort, and ability will be required to assure his success in that effort. The additional financial rewards may well be worth the effort, but success is impossible without that additional attention.

CONSTRUCTING AN INVESTMENT PORTFOLIO

Before you actually initiate your investment program, you should choose one portfolio approach from among all the innumerable portfolio possibilities available to you. There are about as many specific portfolios as there are investors. Since each investor differs from all others in terms of income, age, temperament, and expectations, it is conceivable that each of those innumerable portfolio possibilities is actually being used by at least one investor somewhere. Actually, as indicated in Figure 9–1, all

Figure 9–1   The Portfolio Continuum

Ultra Conservative	— Defensive · Aggressive —	Extreme Speculative

those portfolio possibilities extend across a wide continuum, one that reaches from "ultra-conservative" on one end, to "extreme speculative" on the other. Although there may well be some ultra-conservative investors and some extremely speculative investors, most investment portfolios may be categorized as either defensive or aggressive.

If you decide to construct a defensive portfolio, you may select securities with less risk that require less care and attention, but the return on your portfolio, including dividends and capital gains, will be somewhat less than average. If you decide to construct an aggressive portfolio, you must select securities that have more than average risk which will require more care and attention, but the return on your portfolio may be somewhat more than average. Just exactly what is average, is somewhat difficult to identify, but the average rate of return on stocks as a whole for the last 20 years or more, including dividends and appreciation, is somewhere around 9 percent. Although this is not a very precise definition, it may be sufficient to serve our purposes. For our purposes, a defensive portfolio would be one constructed primarily to conserve the investment funds in that portfolio. The expected rate of return on the defensive portfolio, therefore, would be somewhat less than 9 percent. An aggressive portfolio would be one constructed primarily to earn more than a 9 percent rate of return; the investments selected for inclusion in that portfolio, therefore, would necessarily carry somewhat more than average risk in order to provide that additional return. Whether you decide to construct a more defensive portfolio, or a more aggressive one, will depend primarily upon your own investment objectives, your portfolio goal, and your willingness and ability to manage your portfolio. Each approach has its advantages and disadvantages for an investor, and only you can decide which of those advantages and disadvantages are more pertinent to your own personal situation.

For the relatively young, middle-income, professional man, more than one portfolio approach may be used over the life of his investment program. In the earlier years of his program he might adopt a relatively defensive approach, selecting relatively conservative securities that require relatively little care and attention. Since he will probably devote most of his time and effort to his career during those early years, and since he will have virtually no investing experience, choosing a defensive portfolio approach may be highly advisable. Furthermore, during those earlier years, the dollar size of his portfolio may be small, so that even earning a considerably higher than average rate of return would provide relatively little additional earned dollar income. His additional time and energies would probably be far more productive if they were applied in pursuit of his professional career. On the other hand, someday he will be professionally successful, he will have a sizable portfolio and considerable investing experience; at that time he may very well decide to pursue a more aggressive portfolio approach. With a fairly respectable investment portfolio, even a slightly higher than average rate of return could produce a considerable increase in the dollar return on the portfolio both in terms of income and capital appreciation; a slightly higher return would only require slightly more risk, time, and managerial effort, and might very well be worth them.

SELECTING A PORTFOLIO APPROACH

By no means all investors use a portfolio approach to investing, even though they do have portfolios and are investing. Since a portfolio, by definition, is a list of investments, anyone who has even one investment (assuming that one is a list) has a portfolio. But many such portfolios are the result of no management whatsoever. A portfolio *approach* requires investment management. As indicated earlier, we are primarily concerned in these chapters with securities, particularly stocks, because an investment portfolio can be built with various types of stocks to accomplish almost any investment objective anyone can imagine.

A portfolio approach to investing, as distinguished from merely having a list of securities, assumes that an investor constructs his portfolio with some idea of an appropriate balance among the component parts of the portfolio in the light of some previously selected objectives. The appropriate proportions of these three categories depend upon an investor's portfolio objectives, his investment constraints, how much risk he is able and willing to assume, and what kind of a return he must have from his portfolio. In such a framework, each stock purchase or sale is viewed and reviewed as an integral part in an overall effort to build a list of investments that will provide the desired financial returns on schedule, according to a previously selected portfolio approach. Furthermore, all buying and selling, in fact all potential purchases and sales, fit into the long-range plan guiding the portfolio manager's decisions. This portfolio approach may be either defensive or aggressive, that is, more conservative or more growth oriented, but the portfolio must be managed with some basic plan in mind if most effective results are to be achieved.

If the investor has no inclination or desire to do all this buying, selling, viewing and reviewing himself, and in many cases he should have far more profitable ways to use his time and energy, he can still take a portfolio approach to his investing through the use of such professional portfolio managers who manage mutual funds, trust funds, and variable annuities. More attention will be given to such managers in Chapter Eleven.

Alternative Portfolio Approaches. There is considerable flexibility available to the investor selecting a desired portfolio approach. On the one hand, he can be ultra-conservative, shunning all hint of financial risk in order to protect his initial investment. On the other hand, he may be extremely aggressive, assuming excessive risk with the hope of doubling and redoubling his portfolio through an unusually high rate of return. Although both these extremes may be inadvisable, there is considerable distance between them, and more than enough room to enable a wise investor to build an acceptable, profitable, and manageable portfolio.

Consider the comparison of two portfolio approaches represented in Figure 9–2. A defensive portfolio might be one that included 60 percent conservative stocks, perhaps half bonds and half defensive stock, 30 per-

Figure 9–2 Comparative Portfolio Approaches

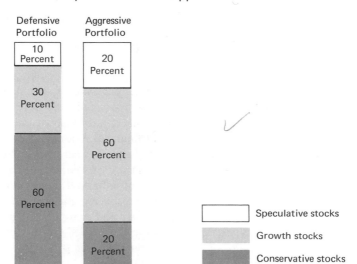

cent growth stocks, and only 10 percent speculative stocks, if indeed any at all, whereas an aggressive portfolio policy might include only 20 percent conservative stocks, 60 percent growth stocks, and 20 percent speculative stocks. One policy is designed to conserve the portfolio, the other to build it.

It is quite possible that an investor's portfolio policies will change considerably over time; for example, as illustrated in Figure 9–3, in his younger years, an investor may be more interested in an aggressive

Figure 9–3 Changing Portfolio Preferences

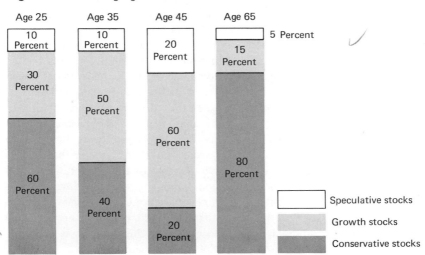

portfolio approach, whereas in his later years he may be more interested in conserving the investment value that he has been able to acquire over time.

Both defensive and aggressive policies assume a portfolio approach. In either case, the investor has seen his investment program as an effort to acquire an organized list of stocks that is designed for a specific purpose. He has considered the component parts of his portfolio as specific means to overcome specific obstacles. The defensive stocks in the portfolio are included to provide cash income and to protect against downside market fluctuations in order to limit the impact of financial risk and market risk. The growth stocks in the portfolio are included to increase slightly the rate of return on the total portfolio, and to overcome the inflation obstacle, and if possible to profit because of inflation. The speculative stocks in the portfolio are included for the specific purpose of taking advantage of developing concepts, industries, and companies that have relatively low present values, and relatively high risks, but at the same time, have some probability of very high returns over the years. With a portfolio approach, an investor can see how all his securities fit into his portfolio. If a stock does not perform as expected, it may be sold. As sales from the portfolio occur, the proceeds from those sales may be invested in new securities that can supplement that particular portfolio component that the investor considers most worthy of strengthening at that particular time. As new investment funds are saved, additional stock purchases will be made to supplement the specific components of the portfolio that most need strengthening.

With a portfolio approach, the investor can decide whether he wants a defensive portfolio policy or an aggressive portfolio policy. He can evaluate the effectiveness of his portfolio in reaching his investment goal. Furthermore, in his annual evaluation, he can determine whether or not his purchases and sales are actually accomplishing his predetermined portfolio policy. If his basic policy is a moderately aggressive one, but he has gradually over the past year drifted into more speculative securities at the encouragement of some more speculative friend or investment adviser or broker, his annual evaluation will show that he has in fact moved to a more aggressive portfolio stance than was his original objective. Conversely, he may find that he is inclined to hold securities that he purchased for growth purposes when they do not grow, or when they do not appreciate in value any more than the market in general. This may mean that the growth securities that he bought were not growth securities at all, but were defensive securities. It may mean that he has simply misjudged the earnings growth of some of the corporations; perhaps they are no longer the growth companies that they once were. If the earnings of a corporation are growing at the rate anticipated, but the stock price has not risen, this may mean that the stock price appreciation that the investor anticipated is yet to come. In this case, he is probably well advised to hold his growth securities with the expectation that the price appreciation will be forthcoming in the next few years. If his stocks in general are not experiencing the rates of earnings growth that had been anticipated, some serious reconsideration may be in order. It may be that he is really more inclined toward a more conservative portfolio than he originally thought was desirable; accordingly, he would leave the portfolio as it is. But he may need to make appropriate adjustments in his portfolio to move it toward the more growth-oriented position that he had originally selected as desirable; accordingly, he would need to sell those securities that he bought for growth, that have not been growing, in order to acquire the funds necessary to buy new growth stocks with better prospects.

Only through a portfolio approach to investing can one establish an adequate method to evaluate a list of securities in the light of desired objectives. Almost all securities are valuable to somebody, and any particular security could be valuable to any individual investor in combination with other securities. However, if a given portfolio is composed entirely of stocks of shoe manufacturing companies, it is highly unlikely that the next purchase should be another shoe stock if the investor is at all interested in avoiding the severe loss that would be associated with any decline in the shoe industry. Similarly, if a given portfolio is composed entirely of speculative stocks, it is highly questionable that the next purchase should be another speculative security. Only if the portfolio policy as stated is to invest only in the shoe industry, or only in speculative stocks, respectively, would these two purchases be appropriate to the portfolio policy. If the investor is at all concerned about protection against risk, or the limitation of risk, his portfolio should be constructed to provide some diversification among various types of stocks, various industries, and various companies.

Diversification. Almost every investment adviser recommends the use of diversification as a means of protecting a portfolio against the various risks necessarily associated with owning only one investment. Most investors do wish to limit risk through adequate diversification. However, no investor needs to buy 50 or 100 stocks to have adequate diversification, although many professional investors do have 100 or more stocks in their portfolios; 10 or 20 stocks may be adequate diversification. But an investor does not necessarily have any real diversification in his portfolio even if he has 50 different stocks if all those stocks have practically the same characteristics. For example, there are numerous investors who really believe that they have provided for themselves much more protection against financial risk by buying 40 or 50 different worthless stocks, than they could have with only one worthless stock. Not so. Any portfolio of 10 stocks, or 50 stocks, is only as good as its average, and if that average value is zero, the portfolio value is zero. It would be better in this case to have only one good stock, and it is a real shame to be deceived into a false sense of security.

Of course, it is possible to gain considerable diversification through the purchase of one stock if that company is itself widely diversified in its manufacturing endeavors. For example, R.C.A. is a highly diversified company engaged in a score of industries. However, there is no certainty that R. C. A. will not have some unique problems at certain times that would cause it to be considerably less profitable than the market as a whole. Owning only one stock, of even a highly diversified company, is a considerable degree of concentration. Although it may be necessary as a first step in a portfolio-building program, it is hardly recommended that all purchases continue to be made in only one company's stock. Nevertheless, ownership of several different stocks of widely diversified companies whose holdings represent 50 to 100 different industries could indeed provide considerable protection against loss due to any specific industry problems. With a diversified portfolio, unexpected losses will be offset by unexpected gains, thereby reducing risk.

Although diversification is primarily designed to minimize market risk, it can also increase some gains resulting from industry or company success. The investor can buy only those companies that have above average corporate earnings records, with above average earnings prospects, in the expectation of above average stock price appreciation. Although some of those companies might not be able to increase their earnings at those high rates consistently, some of them might increase their earnings by much more than 20 percent, and the earnings growth for the portfolio as a whole might be about the 20 percent annual rate. If so, in most years, the portfolio value could appreciate 20 percent or more. Such diversification, based on high historical growth rates of earnings, often can bias the portfolio toward above average price appreciation.

Dollar Cost Averaging.   In addition to diversification, there is another financial principle that may be applied by any investor who is constructing his investment portfolio over time, namely, the principle of dollar cost averaging. By definition, dollar cost averaging implies investing regularly the same amount of money in an investment over a long period of time. By applying this principle, the investor may always sell the stocks purchased through such a plan for more than their average cost. Obviously, many an investor might think that any investment that can always be sold for more than its cost would be worth considering. If a long-term investor has a fairly regular flow of investment funds, all he must do to achieve above average performance is to find a stock that will increase in price over time. Since stocks that are gradually appreciating over time, despite a few fluctuations, are not all that difficult to identify, and since many investors initiating a program may have a fairly steady flow of funds to invest over a long period of time, dollar cost averaging can be a very effective approach to investing.

As an example of how dollar cost averaging works, consider Mr. Seymour Green who is beginning his investment program with $300 a year. He decides to invest in Miscellaneous Shoe Corp. In his first year, the price of Miscellaneous Shoe is $30 a share, and for his $300 he can buy 10 shares. The price of the stock is $30, and his average cost is $30 a share. In the second year, the price of Miscellaneous Shoe has gone to $60 a share, and Mr. Green for his $300 can only buy five shares. After two years of buying Miscellaneous Shoe, investing $300 each year, Mr. Green owns 15 shares of Miscellaneous Shoe at an average cost of $40 a share ($600 ÷ 15 shares = $40 per share). Since the two prices at which he purchased Miscellaneous Shoe were $30 and $60 for the two years respectively, the average price for those two years was $45 ($30 + $60 = $90 ÷ 2 years = $45). Mr. Green's average cost of $40, therefore, is less than the $45 average price. Even if the stock should fall from its present $60 price to its $45 average for the last two years, Mr. Green could still sell his shares for a higher price than his $40 average cost. In theory, dollar cost averaging can be quite profitable. Since the investor always invests the same amount of money each year, he will buy more shares when the price is lower, and fewer shares when the price is higher.

There are three advantages to using dollar cost averaging. First, the investor can buy a very conservative stock with relatively little risk, and thereby benefit through the long-run price appreciation that stocks tend to enjoy. Rather than placing all his savings in a savings account, he may invest those funds in a very conservative stock with very little additional risk in anticipation of a higher rate of return. Second, the investor using dollar cost averaging avoids buying too many shares at high prices. In the midst of rampant enthusiasm and optimism, many investors over-extend themselves at market peaks; obviously, such times will be followed by declining stock prices, disillusionment, and pessimism, during which time the investor may buy too few shares. By investing the same number of dollars each year, the investor always buys more shares at lower prices and fewer shares at higher prices. Third, although any market decline tends to shatter investor confidence, the investor using dollar cost averaging can at least take some cheer from bear markets (that is, depressed markets) because they provided him with opportunities to buy additional shares for his portfolio at unusually low prices. He may even welcome market declines, to some limited extent, knowing that since he continues to buy that same good stock all the time, he is able to buy more shares of that stock at temporarily depressed prices.

There are, however, certain disadvantages to dollar cost averaging. Any investor who attempts to buy at the bottom may learn the hard way that no investor enjoys much success at such an effort. Perhaps, only one investor in the whole country is able to buy at the absolute bottom, and he may have had no intention of doing so. Any investor who postpones his regular stock purchase in an effort to buy at the lowest possible price, may well wait too long, always thinking that any reaction to a low might be followed by a still lower low. After some months of waiting and guessing, he may suddenly discover that the price has moved considerably above earlier prices. Furthermore, if he holds those funds in his checking account too long, he may find himself investing in a pleasure trip to Hawaii, rather than in additional shares of Miscellaneous Shoe. A second disadvantage of dollar cost averaging is the necessity of buying at high prices. As the investor becomes aware that he is paying higher and higher prices for his stock, he may well feel disinclined to buy additional shares at such high prices. But no one really knows how high a stock can go, and if he postpones a regular stock purchase in anticipation of declining prices, he may well find that what he thought was high was really low after all. Also, there is forever the danger that if he does not continue his investment program, the funds he has saved may be spent in Hawaii.

Although dollar cost averaging is especially beneficial to the conservative investor, the aggressive investor may also use dollar cost averaging, slightly modified, to increase the returns on his own portfolio. If an aggressive investor becomes especially concerned about buying stock at such high prices, he can always buy more defensive stocks, such as utilities, at market peaks. Then he can buy more cyclical stocks (those that fluctuate with the business cycle) such as industrial suppliers, that may be especially depressed during market lows. By so doing, he can modify dollar cost averaging in an effort to provide a more aggressive return. The aggressive investor can also modify dollar cost averaging by increasing, perhaps doubling, his dollar purchases after substantial stock price declines, but this policy seriously alters the basic requirement of continuing to invest the same amount of money each year. By using dollar cost averaging, the investor can always buy well-established companies, he can modify his portfolio approach at least to the extent that additional investment funds may be placed in more aggressive, or more conservative, stocks depending upon economic conditions at the time, and he may well be able to achieve considerably better portfolio performance as a result.

CHOOSING YOUR INVESTMENT OBJECTIVES

By no means every investor has the same investment objectives. However, all investors should consider the same alternative investment objectives in order to select that one objective, or that combination of objectives, that fits his own personal situation. Some investors are primarily concerned about the safety of their principal. Others are concerned about the liquidity or marketability of their investments. Still others are concerned about income, or capital gains through price appreciation. Some are primarily concerned about inflation. Since investors vary so greatly by age, health, temperament, portfolio size, and investment experience and interest, it should be apparent that no one portfolio can possibly fulfill the requirements of all investors. Furthermore, since there are thousands and thousands of securities from which to choose, it should be equally apparent that all kinds and varieties of securities are available. Some securities may be exactly right for you, and some are probably absolutely wrong.

If you do not have your own personal investment objectives clearly in mind, how can your broker or investment adviser know what you should buy? And if you have no specific investment objectives in mind, how can you decide whether any specific security could make a significant contribution to your portfolio? No one else can decide your investment objectives for you. Only you can decide how much risk you are willing to assume, and how large a return you require. Until you can determine your own investment objectives, you cannot possibly select your investments properly. One question you must ask, therefore, is what investment objective you want your portfolio to perform. Only when you answer this question, can you proceed to select specific securities that will build a portfolio that will perform according to your desires.

Safety of Principal.   Investing requires the assumption of risk; never doubt it. Nevertheless, investing does not require the assumption of *excessive* risk. In fact, the first and primary requirement of any sound investment portfolio is safety of the funds invested. This objective cannot imply the elimination of risk because investing by its very definition assumes risk. However, this objective does imply a representative selection of quality securities, representing strong companies, purchased at reasonable prices. The selection of speculative securities purchased at excessively high prices cannot provide safety for the investor's principal despite portfolio diversification among a hundred such companies.

The stock prices of even the very best companies will fluctuate. Occasionally, the declining phases of such fluctuations are quite serious for even very sound companies. Nevertheless, safety of principal can be achieved through the purchase of good stocks, representing good companies, managed by capable and responsible people dedicated to the manufacture and distribution of well-known and widely received products. The stocks of such companies are widely owned by both individual and institutional investors (such as universities, life insurance companies, and mutual funds) who continuously scrutinize both the management and the financial statements of such companies. Numerous investment analysts devote considerable time to investigating such companies and writing reports for their investor clientele. Furthermore, in many cases, such stocks are subject to the supervision not only of the Securities and Exchange Commission but the New York Stock Exchange as well.

With all this attention regularly focused on their actions, the managements of such companies must strive to maintain effective stockholder relations as a requisite of their own professional careers. They must exercise some care in the commitment of their corporation's capital; they must maintain the continuous manufacture and distribution of their products; they must maintain their future market position through aggressive research and development programs; they must maintain good employee relations; and they must protect their corporation's earnings and dividend patterns if at all possible. In most cases, such corporations are sufficiently large to permit rather wide industrial diversification within their corporate structures, thereby avoiding any excessive impact on the corporate profits due to temporary problems in any one factory or industry. Although the entire stock market every three or four years experiences an average price decline of 15 to 20 percent or more, relatively few of the good securities representing sound companies experience that large a decline, to say nothing of a 50 percent decline unless their prices have previously risen to unreasonable levels. By investing in conservative stocks of such quality corporations, the investor can assure reasonable safety of his principal except during times of excessive market price appreciation.

Stock prices can rise to unreasonable levels, however. This happens not only to stock prices in general, but also to the stocks of specific companies. Now and then high prices are the result of a conviction that corporate profits will increase dramatically sometime in the future. Occasionally, however, high prices are no more than a reflection of speculative enthusiasm. For example, consider the widely renowned Tried and True Shoe, Inc. whose earnings have increased about 6 percent each year for the last half dozen years, and whose price has rather regularly sold at ten times its earnings. This year, Tried and True Shoe is earning $4 a share, and selling at $40. Most analysts consider it reasonably priced. Next year if the earnings pattern continues, it should earn $4.24 perhaps, and might reasonably sell above $42. On the other hand, if some unusual development should attract unusual attention to the stock, its price could begin to move up rather rapidly in anticipation of rumored higher future earnings. With any dramatic increase in the price, speculative interest in the stock could develop, possibly driving the price as high as $60 or $80 a share. At an $80 price, the total market value of T. & T. S. would have doubled within one year, and might very well be considered unreasonably valued. Although the purchase of T. & T. S. at $40 a share might well be defended as a conservative investment, one that would indeed provide safety of principal, the purchase of that same stock at $80 a share could not be so defended simply because the stock might be unreasonably priced. Although it is possible for a corporation to double its earnings in a very short period of time, the probability of such an occurrence is slight. Consequently, there is considerable likelihood that when the speculative enthusiasm surrounding T. & T. S. begins to wane, the price will fall. If it does, those investors who bought the stock at $80 a share will discover that they have lost a part of their principal. Buying good stocks is not enough; good stocks must be bought at reasonable prices for adequate protection of principal.

Even then, you should diversify to assure safety. Even with careful selection, not all your securities can be expected to perform as your investigations indicated they would. Some of them will be much better bargains than you anticipated, and some will be much worse. To avoid the chance that the only stock you select is the worst possible choice (and some people do seem able to pick only losers), you should select fewer shares each of a representative group of securities, rather than more shares of just one. By thus diversifying your portfolio, you will buy the bad with the good, but you will avoid buying only the bad. On the average, therefore, your aggregate portfolio holdings will be much more likely to reflect the degree of safety you have decided you want. Diversification will not guarantee safety of principal but in combination with the purchase of good stocks at reasonable prices, you go a long way toward providing safety for your investment funds.

One particular misunderstanding about the function of diversification can cancel the entire effort. Some investors apparently believe that diversification reduces or even eliminates all risk, thus permitting them to buy exceedingly speculative securities. They actually believe that by diversifying, they can buy risky stocks at no risk. Consequently, their entire portfolios consist of really worthless or nearly worthless stocks. Such a misunderstanding can be the cause of serious financial losses. Any portfolio will return exactly the average of the securities in that portfolio, no more and no less. If that average represents valuable issues, the return should be satisfactory; but if that average represents worthless securities, in all probability, the results will be negative.

Liquidity.   A second investment objective that is very important to many investors is the liquidity, or ready marketability, of their securities. Even for those investors who have every intention of holding their securities indefinitely, some need occasionally arises to raise additional cash rather quickly. Furthermore, there is always the possibility that an investor might change his investment objectives, or lose confidence in a particular company's ability to perform as he had anticipated; in either case he might want to sell the stock of that particular company. With the prospect of a major stock market decline, an investor might decide to sell all his stocks, and put all of the proceeds of that sale into a savings account. At any rate, relatively few investors are willing to waive their rights to sell securities for any considerable length of time. Any number of things might require the sale of one or more securities in a portfolio.

Liquidity, however, means more than the ability to sell a given stock. Liquidity means the ability to sell that stock quickly without any sacrifice in price. If you are forced to sell an asset, you are almost guaranteed that the price you will receive for that asset will be below its real value. Only those securities for which there is a ready and continuous market can be sold immediately at their current market prices. For those securities that have very thin markets, that is, those for which there is very small demand at any given time, a seller may have to search several days, or even longer, for a buyer who is willing to take the number of shares the investor has to sell at the last quoted market price. Such illiquidity seldom exists in the case of good securities, especially listed securities, because there are usually many available buyers for such securities at any given time. However, in the case of new securities, especially those that are highly overpriced, as well as in the case of unknown over-the-counter stocks, certain real estate investments, privately owned corporations, or unincorporated businesses, ready marketability is often their most serious risk. For those investors who consider liquidity a major investment objective, only those securities for which there are large and active markets should be purchased. Not all investors are so concerned about liquidity. For those who are not, if they understand that they are making relatively long-term commitments that may not be readily turned back into cash, and especially if they have alternative sources of ready cash in the case of emergencies, investments that are not readily marketable may cause them no serious concern.

Income.   A third investment objective is current income. Investments that provide regular and stable income are especially attractive to many investors for two reasons. First, many investors depend upon the income flows from their portfolios to cover such mundane expenses as rent and food. In such cases, regular and stable income is an exceedingly important investment objective. Second, investors are often attracted to securities that pay regular and stable dividends derived from regular and stable corporate profits because the prices of such securities seldom fluctuate as drastically as do the prices of securities that do not pay regular and stable dividends.

Some investors are much more interested in providing current income than they are in capital gains, avoiding inflation, or even safety of principal. For them preferred stocks and bonds that guarantee dividends and interest income may be even more attractive than common stocks. For most investors, however, the possibility of price appreciation is sufficiently attractive to warrant some sacrifice in income stability although income may still be a primary objective. In the case of investors who are accumulating a portfolio, however, dividend income in the place of price appreciation merely creates the problems of paying additional income taxes and reinvesting those dividends. For those investors who must have current income from their portfolios to supplement their other income, this investment objective is of primary importance. For those investors who do not need current income from their portfolios, however, such as younger investors who are still building their portfolios, this investment objective is much less important than those more oriented toward future portfolio values.

Price Appreciation.   A fourth investment objective is price appreciation. In recent years, price appreciation has been viewed as a major investment objective by the great majority of investors, both individual and institutional. Two factors in particular have encouraged such investment for appreciation. First, in recent years income taxes have become a significant determinant in investment decision making. As both income and income tax rates have increased, larger and larger proportions of personal incomes have gone to federal, state, and local governments in the form of taxes. For those investors who are trying to build investment portfolios, any portion of their investment incomes (such as income from dividends) which they lose in the form of income tax payments, merely reduces the total value of those portfolios. Not only do they lose that portion of their incomes, they also lose all future income they would have earned on that reinvested income. The tax laws applied to capital gains are approximately one-half of the investor's marginal income tax rate up to a maximum of 25 percent, if, as, and when securities that have appreciated are actually sold. Since securities can be held indefinitely with no income tax liability resulting from price appreciation, and since even upon eventual sale of those securities, the income tax rate is only one-half the rate incurred on marginal current income, investing for price appreciation has been greatly encouraged.

For example, a small investor with a relatively modest salary might easily lose 25 percent of his dividend income in the form of income taxes, which he could entirely avoid by investing in the stocks of companies that retain all their corporate profits rather than pay out a portion of them in dividends. Furthermore, if that corporation could use those retained earnings profitably, its earnings would continue to rise because of the additional expansion facilitated by the retained earnings. As the corporation's earnings continued to increase, the investor's portfolio would also appreciate in value as a result of corporate profits.

A second reason for recent investor interest in price appreciation as an investment objective is the result of the response of the corporations to investors' indications that price appreciation is now one of their more important objectives. Most corporations are able to expand their operations either through retained earnings, or through the sale of additional securities in the open market. If corporations are indeed making good use of the funds they have already aggregated, investors are willing to buy additional issues of their stocks. As a matter of fact, many of a corporation's existing stockholders would be the very investors who would be most interested in buying additional shares in the company. Since the primary concern of the corporation is to raise additional funds for expansion, the corporation is relatively unconcerned whether those additional funds are acquired through sales of new issues to the investing public, or through additional retained earnings made possible by a low dividend or zero dividend paying policy. From the investor's point of view, it makes relatively little sense to receive dividend income if he intends to reinvest it anyway. Since with a dividend income, he would lose a considerable portion of that income to the government in the form of income tax payments, he would be able to use only the remaining fraction of this income to buy additional shares in the company.

On the other hand, if the corporation followed a low dividend or zero dividend paying policy, all of the funds that would have been received as dividend income can be invested by the corporate officers with no tax loss, the earnings of the corporation per share would increase more rapidly, and the market price of the corporation's stock would rise faster accordingly. Consequently, investors have recently become more interested in good stocks that pay out less of their earnings in dividends. Because of such interest, those corporations that are especially growth-oriented, that is, those that are expanding their operations and earnings at two, three or more times the national growth rate, have been especially inclined toward avoiding or reducing dividend payments in favor of larger retained earnings. Since these corporations' earnings are growing more rapidly than the earnings of most corporations, they have attracted attention. Not only have their earnings increased faster than average, their price-earnings multiples have also increased. So a corporation's stock whose $4 earnings sold at 20 times earnings, that is, for $80, might increase its earnings in four years to $5 and sell at 25 times earnings, that is, $125 per share, which is a high rate of price appreciation. Consequently, investors have looked with considerable favor on those corporations that have retained their earnings, since through this means, stock prices have risen more rapidly than they would have otherwise, and portfolio values increase as a result. For any investor building a portfolio for the future, price appreciation may well be second in importance to safety of principal as an investment objective.

Inflation Hedge.   A fifth investment objective may be to protect the portfolio value against inflation, that is, to protect the safety of principal against loss of purchasing power, or to hedge against inflation. The impact of inflation on an investment portfolio can be either beneficial or detrimental depending upon the securities included in the portfolio. To the extent that bonds and preferred stocks are present in any portfolio, inflation will have an adverse effect on the real value of the portfolio. Since bonds and preferred stocks have fixed-dollar values at maturity, and since those maturity values, or call prices, are paid in the dollars of the day (current dollars) no matter what they will actually buy at the time, any decline in the purchasing power of the dollar will reduce the real value of a fixed-dollar security. In exchange for the safety of principal in terms of dollars plus the income stability that bonds and preferred stocks provide for the portfolio, the investor buys such fixed-dollar investments knowing these investments are susceptible to inflation risk. Even some common stocks are subject to inflation risk to the extent that they are similar to bonds and preferred stocks in terms of their extreme stability of income and market price.

In general, however, common stocks are often bought to provide some protection against inflation. Since many investors are concerned about the impact of inflation on their holdings, one major investment objective they seek is protection against such inflation. Furthermore, the purchase of common stocks is one way to provide such protection. In fact, many common stocks do provide some protection against inflation, and some may actually profit during an inflationary period. If a company can raise the prices of its products sufficiently to permit its earnings to increase with the general rise in all prices, the stock of that company will usually rise in price accordingly, thus maintaining its real value. Or saying the same thing in a different way, as the purchasing power of the dollar declines, the market price of a stock will rise enough to make up the difference if that stock represents a corporation that can raise the prices on its products at the going rate of inflation.

Some stocks actually rise faster because of inflation. In the case of a company whose products are experiencing great demand in a period of general economic expansion, such demand pressure will permit, perhaps even require, unusually rapid price hikes for its products, thus providing unusually fast growth in the corporation's earnings with correspondingly higher stock prices. If variable costs, such as labor and raw materials, represent a relatively small proportion of a corporation's overall costs, its profits can rise exceedingly rapidly. With such higher earnings, especially if they occur at an increasing rate, the prices of those stocks will rise much faster than the rate of inflation. Whereas bonds and savings accounts are fixed-dollar investments, common stocks can rise in price when prices in general rise. Consequently, ownership of common stocks does provide some protection against an inflationary erosion of an investment portfolio. For this reason, common stocks are considered an inflation hedge, that is, a mechanism for offsetting the losses in purchasing power suffered through a general increase in the price level.

Inflation has its greatest impact over longer periods of fairly steady price increases. The higher the rate of inflation, of course, the greater its impact, but the longer the period of time involved, the more serious will be its effect upon fixed-dollar investments. For example, the real value of an asset is cut in half in 40 years with a 1 percent annual rate of inflation. But after all, 40 years is a very long time. However, a 2 percent rate has the same effect in only 20 years. A 4 percent rate of inflation reduces the value of a bond, a savings account, or an insurance policy to only half its purchasing power in only ten years. That is not a very long time. If higher rates of inflation occur over longer periods of time, the impact on a family's income and savings can be absolutely disastrous, especially for those families who have tried very hard to save because they expect to use the income from their investments during retirement to supplement their pension income.

All five of the investment objectives discussed are exceedingly important. No investor will want to ignore any one of them. Nevertheless, each investor must decide for himself which objective or objectives he wishes to emphasize in the construction of his own portfolio. Age, health, financial position, portfolio size, and investment attitude in general must all be considered in selecting the proper combination of objectives. Once those objectives have been selected, however, you can begin to build your portfolio with much confidence. When specific securities are sought with some purpose in mind and selected because they appear likely to accomplish that purpose, portfolio management takes on real meaning. However, without some serious thought about your investment objective, you may just as reasonably buy one stock as any other: your goal then is simply to buy a stock, not to reach a definite objective. When you determine an appropriate investment objective, however, you can proceed to build a portfolio that will enable you to arrive where you want to go. Just where you want to go, that is, the portfolio size that you have selected as your goal, will be significantly affected by the specific investment objectives you wish to emphasize.

SELECTING AN APPROPRIATE PORTFOLIO GOAL

Perhaps everyone is spurred to greater effort if he has a goal worthy of his efforts. This may be especially true in the case of a potential investment portfolio owner. Perhaps the lack of any such goal, in the great majority of cases, will partially explain why so few families have investment portfolios at all, much less a portfolio of any significant size. To the extent that selecting an appropriate goal can be of any help to you in acquiring such a portfolio, assuming that you do indeed consider an investment portfolio worth having, a few comments on what exactly is appropriate may be in order here.

Many an investor, upon deciding to begin an investment program, may say to himself that his goal is an investment portfolio as large as possible. However, with such an ambiguous objective, it is almost a foregone conclusion that he has done relatively little planning, and without such planning, he is unlikely to have very much success. In the case of Mr. Seymour Green, a portfolio objective of $250,000 at age 65 was selected. He thinks this is a reasonable, necessary, and sustainable goal.

However, relatively few investors have been able to reach a portfolio of such magnitude, and many investors may not feel impelled to reach a goal of that size. Actually, the portfolio goal that you might really want to reach could be impossible considering your annual savings, time, and managerial ability. However, by realistically appraising your future needs and your present financial situation, you should be able to determine an appropriate portfolio goal.

The most significant determinant of an appropriate portfolio goal is the income an investor will want from his portfolio when he wants it. For example, if you decide that by age 50 you want a supplemental income from your investment portfolio of $7,000 per year, and you assume that you can get a 7 percent rate of return on your portfolio, your target is $100,000. If you feel that $7,000 might be inadequate as a supplemental source of income, or if you feel that a 7 percent rate of return is more than you could reasonably expect from your portfolio, then $100,000 is too small a target. Your portfolio goal should be determined by the amount of income you expect it to provide. In choosing your goal and your desired income, however, it is exceedingly important that you recognize the impact that inflation will have upon your cost of living some years into the future. Assuming a 3 percent rate of inflation, for example, you must recognize that the value of the portfolio, in terms of purchasing power today, will be approximately one-half of what it is today in only 15 years. In private, personal interviews, Mr. Green has disclosed that he expects a 10 percent rate of return on his $250,000 portfolio, that is, a $25,000 a year supplemental income beginning at age 65. By using his three-stage portfolio approach, he anticipates no difficulty in achieving his goal, nor does he anticipate any difficulty in earning a 10 percent rate of return on his portfolio; his only concern, apparently, is that his $25,000 a year supplemental income may be inadequate to support him in the style to which he wishes to become accustomed.

Whether or not any investor can achieve any given portfolio goal, however, is to a considerable extent determined by his annual saving, the number of years he has in which to reach that goal, and his own managerial ability. Obviously, the more an investor can save each year, the larger his investment portfolio goal can be. If Mr. Green is forever limited to saving only $25 a month, the possibility of achieving his $250,000 goal is extremely slight. On the other hand, if he is able to save twice as much as he originally anticipated, a $500,000 goal might be quite reasonable. Since Mr. Green's proposed annual savings are relatively modest, considering his expected earned income and expenditure plans, the key to his success will be the length of time over which he can build his portfolio, and his own ability as a portfolio manager. By no means all investors have 40 years to build their investment portfolios. Many investors only become convinced of the desirability of an investment program rather late in life, and consequently, have a relatively few years during which to build their portfolios. Unfortunately, even doubling or tripling their annual savings may not permit them to achieve their desired portfolio goals, and they may turn to more aggressive portfolio management as the only possible solution to their problem. By immediately going to a more aggressive portfolio approach, however, they may lose more money in the market than they make, and therefore, fail to reach even a modest portfolio goal.

As discussed in Chapter Two, emotional reaction is an exceedingly important obstacle, one that may seriously interfere with anyone's efforts to achieve financial security. Furthermore, the various investment risks are also serious obstacles that may be especially troublesome to any investor attempting to manage a more aggressive portfolio. Since a more aggressive investor must assume more risk in order to achieve a higher rate of return, greater managerial effort and ability are required for success. The probability of such success is correspondingly lower. If you have relatively modest future income requirements, and if you have a long time in which to achieve your portfolio goal, your annual savings and the annual return on your portfolio need not be very large. Consequently, you may be able to construct and manage a relatively conservative portfolio. On the other hand, if your desired future income is larger, or if the length of time left to you is shorter, your annual savings and your rate of return must be larger to reach any given goal, requiring a more aggressive portfolio approach. Although even a slightly aggressive approach may be excessive for the emotional and managerial characteristics of some investors, most investors who construct their portfolios over longer periods of time, may well be able to manage portfolios which assume slightly more than average risk in exchange for slightly more than average returns. Whether such is necessary and acceptable depends on the investor's portfolio goal and his personal income and temperamental constraints. Whichever basic approach you decide is better for you, there are appropriate portfolio policies for either approach that may facilitate your efforts to overcome all obstacles and reach your chosen goal.

MANAGING AN INVESTMENT PORTFOLIO

Managing a portfolio is a continuous process. Although your portfolio might be constructed in accordance with your objectives, and made up of stocks most appropriately selected, your objectives will change, the securities in your portfolio will change, and the economic, political, and social environment will change. Although it is by no means necessary to devote continuous attention to an investment portfolio, you cannot put your stocks away and forget them. Especially if you are at all inclined toward constructing a somewhat aggressive portfolio, your management efforts must be somewhat greater than would be required by a more defensive portfolio. Although it would be incorrect to assume that a defensive portfolio requires no management effort, a decision to construct an aggressive portfolio carries with it the necessity of selecting specific stocks and watching the portfolio more carefully as requisites of success.

As indicated earlier, innumerable portfolio policies exist upon a continuum from "ultra-conservative" to "extreme speculative." In between the two ends of the continuum, however, those innumerable alternatives can be categorized into two large groupings of portfolio policies, namely, defensive policies and aggressive policies. Generally speaking, the more aggressive your approach, the more risk you must assume; the more conservative your approach, the less risk you must assume. As indicated in Chapter Two, however, the mitigation of one risk may necessarily imply the assumption of another risk. For example, you may wish to buy a high-grade bond in order to avoid financial risk, but in so doing, you assume more inflation risk and interest-rate risk in the process. Conversely, if you wish to avoid inflation risk, you may buy growth stocks; but in so doing, you assume more financial risk and market risk in the process. One of the major advantages of investing through a portfolio approach is that different securities can be selected for the portfolio as a means of overcoming each specific investment risk. Although no one investment may be sufficiently flexible to overcome all investment risks, a portfolio may be constructed and managed to do so. In a very real sense, when an investor selects his particular portfolio approach, he not only chooses the amount of risk he wants to assume, he also chooses the type of risk he prefers. Whichever portfolio approach you take, however, defensive or aggressive, and whichever risks you decide to assume and avoid, all investing requires the assumption of some risk.

DEFENSIVE PORTFOLIO POLICIES

Although all investing necessarily requires the assumption of risk, you may nevertheless manage your portfolio according to policies that tend to reduce risk. Such policies are primarily designed to provide safety of principal, liquidity, and income. They are basically conservative; they require the assumption of less than average risk, and they tend to provide a less than average rate of return. However, they are more likely to provide whatever rate of return they are designed to provide. In fact, they can guarantee you a given rate of return for a short period of time if you ignore inflation. Consequently, there are many investors who are primarily interested in defensive portfolio policies.

Those investors who are just initiating their portfolio-building programs, and investors who have completed the construction of their portfolios, may well be more interested in defensive portfolio policies. In the first case, new investors may recognize that they have a great deal to learn about building and managing their portfolios and therefore might wish to avoid the assumption of above average risk until they have gained more experience. In the case of investors who have already acquired their portfolios, whether they are merely satisfied with the present size of their portfolios, or because of their age, they must be satisfied with their portfolios and the income from them. Therefore, defensive portfolio policies may be considered most appropriate because they are primarily concerned with conserving the portfolios they have already acquired. In either case, there are appropriate assets which may be acquired to facilitate defensive portfolio policies designed to reduce each investment risk. As mentioned in Chapter Two, there are four such investment risks: (1) financial risk, (2) market risk, (3) inflation risk, and (4) interest-rate risk. Each of these risks and the portfolio policies appropriate for reducing such risk will be considered here.

Financial Risk.   Investors who want to avoid financial risk should buy fixed-dollar investments, for example, savings accounts and high-grade bonds. In the case of a savings account, the investor is guaranteed that all the dollars he has placed in that savings account will be available to him anytime he wants them again. In the case of a long-term bond, the investor is promised, although not necessarily guaranteed, that his dollars will be returned to him when the bond reaches its maturity date. In one sense, funds invested in savings accounts do bear some financial risk, since the bank or the savings and loan association in which those funds have been placed could go bankrupt. However, since savings account funds are insured by the Federal Deposit Insurance Corporation and the Federal Savings and Loan Insurance Corporation, the amount of financial risk assumed is extremely slight. Furthermore, although some bonds carry considerably more financial risk than others, the purchase of high-grade bonds, such as United States Treasury Bonds and highly rated state, municipal, and corporate bonds, requires the assumption of very little financial risk. Therefore, for the investor who is willing to accept a 4 or 5 percent rate of return, investing in savings accounts may be the most appropriate defensive policy. But for the investor who desires more return, who is willing to sacrifice liquidity for a few years, but is unwilling to assume greater financial risk, investing in high-grade bonds may be the most appropriate investment policy.

Some additional financial risk must be assumed by the investor who buys common stock. Although some stocks bear relatively little financial risk, any stock issued by a corporation will carry more financial risk than a bond issued by that same corporation simply because the bondholders stand in line before the stockholders in the event that the corporation's earnings should decline. However, the additional financial risk attached to many stocks is extremely slight, and many investors feel that the additional return is more than worth the additional risk. In the case of conservative stocks, sometimes also called defensive stocks or income stocks, the risk is very slight. Because the earnings patterns of the corporations those stocks represent have been so stable for so long, because of the quality of the corporation, its management, the continuing demand for its products, its customers' loyalty, and its widely diversified base of operations, the investor should consider the financial risk associated with the purchase of such a stock relatively slight indeed. Consequently, a defensive investment portfolio policy might require that 60 percent of the total portfolio be placed in conservative securities (perhaps some in savings accounts or high-grade bonds) and the rest in conservative common stocks. All these securities would be purchased because they are quality instruments, and the investor would only sell such securities from his portfolio if the quality of those instruments should fall.

As additional protection against declining earning power of any specific investment, the investor should diversify his portfolio in many ways. In many cases, he may buy conservative common stocks only, but he could diversify by type of instrument by placing funds in several savings accounts, some U.S. Treasury bonds, some high-grade state, municipal, or corporate bonds and several conservative common stocks. Furthermore, he should diversify geographically, perhaps selecting securities issued by eastern, midwestern, and western states, municipalities, and corporations, perhaps even international issues. He should also diversify by industry, perhaps including some securities representing various manufacturing industries, such as the shoe, electronics, and food-processing industries; some extractive industries, such as the aluminum, oil, and steel industries; and some securities representing major retailing corporations. When an investor is just beginning his investment portfolio, of course, he cannot buy all these various securities at one time. Nevertheless, his first investment might very well be a security issued by a very well-diversified corporation, one engaged in perhaps as many as 20 different industries under its corporate structure, with factories and retail outlets all over the country and the rest of the world. R.C.A. was mentioned earlier, but there are many such companies. As additional investment funds became available, however, additional diversification by company and industry would be appropriate.

For the investor who is building a defensive portfolio, dollar cost averaging may also be helpful in avoiding financial risk. Since he is gradually saving additional investment funds, those new funds will become available continuously. Consequently, although the earning power of various corporations may fluctuate slightly from year to year, investing in those same corporations on a regular basis guarantees that the investor will buy more shares of the stocks when their prices are lower, and fewer shares of those stocks when their prices are higher. As a result, the principle of dollar cost averaging automatically facilitates the purchase of more shares at lower prices and fewer shares at higher prices, thereby reducing the impact of financial risk upon the total portfolio. Although any temporary decline in the earning power of a corporation will be reflected in a temporary decline in the price of that corporation's stock, such a lower price may be viewed as a temporary opportunity to acquire still more shares for the same amount of money. Since the investor has invested in high-quality instruments only, any slight fluctuation in earnings or stock prices would not dictate selling that stock; all his investments have been acquired for the purpose of long-run retention. He would only sell when the quality of any particular investment should decline. In this sense, a slight degree of financial risk could be absorbed more readily with the understanding that dollar cost averaging would provide sufficient defense against price declines to make the assumption of that additional risk more than the worth of the extra financial return.

Market Risk.   Market risk implies that the market price of an asset may decline without any decline in the earning power of the asset. Market prices fluctuate in response to changing investor attitudes and changing economic conditions, regardless of the stability of any particular corporation's earnings pattern. Those stocks that have experienced considerable upward price movement in response to stockholder enthusiasm, or falsely rumored earnings increases, are the ones whose market prices may decline rather drastically despite the stability of their earnings patterns. Furthermore, there are times when price-earnings ratios in general have risen rather dramatically, and at such times, market risk for all stocks is especially severe.

Defensive portfolio policies designed to avoid or reduce market risk would call for the selection of fixed-dollar investments and conservative income stocks representing well-established, well-diversified companies, with well-established earnings and dividend patterns, selling at low price-earnings multiples. Especially those stocks that have traditionally maintained rather stable price-earnings multiples, that have neither climbed materially during fits of enthusiasm nor declined materially during fits of depression, would be more attractive to the investor trying to avoid or reduce market risk in his portfolio. Stocks with relatively modest rates of earnings growth tend to sell at more stable price-earnings multiples, whereas stocks with widely fluctuating earnings also tend to experience widely fluctuating price-earnings multiples. Consequently, those stocks with more sustainable earnings growth patterns tend to fluctuate less in market price, and therefore carry less market risk.

Furthermore, by rather liberally applying the principle of diversification to your investment portfolio, you may still further reduce the impact of market risk by neutralizing any temporary fluctuations in the price-earnings multiples of specific stocks. Through diversification, any temporary decline in the price-earnings multiple of one stock would probably be offset by a temporary increase in the price-earnings multiple of some other stock. Consequently, neither change would be reflected in a change in the market value of the total portfolio. For the investor who is accumulating investment funds, the principle of dollar cost averaging would also protect the portfolio against market risk. During periods of temporary market slump, more shares would be purchased with any given dollar figure, whereas at market peaks, fewer shares would be purchased with that same dollar figure. Consequently, whatever market risk had been assumed by the investor would tend to be reduced by his investing on a regular, continuous basis. Essentially, however, market risk may best be avoided by devoting large proportions of the total portfolio value to securities with extremely stable earnings patterns.

Inflation Risk. To avoid or reduce the impact of inflation upon a defensive portfolio, the investor should buy quality stocks that will rise in price as the general price level rises. To the extent that the portfolio is devoted to fixed-dollar investments, such as savings accounts or bonds, and even to the extent that the portfolio is devoted to income stocks whose earnings tend to remain stable if not fixed, inflation risk may be the most serious risk that the conservative investor must face.

In general, conservative investors are usually very conscious of financial risk and market risk and tend to construct portfolios designed to avoid or reduce these risks. However, since such portfolios are designed to avoid or reduce financial risk and market risk, the appropriate defensive portfolio policies require the selection of fixed-dollar investments and conservative stocks. Therefore, conservative investors tend to include high proportions of such securities in their portfolios, exactly the securities they should not include if they are trying to protect themselves against inflation risk. Particularly as inflation risk has become a more significant force in the market, and as financial risk has become a less significant force, conservative investors have tended to protect themselves against the "wrong" risk. Of course, even those investors who are aware of both financial risk and inflation risk, and the degree to which each can reduce the value of their portfolios, may still be more concerned about financial than inflation risk, and should therefore continue to buy fixed-dollar investments. However, for those investors who have not given adequate consideration to the increasing importance of inflation risk and the declining importance of financial risk, such a comparative evaluation is certainly in order.

No one should conclude from these comments that fixed-dollar instruments or conservative stocks should be excluded from the portfolio; financial risk does continue to exist, and the portfolio should be protected against that risk. On the other hand, as inflation risk has become more significant, any investor who wishes to continue to conserve his portfolio must include a larger proportion of stocks in that portfolio that can experience rising earnings and rising prices in response to any general increase in the price level. Since fixed-dollar investments are fixed in terms of dollars, other securities must also be included in the portfolio, namely common stocks, that can increase their earnings and dividends, if the portfolio is to overcome the impact of inflation risk.

As in the case of financial risk and market risk, the principle of diversification can again serve the needs of the conservative investor. Through the purchase of several stocks representing corporations that will probably be able to increase the prices on their products sufficiently to increase their earnings and dividends, and thereby overcome the impact of inflation, the investor can still further protect himself against inflation risk. Although no company can guarantee its own ability to increase its rate of return sufficiently to overcome any inflationary bias in the economy, by including several stocks which represent companies that are likely to protect the real value of their stock the purchasing power of the entire portfolio should be protected more adequately. Although some of the companies' earnings may suffer unexpectedly during periods of inflation, still others will perform better than had been anticipated. Consequently, any portfolio including both would reflect the impact of neither; because of its diversification, the portfolio would reflect a modestly higher rate of return in response to the general inflationary bias in the economy, thus effectively eliminating the impact of inflation risk upon the portfolio's real value.

Interest-Rate Risk.   Since defensive portfolio policies require the purchase of fixed-income securities, the conservative investor's portfolio tends to show the effects of interest-rate risk during periods of rising interest rates.

In recent years, with interest rates rising so rapidly, all individuals' and institutions' conservative portfolios devoted exclusively to fixed-dollar investments have experienced 10 to 20 percent declines in their portfolios' market values. To the extent that any conservative portfolios have included fixed-income instruments, interest-rate risk has hurt the market values of those portfolios. To protect against such risk, the investor should buy quality common stocks that can increase their returns in response to increasing competitive yields on other instruments. If the investor is primarily concerned about conserving his principal, he can also avoid interest-rate risk by buying short-term obligations, such as government bills that mature in three to 12 months, or government notes that mature in one to five years. On such instruments, even with rising interest rates, the market value of bills and notes will not decline very much below par value. On the other hand, when interest rates begin to decline, the income from such short-term obligations will decline, of course, thereby reducing the income from the portfolio. The management problems associated with continuously exchanging maturing bills or notes for newly issued ones can become burdensome. The only way an investor can really avoid the problems caused by interest-rate risk is to buy common stocks or real estate. As is the case of the other three risks, diversification should also be used as a protective measure. If an investor's portfolio is too small to permit diversification through the purchase of several different stocks, he should surely purchase stocks that represent companies that are themselves well diversified.

Since the defensive portfolio policies designed to protect against financial risk and market risk require the purchase of exactly those securities that should be avoided by a conservative investor trying to protect his portfolio against inflation risk and interest-rate risk, the portfolio should include all types of investments if it is to be truly defensive. When you try to reduce the impact of one risk, you necessarily increase the impact of another. There is no way to eliminate completely the effects of all risks. But by maintaining a balanced portfolio, that is, by including both conservative securities and growth stocks, you can protect yourself somewhat against all risks. To the extent that you are more concerned about one risk than another, you may wish to include more of those securities that provide specific protection against that specific risk. But if you wish to invest, you must assume some risk because that is the very essence of investing. Although you can never overcome all obstacles completely through the purchase of any one security, you can manage your portfolio conservatively by selecting a combination of securities according to defensive portfolio policies that reflect your particular concern about each specific risk. However, as your own investment objectives change, as the characteristics of the securities included in your portfolio change, and as the financial characteristics of the general economy change, you may regularly need to make appropriate portfolio adjustments. To be effective in your portfolio management, your portfolio should be regularly reviewed and adjusted to reflect your changing investment attitudes and objectives and the changing economy. By assuming relatively little risk, you may construct and manage a conservative portfolio that will provide a fairly regular annual return of 6 or 7 percent, less than an average stock market return, but more than the guaranteed return on a savings account. Whether the additional return warrants your assumption of slightly more risk and trouble, you alone must decide.

AGGRESSIVE PORTFOLIO POLICIES

Aggressive portfolio policies are designed to include securities in the portfolio with above average risk to permit an above average return on investments. Although some investors are willing to accept a 4 to 7 percent rate of return on their portfolios, still other investors desire a 10 to 12 percent rate, or even more. Although they realize that designing a portfolio with the expectation of higher rates of return requires the assumption of more than average risk and therefore requires above average managerial effort, they are willing to accept that additional risk and provide that additional management in exchange for the higher rates of return. The policies appropriate to a more aggressive portfolio approach differ considerably from the policies appropriate to a defensively managed portfolio, and the securities selected by an aggressive investor may differ considerably from those selected by a more conservative investor. Furthermore, more care and attention must be given to the selection of such securities, and more frequent evaluations of such securities' performance are essential to the success of any aggressive portfolio.

Just as there are innumerable portfolios that can be considered conservative, so there are innumerable portfolios that may be considered aggressive. Some investors construct portfolios that are extremely speculative, so speculative in fact that the investors can hardly be considered investors; they should really be considered speculators, if not gamblers, and their portfolios can hardly be called investment portfolios. By no means all portfolios that are aggressively designed and managed, however, can be considered speculative. If the average rate of return on common stocks continues to be about 9 percent, it should be apparent that any successfully managed defensive portfolio will provide a less than 9 percent rate of return; similarly, any portfolio designed to return anything above that 9 percent rate of return must include stocks that are slightly aggressive. Deciding to be slightly aggressive in your portfolio policies, however, is a far cry from speculating. You do not need to assume unreasonable risks when building a slightly aggressive portfolio. By simply concentrating a larger proportion of a portfolio in growth stocks, the investor can design a more growth-oriented, that is, a more aggressive, portfolio.

The policies discussed in the following section apply to portfolios of various aggressiveness, but reasonably applied may well permit no more than a 14 percent rate of return on the portfolio, that is, approximately 50 percent more than average. Furthermore, even a 14 percent rate of return is indeed difficult to sustain; not impossible, but difficult. For many investors, therefore, especially in their early efforts to build their portfolios, the dollar size of the portfolios may be so small that the additional time and effort required to manage an aggressive portfolio may not be worth the additional dollar income earned. For example, during the first ten years of Mr. Seymour Green's investment program, his portfolio would be considerably less than $10,000. Yet even on a $10,000 portfolio, his additional efforts required to manage his portfolio aggressively, assuming he could make 14 percent rather than 9 percent, would add less than $500 each year to the portfolio's value. During those ten years, Mr. Green might sacrifice his professional success to whatever extent he devoted any significant time and energy to managing his portfolio. He should probably construct his portfolio using rather conservative securities, which do not require substantial management efforts. At some time, however, he will be sufficiently successful in his career to permit some spare time. About that same time, his portfolio may have reached a size that would make more aggressive portfolio management worth his while. At such a time, a more aggressive portfolio stance might be considered, and the following aggressive portfolio policies may indeed be appropriate when he decides to assume more risk.

Financial Risk. In discussing aggressive portfolio policies, financial risk is considered an unusual opportunity to assume greater risk when a corporation's earning power is less than what it may reasonably be expected to be some years in the future. Although many investors are less inclined to pay an average price-earnings multiple for the stock of a company that is new and untried, among such corporations, however, there may well be some that are managed by extremely competent management teams, capable of guiding that corporation to considerable financial success. In many cases, such growth companies continue to increase their earnings rather rapidly over an extended number of years. As those corporations' earnings patterns become well established, investors will be more inclined to pay higher prices, and higher price-earnings multiples, for the stocks. Especially in the cases of corporations whose earnings patterns are increasing more rapidly than average, investors are indeed willing to pay higher price-earnings multiples for the stock. However, above average earnings are difficult to sustain. Many corporations continue to increase their earnings rather rapidly for only a few years, after which they cannot maintain those earnings patterns. In fact, they may not even be able to maintain their peak earnings. If additional competing products are offered to the public by competitors who have been attracted to the industry by such above average earnings, the whole industry may be glutted with output, driving all earnings down. Furthermore, investors who try their very best to buy stocks that will continue to grow, invariably find that some of their growth stock selections fail to meet their expectations. Some companies never really get started, and many run out of gas after a while. However, through regular re-evaluations of the growth stocks held, such situations do become apparent. When a growth stock fails to appreciate, or no longer continues to appreciate, it should either be sold or transferred to the conservative category of an investment portfolio. Furthermore, since one or more such growth stocks may be sold any year, the investor must regularly investigate alternative growth stocks as possible replacements for his existing holdings. Such analyses often require the assistance of an able broker or investment adviser, and even then may require considerable amounts of the investor's time and effort.

Another opportunity for assuming above average financial risk may be found in the form of stocks representing corporations whose earnings have been depressed for one or more years. A number of corporations experience rather widely fluctuating earnings over time. Cyclical stocks may be especially attractive to aggressive investors. Also, some industries have their own cycles of high and low activity. During prosperous economic periods, consumers are buying everything in sight, inventory is low, employment is high, and production is occurring at capacity rates, corporate profits in general tend to be very high, and the stock market rises dramatically creating a bull market. Consequently, prices of cyclical stocks will be especially high. Following such periods of excessive prosperity and speculative enthusiasm, however, declines in business activity cause lower production, higher inventory, higher unemployment, lower profits, and declining stock prices. As indicated in Table 9–1 on page 299 such stock market declines, or bear markets, are fairly frequent, and often continue for 15 months or more from market peak to market trough. Only as corporations bring their costs back under control, as inventories are consumed, and as production again appears on the increase, can investors anticipate higher corporate earnings, and only then will they be willing to pay higher stock prices again. Not all bear markets occur because of depressed earnings, but a great many have in the past. Even if earnings do not continue to fluctuate as widely in the future, investor expectations may well continue to fluctuate, and to the extent that they do, financial risk will continue to affect stock prices adversely.

During periods of depressed corporate earnings, investors are usually unwilling to pay even reasonable prices for stocks. Especially those stocks that have sold at excessively high prices during economic booms will sell at excessively depressed prices during market troughs. Such low prices may be highly attractive to any investor who is inclined toward managing an aggressive portfolio. If he can control his own emotions, such an investor may be able to buy very good, well-established companies whose stocks are selling at very reasonable prices. By buying such stocks at such low prices, the aggressive investor can experience considerably more than average rates of return on his portfolio over time. Of course, he may select stocks whose earnings will continue at depressed levels for some time after he has purchased them, and his patience may wear very thin if the appreciation he anticipates does not materialize as rapidly as he anticipated. Furthermore, he may buy stocks whose earnings and prices continue to decline for a while after he has bought them; in such cases, even his courage may wear thin. Nevertheless, if he can buy a good stock like Tried and True Shoe for $40, after it sold for $80 at the peak of the bull market, and it has really been worth $60 all the time, he has in fact bought a real bargain.

After extended periods of market decline, investors may be able to buy good stocks selling at temporarily depressed prices because of temporarily depressed earnings. For such investors, financial risk may be considered an opportunity to buy unusually good stocks at very low prices. Since the appreciation of stock prices is usually considerably greater than average during the two or three years following a recession, even for quite risky growth stocks, by buying good stocks at depressed prices, the aggressive investor need not assume nearly as much risk as he usually would in order to acquire stocks with considerable possibility for price appreciation. Whether the investor decides to select relative young companies with superior growth potential or more well-established companies at temporarily depressed prices, the purchase of stocks with more financial risk can be exceptionally rewarding if their earnings actually do increase at above average rates.

Market Risk. In addition to the stocks whose prices decline during bear markets because their earnings are depressed, there are also stocks that experience such declines in their market prices despite growth or stability of their earnings patterns. Sometimes such prices decline because investors become disappointed with some specific company or distrustful of a particular industry. After a long period of excessive enthusiasm, anyone, investor or otherwise, will usually experience a period of emotional depression. Some bear markets are purely the result of such emotional depression. However, emotional pessimism and depression often accompany economic recessions, depressing the prices of most stocks, even those whose earnings are growing, along with those whose earnings are declining. In such instances, some stock prices may continue at relatively low levels long after the earnings of such corporations have resumed their upward trend simply because those stocks have long been out of favor with investors.

Any stock that has the loyalty of a large number of investors must have earned that loyalty. Any stock that is currently out of favor probably had such investor loyalty at one time. However, those investors who were most loyal to any given corporation whose earnings collapsed, suffered the most from disastrous declines in its stock price since they are the ones who held their stocks the longest. As a matter of fact, a stock that is seriously depressed below prices at which it once sold, may have caused serious losses to almost all of the investors who have owned the stock. Since no one likes to be hurt, and especially twice by the same stock, investors who were loyal once but got hurt, are often disinclined to buy that stock again. They may yet be trying to sell the stock at some reasonable price. As new investors express interest in the stock because of its earnings growth, they will bid higher prices for the stock, but the existing stockholders may rush to sell at just slightly higher prices because they have no confidence in the stock's ability to hold those higher prices. They cannot believe that the corporation will be able to sustain its improved earnings position. For extended periods of time, therefore, stocks with depressed prices may continue to sell at such depressed prices, simply because the potential supply of stock exceeds potential demand. For aggressive investors who are seeking undervalued securities such depressed market prices can prove to be real bargains.

The primary requirements for success in selecting such securities are a willingness to search for stocks whose earnings have been increasing without proportionate increases in their market prices, and a willingness to hold those stocks patiently, thoroughly convinced that still higher earnings and more rapid price appreciation are just around the corner. Such searching, patience, and conviction can be highly rewarding. However, as in the case of stocks purchased for aggressive portfolios because their earnings are temporarily depressed, so in the case of stocks purchased at temporarily depressed prices despite their stable earnings patterns, when the prices of those stocks have appreciated to more reasonable levels, they should be sold. Rather than holding your stocks indefinitely, as you would in managing a defensive portfolio, when managing an aggressive portfolio, you would purchase stocks in anticipation of unusual price appreciation, and after that appreciation has run its course, sell the stocks to finance the purchase of still other undervalued securities.

There is some danger that an investor managing an aggressive portfolio could become a stock trader, and stock trading can hardly be profitable. However, if the investor is primarily seeking stocks whose prices have been depressed for a year or more for the purpose of holding those stocks for several years, although not indefinitely, the danger of becoming a market trader, or speculator, is relatively slight. Although temporary market fluctuations can be confused with major cyclical swings, and an investor might well misjudge the timing of his purchases somewhat, an understanding of major bull markets and bear markets should facilitate the appropriate implementation of aggressive portfolio policies. As indicated in Table 9–1, from 1900 through the early 1970's, 19 bear markets have occurred. All these bear markets have provided unusual opportunities for the aggressive investor. Since World War II, seven such bear markets have occurred. In each of those instances, market prices in general were significantly depressed, often more than 20 percent below their previous market peaks. On all such occasions, several months of market decline preceded the market trough. The recessions of 1949, 1953, 1957, and 1960 provided the aggressive investor with opportunities resulting from a combination of financial risk and market risk, whereas the bear markets of 1962, 1966, and 1969 were not accompanied by recessions, although some corporate earnings did decline during 1969 and 1970.

Although no investor can know for sure that stock prices will decline another 20 percent every three and one-half years, he may, nevertheless, be fairly certain that frequent market fluctuations will occur in response to fluctuating corporate earnings and fluctuating investor confidence. On those occasions when bear markets do occur, unusual investment opportunities do exist for the more aggressively oriented portfolio manager. Consequently, the assumption of additional market risk is surely one means of achieving a higher than average rate of return on the portfolio.

Table 9-1 Bear Markets from 1900 (as indicated by the Dow-Jones Industrial Average)

	Year	Percentage Decline (from peak to trough)	Length of Decline (in months)
1	1900	32	12
2	1903	38	10
3	1907	45	10
4	1909	26	8
5	1912	24	26
6	1917	40	13
7	1919	47	21
8	1923	19	7
9	1926	17	2
10	1929	90	34
11	1934	24	9
12	1937	52	56
13	1946	25	37
14	1953	14	9
15	1957	20	6
16	1960	18	10
17	1962	29	6
18	1966	26	8
19	1969	36	17
Average		33	16

Source: Harry D. Shultz, *Bear Markets: How to Survive and Make Money in Them* (Englewood Cliffs, N.J.: Prentice Hall, Inc., 1964). Reprinted by permission.

Inflation Risk. When the manager of a defensive investment portfolio considers inflation risk, he is primarily concerned with various means of avoiding that risk, whereas the manager of an aggressive investment portfolio is primarily concerned with selecting those stocks that might promise an above average rate of return because of inflation. Specifically, an aggressive investor may profit from inflation to the extent that he buys growth stocks representing growth companies in growth industries with newer or greater demand, especially if those companies have relatively high fixed-cost structures. In such cases, three distinct forces work together for higher corporate profits. First, inflation is a period in which prices in general are rising. Second, newer companies in newer industries producing newer products, generally face greater demand for their products than they can supply; as consumers become more familiar with those products, and demand increases still more, the prices on such products must naturally rise still more creating even higher profits. During periods of inflation when prices in general are rising, higher prices are rather readily accepted as normal. Consequently, for those corporations producing new products for which there is excessive demand compared to supply, they may be able to raise their prices even faster in periods of inflation than they would during periods of stable prices. Therefore, the profits experienced by such corporations may be considerably greater during periods of inflation than they would have been without such inflation.

Furthermore, growth stocks representing growth companies in growth industries with relatively high fixed-cost structures will make even higher profits because most of their costs are fixed. During periods of inflation, most corporations must raise their prices because they must pay higher prices for such variable inputs as raw materials and other supplies, and higher wages to their employees. But those corporations that have few variable costs inputs, that is, those that have relatively high fixed-cost inputs, such as plant and equipment, do not experience as much cost pressure on their profits. Nevertheless, they may be just as able as any other corporation to raise the prices on their products during periods of inflation. With their prices rising, and their costs rising less rapidly, therefore, their profits may increase even more rapidly during periods of inflation than they would during periods of stable prices.

For the investor who is managing an aggressive portfolio, therefore, inflation is a time to find growth stocks representing growth companies in growth industries, especially those facing newer or greater consumer demand for their products, that have relatively high fixed-cost structures. The profits of such companies should increase more rapidly than average during a period of inflation, and of course, their stock prices should appreciate dramatically. Rather than seeing inflation risk as a possibility of declining purchasing power, the aggressive investor can view inflation risk as a primary cause of unusual buying opportunities in certain select stocks. Not only may he protect his portfolio against inflation risk, he may profit because of it. As inflation has become a more serious risk, all portfolio managers have been forced to recognize its potency in destroying value. The aggressive investor, however, should not ignore inflation just because he does not perceive conservation of value as his primary concern; inflation is undoubtedly destructive in a million ways and simply must be overcome to insure portfolio success.

One warning must be sounded. Although stock prices tend to rise during periods of inflation, stock prices do not automatically rise during all periods of inflation. When inflation becomes quite severe, the monetary and fiscal authorities are forced to initiate tight money policies to restrain the inflationary bias in the economy. When such tight money policies are instituted, corporations and individuals are not able to acquire all the loans from their banks that they want, and thus must turn to the securities markets as their second best source of liquidity. The bear markets of 1966 and 1969 are good examples of serious stock and bond market declines in response to governmental counterinflationary efforts. Although stocks do serve as a hedge against inflation, and some stocks actually do appreciate more rapidly because of inflation, the possibility of a general decline in market prices in response to counterinflationary monetary policies is very real and very serious, especially for the aggressive portfolio manager, but somewhat for the defensive portfolio manager. Rather than experiencing portfolio loss in terms of purchasing power alone, inflation risk may also have a serious impact upon the dollar market value of the portfolio. To whatever extent the aggressive portfolio includes stocks whose market prices should respond better than average during periods of inflation, any counterinflationary monetary policies will cause serious declines in the portfolio value. Although such declines are serious and dramatic, they are relatively short, whereas inflation is certain to be very important. Consequently, the aggressive investor must consider inflation risk as one of the best among those he may assume in his effort to achieve a higher than average portfolio return.

Interest-Rate Risk.   Whereas the defensive portfolio manager would buy common stocks in an effort to avoid interest-rate risk, the aggressive portfolio manager would buy longer term, high-grade bonds in anticipation of declining interest rates. Just as such high-grade bonds decline in market price during periods of rising interest rate, so those same bonds will rise in price during periods of declining interest rates. For example, that same $1,000 bond with a 5 percent coupon that declined to $900 when the current interest rate is at 6 percent, would again climb to its par value if the interest rate were to fall to 5 percent again. In order to aggressively assume interest-rate risk with the hope of better than average portfolio returns, the aggressive investor would buy bonds at depressed market prices in anticipation of declining interest rates. As a matter of fact, some outright speculators consider the purchase of U.S. Treasury bonds at depressed prices to be the very best of all possible speculations.

During bear markets amidst recessionary periods, interest rates fall. The aggressive portfolio manager may be highly attracted to bonds. At such times when corporate production, profits, and stock prices are seriously depressed, stocks are by no means the best investments. At those same times, government spending programs, tax programs, and monetary policies are directed at stimulating employment, production, and income through the introduction of additional money into the economy. Such increases in the supply of money will cause the price of money, that is, the interest rate, to decline. Declining interest rates cause the prices of outstanding bonds to rise. Furthermore, as one of its major means of increasing the money supply, the Federal Reserve System buys government bonds from banks and other institutions; it pays for those bonds with money. As the Federal Reserve System demands more bonds, the prices on those bonds rise still more. Gradually, more and more banks are inclined to exchange their bonds for money; and as the banks acquire more monetary reserves, interest rates fall still further to attract more borrowers who can put those loan funds to productive use. As a counterrecessionary policy, the Federal Reserve System buys bonds from banks to increase the money supply to lower interest rates to attract more borrowers who will use those funds to employ more workers to increase production and to increase income.

As a byproduct of the open market operations of the Federal Reserve System, the aggressive portfolio manager can increase his return by buying high-grade bonds with the expectation that their prices will appreciate as interest rates continue to fall; thus the aggressive investor cooperates with the Federal Reserve System, although incidentally. Actually, he buys those bonds for the purpose of increasing the return on his portfolio at the exact time when the common stocks he holds in the portfolio may experience disastrous declines. By switching some of his portfolio funds from growth stocks into longer term, high-grade bonds, he can reduce the impact of a general stock market decline. After interest rates have declined materially, and bond prices have risen materially, he may then sell those bonds to reacquire his growth stocks at prices perhaps 30 percent or more below their previous peaks. Such portfolio management requires considerable facility in forecasting, timing, and decisive action. By no means all aggressive portfolio managers would be willing to assume such additional interest-rate risk, but some may.

By using a portfolio approach, the aggressive investor may assume several different risks at the same time by holding several different securities. For example, one stock with poor earnings may be acquired; another may be acquired at a low price despite good earnings. At the same time, the portfolio might include some stocks that appear likely to profit rather well because of inflation. All three of these risks, financial, market, and inflation, might be assumed to an above average degree during a period of market expansion, that is, during a bull market. On the other hand, if stock market prices continued to rise rather rapidly, and especially if price-earnings multiples continued to rise, the investor might become less inclined to assume more risk. After three, four, or five years of a bull market, prices and price-earnings multiples are usually above reasonable levels. At such times, the aggressive investor might well choose to sell some of the stocks he bought to assume financial and market risk. Especially if the bull market accompanied a sizable economic expansion, perhaps he should sell many stocks, and buy bonds to assume additional interest-rate risk, in anticipation of declining levels of economic activity, declining stock prices, falling interest rates, and rising bond prices. Although many aggressive investors may be disinclined to assume additional interest-rate risk, total portfolio values may be seriously depressed if an investor continues to hold the same securities during a market decline that he held during the previous market upswing. Consequently, at the very least, the investor might sell several higher-risk stocks, and hold cash in anticipation of future purchases during the next anticipated market trough. Although forecasting such market peaks and troughs accurately is impossible, no special facility is required to anticipate a downturn after four years of rapid appreciation, or an upturn afte 15 months of precipitous decline. To the extent that the aggressive investor can anticipate such major stock swings, the return on his portfolio will be considerably above 9 percent.

SUMMARY

Building an investment portfolio may well be the key to your own personal financial security. Whether you decide to construct a defensive portfolio, or an aggressive one, you should use a portfolio approach in either case. By selecting the appropriate proportions of conservative, growth, and speculative stocks, you can construct whatever portfolio you decide is preferable. By emphasizing conservative securities, using diversification liberally, and using dollar cost averaging, you may reach a modest portfolio goal while maintaining considerable safety of principal, adequate liquidity, and reasonable income. By emphasizing growth stocks, and perhaps speculative stocks to some extent, you may well be able to reach a more ambitious portfolio goal, but you must assume more risk to do so.

The particular portfolio goal that is appropriate for any given investor will depend primarily upon the income that he expects to receive from that portfolio in the future. If he expects a larger portfolio income, the goal must be correspondingly larger. However, an investor may not be able to reach his desired goal; whether or not he can will depend upon the number of years available to him over which he may construct and manage his portfolio, the amount of annual savings he can invest, and the time, effort, and skill he can apply in managing his portfolio. If the investor has more time and annual savings, a considerably more defensive approach may be adequate to enable him to reach his chosen goal. He may not even need an average rate of return. On the other hand, if the investor wants a larger future income from his portfolio, or has fewer years available in which to construct and manage his portfolio, he may have little choice but to adopt an aggressive portfolio approach to earn a higher than average rate of return. Such an aggressive approach, however, will require the application of different, more difficult, portfolio policies requiring additional supervision and management.

For many relatively young, middle-income, professional people, a slightly aggressive portfolio approach, in expectation of a slightly above average rate of return, may well be desirable. Although such an approach does require additional managerial effort, many investors consider the additional rate of return worth the additional effort. A highly aggressive approach, of course, creates truly monumental obstacles in the path to portfolio success. However, if the investor uses a more defensive approach in the earlier stages of his investment program, and only assumes a slightly aggressive approach as he acquires more experience and facility with his investment efforts, the additional reward for a slightly aggressive portfolio effort might well be considerably greater than the additional effort required.

Case Problems

1. Mrs. Martha Jones was recently widowed. Her husband left her 200 shares of XYZ Corporation. He had acquired these shares through profit sharing while working for XYZ. Mrs. Jones is concerned whether these shares are the right investment for her. Her husband never did anything with his portfolio; he merely let the shares accumulate. Mrs. Jones asked her minister for advice. The minister informed her he didn't know much about financial matters, and suggested that she contact you for an explanation of portfolio construction. How about it?

2. Mike Fay, 25, is a college student. Mike has been thinking about what type of portfolio approach would suit him best. He considered his present circumstances, and decided that he will have an aggressive portfolio approach of 20% speculative stocks, 60% growth stocks and 20% conservative stocks. Mike is relieved that he has his portfolio approach solved, and will not have to bother with that again. What advice would you offer Mike?

3. In the past Kevin Sudin has had his entire portfolio in only one stock. Just recently somebody explained the problem with such a portfolio, and advised Kevin to diversify. He is not quite sure how to do so. Explain to Kevin the different ways that one can devise a diversified portfolio.

4. Bernie Downshaw is a relief pitcher for the Chicago White Sox. Despite the team's bad performance last season, Bernie received a big raise. You see Bernie had a big year, three victories, two saves, and only 18 losses. Well, Bernie has two problems. One is his pitching, and the other is investing his money. Bernie may solve one problem by becoming a short-stop, but he wants to solve the other by investing in the stocks. However, Bernie doesn't have a lot of time to fool around with his investments. He is looking for some investing technique that will help him. What would you suggest?

5. Terry Cloth is building an investment portfolio. He has decided a defensive policy is the best for himself at the present. In addition he would like to avoid financial risk. He has read that dollar cost averaging may help avoid financial risk. Terry doesn't understand how this is possible. Try to explain to Terry how dollar cost averaging avoids financial risk.

6. Martha Black and her son Hubert, are classified as very conservative investors. Their primary objective is to maintain the portfolio. Hubert is in charge of managing the funds. Hubert is quite proud. Over the ten years he has been managing the portfolio, its size hasn't gone down one dollar. "Yes sir," he says, "$20,000 ten years ago, and $20,000 today." Considering their goal of simply maintaining value, has Hubert been successful? Please explain.

7. The defensive portfolio manager would buy bonds to avoid financial risk, whereas the aggressive investor would buy growth common stocks to assume more financial risk. Explain why the two approaches are effective for each investor's goals.

8. The defensive portfolio manager would buy common stocks in an effort to avoid interest-rate risk, whereas the aggressive portfolio manager would buy longer term, high-grade bonds in anticipation of declining interest rates. Explain why these approaches are taken and how they are effective.

Selected Readings

Bellemore, Douglas H. *Investments Principles, Practices and Analysis.* 3rd edition. Cincinnati: South-Western Publishing Company, 1966.

Hayes, Douglas A. *Investments: Analysis and Management.* New York: The Macmillan Company, 1966.

Sauvain, Harry C. *Investment Management.* 3rd edition. Englewood Cliffs, N.J.: Prentice-Hall, Inc., 1967.

go to pg 319

CHAPTER **TEN**

SELECTING YOUR INVESTMENTS

Although learning about what a stock is and where, how and why to buy it may be an interesting and entertaining intellectual effort, it is no more than an academic exercise unless at some time you actually decide to buy some specific stock. Even deciding to take a specific portfolio approach to investing, and selecting an appropriate portfolio goal, are no more than academic exercises unless you actually select some specific stock for inclusion in your portfolio. Considering the difficulty that many people have in saving money for investment purposes, you might well expect them to give careful consideration to the various alternative stocks available for purchase. You might expect any investor to give careful consideration to just exactly what kind of performance he wants from his investment portfolio. You might expect him to consider any new purchase in the light of the securities already held in that portfolio. You might also expect him to investigate rather thoroughly the management, competition, and uniqueness of the companies he considers, as well as the financial characteristics of those companies. Especially considering the ready availability of such information, you might expect him to be rather cautious in his selection process, and highly selective in his ultimate decisions. You might expect all this, but you probably know enough about human nature to suspect relatively little investigation prior to selection, and relatively little selection prior to purchase. If this is what you suspect, you are right.

Judging by the way too many investors act, one would suppose that it is exceedingly difficult to determine investment objectives, or that there are no selection tools that could aid an investor in properly selecting securities for his portfolio. One might even suppose that there are no sources of information available to provide the least amount of financial data about corporations. As a matter of fact, the actions of some investors utterly defy explanation. There are identifiable investment objectives; there are widely used qualitative and quantitative selection tools; and there are many publications, many of them free, that provide adequate, even excessive, financial data. Perhaps some investors are unaware of these aids; perhaps still others may be so anxious to invest their $300 that they are psychologically incapable of a five-minute investigation.

For best results, however, for maximum return, you should select your investments in the light of your chosen portfolio approach, your investment objectives, your existing portfolio holdings, and the results of your investigation of the various companies whose stock you have considered for purchase. This is true whether you choose to buy conservative stocks, growth stocks, or speculative stocks. To some extent it is even true if you are planning to buy shares in a ready-made, professionally managed portfolio. Proper selection does not require exhaustive investigations. Most investors could improve their selection process merely by answering a very short check list of questions about each company they consider. In this chapter, such a check list is proposed for the purpose of better enabling you to select your investments. No matter how much you learn about investing, the ultimate results of your portfolio will be determined by the stocks composing that portfolio. The selection of those stocks should not be left to chance. Professional advice should be sought and used, of course, but ultimately each investor must accept some responsibility for managing his own portfolio, and he can only do so intelligently by understanding the selection process and participating in that process himself.

Although there are no techniques guaranteed to enable you to select profitable stocks, there are numerous investment tools that can be of assistance. In the assumption of risk, there is by necessity some possibility of loss. With the use of appropriate selection tools, however, that risk can be reduced with little or no reduction in return, or the return can be increased for any level of risk assumption. This is exactly the purpose of careful selection. Some of these selection techniques are qualitative in nature and are very difficult to measure. Nevertheless, they are exceedingly important and must not be ignored. Particularly important to any corporation are the quality of its management, the competition it faces from other firms, and any unique features, such as patents, consumer confidence, individual leadership, research, and similar items, that distinguish it from other firms. Still other selection tools can be measured rather well, such as expensiveness, profitability, earnings growth, indebtedness, and financial liquidity. These quantitative measures provide valuable clues to a stock's potential success in meeting your financial objectives. By understanding the proper role of each of these factors, and by subjecting each specific stock, either currently held or being considered for purchase, to a check list you may be able to select your investments with more confidence.

QUALITATIVE FACTORS

The importance of qualitative factors in selecting stocks can be easily overlooked in a mass of financial data, analyses, and predictions. Charts, ratios, regression analyses, and moving averages, as well as many other quantitative tools have a rather exotic flavor for some people, and as a result they may overlook such mundane matters as competent management, competitive conditions, or a corporation's unique market position. For many investors, however, the qualitative factors may be the only ones they really understand. Such investors should use those indicators that they do understand, rather than pretend that they understand anything about quantitative security analysis, much less actually make selections on such bases. It is important to keep in mind, however, that good quality to an investor means good, stable, dependable, adequate earnings, dividend, and stock price patterns, rather than just quality brand names or even products.

Actually, there are worse ways to select stocks than on the basis of qualitative factors. Numerous investment clubs have been formed by women simply because their husbands formed similar clubs for men exclusively, and the wives, using only qualitative factors to select their stocks, tend to beat the men who rely upon quantitative factors in choosing their stocks. Although an explanation of why the men tend to perform rather badly in such efforts should probably include more than their use of quantitative selection techniques, the explanation of the women's success appears to lie squarely on their use of qualitative factors. They apparently sit around their coffee tables discussing the youth of the nation, and the new products they have tried recently. When they come across a new cleanser, cosmetic, frozen dinner, or diet drink that they all like, one of them asks the name of the corporation that manufactures the product. Then they buy that stock. Since probably millions of other women also like that same product, the company's sales soar skyward with an appropriate increase in its profits, and a corresponding rise in the price of its stock.

Just exactly which qualitative factors should be considered is a subject of some debate, but among them must be the management, competition, and uniqueness of the corporation. Although even better selection may result from qualitative *and* quantitative analysis, rather than just one or the other, if only one is to be used, the qualitative analysis may be more important, especially for the long-term defensive portfolio manager.

MANAGEMENT

The importance of selecting stocks that represent companies managed by capable people can hardly be overemphasized. In a very real sense, competition and uniqueness are little more than measures of the difficulties and problems that a corporation's management must face. Management is indeed a key factor in the financial success of a corporation. Poor management can ruin a good corporation. Good management can sometimes build a terrible corporation into a real winner. If there were only some simple way to determine the difference between good management and bad management, or even some way to determine when good management is deteriorating or when incompetent management is improving, this might be the only selection technique needed to construct an exceedingly profitable investment portfolio. Unfortunately, there is no such simple method. It is possible, however, to estimate the quality of management by determining the attitudes of those people whom managers serve, specifically, their customers, employees, and stockholders. Furthermore, it may be possible to estimate the quality of management by evaluating the financial results of their activities, through the use of certain quantitative financial tools. In any of these efforts, however, no one measure of financial success should be considered an end in and of itself; each measuring device is merely one technique for estimating the quality of management in an effort to determine the advisability of selecting a particular stock for inclusion in a portfolio. Just as capable management is essential to building a successful investment portfolio, so competent and successful management is essential to corporate profits and higher stock prices. With quality management, acceptable profits will be earned, and stockholders will be appropriately rewarded for the risk they have assumed.

Customer Relations. One of the more direct ways to determine the quality of management for any corporation is to buy its products. Some corporations have built tremendous reputations for satisfying their customers. Others have no such reputation and apparently make little or no effort to build such customer loyalty. Although it may be possible in some cases to operate profitably without good customer relations, at least for a while, the better managements place strong emphasis on selling good products and guaranteeing the performance of those products. They take pride in satisfying customers' desires with all their products, and in producing new and better products. The success of any management's efforts to develop such customer relations is the very heart of its reputation, and ultimately, the source of its survival. By selecting stocks whose managements have long emphasized the importance of satisfied customers, an investor is buying stocks that are very likely to maintain their sales, earnings, and dividend patterns (quantitative factors).

All companies make mistakes, of course. Occasionally, a new product may be a disastrous failure. On the other hand, a company may make a new product that succeeds beyond anyone's wildest dream. When such new products are produced by a major company that is capable of rapid expansion and wide distribution, the impact of that new product upon the profits of that corporation can be as truly heart-warming to a stockholder as the product itself is to a customer. If a new product is produced by an old well-established firm, more customers will be willing to try it more quickly. Furthermore, most people are more than willing to pay reasonable prices for products sold by dependable and customer-conscious manufacturers. Those corporations that over the years have been successful in developing good product lines, that have been well received by millions of happy customers, are indeed blessed with capable management, and the purchases of those happy customers tend to make managers and stockholders happy as well. You can do a whole lot worse than buy stocks in corporations with millions of satisfied customers.

Employee Relations.   A second indicator of a capable and effective management team is the reputation it has for relating well to its employees. Since employees can have a significant impact on corporate profits, and therefore, on stock prices, any investor is well advised to consider the labor-management relations of a company whose stock he is considering for purchase. Although any corporation may occasionally have difficulties with its employees in negotiating wages and working conditions, effective corporate managements are seriously interested in maintaining good labor-relations. However, some corporate managements seem to make little or no effort to maintain good employee morale, and as a result the attitudes of their employees leave much to be desired. Still others apparently try to maintain good relations, but are exceedingly ineffective. In such a corporation, there is little communication and much distrust between management and labor. Some of these problems may derive from difficulties caused years earlier either by management or labor, but at this point it hardly matters. What does matter is that the employees have relatively little respect for the management, and consequently those employees will not do their utmost to make their management successful. Corporations with good management teams are concerned about their employees, their wages and working conditions, and their morale, not just because happier employees help produce better products and profits, but essentially because both management and employees have mutual respect for each other and the functions each performs.

Good employee morale not only indicates effective management, it makes management effective since management must accomplish its work through its employees. On the other hand, poor employee morale tends to have an adverse effect upon workmanship; poor workmanship tends to create waste, increase cost, and produce less dependable products. Furthermore, such an environment tends to result in more frequent and extensive strikes, causing still more waste, still higher costs, and still less dependable product flow to the customer. Corporations with poor employee relations tend to lose many of their better employees, and find it ever more difficult to attract better employees. The impact of such poor employee relations upon product quality, customer attitudes, and corporate profits can hardly be ignored. Although well-enforced cost control measures can indeed do much to maintain product quality and corporate profits for a while, the life of that corporation is somewhat less healthy than it would be if the corporation were managed by more capable men.

The stocks of companies with good employee relations do tend to perform better, and for the stockholder, this may well be a primary concern. Very simply, there is less risk in such stock ownership. Although the stocks of corporations with poor employee relations are often quite reasonably priced, those relatively low stock prices often reflect a conviction on the part of investors that the corporations' problems, and their relatively mediocre earnings in the past, will be continued in the future. If a major shake-up in the management of such a corporation should occur, however, the selection of such a stock might be considered on the basis of potential appreciation due to improved efficiency. Otherwise, the investor should probably avoid the securities of companies whose managements cannot maintain good employee relations, in favor of stocks of those that can. With all the risks that even good companies face, there is little sense in selecting stocks of companies whose managements are creating still more problems for themselves through their inappropriate attitudes toward their employees, or whose employees are dedicated to the general proposition that all managers should be royally abused. In either case, the corporation is in for trouble, and its customers and stockholders are too, whereas, with a good company with good employee relations, production, sales, earnings, and dividends will all have more dependable patterns. An investor can learn a great deal about a company from its employees, and when employees and management are proud of each other and their company, their stockholders are likely to be proud of them, too.

Stockholder Relations.   Stockholders' attitudes toward the management of a corporation are very important to the value of that company's stock. If stockholders have profited in the past from the successful decisions of a management, they tend to have high regard for that corporation and its stock. If management is concerned about its stockholders and communicates that concern, stockholders tend to repay their managers by supporting their managers' requests and decisions. If managers try to protect their stockholders from excessive fluctuations in corporate earnings, dividends, and stock prices, their stockholders tend to value more highly whatever earnings, dividends, and growth their managers are able to provide. All these indications of concern tend to establish good relations between a management and its stockholders, and will go far toward enabling any management to weather a temporary storm.

But not all managements are so concerned about their stockholders. Some make no efforts to stabilize stock prices but rather seem to encourage rampant speculation when it starts. As a result, their stocks' prices rise excessively far beyond anything their earnings could reasonably support, for some time; then those prices fall disastrously, and many stockholders lose all faith in their managements. Some managements mislead stockholders, analysts, and potential investors with wild exaggerations of expected earnings. Consequently, their stocks rise dramatically, only to fall just as dramatically when actual earnings are ultimately reported. Some managements seem to be far more concerned about feathering their own nests through exercising stock option plans at low prices for resale at excessively high prices. Such managers apparently want and expect little stockholder loyalty, and indeed they get exactly that. The stocks of such corporations tend to be valued less per any dollar of earnings and rightly so, since those managements create additional risks for their own stockholders. Occasionally, investors may feel such a stock is a real bargain at its going price, and it may be, but generally speaking, those managers with poor stockholder relations tend to get themselves into serious financial trouble at some time. When they do, years may pass before many investors again trust the corporation enough to buy any more of the stock at even reasonable prices. Good managements try to maintain good relations with their stockholders, just as they do with their customers and employees and earn reputations for such concern. The resulting stockholder confidence tends to be reflected in higher price-earnings multiples and greater resistance to stock-price declines.

There are other groups with whom management must communicate, but stockholders, employees and customers are the most important. If a management can deal sufficiently effectively with them to build a reputation of ability, foresight, and fairness, probably any other group would indicate a similar attitude. Therefore, the attitudes of a corporation's customers, employees, and stockholders can provide a fairly accurate picture of a management's ability to solve its problems effectively, and as such do provide some clue to the advisability of selecting given securities for your portfolio. There may be more accurate ways to select one specific stock in preference to another, but there are worse ways, too.

COMPETITION

A second qualitative factor that may indicate the value of a stock is the amount of competition a firm faces from other firms in its industry, from firms in closely related industries, and from firms in other countries. Some managements face great competition, much resistance to higher prices, considerable cost pressures, and consequently, relatively low profit margins that are forever in danger of becoming losses. Under such difficulties, good management is extremely important, and the degree of competition will indeed determine just how competent each management team really is. Under less competitive conditions, a company can make money, and even expand, with less capable management. However, under extremely competitive conditions, even a very good management team may not be able to maintain dependable earnings and dividend patterns.

Intra-Industry Competition. In recent decades, a number of corporations in the manufacturing industries have grown rather dramatically as smaller companies have merged with larger ones, and in many cases, the huge capital requirements needed to compete with these dominant firms have kept new companies from succeeding or even getting started. In most manufacturing industries, three or four firms manufacture most of the output. They are extremely large, well diversified and well financed. The risk any investor assumes when he buys the stock of such corporations is much less than the risk assumed by investors in those companies or industries in earlier decades. In most manufacturing industries, the investor can find major firms with good managements capable of solving their problems and maintaining their financial positions rather well. In general, management may face relatively restrained competition. On certain occasions, however, an industry composed of only a few large firms such as the chemical fiber or airline industry may experience a rather high degree of competition after a time of unusual expansion that has created a manufacturing capacity that greatly exceeds consumer demand. Furthermore, in the case of certain retail corporations, competitive conditions may continually depress profits regardless of the quality of management.

Adverse competitive conditions might very well cause an investor to select the stocks of corporations whose managements face less competition, such as General Motors, Alcoa, I. B. M. or Xerox. By using such a quality selection device, an investor may select only stocks of large, well-established corporations, perhaps the acknowledged leaders in their industries, with the expectation that such companies will have sufficiently capable managers to solve any problems that might interrupt their established earnings and dividend patterns. Stocks of such corporations tend to be fairly stable around a moderate growth curve permitting reasonably accurate prediction of future value, and providing considerable protection against risk. On the other hand, in stocks of more competitive firms, more fluctuation occurs, more risk exists, and more time, care, and attention must be spent in selecting such stocks.

Inter-Industry Competition. In some industries, there may be one, three, or four well-established corporations whose stocks an investor might reasonably expect to perform rather well over time. However, when well-established corporations in other industries offer substitute products at lower prices, the competitive constraints upon managements are exceedingly severe. The steel industry is an example of such a situation; U.S. Steel and Bethlehem Steel are such corporations. Because of competition by the aluminum, glass, paper, and plastic industries, as well as international competition in steel, the competitive difficulties of even the leading companies in the steel industry have been very severe.

When you consider the cyclical nature of the steel industry (that is, the way the steel industry fluctuates over time), the managements of the various steel companies have some serious problems to solve, indeed. As a result, their earnings and dividend patterns are less dependable than they might be with less inter-industry competition. Because of such uncertainties, investors who might select steel stocks for their portfolios, are less inclined to do so. In fact, steel companies have had real difficulty in maintaining sufficiently high prices of their products to provide adequate funds for needed purchases of new plant and equipment. Furthermore, because of the industry's uncertainties, the steel corporations have faced rather serious problems in raising additional needed funds through the issuance of additional stocks and bonds. As a result, they have not been able to improve the quality of their plant and equipment as rapidly as they should in order to improve their competitive positions. In addition, they have had some rather serious difficulties in negotiating contracts with their employees' unions, in most cases finding themselves forced into paying higher wages without being able to increase productivity. Because of their competitive situation, they have found it extremely difficult to pass these additional wage payments on to their ultimate customers through frequent or sizable steel price increases.

As a result of these problems, the future of the steel companies has been much less bright than the profit pictures of some corporations with which they compete on an inter-industry basis. Some of these other industries have real competitive advantages, and their profit potential seems more attractive. Investors, therefore, have been somewhat disinclined to invest in steel stocks, and rightly so since aluminum and plastics may very well do better. Similarly, in the case of other securities representing companies facing serious inter-industry competition, the risk may exceed the amount some investors are willing to assume.

On the other hand, the time may come when the price of a depressed stock reaches so low a level, that the investor considers it unreasonably depressed. Furthermore, the investor may believe that, regardless of the seriousness of the situation, the quality of management in a given corporation may be sufficient to warrant purchase of that stock with the expectation of above average performance in the future. In such cases as these, the investor might very well decide that a stock representing a company that had faced such inter-industry competition was a desirable purchase. Generally, inter-industry competition can be used as a qualitative measure to aid the investor in selecting stocks. If he wishes to avoid risk, he should sell stocks that suddenly face new competitive problems, and avoid buying those that continually face such competition.

International Competition. One problem that is too often ignored by investors in the United States is that of international competition faced by many corporations. International competition is not usually a serious problem for U.S. industry. In those cases, however, in which international competition is a serious difficulty, investors may be especially hurt because international competition is considered so infrequently. In other countries such as England, Germany or Japan, every citizen may be aware of the importance of international competition as a significant influence upon his life. In this country, there is considerable resistance on the part of many people to goods produced in other countries excluding, of course, those consumer products which we care to exclude, such as bananas, chocolate, coffee, pepper, and rubber. Actually, imports and exports are so small a portion of our total economy that most people are relatively unaware of them and are relatively unconcerned about the problems any firm might face from international competition.

Furthermore, since most of our managers are a product of the economic environment, they are at a comparative disadvantage when dealing with an international problem. When foreign manufacturers are able to produce consumer goods, or industrial goods, that can seriously affect corporate profits of U.S. firms, managers may be somewhat less prepared to deal with this type of competition, than they are to deal with competition from domestic corporations. A similar problem exists for those corporations that are multinational in scope. For example, in the petroleum industry, Gulf, Mobil, Royal Dutch, Texaco, Standard Oil of California, and Standard Oil of New Jersey are examples of such multinational corporations. For all these corporations, international implications have a sizable impact upon their corporate profits.

When corporations face serious competition from other countries, or expand multi-nationally, either in terms of inputs or sales, the managements of those companies assume an entirely different set of limitations, restrictions, and indeterminate relationships. A management that is perfectly capable of handling any difficulties that might arise due to domestic competitors, may suddenly face serious financial, legal, political and social problems about which it has given little or no thought, and for which it has little or no capability. Such a management may be sorely tested when it tries to solve such problems. This is not to say that such obstacles cannot be overcome, or that the considerations of becoming multinational are altogether disadvantageous. On the contrary, there are some very real reasons why some corporations should become multinational in scope; effective handling of their international operations can be exceedingly profitable. Nevertheless, investors who are concerned about the capabilities of a corporation's management to handle problems as they arise, should be especially conscious of unusual conditions that a management might face from international competitors. When a firm has not dealt with international competition but suddenly does face such competition, an investor should be cautious about buying its stock, and if he has previously selected such a stock, he might give serious consideration to selling it.

All of these competitive conditions, whether intra-industry, inter-industry, or international, provide some measure of the problems that any management must face. Those investors who are inclined toward avoiding such difficulties, can use such competition as a measure of desirability in their selection process. By avoiding corporations with unusual problems, an investor assumes less risk since the stocks he does buy will have more earnings, dividend, and price stability. On the other hand, since investors in this country are largely disinclined toward companies facing such competitive problems, the prices of such stocks may sometimes be depressed below their real values, and in such cases an aggressive investor might find an extremely attractive security at a bargain basement price if he can be sure that the managements of such corporations have above average abilities to handle all potential competitive problems.

UNIQUENESS

In the case of some corporations, there may be specific factors that should be given particular emphasis in the selection process. There are many such unique factors that might be considered such as government regulations that can either restrict or guarantee corporate profits; product differentiation that may set apart the products of a particular corporation to the extent that consumers much prefer that particular product even though many others compete with it; patents that may legally prohibit competitors from competing with the patent holders; or some other kind of a monopoly or semimonopoly position that may enable the management of a corporation to profit unusually. In addition to these considerations, a corporation may also be somewhat unique in the consumer demand that it serves. Such factors tend to guarantee the continuous demand by consumers or other manufacturers. In the face of such strong demand, a management might escape any disastrous effects upon its profits, due to cost increases for labor, raw materials, or delivery problems, for example. A decline in the quality of the product or service may even be forgiven simply because there are no competing firms that can satisfy those peculiar consumer demands as well as that unique corporation. Production, sales, earnings, dividends, and stock prices are continuously supported by strong consumer demand for the product.

In addition to the qualitative factors that relate to demand, there are also some similar factors that relate to supply. In particular, those corporations that have considerable control over their costs will not face the excessive cost problems that most corporations face rather regularly. This is particularly true in the case of corporations that have relatively low variable costs, such as raw materials or labor; that is, regardless of the increase in their output, their costs are fairly fixed in nature. If most of the cost of their products has already been incurred—such as the initial cost of research and development, or plant and equipment expenditures—

they can sell more and more quantity without a dramatic increase in production costs. On the other hand, those corporations whose costs are primarily variable, that is, those whose primary inputs are raw materials and labor, may be unable to control costs. In such cases, growth is more costly, rather than more profitable. In the case of those corporations that buy raw materials from a seller who has a monopoly in a raw material, or whose labor belongs to an extremely strong union, profits may forever be on the ragged edge of losses. Any additional profits they make are appropriate targets for their suppliers who are always attempting to raise their prices. The managements of such corporations are indeed hard pressed to maintain their profit margins, their earnings, and their dividend patterns.

An investor who can discover a stock representing a corporation that has all positive, unique characteristics may have found a real investment opportunity. If a corporation has a monopoly position itself, or has government protection for its profits, and at the same time has relatively low labor costs compared to the amount of plant and equipment necessary to produce a product, it may experience steady profit margins, and therefore, dependable earnings and dividend growth patterns. Such securities may be highly attractive. At the very least, they are highly defensive in nature; that is, they experience very little price decline in periods of general economic weakness or depressed stock market prices. Utility stocks are among the best examples of a highly defensive investment; most people will continue to buy electricity and telephone service despite any considerable financial difficulty that their families might face. Although a family in such financial difficulty may well postpone the purchase of a new car, refrigerator, or dishwasher, the purchase of utility services will hardly ever be diminished. Furthermore, the primary costs of such utilities are plant and equipment expenditures, rather than raw materials or labor inputs, and as such, cost pressures are much less than those experienced by automobile or appliance manufacturers. Finally, state utility commissions, charged with the responsibility of supervising utility companies, are much concerned that those firms stay in business, provide additional services, and have the necessary profits to finance normal and required expansion out of retained earnings. If any serious problems should arise, therefore, those commissions should be inclined to permit price increases to guarantee that the services would continue without interruption.

Similarly, those corporations that have acquired patents on major products or manufacturing processes, have often expended huge amounts of money in the research and development necessary to discover and perfect a new product or process, and since those funds have already been spent they are relatively fixed in nature. For example, drug companies may spend huge amounts of money to discover a new drug, but once the process is known, the variable costs of producing a few more pills is slight relative to the initial investment in research. Therefore, as they increase their output and sell the drugs at any price, their profits on those additional sales are very large. Furthermore, if great demand for the new products exists, and if their patents prohibit competition, they may set their prices quite high without fear of losing sales. This monopoly further strengthens profits. Such new products and processes as a Polaroid camera, an I. B. M. computer, or a Xerox copier are all examples of unique positions resulting from exceedingly significant, initial costs in the past but considerable profits once those fixed costs have been paid. With all those profits, a unique company can carry on a truly tremendous research and development program, finding still more and better products and processes, and thereby continue its unique position.

Those investors who are interested in selecting good stocks representing companies with uniquely profitable manufacturing processes or products, may well find that such a selection process may enable them to construct an investment portfolio with more than adequate performance. In fact, using uniqueness as the only selection determinate would insure the placement of some very fine stocks in a portfolio. In addition to all the above qualitative factors, there are still some others not quite as readily identifiable. For example, the unique position of a corporation may well be the result of unusually imaginative and capable management. Those managers may also enable that corporation to attract new people of unusually imaginative capabilities. Since such corporations make a great deal of profit, exceptional people may be more willing to work for such corporations; and to the extent that this is true, they may be able to select their new employees from among exceedingly good applicants. As a matter of fact, this does indeed seem to be the case. To the extent that it is, the futures of such corporations may be as bright as their present since such imaginative and capable people are the basic source of such unique qualitative characteristics.

The qualitative factors are not the only ones to which an investor can look to provide clues to selecting securities, but surely such factors are very important. No investor should ignore such factors as capable management; customer, employee, and stockholder relations; intra-industry, inter-industry, and international competition; protected profits, if not guaranteed profits, resulting from highly differentiated products, patent holdings, government regulations, monopoly or semimonopoly positions. There are, indeed, quantitative tools that may enable the investor to identify an outstanding security; but even without such quantitative tools, the qualitative factors just discussed may enable any investor to select securities that will yield higher than average returns. In a very real sense, the quantitative tools are merely efforts to measure more accurately the historical financial results of the qualitative factors affecting the success of any given corporation. Although there is some probability that better portfolio results can be achieved through the use of quantitative tools along with qualitative tools, better than average results may well follow a selection process that gives serious attention to qualitative factors only. Especially for those investors who are looking to the long run, perhaps even to the exclusion of any short-run fluctuations, they might depend upon qualitative factors alone with considerable success.

Although the qualitative factors discussed should be applied to all corporations in making a selection of a security, there may very well be some specific consideration about a corporation that strikes you as so very important that nothing else really matters. This unusual consideration should be recognized as a uniqueness in your general qualitative evaluation, of course, but sometimes the unusual is so important that all other considerations fade into nothingness. This will seldom happen, but if it happens to you, if you are part of such a corporation, if you are in a position to make the unusual happen, or if you are sufficiently close to such a situation to see the beginning of a truly unique creation, you might very well emphasize such a qualitative factor sufficiently to overlook any other weaknesses in that stock. In any event, the qualitative factors are indeed important to any investor as tools to facilitate appropriate selection of specific stocks. The investor who ignores such factors must surely do so at some serious additional risk. On the other hand, the investor who discovers and recognizes such qualitative factors, will often find them extremely valuable tools in selecting exactly those investments that most appropriately reflect his investment portfolio approach.

QUANTITATIVE FACTORS

Although qualitative factors should play a significant role in the selection of one's investments, many investors want to know more about a given stock. Most investors want to know at least something about the price of the stock, its earnings, its dividends, its growth potential, and perhaps even something about its financial structure. Indeed, financial data are quite important to the selection process of many investors. One need not be a professional investor, however, to appreciate and use some of the more common quantitative selection tools. On the contrary, these tools are so commonly used that they are readily available in published form, and readily understandable and usable by any investor who cares to take advantage of them. (The Appendix to this chapter contains sample data from three widely used financial publications.)

Quantitative factors are especially useful in determining which stock is the best among various good stocks. Even when one restricts his investments to quality stocks, some good companies are better investments than others at particular times. Even good stocks may be overpriced; even those with good profit ratios, and good growth rates can be too expensive. By considering quantitative factors as well as qualitative factors in your selection process, you may be even more successful in your effort to select valuable securities. Essentially, the success of any investor's program will depend upon his ability to buy valuable investments. Five quantitative factors are discussed in this section that may be helpful to you in selecting more valuable investments. By understanding the significance of such quantitative factors as expensiveness, profitability, growth, indebtedness, and liquidity, your selection check list may enable you to compare investment alternatives more effectively and select valuable investments more successfully.

The use of such quantitative tools need not require extensive calculations using volumes of financial data; in many cases, brokerage reports and publications, as well as the annual reports of the corporations themselves, may provide adequate, even excessive, analyses for most investors' purposes. For example, particularly important in any investor's mind is how much he should pay for a stock; that is, is the current price of even a good stock more than it is really worth? Whether or not a stock is too expensive may be determined by using a quantitative tool. Most often, the expensiveness of a stock is measured in terms of the corporation's earnings, either using a price-earnings ratio, or some other valuation technique. Furthermore, most investors are concerned with the past and future profitability of the corporation, and such a profitability measure is usually expressed in terms of an earnings flow related to the total funds invested in the corporation. Another indicator many investors often use is earnings appreciation over time; such a growth in earnings is usually expressed as a percentage change in a corporation's earnings over the last year or several years. In addition to the expensiveness, profitability, and growth indicators, some investors are also much concerned about indebtedness and liquidity measures, which provide some clues to the stability and quality of corporate earnings.

In addition to these five quantitative techniques, which will be discussed in some detail, a whole host of other financial tools could be used to determine the fundamental financial position of a corporation. Some of them are very helpful. In addition to these fundamental analytical tools, there are also several other quantitative techniques that are sometimes used to determine the technical, or market position of a stock; that is, whether or not its present market price shows strength or weakness. Such technical analyses as moving averages, point and figure charts, volume indicators, and price patterns are occasionally used by many, more sophisticated investors. Such technical tools are difficult to interpret at best, and have been rather seriously criticized as thoroughly worthless at worst. There are still other tools, such as regression analyses, that may be used to project various data into the future, for example, earnings and dividend data.

Some quantitative tools duplicate one another, some are of only occasional value, and some may be worthless. Whatever tool an investor uses, if it improves the return on his portfolio, it may be worth the trouble. No one can master all quantitative techniques at once, however, so in this section, the quantitative tools presented are the five fundamental indicators that will facilitate a selection process. If you are interested in still other techniques, or additional explanation of even the five given, to say nothing of an extensive explanation in support of technical indicators, there are many other books on investments that may satisfy your curiosity and interest. If you can come to appreciate the five quantitative tools presented in this section, you should have acquired sufficient understanding to considerably facilitate your selection process. By selecting your investments, using not only quantitative techniques but qualitative ones as well, you should considerably improve the performance of your investment portfolio.

EXPENSIVENESS

The most significant quantitative characteristic of an investment is its expensiveness. This does not mean its price. A $4 stock may be extremely expensive, excessively costly, unreasonably priced whereas a $40 stock, or a $400 stock, may be a real bargain. Anything you buy is only expensive in terms of available alternatives, and the respective abilities of all those alternatives to accomplish your objectives. Just as a $400 car may be overpriced, and a $4,000 car may be a bargain, a $4 investment may be many times more expensive than a $40 investment.

In the case of stock, this may be even more true since all shares of a given stock are identical. Consequently, ten shares of a $4 stock are quite comparable to one share of a $40 stock. The pertinent question is whether or not the ten shares of the $4 stock will accomplish your objectives better than one share of the $40 stock. The fact that one stock has a low price whereas the other has a higher price is utterly irrelevant. Any corporation can split its stock ten shares for one by simply issuing to all its stockholders nine additional shares for each share held; therefore, any $40 stock would become a $4 stock. No one believes that a pie cut into ten pieces is more valuable than a pie that is not cut; the pie cut into ten pieces may be more valuable to you if you like that kind of pie better. Similarly, ten shares of a $4 stock may be better than one share of a $40 stock, but only if those ten shares better enable you to reach your objective, presumably a relatively certain financial return on your portfolio. It all depends on the particular stocks. If AOK sells at $4 and XYZ sells at $40, they may both be fairly priced and equally expensive; whereas two other stocks, selling at $4 and $40 respectively, could be outrageously priced.

Essentially then, expensiveness is a measure that compares the price of a stock and the financial return from owning that stock. Therefore, two questions must be answered to determine the expensiveness of an investment:

1. What is the price of a stock?
2. What is that stock expected to earn?

By asking these two questions about any stock, or any other investment for that matter, a measure of expensiveness can be computed that permits a comparison of all investments. This measure of expensiveness is called a price-earnings ratio (P/E ratio), or a price-earnings multiple (P/E multiple). By dividing the price of a stock by the expected earnings of that stock, each investment can be valued in terms of how expensive that stock is compared to any dollar's worth of earnings, that is the relative willingness of investors to pay a higher or lower price for any corporation's earnings.

For example, if AOK Corp. is expected to earn 40¢ a share this year, the price-earnings ratio would be 10 ($4/$.40 = 10); that is, for every dollar's worth of AOK earnings you want, you must pay $10. Now assume that XYZ Corp. is expected to earn $4 a share. Since it is selling at $40, its price-earnings ratio is also 10 ($40/$4 = 10); that is, for every dollar's worth of XYZ Corp. earnings you want, you must pay $10. By comparing the price-earnings ratios of AOK and XYZ, you can see that neither corporation is more expensive than the other; they are equally priced.

But now consider another $4 stock, Lack Luster Unlimited, Inc., from which no earnings are expected. This corporation has lost money every year for the last ten years, but despite this record, its stockholders believe that someday it will make a profit. No one knows exactly when, and in the immediate future no earnings can be sighted. For the sake of argument, we might grant that five years from now Lack Luster could earn two cents a share. Ignoring the fact that we must wait five years to get our pennies, we could compute a price-earnings ratio for Lack Luster of 80 ($4/$.02 = 80); that is, for every dollar's worth of earnings that you might get from Lack Luster five years from now, you must pay $80 today. Compared with AOK and XYZ, Lack Luster is a very expensive stock. If its profits one day do materialize, and especially if those profits were to increase someday in the future at a significant rate of growth, Lack Luster might be a bargain; and it is exactly on this premise that speculators buy shares of such companies. As an investment today, however, Lack Luster, and all stocks like it, leave a great deal to be desired. When compared with companies with more established earnings patterns, they can hardly be considered investments at all.

Expensiveness, then, can be measured with a price-earnings ratio. However, not all stocks with low P/E ratios are better purchases than all stocks with high P/E ratios. This is particularly true when the P/E ratios being compared have been computed using current prices and current reported earnings. It is less true when the P/E ratios used have been computed using current prices and estimated future earnings. To a considerable extent, a high P/E ratio is an indication of investors' respect for a given management's ability to maintain or increase earnings in the future. If investors doubt a given management's ability to maintain or increase its earnings, those investors are not likely to pay a very high price for any dollar's worth of earnings. On the other hand, if investors in general are convinced that a given corporation has a superior management, capable of satisfying its customers, employees and stockholders with above average performance in every way, those investors will anticipate above average earnings and will be willing to pay a premium price for the stock of that company. If the corporation has been able to increase its earnings at two or three times faster than the increase in the gross national product, such a company would be considered a growth stock, and the P/E ratio of that corporation could well be two or three times the P/E ratio of a more static corporation. There may well be more uncertainty about exactly what the future earnings of such a corporation may be, but there may be relatively little uncertainty that the earnings of the corporation will continue to increase at an above average rate. Since the uncertainty, or the risk, of owning that stock is less than average, it may well be inexpensive at a P/E ratio of 20 or 30. Indeed, some corporations sell for P/E ratios of 40, 50, 60, and above, and do so because investors are convinced that the earnings of those corporations will continue to increase at above average growth rates in the future.

A capitalization rate, or a discount rate, can be used as an alternative to the P/E multiple as a way to evaluate the expensiveness of a stock. A capitalization rate measures value because it is the rate of return investors expect to earn on an investment. With an earnings figure and a capitalization rate, therefore, you can determine value. For example, using AOK Corp, again, investors indicate that they want to earn a 10 percent rate of return on AOK and since they expect AOK to earn 40¢ a share, they will pay $4 per share ($.40 ÷ .10 = $4). Some investors prefer to use a capitalization rate rather than a P/E ratio in their valuation efforts, but actually, either the P/E ratio or the capitalization rate may be used to accomplish the same purpose, since one is merely the reciprocal of the other. (That is, if you divide 1 by a given capitalization rate, you get the appropriate P/E ratio; 1 ÷ .05 = 20. A capitalization rate of .05 is equal to a P/E ratio of 20.) The important point is not whether you use one or the other, but that you realize the relationship of each to risk or uncertainty. Table 10–1 presents a series of capitalization rates and price-earnings ratios as they relate to risk or uncertainty. The greater the uncertainty of any earnings flow, the higher rate of return necessary to attract any investor or, to say it another way, the lower the price per dollar's worth of earnings any investor will pay. On the other hand, the greater the certainty of a stock's earnings, the lower the necessary capitalization rate and the higher the price-earnings multiple will be.

Most large, stable, well-established companies will sell at P/E ratios of between 10 and 20. Occasionally, their P/E ratios may fall below 10,

Table 10–1 Selected Capitalization Rates Translated into Equivalent Price-Earnings Ratios and Degree of Risk

Capitalization Rate (%)			Equivalent Price-Earnings Ratio
1		High	100 to 1
2	{	degree of	50 to 1
4		certainty	25 to 1
5			20 to 1
6		Normal	16.7 to 1
8	{	degree of certainty	12.5 to 1
10		or uncertainty	10 to 1
15			6.7 to 1
20		High	5 to 1
25	{	degree of	4 to 1
33 1/3		uncertainty	3 to 1
50			2 to 1

Source: Frederick Amling, *Investments: An Introduction to Analysis and Management,* 2nd ed., p. 230 © 1970. Reprinted by permission of Prentice Hall, Inc., Englewood Cliffs, N. J.

and occasionally, they may rise above 20, but these occasions are relatively infrequent, and the stocks that experience such excesses are relatively few. For example, consider the stocks in the Dow-Jones Industrial Average, which is a widely used indicator of stock market levels and fluctuations. It consists of 30 large, stable companies, and represents rather well the market performance of such conservative stocks. As the prices of the stocks in the Average change, the Average itself changes; thus the Dow-Jones Industrial Average is an indicator of stock price changes in general. Table 10–2 presents each of the companies included in the Dow-Jones Industrial Average, and presents each company's average P/E ratio for the periods, 1953–1962 and 1957–1966. Those companies whose earnings have been more stable, such as American Tobacco, International Harvester, and Standard Oil, (Calif.), have relatively low P/E ratios, whereas those companies whose earnings have tended to increase more rapidly, such as Alcoa, Eastman Kodak, General Electric, and Westinghouse, sell at somewhat higher than average P/E ratios. Furthermore, higher P/E ratios tend to indicate companies whose earnings are expected to increase in the future more rapidly than normal. Therefore, an investor might expect to pay a higher price relative to a corporation's current earnings if its earnings were increasing faster than average, whereas those companies whose earnings tend to be more stable, will normally sell at lower P/E ratios. Consequently, if you expect American Tobacco to sell around 12 times earnings, and Alcoa to sell around 25 times earnings, you might feel that Alcoa at 18 times earnings was inexpensive, whereas American Tobacco at 18 times earnings was

Table 10–2 P/E Ratios for the Individual Dow-Jones Industrial Companies 1953–1962 and 1957–1966

Company	Average P/E Ratio 1953-1962	Average P/E Ratio 1957-1966
Allied Chemical	18.5	19.7
Alcoa	26.9	29.2
American Can	16.0	16.1
AT&T	15.5	18.1
American Tobacco	11.6	12.3
Anaconda	11.6	11.6
Bethlehem Steel	12.9	15.2
Chrysler	15.7	13.1
du Pont	23.2	18.9
Eastman Kodak	22.6	28.6
General Electric	23.3	26.4
General Foods	16.8	21.3
General Motors	13.1	14.7
Goodyear	13.3	16.6
International Harvester	12.0	12.2
International Nickel	16.2	20.2
International Paper	16.3	23.1
Johns-Manville	14.4	16.0
Owens-Illinois	16.5	19.2
Procter & Gamble	19.5	23.9
Sears, Roebuck	16.6	22.6
Standard Oil (Calif.)	11.0	12.8
Standard Oil (N.J.)	13.5	15.7
Switft	15.9	16.1
Texaco	11.7	14.3
Union Carbide	23.3	21.9
United Aircraft	13.9	16.6
United States Steel	13.9	16.4
Westinghouse Electric	20.0	21.6
Woolworth	14.2	13.4

Source: *The Value Line Investment Survey,* October 25, 1963, pp. 118, 119, 140, and 145; November 8, 1963, pp. 321, 322, and 324; November 15, 1963, pp. 406, 410, and 422; November 29, 1963, pp. 618 and 637; December 6, 1963, pp. 713, 732, and 734; December 13, 1963, pp. 807, 823, 826, 828, and 837; December 27, 1963, pp. 1009, 1017, and 1020; October 4, 1963, pp. 1113 and 1120; and October 11, 1963, pp. 1208, 1216, 1223, and 1229. Arnold Bernhard & Co., Inc., New York. Standard and Poor's *Industry Survey—Aerospace,* April 25, 1963, p. A31 for United Aircraft, *Moody's Handbook of Common Stocks,* 1968 (First Quarter), pp. 25, 32, 40, 66, 67, 73, 122, 206, 314, 327, 400, 401, 405, 429, 511, 513, 515, 533, 721, 765, 830, 868, 870, 896, 908, 938, 945, 962, 996, and 1007.
From: Frederick Amling, *Investments: An Introduction to Analysis and Management,* 2nd ed., p. 498, © 1970. Reprinted by permission of Prentice-Hall, Inc., Englewood Cliffs, N. J.

excessively expensive. Since an investor assumes risk in expectation of a financial return, the amount a given stock is earning, and how fast its earnings are increasing, provide the keys to whether any given price is reasonable or too much to pay for the stock. Just as paying $40 a share may be cheap for one company and $4 a share may be expensive for another, paying 25 times earnings may be inexpensive for one company and exceedingly expensive for another.

Whether or not a stock is expensive depends upon whether its current market price is above or below its computed value, sometimes called intrinsic value, or real value. The market value is the price you read in the newspaper. The real value is its computed value determined by capitalizing its earnings. For example, consider the case of Altogether, Inc. selling at $25 a share, this year expected to earn $2 a share, with a P/E ratio based on this year's earnings of 12.5. This price could also represent the real value of a share of Altogether stock, and Investor A thinks it does. He assumes that a share of Altogether carries with it sufficient risk to require an 8 percent rate of return; therefore, he will expect to earn 8 percent on his investment ($25 × .08 = $2). Thus, the valuation process can be presented either in terms of a P/E multiplier (what the investor will pay for earnings) or a capitalization rate (the rate of return the investor expects to earn on an investment). For example, using the P/E multiplier, the valuation formula would be as follows:

$$V = ME$$

In this formula V refers to the value of the stock; M refers to an average historical P/E multiplier, or the normal P/E multiplier, of the stock, and E refers to the expected earnings of that stock. Using Altogether, Inc. as our example, you would compute the value as follows:

$$V = ME; \$25 = 12.5 \times \$2$$

As stated earlier, value can also be presented as a capitalization of earnings, which is merely presenting risk or uncertainty as a devisor rather than a multiplier. Using a capitalization rate, the valuation of Altogether would be as follows:

$$V = E \div K \qquad \text{or} \qquad V = E/K$$
$$\$25 = \$2 \div .08 \qquad \text{or} \qquad \$25 = \$2/.08$$

In this formula V and E refer to value and earnings, of course, and K refers to the capitalization rate or the rate of return investors expect to earn on this investment. Using either valuation formula, a share of Altogether stock is valued at $25 per share.

However, by no means every investor will agree with Investor A that a share of Altogether, Inc. is worth $25. For example, Investor B may believe that there is more uncertainty of risk associated with Altogether than an 8 percent rate of return would justify; therefore, he would expect a higher rate of return, perhaps 10 percent, whereas, Investor C might believe there is less uncertainty associated with Altogether than an 8 percent rate of return would require. Therefore, he might expect to earn no more than a 5 percent return. Yet all investors might expect Altogether to earn $2 next year. In the case of Investor B, who expects a 10 percent rate of return, he would be willing to pay no more than $20 per share ($20 = $2 ÷ .10). Expressing this same value in terms of a P/E ratio, Investor B would expect to pay no more than ten times a dollar's worth of earnings for a stock as risky as Altogether ($20 = 10 × $2). Similarly, Investor C, who considers Altogether less risky and requires only a 5 percent rate of return, would be willing to pay as much as $40 per share for the stock ($40 = $2 ÷ .05). Expressing the same value using a P/E multiplier, he would be willing to pay $40 for every dollar's worth of earnings $40 = 20 × $2).

Both the capitalization rate and P/E multiples are reflections of the degrees of uncertainty that investors believe are applicable to various investments. As is indicated in Table 10–1, capitalization rates are inversely related to P/E ratios, but both are closely related to investors' attitudes toward certainty and uncertainty. Since the current market price of Altogether stock is $25 a share, Investor A would consider it fairly valued, Investor B would consider it overpriced, and Investor C would consider it a real bargain. If Investor A decided to sell it in order to buy an undervalued security, Investor B would not buy it, but Investor C might be happy to do so. But all three investors using the same valuation process would make their decisions in the light of their investment objectives.

Considering the differences of opinion on both degree of uncertainty, and the necessary capitalization rates or P/E multipliers, to say nothing about any differences of opinion on estimated earnings, one other valuation formula is worth considering. Especially if you use a normal or historical P/E rate, or capitalization rate, and an earnings figure estimated by someone else, there may well be some question in your mind about the accuracy of either the multiplier or the earnings estimate. You might decide that you would buy no stock whose price was currently no more than 75 percent of its real or computed value. Such a valuation formula would appear as follows:

$$V = .75 \text{ ME}; \quad V = .75 \text{ E/K}$$

For example, Investor C might truly believe that Altogether would earn $2 a share and should be capitalized at 5 percent, i.e., sell at a 20 times multiple. Nevertheless, because he might be somewhat uncertain about both the earnings estimate and the appropriate risk or uncertainty, he might wish to protect himself a bit. In fact, all three of our hypothetical investors might be somewhat unsure of the appropriate risk and earnings figures. Therefore, they might choose to compute the real value of Altogether stock using the historical or normal P/E multiple or capitalization rate, and a generally accepted earnings estimate, but also protect themselves against uncertainty and error by requiring an arbitrary 25 percent discount in current market price below real value before they would buy the stock. Using a P/E multiple, the valuation formula would be as follows:

$$V = .75 \ ME; \$30.00 = .75 \times 20 \times \$2$$

Or using a capitalization rate, the valuation formula would be as follows:

$$V = .75 \ E/K; \$30.00 = .75 \times \$2/.05$$

Consequently, if Altogether can be purchased, for $30 or less, it may be considered reasonably priced. By using this short-cut method of valuing stocks, you can considerably reduce the risk that your own estimates, or the estimates of someone else, are in error. Although you may miss some excellent purchases because you set your real value below the current market price, you will avoid unwise purchases made on the basis of excessive optimism.

One other comment here may be appropriate. Although most investors are more concerned about the expensiveness of a stock than they are about dividends, some reference to the relationship between stock prices and dividends should be made. The measure that relates price to dividends is called yield. Again assuming Altogether is selling for $25 per share, the investor would receive a 4 percent rate of return since Altogether pays a $1 dividend ($25 × 4% = $1). Yield is significant primarily to investors who are especially interested in dividend income. Although dividend yield is relatively unimportant to most young, middle-income professional people, dividend income can be crucial for investors dependent upon their investments for supplemental income to pay the landlord and grocer. Actually, all defensive investors are somewhat interested in yield because higher yields may indicate more dependable earnings patterns, and greater stock price stability. Even to younger, more aggressive investors, however, yield may serve a valuable function, because a relatively low yield on a stock with a relatively high P/E multiple may indicate corporate expansion through retained earnings, substantial earnings growth, and substantial investor confidence in the superior managerial abilities within the corporation.

Expensiveness is truly an important consideration. Even good stocks can be overpriced; occasionally, stocks are overpriced because they are quality investments. If you pay too much for any investment, the return from that investment will not be adequate to enable you to reach your goal, and will therefore not be enough to justify the purchase. Furthermore, if you pay too much for an investment, there is the very real possibility that other investors will shortly determine that the market price is above its real value, and that price will come tumbling down. Therefore, by avoiding investments that are currently more expensive than they should be, you should increase the rate of return on your portfolio, and avoid price declines resulting from market adjustments.

PROFITABILITY

A second quantitative factor is profitability which is a measure of a corporation's net profit. Since any stock may be valued by using corporate earnings (or net profits) as one of the two primary determinants, it should be fairly evident that corporate profitability is an exceedingly important topic. When you consider that there are so many different uses for a term like earnings, some serious consideration should be given to the various alternative ways of using the term and the different methods of estimating earnings in the future.

Total earnings may be related to: (1) total assets, (2) total long-term capital, or (3) total equity, that is, stockholder's capital. Each of these three measures provides a different rate of return, but in terms of comparing one corporation to another, they basically show nothing different about corporations than how the corporation has been financed. For example, consider the balance sheet and income statement of Altogether, Inc. in Table 10–3. Since total assets of Altogether are $90 million, and total earnings are $6 million, the rate of profitability would be 6.7 percent ($90M × 6.7% = $6M). The second measure of profitability relates total earnings to total long-term investment. Since $10 million worth of Altogether's total assets are financed using short-term debts (money owed to suppliers and current bank loans), the total long-term investment in Altogether is $80 million. Of this, $20 million has been supplied by bondholders, and $60 million has been supplied by stockholders. The rate of profitability using earnings divided by total investment, is 7.5 percent ($80M × 7.5% = $6M). Despite the fact that 7.5 percent is greater than 6.7 percent, Altogether is obviously no more profitable using the second method of measuring profitability than it is using the first. Total profit is still $6 million. Similarly, the third measure, earnings divided by equity, is just one more way to determine the same thing. Since stockholders have supplied $60 million, and the earnings are $6 million this year, the rate of return on stockholders' equity (then capital) is 10 percent ($60M × .10 = $6M). Regardless of which of these measures of profitability you choose to use, you will derive a rate of profitability that will permit you to compare the profitability of Altogether with that of other companies. Each of these three figures is important for different purposes; but actually, all three are simply different ways to relate total earnings to the whole corporation. They measure the profitability of the corporation in terms of the total funds invested in that corporation.

Table 10-3   Altogether, Inc. Financial Statements

Balance Sheet *(in millions)*	

Assets:	
Current Assets	$20
Fixed Assets	70
Total Assets	$90
Debts and Equity:	
Current Debts	$10
Bonds	20
Stockholders Equity	60
Total Debts and Equity	$90

Income Statement *(in millions)*	

Sales	$50
Expenses	38
Total Earnings	$12
Taxes	6
Net Earnings	$ 6

Per Share Earnings: $2.00 (3 million shares outstanding)
Per Share Dividend: $1.00

Just exactly which measure of profitability any given investor decides to use may be a matter of personal choice or available data. It is indeed important, however, that profitability be recognized as a significant quantitative tool. Whichever measure of profitability is used, the investor can compare the profitability of Altogether, Inc. with the profitability figure of all the other stocks he is considering. Through such comparisons, he will be more able to select those securities that can provide those rates of return that he requires for his investment objectives. By either estimating future earnings for himself, or using the estimates of professional analysts, the investor may determine a future earnings figure that he can use in his valuation process. It is rather important to note, however, that historical earnings patterns do change. Although it may be helpful to use historical earnings patterns as a clue to future profitability, change is inevitable. Just because a corporation has continued to increase its earnings 10 percent each year, there is no guarantee that it will be able to maintain that earnings growth pattern. Those corporations whose earnings are growing at fairly reasonable rates, however, are much more likely to sustain their earnings patterns than are the corporations whose earnings have been growing very rapidly. Nevertheless, while high growth rates continue, growth can be the primary determinant of present and future profitability.

If you can estimate earnings and price-earnings multiples more accurately, you can select your investments with greater certainty, and reduce your overall portfolio risk for any given rate of return. If you take an aggressive approach, appropriate selection of undervalued investments will be primarily determined by your ability to estimate earnings and price-earnings multiples more accurately than investors in general. To the extent that you can do so, however, you will be rewarded with an above average rate of return. Throughout your portfolio management effort, you can experience greater certainty in the progress you are making; you can experience the ultimate satisfaction of having achieved your investment goal.

GROWTH

Growth is another term that can be used in any of several ways. Growth may mean more sales. Growth may also mean higher market prices, or higher total market value. Since we are primarily concerned with selecting valuable securities, however, and since our concept of value is based upon earnings, growth in this context refers to an increase in earnings (percentage change in earnings).

Actually, any increase in earnings may be considered growth. However, those corporations whose earnings are increasing very gradually, perhaps 1 to 6 percent a year, would not usually be considered growth stocks. Only those stocks whose earnings are increasing at above average rates are growth companies. Particularly those with earnings growth rates of 10 to 15 percent, i.e., two or three times the increase in the gross national product, are usually considered growth stocks. For example, if the gross national product is increasing at 5 percent a year, and Tried and True Shoe is experiencing annual earnings increases of about 5 percent a year, that would hardly be considered a growth situation. On the other hand, if Miscellaneous Shoe is experiencing an annual earnings increase of 15 percent a year, that would be considered a growth situation.

Any amount of earnings growth will support a higher P/E ratio, or a lower capitalization rate, than could be supported without any expected increase in earnings. Table 10–4 indicates the extent to which current P/E multiples will be influenced by various growth rates. Particularly noteworthy, are the higher current P/E multiples that may be justified with higher expected growth rates. Table 10–5 indicates the importance of longer periods of even nominal increases in per share earnings upon current P/E multiples.

Table 10–4   Growth Rates and Price-Earnings Multiples

Expected Rate of Growth (For 7 years)	Multiplier of Average (Fourth-Year) Earnings	Multiplier of Current Earnings
3.5%	13	15.0
5.0	14	17.0
7.2	15	20.0
10.0	16	23.5
12.0	17	27.0
14.3	18	31.0
17.0	19	35.5
20.0	20	41.5

From *Security Analysis*, 4th edition, p. 537, by Benjamin Graham, David L. Dodd, and Sidney Cottle. Copyright 1962 by McGraw-Hill Book Company. Used with permission of McGraw-Hill Book Company.

In previous years before such significant rates of inflation had become well established, growth stocks were often defined as those whose per share earnings had increased at the rate of at least 7.2 percent for some years in the past, and were expected to continue at that rate for some years into the future. With at least a 7.2 percent annual increase, earnings would at least double in ten years. Such rapid increases in earnings are important for two reasons. First, since earnings are expected to increase quite rapidly, dividends are a relatively less significant consideration in any growth stock valuation process. Secondly, since companies whose earnings are growing quite rapidly are those in greater need of additional funds to facilitate expansion, many such corporations finance much of their expansion through retained earnings and pay out relatively small percentages of those earnings in the form of dividends. Consequently, in any growth stock valuation process, dividends are a relatively less significant factor, and in fact, are dropped from the valuation process in many cases. For example, if you use a table similar to Table 10–4, you may estimate earnings for the next seven years. Assume that the average earnings for the next seven years would be about equal to the middle or fourth year's earnings, and apply an appropriate multiplier to that earnings figure. Since the significant factor in this valuation method is expected rate of earnings growth, the appropriateness of any multiplier depends upon a specific growth rate. These various relationships between such expected growth rates, the multiplier for the average earnings over the next seven years, and the appropriate multiplier for current earnings are all indicated in Table 10–4.

Although one might expect that forecasting earnings and growth rates four years into the future, to say nothing of seven years hence, would be sufficiently difficult to challenge almost anyone, some analysts are, nevertheless, regularly tempted to estimate growth rates ten years into the future, sometimes even 20 years. Indeed, it is highly doubtful that the company that has maintained an earnings growth rate for several years, would suddenly cease to increase its earnings at all. However, projecting growth rates very far into the future is an extremely tricky business. To the extent that earnings growth can be anticipated farther into the future, investors are certainly willing to pay higher current prices for that expected growth. Consequently, it may be of interest to consider just what P/E multiples might be justified for several growth rates for longer periods of time. Table 10–5 indicates such P/E multiples. Although the P/E multiples at the higher growth rates for the longer periods in Table 10–5 appear quite high, much higher growth rates are regularly projected for some companies. Assuming an expansion of Table 10–5, therefore, an annual growth rate of 30 percent for the next ten years would call for a price earnings multiple of 104, a truly astronomical figure. It is certainly obvious, however, that with higher expected rates of increase, any multiple applied to current earnings must be very high, simply because current earnings are so much below what future earnings are estimated to be.

Despite the difficulty of estimating future earnings, future earnings must be estimated. Similarly, despite the difficulty in estimating growth rates, growth rates simply must be estimated. Earnings growth is so significant a factor in determining the real value of any investment, it simply cannot be ignored. This necessity for estimating future earnings, however, does not require that estimates be made too far into the future. In many cases, future earnings estimates only three years into the future

Table 10–5   P/E Ratios and Growth Rates for Longer Periods

Annual Increase in Per-Share Earnings, Percent	Justified Price-Earnings Ratios (Number of Years of Earnings Increase*)				
	5 years	*7 years*	*10 years*	*15 years*	*20 years*
2	15	15	13	12	10
4	17	17	16	16	15
5	18	18	18	18	18
6	19	19	20	21	22
8	21	22	24	28	30
10	23	25	28	35	45
12	25	28	33	48	—
14	27	32	40	—	—

*Assumes earnings growth rate continues at 5 percent at the end of period.

can be considerably helpful in facilitating your selection process. Because there is additional risk associated with growth stocks, however, defensive investors who are more inclined toward safety of principal and income, should place less of their investment funds in growth stocks. On the other hand, more aggressive investors who are more inclined toward long-term capital appreciation, should emphasize growth stocks in their investment portfolios. Such growth stocks require more careful and frequent evaluation than most conservative investments, but in the long run, the investor will enjoy a greater return resulting from greater emphasis upon growth stocks, if he can afford the additional management effort.

INDEBTEDNESS

A fourth quantitative factor that is quite significant for some investors is the extent to which the corporation has been financed through the use of bonds or debt securities. Since bondholders have claims on corporate assets prior to stockholders, there may be significantly less risk attached to bonds than stocks if both are issued by the same corporation. Furthermore, when a corporation finances any of its financial structure through issuing relatively risk-free bonds, more risk is shifted to the stockholders of that corporation, since all of the risk of that corporation must fall on someone. The larger the proportion of the financial structure financed through bonds, the more risk is shifted to the stock. For example, if a corporation can sell bonds with 5 percent coupons and earn 10 percent on the funds invested, the stockholders receive the difference, but if the corporate management is unable to make a profit on the borrowed funds, the bondholders must still be paid their interest, which reduces stockholders' profit.

This may be more understandable if you relate it to borrowing on your home. If you buy a $20,000 home in a neighborhood where real estate values are appreciating about 10 percent a year, you might expect the value of your home to rise to $22,000 after the first year. If you had paid for your home outright, you would make 10 percent on your funds ($20,000 × 10% = $2,000). On the other hand, if you bought your home with a $2,000 down payment, and an $18,000 mortgage, you would make 100 percent on your money. Your down payment was $2,000, and the value of your property increased $2,000; you still owe roughly $18,000, but the value of your property is now worth $22,000. On the other hand, if the value of your home falls to $18,000, you would lose 10 percent of your money, if you had bought the home outright for $20,000 with no mortgage, whereas, if you used an $18,000 mortgage, that $2,000 loss would have completely eliminated your equity. By guaranteeing the return to a creditor, all the risk is shifted to the owner.

Issuing bonds to acquire funds to buy assets is highly desirable from the viewpoint of some stockholders; however, others are not so inclined. The process of corporate borrowing is called trading on the equity, or leverage. As long as the corporation is making a profit, leverage increases the per share earnings for the stockholders. The larger the proportionate indebtedness, the larger the percentage return to the stockholders. In the case of losses, however, larger indebtedness, i.e., more trading on the equity, or more leverage, increases the losses for the stockholders since those stockholders are the only ones to absorb the losses, having guaranteed to the bondholders that they would have a fixed rate of return.

For example, if the stockholders invest $60 million in Altogether, Inc. and the bondholders invest $20 million, the debt to equity ratio is ⅓ or .33. Stated another way, the debt to total investment is ¼ or .25. Assuming that the bondholders in this example are guaranteed a 5 percent rate of return on their bonds, the total interest payment is $1 million each year. After having paid that $1 million interest expense, in addition to the other $37 million in expenses, Altogether earns $12 million, pays federal income taxes of $6 million, leaving for the stockholder a net earnings of $6 million, or a 10 percent rate of return on their $60 million equity. If there were no bonds, the stockholders would have invested the additional $20 million, so that stockholders' equity would be $80 million. Total earnings would then have been $13 million, since they would not pay the $1 million interest expense. Federal income taxes would have been $6.5 million, leaving a new earnings of $6.5 million for the stockholders. The return then of $6.5 million earnings on $80 million stockholders equity would be 8 percent. Therefore, the stockholders would make 20 percent less without the bondholders than they would with them, assuming no other changes; that is, by using indebtedness, the stockholders increase their earnings 25 percent.

As long as those earnings continue to increase, the stockholders will profit even more handsomely because of that indebtedness. If at any time earnings decline, the stockholders will suffer more than proportionate per share reductions in earnings because of that indebtedness. Consequently, the price of a common stock representing a corporation with significant indebtedness, tends to fluctuate more because of that indebtedness. For those investors who are concerned about safety of principal, liquidity, and income, indebtedness is a serious handicap. It adds additional risk to the stock, over and above any uncertainty associated with the business itself. On the other hand, for those stockholders who are especially concerned about capital appreciation and are willing to accept temporary fluctuations in the market price of their stocks, higher debt to equity ratios may be preferable. For growth stocks, indebtedness may be highly attractive, because the earnings growth may be quite likely to continue, and the difference between the rate of interest on the bond and the profitability of the company may be tremendous. In such cases, leverage is highly desirable to aggressive investors. For defensive investors, who are trying to avoid risk, however, leverage is undesirable because it does increase risk. But for either defensive or aggressive investors, the indebtedness ratio can provide a quantitative measure of various investments being considered for selection.

LIQUIDITY

A fifth quantitative factor that is often given serious consideration in any selection process is liquidity, i.e., the ability of a corporation to meet its financial obligations on time. Actually, for many less well-established firms or more rapidly growing firms, the relationship between highly liquid assets, called current assets, and the amount of the current bills, or liabilities, is an exceedingly important one. The most liquid asset of all, of course, is cash. There are other current assets, however, that can be fairly easily turned into cash such as accounts receivable that are owed to the corporation by customers, and current inventory holdings. In many cases, current inventory holdings are purchased on credit, and those debts are listed as current debts or accounts payable. But current debts must be paid currently, if a firm is to avoid any financial problems. Regardless of whether or not corporations' customers send in their checks on time, current debts must be paid on time to maintain one's credit standing. Occasionally, a corporation does run into some difficulty because its customers do not pay their bills on time, and the corporation must have some cash reserves in order to maintain its good name by paying its own bills when due. Less seasoned corporations, with less established lines of credit at their banks, may have such liquidity problems. For larger corporations, liquidity would not ordinarily be a problem; however, even for larger corporations, in periods of tight money when bank credit lines are not honored, liquidity could even be a problem for them.

There are many measures of liquidity, but two measures in particular are of special importance. The first of these is called the current ratio. The current ratio expresses the relationship between current assets and current liabilities, and is determined by dividing the former by the latter. Using Altogether, Inc. as an example, if current assets are $20 million, and current liabilities are $10 million, the current ratio would be 2 to 1. Since not all current assets can be readily turned into cash, some delay might be experienced before some of those current assets could be used to pay current bills. For example, some of Altogether's customers might not pay their accounts on time, and the company might not be able to sell their inventory as fast as they wanted to. Therefore, current assets should exceed current liabilities in order to guarantee that the corporation's financial obligations could be met when due. Whether the current ratio is 2 to 1, 1.2 to 1, or 3 to 1, current assets should exceed current liabilities sufficiently to avoid any liquidity problems. Such a ratio may be of special value to an investor who is somewhat concerned about the financial position of a given corporation.

A second liquidity measure that is of more immediate value is the cash ratio. A cash ratio compares only cash, plus short-term marketable securities, to current liabilities, thereby excluding such current assets as accounts receivable and inventory, which may be somewhat less liquid than they appear. Cash, of course, is the most liquid asset, but short-term marketable securities can be converted into cash very quickly. If Altogether has $5 million in cash and marketable securities, and $10 million in current liabilities, the cash ratio would be .5 to 1. The corporation would not be able to pay off completely its current liabilities out of these cash holdings, but after all, it really expects to pay its current liabilities as it collects its accounts receivable; it does not really expect to reduce its cash position at all. Whether a corporation has a cash ratio of .5 to 1, .3 to 1, or 1 to 1 is not nearly so significant as the change in that cash ratio over a one- or two-year period. If the cash ratio has continually declined, the corporation may be facing serious liquidity problems, and this ratio may be an indication of still greater financial problems in the future.

Liquidity is not nearly so important a quantitative factor as expensiveness, profitability, growth, and indebtedness, except in the case of less well-established, or more speculative corporations. Such corporations are the very ones that may expand too rapidly, using current debt as a primary means of financing. Such current debt may be highly desirable from the viewpoint of the corporation, since it may be readily extended by supplier corporations, and may not carry any interest charges. In one sense, current liabilities may be considered interest-free debt. Because more speculative corporations might have difficulty in issuing bonds and might even have difficulty in issuing additional stock, current debt from suppliers can be an exceedingly important source of financing. Such corporations can become over-extended, however, if they have bought supplies and produced inventory in anticipation of immediate sales for cash, but their customers have demanded credit. Furthermore, if they have bought additional supplies in anticipation of rather quick collection of their own customers' accounts, and their customers delay somewhat in paying those accounts, cash may not come into the corporation fast enough to meet the current liabilities incurred. Most large well-established corporations do not have such difficulties except in periods of tight money when all corporations have liquidity problems. For smaller corporations, however, liquidity can be a very serious difficulty, and any investor considering the selection of such securities for his portfolio is well advised to give such a liquidity ratio at least some consideration.

All five of the quantitative factors we have considered, expensiveness, profitability, growth, indebtedness, and liquidity, are more significant for some corporations than for others. Expensiveness is always a serious consideration since it is possible to pay too much for even the very best quality security. Profitability is also an extremely important factor; every investor is especially concerned about earnings, and they should be given serious consideration. Especially for younger investors, growth may be the most important quantitative factor, even including expensiveness, because if a corporation's earnings are growing at a sufficiently rapid rate, extremely high price-earnings ratios, based on current earnings, can well be justified. Growth rates do tend to change, however; and when earnings begin to grow at less rapid rates than they have in the past, investors tend to sell those stocks with resulting declines in the stock prices of such growth companies. For investors who are especially concerned about safety of principal, liquidity, or income, indebtedness may be a significant factor. Even for those investors who are not so much interested in safety of principal, however, indebtedness can serve as a significant quantitative indicator. Since indebtedness, or leverage, does increase the rate of return on a common stock, facilitating a profit above what it would be without such indebtedness, investors who are interested in above average returns may be interested in those corporations with larger debt positions. Liquidity may be of special importance to any investor when he is considering buying a more speculative stock for inclusion in his portfolio. Especially important is any change in a corporation's liquidity ratio over time, because such a change may indicate greater liquidity problems for that corporation in the future.

Each of these quantitative factors can serve as a selection tool. Just as no qualitative factor can solve all the investor's problems each quantitative factor has its place, and each may be of value in particular situations. Overall, by using qualitative and quantitative factors, and by accepting the contributions that each factor has to make, the investor may be better able to select valuable securities. If he uses only the qualitative factors, his selection process may be somewhat less accurate than it could be if both sets of indicators were used. If he uses only the quantitative factors, he could be, misled if those financial data do not accurately reflect the quality of the company. By using both qualitative and quantitative factors, the investor can construct a selection check list that will reflect short-run and long-run prospects.

SELECTING SPECIFIC STOCKS

After considering various qualitative and quantitative factors some specific stock must actually be selected if you are indeed to develop an investment portfolio designed to accomplish your investment objectives and reach your goal. By incorporating all of these selection factors into a selection check list, you may subject any corporation to a relatively quick yet thorough analysis to see if this particular stock meets your requirements. Some qualitative and quantitative factors not discussed in the previous pages may be especially important to you, and if so, you can modify the check list to your heart's content. As you gain analytical experience, you will find that some data are much more meaningful to you than others, and you will need to modify your check list accordingly. Initially, however, just those qualitative and quantitative factors we have discussed should be enough. Table 10–6 provides an example of such a selection check list.

Table 10–6   Stock Selection Check List

Corporation:			
	Favorable	**Acceptable**	**Questionable**
Qualitative Factors:			
Management			
Competition			
Uniqueness			
Quantitative Factors:			
Expensiveness			
Profitability			
Growth			
Indebtedness			
Liquidity			

Comments:

Keeping in mind your portfolio structure, you may wish to include some specific stocks that are conservative, some that are growth stocks, and some that are speculative stocks. Although it is highly inadvisable to buy a speculative stock as your very first investment, perhaps you will want to choose between a conservative or growth security. Perhaps your best approach would be to make a decision regarding the respective proportions of conservative and growth stocks you decide to include in your portfolio. If you decide to include more conservative stocks than growth stocks, perhaps your first selection should be a conservative investment, whereas if you plan to have more growth stocks than conservative ones, perhaps your first selection should be a growth stock. As you continue to build your investment portfolio, the specific securities that you select should strengthen that particular section of the portfolio that you think is weaker at that time.

CONSERVATIVE STOCKS

Assuming that you are basically a conservative investor, or that at this particular time you feel that the conservative section of your portfolio needs strengthening, several alternative conservative stocks should be considered. Such alternatives may come to your attention from many sources. Your broker is always available to you for suggested securities, and by telling him that you are especially interested in a conservative stock at any given time, he would be ready, willing, and able to make several suggestions. If you have already selected an industry from which you wish to make your selection, he can be of additional assistance to you.

For example, if you tell your broker that you are interested in the shoe industry and wish to buy a conservative stock, he may recommend Tried and True Shoe, Inc. as one of the alternatives you should consider. Or perhaps someone else has called T. & T. S. to your attention. Perhaps you have been thinking about it without anyone else's suggestion. You may have been familiar with T. & T. S. for a long time; perhaps you have purchased several of their products over the years; at the very least, you have heard no adverse comments about the company. The broker can send you an analysis on the shoe industry, and an analysis of Tried and True Shoe prepared by his firm's research staff. If you have not already known, you will learn that Tried and True is a leader in the shoe industry, and has been a leader for a long time. By checking the financial data, you note that the stock is selling for a recent price-earnings multiple of 12 times earnings; the stock is earning 8 percent on total investment, and 10 percent on stockholders' equity; its earnings have been increasing at about 6 percent a year for several years, and such a rate is expected to continue; 20 percent of its total investment is financed through bonds for a 1:4 debt to equity ratio; its current ratio is 2 to 1. You gather all this data together and record it on your check list as indicated in Table 10–7.

After making such check lists for several other alternatives, you can compare Tried and True Shoe with all the rest, and select whichever one you feel most appropriately reflects the kind of stock you want to buy, and the one that is most reasonably priced at the time. You cannot really weigh all factors equally, but all should be considered. If the growth rate is unusually high, several other weaknesses may be ignored. If the stock is too expensive, you may pass it by despite good management, earnings record, or what have you. Your investigation may show that a given stock you thought would be a good conservative security, is in reality a growth stock, and should not be considered for the conservative section of your portfolio at all. In considering conservative securities, you may wish to add dividend or interest income, either to the check list proper or at the bottom. You may also wish to add any general comments about the company, the industry, or the management of the company.

GROWTH STOCKS

If you are more interested in purchasing a growth than a conservative stock, the same general process can be followed. Although there is rela-

Table 10–7 Stock Selection Check List

Corporation: Tried and True Shoe, Inc.

	Favorable	Acceptable	Questionable
Qualitative Factors:			
Management	X		
Competition	X		
Uniqueness	X		
Quantitative Factors:			
Expensiveness	12X		
Profitability	10%		
Growth		5%	
Indebtedness	1:4		
Liquidity	2:1		

Comments: A leader in the industry; numerous patents. Current dividend is $1.00, increasing about 10¢ a year.

---

tively little difference in the process you follow in considering growth stocks, the emphasis upon various factors is decidedly different. Rather than looking for stability, you are looking for growth. Although you would look at past earnings, you are more interested in future earnings. Rather than looking for current income, you are looking for capital gains.

Assuming that you are still interested in the shoe industry, one of the alternatives which your broker would surely recommend to you is Miscellaneous Shoe Corp. Miscellaneous Shoe is especially interesting because its management has been aggressively buying smaller shoe companies; this acquisition has rapidly increased its position in the industry. As smaller competitors have been acquired, Miscellaneous Shoe has applied improved managerial techniques that have increasingly produced lower costs and better products, controls, and profits. It has been earning 10 percent on total investment and 15 percent on stockholders' equity. Its earnings have been increasing at about 15 percent a year. However, one-third of its total investment is financed through debt instruments, and its current ratio is only 1 to 1. Table 10–8 represents a check list for Miscellaneous Shoe Corporation.

Table 10–8   Stock Selection Check List

Corporation: Miscellaneous Shoe Corporation

	Favorable	Acceptable	Questionable
Qualitative Factors:			
Management	X		
Competition		X	
Uniqueness	X		
Quantitative Factors:			
Expensiveness		20X	
Profitability	15%		
Growth	15%		
Indebtedness		1:2	
Liquidity		1:1	

Comments: Growing rapidly due to aggressive acquisition policy.

Without doubt there is more risk associated with Miscellaneous Shoe than with Tried and True Shoe, but after all, you are looking for a growth stock. Miscellaneous Shoe has a 15 percent growth rate in earnings, somewhat less sustainable than a 5 percent growth rate, to be sure, but at present, Miscellaneous Shoe shows no signs of decreasing its rate of earnings growth. Its debt position adds risk, and its liquidity position is somewhat less secure, but neither of these ratios indicates serious diffi-culty. All in all you are impressed with Miscellaneous Shoe as a growth stock possibility. By comparing your check list on Miscellaneous Shoe with similar check lists on several other alternative growth stocks, you may conclude that Miscellaneous Shoe is the best buy. As a growth stock, it is reasonably priced. As its earnings continue to grow at 15 percent each year, its market price should rise substantially. If its earnings show signs of weakening, or even reach some target price you have forecasted in three-years time, you will sell it anyway. Although more frequent evaluations of Miscellaneous Shoe must be made than of Tried and True Shoe, you may well consider the additional expected rate of return to be worth the additional time and effort required. All things considered, Miscellaneous Shoe should continue to sell at 20 times earnings.

SPECULATIVE STOCKS

Assuming that your portfolio presently consists of an adequate number of both conservative securities and growth stocks, you might well be considering a speculative stock, or you might be planning to sell a speculative stock and replace it with another one. One such stock that you can hardly help but consider is Plastic Shoe, Inc. Plastic Shoe has been attracting a great deal of attention recently. Its management claims to have a product with so much potential that the whole leather shoe industry may one day be replaced. Its shoes are imaginatively designed, and its costs are remarkably low. If sufficient consumer demand can be stimulated, Plastic Shoe could be fantastically profitable. The management seems to be reasonably good; in fact, several of the officers in Plastic Shoe were former officers in other shoe companies. But whether or not they can profitably produce a shoe that the public will buy is yet to be determined. Plastic Shoe has made no profits to date, and in the next five years may make none. Such a pattern is not too unusual. However, if five years from now, additional research on the product has provided the know-how to produce a plastic shoe that the public will buy, the stock's price could go from its present $3 to $300 a share. By comparing your check list on Plastic Shoe, as indicated in Table 10–9, with the check lists on the various other speculative stocks that you have been considering, you may well decide to sell your present speculative holding and put the proceeds of that sale into Plastic Shoe.

Whether or not you buy Plastic Shoe, or any speculative stock for that matter, should depend upon how well such a stock fits your investment objectives and your present portfolio holdings. Although there are times when you might well wish to sell some of your conservative stocks in order to buy growth or speculative securities, you should recognize that by so doing, you make a major change in your portfolio position. Switching from one conservative stock to another conservative stock may upgrade your portfolio, but it does not drastically change your portfolio policy, that is, it does not change the proportions of conservative, growth, and speculative stocks in your portfolio. There may be times when you should hold more growth and speculative stocks, just as there may be times when more conservative stocks should be held. During those times, a major change in your portfolio policy may very well be appropriate. For example, when the whole market seems to be overpriced, more of the portfolio might be placed in conservative stocks. At times when the whole market seems to be underpriced, perhaps a larger proportion of your portfolio should be placed in growth and speculative issues. Regardless of the portfolio policy you follow, and regardless of the particular market conditions at any given time when you are evaluating various securities, the process of selecting those specific stocks should be one that permits you to compare the various qualitative and quantitative factors that are important to you and other investors, since ultimately, such evaluations determine investors' attitudes toward all stock values. With

Table 10–9   Stock Selection Check List

Corporation: Plastic Shoe, Inc.

	Favorable	Acceptable	Questionable
Qualitative Factors:			
Management	X		
Competition			X
Uniqueness	X		
Quantitative Factors:			
Expensiveness		?	
Profitability			0
Growth	?		
Indebtedness		0	
Liquidity		1:1	

Comments: Research efforts could be fantastically profitable. High risk, but tremendous potential. Might be acquired by a major shoe company.

only slightly more than average managerial effort, the return on your portfolio should make the additional rewards worth far more than the additional efforts.

SUMMARY

Selecting specific investments is truly a challenging experience. You have hundreds of alternative investments from which to choose. You have many constraints with which you must work, and you must consider your investment objectives, how much safety, liquidity, income, and capital appreciation you expect from your portfolio. You must also consider your investment goals, the ultimate income you expect to derive from that portfolio, the annual savings you anticipate, and the time and effort you are willing and able to devote to managing your portfolio. Although specific securities must be selected for even the most defensive investment portfolio, considerably less time and effort must be expended in the selection of such securities, and in the subsequent evaluations of those securities, because conservative stocks of well-established corporations tend to have relatively stable earnings and dividend patterns. In a more aggressive portfolio effort more care and attention must be given to the appropriate selection of securities in order to assure that you assume no more risk than is justified by the prospective rate of return. Although no investor starting from zero can have very much of a portfolio initially, he must begin with a selection of some specific security. His most appropriate approach probably is to select one investment that represents fairly well the largest proportion of his planned portfolio. If he is primarily defensive in his approach, he should select a conservative security first, whereas, if he is primarily aggressive in his approach, he should select a growth stock first. Whatever specific securities are being considered for inclusion in the portfolio, however, there are certain qualitative and quantitative factors that should be considered in each and every case.

Hopefully, the investor would use both qualitative and quantitative factors in his selection process. To the extent that he uses only one or the other, the effectiveness of his selection process will be reduced. Several qualitative factors should be considered in selecting a stock. These include the quality of its management indicated chiefly by its relations with customers, employees, and stockholders; competition—whether intra-industry, inter-industry or international—and the uniqueness of its position in the economy. For example, by investigating the competitive problems that a given corporation's management must face, the investor can find clues to facilitate his stock selection process. Furthermore, there may be certain unique features about some corporations that especially attract an investor's interest: a unique process or product for which there is much consumer demand, a monopoly or semimonopoly position resulting from either government regulation, customer loyalty, patent provisions, or highly differentiated products, or a relatively high fixed cost structure. All in all, the qualitative factors of effective investment selection are extremely important. For those investors who are willing to make the additional effort, quantitative evaluation may facilitate an even better portfolio performance. Such factors as expensiveness, profitability, growth, indebtedness, and liquidity may be appropriate considerations for any investor.

Regardless of the particular type of investment being considered, each one may be subjected to a check list of questions to determine the appropriateness of a stock for a portfolio. Through more careful selection of your investments, and through periodic evaluations, you should be able to reduce the amount of risk you assume for any given rate of return, or increase the rate of return on your portfolio for any amount of risk you decide to assume.

Case Problems

1. Richard Young is a recent graduate of a large eastern university. Rich majored in finance while in college. He learned many methods and tech-

niques for evaluating and selecting stocks. Rich feels he is quite good at stock selection even though he has never invested any money in the stock market. A friend, who never went to college, is dong quite well in the stock market. The other day Rich asked his buddy where he had learned about such things as ratios, liquidity, dividend payout and other factors about stocks. His buddy told him he knew nothing about these things. He said he judged stocks solely by the quality of their managements and their relations with customers, employees, and stockholders. Rich felt this was unwise. Do you agree or disagree with Rich? Why?

2. Homer Berry is a rainmaker in central New Mexico. It has been very dry recently so Homer has had quite a bit of work. In fact he has saved enough money that for the first time in his life he is considering some security investments. Since Homer has never bought securities before, he has little confidence in his ability to select stocks for a portfolio. Homer feels he is unable to utilize charts and figures; in effect he can't use quantitative factors. Since a friend of Homer told him that quantitative factors are very important, but qualitative factors are useless, Homer has decided to bury his money. Evaluate what Homer's friend has done.

3. John and Bob have decided to invest their money together. They have agreed to examine a number of factors before they select a stock for their portfolio. John and Bob have two stocks under consideration. It seems that both stocks have price-earnings ratios of 20. In addition all other factors are similar. Stock A is selling for $50 and Stock B is selling for $45. John feels that there is no doubt about which stock is better. He feels that Stock B is less expensive than Stock A and is better. Bob feels that the two stocks are practically equal according to all the factors that he and John have considered. Do you agree? Why?

4. Betty is trying to select a stock for her portfolio. She has limited her possible choice down to two companies. The stocks are similar in most respects. However, she still would like to see which stock has the better return on equity. Both companies have $500,000 in assets and earn about $50,000 yearly before interest and dividends. However, one company is solely financed by stock while the other is financed by stock and $250,000 in 6% bonds. Which company would you recommend? Why?

5. Mary Ann is new to the investment world. She realizes that both qualitative and quantitative factors are important. Her boyfriend has agreed to help her compile some quantitative data for her on several different companies. However, he will not advise her. He has the figures broken down into five different areas. Under profitability he has six different rates of return for each company. Mary Ann is not quite sure what all this means. She expected to get rates of return but only expected one for each company. Explain these different rates to her and how they might be useful in selecting stocks.

6. Assume that you are investigating several stocks with anticipation of starting an investment portfolio of your own. The information that you have been able to find is partially incomplete. Below is a list of the stocks and the information that you have been able to find. Please fill in the incomplete blanks with your educated estimates.

Stock	Growth Rate	Expected Earnings	Current Earnings	Current Value
A	10%	$5	—	$47
B	25%	$5	$4	—
C	—	$4	$3	$81

Selected Readings

Bellemore, Douglas H. *Investments Principles, Practices and Analysis.* Cincinnati: South-Western Publishing Company, 1966.

Mayer, Martin. *Wall Street: Men and Money.* New York: Collier Books, 1966.

Hayes, Douglas A. *Investments: Analysis and Management.* New York: The Macmillan Company, 1966.

Moody's Stock Survey. Published weekly by Moody's Investor's Survey, 99 Church Street, N.Y., N.Y.

Moody's Handbook of Common Stock. Published by Moody's Investors Service.

Standard & Poor's Industry Surveys. Published by Standard & Poor's Corp. 345 Hudson St., N.Y., N.Y.

Value Line, Investment Survey. Published by Arnold Bernhard & Co., 5 East 44th St., N.Y., N.Y.

West, David A. (ed.). *Readings in Investment Analysis.* Scranton, Penn.: International Textbook Company, 1969.

APPENDIX: PUBLICATIONS ON STOCK INFORMATION

Although there are hundreds of sources of information available about corporations and financial data, many of them free, extracts from three widely used and readily available publications are presented in this section. They are the Standard & Poor's *Stock Guide, Stocks on the Big Board* provided by the New York Stock Exchange, and a series of reports on individual companies also prepared by Standard & Poor's. Each of these publications includes similar data; however, each publication has certain special features. In addition to these three publications, there are many other similar publications that provide a great deal of financial information about many companies. One, if not all, of these publications is available at most brokerage firms for most investors. If not, many similar publications may be available that may serve your purposes just as well.

STANDARD & POOR'S *Stock Guide*

Stock Guide is perhaps the best known, and certainly the most widely used, of the Standard & Poor's publications. The *Stock Guide* includes many corporations, not only those listed on the New York Stock Exchange, the American Stock Exchange, and certain of the regional exchanges, but also a number of corporations that are traded over the counter. The stocks are listed alphabetically, giving the ticker symbol, much quantitative information about each stock, and a rating for many of the corporations. Table 10–10 provides an example of a *Stock Guide*. Notice that the various columns provide the following data about the corporations listed:

1. The page index number
2. Ticker symbol
3. The name of the stock
4. Market where the stock is traded
5. A ranking or rating
6. The par value
7. The number of institutions holding the stock
8. The number of shares held by institutions
9. The principal business of the corporation
10. The price ranges for a 30-year period, last year, and the current year
11. The number of shares traded in the previous month
12. The high, low, and last bid prices on the stock
13. The dividend yield
14. The price-earnings ratio
15. The year in which some annual dividends have been paid
16. Last paid dividends
17. The dividend payment date
18. The financial position of a corporation, giving cash, current assets, current liabilities, and the balance sheet date
19. The capital structure, giving long-term debt, preferred stock outstanding, and common stock outstanding
20. Earnings for each year for the past five years
21. Earnings in the last 12 months
22. Earnings still more recently

In addition to this data, there are various symbols indicating such unusual occurrences as stock splits and stock dividends. Indeed, the Standard & Poor's *Stock Guide* is a wealth of financial data about a great many corporations. Furthermore, at the front of the booklet, this little publication includes comments about recent market developments; and at the back, it lists the major industries, and the major corporations in those industries, indicating a stock ranking for each corporation. It also provides information on commission charges on the various exchanges and directions on how to use the *Stock Guide*. All in all the *Stock Guide* can be an exceedingly helpful selection tool to any investor who will take the time and effort to familiarize himself with what it includes, and will use the available data in constructing his stock selection check list.

Table 10-10 Extracts from Standard & Poor's Stock Guide, Year-End 1970

10 AAA-AGM

STANDARD & POOR'S CORPORATION

INDEX	Ticker Symbol	STOCKS NAME OF ISSUE (Call Price of Pfd. Stocks)	Market	Par Val.	★ Inst. Hold. Cos (000)	STOCK CHARACTERISTICS Principal Business	1936-68 High	1936-68 Low	PRICE RANGE 1969 High	1969 Low	1970 High	1970 Low	Dec. Sales in 100s	December, 1970 O-C Recent Bid Ask High	Low	Last	% Div. Yield	P-E Ratio
1		AAA Enterprises, Inc.	UNL	13¢		Mfr mobile; modular homes						3⅜			4⅝B	1A		d
2		AAI Corp.	UNL	B—		Electronic ordnance; gov't.	30	3⅜	11	8⅜		4⅝B	1A				41
3	AIR	AAR Corp.	MW	B—		Overhauls, mfrs. nav/com eq	23⅜	9¼	17⅛	5	6⅞	2⅝	64	18⅛	16⅛	17⅝A		31
4	ABJ	Abacus Fund	NYS	B—	1	Closed-end investment co.	39⅜	8⅞	21⅛	9¼	19⅜	9½	770	14¼	12⅝	14⅜	1.6	
5	ABT	Abbott Laboratories	NYS, Ci, MW, PB, PC	No	148 1360	Leading ethical drug producer	75¾	a2¼	78½	64¼	26¾	9¼	1625	77	70	75½		26
6	AMC	Aberdeen Manufacturing	ASE	1	15	Curtains, umbrellas; lawn furn	a15⅛	a5⅜	15	4⅞	10¾	6¼	137	10¼	8⅛	10¼	3.9	8
7	APT	Aberdeen Petroleum, Cl A	ASE	1		Heat tr equ; oil & gas leases	17⅝	⅛	14⅞	4⅛	7¼	3⅜	234	5⅞	4	5	‡	13
8		Aberle Industries, Inc.	UNL	1¢	1	Mfr hosiery; bus forms; mchy		a3½	18⅛	a4¼	9	2⅝		7¼	2¾	3¼A		15
9	A	Abitibi Paper Co., Ltd.	TS, MS, VS	No	28 1112	A leading newsprint mfr	16⅛	a3¼	13⅜	8⅜	13	6⅝	3562	8⅛	7	8⅝	2.5	27
10	ACF	ACF Industries, Corp.	NYS, Bo, PB, PC	No	53 1725	Mfr & lease RR cars; auto eq.	68⅞	a2⅜	66⅛	41⅜	51½	35½	1136	46	44	45½	5.3	14
11	AMT	Acme-Cleveland Corp.	NYS	1	3	Mfr automatic mach tools	a30⅛	a1⅛	30⅞	21	24	12	541	15¾	12¾	13¾	6.0	11
12		Acme Electric Corp.	UNL	1	1	Contr pwr sup; transform's	25¼	a3⅜	15⅝	8	11	4½			5⅞	6⅜	2.5	11
13		Acme General Corp.	UNL	No		Door hardware systems			14⅛	7	9¾	4½		6⅜	6⅜	7A		8
14	ACE	Acme-Hamilton Manufacturing	ASE	50¢		Rubber hose; other items	a25⅛	1⅞	9¼	4⅛	9¼		237		2⅝	2¾	2.7	22
15	ASC	Acme Markets, Inc.	NYS, PB	1	14 160	Major food supermk chain	107⅛	6¼	54¼	37¼	46	36	792	44	39⅜	43⅜		10
16	ACL	Acme Precision Products	ASE	1		Dies, cast parts, mtl hdlg eq	22	1⅜	11¼	3½	5¼	2½	154		2½	3⅞	‡4.6	13

Uniform Footnote Explanations—See Page 1. Other: ¹Bo, Ci, De, PB, PC, TS. ²Bo, MW, PB. ³As computed by Standard & Poor's. ⁴‡$0.72, '70; ‡$1.09, '69. ⁴@$2.58, '69. ⁷@$1.16; @p⁴1.01, '69. ⁸$Scale to $45 in '79. r—As reported by company. s—Fiscal Dec '67 & prior. t—9 mo Sep '66; prior fiscal Dec. '68. v—Fiscal Dec '68 & prior. w—No recent report. x—Fiscal Apr '67 & prior.

COMMON AND PREFERRED STOCKS

AAA-AGM 11

Same Div. Ea.Yr. Since	DIVIDENDS Latest Payment $	Ex. Div.	Date	So Far 1970	Total Ind. Rate	$ Paid 1969	FINANCIAL POSITION Mil-$ Cash & Equiv.	Mil-$ Carr. Assets	Mil-$ Carr. Liabs.	Balance Sheet Date	CAPITALIZATION Long Term Debt Mil-$	Pfd.	Com. Shs. 000		$ Per Shr 1966	EARNINGS—$ Per Shr Years 1967	1968	1969	1970	$ Per Shr Last 12 Mos.	INTERIM EARNINGS OR REMARKS Period $—Per Share—$ 1969	1970	INDEX
	None paid			Nil	Nil		0.38	6.51	7.87	12-31-69	1.23		3120	Dc	−0.01	0.07	0.24	d0.89		d0.89	6 Mo Jun	d0.33	1
	None paid						0.15	11.9	7.35	12-31-69	1.19		877	Dc	0.24	−0.90	0.34	0.11		0.11	6 Mo Nov		2
	2½% Stk 2-9-71	1-6	7⅛%Stk 5%Stk				0.33	8.23	4.58	5-31-70	1.59		764	My15	a0.73	a0.55	a0.10	a0.53	a0.41	0.58	6 Mo Nov	0.21	0.38	3
1926	h. 2% Stk 10-28-70	9-15	h2%Stk Stk h				Net Asset Val $14.58		88.8	9-30-70	52.4	171	3800	Mr13	#18.8	v#21.0	#19.8	#17.4		#2.82	0 Mo Sep	@1.80	@2.04	4
	Q0.27½ 2-15-71	1-18	1.10 1.10	1.07½			16.4	197		12-31-69	2.03		13495	Dc	2.35	2.10	2.59	E2.90	@2.82	@2.82	0 Mo Sep	@1.80	@2.04	5
1965	Q0.10 12-21-70	11-23	0.40 0.40	0.39			0.30	22.7	12.8	12-31-69	6.86		857	Dc31	1.13	a0.13a	a1.21	a1.21		1.25	9 Mo Sep	*1.13	⁵1.17	6
	2% Stk 12-11-70	1-11	2%Stk Stk	0.07			0.29	2.72	1.73	9-30-69	2.02		*1093	8p	*0.19	0.15	*0.23	*0.08		0.38	9 Mo Jun	*0.18	0.28	7
	None paid			Nil			3.35	2.35	1.89	9-30-69	1.33		*863	8p	a0.06	a0.12	a0.34	0.68	P*0.22	0.22	9 Mo Sep			8
1949	gQ0.05 1-1-71	11-27	g0.32 0.20	g0.36			5.75	114	49.0	j12-31-69	110	200	17863	Dc	0.92	0.72	0.64	3.90	E3.25	0.30	9 Mo Sep	0.47	0.13	9
1951	Q0.60 12-15-70	11-20	2.40 2.40	2.40			11.7	126	46.1	12-31-69	‡173		5614	Dc	5.13	x3.80	3.79	3.80	E3.25	3.87	9 Mo Sep	2.68	2.65	10
1936	Q0.20 11-20-70	10-30	1.15 0.80	1.40			3.02	58.4	20.2	9-30-69			3843	8p11	p2.67	2.32	*2.22	2.05	P*1.18	1.18			11
1939	Q0.04 12-14-70	11-9	0.16 0.16	0.16			0.44	7.97	2.18	6-30-70	1.54	2	515	Je27	1.26	a1.72	0.78	0.07	2.05	0.59			12
1967	Q0.05 11-13-70	10-19	0.20 0.20	0.16			1.28	3.41	2.08	10-28-69			940	Oc	0.32	0.42	0.74	*0.83		0.89	9 Mo Jul	0.56	0.62	13
	None since 1946			Nil			0.15	7.83	5.01	10-31-69	‡3.54	263	1333	Oc	*0.27	*0.23	*0.29	*0.37		0.11	9 Mo Jul	*0.27	0.01	14
1939	Q0.50 1-4-71	11-30	‡2.00 2.00	‡2.00			40.5	194	135	3-28-70	‡37.2		3239	Mr17	a2.96	a2.68	a3.41	E4.20	3.87	4.03	6 Mo Sep	1.55	1.71	15
	Q0.10 12-15-68	11-24		Nil			0.18	2.84	1.96	9-30-70	1.91		901	8p	c0.35	cd0.83	c*0.30	0.32	0.22	0.22	6 Mo Sep			16

▼Stock Splits & Divs: ¹²³-for-1, '66. ¹³³-for-1, '66; to 5%, '69. ¹⁴³-for-1, '66. ¹⁵Adj to 2½%, '70. ¹⁶Adj to 5%, '70. ¹⁷Adj to 4%, '70. ¹⁸4-for-3, '68. ¹⁹2-for-1, '68. ²⁰²-for-1, '68.
²⁶6-for-1, '66; adj to 2% Jan, '69. ²⁴²2 for-1, '66. ²⁷100%, '67. ²⁸²-for-1, '68. ²⁹2-for-1, '68. ³⁰7-for-5, '70. ³¹4-for-3, '68.

Reprinted with permission from Standard & Poor's Corporation.

Stocks on the Big Board

This pamphlet is provided periodically by the New York Stock Exchange, at irregular times throughout each year. It arranges data somewhat differently than the Standard & Poor's *Stock Guide,* and limits its stock information to stocks traded on the New York Stock Exchange. Table 10–11 is a page from *Stocks on the Big Board.* The information provided by column is as follows:

1. The name of the company
2. The number of institutions holding the stock
3. The price range for the year
4. A recent closing price
5. The dividend yield
6. The price-earnings ratio
7. The year since which cash dividends have been paid
8. Dividend information
9. Dividend increases in the last ten years
10. Percentage dividend payout on a five-year average
11. Earnings per share for recent years
12. The growth rate as a trend for the latest five years
13. The growth rate for the last year recorded

Especially significant in *Stocks on the Big Board,* for each stock on the same page are two figures, a growth rate and a P/E multiple. These are especially important to more aggressive investors who are concerned about capital gains. Although many publications have P/E ratios for many companies, and several have earnings data for several years, *Stocks on the Big Board* has both computed growth rates and P/E multiples for all those companies side by side. This is especially helpful to investors who place primary importance upon growth as a quantitative selection tool. As a matter of fact, this is one of the few publications that include growth rates for the latest five years and the last year. The information is arranged so that the investor can easily compare data about various stocks within a particular industry. In addition to all these data for each of the stocks on the exchange, the booklet includes a number of unusual data at the beginning of each issue, sometimes listing favorite stocks of institutional investors, sometimes listing those companies that have increased dividends in each of the last ten years, and periodically providing other interesting data. At the end of this booklet, those corporations that have had consecutively higher earnings for the past three years are listed with financial data about each corporation; following that, *Stocks on the Big Board* provides graphic data about the New York Stock Exchange Index, the Standard & Poor's Industrials Index (425 stocks) for the last four years, and various price patterns for the stocks in various major industries. This financial data can be exceedingly helpful to any investor who is attempting to improve his selection process.

Table 10–11 Page from *Stocks on the Big Board—Winter 1971*

COMMON STOCKS SHOWING 5-YEAR COMPOUND GROWTH RATE IN EARNINGS PER SHARE, GROUPED BY INDUSTRIES.

ISSUE	No. Insts. Hldg. Stk.	1970-71 Price Range		Closing Price Jan. 18	% Yld. on Ind. Div.	P-E Ratio	Cash Divs. Ea.Yr. Since	DIVIDENDS Ind. Rate $	Paid 1970 $	% Increase Last 10 Yrs.	% Payout 5-Yr. Av.	EARNINGS ($) Per Sh. Yr. End.	1968	1969	¶ Last 12 Mos.	GROWTH RATE % Trend Latest 5 Yrs.	Last Yr. Rep'td
1—AEROSPACE																	
AMBAC Industries	13	20⅞	7½	13⅛	3.8	12	1965	0.50	0.50	‡100	25	Dc	1.50	1.52	[9]1.11	24	11
Amtel, Inc.	2	15⅝	5⅝	7¼	4.4	14	1964	0.32	0.32	♦167	29	Dc	1.04	0.93	[9]0.52	36	—
•Aro Corp.	0	20¼	13	19½	4.6	11	1931	0.90	0.90	122	39	Nv	2.01	1.92	[8]1.80	11	—
•Curtiss-Wright	5	18⅞	10⅛	12⅜	4.8	29	1940	0.60	0.90	13	75	Dc	1.30	1.36	[9]0.43	14	5
•Grumman Corp.	23	26¼	12¾	23⅞	4.2	8	1933	1.00	1.00	104	25	Dc	2.67	3.10	[9]2.89	8	16
Kidde (Walter) & Co.	42	46¾	15	28¼	s—	10		2½%Stk	2½%Stk	—	—	Dc	3.15	3.61	[9]R2.70	27	15
Martin Marietta	48	20⅞	11⅛	20⅜	5.4	11	1954	1.10	1.10	29	55	Dc	2.08	2.21	[9]1.93	10	6
McDonnell Douglas	61	28	13	24½	1.6	8	1950	0.40	0.40	310	y17	Dc	3.47	4.27	[9]R2.93	11	23
Northrop Corp.	25	35¾	15⅝	25¾	3.9	7	1951	1.00	1.00	25	30	Jy	‡3.80	‡4.06	[10]3.93	14	7
Rohr Corp	14	26½	14¼	17⅜	4.6	7	1950	0.80	0.80	19	35	Jy	‡2.81	‡2.92	[10]2.59	16	4
Southwest Airmotive	17	26	11	15⅞	s—	17	—	3%Stk	3%Stk	—	—	My	‡0.91	‡1.08	[11]R0.95	27	19
•Sundstrand Corp.	38	30¼	12⅛	25½	3.1	14	1940	0.80	0.80	67	32	Dc	2.90	□2.01	[9]1.82	22	—
Systron Donner	5	28⅝	7⅞	10⅝	—	15	—	Nil	—	—	—	Jy	‡△1.05	‡△0.82	[10]0.71	5	—
Talley Industries	12	38¼	6¾	11½	—	—	—	Nil	—	—	—	Mr	2.68	■0.08	0.08	15	—
Thiokol Chemical Corp.	4	14⅛	7	11	3.6	11	1966	0.40	0.40	#60	x32	Dc	1.19	1.20	[9]1.01	7	1
•TRW, Inc.	78	38½	22¾	35⅛	3.0	14	1936	1.05	1.05	231	39	Dc	2.23	2.44	[9]R2.47	14	9
•United Aircraft Corp.	137	40½	23⅝	38⅝	4.7	12	1936	1.80	1.80	35	36	Dc	5.10	4.21	[9]3.31	8	—
Watkins Johnson	22	23⅛	9⅜	23⅛	—	29	—	Nil	—	—	—	Dc	1.14	0.64	[9]0.81	19	—
Whittaker Corp.	29	19⅜	5	7¾	—	28	—	Nil	—	—	—	Oc	‡R△1.42	R□0.28	R0.28	10	—
2—AIR TRANSPORT																	
Delta Air Lines	133	38½	24⅛	37¾	1.3	16	1949	0.50	0.45	400	17	Jn	‡2.05	‡2.33	[9]2.34	10	14
Emery Air Freight	21	62	41	60	1.7	38	1952	1.00	0.92½	517	67	Dc	1.13	▲1.23	[9]1.58	18	9
KLM Royal Dutch Air	7	56¼	28	55¼	4.0	8	1967	☆2.22	☆2.22	—	—	Mr	▲9.86	6.93	[9]7.10	27	—
Northwest Airlines	197	29	14⅜	23⅜	1.9	9	1955	0.45	0.45	350	12	Dc	▲2.74	2.55	[6]2.56	9	—
World Airways, Inc.	0	11⅞	5	8	—	23	—	Nil	—	—	—	Dc	1.20	0.93	[9]0.35	19	—
3—AMUSEMENTS — Motion Pictures																	
Columbia Pictures Ind.	21	31½	8⅝	13⅜	s—	16	1967	3%Stk	0.45s	—	—	Jn	‡1.00	‡1.02	[9]0.84	22	2
Disney (Walt) Prod.	53	82	45	79	0.2	41	1957	0.15s	0.15s	97	8	Sp	‡1.67	‡1.88	[12]1.92	7	13
4—Radio & TV Broadcasters																	
Capital Cities Broadcasting	43	36½	19½	34¼	—	21	—	Nil	—	—	—	Dc	1.55	1.84	[9]R1.60	28	19
Cox Broadcasting	13	24⅝	10¼	20½	1.5	17	1964	0.30	0.30	♦200	20	Dc	1.19	1.23	[9]1.23	12	3
Taft Broadcasting	29	29¾	13⅞	27⅞	2.2	15	1959	0.60	0.60	233	29	Mr	2.02	△1.85	[12]1.88	5	—
5—Other																	
•AMF, Inc.	59	29½	16⅝	28½	3.2	14	1927	0.90	0.90	30	62	Dc	□1.54	1.85	[9]2.00	11	20
•Bell & Howell Co.	37	57⅜	22½	33½	1.8	17	1936	0.60	0.60	50	24	Dc	△2.45	△2.07	[9]R1.93	14	—
Berkey Photo	25	18⅛	5⅛	8¾	—	19	—	Nil	—	—	—	Dc	△1.17	△0.84	[9]0.45	5	—
Brunswick Corp.	33	21⅞	9⅞	21½	0.6	23	1969	0.12	0.10	—	—	Dc	△0.68	0.78	[9]0.96	⊕120	15
•Eastman Kodak Co.	742	84⅝	57⅝	75¼	1.8	30	1902	1.32	1.28	164	48	Dc	2.33	2.49	[9]2.52	16	7
Hunt (Phil A.) Chem.	11	23⅛	13	16½	0.7	30	1964	0.12	0.12	♦100	29	Dc	0.41	0.52	[9]0.55	32	27
Mattel Inc.	39	41	24⅛	40	0.3	35	1960	0.10	0.10	233	21	Ja	0.64	0.91	[10]1.14	29	42
Milton Bradley	18	26½	13¾	23⅜	2.6	17	1951	0.60	0.60	z999	38	Dc	1.11	1.32	[9]1.38	10	19
•Polaroid Corp.	304	130¾	51	85⅞	0.4	48	1952	0.32	0.32	z999	13	Dc	1.86	*1.90	[9]1.80	26	2
6—AUTO PARTS																	
Bearings, Inc.	7	50¼	33½	42⅛	2.4	11	1957	1.00	1.00	67	25	Jn	‡3.76	‡4.10	[9]4.01	9	9
Budd Co.	15	18¼	6	12⅝	—	def	1947	Nil	0.45	—	—	Dc	1.89	1.75	[9]Rd0.42	16	—
•Champion Spark Plug	44	31½	19¾	31⅜	3.8	13	1919	1.20	1.20	33	58	Dc	2.14	2.24	[9]2.37	10	5
•Dana Corp.	17	29¾	18¾	27	4.6	13	1936	1.25	1.25	40	47	Au	‡2.50	‡2.60	[11]2.15	5	4
•Eaton Yale & Towne	83	40⅝	22¼	35⅞	3.9	13	1923	1.40	1.40	56	42	Dc	2.86	3.46	[9]2.75	5	21
Echlin Mfg. Co.	17	33⅜	15½	30⅞	1.7	22	1950	0.52	0.51	285	43	Au	‡1.00	‡1.32	[11]1.40	15	32
Gateway Industries	1	11½	4⅞	6	—	7	—	Nil	—	—	—	Dc	1.60	1.06	[9]0.83	31	—
Genuine Parts	9	37½	21¾	37⅜	2.0	24	1948	0.75	0.72⅞	265	40	Dc	1.29	1.47	[9]R1.57	12	14
Houdaille Industries	6	15⅞	8⅝	13	4.6	14	1947	0.60	0.75	219	45	Dc	1.55	1.52	[9]0.93	11	—
McCord Corp.	7	30	18⅞	28	4.3	9	1946	1.20s	1.20s	20	35	Au	‡4.27	‡△3.31	[11]2.95	14	—
Monroe Auto Equipment	43	50⅜	27	45⅝	1.3	20	1958	0.60	0.60	♦200	22	Jn	‡1.92	‡2.19	[9]2.32	35	14
•Purolator Inc.	16	76	42	75¼	2.1	18	1941	1.60	1.60	240	43	Dc	3.78	3.84	[9]4.17	10	2
•Smith (A. O.) Corp.	5	49	25½	46¼	3.0	10	1940	1.40	1.40	—	27	Dc	4.68	5.84	[9]4.84	43	25
•SOS Consolidated	0	21⅜	10	16⅞	2.6	10	1943	0.44	0.44	z999	21	Au	‡1.96	‡1.75	[11]1.75	18	—

For explanation of items in tables see page 7. Footnote information is on page 30. ☆Div. excludes 15% tax withheld at source for which refund can be claimed. ‡ Comparison 1969 versus 1970. ¶ Period ended indicated by superior number: [1] for Jan., [2] for Feb., etc.

Reprinted with permission from *Stocks on the Big Board — Winter 1971* (New York: New York Stock Exchange, February 1971) p. 13.

STANDARD & POOR'S COMPANY REPORTS

A third publication that is readily available, and especially appreciated by many investors, is the series of company reports prepared by Standard & Poor's. Table 10–12 shows the U.S. Steel report. The data was up to date at the time of its publication. Obviously subsequent reports issued

Table 10–12   Example of an Individual Company Report

X[1]

U. S. Steel   2358

Stock—	Price Feb. 1'71	Dividend	Yield
COMMON	33¼	[2]$2.40	[2]7.2%

RECOMMENDATION: This large integrated company sustained a decline in its leading market share of the steel industry along with a relatively poor earnings record within the past decade. However, a massive capital program designed to effect major economy moves and emphasize expansion in flat rolled steels together with diversification efforts should be beneficial. The stock is viewed as reasonably priced on near-term earnings expectations, but increased domestic and foreign competition and the less-than-impressive growth prospects for the steel industry are restrictive factors in the longer-range outlook.

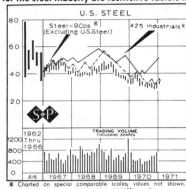

TOTAL REVENUES (Million $)

Quarter:	1970	1969	1968	1967	1966
March	1,177	1,081	1,095	965	950
June........	1,298	1,266	1,438	1,037	1,194
Sept........	1,265	1,170	1,076	1,013	1,215
Dec.	1,143	1,308	1,001	1,053	1,076

Based on a preliminary report, revenues for 1970 edged up slightly (1.2%) from those of the preceding year, aided by higher selling prices on most major products, and a higher level of export shipments. The gain was restricted by the general economic slowdown, plus the adverse effect of the GM strike in the fourth quarter and the trucking and steelhaulers' strikes during the second quarter. Margins came under pressure from rising labor and raw material costs (particularly for scrap) and a less favorable product mix; pretax income fell 43%. After lower taxes at 9.8% (aided by investment tax credits and mineral production payments), versus 23.8%, net income declined 32%. Share earnings were $2.72, compared with $4.01 in 1969.

PROSPECTS

Near Term— Aided by a general economic recovery and the contribution of sales deferred as a result of the GM strike, revenues for 1971 are likely to exceed the $4.88 billion of 1970. Volume through the first seven months should be disproportionately heavy as customers build stockpiles in advance of the August 1, 1971 expiration of the present union contract. Sales could decline sharply after that date.

Despite rising labor and raw material costs, margins are likely to benefit from the higher volume and substantial price increases. Thus, barring a long strike, earnings for 1971 could modestly exceed the $2.72 a share of 1970. Dividends at $0.60 quarterly are not considered completely secure.

Long Term— Secular growth in steel consumption is expected to be at a slower rate than the projected expansion in the general economy. Diversification moves, improved cost controls, and a better competitive position are prerequisites to realization of the company's profit potential.

RECENT DEVELOPMENTS

In January, 1971 the company raised prices an average of 6.8% on structural shapes, carbon plates, and piling. The new prices, which are effective March 1, 1971 do not carry a 12-month price maintenance guarantee, as did the 1970 price increases. Extra charges which are added to the base price were not changed, which effectively reduced the delivered cost to less than the average increase.

The second phase of development of the Mt. Wright iron ore body in Quebec, Canada has commenced. An annual capacity of 16 million gross tons of concentrates is contemplated by 1975. Cost of the project is estimated at $300 million.

DIVIDEND DATA

COMMON SHARE EARNINGS ($)

Quarter:	1970	1969	1968	1967	1966
March	0.66	0.94	1.29	0.76	0.93
June........	0.72	0.98	1.90	0.80	1.43
Sept.	0.62	0.87	0.61	0.67	1.13
Dec.	0.72	1.22	0.89	0.96	1.11

Dividends in the past 12 months were:

Amt. of Divd. $	Date Decl.	Ex-divd. Date	Stock of Record	Payment Date
0.60...	Apr. 28	May 4	May 8	Jun. 10'70
0.60...	Jul. 28	Aug. 3	Aug. 7	Sep. 10'70
0.60...	Oct. 27	Oct. 30	Nov. 6	Dec. 10'70
0.60...	Jan. 26	Feb. 1	Feb. 5	Mar. 10'71

[1]Listed N.Y.S.E.; also listed Midwest & Pacific Coast S.Es. & traded Boston, Cincinnati, Detroit, Phila.-Balt.-Wash. & Pittsburgh S.Es.   [2]Indicated rate (see text).

Table 10–12 (continued)

2358   UNITED STATES STEEL CORPORATION

INCOME STATISTICS (Million $) AND PER SHARE ($) DATA

Year Ended Dec. 31	Net Sales	% Oper. Inc. of Sales	Oper. Inc.	¹Deprec. & Depl.	Net Bef Taxes	Net Inc.	Common Share ($) Data — Earns.	Divs. Paid	Price Range	Price-Earns. Ratios HI LO
1971--	----	---	----	----	----	----	---	0.60	--------	
1970--	----	---	----	----	²163.5	²147.5	²2.72	2.40	39½-28⅛	15-10
1969--	4,754	12.1	574.5	297.7	285.2	217.2	4.01	2.40	49 -32¾	12- 8
1968--	4,537	13.3	601.3	256.0	353.7	253.7	4.69	2.40	45½-38	10- 8
1967--	4,006	14.9	595.9	357.2	248.5	172.5	3.19	2.40	50¼-38	16-12
1966--	4,355	17.6	766.8	349.4	445.2	249.2	4.60	2.10	55¾-35	12- 8
1965--	4,400	18.2	800.5	328.4	510.5	275.5	4.62	2.00	55⅞-46	12-10
1964--	4,077	18.9	770.1	339.7	451.8	236.8	3.91	2.00	64½-50½	17-13
1963--	3,599	18.7	674.0	316.1	368.5	203.5	3.30	2.00	57½-43½	17-13
1962--	3,469	16.3	566.9	270.9	295.7	163.7	2.56	2.75	78⅞-37¾	31-15
1961--	3,302	16.9	556.8	212.3	351.2	190.2	3.05	3.00	91¼-75¼	30-25
1960--	3,649	20.6	749.9	214.2	574.2	304.2	5.16	3.00	103¼-69¼	20-13

PERTINENT BALANCE SHEET STATISTICS (Million $)

Dec. 31	Gross Prop.	Capital Expend.	Cash Items	Inven-tories	Receiv-ables	Current Assets	Current Liabs.	Net Workg. Cap.	Cur. Ratio Assets to Liabs.	Long Term Debt	($) Book Val. Com. Sh.
1969--	9,051	601.8	349.0	868.6	647.6	1,865.2	1,331.6	533.6	1.4-1	1,434.67	66.47
1968--	8,581	697.4	729.8	813.5	467.2	2,010.6	1,135.2	875.3	1.8-1	1,571.26	64.87
1967--	8,011	574.7	430.8	842.8	398.5	1,672.0	1,016.8	655.2	1.6-1	1,200.73	62.59
1966--	7,553	440.7	787.8	726.5	379.3	1,893.6	1,069.6	824.0	1.8-1	1,252.80	61.32
1965--	7,196	353.6	764.2	641.8	344.5	1,750.6	860.0	890.6	2.0-1	705.09	62.94
1964--	6,902	292.6	583.0	700.4	390.5	1,673.9	847.5	826.4	2.0-1	745.42	60.09
1963--	6,669	244.7	857.4	641.5	279.3	1,778.3	766.6	1,011.6	2.3-1	770.57	57.95
1962--	6,553	200.6	691.3	743.3	252.0	1,686.6	723.3	963.3	2.3-1	833.44	56.66
1961--	6,549	326.8	642.2	793.3	267.6	1,703.1	755.7	947.5	2.3-1	893.40	56.60
1960	6,303	492.4	451.7	725.6	218.5	1,395.8	787.7	608.1	1.8-1	422.78	56.56

¹Incl. amort. ²Preliminary.

Fundamental Position

U. S. Steel produced 34.7 million tons of steel in 1969 (24.6% of the industry total), and shipped 22.4 million tons of finished products (23.8% of the industry). Steelmaking capacity is over 42 million tons. Operations are fully integrated, embracing vast iron ore, coal and limestone reserves as well as railroad, shipping, ironmaking, finishing, fabricating and structural sheet erection operations. The company is one of the largest sellers of iron ore, and a major cement producer, but steel is believed to account for about 85% of dollar volume.

Steelmaking capacity is located as follows: Chicago area 33%, Pittsburgh district 30%, Youngstown and Lorain, Ohio 13%, Alabama 10%, eastern Pa. (Fairless works) 7%, Utah and California (Columbia-Geneva division) 7%. The corporation's product mix in the heavier weight steels is proportionately much higher than the industry average but expansion in lighter, flat-rolled products is now being emphasized. The latest available breakdown of finishing facilities by products is: sheet and strip 28%, plates and structurals 25%, bars 13%, tubular products 12%, tinplate 10%, wire 9%, rails and others 3%.

Iron ore mined in 1969 totaled 44 million tons, with more than three quarters of output used for internal operations and the remainder sold commercially. Iron ore reserves exceed 2 billion tons; about half is in the United States and the rest consists of high grade deposits in South America and concentrated grades in Canada.

The American Bridge division, fabricates and erects bridges, buildings, barges and related structures. A broad line of machinery and equipment for the petroleum industry is distributed through the Oilwell division, and numerous varieties of steel drums and pails are manufactured by the U. S. Steel Products division.

The U. S. Steel Supply division operates 28 steel service centers in 22 states.

Chemical products, which consist primarily of coal by-product chemicals, are conducted through USS Agri-Chemicals, serving the agricultural chemical field, and USS Chemicals, serving industrial chemical, tar product and plastic markets. A joint-venture for the production of a polyethylene resin is planned.

Production of specialty cements is conducted through the Universal Atlas Cement division and the Bahama Cement Co.

Other operations include engineering and consulting services, housing and real estate, aluminum products, titanium and financing services. USS is also actively engaged in world-wide mineral exploration.

Common dividends, paid since 1940, averaged 61% of earnings in 1966-70.

Finances

Capital outlays for 1970 totaled $514 million, down from $602 million in 1969. Authorizations for new plant and equipment made during 1970 totaled $634 million. U. S. Steel could be required to pay up to $200 million in back taxes as a result of a recent unfavorable court ruling.

CAPITALIZATION

LONG TERM DEBT: $1,398,700,000.
COMMON STOCK: 54,169,462 shares ($30 par).

Incorporated in N.J. in 1901; reincorporated in Del. in 1965. **Offices**—71 Broadway, NYC 10006; 525 William Penn Place, Pittsburgh, Pa. 15230. **Pres**—E. B. Speer. **Secy**—B. L. Rawlins. **VP-Treas**—R. W. Hyde. **Dirs**—E. H. Gott (Chrmn), R. M. Blough, H. Branch, Jr., H. T. Heald, A. A. Houghton, Jr., T. V. Jones, R. H. Larry, F. J. Lunding, W. M. Martin, Jr., G. M. Metcalf, J. M. Meyer, Jr., G. S. Moore, H. I. Romnes, S. I. Saunders, E. B. Speer, R. C. Tyson, W. A. Walker, H. S. Wingate, L. B. Worthington. **Transfer Agents**—Company's offices; Continental Illinois National Bank & Trust Co., Chicago. **Registrars**—First National Bank of Chicago; Morgan Guaranty Trust Co., NYC.

From the N.Y.S.E. Stock Reports. Reprinted with permission of Standard & Poor's Corp.

on U.S. Steel have revised the data. Notice that these reports give the following information:

1. Recent price, dividend, and yield
2. Recommendation
3. Total revenue data
4. Comments on prospects
5. Comments on recent developments
6. Earnings and dividend data
7. Income statement data
8. Balance sheet data
9. Comments on numerous qualitative factors
10. Capitalization data

These reports are available for thousands of individual corporations, those listed on organized exchanges and many traded over the counter. These reports are available at brokerage firms along with reports prepared by the brokerage firm's research staff.

Certainly, with all three of these publications, any investor can consume several hours of time and several pounds of energy. Even with only one, any one, the investor will have sufficient data to improve his selection process. The P/E ratio is readily available; several profitability rates of return can be quickly determined; growth rates are given in *Stocks on the Big Board,* and can be readily computed from data in the other two. Although no indebtedness ratio is computed, the capitalization data necessary to compute either a debt to equity ratio, or debt to total investment ratio, are presented in both the *Stock Guide* and the company reports; similarly, although neither the current ratio, nor the cash ratio, is computed in the three publications, the cash data, current assets data, and the current liability data are presented in both the *Stock Guide* and the company reports. With only these three free publications, the investor can check the quantitative data on thousands of specific corporations, finding many of the quantitative measures already computed, and all the other necessary data ready for rapid calculation. As you acquire some facility in your selection efforts, some tools will be more helpful to you than others. You may even decide you need considerably more detailed information. To initiate your efforts, however, these tools will surely be more than adequate.

CHAPTER ELEVEN

USING PROFESSIONAL PORTFOLIO MANAGEMENT

Professionally managed investment portfolios are an alternative to constructing and managing your own portfolio. Particularly for an investor who has a relatively small investment portfolio and perhaps for anyone who is just beginning an investment program, the time and energy required to construct and manage a personal investment portfolio may not be worth the return. If you accept the definition that investing is the acquisition of assets of reasonable risk in anticipation of a financial return, you might be hard-pressed to justify managing your own portfolio for only a few dollars return each year. Furthermore, some investors find it very difficult, if not indeed impossible, to manage their own portfolios effectively, regardless of how hard they try. If you are really concerned about receiving an acceptable rate of return on your portfolio, and you find it difficult to earn that rate of return through your own efforts, you should seriously consider using professional portfolio management to make sure that you achieve your investment goal.

Most relatively small investors who choose to use professional portfolio management do so through the purchase of mutual funds. Another alternative quite similar to the mutual fund is the closed-end investment company. Furthermore, as indicated in Chapter Eight some investors might be interested in a real estate investment trust. In recent years, variable annuities have been attracting considerable investor attention. For larger investors, common trust funds offered by various commercial banks might also be considered. All of these funds exist because many investors are interested in buying stocks, bonds, or real estate, but do not choose to select their own securities and manage their own portfolios. Professionally managed investment funds are established for the express purpose of aggregating the funds of many investors, individuals and institutions, to construct a sizable investment portfolio, consisting of millions of dollars (one sufficiently large to attract capable, competent, professional analysts and portfolio managers). Although no individual investor with a small investment program could afford the professional investment advice and management he might desire, when millions of individual investors and institutions pool their funds under the supervision of such professional investment management, the cost per investor is relatively slight.

(A mutual fund is an investment company that continues to offer its shares to additional investors, and stands ready to buy back those shares at their net asset value at any time) All the money received from the sale of such mutual fund shares is then invested in stocks and bonds of various corporations according to the agreement between the fund management and its shareholders. As those corporate stocks and bonds pay dividends and interest, the fund management distributes them to the fund shareholders. As the stocks in the mutual fund portfolio appreciate in market price, the net asset value of the fund shares appreciates. (Net asset value is the total fund portfolio divided by the number of fund shares outstanding.) As the fund management sells stocks that have appreciated in price, the capital gains are distributed to the fund shareholders. The management continuously evaluates the fund investments as well as alternative investments, sells stocks that should be sold, and reinvests the proceeds of such sales along with all additional money received from the sale of additional fund shares. For this professional portfolio management, the mutual fund managers are paid an annual fee of about one-half of 1 percent of the total portfolio value.·

The closed-end investment company issues a fixed number of shares permanently, and proceeds to manage the portfolio acquired through the sale of those shares. It does not continually issue new shares, nor will it redeem its outstanding shares. Any investor who owns shares in a closed-end investment company, who wishes to sell those shares, must find a buyer for them just as is the case of any investor owning any stock of any corporation. Several closed-end investment companies have listed their shares on organized exchanges, however, so resale is feasible, although not necessarily at the net asset value. The seller of closed-end investment company shares can receive no more than what the highest bidder is willing to pay, regardless of the net asset value of the fund shares, and occasionally he must sell at sizable discounts below the par share value of the total portfolio. Although there are several basic differences between closed-end funds and mutual funds (open-end funds) the management of a closed-end investment company performs most of the same portfolio operations that a mutual fund management performs.

Variable annuities offer another ready-made, professionally managed portfolio. They are sold by life insurance companies, primarily to provide retirement income. They differ from ordinary annuities in that they do not guarantee to the annuitant a lifetime payment of a given number of dollars each month after retirement; rather, they guarantee to the annuitant a lifetime payment of a fixed number of units of the fund, based on the fluctuating value of the investments included in the fund. Traditionally, fixed annuities have invested their premiums received in bonds and mortgages because fixed annuities do require a guaranteed lifetime dollar payment to annuitants. However, with the significant increase in inflation, dollar guarantees have become increasingly less attractive. Therefore, life insurance companies have created variable annuities in an effort to guarantee the purchasing power of retirement dollars. With variable annuities, life insurance companies invest their premiums received in common stocks with the expectation that stock price appreciation will provide a better rate of return than they could earn on only fixed income investments, certainly a rate of return adequate to overcome inflation. Variable annuities do continue to sell additional units at a price equal to the net asset value of existing units. The fund management continuously invests those additional dollars along with the proceeds on any sales of portfolio holdings that may result from continuous portfolio adjustments. Under most variable annuity plans, the investor can cash out his portfolio value, although under some, he may be able to cash out only fractions of his total holding.

Many commercial banks have recently created common trust funds to provide professional portfolio management for their clients. Although investors who have sizable portfolios may still receive personalized investment trust management from most banks, portfolios of $100,000 or more are increasingly necessary to acquire that personalized attention. On the other hand, by commingling all funds held in trust into one or a few large investment portfolios, perhaps one or two rather conservative trust funds and one or two growth trust funds, considerable care and attention may be devoted to those few portfolios by very capable analysts and portfolio managers at relatively little cost for any one investor. Bank common trust funds seem to be increasing in popularity. In most cases, however, they are used by larger investors who have accumulated an investment portfolio that they want to place in trust for someone else. The funds are placed in trust with the bank as trustee, and the bank manages the portfolio for the beneficiary of the trust who may receive no return from the trust for many years, depending upon the terms of the trust.

Real estate investment trusts, likewise, are designed to provide that same professional management that the other funds provide, but the money placed in a real estate investment trust is invested in real estate rather than in securities. By investing in a real estate trust, the investor has the advantages of real estate investing, and the managers of the trust assume all the management problems. Real estate investment trusts also seem to be increasing in popularity, and may well be more important investment vehicles in the future.

Although each of these alternative funds provides many advantages to many people and may well deserve considerable emphasis, most investors who choose to build their investment programs through the use of a ready-made, professionally managed investment portfolio do so through mutual funds. Consequently, this chapter will be devoted primarily to buying mutual funds. There are many alternative mutual funds available with widely different investment approaches, securities held, portfolio income, price appreciation, and numerous special features. With the development of the mutual fund industry in recent decades, many investors have discovered solutions to their investment problems through the purchase of mutual fund shares.

BUYING MUTUAL FUNDS

In recent years, mutual funds have increasingly offered additional services, some have earned surprisingly large rates of return, and as a whole they have become increasingly popular as an investment medium. With the creation of several hundred new mutual funds over the last ten to 15 years, investors are now much more likely to find the kinds of funds they want with professional management attitudes that more closely represent their own investment attitudes. Traditionally, mutual funds were designed to represent the market as a whole. Most funds included some bonds, some preferred stocks, defensive common stocks, and a few aggressive common stocks. In short, most mutual funds had balanced portfolios. More recently, many mutual funds have invested all their holdings in just one type of security, such as growth stocks or municipal bonds; or in one industry, such as the electronics industry, the space industry, or the oceanography industry. Consequently, investors who are interested in one particular type of stock or industry but do not have the inclination to investigate all those alternative stocks of that type or in that industry may invest in a mutual fund managed by professional portfolio managers who have promised to invest all their shareholders' funds according to that particular portfolio approach. Although considerable diversification within the fund may exist, the investor may nevertheless assume a high degree of investment concentration in a specific type of stock or a specific industry.

Basically, there are three types of mutual funds: (1) balanced funds, (2) growth funds, and (3) specialty funds. The balanced funds attempt to diversify their portfolios among many kinds of bonds (corporate, municipal, state and federal), and stocks from many industries. Although balanced funds do emphasize particular industries they nevertheless represent considerable diversification. Furthermore, although they own both bonds and stocks, they may vary the proportions of their portfolios in bonds and stocks, depending upon specific economic and market conditions. When the stock market appears to be generally overpriced, more bonds may be held, whereas when the market appears underpriced a much larger proportion of the portfolio may be placed in stocks, perhaps even in some aggressive common stocks. In general, balanced funds are quite conservative; they are constructed and managed to earn about an average rate of return of 9 percent but to assume less than an average amount of risk.

Growth funds are invested almost exclusively in common stocks, and specifically in common stocks that are expected to appreciate at considerably more rapid rates than the market in general, perhaps with a goal of 14 percent return. Because growth fund managers construct their portfolios using growth stocks, however, considerably larger fluctuations in their portfolio values may occur. During bear markets, growth funds may fall considerably more than either the market as a whole, or balanced funds in general whereas during bull markets they may appreciate in value considerably more than either the market in general or balanced funds. Consequently, the investor who has growth as a primary investment objective, if he is willing to accept larger portfolio fluctuations, may place most of his portfolio in growth funds.

Specialty funds are constructed and managed in an effort to accomplish some more specific portfolio objective. Some are designed to provide current income; therefore, funds are invested primarily in bonds, preferred stocks, and common stocks with high yields. Although specialty funds may give the appearance of balanced funds, they are actually designed to provide considerably more current income than price appreciation. In fact, some of them are devoted exclusively to various types of bonds. Some other specialty funds are built using only very speculative common stocks; therefore, they may hold only very low priced stocks, or only stocks representing one specific industry. These specialty funds, therefore, may be very conservative or extremely speculative, depending upon their portfolio objectives. In addition to these three basic types of mutual funds, there are many others. For example, there are differences in management costs; some offer numerous special features and services, whereas others do not; some differ greatly in their investment philosophies although their basic objectives may be quite similar; and they differ in the abilities of their managers.

Since the investment characteristics of various mutual funds differ so much, the individual investor can select from many available mutual funds only those funds that offer the services and features he wants, and whose objectives most closely match his own. If he is more interested in a conservative approach, he may invest more of his portfolio in balanced fund shares. If he is more interested in aggressive performance, he may invest more of his portfolio in growth fund shares. If he is inclined to include some speculative stocks in his portfolio, he may wish to buy some specialty fund shares. In each and every case, however, his mutual funds are managed by professional portfolio managers who devote their full time and energy to managing their funds. By varying the proportions of his portfolio devoted to different risk categories, the investor can construct his own portfolio in the light of his own risk and return requirements. He can still determine his basic portfolio approach; yet he can turn over the problems of managing securities to his professional portfolio managers.

BUYING A PORTFOLIO APPROACH

Throughout the previous three chapters, considerable emphasis has been placed upon the importance of using a portfolio approach to investing. By investing in mutual funds, the investor buys a portfolio approach which meets his investment objectives. For example, an investor can invest all his money in a balanced mutual fund designed to provide considerable market representation with considerable diversification at considerable risk reduction. In so doing, he accepts that one fund as his portfolio approach. On the other hand, an investor may not wish to buy shares in only one fund, even one that represents his personal investment objectives rather well. As an alternative, he may prefer to invest in several mutual funds at once, placing perhaps 50 percent of his portfolio in one or more balanced funds, 40 percent of his portfolio in one or more growth funds, and 10 percent of his portfolio in one or more speculative mutual funds. By so doing, he still constructs his portfolio in accordance with his previously selected investment objectives, but he avoids the problems of selecting individual securities for his portfolio, and the problems of managing and evaluating his portfolio regularly. Furthermore, he even avoids the risk of relying upon only one mutual fund management. Subsequently, his own personal evaluations would be comparisons between the performances of the mutual fund managers who manage his portfolio, and the performances of those investment managers who manage the mutual funds he does not own. His own personal portfolio management efforts would be limited to adjusting the proportions of his portfolio invested in his various mutual funds as well as continuing to invest his additional savings according to his investment program. By reducing his own personal portfolio responsibilities, and depending upon professional portfolio managers to select specific securities, he may well increase the probability that his investment approach will achieve his ultimate investment goal.

As a specific example, consider again the case of Seymour Green. He knows his investment goal is $250,000. He knows that he wants a 9 percent rate of return. He knows that he must take a somewhat aggressive approach to earn that 9 percent rate of return. He also knows some of the constraints with which he must work; specifically, he has only $300 a year to invest, he has no investment experience, and he has already committed time and energy to his professional career. Certainly, any investor such as Seymour Green might seriously consider buying into a mutual fund, or several mutual funds, that represent his own portfolio approach to avoid the necessity of managing his own portfolio. In Seymour's case, he has already decided that he wants to invest 30 percent of his portfolio in conservative stocks, 60 percent in growth stocks, and 10 percent in speculative stocks. However, he has also considered all the problems involved in selecting specific securities and managing his own portfolio, and is seriously questioning whether he should go to all that trouble. As an alternative, he is considering buying three mutual funds, Consolidated Balanced Fund, Hallelujah Growth Fund, and Possible Bonanza Fund, each representing one of the three components of his portfolio. As long as the managers of his three funds continue to perform their functions well, he may need to make no changes in his portfolio. If one or more of the funds should fail to perform according to his expectations, of course, he may wish to make a change. Furthermore, if he should decide to change the proportions of his conservative, growth, and speculative holdings, in response to changing market conditions, he may also wish to make some portfolio adjustments for that reason. At no time, however, must he be concerned about selecting specific securities since his three fund managers have assumed that responsibility.

In the beginning his investment program will be only $300 a year. The dollar return on his portfolio will be very, very small regardless of his managerial efforts. If through some considerable effort on his part, he were able to earn a 15 percent rate of return on his portfolio rather than perhaps 10 percent through mutual funds, he would still earn only $45 on his portfolio that first year; with little or no effort, he might earn $30. Just how much time and effort is that additional $15 worth? Considering Mr. Green's inexperience, there may be some serious question whether he can achieve a 15 percent rate of return on his portfolio; he might not even hold his own. Therefore, at least initially, Mr. Green may well decide that he should invest his $300 a year in a ready-made portfolio managed by professional investment managers.

WHY BUY MUTUAL FUNDS?

In recent years, many investors have chosen to use mutual funds. As indicated in Table 11–1, mutual fund sales have been rather startling. Especially so when you consider that all mutual fund shares have been purchased voluntarily. Although pension fund assets are almost twice as large as those of mutual funds, almost all pension funds are nonvoluntary whereas mutual funds have grown because individual investors have voluntary chosen that means to build their investment portfolio. Investors buy mutual fund shares for many reasons, and perhaps no list however long could really be all-inclusive. However, six specific reasons are common to many investors. First, investors buy mutual funds because

Table 11–1   Growth of Mutual Fund Assets

Year	Mutual Funds
1969	$52,621,400,000
1968	56,953,600,000
1966	36,294,600,000
1964	30,370,300,000
1962	22,408,900,000
1960	17,383,300,000
1958	13,242,388,000
1956	9,046,431,000
1954	6,109,390,000
1952	3,931,407,000
1950	2,530,563,000
1948	1,505,762,000
1946	1,311,108,000
1944	882,191,000
1942	486,850,000
1940	447,959,000

From *Investment Companies 1970,* 30th edition. (New York: Wiesenberger Services, Inc. 1970), p. 13. Reprinted with permission of Wiesenberger Services, Inc.

they want to invest in common stocks in anticipation of a higher rate of return than they could receive from a savings account, but they do not want the responsibility of selecting specific securities. Second, they buy mutual funds because they believe that a professional portfolio manager might manage their portfolio funds more effectively with less risk than they could manage them themselves. Third, they buy fund shares because they want diversification as a means of protecting their portfolios, but they do not have sufficiently large portfolios to permit the purchase of more than one or two stocks. Fourth, investors buy funds because they believe dollar cost averaging is an effective financial aid to portfolio accumulation, but in many cases, the annual savings figure is inadequate to support the continuous and regular purchase of more than one or two individual securities. Fifth, investors buy funds because it is very convenient to let a professional portfolio manager assume all the responsibility of selecting specific securities and adjusting the portfolio in response to changing economic and market conditions. Sixth, many investors buy funds to provide themselves with an appropriate measure of their own portfolio performance; i.e., if they manage part of their investment funds and that part performs better than the portion of their portfolios that they have invested in mutual fund shares, they may take some additional satisfaction from having competed successfully against the professionals. Although there may be many other reasons that any individual investor might emphasize, probably all mutual fund investors would explain their purchases of mutual fund shares, at least in part, on these six bases.

Financial Return.   Since anyone who invests does so in anticipation of a financial return, it should come as no surprise that a buyer of mutual fund shares is interested in financial return. Actually, perhaps most investors who buy mutual funds shares do so because they expect to receive a higher rate of return on their investment portfolios through mutual funds than they could achieve through their own personal portfolio management efforts.

There are three sources of such returns on mutual funds: (1) dividends, (2) realized capital gains, and (3) unrealized capital gains that take the form of rising per share net asset values. In a great many cases, investors are perfectly correct in expecting a higher rate of return on their investment through mutual funds than they could achieve through their own personal management effort. Because mutual funds are managed by professional investors who devote all their time and energy to managing those funds, the fund investor could indeed hope to achieve a higher rate of return for any given amount of risk assumed. Furthermore, because thousands of individual investors have placed their funds under the supervision of professional portfolio management, the annual management fee for such service is often only one-half of 1 percent. If the professional management of the fund can indeed select securities more effectively than an individual investor, the dividends and price appreciation on the securities held in his fund should be greater than he would be able to achieve by himself.

When the fund receives dividends on the stocks it holds, those dividends are forwarded to the shareowners of the fund. As the stocks held by the fund appreciate in market value, those higher prices are reflected in higher net asset values of the fund shares. If and when the fund manager sells stocks out of the fund that have appreciated in value, the capital gains realized through that sale are also forwarded to the shareowners of the fund. The mutual fund owner, therefore, profits through dividends received, capital gains realized, and share value appreciation. As the stocks held by the fund appreciate in market price, the investor enjoys an increase in his fund shares' net asset value. The performance of his investment portfolio, therefore, would be determined by adding the three figures together: dividends, realized capital gains, and unrealized capital gains. In any given year, if an investor had a 3 percent dividend, a 4 percent realized capital gain, and a 4 percent unrealized capital gain, his total rate of return for the year would be 11 percent before taxes. By comparing that total annual rate of return against the performance of other mutual funds, or his personally managed portfolio, the investor may evaluate the effectiveness of his mutual fund's management.

Professional Management.   Considerable emphasis has already been placed upon the importance of professional portfolio management. Perhaps too much has been said, or at least implied, about the inevitable superiority and success of a professional over an amateur. Certainly, nothing said so far was meant to imply that all professionals are of equal talent or that no amateur can ever succeed. Professionals in any field do vary in their capabilities, and portfolio managers are surely no exception. Portfolio rates of return, however, must not be the only basis of judging a management's performance. All mutual funds have stated investment objectives, but some emphasize safety of principal, stability, and income, rather than above average rate of return. If a fund management accomplishes its objectives, it has performed well. If you buy shares in a fund whose objectives are the same as your own, you will achieve your investment goals as your fund manager succeeds in achieving his.

Diversification.   Many investors who are convinced that diversification is desirable, but do not have adequate investment capital to buy enough shares in several companies, choose mutual fund shares as a solution to their dilemma. Since a fund may include 50 or 100 different stocks, any fund share you buy provides you with a diversified portfolio since your one mutual fund share reflects the total number of stocks held by the mutual fund. Again, however, you should be cautioned about the misuse of diversification. Just because you own shares in a fund that has 50 or 100 different stocks in its portfolio, you do not necessarily have adequate diversification against all investment risks. Particularly, if you buy shares in a very speculative fund, you may have assumed tremendous risk. Even by investing in a well-diversified growth fund, you may assume more risk than you are aware. In bear markets when stocks in general decline 15 to 20 percent, growth funds may decline 30 percent and speculative funds may lose over half of their value. On the other hand, if you buy shares in a well-diversified balanced fund, you may indeed acquire adequate diversification through the purchase of only one share.

Whether or not any mutual fund is sufficiently diversified to protect you against all the investment risks will depend upon your own personal investment objectives and the investment objectives of the fund itself. Very often, you may determine the adequacy of such diversification by consulting the fund's prospectus which lists the assets held by the fund. Subsequently, if the fund shares decline more in the next bear market than you think acceptable, perhaps you should consider switching to a more fully diversified, better balanced fund. With almost 1,000 mutual funds from which to choose, you should be able to find many that offer a sufficiently well-diversified portfolio to meet your own personal requirements.

Dollar Cost Averaging.   Dollar cost averaging is a financial technique capable of increasing your portfolio rate of return. But as you will recall, dollar cost averaging requires the investment of the same amount of dollars in a stock regularly, over an extended period of time. By investing $25 each month, or $300 each year, dollar cost averaging does guarantee an above average rate of return, if you are investing in a security that gradually appreciates over time with some periodic fluctuations. However, since many investors can only save relatively small amounts each year, using dollar cost averaging requires the concentration of savings in only one investment. Although you may select a large, well-diversified corporation in which to invest, your portfolio would still consist of only one security, probably much more concentration than you would desire. On the other hand, if each year you invest in a different stock, you can diversify but you cannot use dollar cost averaging.

As an alternative, you might well consider the purchase of shares in a well-diversified fund, thereby avoiding the risk of concentration. By investing the same number of dollars each month or each year, you would obtain a better than average rate of return through dollar cost averaging, if these fund shares are appreciating over time yet fluctuating periodically. Most mutual funds' shares meet these two requirements, although some do not appreciate very rapidly, and still others may fluctuate far more than what you have in mind. Since there are so many funds available, however, you might well find several that are exactly what you are seeking. If you can decide on one, or a few, and can regularly invest the same number of dollars in those funds over an extended period of years, dollar cost averaging and diversification can both be used to increase your portfolio rate of return with less risk.

Convenience.   In addition to all the potential return and risk considerations involved in the purchase of mutual funds, many investors decide to buy funds simply because funds are such a convenient means of investing. Although a great many people are interested in initiating investment programs, by no means all of them are interested in analyzing alternative investments, evaluating stock performances, buying and selling individual stocks to adjust their portfolios in responses to changing stock values and changing economic and market conditions. For the small investor, being limited to only one, two, or a few stocks at the very most, he may not feel that his portfolio could provide him with a sufficient dollar return or with sufficient diversification to reward his risk assumption, time, and effort. In a few funds, it is possible to invest as little as $25 a month; in many, it is possible to invest as little as $300 a year. By continuously investing in a well-diversified, professionally managed portfolio without any inconvenience of periodic stock analyses and evaluations, the investor can build his portfolio to his desired goal with almost no time or effort. If any investor places a value on his own time, the management fee required by mutual fund managers is really insignificant; surely, for any investor with a relatively modest investment portfolio, the management fee is far less than the cost involved in managing his portfolio himself. Especially if he is at all concerned about his own ability to manage his portfolio well enough to receive an average rate of return, the investor many very well prefer to use professional investment management to achieve his investment goal. However, even if he could achieve a slightly higher rate of return on his portfolio by managing it himself, which might be possible in some cases, the convenience of letting someone else do it could be worth far more than the extra return.

Performance Measure.   Although probably few investors buy mutual funds only to provide a measure of their own investment acumen, nevertheless, many fund shareowners may use fund performance as a measure of their management abilities. Although some market index could serve the same function, for example, the Dow-Jones Industrial Average, a better performance measure should be provided by a fund because the objectives of that fund closely resemble the investor's own investment objectives.

Many investors wonder whether they should manage their own portfolios or let some professional fund manager do it for them. Knowing which is better is very difficult to determine. One solution is to do both for a while, and compare the performances on the mutual fund portfolios with the performance of the self-managed portfolio. In Mr. Green's case, for example, he might continue to buy shares in Consolidated Balanced Fund, Hallelujah Growth Fund, and Possible Bonanza Fund until age 40. At that time, when he redoubles his monthly savings to $100 each month, he might well decide to invest that extra $50 a month in a portfolio of his own. After all, by then he will have achieved considerable success in his career; he will have built a sizable portfolio, and observed the financial markets for 15 years, although perhaps somewhat irregularly. By then, he may feel that he has sufficient familiarity with the stock market, sufficient free time, and sufficient investment funds to permit the construction and management of his own portfolio by selecting his own stocks. By beginning his own portfolio at the same time that he continues the regular investments in his funds, he will have a ready-made bench mark against which to judge his own personal performance. After a year or two of managing his own portfolio he may determine that he can indeed manage his own stocks better than his fund shares have performed. In such a case, he might well decide to invest all his $1,200 annual savings in his own portfolio. On the other hand, if he cannot perform as well as his professional managers can, he might well decide that a larger financial return on his portfolio is more important to the success of his investment program than the psychological return to his ego that he enjoys through managing some of his portfolio himself. Consequently, he might sell the stocks he has purchased, and invest the proceeds of those sales in additional mutual fund shares. Whatever his decision, the performance of his mutual funds would provide him with a means of measuring the performance of his portfolio since the investment objectives of each would be the same. This reason may be relatively unimportant to some investors, but in conjunction with all the other reasons for investing in a mutual fund, it might be enough to attract you to mutual funds, even without the various special features they offer.

HOW TO BUY MUTUAL FUNDS

Mutual funds may be purchased in several different ways. In most cases, an investor buys mutual fund shares from his broker just exactly the same way he would buy any corporate stock. Similarly, he might get the suggestion to buy mutual fund shares from any of the same sources that suggest various corporate stocks to him. His broker or investment adviser may suggest mutual funds; some colleague or investor friend may suggest them; he may read an article or advertisement about mutual funds in some financial paper or magazine. Two of many valuable sources of information are *Forbes Magazine* and Wiesenberger Services' *Investment Companies. Forbes* annually devotes its August 15 issue to evaluating many specific mutual funds. Wiesenberger Services annually publishes *Investment Companies,* which includes a truly enormous amount of data on hundreds of specific funds. Mutual fund prices, articles, and advertisements are published daily on the financial pages of most newspapers. Most brokers have available the prospectus of many funds just for the asking since most funds distribute their shares through such brokers. Since most funds carry a larger commission, or load, than the buying or selling of listed common stock most brokers are quite pleased to sell fund shares to investors.

However, some funds do not distribute their shares through brokers and dealers, and have no commission, or load, provision. Consequently, the investor interested in buying shares in a no-load mutual fund would buy his shares directly from the fund itself either by telephone or mail. In still other cases, funds have their own sales organizations; they do not distribute their shares through brokers and dealers in general, nor do they sell on a no-load basis by telephone or mail. Such funds have their own private sales organizations and emphasize the importance of selling their shares in their investors' homes, often under a contractual arrangement. Under a contractual plan, the fund salesman receives his largest commission on the front end of the plan, thereby making it feasible for him to expend considerable effort and energy in convincing potential investors that they should buy shares through him. Whether an investor buys load funds, no-load funds, or front-end load funds, each has its advantages and disadvantages; therefore, the investor should understand each method to decide which particular approach might be most appropriate in his own case.

Load Funds.   The distribution of most mutual fund shares is handled quite similarly to the distribution of any other publicly offered new issue of stock. The broker-dealer through whom the investor buys his shares is the last link in a chain of underwriters (investment banks) through which a fund distributes its shares. Although the commission on fund shares is somewhat less than the typical 15 percent commission on other offerings of new issues, most mutual fund commissions are higher than the typical 1 to 2 percent commission on a purchase of listed stock, and slightly more than the commission charged for buying common stock over the counter. Comissions, or loads, on most funds vary from 7.5 to 8.5 percent. About a third of that commission goes to the broker, about a third to his brokerage firm, and about a third to other members of the underwriting team. Some funds have slightly lower commissions, and all funds offer progressively larger quantity discounts for progressively larger dollar purchases. In general, however, most load funds charge about 8 percent commission for purchases of under $10,000. In contrast to all other security ownership, the investor who owns mutual funds pays no commission when he sells his shares.

The commission, or load, on any given fund is readily identifiable in the daily newspaper as the difference between the asked price and the bid price. For example, consider the following rather typical newspaper quotation:

	Asked	*Bid*	*Prev. Bid*	*Bid Chg.*
Con. Bal.	20.00	18.40	18.36	+.04

According to this quotation, Consolidated Balanced Fund may be purchased at $20 per share and sold for $18.40, which is its net asset value. Eight percent of $20 is $1.60 commission per share. On the previous trading day, Consolidated Balanced Fund had a net asset value of $18.36, so today's closing bid price, or net asset value, is up four cents a share. Any investor wishing to buy less than $10,000 worth of Consolidated Balanced Fund's shares must pay $20 per share today, and any investor wishing to sell his shares back to the fund could receive $18.40 for each share.

In exchange for his commission, the broker performs several functions. He should familiarize himself with the various funds available, so that upon request, he can suggest several alternative funds which might fit anyone's investment objectives very closely. He should have various fund prospectuses readily available or be able to procure them quickly. In addition, he should have various other sources of information pertaining to fund objectives, performances, and assets held. Although your broker cannot be expected to provide you with unlimited published information for one-third of a small commission, his brokerage firm should also be willing to provide him with several sources of published information, in exchange for a third of the commission, and you might very well have access to the firm's investment library. The last third of the commission is paid to various other members of the underwriting team; specifically, to various research houses and publishing houses that make much information available to the investor, his broker, and also to his portfolio manager. In part, one reason why the annual management fee is as low as one-half of 1 percent for load funds, is that such funds continue to receive new commission dollars resulting from new fund share sales to defray various expenses of operating the fund. Load funds usually have lower expense ratios than no-load funds, in many cases less than half.

There are various other services that may be made available to the mutual fund investor, either through the fund itself or the broker. Certainly, the broker should aid the investor in selecting the most appropriate funds for him. As indicated earlier, there is no additional commission if the investor should ever decide to sell his fund shares. Depending upon the size of the investor's investment program, the broker may be willing and able to spend considerable time and effort to help plan an effective and sustainable financial plan. Obviously, the investor who chooses to buy no-load funds can hardly expect the same "royal treatment" from a broker who must make his living from commissions.

No-Load Funds. There are some investors, however, who buy only mutual funds that do not have commission charges. In most cases, an investor buying a no-load fund will do so directly from the fund either by telephone or mail. It's possible that some brokers may be willing to buy no-load fund shares for an investor, but they will probably charge their firm's minimum fee to do so. Since no-load funds choose to distribute their shares without the benefit of brokers and dealers, however, you should probably know your broker fairly well before you ask him to buy a no-load fund for you.

There are about 100 no-load funds. If you know which fund shares to buy, there is no need to use a broker for the purchase of no-load funds. Any investor can determine very readily which mutual funds are no-load funds. For example, consider the following typical newspaper quotation:

	Asked	*Bid*	*Prev. Bid*	*Bid Chg.*
Tru. Blue	11.23	11.23	11.19	+.04

You will notice that Truest Blue Trust Fund shares have exactly the same asked and bid prices, indicating that there is no commission or load. All funds quoted in the newspaper with identical asked and bid prices are no-load funds. Furthermore, no-load funds advertise regularly in various financial publications, and they advertise quite often in daily newspapers.

Their performances are reported in various business and financial publications, including *Forbes* and Wiesenberger Services' *Investment Companies*. By identifying various no-load funds, investigating their characteristics, objectives, performances, and expense ratios for yourself, you may well be able to identify a no-load fund that meets your requirements.

Although no-load funds compose considerably less than 10 percent of the mutual fund industry in terms of total assets, they are indeed a thriving portion of the industry. Despite the fact that they have no underwriters and dealers selling their shares, many investors have bought their shares, at least in part, because they have no sales charge. In most cases, no-load funds are operated either by portfolio managers who serve primarily as investment advisers and trustees, or by brokerage firms that can handle their own portfolio transactions. In the first case, the investment advisers who serve large investors may establish a no-load fund because there is relatively little additional research or trouble involved in managing one more large trust fund made up of the funds from many small investors. Although such investment advisers could not afford to manage the investment funds of small investors, or rather the small investors could not afford to pay the investment advisers' fee, they can do so collectively through a no-load fund. Many small investors do approach such investment advisers for their services, even those that have no arrangement for handling smaller accounts. By establishing a no-load trust fund, the investment advisers can accept the funds of all investors who come to them to request their services if those smaller investors agree to place their funds in one large portfolio; then that portfolio can be managed just as would a portfolio for one large investor. In the second case, brokerage firms may establish no-load funds because they can supplement their annual management fees with the profits they make from handling their funds' portfolio transactions. Furthermore, many brokerage firms are approached by investors, large and small, who request that the firms manage their portfolios. Some even establish load funds for such purposes, but some establish no-load funds specifically to serve such customers. In either case, the annual expense ratios on no-load funds do tend to be somewhat higher than the expense ratios on load funds.

Despite the fact that no-load funds do not distribute their shares through brokers and dealers, they continue to attract investor attention. Although no-load fund portfolios in general are relatively small, a few have more than $100 million in assets and have become quite well known. In most cases, no-load funds have grown very rapidly only when they have achieved rather remarkable performance records. As in any other case, when some outstanding year comes along for a no-load fund, numerous magazine articles announce their unusual performance, and many more investors become aware of that fund. Consequently, many more investors invest their money with that fund. The growth in mutual funds, however, has not been generated by no-load funds. Since the sales efforts of thousands of brokers and dealers, with commissions as their incentives, have been of primary importance in the growth of the mutual fund industry, the larger growth has been in the load fund industry.

One word of caution might well be in order. Some investors seem to find no-load funds attractive for the wrong reason. Any investor who finds a fund's management attractive may well wish to buy shares in that fund; any investor who finds that a given fund's objectives agree with his own personal objectives may well wish to buy shares in that fund; any investor who finds any fund's performance to be attractive, or even acceptable, may well wish to buy shares in that fund. However, those investors who buy shares in a no-load fund simply because there is no commission charge, regardless of its management, objectives, or performance, may well have bought the wrong fund. To buy the wrong fund because it has no commission or load charge is a highly questionable practice. Furthermore, to forfeit better management or performance just to avoid a one-time commission is a highly questionable practice. Even a slightly better annual performance of the fund would shortly overcome that load charge. On the other hand, any investor who does not want the services that his broker may provide, who is willing to do his own investigating and evaluating, who finds a no-load fund that is just as attractive as a load fund in terms of management, objectives, and performance, might well consider the purchase of such no-load fund shares.

Front-End Load Funds. About 100 mutual funds are now offering front-end load plans, or contractual plans. The larger mutual funds offering such front-end load plans distribute their shares through their own sales organizations, although some mutual funds also sell their shares through independent investment dealers. Actually, there is no specific contract that the investor must sign requiring that he complete a contractual plan; however, the front-end load provides considerable incentive to the investor to complete his plan, just as it provides considerable incentive to the mutual fund salesman to sell the plan. Since the investor pays most of the commission in the first year of purchase, and relatively less in subsequent years, he must accept considerable loss if he withdraws his money after the first year or two of his investment plan. If he withdraws early, a large portion of his savings will have gone to pay the salesman's commission. On the other hand, since a relatively large portion of the commission is paid to the salesman in the first year, fund salesmen selling front-end load plans are willing to spend much more time and effort trying to sell fund shares to smaller investors. In many ways, the front-end load on a contractual fund plan is similar to the front-end load on a life insurance policy, although life insurance commissions are higher. In both cases, a large portion of the first year's investment or premium goes to the salesman, thereby enabling him to afford much more personal attention to any potential customer.

For example, consider the small investor who might want to begin an investment program, but hardly knows how to begin with only $300 a year. To whom can he turn? Who would be willing to accept his $25 each month for investment purposes? After all, 8 percent of $25 is only $2, and 8 percent of $300 is only $24. Just how much personal attention can any uninformed potential investor expect to buy for $2 or even $24? With the front-end load plan, any investor may begin a ten-year investment program to invest $3,000 over that ten-year period at the rate of $300 each year. The total commission charge for the $3,000 at 8 percent, therefore, would be $240. Under some contractual plans, the first year's commission could be as high as $150, or 50 percent of the first year's investment; in other cases, the first year's commission might be $100 or 33 percent of the first year's investment. The remainder of the total commission would then be spread over the life of the plan. Although $2 or $24 would be not enough to make it profitable for a mutual fund salesman to spend very much time with such an investor, $100 or $150 might be. Certainly, with this front-end load, any mutual fund dealer can find it possible to spend considerably more of his time and effort in explaining the advantages of an investment program to potential investors who might be interested in establishing small investment programs. Although the small investor who does not continue with a contractual plan must forfeit a much larger commission in his earlier years, there is some evidence that small investors are more successful in reaching their investment goals when they use contractual plans rather than voluntary plans.

Because of the relatively high commissions in the first years of contractual plans, however, there has been considerable criticism of front-end loads. There has been much feeling that small investors have been abused when mutual fund dealers have sold them front-end load investment plans particularly those small investors who have been forced to liquidate their investment plans after making only a few payments. In 1967, the Securities and Exchange Commission recommended that Congress prohibit front-end loads to protect small investors from such loss. In October, 1967, sponsors of contractual plans announced a new feature providing that any investor experiencing provable financial hardship could withdraw from his investment program during the first 12 months, and be refunded the full amount of the commission he had paid. In addition to this feature, many funds have long offered to any investor the privilege of reneging within the first 60 days after purchasing a contractual plan, and having his entire investment refunded to him. Future legislation may further alter the provisions of the front-end load plans; one proposed bill suggests a maximum single-year commission of

20 percent. Of course, front-end loads could be eliminated entirely. If they are, some small investors may be eliminated along with them.

Certainly, some criticisms of front-end loads may be justified. However, front-end load plans do offer advantages to some investors. Perhaps the primary advantage is that without such a front-end load provision, many small investors would never be approached by any mutual fund dealer, and an investor could hardly expect to receive very much personal attention considering the value of any broker-dealer's time, and the amount of commission they could expect in return. Although the commission on a front-end load plan is indeed quite high during the first few months of such a program, the value of a sustainable long-term investment program can hardly be denied. To the extent that any investor is enabled to establish such a sustainable investment program through the sales efforts of any fund dealer, that investor may himself feel that the commission he has paid is more than worth the return. Furthermore, contractual plans do have the advantage of establishing specific investment goals. Apparently, some investors are much more successful in sustaining an investment program that provides for specific monthly investments leading to a specific investment goal some ten years into the future.

Furthermore, plan completion insurance is also offered by many mutual funds that sell contractual plans. Under a completion insurance policy, if a planholder should die before completing his contractual plan, the insurance company would pay to the fund the difference between what the investor had already paid into the program and his ultimate goal. The insurance rates are computed on a group-term policy basis, and are deducted from his regular plan payments. Although a few voluntary plans also offer such completion insurance, most voluntary plans do not establish a specific investment goal, and do not offer plan completion insurance in conjunction with their fund sales. All these features, and various other special services as well, may be entirely unknown to new small investors, but they might be of value.

Regardless of how an investor buys mutual funds, there are advantages and disadvantages to each method. Apparently, there are sufficient advantages to some investors to overcome the respective disadvantages of each method because load funds, no-load funds, and front-end funds continue to sell. For the investor who wishes to have considerable alternative funds from which to choose, and who wishes to have the advice of his broker on which of those many funds might be more appropriately purchased in his particular case, that investor probably should use load funds sold through thousands of brokers in hundreds of brokerage firms. Consequently, he would buy his fund shares in exactly the same way that he would buy any other common stock. On the other hand, for the investor who is willing to investigate many alternative funds for himself, and who is willing to select for himself one or more funds that he considers more appropriate in his particular case, no-load funds may be purchased directly from the funds themselves either by telephone or mail. For the investor who is in need of considerable investment advice, who understands little if anything about mutual funds, or who needs considerable incentive to continue his investment program, front-end load funds may be the most appropriate way to begin his investment program despite their rather high initial commission charges.

Regardless of which of these three methods an investor uses, he should select a truly professional, capable, effective management with acceptable investment objectives and an acceptable performance record. If this portfolio management is managing a mutual fund successfully, the annual management fee and the initial dealer commission may be of less importance to any investor. If he initiates a sustainable mutual fund investment program, that investor's primary concerns are making his regular monthly, quarterly, or annual contributions to his portfolio, and occasionally evaluating the relative performance of his fund or funds. Regardless of the specific fund, he need assume no responsibility for selecting specific investments to be included in that portfolio. He need not be concerned with making appropriate portfolio adjustments in response to changing economic or market conditions. In whichever way he buys shares in a mutual fund, he assumes that his fund will be managed by professional portfolio managers. As long as those portfolio managers continue to perform in accordance with his expectations, he may continue to invest additional savings in additional shares of that fund indefinitely. If his fund managers should not perform according to his expectations, or if they should change their objectives or investment approaches, or if the investor himself should change his investment attitudes or objectives in response to any number of things, then he might well wish to alter his fund contributions in some way or even sell some of his share holdings in order to buy other fund shares more to his liking. By continuing to invest on a regular basis in one or more funds that are performing according to his expectations, the investor can be much less concerned about the many problems of portfolio management, much more assured of achieving his ultimate investment goal, and much more assured of achieving his ultimate financial goal of financial security.

SPECIAL MUTUAL FUND FEATURES

In addition to the characteristics already indicated, there are other numerous special features of funds. For example, there are various kinds of special funds in addition to the balanced funds, growth funds, and speculative funds. There are hedge funds, that provide tremendous flexibility to the hedge fund managers, permitting high degrees of concentration, fund borrowing, short selling, and various other unusual fund practices. There are municipal bond funds that invest only in municipal bonds to provide diversification for investors who are especially attracted to municipal bonds by their income tax exempt feature, but do not wish to assume the responsibility involved in selecting specific municipal bonds. Similarly, there are convertible bond funds that invest only in convertible bonds.

There are also dual funds, or split funds, that sell two different types of shares in the same fund, one type providing current income only, and the other providing capital appreciation only; thus, whichever part of a portfolio's performance, either dividends or capital gains, an investor prefers, can be emphasized by the choice of the shares he buys. If he wants to emphasize current income, he may buy the income shares and receive twice as many dividends (since his allotted capital gains are converted into dividends as well) whereas, if he wants to emphasize capital gains he may buy the capital shares and receive twice as many capital gains (his and those that would have gone to the income shareowners if they had not agreed to give them up in exchange for twice as much income). Then too, there are the various kinds of performance funds, the so called, go-go funds, using unusual, sometimes rather exotic, approaches in an effort to achieve unusually high rates of return. There are even fund funds that invest their entire portfolios only in other mutual funds managed by still other fund managers; their special service is to select specific mutual funds that are managed by especially capable portfolio managers.

There are some special features, however, that should be emphasized for the relatively young middle-income professional man. First, funds offer periodic investment plans that are especially designed to enable the investor to accumulate a portfolio by investing only a few hundred dollars regularly each year. Second, funds offer automatic reinvestment plans that enable the investor to reinvest all his dividends in additional shares. Third, many funds offer the privilege of within-group conversion, whereby the investor may exchange all his investment funds in one fund within a group of funds for shares of another fund within that same group at little or no charge. Especially for the aggressive investor who might wish to invest in growth fund shares during prosperous times, but invest in more conservative fund shares at times of high market prices, within-group conversion permits exchange of growth fund shares for balanced fund shares, or visa versa, at his discretion.

Funds offer periodic withdrawal plans which permit the investor to receive monthly checks of any desired size from his portfolio regardless of whether or not the fund receives that much in dividends or capital gains in any given month or year. If dividends and capital gains are less than his requested withdrawals, the fund will return to him a portion of his portfolio capital. Consequently, the investor may request $6,000 a year, and receive those $500 checks monthly, despite the fact that stock prices and mutual funds' net asset values may be declining throughout any given year. Investors can be relatively unconcerned during any given year about the market in general, or the mutual fund performance in particular, as long as his fund earns over an extended number of years approximately what he withdraws from his fund. He could even choose to gradually reduce his fund portfolio through a periodic withdrawal plan, knowing that by using such a plan, he will slowly deplete his portfolio.

Mutual funds offer a redemption privilege at no charge whereby the investor may sell his shares back to the fund at the per share net asset value at that time. If ever he should need his money, or if he should simply decide he no longer wants to own shares in that particular fund, the investor can redeem his shares for his equivalent share of the total portfolio's market value at no cost.

PERIODIC INVESTMENT PLAN

Through the use of a periodic investment plan, sometimes called an accumulation plan, an investor can regularly invest a relatively small amount of savings on a monthly or quarterly basis. Most of these are voluntary plans although some funds offer contractual plans as well. In most cases, the funds require a minimum initial investment, quite often $250 or $500, although sometimes as large as $25,000. Also, many of these funds require minimum monthly or quarterly payments, often $25 or $50, although some are quite substantial. Some funds are available, however, that require no minimum initial investment, and permit periodic investments of any amount. In most cases, periodic investment plans establish specific dollar amounts to be invested periodically, for example $25, $50, or $100 per period, and the fund may not accept checks written for irregular amounts. Under such plans, the dividends and capital gains earned are automatically reinvested for the investor, but this is not always required. Although the fund may permit some flexibility, if the investor does not continue to make his regular monthly or quarterly payments, the fund will terminate the plan.

For investors such as Seymour Green, the periodic investment plan could be an ideal situation. Since it is difficult to invest $25 a month, or even $50 a month, directly in corporate securities (although the investor could use the New York Stock Exchange monthly investment plan), a mutual fund that offers a periodic investment plan may greatly simplify a small investor's efforts. He simply sends his monthly or quarterly checks to the fund for purchase of additional shares on a regular basis; all his dividends and capital gains accruing from the portfolio will be automatically reinvested in additional shares of the fund. Through such a plan, any investor can accumulate a sizable portfolio over time. By regularly investing his additional savings, and by automatically reinvesting all his dividends and capital gains, Mr. Green could be assured of achieving his $250,000 investment goal, if the fund management were able to earn 9 percent on the portfolio over time, and if Mr. Green can make sure that his regular monthly payments arrived on schedule. He need not assume any other investment responsibilities. The simplicity of the periodic investment plan alone has attracted many investors to mutual funds, and about half of all such investors use accumulation plans.

AUTOMATIC REINVESTMENT PLAN

Many investors prefer to have greater flexibility in their investment programs than a periodic investment plan permits. Some wish to double their investment contributions some years, and invest little or nothing in others. Consequently, almost half of all fund investors prefer to have regular or open accounts with their fund managers. Thereby, they may make any investment purchases above the minimum amount at any time. Nevertheless, they may wish to have their dividends automatically reinvested in additional shares of the fund. In some cases, dividends can be reinvested at net asset value, rather than at the offering price. Obviously, the investor would prefer to reinvest his dividends at net asset value, since with no commission charge, the portfolio would grow slightly faster.

Although some investors do prefer to receive their dividends in cash, and some may even choose to accept their realized capital gains in cash, many investors who are building an investment portfolio may not want to receive their dividends at all. For many people, any check received will be automatically deposited in their checking accounts, and once there anything in the world can happen to that money. Since the investor is primarily depending upon the return from his portfolio to help build that portfolio, he might very well appreciate a plan whereby all the return on his portfolio would be automatically reinvested. If he does not receive his dividends in cash, he may never miss them, and they will certainly facilitate the growth of his portfolio over time.

Whether or not the investor receives his dividends and capital gains in cash or reinvests them automatically or otherwise, he must still pay his income tax obligations. Dividends are taxable at the marginal income tax rate, and capital gains are taxable at half that rate for the average small investor. If an investor uses an automatic reinvestment plan, he must be prepared to pay his income taxes out of other income, and in effect, he is investing slightly more than his periodic investment contributions.

WITHIN-GROUP CONVERSION

A special feature that may be especially attractive to the aggressive investor is provided by fund managements that manage a group of funds. Increasingly, fund managements are managing several different types of funds: one or two conservative funds, two or three growth-oriented funds, and perhaps a speculative fund or two. Since such managements continuously investigate all types of corporations, they regularly discover various investment opportunities that might not be acceptable for any given fund. For example, a more speculative stock might well be acceptable to a more conservative fund, but no conservative portfolio manager would be willing to include it in his conservative fund. Consequently, fund managers who manage only one fund, must exclude from their portfolios numerous securities that would be acceptable to a different type of fund. For relatively little additional effort, therefore, a management can manage several funds of different types at the same time. Furthermore, a fund management that is successful in managing a growth fund, will discover after several years that the fund has become a conservative or a balance fund, simply because it has grown so large that it can only buy stocks of very well-established corporations. If it still wants to manage a growth fund for its clients, it must create a new growth fund. In such ways, fund managements tend to acquire several funds of different types that they can manage continuously.

Investors who have invested in a growth fund that has experienced considerable market appreciation in the past, may come to feel that the stock market has risen to unsustainable heights. Therefore, they might very well be interested in exchanging some of their growth fund shares for shares in a more conservative fund, with the thought that a more conservative fund would decline less than a growth fund during any subsequent period of general market decline. Since most mutual funds are load funds, that have 8 percent commissions or thereabouts, the sale of $10,000 worth of growth fund shares, for reinvestment in a balanced fund, would cost $800 in commission. Assuming that a market decline did occur, and growth fund shares did decline precipitously, the investor might later wish to sell his conservative fund shares at the market trough, and buy back into the growth fund. Again, he would have to pay another $800 commission. When the investor buys shares in a fund that is part of a group, however, he may exchange the shares of one fund in that group, for shares in another fund in that same group, for only five dollars. Usually, he must hold his shares for six months or longer.

As an example of how within-group conversion operates, assume that Mr. Green does decide to invest 30 percent of his portfolio in Consolidated Balanced Fund, 60 percent in Hallelujah Growth Fund, and 10 percent in Possible Bonanza Fund. He could continue to maintain those proportions regardless of market conditions, of course; but there might be certain occasions when market prices appear very high to him, and he might feel rather uneasy about owning so much Hallelujah Growth and Possible Bonanza. At such times, he might prefer to have a much larger proportion of his portfolio invested in Consolidated Balanced shares. Since Consolidated Balanced and Hallelujah Growth are managed by the same management, he can exchange half of his Hallelujah Growth shares for an equal dollar amount of Consolidated Balanced shares.

Consequently, 60 percent of his portfolio would be invested in Consolidated Balanced, 30 percent of his portfolio in Hallelujah Growth, and 10 percent in Possible Bonanza. Actually, he might wish to sell his Possible Bonanza shares too, and he might well decide to do so. However, since Possible Bonanza is not part of any group, he cannot exchange his Possible Bonanza for any other fund shares without paying the commission. He could decide to sell his shares in a more conservative fund, paying the commission, of course. He could sell, and hold the proceeds in cash. On the other hand, he might continue to hold his Possible Bonanza shares despite his concern about a possible market decline; and if he does, Possible Bonanza shares might decline twice as much as the whole market.

Assuming a stock market decline of 20 percent, Consolidated Balanced might well decline 10 percent; Hallelujah Growth might decline 30 percent; Possible Bonanza might fall 50 percent. At somewhere near the market trough, Mr. Green, or any other slightly aggressive investor, might choose to exchange some of his Consolidated Balanced Fund shares for Hallelujah Growth Fund shares, since in the subsequent recovery period, Hallelujah Growth should appreciate in value much faster than Consolidated Balanced. Again, such exchange on a group basis would cost Mr. Green only five dollars, rather than $800 or 8 percent of whatever the amount of his portfolio he decides to convert. Within-group conversion is only possible when an investor owns shares in a fund that is part of a group of funds that includes the fund which he wishes to own. Several groups have formed in recent years, and the trend is likely to continue. Especially for the more aggressive investor, within-group conversion may be an attractive feature that might very well influence his selection of a specific mutual fund in which to invest.

PERIODIC WITHDRAWAL PLANS

With a periodic withdrawal plan, sometimes called a check-a-month plan, the investor withdraws the money he has invested in a fund over an extended period of time. Usually there is a minimum amount that he must have accumulated over time, perhaps $10,000, but any investor who has accumulated a sizable investment portfolio can initiate a periodic withdrawal plan at any time. Furthermore, an investor may buy shares in a fund for the express purpose of creating a periodic withdrawal program. He may have accumulated money through a small business, through real estate investing, or through his own portfolio management efforts; after some years, he could well decide he wants to invest in a well-diversified, professionally managed fund, sit back without any management responsibilities, and receive a regular return from his investment portfolio. Similarly, he might wish to establish a periodic withdrawal plan for his family if he were to die to provide a monthly income for them.

However he has accumulated his portfolio, one day he may well wish to receive some cash income from his investments.

For example, an investor might wish to receive $500 each month from his portfolio. If he has a sufficiently large portfolio, his dividends alone might be more than $6,000 a year. However, assuming a 3 percent dividend rate of return, the portfolio would have to be $200,000 or more to provide $6,000 in dividends each year. If he has a portfolio of only $100,000, his dividends and realized capital gains might equal $6,000 a year; by receiving his monthly checks of $500 each, therefore his portfolio would continue to appreciate through unrealized capital gains. But if the portfolio is only $60,000, and the fund has been earning a 10 percent rate of return, 3 percent from dividends, 3 percent from realized capital gains, and 4 percent from unrealized capital gains, his periodic withdrawal plan would sufficiently deplete his portfolio each year to prohibit any further growth. Furthermore, in some years, his portfolio will not earn 10 percent. In fact, in some years, his portfolio will decline in value. With an automatic withdrawal plan, the investor will continue to receive his $500 monthly checks regardless of the dividends, realized capital gains, or unrealized capital gains of the total fund. Regardless of the market conditions in any one year, whether the portfolio is appreciating far above average or is declining substantially amidst a catastrophic bear market, the investor will continue to receive his $500 each month. As long as the portfolio continues to earn its 10 percent average annual rate of return over time, $6,000 can be withdrawn from the fund each year without depleting the principal.

In some cases, an investor may wish to receive larger payments than could be sustained by the average annual rate of return on his portfolio; that is, the investor may wish to receive payments that do deplete his portfolio over time. For example, an investor with a $50,000 portfolio earning an average rate of return of 10 percent, may wish to receive $6,000 each year despite the fact that his mutual fund holdings only earn $5,000 a year. Nevertheless, by using a periodic withdrawal plan he may continue to receive his $500 each month for a very long time since his portfolio will continue to work for him throughout the withdrawal period. Eventually, of course, the portfolio would be exhausted since he is annually depleting the portfolio by withdrawing more than he is earning on his investments.

REDEMPTION

The redemption privilege is one unique feature that mutual funds make available to their shareowners. The fund will redeem shares for their cash value at no charge. In almost any other investment situation, when an investor wants to sell his investments in order to raise cash quickly, he can only do so if he can find some other investor who is willing to buy exactly what he has to sell. Surely no corporation will buy back its own stocks since they are perpetually issued; but even then, most stocks are more readily salable than many other investments. Even when investors can find many other investors who are interested in buying their shares, if they need to raise cash quickly, they cannot be assured that anyone else will be willing to buy their specific holdings at anything near their true value. Of course, common stocks listed on organized exchanges are very liquid investments because investors are always interested in a bargain. Nevertheless, even listed stocks often sell at rather depressed market prices. Mutual fund shares also experience depressed prices, just as do the shares in other portfolios or stocks in general. But at least through the redemption feature, mutual fund investors do have a guaranteed buyer at cash value, whereas closed funds, for example, do not. Mutual funds promise to redeem their shares at any investor's option at current net asset value. On any business day, the fund shareowner may exchange all or any part of his shares for cash at the net asset value computed on the basis of market prices that day of securities held in the portfolio. Consequently, the investor in such funds knows that he can always raise cash quickly without any undue loss resulting from a forced sale.

No investor is guaranteed a profit when he sells his shares, of course. If the market in general is depressed at the time he is forced to sell, the net asset value of the fund shares will be considerably below the price at which they have recently sold. If an investor has only recently purchased his fund shares, he might receive an amount considerably below the price for which he purchased them. Furthermore, in the case of load fund shares, any sale shortly after purchase almost certainly would be below the purchase price because of the 8 percent commission charge. Only if his shares had appreciated more than 8 percent would the investor's net asset value at redemption be higher than his original purchase price, which included the load charge. Consequently, fund investors tend to be long-term investors. But if anyone for any reason should decide to sell his shares, he may do so at any time. By either selling his shares directly to the fund itself, or by taking them back to the local broker-dealer through whom he bought them, the shareowner can tender his shares for redemption and receive a check within four or five days. Although other corporations occasionally buy back their own shares for their own purposes, only mutual funds stand ready, willing, and able to redeem their shares at their shareowners' option. Consequently, the investor in funds is in the unique position of being able to exchange his investment shares for cash at any time at their current net asset value at no commission charge.

REGULATION

As in the case of corporate securities, mutual fund shares are subject to the provisions of the Securities Act of 1933, the Securities Exchange Act of 1934, and many state security laws. Since most funds sell their shares through brokers and dealers who also sell other securities, the provisions that apply to most other brokers and dealers apply to those who distribute fund shares as well. In addition, funds are also regulated by the provisions of the Investment Company Act of 1940. Congress, after an extensive study of investment companies and their practices during the 1930's, passed the Investment Company Act of 1940 to further regulate investment companies and directed the Securities and Exchange Commission to administer the provisions of the law. These various statutory efforts, as well as many industry efforts, provide the investor with considerable protection and information.

The Securities Act of 1933 requires that mutual funds submit registration statements to the S.E.C., and that they provide complete and accurate financial information to potential investors through a published prospectus and regular reports. The Securities Exchange Act of 1934 establishes minimum standards for brokers and dealers engaged in the sale of funds. The Investment Company Act of 1940 goes still further. Specifically, all mutual funds must inform their potential shareowners of the objectives of the fund, its investment policy, and the specific securities held in the fund on a regular basis. Mutual funds are also regulated to assure that the portfolios are managed in the best interest of all the shareowners rather than merely for the officers, directors, and investment advisers of the fund, Adequate diversification is required for all funds claiming to be diversified, and adequate reserves are required to assure the proper conduct of business.

Although several federal and state security laws, and the S.E.C. as well as many state commissions, regulate and supervise funds, dealers, and managers, no law and no commission can guarantee the accuracy, completeness, or clarity, of any fund prospectus. Furthermore, no law, commission, dealer, or management can ever guarantee the value of any investment. Each investor must make his own judgments about the values of various alternative investment opportunities. Nevertheless, when any investor considers the use of professional portfolio management as a means to facilitate his financial objectives and reach his investment goal, he must be concerned about the honesty and integrity of any such investment management. In many cases, investors have lost substantial portions of their investment portfolios (in some cases, their entire portfolios), because the investment advisers they selected were not subject to appropriate regulations. Because funds are regulated under a variety of laws administered by numerous regulatory commissions, the investor can thereby be assured of public scrutiny and supervision. Anyone, professional or amateur, can make honest mistakes, and no regulations can protect against such matters. On the other hand, there is a vast difference between honest error and outright dishonesty. Through the use of mutual funds, the investor knows that his chosen professional management is responsible under such appropriate regulation to conduct himself in a prudent professional manner.

All these special features have helped to attract investors to mutual funds. Although some investors may not be interested in using such features as a periodic investment plan or an automatic reinvestment plan, all investors should appreciate the redemption feature and the regulatory efforts of the public commissions. Furthermore, many investors become more interested in a periodic withdrawal plan when they reach or approach their investment goals. Those investors who prefer to use a slightly aggresive approach to investing may occasionally find within-group conversion helpful in facilitating their above average portfolio returns. These extra features plus a potentially higher rate of return, adequate diversification, and the peace of mind and convenience of using professional portfolio management have been quite effective in attracting investors.

SELECTING SPECIFIC MUTUAL FUNDS

As indicated earlier, a great many investors have selected funds as a means of achieving their investment objectives and goals. In the 1960's, investors quadrupled their mutual fund holdings, and by 1970 mutual funds held over $50 billion worth of investments in their portfolios. However, just as no investor can buy all the stocks on the New York Stock Exchange, no investor can buy all mutual funds. The investor must buy one or a few specific funds, and which ones he buys will make a big difference. No two fund managers take exactly the same approach, and no two funds hold exactly the same securities. Different funds have different managements, different objectives, and consequently, different performance records.

The following table may help clarify the importance of selecting specific securities. Table 11-2 lists the 30 stocks in the Dow-Jones Industrial Average ranked in order of their price change during the 1960's. As you can readily see, any investor holding Eastman Kodak from December 31, 1959, to December 31, 1969, would have more than doubled his money, ignoring dividends. However, of all the Dow Jones stocks, only Eastman Kodak performed so well. For nine of the 30 stocks, their prices were actually lower at the end of 1969 than they were at the beginning of 1960. A mutual fund manager might have diversified his portfolio at the beginning of the decade among those bottom nine performers with considerable expectation that he had guaranteed his portfolio against loss over the next ten years since the corporations comprising the Dow Jones Industrial Average are well-established firms with good management teams. But such is not the case. What the list will look like in 1980, no one can imagine. It is highly probable, however, that in 1980 some of those same 30 stocks will have appreciated over

Table 11-2 Percentage Changes in the Dow-Jones Industrial Stocks, December 31, 1959–December 31, 1969

Eastman Kodak	+207%	American Tel. & Tel.	+22%
Sears Roebuck	+169	Johns-Manville	+22
Procter & Gamble	+144	Owens-Illinois	+18
Chrysler	+102	Westinghouse Elec.	+ 6
Internat'l Nickel	+ 97	Std. Oil of Calif.	+ 2
Woolworth	+ 70	Internat'l Harvester	0
General Foods	+ 59	American Can	− 5
United Aircraft	+ 48	Anaconda	− 6
Texaco	+ 43	General Electric	−22
American Brands	+ 34	Aluminum Co.	−33
Goodyear Tire	+ 34	duPont	−35
Swift & Co.	+ 33	Union Carbide	−50
Internat'l Paper	+ 29	Bethleham Steel	−50
General Motors	+ 27	Allied Chemical	−58
Standard Oil (N. J.)	+ 24	U.S. Steel	−66

Note: All figures have been adjusted where necessary for splits and stock dividends distributed.
From *Investment Companies*, 1970, 30th edition, p. 53 (New York: Wiesenberger Services, Inc., 1970). Reprinted with permission of Wiesenberger Services, Inc.

the decade while others will have declined. Which of those 30, or any other 30, any given portfolio manager selects will make all the difference in his portfolio's performance.

Although all portfolio managers attempt to appropriately time their investments, most professional portfolio managers are much more concerned about proper selection of individual stocks than they are about overall market fluctuations. Just by looking at the specific stocks in a given fund's portfolio as listed in its prospectus, the individual investor may be able to determine a great deal about that manager's attitudes toward appropriate security selection. Furthermore, portfolio performance is directly related to portfolio objectives. If the sole investment objective is maximum capital gains—an increasingly important portfolio objective for mutual funds in general—the portfolio manager may then be judged solely on long-term portfolio appreciation, regardless of the risks that the portfolio manager assumes. On the other hand, if the primary investment objective is to provide an adequate rate of return with minimum risk assumption, the performance of the portfolio manager would be judged on an entirely different basis. Performance must be seen as the achievement of desired objectives.

Consequently, the selection of specific funds to accomplish specific objectives is extremely important. The investor must first determine his own objectives and put relative weights on those various objectives. Then he can select specific funds to achieve those objectives. If you are more inclined to emphasize safety of principal and income. you should direct your attention toward balanced funds. If you are more inclined to emphasize capital appreciation, you should direct your attention toward growth funds. Upon determining your own objectives, you can then seek specific funds whose objectives are comparable to your own.

DETERMINING MUTUAL FUND OBJECTIVES

Since each fund must state its investment objectives in its prospectus, any investor can determine a given fund's objectives for himself if he is willing to take the time and trouble. In many cases, the name of the fund indicates its investment objectives, and certainly, any broker can determine any given fund's investment objectives. However, to facilitate comparisons among various funds, the investor may wish to consider various publications that regularly publish a great deal of mutual fund data. Most brokers and dealers can make various publications available to their customers; and some are so inexpensive, the investor may wish to buy them himself.

As an example, consider Table 11-3 which is the beginning of Wiesenberger's alphabetical list of all mutual funds in the United States at the end of 1969 for which information could be obtained. Notice the various columns in which data are provided. For example, consider the first mutual fund, Aberdeen Fund, by column:

1. Name of the fund—Aberdeen Fund
2. Year of origin—1933
3. Primary Objectives—growth (as compared to maximum capital gains, fixed income, or speculation)
4. Policy—common stocks (as compared to fixed income, speculation, or a balanced portfolio)
5. Total net assets—$36.5 million
6. Number or shareholders—5.5 thousand
7. Net asset value—$2.10 (which is the cash or redemption value)
8. 12-month change in net asset value—(−17.3)
9. Number of issues held—57
10. Expense ratio—.76
11. Offering price—$2.30
12. Sales charge—8 percent (which is the commission or load)

The second, third, and fourth funds are all members of the same group: Admiralty Fund-Growth Series seeking maximum capital gains, Admiralty Fund-Income Series seeking income through fixed-income securities, and Admiralty Fund-Insurance Series seeking growth through speculative securities. The seventh fund, Afuture Fund, established in 1968 with maximum capital gains through common stocks as its investment objective, has no sales charge; that is, it is a no-load fund; its net asset value in column seven, and its offering price in column 11, are $10.40 each. The fifteenth fund, American Business Shares, is a balanced fund

Table 11-3 Mutual Fund Objectives

Fund	Year Org.	Primary Objective	Policy	Total Net Assets (000,000) Dec. 31. 1969	Number of Shareholders (000) Dec. 31. 1969	Net Asset Value Per Share Dec. 31. 1969	12 Mos. % Change in Net Assets Per Share	Number of Issues Held 12/31/69	Expense Ratio- Latest Fiscal Year	Offering Price 12/31/69	Sales Charge % Range
Aberdeen Fund	1933	G	CS	$ 36.5	5.5	$ 2.10	-17.3	57	0.76	$ 2.30	8-0.95
Admiralty Fund—Growth Ser. (a)	1956	MCG	CS	47.0	21.3	9.38	-35.0	84	0.99	10.28	8.75-1
Admiralty Fund — Income Ser. (b)	1957	I	FI	8.0	2.2	3.69	-24.4	42	0.99	4.04	8.75-1
Admiralty Fund — Insurance Ser. (c)	1956	G	Spec	4.3	2.2	7.84	-10.5	22	0.99	8.59	8.75-1
Advisers Fund	1950	G-I	CS	3.3	2.0	7.23	-16.9	34	0.59	7.90	8.5-1
Affiliated Fund	1934	G-I	CS	1,595.0	235.0	7.21	-17.7	160	0.31	7.80	7.5-1.9
Afuture Fund	1968	MCG	CS	13.3	8.5	10.40	-20.7	51	1.50	10.40	None
AGE Fund	1969	G	CS	0.4	1.3	4.64	–	28	–	4.73	2-1
All American Fund	1962	G	CS	3.0	10.0	0.81	-41.7	100	0.66	0.89	8.5-0.5
Allen (Leon B.) Fund	1952	G	CS	2.7	0.4	6.51	-12.7	17	1.52	6.58	1.0
Alpha Fund	1968	MCG	CS	20.0	4.1	11.91	- 8.8	53	1.40	13.02	8.5-1
Alpine Equity Fund	1969	G	CS	0.2	◄	9.90	–	8	–	9.90	None
Alpine Growth Fund	1969	MCG	CS	0.9	◄	10.10	–	13	–	10.10	None
AMCAP Fund	1966	G	CS	76.5	4.3	6.02	- 8.0	75	0.69	6.58	8.5-1
American Business Shares	1932	I-S-G	Bal	24.5	16.9	3.06	-14.0	102	0.80	3.32	7.5-1.9
American Diversified Investors Fund	1964	G-I	CS	2.3	2.5	10.26	-14.0	34	1.09	11.21	8.5-0.75
American Enterprise Fund	1958	G	CS	0.8	0.4	14.52	-25.8	21	2.45	14.52	None
American Equity Fund	1969	G-I	CS	1.0	1.5	4.58	–	57	–	5.01	8.5-0.75
American Express Special Fund	1969	G	CS	78.0	37.0	10.04	–	62	–	O-T-C	O-T-C
American Growth Fund	1958	G	CS	14.5	7.3	5.87	-20.5	43	1.00	6.42	8-0.75
American Insurance Inv. Stock Fund	1965	G	Spec	0.7	0.3	12.66	- 4.5	24	1.00	13.84	8.5-1
American Inv. Counseling Fund	1965	G	CS	4.0	0.4	10.81	-17.5	29	1.00	10.81	None
American Investors Fund	1957	MCG	CS	295.3	142.0	7.51	-29.7	206	0.95	7.51	None
American Mutual Fund	1949	G-I	CS	371.2	48.1	8.99	-16.4	101	0.58	9.83	8.5-1
American National Growth Fund	1953	MCG	CS	7.2	5.9	3.01	-15.4	46	0.98	3.29	8.5-1

Table 11-3 (continued)

Fund	Year Org.	Primary Objective	Policy	Total Net Assets (000,000) Dec. 31. 1969	Number of Shareholders (000) Dec. 31. 1969	Net Asset Value Per Share Dec. 31. 1969	12 Mos. % Change in Net Assets Per Share	Number of Issues Held 12/31/69	Expense Ratio- Latest Fiscal Year	Offering Price 12/31/69	Sales Charge % Range
Anchor Capital Fund	1968	MCG	CS	$ 78.4	21.0	$ 8.93	-15.7	54	0.75	$ 9.79	8.75-1
Anchor Growth Fund (d)	1952	G	CS	519.0	111.2	12.22	-17.4	91	0.61	13.39	8.75-1
Anchor Income Fund (e)	1944	I-S-G	Bal	139.0	24.4	7.96	-18.3	123	0.65	8.72	8.75-1
Apollo (f)	1960	MCG	CS	0.3	0.8	7.22	+3.0	6	n.s.	§	8.5-1
Argonaut Fund	1968	MCG	CS	1.0	0.1	9.77	-14.4	17	1.00	9.77	None
Associated Fund Trust	1939	I-G	FI	60.4	21.2	1.22	-26.9	85	0.78	1.34	8.75-1
Astron Fund	1968	MCG	CS	8.6	4.2	5.93	-28.1	44	0.97	6.48	8.5-1
Atlantic Fund	1961	S-I	Spec	3.3	0.4	25.84	+0.9	N.M.	N.M.	25.84	None
Audax Fund	1969	G	CS	2.6	1.7	9.14	–	15	–	9.99	8.5-0.5
Axe-Houghton Fund A	1938	G-I-S	Bal	67.7	12.2	6.22	-29.1	134	0.89	6.76	8-1
Axe-Houghton Fund B	1938	S-I-G	Bal	247.5	58.1	7.82	-27.7	387	0.72	8.50	8-1
Axe-Houghton Stock Fund	1932	MCG	CS	80.7	23.1	6.15	-26.7	197	1.07	6.72	8.5-1
Axe Science Corporation	1954	MCG	CS	50.3	22.3	4.91	-31.6	129	0.78	5.34	8-1
Babson (David L.) Investment Fund	1959	G-I	CS	29.7	7.8	9.02	- 0.3	69	0.91	9.02	None
Balanced Income Fund	1964	I-G	Bal	8.0	1.2	8.11	-15.7	56	0.51	8.89	8.75-1
Bank Stock Fund	1965	G	Spec	0.2	0.1	4.50	- 8.7	19	2.30	4.92	8.5-1
Barclay Fund	1968	MCG	CS	7.0	1.0	10.58	-15.6	29	1.00	10.58	None
Beacon Hill Mutual Fund	1964	G	CS	1.3	1.3	10.30	-10.5	34	1.00	10.30	None
Becker Fund	1969	G	CS	2.3	0.6	10.93	–	41	–	11.95	8.5-1
Berger-Kent Special Fund	1969	MCG	Hedge	29.0	4.0	9.71	–	40	–	O-T-C	O-T-C
Berkley Dean Special Fund	1969	MCG	CS	2.1	0.5	8.51	–	25	–	9.30	8.5-1
Berkshire Capital Fund	1968	G	CS	0.6	0.2	8.39	8.2	30	0.25	9.17	8.5-1
Berkshire Growth Fund	1968	MCG	CS	1.4	1.7	9.14	0.8	27	1.38	9.99	8.5-1
Blair Fund	1966	MCG	CS	23.8	4.2	11.80	6.6	40	1.09	12.90	8.5-1
BLC Growth Fund	1969	G	CS	3.0	0.2	10.61	–	30	–	C.P.	8.5-1

From *Investment Companies 1970*, 30th edition, p. 104. Reprinted with permission of Wiesenberger Services seeking income, safety, and growth in that order. You might further note that Admiralty Fund-Growth Series, seeking maximum capital gains, lost 35 percent in the 1969 bear market, whereas, American Business Shares, seeking income, safety, and growth through a balanced portfolio, lost only 14 percent, a significant loss but much less than average for that year.

When an investor has determined his own investment objectives, he can indicate to his broker the type of fund in which he is interested, and his broker may suggest several mutual funds with investment objectives similar to that of his client. In many instances, publications such as Wiesenberger's *Investment Companies* are included in the broker's research library for use by the firm's various clients, if anyone cares to use them. Even when the investor has identified the investment objectives of various funds, and has selected numerous alternative funds with stated investment objectives comparable to his own, he still must select one or two specific funds. Certainly, a major determinant in the selection of specific funds will be the investor's conviction that the management of those funds will be able to achieve their stated investment objectives. Although past performance never guarantees future performance, the ability of any management to perform in the future is to some extent indicated by its past performance record.

EVALUATING MUTUAL FUND PERFORMANCE

Evaluating performance is a great deal more difficult than determining objectives. For example, since growth funds are managed to seek above average rates of return, they must invest in more growth-oriented common stocks; consequently, such funds assume more risk and experience larger price fluctuations. On the other hand, balanced funds are designed to provide safety of principal and income; thus they experience smaller price fluctuations. In evaluating the performance of any given fund, therefore, the objectives of that fund are of major importance. Growth funds should be compared with other growth funds rather than with balanced funds, and balanced funds should be compared with other balanced funds rather than with growth funds. In the first case, more price appreciation with larger fluctuations might be expected whereas, in the second case, smaller fluctuations with less long-run appreciation might be expected. Any portfolio manager has performed well if he succeeds in achieving his predetermined investment objectives, regardless of the income, price appreciation, or fluctuations that his mutual fund experiences. The investor's job is to determine which particular objectives are most important to him, and whether or not any given management can succeed in accomplishing his objectives, and the stated objective of the fund.

In the following three tables, data are presented for several mutual funds indicating the approximate percentage changes in their net asset values per share. These changes indicate return on investment except for dividends. Change in net asset value is certainly one way to evaluate mutual fund performance; in fact, this is often the only measure used. Table 11–4 presents the performance data for smaller growth funds that have long-term growth of capital and income as their objectives. Table 11–5 presents the data on balanced funds. Table 11–6 presents the data on large growth funds. As you may recall from Chapter Nine, 1960, 1962, 1966 and 1969 were periods of general stock market weakness. In evaluating various fund performances, therefore, you would normally expect declines in those years. Furthermore, since the growth funds assume more risk than the balanced funds, you would normally expect more serious percentage declines for growth fund net asset values than you would for balanced funds.

Referring to Table 11–4, and again using Aberdeen Fund as an example, the fund did decline in each of those four years. Furthermore, Aberdeen declined more than the average of the group in each of those four years. In the other six years which experiencd marked stock market appreciation, Aberdeen Fund appreciated in value each year; but in only one of those six years, 1965, did it appreciate more than the group average. Nevertheless, an investment in Aberdeen Fund in 1960 held for the decade would have returned a total price appreciation of 65 percent, assuming that capital gains were reinvested but that dividends were not.

The first fund in Table 11–5 is American Business Shares. In three of the four years of market decline in the 1960's, American Business Shares also declined in per share net asset value; in each case, however, less than the average decline of the group. In each of the six years of general market appreciation, American Business Shares also appreciated; and in three of those six years, its shares appreciated more than the group average. An investment in American Business Shares in 1960 held throughout the decade would have returned a total price appreciation of 86 percent, assuming that capital gains were reinvested but that dividends were not.

Table 11–6 provides data on large growth funds. The first fund in that group is Anchor Growth Fund. In Anchor's case, in only two of the four periods of market weakness, did Anchor shares decline in net asset value, but in both those years the declines exceeded the group average. In the six years of general market appreciation, Anchor's shares appreciated each year; but in only two of those six years, did Anchor's shares appreciate more in value than the average of the group. Nevertheless, if an investor had bought Anchor Growth Fund shares in 1960 and held them throughout the decade, his investment would have appreciated 106 percent, assuming that capital gains were reinvested but that dividends were not. By evaluating each of the funds within each group, the investor may evaluate the performance of the various management efforts, and

Table 11-4 Performance of Smaller Growth Funds (objective: long-term growth of capital and income; volatility: moderately above average)

Approximate Percent Change in Net Assets per Share

Records for Individual Years

Annual Results

Fund	1969	1968	1967	1966	1965	1964	1963	1962	1961	1960
Aberdeen Fund (1967)	- 14.8	+ 9.2	+23.6	- 7.8	+20.2	+11.0	+20.5	- 15.4	+20.3	- 2.0
AMCAP Fund	- 6.5	+22.0								
American Growth Fund	- 18.8	+14.8	+30.5	- 6.5	+17.4	+13.7	+27.0	- 13.9	+37.7	+4.3
Babson (David L.) Investment Fund	+ 1.3	+19.1	+21.0	- 6.5	+18.1	+11.0	+20.2	- 14.6	+14.6	+6.1
Boston Common Stock Fund (1968)	+ 2.1	+25.8	+ 9.6	- 11.3	- 0.4	+24.8	+10.8	- 3.8	+23.0	- 6.1
Capital Shares (1969)	- 15.7	+30.6	+ 3.1	- 26.8	- 4.7	+ 4.3	+18.0	- 8.8	+82.7	
CG Fund	- 15.8									
Colonial Growth Shares	- 16.0	+ 6.7	+55.9	+ 2.7	+23.7	+13.9	+11.2	- 14.3	+18.9	+5.8
Commerce Fund	- 13.0	+22.0	+22.7	- 9.2	+11.0	+14.0	+17.6	- 5.4	+32.4	+6.7
Common Stock Fund of St. Bd. & Mtg.	- 6.9	+17.9	+33.2	- 1.2	+20.6	+17.4	+21.0			
Consultant's Mutual Investments	- 13.6	+20.8	+32.4	- 1.7	+26.0	+17.8				
deVegh Mutual Fund	- 14.7	+26.0	+26.1	+ 6.8	+27.5	+11.7	+15.6	- 12.5	+18.9	- 4.5
Dodge & Cox Stock Fund	- 13.8	+24.1	+28.1	- 11.6	+17.7					
Eberstadt Fund	- 8.5	+24.8	+31.9							
EGRET Growth Fund	- 13.5	+12.6	+30.9	- 5.1						
Energy Fund	- 14.7	+ 6.1	+38.8	- 0.7	+28.7	+ 9.1	+21.4	- 17.9	+20.2	+6.0
Federated Growth Fund (1960)	- 13.0	+13.9	+37.7	+ 1.8	+30.4	+ 9.7	+ 9.5	- 20.2	+18.2	- 6.1
Foursquare Fund	- 19.7	+ 5.8	+31.9	- 2.9	+33.3	+ 6.0	+17.1			
Franklin Custodian—Growth Series	- 2.3	+10.1	+27.4	- 3.7	+19.7	+10.3	+20.2	- 15.1	+24.5	+7.9
Group Sec.–Apex Fund (1963)	- 17.1	- 3.7	+38.9	0.0	+56.9	+ 8.1	+ 5.7	- 25.1	+10.0	- 2.6

Table 11-4 (continued)

Approximate Percent Change in Net Assets per Share

Records for Individual Years

Annual Results

Fund	1969	1968	1967	1966	1965	1964	1963	1962	1961	1960
Growth Industry Shares	- 2.1	+ 4.5	+28.3	- 7.2	+18.6	+11.9	+17.9	- 21.5	+23.2	+ 5.4
Johnston Mutual Fund	+ 0.5	+ 7.7	+30.1	+ 6.1	+23.3	+12.3	+18.5	- 16.1	+23.1	+14.1
Keystone (S-3) Growth Common	- 13.8	+ 8.5	+32.2	0.0	+36.6	+17.1	+22.7	- 14.7	+26.7	- 5.9
Loomis-Sayles Capital Development	- 16.4	+14.1	+39.6	+ 4.3						
Mairs & Power Growth Fund	- 7.7	+19.7	+43.3	- 3.9	+19.7	+10.1	+16.0	- 14.4	+33.0	+ 4.7
Mid America Mutual Fund	- 10.9	+ 7.0	+27.6	- 0.1	+19.2	+12.8	+15.8	- 24.4		
Mutual Invest. Foundation—MIF Growth	- 9.6	+13.4	+28.1	- 6.4	+18.9	+16.4	+19.4	- 17.8		
Mutual of Omaha Growth Fund	- 14.6									
National Industries Fund	- 21.1	+ 4.1	+36.3	- 2.5	+33.4	+15.2	+19.1	- 17.0	+39.4	
National Sec.—Growth Stocks Series	- 11.7	+13.6	+40.1	- 1.1	+24.3	+11.2	+17.1	- 19.3	+16.2	+ 2.0
NEL Growth Fund	- 4.0									
Philadelphia Fund	- 3.2	+ 9.0	+23.4	- 4.9	+19.6	+13.4	+20.7	- 11.3	+21.0	+ 5.9
PRO Fund	- 0.6	+48.0								
Putnam Investors Fund	- 0.3	+13.3	+30.2	- 2.0	+12.4	+12.4	+15.6	- 17.5	+16.1	- 8.4
Steadman Fiduciary Investment Fund	- 16.7	+ 8.1	+31.7	- 12.5	+15.5	+11.9	+18.4	- 12.0	+21.6	- 4.0
Stein Roe & Farnham Capital Oppor. (1969)	- 6.6	+28.0	+30.5	- 12.8	- 0.7	+15.2	+ 8.8	- 14.6	+24.3	+ 3.9
Stein Roe & Farnham Stock Fund	- 7.5	+15.4	+27.0	- 4.5	+16.4	+13.1	+17.8	- 14.8	+24.1	+ 6.9
Teachers Association Mutual Fund	- 20.9	+ 1.3	+36.4	- 6.4	+29.0	+10.4	+11.4	- 14.2	+31.6	+ 2.7
Value Line Fund	- 21.1	+16.7	+68.4	+ 0.6	+27.4	+ 8.1	+34.5	- 7.8	+28.2	- 3.2
Windsor Fund	- 3.7	+21.1	+31.4	- 3.3	+29.0	+13.9	+12.7	- 25.1	+29.6	+11.0
AVERAGES	- 10.7	+14.1	+31.7	- 4.1	+21.5	+12.5	+17.4	- 15.3	+26.1	+ 1.9

From *Investment Companies 1970*, 30th edition, p. 126. Reprinted with permission of Wiesenberger Services, Inc.

Table 11-5 Performance of Balanced Funds

Fund	Approximate Percent Change in Net Assets per Share — Records for Individual Years — Annual Results									
	1969	1968	1967	1966	1965	1964	1963	1962	1961	1960
American Business Shares	-9.7	+16.0	+11.4	-2.7	+6.0	+10.5	+14.5	-2.9	+21.9	+8.7
American Express Investment Company	-10.2	+12.0	+19.9	-6.9	+11.6	+12.2	+12.2	-6.4	+16.1	+3.4
Axe-Houghton Fund A	-27.5	+19.3	+58.1	-0.4	+19.0	+17.6	+18.8	-5.2	+15.4	+2.0
Axe-Houghton Fund B	-24.7	+14.1	+32.4	-5.6	+16.3	+14.0	+17.5	-8.8	+21.9	+1.9
Balanced Income Fund	-11.4	+22.9	+22.5	+4.5	+10.3					
Boston Foundation Fund	-15.0	+19.2	+23.6	-4.7	+18.1	+11.6	+10.5	-11.2	+18.9	+2.9
Boston Fund	-9.0	+11.8	+7.4	-9.5	+4.2	+13.7	+11.1	-3.8	+19.3	+9.1
Channing Balanced Fund	-13.2	+10.8	+18.9	-4.6	+13.2	+14.2	+14.9	-4.7	+22.8	+3.9
Composite Bond & Stock Fund	-15.8	+15.5	+35.1	-8.6	+15.0	+8.9	+10.2	-2.6	+14.5	+9.1
Dodge & Cox Balanced Fund	-8.0	+14.7	+16.7	-5.2	+15.1	-9.8	+12.7	-7.7	+20.8	+2.7
Eaton & Howard Balanced Fund	-9.3	+14.7	+6.9	-5.0	+2.9	+11.5	+11.4	-2.7	+20.0	+3.6
Group Sec.–Balanced Fund	-8.5	+18.7	+9.9	-7.6	+8.7	+15.0	+15.1	-7.8	+22.0	+3.6
Investors Mutual	-6.4	+7.3	+12.5	-7.9	+5.7	+11.7	+13.9	-4.2	+18.3	+4.0
Loomis-Sayles Mutual Fund	-7.5	+15.0	+15.8	-4.4	+6.5	+13.6	+15.7	-9.8	+22.3	+6.4
Massachusetts Fund	-10.5	+12.4	+18.0	-2.9	+10.0	+10.9	+11.9	-4.5	+19.0	+3.9
Nation-Wide Securities Company	-8.0	+15.9	+9.3	-6.9	+7.2	+12.7	+13.6	-3.2	+23.0	+9.8
George Putnam Fund of Boston	-6.6	+10.6	+18.7	-3.8	+13.0	+11.4	+12.6	-11.9	+24.2	+8.9
Scudder, Stevens & Clark Balanced Fund	-6.2	+6.5	+7.3	-9.2	+8.3	+13.5	+14.3	-4.9	+20.1	+2.0
Shareholders' Trust of Boston	-18.8	+27.1	+38.6	-6.6	+14.0	+12.0	+13.7	-3.8	+12.8	+4.7
Sigma Trust Shares (1966)	-15.9	+8.6	+12.0	-4.2	+8.4	+11.9	+8.5	+1.4	+20.2	+8.2
Stein Roe & Farnham Balanced Fund	-7.7	+13.6	+21.0	-3.2	+11.6	+11.1	+13.7	-6.6	+18.7	+6.4
Wellington Fund	-7.7	+7.8	+8.1	-6.6	+5.4	+10.7	+11.7	-5.3	+18.8	+5.0
Whitehall Fund	-2.2	+16.3	+28.3	-5.4	+8.5	+10.7	+12.3	-1.9	+18.3	+2.6
AVERAGES	-11.3	+14.4	+19.7	-5.5	+10.4	+12.2	+13.2	-5.4	+19.5	+5.1

From *Investment Companies 1970*, 30th edition, p. 128. Reprinted with permission of Wiesenberger Services, Inc.

Table 11-6 Performance of Large Growth Funds (1969 year-end assets over $300,000,000)

Approximate Percent Change in Net Assets per Share

Records for Individual Years

Annual Results

Fund	1969	1968	1967	1966	1965	1964	1963	1962	1961	1960
Anchor Growth Fund	- 16.4	+ 2.1	+ 51.6	+ 1.5	+38.8	+12.1	+16.7	- 28.7	+18.3	+ 4.8
Chemical Fund	+ 5.8	+ 6.3	+ 30.7	- 1.9	+27.4	+14.2	+29.4	- 15.4	+19.4	- 0.2
Delaware Fund	- 16.3	+14.3	+ 31.0	+ 2.6	+35.5	+15.4	+19.3	- 15.1	+27.7	- 2.0
Dreyfus Fund	- 11.9	+11.6	+ 26.5	+ 1.7	+29.6	+16.7	+24.8	- 13.7	+26.1	+ 6.5
Enterprise Fund	- 25.9	+44.3	+116.9	+ 4.0	+43.3	+24.5	+27.9	**	**	**
Fidelity Capital Fund	- 14.0	+ 0.4	+ 32.2	+ 3.4	+49.5	+15.3	+37.0	- 23.9	+33.1	+28.6
Fidelity Trend Fund	- 12.1	+ 1.9	+ 35.1	- 3.2	+56.9	+14.9	+46.4	- 19.0	**	**
Investors Variable Payment Fund	- 14.1	+ 8.5	+ 32.8	- 5.2	+18.7	+14.6	+18.5	- 17.1	+24.8	+ 1.1
Keystone (S-4) Lower-Priced Common	- 20.8	+12.1	+ 66.0	- 6.7	+30.1	+21.1	+14.7	- 23.0	+29.1	- 3.8
Mass. Investors Growth Stock Fund	+ 0.2	+ 1.7	+ 29.1	+ 1.6	+24.9	+10.1	+18.6	- 17.3	+25.4	+ 8.5
National Investors Corp.	+ 4.4	+ 8.3	+ 31.6	- 1.3	+23.0	+11.5	+19.1	- 15.3	+20.7	+12.2
Oppenheimer Fund	- 16.0	+22.1	+ 37.2	+ 1.1	+35.5	+22.6	+24.5	- 21.4	+51.5	+10.3
Price (T. Rowe) Growth Stock Fund	+ 3.4	+ 8.4	+ 26.8	- 0.9	+25.6	+11.9	+18.5	- 12.7	+24.7	+ 8.0
Putnam Growth Fund	- 13.3	+10.8	+ 40.9	- 5.3	+31.3	+11.7	+13.3	- 21.0	+39.3	+19.9
Technology Fund	- 9.3	+ 8.3	+ 32.4	- 4.2	+30.2	+13.0	+16.0	- 16.7	+21.5	+ 1.5
United Accumulative Fund (1967)	- 10.3	+ 6.9	+ 12.9	- 6.0	+14.8	+16.6	+18.2	- 11.1	+27.5	+ 3.3
United Science Fund	- 10.2	+ 3.4	+ 31.8	- 9.1	+36.1	+ 9.2	+19.1	- 18.1	+18.9	- 2.2
AVERAGES	- 10.4	+10.1	+ 39.1	- 1.6	+32.4	+15.0	+22.5	- 18.1	+27.2	+ 6.4

From *Investment Companies 1970*, 30th edition, p. 122. Reprinted with permission of Wiesenberger Services, Inc.

thus project their abilities to perform in the future. Assuming that the investor can determine his own objectives, and thereby can determine which group of funds in which to search, such an evaluation of the performance data may better indicate which specific mutual fund he might most prefer to buy.

Table 11–7 and 11–8 indicate annual mutual fund ratings by *Forbes*. *Forbes* indicates each fund's performance ratings, price changes, dividend, assets, sales charge, expense ratio. You might make special note of the consistency ratings in up markets (bull markets) and down markets (bear markets). If a given fund has performed better than average in the past three up markets, *Forbes* gives that fund an above average rating, whereas if it performs less well it receives a lower rating. Therefore a growth fund would rate higher in up markets and lower in down markets, whereas a balanced fund would rate lower in up markets and higher in down markets.

In Table 11–7, notice Aberdeen Fund. *Forbes* rates its consistency in up markets and down markets, respectively, as B and D. Since growth funds are managed to appreciate, the investor would expect better performance in up markets than he would in down markets. In Table 11–8, notice American Business Shares. *Forbes* rates its consistency in up markets and down markets, respectively, as D and A. Since balanced funds are managed to provide safety of principal and income, the investor would expect balanced funds to appreciate less in up markets, but decline less in down markets. From 1962–70, Aberdeen Fund appreciated from $100 to $136.88, whereas American Business Shares appreciated only from $100 to $115.83. But American Business earned a dividend of 5.5 percent, whereas Aberdeen's dividend was 3.0 percent. Although neither Aberdeen nor American Business Shares may have achieved its stated objectives as well as might be desired, their respective managements do seem to be achieving their rspective investment objectives.

By investing in funds with investment objectives comparable to your own, you should be assured that their respective managements will select only those securities to include their portfolios that carry the appropriate risk and return which you want. By evaluating the performance of various funds annually, or more or less regularly, you should be able to determine whether or not your mutual fund managements are performing up to your expectations. As long as they are, you may well stay with them indefinitely, periodically buying additional shares as you accumulate savings. If your specific funds do not perform according to your expectations, not necessarily in any one year but over several years' time, you may well choose to select some other portfolio manager who may be better able to achieve your investment objectives and goals.

No portfolio manager can be expected to perform better than all other portfolio managers in every respect. Similarly, no portfolio manager can

Table 11–7   *Forbes* Fund Ratings 1970

▬▬▬▬ *Forbes* ▬▬▬▬
Fund Ratings 1970

PERFORMANCE RATINGS

DOLLAR RESULTS

In UP Markets	In DOWN Markets		1962-70	Recent Market Decline	Dividend Return	Assets in Millions	Maximum Sales Charge	Annual Expenses (Cents per $100)
		$100 ENDED AS . . .						
—	—	Standard & Poor's 500 Stock Average	$132.82	$63.94	4.4%			
B	C	FORBES Stock Fund Average	$146.06	$61.34	3.3%			
		STOCK FUNDS (LOAD)						
B	D	Aberdeen Fund	$136.88	$59.33	3.0%	$ 30.2	8.75%	$0.78
		Admiralty Funds (formerly B.C. Morton Fund)						
A	F	Growth Series	125.09	31.99	0.2	24.6	8.75	0.99
D	A	Income Series	125.73	69.62	5.6	7.8	8.75	0.99
B	C	Insurance Series	103.66	63.53	1.7	3.3	8.75	0.99
C	F	Advisers Fund	107.77	49.32	2.7	2.7	8.50	0.59
C	B	Affiliated Fund	131.82	61.60	5.4	1,307.1	7.50	0.31
• B	F	American Express Capital Fund (formerly Commonwealth Capital Fund)	157.28	50.03	3.0	145.5	8.50	0.67
B	D	American Express Stock Fund (formerly Commonwealth Stock Fund)	141.78	59.85	4.0	55.1	8.50	0.66
A	D	American Growth Fund	156.09	58.83	2.8	11.5	8.50	1.00
C	B	American Mutual Fund	143.54	64.34	5.5	297.7	8.50	0.58
B	F	American National Growth Fund	166.55	56.05	3.3	5.8	8.50	0.98
A	F	Anchor Growth Fund (formerly Diversified Growth Stock Fund)	171.87	50.91	2.2	354.8	8.75	0.61
D	C	Associated Fund Trust	115.24	62.57	7.6	52.6	8.75	0.75
A	D	Axe-Houghton Stock Fund	251.67	57.36	1.8	66.4	8.50	1.02
B	F	Axe Science Corp.	181.52	49.59	4.0	38.8	8.00	0.76
C	C	Bondstock Corp.	143.00	60.07	4.0	22.1	8.50	0.70
D	B	Broad Street Investing Corp.	138.11	68.81	4.1	304.0	8.50	0.23
B	B	The Brown Fund of Hawaii	139.65	74.02	. 2.6	4.1	8.50	0.88
C	B	Bullock Fund	140.42	62.28	4.1	123.9	8.67	0.40
A+	F	Businessman's Fund (formerly McDonnell Fund)	150.09	52.51	2.7	14.4	8.75	0.77
A	F	Capital Investors Growth Fund	133.72	44.69	0.9	2.7	8.75	1.00
B	F	Capital Shares	82.10	53.03	1.5	42.0	8.75	1.00
B	C	Century Shares Trust	103.00	66.02	2.9	74.0	8.50	0.44
		Channing Funds						
C	B	Common Stock Fund	142.01	65.45	4.2	26.1	8.50	0.74
A	F	Growth Fund	144.08	41.63	2.3	188.7	8.50	0.63
A+	F	Special Fund	154.19	33.70	1.8	85.2	8.50	0.72
A	F	The Chase Fund of Boston	175.01	42.56	3.2	67.5	8.50	0.68
A	B	Chemical Fund	221.53	71.65	2.4	437.2	8.50	0.39
D	B	The Colonial Fund	130.10	61.55	5.2	191.5	8.50	0.50
B	F	Colonial Growth Shares	169.07	52.95	2.5	54.0	8.50	0.71
B	D	Commerce Fund	144.18	58.69	3.5	74.0	8.50	0.65
• A	• B	Common Stock Fund of State Bond and Mortgage Company	203.46	63.87	2.1	21.4	8.00	0.86
D	D	Commonwealth Fund Indenture of Trust Plans A & B	115.97	58.22	5.4	26.2	7.65	0.60
D	C	Commonwealth Fund Indenture of Trust Plan C	117.52	61.28	5.2	42.0	7.50	0.74
B	B	Composite Fund	156.00	61.55	4.5	35.1	8.00	0.75
B	F	Consumers Investment Fund	162.04	45.88	1.2	7.2	8.50	0.75
D	B	Corporate Leaders Trust Fund Certificates, Series "B"	98.47	69.19	5.0	51.3	7.64	0.18
		Crown Western Investments						
C	F	Dallas Fund	130.52	37.52	2.5	7.2	8.50	1.00
B	D	Diversified Fund	133.26	57.18	2.8	14.9	8.50	1.00

• Fund rated for two periods only; maximum allowable rating A.

WHAT THE RATINGS MEAN

FORBES rates mutual funds on the basis on their performance in three rising markets and three falling markets. We rate funds against each other rather than on an absolute scale. In **up** markets the top 12.5% get an A+; the next 12.5% get A, the next 25% get B; the next 25% get C; the lowest 25% get D. In **down** markets, reflecting the poor performance in the recent crash, we also give F ratings. As a result, a fund gets a B rating in **down** markets only if its average performance over three **down** markets was better than the S&P's 500. Funds that did an outstanding job in the recent crash got an A. Those that didn't beat the averages at all got a C, D, or F depending on how poorly they fared, giving particular weight to the most recent **down** market.

From Forbes Magazine, August 15, 1970, p. 51. Reprinted with permission of Forbes Inc., N.Y., N.Y.

Table 11–8   *Forbes* Fund Ratings 1970

■ *Forbes* ■
Fund Ratings 1970

PERFORMANCE RATINGS — DOLLAR RESULTS

In UP Markets	In DOWN Markets		1962-70	Recent Market Decline	Dividend Return	Assets in Millions	Maximum Sales Charge	Annual Expenses (Cents per $100)
		$100 ENDED AS . . .						
—	—	Standard & Poor's 500 Stock Average	$132.82	$63.94	4.4%			
B	C	FORBES Stock Fund Average	$146.06	$61.34	3.3%			
C	D	FORBES Balanced Fund Average	$109.77	$67.18	5.0%			
		BALANCED FUNDS (LOAD)						
D	A	American Business Shares	115.83	74.18	5.5	23.0	7.50	0.84
C	F	American Express Income Fund (formerly Commonwealth Income Fund)	110.12	64.83	6.1	109.0	8.50	0.61
B	F	American Express Investment Co. (formerly Commonwealth Investment Co.)	112.99	67.29	5.1	136.1	8.50	0.62
B	F	Anchor Income Fund (formerly Diversified Investment Fund)	108.65	62.77	5.6	115.1	8.75	0.65
A+	F	Axe-Houghton Fund A	159.62	51.06	4.1	49.9	8.00	0.89
A+	F	Axe-Houghton Fund B	116.96	56.33	6.0	198.6	8.00	0.69
B	F	Boston Foundation Fund (formerly Income Foundation Fund)	118.14	64.09	7.2	34.1	8.50	0.92
D	C	Boston Fund	95.68	69.41	4.7	206.5	8.50	0.62
		Channing Funds						
B	C	Balanced Fund	126.39	68.73	4.4	83.4	8.50	0.66
B	B	Income Fund	141.33	70.94	6.0	60.1	8.50	0.69
A	D	Composite Bond & Stock Fund	$121.68	$67.01	5.5%	$10.9	8.00%	$0.79
D	C	Eaton & Howard Balanced Fund	100.66	68.29	5.4	135.7	8.50	0.59
C	D	Eaton & Howard Income Fund	105.85	65.54	6.4	15.1	8.50	0.74
A+	F	Financial Industrial Income Fund†	178.90	60.36	5.4	83.1	8.50	0.73
D	D	Franklin Custodian Funds—Income Series Shares	97.13	65.79	8.1	3.8	8.75	0.94
C	A	Group Securities—Balanced Fund (formerly Fully Administered Fund)	114.60	77.51	5.9	16.4	8.50	0.94
D	B	Income Fund of Boston	103.01	72.57	7.4	34.4	8.75	0.85
D	B	Investors Mutual	99.75	71.24	4.9	2,278.3	8.00	0.30
D	C	Keystone Custodian Funds—K-1	99.98	68.37	7.2	92.7	8.30	0.52
B	F	Massachusetts Fund	116.13	63.43	4.4	156.9	8.75	0.57
		National Securities						
C	D	Balanced Series	106.58	66.67	5.4	3.4	8.50	0.69
A	F	Dividend Series	141.68	63.49	6.8	79.6	8.50	0.65
C	B	Income Series	107.30	69.80	6.9	67.2	8.50	0.66
D	A	Nation-Wide Securities Co.	112.66	74.23	5.5	67.4	7.50	0.45
A+	F	Provident Fund for Income	144.11	60.77	7.8	69.8	8.50	0.80
B	C	The George Putnam Fund of Boston	125.87	69.93	4.3	342.3	8.50	0.46
D	F	Putnam Income Fund††	91.83	64.45	7.0	115.7	8.50	0.50
D	D	Sigma Trust (formerly New England Fund)	91.97	62.04	5.4	15.0	8.50	0.73
D	C	Wellington Fund	94.94	68.60	4.8	1,151.8	8.50	0.44
B	B	Whitehall Fund	125.60	69.28	4.2	14.0	8.50	0.46

†Transferred from stock section in 1970; would have ranked B, C as a stock fund.
N.A. Not available.
††Transferred from stock section in 1970; would have ranked D, B as a stock fund.

WHAT THE RATINGS MEAN

FORBES rates mutual funds on the basis on their performance in three rising markets and three falling markets. We rate funds against each other rather than on an absolute scale. In up markets the top 12.5% get an A+; the next 12.5% get A, the next 25% get B; the next 25% get C; the lowest 25% get D. In **down** markets, reflecting the poor performance in the recent crash, we also give F ratings. As a result, a fund gets a B rating in **down** markets only if its average performance over three **down** markets was better than the S&P's 500. Funds that did an outstanding job in the recent crash got an A. Those that didn't beat the averages at all got a C, D, or F depending on how poorly they fared, giving particular weight to the most recent **down** market.

From Forbes Magazine, August 15, 1970, pp. 55 and 58. Reprinted with permission of Forbes, Inc., N.Y., N.Y.

be expected to perform better than all other portfolio managers in achieving any one objective every year. Therefore, any investor who expects perfection is doomed to disappointment. If an investor annually evaluates the performance of his mutual funds in the light of other funds and forever finds his holdings unacceptable, he might be tempted to switch to the funds that performed best in each preceding year. Although annual evaluations are indeed appropriate, annual switching to the front runners is hardly advisable. As a matter of fact, it seems hardly reasonable to expect the front runner in any one year to be able to perform much better than average the next, simply because of the problems that have been created due to the great influx of new investor money responding to that top performance record. If the investor has been able to identify his own investment objectives appropriately, and has invested in mutual funds with investment objectives that accurately reflect his own, he should evaluate those funds over time. Although superiority in any one year speaks very well for any management, consistency over an extended period of time may well be far more important for the long term investor. By selecting specific funds by their investment objectives and their consistent performance, the investor need not make many changes at all. Any portfolio management that can consistently achieve its stated objectives is a truly professional management, one upon which any investor may depend to assure regular progress toward his ultimate investment goal.

SELECTING SPECIAL FEATURES

Many investors are especially interested in specific fund features. Some are very interested in a periodic investment plan, or an accumulation plan. Some are interested in an automatic reinvestment plan, or an automatic dividend reinvestment plan. Some are interested in within group conversion. Some are interested in a periodic withdrawal plan. Still others may be interested in a no-load fund, or even a front-end load fund. These and other special features are offered by various mutual funds, but not by all. Consequently, some investors may wish to investigate the specific special features that various mutual funds offer, and make their selection of specific mutual funds partially on the basis of the special features offered. In Tables 11–9, 11–10, and 11–11, three specific mutual funds are presented: American Investors Fund, Fidelity Capital Fund, and United Income Fund. Each fund offers different special features, and each differs substantially from the others.

Table 11–9 presents considerable information about American Investors Fund. American Investors has been one of the more widely distributed no-load funds. It has about $300 million in total assets. It emphasizes capital appreciation through common stock investing and high portfolio turnover. It offers a voluntary accumulation plan, permits periodic payments in any amount, provides for automatic dividend reinvestment, and provides a periodic withdrawal plan for accounts valued

Table 11–9 American Investors Fund, Inc.

AMERICAN INVESTORS FUND, INC.

88 Field Point Road, Greenwich, Connecticut 06830

Organized in 1957, this fund is managed by Chestnutt Corporation, which publishes weekly stock market reports and also manages individual accounts. All of the fund's officers are either officers or directors of the investment adviser.

Investment policy of the fund places primary emphasis on selection of securities believed to have good prospects for better-than-average capital appreciation, consistent with reasonable preservation of principal. Technical market analysis is used extensively in determining portfolio action. Assets will ordinarily be invested in common stocks, but senior securities may also be held.

Selective, rather than broad, diversification is a basic policy; there is no limit on concentration of assets in any one industry. Five industries accounted for slightly more than 42% of year-end 1970 assets: financial savings & loan (13.4% of assets), machinery (7.9%), business machines and oil (each 7.4%), and drug (6.9%). First Charter Financial was the fund's largest individual common stock holding, at 6.3% of assets, followed by Combustion Engineering (3.9%), Great Western Financial and National Cash Register (each 3.4%), and Revlon (3.3%). Unrealized depreciation was 14.4% of year-end assets.

Special Services: The voluntary *accumulation plan* requires a $400 minimum initial investment; subsequent periodic payments may be of any amount. Shareholders may arrange for *automatic dividend reinvestment.* A monthly or quarterly *withdrawal plan* is available without charge to accounts valued at $10,000 or more. The minimum regular withdrawal payment is $25. A *Keogh Plan* custody agreement and master corporate retirement plan are available.

Statistical History

| | | | AT YEAR-ENDS | | | | | ANNUAL DATA | | | | |
| | | | % of Assets in— | | | | | | | | Offering Price— | |
	Total Net Assets	Number of Shareholders	Cash & Equivalent	Bonds & Preferreds	Common Stocks	Net Asset Value Per Share	Yield	Income Dividends	Capital Gains Distributions	Expense Ratio	High	Low
1970	$227,451,860	153,216	1%	4%*	95%	$5.31	0.5%	$ .04	$	0.88%	$ 7.66	$4.01
1969	295,264,446	142,432	6	4*	90	7.51	0.1	.07	.30	0.86	10.68	7.23
1968	342,341,295	102,827	8	3*	89	10.68	0.1	.0225	.8375	0.86	11.57	8.04
1967	242,884,890	59,000	10	1*	89	9.975	0.2	.035	.245	0.88	10.68	7.37
1966	86,590,000	19,000	5	1	94	7.427	0.5	.035	.245	1.09	8.987	5.89
1965	58,285,431	12,000	1	....	99	7.45	0.2	.0075	.2425	1.29	7.67	4.96
1964	25,034,477	7,500	1	....	99	5.177	0.2			1.23	5.35	4.78
1963	11,044,110	5,500	1	....	99	4.172		.0285	.474†	1.42	4.74	3.44
1962	6,658,198	4,700	1	....	99	3.445	0.8	.0025	.2525	1.50	4.635	2.66
1961	5,746,469	4,000	2	....	98	4.495	0.8	.02	.1225	1.51	4.935	3.53
1960	4,225,669	3,800	4	9*	87	3.577	0.6			1.41	3.815	3.10

* This percentage includes a substantial proportion in convertible issues.
† Includes $0.04 return of capital.

Note: Figures adjusted for 4-for-1 stock split effective July 16, 1968.

Directors: George A. Chestnutt, Jr., Pres.; Stanley Law Sabel, V. P. and Sec.; Warren K. Greene, V. P.; John Currier; Frank G. Fowler, Jr.; William A. Semmes; Francis L. Veeder.

Investment Adviser: Chestnutt Corporation. Annual compensation to the Adviser is 4/5 of 1% of the first $50 million of net assets of the fund, computed quarterly; 3/5 of 1% of the next $50 million; 2/5 of 1% on the next $200 million; and 7/20 of 1% on the next $200 million.

Custodian and Transfer Agent: The Bank of New York, New York, N. Y.

Distributor: None. Shares are sold directly by the fund.

Sales Charge: None. Shares are issued at net asset value. There is a $400 minimum purchase and a 60-cent bank charge on all purchases.

Dividends: Payments from investment income and realized capital gains, when available, are made each year. There are no fixed distribution dates.

Shareholder Reports: Issued quarterly. Fiscal year ends December 31. The 1970 prospectus was available in April.

Qualified for Sale: In all states and D.C.

An assumed investment of $10,000 in this fund, with capital gains accepted in shares, is illustrated below. The explanation on page 145 must be read in conjunction with this illustration.

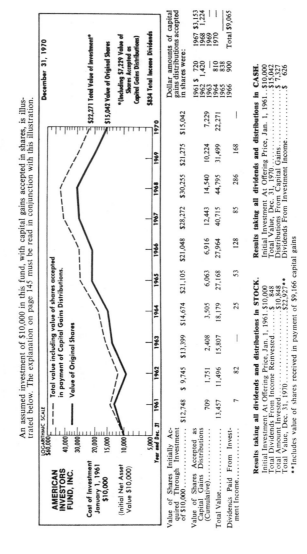

AMERICAN INVESTORS FUND, INC.

LOGARITHMIC SCALE

- - - - Total value including value of shares accepted in payment of Capital Gains Distributions.

—— Value of Original Shares

Cost of Investment January 1, 1961 $10,000
(Initial Net Asset Value $10,000)

December 31, 1970

$22,271 Total Value of Investment*

$15,042 Value of Original Shares

*(Including $7,229 Value of Shares Accepted as Capital Gains Distributions)

$834 Total Income Dividends

Dollar amounts of capital gains distributions accepted in shares were:

1961	$ 720		1967	$3,153
1962	1,420		1968	1,224
1963	—		1969	—
1964	810		1970	—
1965	838			
1966	900		Total	$9,065

Year end Dec. 31	1961	1962	1963	1964	1965	1966	1967	1968	1969	1970
Value of Shares Initially Acquired Through Investment of $10,000	$12,748	$ 9,745	$13,399	$14,674	$21,105	$21,048	$28,272	$30,255	$21,275	$15,042
Value of Shares Accepted as Capital Gains Distributions (Cumulative)	709	1,751	2,408	3,505	6,063	6,916	12,443	14,540	10,224	7,229
Total Value	13,457	11,496	15,807	18,179	27,168	27,964	40,715	44,795	31,499	22,271
Dividends Paid From Investment Income	7	82	—	25	53	128	85	286	168	—

Results taking all dividends and distributions in STOCK.

Initial Investment At Offering Price, Jan. 1, 1961. $10,000
Total Dividends From Income Reinvested..... $ 848
Total Amount Invested..... $10,848
Total Value, Dec. 31, 1970..... $22,927**

**Includes value of shares received in payment of $9,166 capital gains

Results taking all dividends and distributions in CASH.

Initial Investment At Offering Price, Jan. 1, 1961. $10,000
Total Value, Dec. 31, 1970. $15,042
Distributions From Capital Gains. $ 7,327
Dividends From Investment Income. $ 626

Table 11-10 Fidelity Capital Fund, Inc.

FIDELITY CAPITAL FUND, INC.

35 Congress Street, Boston, Massachusetts 02109

This fund was organized in December 1957 by Fidelity Management & Research Company, the same management which supervises Fidelity Fund, Fidelity Trend Fund, Puritan Fund, Salem Fund and Everest Fund, as well as several funds not continuously offered.

Long-term growth of capital is the primary objective of the fund. Basically a common stock fund, it has restrictions as to the proportion of assets to be invested in any one type of security or industry. Flexibility is the keynote of the fund's investment policy.

At the 1970 fiscal year-end, November 30, more than one-half of the fund's common stock investments were in five industry groups: chemicals and communications (each 10.2% of assets), financial services (10.1%), oils (8.8%), and foods, household products & drugs (8.1%). Procter & Gamble, at 5.6% of assets, was the largest individual common stock holding. Other large investments included duPont (5.3%), American Telephone (4%),

General Telephone (3.7%), and BankAmerica Corp. (3.1%). Unrealized depreciation was 3.5% of fiscal year-end assets.

Special Services: The voluntary *accumulation plan* requires an initial minimum investment of $500; subsequent periodic payments must be at least $50 and total $300 annually. Income dividends are invested at offering price. Investors may arrange for payments to be made by bank draft against their checking accounts. *Contractual plans* (10- or 15-year payment period) with optional completion insurance are available through Crosby Plans Corp. The *withdrawal plan* is available without charge; the account must be worth at least $10,000 for a monthly plan, $5,000 for a quarterly plan. Shares held at least six months may be *exchanged* at asset value for those of Fidelity Fund, Fidelity Trend Fund, Salem Fund, Everest Fund or Puritan Fund for a $5 service fee. A *Keogh Plan* custody agreement is available.

Statistical History*

| | Total Net Assets | Number of Share-holders** | AT YEAR-ENDS % of Assets in— | | | Net Asset Value Per Share | Offer-ing Price | Yield | ANNUAL DATA Income Divi-dends | Capital Gains Distribu-tions | Expense Ratio | Offering Price— | |
			Cash & Equiva-lent	Bonds & Pre-ferreds	Common Stocks							High	Low
1970	$610,698,624	129,800	8%	6%***	86%	$11.26	$12.31	3.1%	$0.38	$...	0.53%	$12.59	$ 9.34
1969	599,502,272	137,300	4	6***	90	11.34	12.39	2.8	0.35	0.16	0.55	15.08	12.01
1968	723,996,130	134,600	4	2***	94	13.78	14.98	1.6	0.25	0.88	0.56	16.82	13.53
1967	727,296,912	130,000	7	5	88	14.82	16.11	1.2	0.21	1.44	0.56	17.79	13.35
1966	424,438,882	95,000	15	3	82	12.47	13.55	1.3	0.20	2.10	0.64	18.66	13.33
1965	332,032,991	73,700	5	...	95	14.22	15.46	0.8	0.14	2.64	0.65	18.55	11.74
1964	221,257,713	71,500	3	...	97	11.42	12.41	0.9	0.12	0.27	0.65	13.08	11.13
1963	174,207,957	70,100	5	...	95	10.24	11.13	0.9	0.10	...	0.66	11.17	8.16
1962	136,025,456	71,300	10	1	89	7.55	8.21	1.2	0.10	0.405†	0.71	10.93	7.13
1961	160,035,792	56,000	...	...	99	10.05	10.92	0.5	0.055	...	0.72	11.77	8.46
1960	25,012,291	8,500	4	...	96	7.90	8.58	0.9	0.075	0.37	0.67	8.60	6.33

* For years prior to 1966, data for total net assets, number of shareholders and portfolio holdings are as of November 30. Expense ratios are for fiscal years ended November 30; other figures are for calendar years.
** Includes contractual planholders starting in 1961.
*** Includes substantial proportion in convertible issues.
† Represents profits realized in the previous year.
Note: Figures adjusted for 2-for-1 stock split effective March 29, 1962.

Directors: Edward C. Johnson 2d, Chmn.; D. George Sullivan, Pres.; Edward C. Johnson 3d, Exec. V. P.; C. Rodgers Burgin; Alfred B. Cornell; Gilbert H. Hood, Jr.; George K. McKenzie; Horace Schermerhorn. Director Emeritus: George R. Harding.

Investment Adviser: Fidelity Management & Research Company. Compensation to the Adviser is ½ of 1% on first $200 million of average daily net assets; 0.45% on next $100 million; 0.40% on the next $400 million; 0.35% on assets up to $1 billion; and 0.30% on assets of $1 billion and over.

Custodian and Transfer Agent: The National Shawmut Bank of Boston, Boston, Mass.

Distributor: The Crosby Corporation, 225 Franklin Street, Boston, Mass. 02110, and 134 South La Salle Street, Chicago, Ill. 60603.

Distributor for contractual plans: Crosby Plans Corporation, 225 Franklin Street, Boston, Mass. 02110.

Sales Charge: Maximum is 8.5% of offering price; minimum is 1% at $1 million. Reduced charges begin at $10,000 and are applicable to combined purchases of two or more of specified funds in the Fidelity group. See page 140 for details. Minimum initial purchase is 10 shares.

Dividends: Income dividends are paid semi-annually in the months of May and November. Capital gains, if any, are paid optionally in shares or cash in January.

Shareholder Reports: Issued quarterly. Fiscal year ends November 30. New prospectus usually effective in March.

Qualified for Sale: In all states, D. C. and Puerto Rico.

An assumed investment of $10,000 in this fund, with capital gains accepted in shares, is illustrated below. The explanation on page 145 must be read in conjunction with this illustration.

FIDELITY CAPITAL FUND, INC.

LOGARITHMIC SCALE — $40,000 / 30,000 / 20,000 / 15,000 / 10,000 / 5,000

- - - Total value including value of shares accepted in payment of Capital Gains Distributions.
——— Value of Original Shares

Cost of Investment January 1, 1961 — $10,000 (Initial Net Asset Value $9,150)

Year end Dec. 31	1961	1962	1963	1964	1965	1966	1967	1968	1969	1970
Value of Shares Initially Acquired Through Investment of $10,000...	$11,645	$8,749	$11,866	$13,233	$16,477	$14,450	$17,173	$15,968	$13,140	$13,048
Value of Shares Accepted as Capital Gains Distributions (Cumulative)...	464	348	472	850	4,399	6,839	10,615	11,452	9,747	9,678
Total Value...	12,109	9,097	12,338	14,083	20,876	21,289	27,788	27,420	22,887	22,726
Dividends Paid From Investment Income...	64	120	121	145	173	294	359	469	696	767

December 31, 1970

$22,726 Total Value of Investment*
$13,048 Value of Original Shares
*(Including $9,678 Value of Shares Accepted as Capital Gains Distributions)
$3,208 Total Income Dividends

Dollar amounts of capital gains distributions accepted in shares were:

1961	$ 469		1967	$2,458
1962	—		1968	1,650
1963	—		1969	318
1964	325		1970	—
1965	3,256			
1966	3,083		Total	$11,559

Results taking all dividends and distributions in STOCK.
Initial Investment At Offering Price, Jan. 1, 1961. $10,000
Total Dividends From Income Reinvested...... $ 3,459
Total Amount Invested...... $13,459
Total Value, Dec. 31, 1970...... $26,355**
**Includes value of shares received in payment of $12,271 capital gains.

Results taking all dividends and distributions in CASH.
Initial Investment At Offering Price, Jan. 1, 1961. $10,000
Total Value, Dec. 31, 1970...... $13,048
Distribution From Capital Gains...... $ 9,148
Dividends From Investment Income...... $ 2,207

From *Investment Companies 1971*, 31st edition, p. 203. Reprinted with permission of Wiesenberger Services, Inc.

Table 11-11 United Funds, Inc.

UNITED FUNDS, INC.

20 West 9th Street, Kansas City, Missouri 64105

Organized in 1940, United Funds, Inc., now comprises four classes of shares: the Accumulative Fund, the Income Fund, the Science Fund and the Bond Fund. These four funds, with combined assets at the end of 1970 of $2.3 billion, are managed and distributed by Waddell & Reed, Inc., which has its own nation-wide retail sales organization. The funds are also available through a limited number of securities dealers. In 1969, the management company was acquired by Continental Investment Corporation, a Boston-based financial organization.

The three largest United Funds are described on this and the following pages. The fourth, United Bond Fund, was initially offered in March 1964 and is designed for investors whose primary objective is preservation of capital through investment in a portfolio of fixed-dollar-type securities; year-end assets of this fund totaled over $5.7 million.

A Canadian subsidiary of Waddell & Reed, Inc., acts as investment adviser to United Funds Canada–International Ltd., shares of which are not currently being offered.

Special Services: There are voluntary *accumulation plans* for Accumulative and Science Funds; the minimum initial investment required is $150. Subsequent periodic payments must be at least $25. *Contractual plans* with optional completion insurance are available for United Science Fund. *Automatic dividend reinvestment* is available for all funds; income dividends are invested at asset value.

A monthly or quarterly *withdrawal plan* is available without charge (all funds) to accounts (all funds may be combined) worth at least $10,000. Payments may be: level-dollar amounts ($50 monthly minimum); variable amounts based on a fixed percentage of asset value; or, also variable, the proceeds from the sale of a fixed number of shares (minimum of 5). Shares of any fund held for sixty days may be *exchanged* without charge at asset value for those of any other; a small service charge applies to transfers of shares held less than sixty days. *A Keogh Plan* custody agreement is available for all funds.

UNITED INCOME FUND

Second largest of the United Funds, this fund had year-end assets of $778 million. It has been in operation since 1940, and is intended for those who are primarily interested in dividends from net investment income. Emphasis at all times is on the production of a satisfactory rate of current income. During normal periods of business, companies which provide opportunities for reasonable capital growth will be stressed. At times of business recession, management will seek out companies whose earnings and dividends have historically shown resistance to changing economic conditions.

Present policy is to invest largely in common stocks, although bonds and preferred stocks may be held in any proportion management deems advisable. Common stock investments comprised 83% of assets as of December 31, 1970, below average for the past 10 years. Bond and preferred stock commitments were closer to their average position during the period.

About 36% of total assets comprised investments in five major industry groups: petroleum, geology & related (11.4% of assets), tobacco (6.9%), retail trade (6.7%), electric utilities (6.3%), and food products & services (4.8%). The five largest individual common stock holdings, ranging from 2.5% to 2.2% of assets, were IBM, Revlon, S. S. Kresge, Philip Morris, and Reynolds Industries, in that order. Unrealized appreciation was 13.2% of year-end assets.

Statistical History

	Total Net Assets	Number of Share-holders	AT YEAR-ENDS — % of Assets in			Net Asset Value Per Share	Offer-ing Price	Yield	ANNUAL DATA				
			Cash & Equiva-lent	Bonds & Pre-ferreds	Common Stocks				Income Divi-dends	Capital Gains Distribu-tions	Expense Ratio	Offering Price High	Low
1970	$778,296,648	104,200	9%	8%*	83%	$12.86	$14.09	2.9%	$0.43	$0.58	0.38%	$15.13	$10.84
1969	775,741,718	101,450	4	7*	89	13.68	14.95	2.1	0.33	0.33	0.39	17.65	14.46
1968	852,465,069	97,250	6	11	83	16.22	17.73	1.6	0.30	0.66	0.37	19.10	14.32
1967	759,169,696	96,350	5	2	97	14.93	16.32	2.0	0.34	0.58	0.39	16.96	13.99
1966	633,017,845	95,950	11	8	81	12.84	14.03	2.6	0.37	0.50	0.41	16.44	12.92
1965	684,766,416	87,800	2	2	96	14.69	16.05	2.3	0.37	0.43	0.47	16.43	14.40
1964	581,066,814	87,000	2	3	94	13.80	15.08	2.3	0.35	0.41	0.50	15.97	13.55
1963	449,470,976	78,000	3	3	94	12.40	13.55	2.5	0.35	0.39	0.56	14.15	12.28
1962	342,941,591	71,200	5	5	90	11.27	12.32	2.8	0.35	0.39	0.57	14.66	10.71
1961	353,765,940	72,000	1	5	94	13.41	14.66	2.3	0.34	0.40	0.56	15.36	11.82
1960	262,443,425	60,500	4	3	93	10.93	11.95	2.8	0.35	0.39	0.59	12.15	11.02

* Includes a substantial proportion in convertible issues.

An assumed investment of $10,000 in this fund, with capital gains accepted in shares, is illustrated below. The explanation on page 145 must be read in conjunction with this illustration.

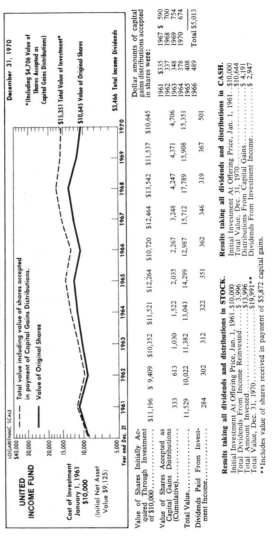

UNITED INCOME FUND

LOGARITHMIC SCALE

$40,000
30,000
20,000
15,000
10,000
5,000

Cost of Investment January 1, 1961 $10,000
(Initial Net Asset Value $9,125)

--- Total value including value of shares accepted in payment of Capital Gains Distributions.

— Value of Original Shares

December 31, 1970

*(Including $4,706 Value of Shares Accepted as Capital Gains Distributions)

$15,351 Total Value of Investment*

$10,645 Value of Original Shares

$3,466 Total Income Dividends

Year end Dec. 31	1961	1962	1963	1964	1965	1966	1967	1968	1969	1970
Value of Shares Initially Acquired Through Investment of $10,000	$11,196	$9,409	$10,352	$11,521	$12,264	$10,720	$12,464	$13,542	$11,537	$10,645
Value of Shares Accepted as Capital Gains Distributions (Cumulative)	333	613	1,030	1,522	2,035	2,267	3,248	4,247	4,371	4,706
Total Value	11,529	10,022	11,382	13,043	14,299	12,987	15,712	17,789	15,908	15,351
Dividends Paid From Investment Income	284	302	312	322	351	362	346	319	367	501

Results taking all dividends and distributions in STOCK.

Initial Investment At Offering Price, Jan. 1, 1961..$10,000
Total Dividends From Income Reinvested.....$ 3,996
Total Amount Invested.....$13,996
Total Value, Dec. 31, 1970.....$19,991**

**Includes value of shares received in payment of $5,872 capital gains.

Results taking all dividends and distributions in CASH.

Initial Investment At Offering Price, Jan. 1, 1961..$10,000
Total Value, Dec. 31, 1970.....$10,644
Distributions From Capital Gains.....$ 4,191
Dividends From Investment Income.....$ 2,947

Dollar amounts of capital gains distributions accepted in shares were:

1961	$335	1967	$ 590
1962	337	1968	700
1963	348	1969	754
1964	378	1970	674
1965	408		
1966	489		Total $5,013

From *Investment Companies 1971*, 31st edition, pp. 296, 297. Reprinted with permission of Wiesenberger Services, Inc.

at $10,000 or more. Furthermore, it offers a Keogh plan, which is a tax-sheltered pension program. As indicated in the chart, a $10,000 investment in American Investors Fund at the beginning of 1960 would have appreciated to $30,067. In addition, $824 in total dividends were distributed. As a very rough rate of return, ignoring compounding, ignoring dividend reinvestment, and ignoring income taxes, the investor might view his portfolio as having grown from $10,000 to a total of $30,891, for a return of $20,891, or about a 20 percent annual rate of return over the ten-year period.

Table 11–10 presents data on Fidelity Capital Fund. The Fidelity group is one of the best-known and most highly regarded investment groups of mutual funds. Fidelity Capital has about $600 million in total assets. It emphasizes long-term growth through common stocks. It also offers an accumulation plan, but the minimum initial investment must be $500 with subsequent periodic payments of at least $50 and $300 annually. Automatic dividend reinvestment, a withdrawal plan, and a Keogh plan are also offered. In addition, Fidelity Capital offers a contractual plan with optional completion insurance. Furthermore, Fidelity Capital Fund shareowners may convert their shares within the Fidelity group to Fidelity Fund, Fidelity Trend Fund, Salem Fund, Everest Fund, or Puritan Fund. Fidelity Capital is a load fund with a maximum commission of 8.5 percent of the offering price. As indicated in the chart, $10,000 invested in Fidelity Capital at the beginning of 1960 would have appreciated to $29,190 assuming that capital gains had been reinvested. In addition, $3,216 in total dividends were distributed. Consequently, an investor might compute a very rough portfolio return by adding his total dividends to his total appreciation by the end of 1969, a total of $22,406. Ignoring all complicating factors, this is about a 22 percent annual rate of return over the ten-year period.

Table 11–11 presents data on United Income Fund. It has about $800 million in total assets. As the name implies, United Income Fund emphasizes income, primarily through common stock dividends. United Income is one of a group of United Funds distributed through Waddell Reed, Inc., a private sales organization. United has front-end load plans, or contractual plans, with optional completion insurance. United also offers an accumulation plan with a minimum investment of $150 and subsequent periodic investments of $25, an automatic dividend reinvestment plan, a periodic withdrawal plan, a Keogh plan, and within-group conversion to any other fund within the United group. Note, especially, that the dividend income on United Income Fund has been very consistent, almost 3 percent at the beginning of the decade and gradually rising to 3.75 percent in 1969, for a total dividend figure of $3,316. Over the decade, the fund appreciated to $16,250. A very rough rate of return, therefore, might be computed by adding the dividends and the appreciation through the end of 1969 for $9,566 total return, or a

9.5 percent annual rate of return over the ten-year period. Although Fidelity Capital's total dividends for the whole decade were almost equal to those of United Income Fund, you might note that almost all of Fidelity Capital's dividends came in the last few years of the 1960's, as a result of its considerable appreciation in total value. You might also note that American Investors and Fidelity Capital had considerably greater price volitility than United Income Fund.

In comparing these three funds, each offers some of the same special features as the others, but each differs considerably from the others as well. American Investors is a no-load, common stock, growth fund. Fidelity Capital is a load fund within a group, but again seeking growth as a primary investment objective. United Income Fund is a front-end load fund with completion insurance within a group, but it stresses income primarily through common stock dividends. All three offer periodic investment plans, automatic reinvestment plans, and periodic withdrawal plans. Furthermore, all three are very large, well established mutual funds. In addition to examples such as these three, many new small specialty funds offering all kinds of more speculative portfolios, and more speculative special features are available for the mutual fund investor who prefers the rare and exotic. The individual investor's job is to determine which particular investment objectives and which special features he desires, and select specific mutual funds that may satisfy those desires. The professional portfolio manager's job is to construct and manage an investment portfolio that will achieve his stated investment objectives. When the investor does his job, he will select those specific funds that are more likely to perform according to his wishes and expectations. When the professional portfolio manager does his job right, he will so manage his fund that the investor's wishes and expectations are fulfilled. It is conceivable, of course, that the individual investor might beat the professional portfolio manager at his own game; however, that might take a bit of doing. If the investor does not care to take up the challenge, he may decide to use the professional's abilities to his own advantage by selecting the professional's portfolio as his own. By so deciding, the individual may devote more of his time and energy to his own career, while the professional portfolio manager devotes his time and energy to making those investment dollars so perform that the investor achieves his desired rate of return with the least risk possible. Through such a combination of efforts, both the individual and the professional may benefit, each contributing to the other's professional progress and ultimate financial security.

SUMMARY

For an investor who wants to build an investment portfolio but cannot devote very much of his time, the use of professional portfolio management may be the best means of achieving his investment objectives and goals. Numerous types of professionally managed investment portfolios are available. In most instances, the small investor has turned to open-end investment companies, i.e., mutual funds. Others have turned to either closed-end investment companies, variable annuities, real estate investment trusts, or commercial bank common trust funds. Each of these professional portfolios offers special advantages to any investor, and variable annuities in particular may assume a substantially more significant role in the future. In recent years, however, mutual funds have been the primary medium through which investors have used ready made, professionally managed investment portfolios to achieve their objectives and goals.

Basically, there are three types of mutual funds, i.e., balanced funds, growth funds, and specialty funds. Balanced funds emphasize safety of principal and income through wide diversification. Growth funds emphasize price appreciation through growth common stocks. Specialty funds vary in their portfolio objectives; some seek greater current income through fixed-income investments, and some seek higher rates of return through more speculative common stocks. Since the investment characteristics of various funds differ so much, the individual investor may select from many portfolio approaches, services, and features, in an effort to match his own investment objectives to those of a professionally managed portfolio. Rather than constructing and managing his own investment portfolio by selecting specific conservative, growth, and speculative stocks in accordance with his investment objectives, the investor may buy shares in a ready made, professionally managed mutual fund whose investment objectives coincide with his own personal investment objectives. Thereby, he instantly acquires adequate diversification and continued portfolio supervision.

There are many reasons for the popularity of mutual funds in recent years. Particularly, investors have increasingly bought mutual fund shares because they sought higher rates of return through common stock investing without the responsibility of selecting specific securities. Furthermore, many investors believe that a professional portfolio manager might manage their portfolios more effectively with less risk than they could manage them themselves. Through mutual funds, the investor may reduce his risk and increase his rate of return through adequate diversification and dollar cost averaging. Furthermore, many investors buy funds because they find it so very convenient to let a professional portfolio manager assume all the responsibility of selecting specific securities and adjusting the portfolio in response to changing economic and market conditions. Some investors buy funds to provide themselves with an appropriate measure of their own portfolio performance, feeling that a professionally managed portfolio with objectives closely resembling their own may be the most appropriate means for determining whether they should manage any portion of their own portfolios themselves.

Mutual funds may be purchased in several different ways. The investor may buy mutual fund shares from his broker in just exactly the same way he would buy any common stock. He may also buy shares directly from a fund by telephone or mail. Furthermore, he may buy shares from a fund with its own sales organization through a fund salesman who calls on his potential customers in their own homes. In the first case, the investor would buy shares in a load fund, that is, in a mutual fund which distributes its shares through brokers and dealers across the country, for which service the investor pays a load, or commission. In the second case, the investor would buy shares in a no-load fund, one that is not sold through brokers and dealers, and therefore has no load, or commission. In the third case, the investor would buy shares in a front-end load fund, one that concentrates the load charge in the early months of an investor's contractural investment program; thereby, the mutual fund salesman can justify considerably larger expenditures of time and energy in explaining to the small investor the various alternative approaches and features that may be available.

Mutual funds offer special features such as: a periodic investment plan, an automatic reinvestment plan, within-group conversion, a periodic withdrawal plan and a redemption privilege at no charge. Since mutual funds are regulated under various state and federal laws, and supervised by various regulatory commissions, an investor may feel more assured that his portfolio is being handled by a truly professional portfolio management. Because mutual funds offer these various advantages and special features, many investors have chosen the funds as their means of achieving their investment objectives and goals.

Case Problems

1. Robert Widmark is a young family man starting an investment program. This year he is able to put $400 into the investment program. Robert hopes to earn 10 percent on his investments. In this way he feels he can accumulate a sizable retirement nest egg. At this point in his career Robert is very busy. Being a young lawyer, he has to work many hours. Robert realizes that it is not worth much of his time to earn $40 of his investment portfolio. So, he would like to hire out his portfolio managing. What alternatives can you suggest to Robert?

2. Larry Ross is a very busy man. Larry's construction business takes a lot of his time. With this in mind, Larry has decided that it's not worth his time to manage his own investment portfolio. Larry has heard that mutual funds are one way to have his portfolio managed by someone else. He has looked into the funds but wasn't aware that there were several types. His problem is that he doesn't know what type of mutual fund represents his desired portfolio approach. He has found that there are balanced, growth

and specialty funds. Larry would like you to explain each so he can determine which best fits his investment goals.

3. Dick Ottumwa realizes that he doesn't have the time or skill necessary to manage his own investment program. Dick is definitely sold on the idea of mutual funds. He has decided that a growth fund fits his portfolio approach best. However, Dick realizes there are different ways to buy different funds. Please help Dick and explain the advantage to each type of commission arrangement.

4. Bud Welch is the owner of a small business in Central California. Bud has decided to retire. He put his business up for sale, and sold it for $100,000 to a big chain. Bud realizes that $100,000 will not last long the way he and his wife spend money. So, he knows he should invest the money. Bud has decided that a mutual fund is his best alternative. He is particularly interested in some of their special features. He is trying to explain the mutual fund special features to his wife, but she doesn't understand the advantages of the special features. What are the advantages to each of the special features?

5. Marvin Butterfield is reading the *Wall Street Journal* for the first time in his life. He enjoys looking at all the quotations. However, he is puzzled by the quotation of the mutual funds. He doesn't know what to make of the numbers or what they show. Below is a sample listing. Please explain to Marvin what the figures show. Also what is the absolute and percentage load of the fund?

	Asked	*Bid*	*Prev. Bid*	*Bid Ch.*
Con. Bal.	30.00	27.40	27.60	−.20

6. Snoopy McKee started an investment portfolio 10 years ago. He now is 50 years old and would like to retire. His portfolio is worth $75,000. He is considering a periodic withdrawal plan. He feels that he needs $750 a month to live on during retirement. His fund is earning 10 percent return a year. Snoopy realizes that he will be withdrawing more than his fund earns. He has figured out all the details. His question is why does the fund deplete at a faster rate each year when he takes out the same amount each year?

Selected Readings

"Forbes Mutual Fund Survey." Annual performance ratings. Published annually in the August 15 issue of *Forbes Magazine.*

Investing Made Easy. Published by the Investment Company Institute, 61 Broadway, N.Y., N.Y. A free copy is available on request.

Mutual Fund Fact Book. Published annually by the Investment Company Institute.

Wiesenberger Services. *Investment Companies, Mutual Funds, and Other Types.* Latest edition of this annual publication. Wiesenberger Services, 61 Broadway, N.Y., N.Y.

CHAPTER **TWELVE**

OWNING A BUSINESS

It may be difficult for you to imagine yourself as the owner of a small business. But almost everyone, at some time, thinks about the possibility of being the owner and manager of a company. And a surprising number of people actually carry through with their ideas. About 95 percent of all the companies in the country are classified as "small," and many large companies started out as nothing more than the ambitions of one individual.

In the United States, because of our free enterprise system, a person has the right to start his own company and compete against others. This is why it is said that part of the "American Dream" is the possibility of starting a company from scratch and developing it into a successful business operation. Business ownership offers independence and freedom that is unattainable as an employee, and it can provide a virtually unlimited horizon for fulfilling dreams and ambitions. In the process, business ownership can provide an important means by which a person can improve his financial position.

If the possibility of owning a business intrigues you, perhaps you should examine the possible rewards and problems of owning a company. Although the reasons for owning a business can be very appealing, no one should attempt to own a company until he has studied the major problems that might be involved. When a person establishes his own business, he must decide which type of business he wants to own, and he should appraise his qualifications and chances of success. Once he decides that he is qualified the real problems begin: a businessman must decide how his company will be owned, how the financing will be arranged, and how the company will be managed. You should know something about these problems—*not* because you necessarily need to know how to manage a small business—but because you should be aware of the opportunities and problems of owning a company.

DECIDING TO OWN A BUSINESS

Before a person can decide whether or not he should own a small business he should consider the advantages of owning a company, study his chances of success, and examine his qualifications. If a person finds that his reasons for wanting to own a company are not sufficient to risk failure, he can decide against business ownership. Or, if a person believes he is not qualified to own a company he can continue to work as an employee rather than an owner. But when a person has good reasons for wanting to own a company and he believes that his qualifications promise a good chance of success, he may be well on the path to improving his financial position.

REWARDS OF BUSINESS OWNERSHIP

One of the primary reasons for owning a business is the opportunity for financial gains. The profits from a well-managed, prosperous business can provide a tremendous income to the owner. For all practical purposes, there is no limit to the income that might be provided by a company. This is in sharp contrast to the typical employee's salary which has definite limits.

But not every business owner expects to get rich—and it is a mistake to assume that every entrepreneur is trying to amass a personal fortune. Some people go into business with the realization that their income will not be substantial. Consider, for example, the owner of a service station, small bakery, or small automobile repair shop who may earn only a reasonable income. The income might still be higher than the person would earn as an employee. In other words, an individual may have financial reasons for owning his own business even if he believes the monetary rewards will not be great.

Financial reasons, as important as they are to businessmen, are not the only incentives for owning a company. The desire to be independent —to be your own boss—is another reason that leads many people to business ownership. Some people are simply unhappy when they are subject to authority and control. Unfortunately, a person who works in a large organization sometimes has little free time and perhaps only a small degree of independence. But it is important to realize that while the owner of a small business has much greater independence than a typical employee, an owner is still not perfectly free to follow his own desires. A small businessman must work with and generally satisfy his customers, suppliers, employees, the government, and even competitors to some extent. A businessman who neglects his responsibilities to these groups is not likely to remain in business long.

The owner of a small business is also likely to be motivated by a sense of pride and satisfaction. A person who has the drive, initiative, and ambition to own a business is generally respected in the business community, and he can readily measure his accomplishments. Employees, on the other hand, usually cannot be as proud of the business, and they cannot always see the fruits of their labor.

CHANCES OF SUCCESS

One of the great dangers in owning your own company is the fact that young, small companies have a high rate of failure. This is shown clearly in Table 12–1. Table 12–1 indicates that the majority of business failures are firms that are young (five years old or less) and small. And over 80 percent of the failing firms have liabilities under $100,000. Only a very small percentage of the failures are companies that have over $1,000,000 in liabilities.

Table 12–1 Business Failures, by Age and Size of Company

Age of Company	Percentage of Failing Companies	Size of Liability[a]	Percentage of Failing Companies
5 years	53.9	Under $5,000	5.0
6-10 years	23.3	$5,000-$25,000	34.6
10 years and over	22.8	$25,000-$100,000	41.7
		$100,000-$1,000,000	17.5
		Over $1,000,000	1.2

[a] Liability refers to current liabilities and does not include long term, publicly held obligations. Offsetting assets are not taken into account.
Source: Dun and Bradstreet, *The Failure Record* (New York, 1969) pp. 7 and 11. Used with permission.

Obviously, a person who starts his own business (or buys an existing company) must be willing to accept the possibility that he may not be successful. A businessman, however, might be able to minimize his chance of failure if he is familiar with the failure rates of various types of firms. Table 12–2 can be helpful in this regard.

Suppose you enjoy photography and would like to open a camera store. This might be a wise decision, but you should know that camera stores have a high rate of failure. Table 12–2 shows that camera stores have the highest rate of failure of any type of retail store shown in the table. Jewelry stores have the lowest rate of failure.

It is also helpful to know that failure rates differ considerably in different parts of the country. As a general rule, failure rates are lower in the South and Midwest and higher in the West. Specifically, the rates of failure have been high in California, Arizona, and Oregon. This is probably a result of rapid population growth and extreme competition.

Failure rates are also much higher during some years than others. Of course, many companies failed during the Great Depression of the

Table 12–2   Failure Rates in Retail and Manufacturing Lines

Retail Failures Ranked by Failure Rates *Line of Business*	Failure Rate per 10,000 Operating Concerns
Cameras and photographic supplies	67
Books and stationery	58
Women's ready to wear	58
Appliances, radio and television	54
Furniture and furnishings	52
Men's wear	50
Gifts	50
Infant's and children's wear	49
Toys and hobby crafts	49
Sporting goods	47
Lumber and building materials	40
Bakeries	35
Women's accessories	30
Auto parts and accessories	29
Drugs	28
Eating and drinking places	27
Dry goods and general merchandise	24
Shoes	22
Hardware	21
Automobiles	21
Farm implements	19
Groceries, meats and products	16
Jewelry	16
Manufacturing Industries Ranked by Failure Rate *Line of Industry*	
Furniture	117
Transportation equipment	90
Textile	75
Leather and shoes	70
Electrical machinery	51
Apparel	50
Machinery	48
Paper	47
Metals, primary and fabricated	45
Chemicals and drugs	44
Printing and publishing	36
Food	32
Stone, clay and glass	30
Lumber	20

Source: Dun and Bradstreet, *The Failure Record* (New York, 1969), p. 6. Used with permission.

1930's, but the rate of failures was also high in 1961 and a rash of failures developed in 1970. This means that a person who is considering the possibility of owning his own business should give some thought to economic conditions.

CAUSES OF FAILURES

What causes business failures? In view of the high rate of failures of small businesses, this question deserves the serious attention of anyone who is contemplating business ownership.

Table 12–3 is useful because it shows that the apparent causes of failure can be traced to underlying causes. According to this table the basic causes of business failures—contrary to common belief—are seldom attributable to business recessions, fraud, or disasters. Almost 90 percent of all business failures result from lack of experience, unbalanced experience, and incompetence, in other words, poor management and inadequate experience.

The pitfalls in managing a small business have been set forth specifically in a recent study by Dun and Bradstreet. This study states the leading pitfalls as follows:

1. Lack of experience
2. Lack of money
3. Wrong location
4. Inventory mismanagement
5. Too much capital going into fixed assets
6. Poor credit granting practices
7. Taking too much money out of the business
8. Unplanned expansion
9. Having the wrong attitudes

Since these pitfalls can all be traced to poor management, it is obvious that management is the key to a successful small company. More will be said about this topic later in the chapter.

QUALIFICATIONS

It should be clear now that not everyone should attempt to own a business. Some businesses are probably doomed from the start because the owner is just not qualified. Experts in the business management know that the owner of a small business has a much greater chance to succeed if he meets four major qualifications: (1) appropriate personal characteristics, (2) proper experience and education, (3) an adequate degree of management ability, and (4) sufficient financial capacity.

Personal Characteristics.   A proprietor can usually achieve greater success if he has a personality that enables him to get along well with customers, employees, and business associates. The problem is that it is hard for a person to evaluate objectively his own personality. However, published forms are available that will help a person determine if he has the personal characteristics that are helpful in owning a business.[1]

---

[1] See, for example, H. N. Broom and Justin G. Longenecker, *Small Business Management* (Cincinnati: South-Western Publishing Co., 1966), p. 112.

Table 12–3   Causes of Business Failures

Manufacturers	Wholesalers	Retailers	Construction	Commercial Service	Total All Concerns	Underlying Causes
2.1%	3.0%	3.0%	2.9%	2.3%	2.8%	NEGLECT
1.3	2.7	1.0	0.7	1.3	1.2	FRAUD
8.9	8.0	12.4	8.3	11.5	10.6	LACK OF EXPERIENCE IN THE LINE
13.4	12.3	16.2	18.5	17.7	16.0	LACK OF MANAGERIAL EXPERIENCE
17.8	18.1	18.6	18.6	16.7	18.2	UNBALANCED EXPERIENCE*
51.7	52.3	41.9	45.4	41.3	45.0	INCOMPETENCE
1.6	1.2	2.0	0.7	1.2	1.5	DISASTER
3.2	2.4	4.9	4.9	8.0	4.7	REASON UNKNOWN
100.0	100.0	100.0	100.0	100.0	100.0	Total Percent
1,513	981	4,366	1,670	1,106	9,636	Number of Failures
$192,795	$131,829	$50,440	$127,220	$78,923	$97,654	Average Liabilities per Failure

*Experience not well rounded in sales, finance, purchasing, and production on the part of the individual in case of a proprietorship or of two or more partners or officers constituting a management unit.

A businessman who owns his business needs a high degree of drive, ambition, and willingness to work long hours. Some people who enjoy the freedom and independence that are associated with business ownership are just not capable of forcing themselves to work.

Education and Experience.   You have probably heard stories about the poor boy who had to quit school at an early age and later developed a multi-million dollar business. But you should realize that it was easier in the past to become a business success without an education than it will be in the future. As Chapter Seven pointed out, education plays an important role in determining a person's occupation, and it would be a mistake to believe that a self-employed person does not need an education. Indeed, since the owner of a business usually must manage the entire business operation, he may have a greater need for education than an employee who works at a specialized job. A high school education, at least, is a necessity for business ownership, and a college degree is

Apparent Causes**		Manufacturers	Wholesalers	Retailers	Construction	Commercial Service	Total All Concerns
Due to:	bad habits	0.6%	0.7%	0.9%	1.0%	0.5%	0.8%
	poor health	1.3	1.8	1.3	0.9	1.0	1.2
	marital difficulties	——	0.1	0.3	0.4	0.4	0.3
	other	0.2	0.4	0.5	0.6	0.4	0.5
On the part of the principals, reflected by:	misleading name	——	0.2	0.0	——	0.1	0.0
	false financial statement	——	0.4	0.4	0.2	0.4	0.3
	premeditated overbuy	0.1	0.4	0.2	——	——	0.1
	irregular disposal of assets	0.7	1.5	0.3	0.5	0.6	0.6
	other	0.5	0.2	0.1	0.0	0.2	0.2
Evidenced by inability to avoid conditions which resulted in:	inadequate sales	44.4	39.7	44.6	25.2	38.0	40.0
	heavy operating expenses	15.9	11.4	8.3	26.4	19.0	14.2
	receivables difficulties	12.9	13.3	4.9	14.6	5.5	8.7
	inventory difficulties	3.1	6.8	6.8	1.3	2.4	4.8
	excessive fixed assets	6.1	3.3	3.4	3.8	7.7	4.4
	poor location	0.7	1.8	5.9	0.6	2.2	3.3
	competitive weakness	19.5	23.1	22.3	23.8	19.3	21.9
	other	2.2	3.4	1.7	5.4	1.5	3.6
Some of the occurrences could have been provided against through insurance	fire	1.3	0.4	0.9	0.3	0.3	0.7
	flood	0.1	0.1	——	0.0	0.0	0.0
	burglary	——	0.1	0.3	0.0	0.1	0.2
	employee's fraud	——	0.2	0.2	0.1	0.3	0.1
	strike	0.1	0.2	0.0	——	0.1	0.1
	other	0.1	0.2	0.6	0.3	0.4	0.4
Percent of Failures		15.7	10.2	45.3	17.3	11.5	100.0

**Because some failures are attributed to a combination of apparent causes, the totals of these columns exceed the totals of the corresponding columns on the left.

Source: Dun and Bradstreet, *The Failure Record*, (New York, 1969) pp. 7 and 11. Used with permission.

valuable. In some types of businesses a graduate degree is ideal preparation.

But few people are able to handle a company (even a small company) immediately after they graduate from school. Experience is important, but experience—by itself—does not necessarily prove that you can manage a business. The *kinds of experience* you have had are critical. Consider Joe Stiles' case. When he graduated from college he started selling and found that he had the ability to sell. In fact, he was an extraordinary salesman. But Joe decided that he should not have to pay an "overriding commission" to his superiors, so he started his own sales organization. Joe believed he would have little trouble because he had a good education, five years' experience, and a proven ability to sell. But Joe's company failed within a year. Why? Because Joe did not know how to manage his company's bookkeeping problems, tax questions, legal difficulties, and financial problems. He had no experience along these lines. A person should have a wide range of experience with the major problems he will encounter in his business. It is not enough to have extensive experience in a specialized area. For purposes of owning a business, it is more valuable to have five years' experience than to have one year's experience five times.

Management Ability.   Strangely enough, many people know the operation of a business very well and yet they cannot manage their own company. At the same time, many of the most successful companies are managed by people who know practically nothing about the day-to-day operations of their company. Apparently the ability to manage is fairly separate and distinct from education and experience.

An effective manager must have the ability to plan, organize, direct, and control his company. Normally this requires a good general knowledge of business practices, and perhaps more importantly, an ability to work with others. Every businessman must work with other people, and as a business grows, a manager must be more and more able to delegate responsibility to others. Many small businesses are stifled because the owner only lets the business grow to the extent that *he* can handle the day-to-day work.

FINANCIAL CAPACITY

A person cannot start his own business or buy an existing company without money. Funds may be needed for rent, inventory, machinery, equipment, salaries, taxes, insurance premiums, and legal fees. And when the total expense of starting a business is calculated, it usually is a surprisingly large amount. This is probably one of the major reasons why many people decide they should not own a business.

While it is true that a businessman may need a substantial fund to start his business, most people who meet the other qualifications reasonably well can probably raise enough money to get a business started. In addition to a prospective business owner's money, funds may be raised for a promising business venture from many different sources. Since the problem of raising adequate capital is a fundamental problem of owning a business, this problem is given separate treatment in this chapter.

CHOOSING THE RIGHT BUSINESS

After making the decision (or tentative decision) to own a business, the next logical step is to determine what kind of business you should own. In doing this, you should keep firmly in mind the importance of your experience.

THE FIELDS OF SMALL BUSINESS

Only large firms can normally operate profitably in certain fields of business. In the field of transportation, communications, and public utilities the required investment in physical facilities is usually so great that only large companies can succeed. Table 12–4 can be very helpful in studying the fields that are most attractive for small businesses.

Table 12–4 shows that mining and manufacturing tend to be dominated by large companies. This does not mean that a small company has no chance of success in these fields. But the chances of success are much greater in other lines of business.

The fields of business that are most commonly populated by small companies are agriculture, forestry, and fishing; finance, insurance, and real estate; and the service industry. Companies in the service industry include a wide variety of companies such as those that provide business services (for example, accounting firms, advertising agencies, employment agencies, and tax consultants), personal services (such as barber and beauty shops, laundries, travel agencies, and music teachers), automobile and repair services, entertainment and recreation services, and hotels and motels. The financial field is dominated by many small companies because of the great number of real estate and insurance agencies.

FINDING A SPECIFIC BUSINESS

Although it is helpful to know that certain fields of business offer greater chances of success than others, a person who is interested in owning a business is faced with the practical problem of choosing a specific business. He must either find a business that can be bought or start his own company.

Finding an existing business usually is not much of a problem. In fact, the problem is that there are so many businesses for sale. These can be found in the classified sections of large newspapers, in trade press publications (magazines and journals in specific lines of business), from trade associations, and business brokers. Business brokers are firms that specialize in matching buyers and sellers of companies. Normally, a business broker receives a commission from the seller rather than the buyer. Not only do business brokers match buyers and sellers, they also provide help in evaluating a company that is for sale.

THE PROBLEM OF RAISING CAPITAL

As we have seen, many would-be entrepreneurs are stymied by the problem of raising enough money to get started. Many people undoubtedly give up before they really know if they can raise enough money. Actually the only way a person can determine whether he can raise sufficient capital is to study his need for funds and investigate the possible sources.

CAPITAL NEEDS

A small business usually has a need for four different types of funds. The first is working capital. Although the term "working capital" is defined

Table 12-4 Size of Businesses in Various Industries

	Percentage of Companies Classified by Number of Employees								
	1 to 3	4 to 7	8 to 19	20 to 49	50 to 99	100 to 249	250 to 499	500 or more	Total
Agriculture, forestry, fisheries	64.0%	19.4%	12.0%	3.6%	0.8%	0.2%	0.0%	0.0%	100%
Mining	39.4	18.2	22.1	12.1	4.3	2.4	0.7	0.4	100
Construction	54.0	20.8	15.6	6.4	2.0	0.9	0.2	0.1	100
Manufacturing	25.4	16.3	22.0	16.8	8.4	6.5	2.6	2.0	100
Transportation, communication, electrical, gas and sanitary services	44.9	18.1	19.3	10.2	3.9	2.3	0.7	0.6	100
Wholesale and retail trade	41.4	22.4	22.6	10.0	2.6	1.0	0.2	0.1	100
Finance, insurance and real estate	65.9	15.6	11.1	4.6	1.5	0.9	0.2	0.2	100
Services	65.0	17.2	11.2	4.2	1.3	0.7	0.2	0.2	100

Source: *Statistical Abstract of the United States*, 1968, p. 476.

in several ways, businessmen normally use the term to mean total current assets. Most businesses need working capital in the form of cash, accounts receivable, and inventory in order to operate.

The second type of capital needed is fixed asset capital. Fixed assets are the long-term, reasonably permanent assets that are used in the business. Unlike current assets, they are not normally sold or converted into cash. The most common examples of long-term fixed assets are land, buildings, machinery, equipment, and automobiles or trucks. Often a small business can reduce its needs for fixed asset capital by renting, leasing, or sub-contracting.

Promotional expense capital is usually needed .by a small business which includes funds for legal fees, state organizational taxes, expenses of finding an appropriate location, and advertising costs. In other words, these are the start-up costs that are not included in the other needs for funds.

In most small businesses, there is a fourth need for capital—funds for personal expenses. Although this is technically not a part of the business capital, as a practical matter most new business owners need money for personal living expenses while the company is getting started. Many companies cannot immediately operate at a profit, even though they will be able to generate profits after the company is firmly established.

Every company is unique, to some extent, and therefore the needs for capital depend on the characteristics of each company. Furthermore, the need for working capital may be seasonal. Consequently, when capital needs are projected into the future, a businessman must realize that he cannot get a precise answer. The best he can hope to do is arrive at a reasonable *estimate* of capital needs.

The first step in estimating capital needs is to forecast the volume of sales. This can be done in several ways. If the business has been operating in the past, its sales record can be used. Another approach involves a study of similar companies. For example, if you are considering the possibility of opening a shoe store, you might be able to get estimates of your sales volume from existing shoe stores that are similar to the one you are considering. Another approach is to start with a desired profit figure and work backwards to a sales prediction. Suppose you are aiming for an annual profit of $15,000 and you learn that a shoe store typically earns 3 percent on sales. If this is the case, you would know that you must have sales of $500,000 to achieve your profit goal. Then you could study the question of whether or not it is reasonable to expect sales of $500,000. Obviously this approach can be dangerous and should be checked carefully.

After sales are forecast, the next step is to determine the amount of assets that are necessary for that volume of sales. One method of doing this is to use standard ratios. A number of organizations, such as

Dun and Bradstreet, banks, and trade associations publish such ratios. Table 12–5 shows several important ratios for different types of companies.

Now, following our example of a shoe store, Table 12–5 should help us arrive at some useful conclusions. The table shows that the average ratio of net sales to net working capital for a shoe store is 3.84 percent. Therefore, if we expect sales of $500,000, we will need $19,200 (3.84 percent of $500,000) in net working capital (if we have an average amount of net working capital).

Table 12–5 shows the average ratio of net sales to inventory. If we have a predicted sales figure we can use this figure to estimate the amount of inventory a company needs. For a shoe store, the table indicates that an average inventory for a company with $500,000 in sales is $17,000 (3.4 percent of $500,000). Although Table 12–5 shows only three ratios for each type of business, other ratios are available.[2] These other ratios can be used to determine the coverage amount of accounts receivable, cash, and other assets that a company might require.

The use of average ratios can be very helpful in estimating a company's need for capital. However, it should be emphasized that using ratios in this manner can be deceiving. At best, the ratios indicate the amount of capital needed by an *average* company. Since all companies are different, the ratio approach may not provide reliable answers for all companies.

Estimates of capital needs should be checked with other individuals. Suppliers, for example, can often provide helpful estimates concerning the amount of working capital a new firm needs. In some cases, estimates might be provided by similar companies.

SOURCES OF FUNDS

After arriving at an estimate of capital needs, a person must investigate the sources he can use to raise the needed capital. A new business can be financed in a number of ways, and a person who is interested in owning a business should explore all possibilities.

Seymour Green once had an experience that can teach us something. He wanted desperately to open a shoe store and he decided that he needed $20,000. But he had only $2,000 in his savings account. Apparently Seymour was $18,000 short and it seemed as though he had no chance to raise the necessary funds. But Seymour was determined. After checking further, he found he had an extra $500 in his bank account and $1,500 in cash value in his life insurance policy. This brought his total savings to $4,000. Then Seymour sold one of his cars for $2,000 and his camping trailer for the same amount. He now had $8,000—but still

---

[2] Numerous sources of information (broken down by type of business) are listed in "How to Build Profits by Controlling Costs," Dun and Bradstreet, Inc., 99 Church Street, New York, New York 10007.

Table 12–5 Important Financial Ratios

	Net Profits on Net Sales	Net Sales to Net Working Capital	Net Sales to Inventory
Retailing			
Children's and infants' wear stores	1.70	4.36	4.4
Discount stores	2.00	8.26	5.2
Farm equipment dealers	1.63	5.92	2.9
Gasoline service stations	2.42	6.80	12.7
Jewelry stores	4.48	2.21	3.1
Paint, glass and wallpaper stores	3.23	4.84	6.5
Shoe stores	3.00	3.84	3.4
Wholesaling			
Air condtg. and refrigtn, equipt. and supplies	1.82	5.83	6.5
Chemicals and allied products	1.89	7.45	11.3
Commercial machines and equipment	1.62	5.40	6.5
Drugs and druggists' sundries	1.05	7.00	6.6
Electronic parts and equipment	2.04	4.38	4.1
Fresh fruits and vegetables	1.32	14.17	57.5
Hardware	1.35	4.22	4.6
Meats and meat products	0.49	21.75	39.6
Paper and its products	1.17	6.41	8.1
Plumbing and heating eqpt. and supplies	1.75	4.80	5.5
Tires and tubes	2.39	4.80	5.3
Manufacturing and Construction			
Agricultural chemicals	2.22	5.07	7.4
Books; publishing, publishing and printing	3.45	3.78	4.2
Commercial printing except lithographic	2.63	6.43	**
Confectionery and related products	1.81	7.03	7.7
Dairy products	1.43	17.88	32.6
Drugs	7.11	3.89	6.4
Electrical work	2.39	7.45	**
Engineering, laboratory and scientific instruments	3.59	2.69	4.3
Fur goods	1.04	6.47	6.7
Grain mill products	1.72	8.96	12.0
Apparatus and plumbing fixtures	2.97	3.66	5.6
Household appliances	3.16	4.50	5.1
Iron and steel foundries	2.92	5.40	12.3
Meat packing plants	0.73	17.98	30.0
Millwork	2.36	4.89	6.8
Motor vehicle parts and accessories	4.49	4.13	6.1
Paints, varnishes, lacquers and enamels	2.95	4.50	6.5
Passenger car, truck and bus bodies	1.84	5.50	5.7
Plumbing, heating and air conditioning	1.82	8.33	5.5
Soap, detergents, perfumes and cosmetics	4.50	4.61	8.3
Soft drinks bottled and canned	4.62	9.78	13.6
Special industry machinery	3.27	3.59	4.7
Surgical, medical and dental instruments	4.38	3.44	4.8
Work clothing, men's and boy's	2.57	3.82	3.8

**Not computed. Printers carry only current supplies such as paper, ink, and binding materials rather than merchandise inventories for resale. Building Trades contractors have no inventories in the credit sense of the term. As a general rule, such contractors have no customary selling terms, each contract being a special job for which individual terms are arranged.

far short of his goal of $20,000. When Seymour told his brother about his problem his brother offered to loan him $1,000 if he could raise enough money to get the company started. At this point, Seymour decided to ask his bank for a loan. His bank came through with a $6,000 loan. Seymour was now only $3,000 short of his required $20,000. At this stage a shoe manufacturer offered to lend the remaining $3,000 and Seymour was in business.

Seymour's experience illustrates several important ideas. First, in many cases it is not impossible to raise a large amount of money, even if it appears hopeless. Secondly, a person may have a number of sources of funds. Actually, there are several ways money can be raised to start a new company.

Personal savings are the most important source of funds for a small business. And, as shown in Seymour's case, a person might be able to convert some of his assets into cash to start his business. It is almost impossible to start a business with absolutely no financial contribution from the owner. But if a person is willing to put up his own money, he may be able to obtain funds from others.

Loans from relatives and friends provide a common source of funds for a new business. If loans of this type are used, however, they should be handled carefully. It is easy for family disputes and emotions to create problems.

Another source of funds, which is often overlooked, are loans from previous owners. Suppose you decide to buy an existing shoe store but cannot seem to raise the necessary funds. It is quite possible that the owner of the store will be willing to lend money to you, so that you can buy his business. You can then repay him from future earnings of the company. Insurance agencies and other types of businesses are frequently purchased in this manner.

Commercial banks (and other financial institutions) usually prefer to limit their lending to the working capital needs of existing businesses, rather than providing initial capital. But a fair amount of initial financing is provided through financial institutions.

Trade credit is another important source of funds—that is, loans made by suppliers. In other words, a supplier may be willing to provide inventory (or a portion of needed inventory) for a company and not require immediate payment. Suppliers are usually an excellent source of credit because they may be more liberal in the terms of their loans, and they may be fairly eager to extend credit. The reason, of course, is that suppliers are anxious to develop new customers. By helping customers get started in business, they benefit from a solid business relationship (and a possible source of profits) that may last for years.

Equipment supplier loans are also used by some types of new companies. If you are starting a business that requires equipment, you can normally purchase the equipment on an installment basis. A restaurant, for example, may need some expensive cooking and cooling equipment, but a new business owner may not have to pay cash for the equipment.

Life insurance can also be used as a source of capital. Suppose you are a young employee but you would like very much to own the business. The problem is that you do not have quite enough experience and you cannot raise enough money. The present owner has no great desire to sell the company at the present time, but he will want to sell it when he retires. He is also a little concerned about the future of his business in the event of his death. Why not enter into an agreement with the owner to buy the business when he dies? This type of agreement (called a buy-and-sell agreement) obligates you to buy the business and the owner's heirs to sell the business to you upon the owner's death. This type of agreement is usually funded with life insurance on the owner's life. It is an ideal way to provide funds to buy a business because life insurance makes money available just at the time the funds are needed (when the owner dies). The premiums on the life insurance policy can be paid in several ways. Perhaps you (as an employee who wants to buy the business) will agree to pay the premiums. Sometimes an employer agrees to pay the premiums himself, particularly if he can pay the premiums in lieu of salary increases. Or sometimes an employer will pay the premiums because he wants the assurance that the business will be sold promptly and at a fair price when he dies. The buy-and-sell agreement can be arranged in different ways, but it is common (in this type of situation) to postpone the *actual* transfer of the business until the owner dies. If the owner lives past the age when he wishes to retire, he can retire and let the employee who wants the business serve as a manager. It is clear that buy-and-sell agreements can become very technical and confusing; if such an arrangement is considered, an attorney is necessary.

CHOOSING THE LEGAL FORM OF ORGANIZATION

After deciding to own a certain type of business, one of the immediate problems is to determine *how* the business will be owned. In other words, a legal form of organization must be selected. A businessman can choose any one of at least six or seven legal forms, but most businesses operate as a sole proprietorship, partnership, or corporation.

It is well to keep in mind that the size of the company and the industry are important factors in selecting a form of organization. Table 12–6 shows these factors clearly. Notice that sole proprietorships are the most common form of organization in every industry except manufacturing. The corporate form of organization is the most popular for manufacturers. Notice that Table 12–6 shows that sole proprietorships are the most numerous type of business. But this can be deceiving. Corporations are not as numerous but because they tend to be large, they actually do more business than other types of companies.

Table 12-6 Percentage of Companies Operating as Sole Proprietorships, Partnerships and Corporations

	Proprietorships			Partnerships			Corporations			Total
	A	B	C	A	B	C	A	B	C	
Agriculture, forestry, fisheries	93.0%	1.7%	0.7%	3.0%	0.5%	0.3%	0.4%	0.1%	0.3%	100
Mining	50.0	3.1	3.1	18.8	1.6	3.1	9.4	3.1	7.8	100
Construction	69.9	5.7	4.8	4.0	1.3	1.5	3.4	1.8	7.6	100
Manufacturing	37.0	4.4	4.2	4.7	1.5	2.5	8.9	4.7	32.1	100
Transportation, communication, electrical, gas, and sanitary services	74.1	2.9	2.1	3.5	0.8	0.8	7.0	2.4	6.4	100
Wholesale and retail trade	53.0	10.8	9.5	4.2	2.0	3.2	3.6	2.5	11.2	100
Finance, insurance and real estate	43.8	1.3	0.7	19.0	1.2	0.9	24.2	3.8	5.1	100
Services	81.0	4.0	1.0	4.3	1.0	1.3	3.8	1.3	2.3	100

Note: A = less than $50,000 gross income

B = $50,000 to $99,900 gross income

C = $100,000 or more gross income

Source: *Statistical Abstracts of the United States,* 1968, p. 475.

Choosing the form of organization is an important decision. A sole proprietorship, partnership, and a corporation are substantially different from one another. There are advantages and disadvantages to each form of organization, but there is usually one form that is most appropriate for a certain situation. Selecting the appropriate form of organization, therefore, is a necessary requisite to financial success.

SOLE PROPRIETORSHIPS

A sole proprietorship is a business that is owned by one person. In most cases a sole proprietor also manages his company, but it is individual *ownership* that distinguishes a sole proprietorship.

Sole proprietorships are the most popular type of organizations. There are more sole proprietorships than corporations (or partnerships), but most individually owned companies are small. As a general rule, the sole proprietorship approach is most appropriate for small companies and normally inappropriate for large businesses. This, however, is not always true because some fairly large companies (as shown in Table 12–6) are sole proprietorships.

Advantages of Sole Proprietorships. A sole proprietorship is the simplest and least expensive type of company to organize. A sole proprietorship is established when you start selling a product or a service. You may have to pay a license fee or a small charge to the city or state government, but a sole proprietor is not required to go through a detailed, time-consuming, expensive legal process to get his company started.

This is not to say that the government does not get involved in the regulation or supervision of sole proprietorships. It does. A sole proprietor is required by the government to follow numerous laws and regulations. For example, a sole proprietor may be required to keep records and pay social security taxes for employees, pay employees minimum wages, and provide disability benefits for employees. But these are problems in operating a going concern (not in starting the company) and they are not unique to sole proprietorships. In fact, governmental regulation is relatively light. An individually owned company is not regulated or controlled as stringently as other types of companies. The great majority of laws and regulations imposed on businessmen are directed to corporations rather than sole proprietorships.

Since a sole proprietor owns everything the business owns, he receives all the profits from the company. The profits are not divided among partners or stockholders. Furthermore, an individual owner has greater control and freedom of action than partners or managers of a corporation. A sole proprietor can make business decisions without consulting with other owners. This means an individual owner can work with maximum speed and a minimum amount of friction with other personalities.

Compared to a corporation, a sole proprietorship normally provides federal income tax advantages to the owner of a small business. Since the law makes no distinction between the business assets and personal assets of a sole proprietor, there is no difference (for tax purposes) in a sole proprietor's business income and his personal income. In other words, there are no special income tax rates that apply to sole proprietors. The owner of a small business simply includes the business income (and business expenses) when filing his tax return.

Disadvantages of Sole Proprietorships.   A person who starts his own business will probably have greater difficulty in raising capital than if he were willing to bring in a partner or sell stock in the company. Raising capital is a common problem for most small business firms, whatever their legal form of organization, but the problem is naturally greater when capital must be raised by one individual.

Another major disadvantage of a sole proprietorship is that there may be fewer individuals with experience and management ability than in another form of business such as a corporation which uses the resources of many managers. A sole proprietor can make quick business decisions but he does not always have the advantage of consulting with other owners.

Sometimes a sole proprietorship is unable to keep the best employees. Good employees who contribute greatly to the success of a company may want to share in the profits of the company. Unless some type of profit-sharing plan can be established, employees may be tempted to start their own company or join another company that eventually offers them some type of ownership.

A sole proprietorship is not a permanent form of organization. When a sole proprietor dies, the business is dissolved. But—you may ask yourself—what about the cases where a sole proprietor dies and the business continues? Is a sole proprietorship permanent or not? The answer is that legally the business dies with a sole proprietor, but as a practical matter, the operations and even the name of the company might be continued. In fact, the business is *not* continued—a new business has taken its place. Sometimes it is easy to pass along a business after the owner's death, but frequently it may be impossible because of financial and legal problems.

Perhaps the most serious disadvantage of a sole proprietorship is the unlimited liability of the owner. Because the law makes no distinction between the personal assets and business assets of a sole proprietor, business debts are regarded as personal debts. That is, a sole proprietor places *all* his assets at stake when he goes into business. This means creditors may be able to take a sole proprietor's *personal* assets as well as his business assets.[3]

---

[3] However, there are laws that prevent creditors from taking certain types of assets. For example, in some cases a person's home and his life insurance cannot be taken by creditors.

PARTNERSHIPS

A partnership is an association of two or more persons to carry on as co-owners of a business. Most partnerships involve two partners, but some involve, three, four or even a greater number of partners.

In a *general partnership,* all the partners participate actively in running the business. The partners may not contribute an equal amount of time, capital, material, and they do not necessarily receive an equal amount of income from the business, but each partner has some degree of control in the partnership.

In a *limited partnership,* at least one partner has limited liability and no voice in the management of the company. This type of organization usually results when one person contributes money or materials and another contributes his labor. A partner who has no voice in the management of the company (a limited partner) may or may not receive an equal income from the business.

Advantages of Partnerships. A partnership is fairly easy to organize. Basically, all that is required is an agreement between the partners. Some states require a written agreement, but in other states an oral agreement is sufficient. Even if the law does not insist on a written agreement, it is always desirable to have a carefully developed, written agreement between the partners. The agreement should spell out the company's name, names of partners, duration of the agreement, incomes to be paid to each partner, procedure for bringing in new partners, procedure for dissolving the partnership, and each individual's duties and authority. The written agreement is often overlooked by partners, but history shows that misunderstandings and problems often develop without a carefully constructed agreement.

Another advantage of a partnership is that it combines the management abilities and financial capacity of the partners. It is usually easier to gather more capital than one person could contribute by himself. And a partnership might make it possible for partners to specialize in areas of their competence. One person, for example, might be an excellent office manager and another a great salesman. Together they might be able to build a business firm that would be much more than twice as successful as a firm either one could develop.

Partners are usually taxed as individuals. Even though partnerships are required to file a federal income tax form for informational purposes, the partnership itself pays no federal income taxes. Instead, each partner pays taxes on the income he receives from the business.[4]

Disadvantages of Partnerships. One of the potential disadvantages of a partnership is divided management. While this can be an advantage, it

---

[4] Partnerships may, in some cases, elect to be taxed as a corporation.

sometimes proves to be a disadvantage. Partners are not likely to agree at all times on how the business should be operated. Disagreements are certain to occur between partners. While this is not always disadvantageous, if agreements arise over fundamental decisions, the partnership may have to be dissolved.

While limited partners may have limited liability, the liability of general partners is unlimited. Furthermore, each general partner is responsible for the business debts of all partners. As a result, it is not too difficult for a dishonest or incompetent partner to ruin the entire business.

Another disadvantage of the partnership form of organization is that partnerships have a limited life. In fact, partnerships are even less permanent than sole proprietorships. Consider this situation: four men have the option of forming a partnership or operating individually. If they operate as sole proprietors and one person dies every ten years, the first proprietorship would last ten years, the second 20 years, the third 30 years and the last 40 years. But if a partnership had been formed, the entire partnership would be dissolved when the first partner dies. Of course, the remaining partners might be able to start a new partnership, but the financial and legal problems caused by the death of a partner would have to be solved. Furthermore, lenders are aware of this characteristic of partnerships and long-term loans may be difficult to arrange.

CORPORATIONS

A corporation is an interesting and important form of organization. It is an *artificial* entity—an invisible, intangible being that is created by law. In other words, a corporation is treated for many purposes as an individual, but it actually exists only in the eyes of the law.

The rights of a corporation are derived from the law under which it is organized. And the law can give a corporation almost all the rights an individual may have. A corporation, for example, may have the right to buy and sell property, hire employees, sue other business firms and individuals, and pay federal income taxes.

Advantages of Corporations.   The corporate form of organization provides limited liability for its owners. This is an important advantage of corporations over partnerships and sole proprietorship. An owner (or part owner) of a corporation cannot lose more than he has invested. Even if a corporation goes bankrupt and its assets are insufficient to pay off its debts, the company's creditors cannot look to stockholders for additional money.

Even though limited liability is one of the important and essential features of a corporation, it is still possible for stockholders to incur unexpected liabilities. A series of court decisions in recent years has made it quite clear that *officers and directors* of corporations can be held responsible to *stockholders* for losses caused by negligence or careless management. This new development is especially important for small corporations. If you organize a corporation or even participate in developing a new corporation, you may very well become an officer of the corporation or a member of the board of directors as well as a stockholder. If so, your personal assets could be subject to lawsuits—not from outsiders —but from other stockholders. The limited liability feature does not prevent stockholders from suing the officers who manage a corporation.

Despite the fact that corporations are the most common form of business for large companies, the corporate form of organization offers an advantage that is particularly valuable for small, growing companies. It is relatively easy to raise capital in a corporation. While there may be financial and legal problems, a corporation can usually raise additional funds simply by issuing more stock. The ability of a corporation to raise funds in this way depends, of course, on how prospective investors view the firm.

A corporation has perpetual life. It does not cease to exist when one of the stockholders dies. If a stockholder dies, becomes disabled, or retires the corporation can continue to do business. This promotes a sense of security and confidence in corporate organizations.

Another advantage of a corporation is that ownership can be transferred quickly and easily. In fact, a stockholder can normally buy or sell (at a price) a large amount or a small amount of stock.

Disadvantages of Corporations.   It is more difficult to organize a corporation than it is to organize a sole proprietorship or a partnership. Each state has a detailed set of laws and procedures that must be followed. As a result, the process of getting started can be expensive and time-consuming. Even after it is organized, a corporation is strictly regulated. Corporations must file special reports and notices, and abide by a detailed set of regulations.

The tax treatment of small corporations is usually a disadvantage of this form of organization. The corporation itself pays income taxes, and when dividends are paid, stockholders must again pay income taxes (subject to some exceptions noted in Chapter Six). Corporations must also pay annual franchise fees, real estate taxes, capital stock taxes, and other special taxes on assessments. Actually, however, corporations are heavily taxed when the income of the company is not great, but personal income tax rates are higher when the income is extremely large. The highest tax bracket for a corporation is approximately 52 percent, but personal income taxes may go as high as 70 percent. Therefore, large companies have a tax incentive to incorporate but small companies may be in a better financial position under the personal tax rates applied to partnerships and sole proprietorships.

OTHER BUSINESS FORMS

If you want to own a company, it is unlikely that you would choose some form of organization other than a sole proprietorship, partnership, or corporation. However, there are other forms, and you should at least be aware of them.

A joint stock company is a voluntary association of persons. It has characteristics of partnerships and corporations. Essentially it is a corporation. Ownership is evidenced by shares, and the shares may be bought and sold without the consent of other members of the association. The business is managed by directors, who are elected by the owners. In most cases, the business is taxed as a corporation, and the business is not terminated by the death of an owner. These are all important characteristics of corporations. But a joint stock company differs in two ways from a corporation. On the one hand, it is easier to organize and start a joint stock company. The primary disadvantage when compared to a corporation is that the members of a joint stock company have unlimited liability. The amount they can lose is not limited to the amount of their investment. This, of course, is the main reason why joint stock companies are not very popular.

In some situations it may be wise to organize a trust to hold and manage property. Joint ventures and syndicates may also be used as a form of business ownership, and cooperatives are sometimes used for groups of consumers or farmers and financial institutions. These specialized forms of business are not very important for small companies.

ACQUIRING YOUR OWN BUSINESS

BUYING AN EXISTING BUSINESS

The advantage of buying an existing concern is that it should be less risky than starting a new company. When a new company is started, the sales forecast (no matter how carefully constructed) may not be very reliable and, consequently, the profit earned by the owner of a new company is largely unpredictable. But an existing business has an actual operating record that can be studied, and as a result, sales and profits are much more predictable. True, when the ownership of a company changes, the newcomer may not be able to do as well as the previous owner—or he may be able to do better. But in any event, a person who buys an existing business should have some idea of how successful the company will be.

An existing business has a location that has proven its value. And location can be a critical factor for a small business. Service stations, for example, obviously earn much more in a good location. When a new company is started, generally a location must be selected. The location of the new company might be excellent or the location may prove to be less desirable than the owner believed it would be. The point is simply that there is less risk in the existing location.

Another important reason why there is less risk associated with an existing business is that a going concern has already established a group of customers, and often the clientele will remain loyal to the business even after it has changed ownership. In addition, an existing company may have valuable relationships with others, such as employees, suppliers, and union officials.

Apart from the idea of risk, there is another major advantage of buying an existing company rather than starting a new one. The time, effort, and cost of starting a new business may be avoided or minimized by buying a going concern. Of course, time and effort must be devoted to financial and legal problems when a company is purchased, but the problems should be fewer because an existing company normally has inventory, physical facilities, employees, and other necessities.

If you become interested in buying a business and you discover one for sale, one of the first logical questions you should ask yourself is, "Why is the present owner interested in selling the business?" This is not only a logical question, but an important one. The seller may tell you that he is retiring because of poor health, old age, or a desire to live elsewhere. But these may not be the real reasons for selling, or they may be only part of the true reasons. The owner may be having trouble from competition, rising costs, increasing taxes, or labor problems. Since there is always the possibility that the owner has hidden reasons for selling, a prospective buyer should always probe carefully into the business for possible problems. This may be done by talking to competitors, employees, suppliers, and others who may know something about the business.

The factor that is of crucial importance in buying a business is the price to be paid. But how can a buyer determine if he is paying a reasonable price? Since a business is bought to obtain future net income, the basic problem is how to place a value on future profits.

The usual method of calculating the value of a business is to capitalize the company's net income. Capitalization simply refers to the process of translating a series of future profits into one lump sum. For example, assume that a company produces an annual net profit of $12,000. If the prospective buyer believes 10 percent is a satisfactory return, the business is worth $120,000. (This figure, $120,000 was arrived at by dividing $12,000 by 10 percent.) In practice, the capitalization process may not be so simple. The annual net profit figure that is relevant for the calculation is not the company's average *past* net income, but the company's net income in the future. This means that the projected profits of the company are the important figures, but expected profits are sometimes hard to estimate.

The rate at which profits are capitalized makes a big difference. If you capitalize $12,000 at 5 percent, the answer is $240,000. And at 20 percent, a future income of $12,000 is worth only $60,000, or one-fourth as much. Theoretically, the capitalization rate should depend on the amount of risk in the business. If a business has little risk, a buyer may be willing to settle for a low rate, but a higher rate should be used when assuming more risk. Still, the rate used to capitalize earnings is largely subjective and a reliable answer is not always available.

Another problem with the capitalization approach is that goodwill may have to be recognized. Consider this example: the "ABC" Company has $120,000 in assets (true market value) and a reasonable capitalization rate is believed to be 10 percent. This would mean the company should produce a net annual profit of $12,000. But the company regularly generates $14,000 in annual profits. This can only be done because of goodwill. (Goodwill is the intangible factor that results from customer loyalty or some other advantage permitting a company to earn a higher profit than seems reasonable in terms of the company's physical assets.) Apparently goodwill is producing $2,000 each year in profits for the "ABC" Company. Because goodwill is intangible and, therefore, probably more risky, it is usually capitalized at a high rate, often 20 percent. If this is done, the ABC Company is worth $130,000 ($120,000 ÷ 10 percent plus $2,000 ÷ 20 percent).

In considering the purchase of a company, a prospective buyer should always conduct a careful and detailed analysis of the financial records of the company. Unfortunately, many small business owners do not keep adequate financial records. When this is the case, a buyer may be restricted by the quality of the financial statements. In any event, a buyer should insist upon sales and profit figures for at least the three preceding years. If the owner will not supply these figures, a buyer should be cautious. If the owner has the figures and will not make them available, the buyer should suspect a major problem. And if the owner cannot show his business figures because he has not kept adequate records, the buyer should realize that he may be buying something less than a genuine business firm.

In analyzing the company's financial statements, a buyer should study the company's sales figures, expenses, profits, the company's working capital, inventory turnover, and contingent liabilities. In these studies he should investigate the *quality* of the company's assets and determine whether or not they are valued accurately. The same applies to business liabilities. In most cases, it would pay a buyer to hire an independent auditing firm for a professional financial analysis of the company. If the company appears to be a wise purchase, it is always advisable to have an attorney check the company's contracts and help transfer the company to you.

STARTING A NEW COMPANY

There are three major reasons why many people prefer to start their own company rather than to buy a going concern. First, if you start your own company you can select your own location, inventory, employees, bankers, and products. In other words, you can avoid the mistakes of previous owners. There will be more risk in a new company, but also greater opportunity if you manage the company well.

A second reason, which is similar to the first, is that it is sometimes difficult to find a suitable existing company. It is easy to find companies for sale, but there are probably more unsuccessful than successful companies for sale. Do you want to buy a company that is operating more and more in the red each year, or, do you want to buy a well-managed, successful company? If so, the price will probably be high. Thus, there is a basic dilemma. As a general rule you can buy a poor company cheaply or a good company at a high price. This dilemma naturally leads many people to start their own business.

Sometimes it is absolutely necessary to start a new company if you want to go into business for yourself. This is the case when you want to sell a product or service that has just been created and there are no other companies in the field.

Starting a new company, we have seen, involves a considerable amount of risk. Ideally, a person should only start a new company after he has investigated and planned carefully. Some of the problems of starting a new business have already been discussed, such as raising capital and selecting the proper form of organization. But, in addition, a person who starts a new business should be convinced that there is a genuine need for his product or service and that he can meet these needs effectively and economically. If the product or service is already being provided by other companies, a new company should not be started unless there is evidence that the demand for the product or service has expanded or existing companies are not being managed effectively. In other words, a company should not be started simply "to get into business." And if a new company is organized to sell a new product or service, a prospective businessman should realize that competition may be fierce if the product or service is well accepted.

OBTAINING A FRANCHISE

Franchising is not a new idea—it has existed since the Middle Ages—but it was only in recent years that franchising has enjoyed great popularity. A few companies, such as General Motors and Rexall Drugs, used the franchising idea around 1900, but it was not until the late 1950's that franchising started to develop on a large scale. In the 1960's there was a tremendous boom in franchising.

A franchise is simply an agreement between a company and an individual that gives a person the right to sell the company's product or service using the company's name, reputation, selling techniques, and possibly other services. The company that grants the franchise is the *franchisor* and the person who buys the franchise is the *franchisee*.

A franchisor usually offers a proven method of operation to a franchisee. While the services provided vary somewhat, many franchisors provide the following: an established name and reputation, advertising, help in locating the business, an effective store design, training, centralized purchasing, and financial assistance. The franchisees (who operate under a common name such as McDonalds, Dairy Queen, or Colonel Sanders Kentucky Fried Chicken) agree to abide by specific rules and operate with the standardized procedures established by the franchisor.

There are an amazing variety or franchises. Table 12–7 does not include all the possible types of franchises, but it illustrates the wide variety that is available. After glancing at the table, it is obvious that you can get a franchise for almost any type of business.

A person who is interested in learning about franchises in a specific field should have no trouble. There are many franchise directories published annually. One of the most authoritative and inclusive lists of franchises is contained in the *Franchise Journal* (National Franchise Reports, 333 North Michigan Avenue, Chicago, Illinois 60601). This directory is published each January and contains over 1,000 listings.

Table 12–7   The Variety of Franchises

Art Galleries	Lawn and Garden Care
Automotive Products	Motels
Automotive Services	Nursing Homes
Automotive Washes	Painting
Automotive Repairs	Pet Shops
Beauty and Slenderizing Salons	Printing
Building and Construction	Publishing
Business Aids	Rentals and Leasing
Business Services	Safety Equipment
Campgrounds	Sales Schools
Children's Products	Signs
Chemical Coatings	Sport and Recreation
Chemical Repair	Stores (retail)
Cleaning and Maintenance	Swimming Pools
Cosmetics	Training Schools
Dance Studios	Travel Agencies
Employment Services	Tree Services
Entertainment	Vending Machines
Food Operations	Water Conditioning Systems
Fund Raising	Weight Control
	Wigs and Hairpieces

The Franchise Fee.   Just as there is a great variety in types of franchises, there are many variations in franchise fees. A franchisee may pay a lump sum when the agreement is signed, he may periodically pay a percentage of his gross sales, he may agree to buy the franchisor's supplies and equipment, or he may make payments to the franchisor based on any or all of these methods. These charges differ greatly according to the company and type of business. The minimum franchise investment may be as low as a few hundred dollars or it may be as high as $20,000 or even higher. A franchisee should know if additional charges can be made. Some companies, for example, make extra charges for "special" services (and their concept of "special" services becomes important) or assessments for such things as a national advertising program. Obviously, it is important for a potential franchisee to know exactly how much the total payments paid to the franchisor can amount to. More importantly, a franchisee must know if the services he receives are worth the payment he makes to the franchisor.

SERVICES FOR FRANCHISEES

One of the important services provided by some franchisors is help in selecting a site. A person who is not an expert in business location is likely to put too much weight on unimportant factors when he selects a location. But many franchisors have experts who select locations only after a careful study is made. These studies may involve a number of factors such as climate, public utilities, taxes, protective services, labor problems, pedestrian and highway traffic, population growth and many other variables.

If a franchisor makes location studies, these are normally very helpful. But some companies provide little or no help with this problem. Others retain the right to approve a location selected by a franchisee, but they provide no assistance themselves.

Help in selecting a location is not the same as protection for a market area that is given by some companies. The better franchisors include in their agreements a provision that guarantees a franchisee the exclusive right to represent the parent company in a given area. The protected area can extend over part of a city, an entire city, a county, or even an entire state. An important consideration is the duration of the protection. Some companies only guarantee that another franchisee cannot operate in the area during the first five years of operation. When the guarantee expires, the company can sell another franchise in the same area. Even this, of course, is better than the agreements that provide no protection at all.

Most franchisors provide some type of training for new franchisees, but the quality of the training differs greatly among the companies. Some have formal courses that last several weeks; others simply provide a manual that tells how the business venture should be managed. Some

franchisors provide regular "refresher" courses, but others give no training or assistance after the business is started. Many franchisors will not
pay a salary or pay expenses for training courses, but others pay some
of the training costs.

Reputable franchisors usually advertise widely. Their advertising
programs often extend beyond radio and television into newspapers and
national magazines. In addition, many companies direct mail material,
display signs, and other types of promotional material. Franchise agreements should spell out exactly how much advertising and promotional
services will be provided and how they will be financed. Some companies
pay for national advertising, but local advertising is left to the franchisee.

Before a franchise contract is signed, it is always helpful to have an
attorney examine the agreement. In addition to the points previously discussed, a franchise agreement should cover the following:

1. Conditions under which the franchise can be terminated. These conditions are needed to protect both the franchisor and the franchisee.
2. Transfer of rights. The agreement should spell out the duration of
   the contract and state exactly how ownership of the business can be
   transferred.
3. Direct purchases. These clauses make clear the obligation, if any,
   the franchisee has to buy products and equipment from the franchisor.
4. Protection against third-party claims. Franchisors often require franchisees to carry a certain amount of liability insurance.
5. Quota clauses. These provisions place requirements on a franchisee
   to sell a stated amount during each period.
6. Product restrictions. Most franchisors limit the products that can be
   sold and many companies require their prior approval.
7. Price controls. Some franchisors specify maximum prices, some issue
   a suggested price list and others let the franchisee set his own prices.
8. Record-keeping requirements. The agreements of some companies
   include provisions to maintain certain records, sometimes on forms
   supplied by the franchisor.
9. Mandatory working hours. Sometimes a franchisee is required to
   devote his full time and "best efforts" toward the business. Others
   may have more stringent requirements.
10. Physical appearance. Agreements customarily include requirements
    for the appearance of the facilities and possibly employees. Main-
    tenance requirements are common. For example, some companies
    require the building to be painted every two years.

It should be clear now that there are many varieties of franchises.
Some companies have established fine reputations, but others are undoubtedly designed to make a profit at the expense of franchisees. A
person who is interested in a franchise should follow one basic rule:
investigate carefully before investing. A franchise can offer many advan-

tages associated with business ownership, but the costs and lack of freedom can be substantial.

MANAGING YOUR COMPANY

Getting a company started is a big hurdle, but managing a "going concern" also involves many problems. There is much more to running a company than is obvious at first glance. As a result, it is easy for a person to believe that he can operate a business even if he has no management ability.

The abilities required of an employee differ from those required to manage a company. An employee must be able to accomplish certain types of work, usually of a fairly narrow and routine nature. But an effective manager must be able to: (1) plan, (2) organize, (3) direct, and (4) control the business. Since management can be broken down into these parts (planning, organizing, directing, and controlling), they are sometimes called the basic functions of management.[5]

The management functions are often confused with management positions. In other words, some people believe that one person handles one function, another person carries out another function, and so forth. But this is not the case. Each management function could conceivably be allocated to individuals but usually they are not. And many individuals may be involved in only one of the management functions. In large companies, for example, an entire department of the company may be devoted to planning.

The management functions are simply parts of the management process; they are not necessarily divided among individual employees. Stop and consider what this means. To take an extreme case, a sole proprietor who has no employees must perform *all* the management functions himself if he wants to manage his company effectively. Furthermore, the management functions apply to all business firms regardless of size and type of business. The owner of a small business who gets too involved in day-to-day work and neglects the management functions is almost certain to be unsuccessful. A successful manager is a person who performs the basic management functions effectively.[6] It is of some importance, therefore, for a small business owner to have a clear understanding of each of the basic management functions.

PLANNING

The first function of management (and perhaps the most important management function for small companies) is planning. It involves the selec-

---

[5] Some management authorities classify the basic management functions in different ways, but the breakdown given is the most common.

[6] Of course, not all small businessmen *recognize* that they are performing management functions.

tion of *future* courses of action. In other words, planning is making decisions *before* they are required.

Advantages of Planning.   Unfortunately, the owners of small companies tend to neglect the planning function. They neglect it for several reasons. First, to some people there is just not much *fun* in making "unreal" preliminary decisions. Secondly, small businessmen often have considerable pressure for day-to-day work. Planning can be postponed, they believe, but some jobs must be done immediately. Another reason is that the value of planning is underestimated.

Planning should not be neglected. When a manager plans, his decisions are likely to be improved. If decisions are postponed until they are absolutely necessary, mistakes will be made. Planning will not avoid all mistakes, but better decisions should be made if the problem is studied carefully in advance. Planning also encourages coordinated thinking. Suppose you start a company with a partner and one employee. If you insist upon planning, all three of you should be able to strive for the same goal and work together. But if you fail to plan, each person may act independently and you may not be working toward a common goal as a team. Another benefit of planning is that it develops standards for future performance. If you plan to have sales amounting to $100,000 and your company sells less, you have a reason for being disappointed and corrective action can be taken. But if you fail to forecast sales, how can you evaluate your progress? Selling more than you did in the previous year might be a poor method of measuring your success. You can actually sell more than you did in a previous year and still be losing ground to your competitors.

Types of Plans.   There are many types of plans. They can be specific or broad, short range or long range; they can be formal or informal. And of course, plans can be concerned with important company activities or some that are not so important. Naturally, the owner of a business should be greatly concerned only with the important future courses of action.

The most fundamental type of plan is concerned with the objectives of the company. Since these are so important, every company, large or small, should have carefully defined objectives. Usually the main objective of a company is to maximize profits or to maximize the owner's wealth. Notice that this means a company will not necessarily want to maximize sales, income, or some other figure. In some cases a company can increase its sales and actually decrease its profits. For a company to earn the greatest profit possible, several types of plans are needed. The most critical plans for a small business are: (1) sales planning, (2) the cash budget and (3) projected financial statements.

(1) Sales plans.   Unless your company can *sell* a product or a service, you cannot stay in business. This is an obvious fact, but the "marketing

concept" is a rather modern development in management-thought. According to this concept, a company can maximize its profits only when it is directing its attention to the needs and wants of customers. Although the desires of employees, business owners, and others may be important, to the ultimate success of the company they must always be subsidiary to the desires of customers.

Following the marketing concept, sales planning revolves around decisions to:

1. Select products or services that will appeal to consumers.
2. Package products so that they will be attractive to customers.
3. Price the product or service so that customers will buy.
4. Advertise and promote the products or services so that consumers will want to do business with your company.

Sales planning, then, is not a simple process of estimating how much you will sell. A sales forecast is of great importance to a small company, but sales can be planned only after each of the four problems listed above have been studied carefully.

(2) *Cash budget.*   In trying to gain the maximum profits from a company, it is important to keep in mind that there is a distinction between the inflow of cash and profits. An expenditure may not reduce profits, and profits might not be increased by cash income. But even though the owners of a business are ultimately concerned most directly with profits, planning the cash inflow and outflow is a critical problem.

The first step in planning cash flows is to prepare a cash budget. Although cash budgets are developed in several ways, one of the most popular methods is called the cash receipts and disbursements method. It is illustrated in Table 12–8.

A cash budget has many uses. Basically it enables a company to arrange its cash inflows and outflows so that debts can be met without difficulty. But a budget also indicates when excessive cash may be accumulating or when borrowing might have to be arranged. For the owners of small businesses, the cash budget can indicate when funds will be available for payments to owners. It would be unwise for a businessman to withdraw cash from the company just before cash will be needed to pay debts. Clearly, a cash budget is essential to the sound management of a small company.

(3) *Projected financial statements.*   Regardless of the different types of budgets that are prepared, the last step in the budgeting process should be to forecast the financial position of the company. Usually this is done by projected (sometimes called *pro forma*) financial statements. The two statements that are most important in making a projected financial statement are the income statement (which shows the profit or loss of the company during a period of time) and the balance sheet (which shows the financial condition of the company on a certain date).

Table 12–8   Forecast of Cash Receipts and Disbursements

	January		February	
	Forecasted	*Actual*	*Forecasted*	*Actual*
Estimated receipts:				
Cash sales				
Collections from accounts receivable				
Miscellaneous income				
Total cash income				
Estimated disbursements:				
Salaries				
Accounts payable				
Advertising				
Interest				
Rent payments				
Other expenses				
Total disbursements				
Estimated excess of cash inflow over disbursements				
Cash balance (end of month)				

Examine Table 12–9 which is an illustration of a projected income statement. The table shows that the owner of the company is projecting a net profit (after income taxes) of $21,000. This is not necessarily the amount the owner *hopes* to make; it is the amount he *expects*. The expected profit should always be based on the most realistic estimates pos-

Table 12–9   Pro Forma Income Statement (January 1–December 31)

Sales		$306,000
Less: Returns, allowances, and discounts		6,000
Net sales		$300,000
Cost of goods sold		100,000
Gross profit		$200,000
Administrative expenses	$ 60,000	
Selling expenses	110,000	$170,000
Net profit (before income taxes)		$ 30,000
Taxes		9,000
Net profit (after income taxes)		$ 21,000

sible. This means each of the figures in the income statement is not necessarily the amount the owner will draw out of the company. In a small company it is likely that the owner will want to reinvest some or all of the profit in the company.

Since an income statement shows what happens (or may happen) to a company during a period of time, a projected statement involves only one set of figures. But a balance sheet is a financial picture of a company at a point in time. Therefore, a pro forma balance sheet compares figures on two different dates. This is shown in Table 12–10. If you study Table 12–10 for a moment, you will see how the owner of the company expects the company to change during the year. Apparently he is planning to invest additional money in inventory, machinery, and equipment, and he is expecting to pay off some of the notes payable, although he will let his accounts payable increase a little. The important feature of the statement is the fact that the owner expects to increase considerably his capital in the company. His investment in the company (as measured by the capital account) is expected to increase to $32,000 from $20,000.

Table 12–10   Pro Forma Balance Sheet

Assets	December 31	
	1972	*1973*
Cash	$ 3,600	$ 3,700
Accounts receivable	4,400	4,800
Inventory	42,000	48,000
Machinery and equipment	10,000	13,500
Total Assets	$60,000	$70,000
Liabilities and Capital		
Notes payable	$20,000	$15,000
Accounts payable	15,000	18,000
Taxes payable	5,000	5,000
Capital	20,000	32,000
	$60,000	$70,000

ORGANIZING AND STAFFING

A business organization is a group of people and a businessman must constantly keep in mind that he is organizing the work of people.[7] Organizing is an important function of management because a manager must organize the work of different people so they work together effectively toward the company's goals. Without proper organization there

---

[7] Unless, of course, the business owner is a sole proprietor who has no employees.

will be personal frictions, frustrations, and confusion among employees. It is absolutely necessary, therefore, for a business owner to set up an organization properly so that good employee morale and teamwork can be achieved.

Selecting the Type of Organization.   Although a business can be organized in several ways, there are only two basic organizational patterns that are practical for small companies. Very small companies normally use a *line* organization. This type of organization makes each employee responsible to only one superior.

Figure 12–1 shows a line organization with 13 employees under the president. Notice that each salesman reports to the sales manager and no other person. The same is true of all employees. When a person has more than one boss to whom he reports and from whom he receives orders, confusion and friction are likely to result.

Figure 12–1   Line Organizational Structure

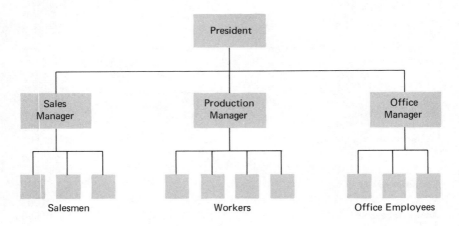

Another basic type of organizational structure is the line and staff organization. In this type of structure, employees in staff positions provide service and advice to other employees. Orders cannot be given by staff advisers—these must come from line employees. Figure 12–2 can help your understanding of a line and staff organization. The connecting lines show that each staff member communicates directly with the company president, but this is also true of the three line managers.

There is no easy formula that can tell a business owner which type of organization he should use. If staff specialists are needed, the company should use them. As a general rule, however, very small companies (perhaps fewer than ten employees) can use a simple line organization, and as the company grows, staff advisers, such as lawyers or assistants to the president, may be added.

Figure 12–2   Line and Staff Organizational Structure

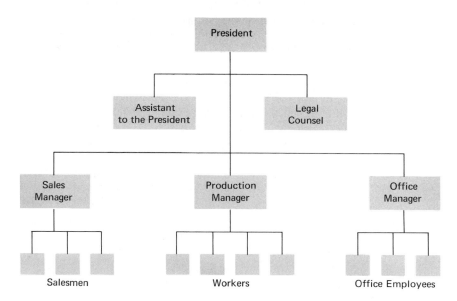

The Value of Organization.   Many owners of small businesses doubt the value of a formal organizational chart. This is because they misunderstand its use. Preparing an organizational chart is not the same as creating an organizational structure for the company. An organizational chart is only a device used to illustrate the organization; it is nothing more than a symbol. The true organizational structure is the pattern of relationships that exist among employees.

One of the greatest benefits of an organizational chart is that it forces the business owner to think through and analyze the relationships that he wants in his company. In the process of developing the chart, the owner can ask himself, for example, if he really wants John to work under Paul's direction. Maybe it would be better for John to work under someone else. This kind of thinking can be extremely helpful.

Another valuable benefit of organizing is that it sets up clear lines of authority and responsibility. The lines of authority should be definite, and well known to all employees. By making the authority-responsibility lines clear, there should be minimum uncertainty about who should make a decision or do a certain job.

Too often the owner of a small business will establish a formal line of authority and then violate it himself. The president of the company should not get involved in the immediate supervision of workers; this is the job of the supervisor. The president should communicate his business orders through the proper channels just as everyone else does. Otherwise, employees will be inclined to follow the example set by the president and ignore the proper channels for business actions.

Delegation of Authority.   An important principle of management is that a manager should delegate authority to make business decisions to the greatest extent possible on the basis of employee competence. In other words, a manager should try to give every employee authority that is commensurate with his ability. By delegating authority, a manager frees himself for more important work.

Although managers in all companies may fail to delegate authority as much as they should, the problem may be particularly important to managers of small companies. In fact, the failure to delegate may be the greatest management weakness in small businesses. The owner of a small business is naturally the person who knows more about the company than any other person. And as a result, he may be inclined to try to make all the business decisions. But this creates several problems. First, the owner may not have the time to get involved in every business problem and also tend to his managerial functions. Too often business owners complain about not having enough time to handle their day-to-day problems and still have time for planning. When a manager makes this complaint, it is almost a certainty that he is misplacing his priorities—giving too much weight to daily problems and not enough attention to important functions. Furthermore, employees will tend to become discouraged if they have to go to the owner for a decision on every problem.

Delegation of authority is important in the management of a small company, and it is absolutely necessary for growth. Undoubtedly many small companies are limited in their growth because the owner refuses to delegate authority. One person, no matter how capable, simply cannot handle all the management problems that arise in a rapidly growing, successful company. This means that the owner of a small company must learn to delegate authority, even if employees cannot handle the problem as well as it could be handled by the owner.

Staffing the Company.   The selection of employees is a problem common to all companies, but it is especially critical for small businesses. A small business normally relies heavily on each and every employee. And consequently, a single ineffective employee can easily destroy a small company.

But how can the owner of a small company attract good employees? Large companies usually have advantages in training programs, fringe benefits, greater prestige, and other factors. Therefore, unless the small business owner can offer some counterbalancing advantages, he may find himself with ineffective employees. The most common advantage that can be offered to prospective employees is the opportunity to progress in the company without too much competition from other employees. In some cases, employees may look forward to becoming the owner or part-owner of the business. Another possible advantage that small business owners should stress is the freedom and flexibility that can be offered by a small company. Employees in a large company are frequently placed in a narrow, routine job. But in a small company, employees are more likely to be given broader responsibilities.

DIRECTING

The word "directing" may carry a rigid and harsh implication. But this is misleading. The management function of directing simply refers to the execution of managerial plans. Basically, it can be thought of as a communication process. The owner of a business must communicate effectively with employees to obtain results. But good direction involves more than simple communication. A business manager who gives orders to employees may communicate but he may not get very good performance. Usually, it is necessary to communicate *and motivate* employees to go a good job. Viewed in this light, the management function of directing can be seen as a difficult, but important problem.

Approaches to Directing. How would you communicate with employees and motivate them to do their job to the best of their abilities if you owned a small business? Some businessmen follow the *autocratic* approach to leadership. This method stresses commanding and order-giving. An autocratic leader handles most of the important decisions himself and delegates only a small amount of authority to employees. At the other extreme, some managers follow the *laissez-faire* approach. This approach permits the manager to let employees handle the entire problems or projects with virtually no direction. Employees may have the right to set their own objectives and develop their own plans for reaching their objectives. Somewhere in between these two types of leadership is *participative management.* This is a type of democratic leadership in which the manager shares some of the important decision-making responsibilities with his employees. Of course, employees can participate in various degrees and in different ways.

The owner of a small business is usually not too concerned with what different types of leadership are called. He is simply interested in getting results. But the important point is that every business manager must follow some leadership pattern (even if he does not know what it is called), and there are advantages and disadvantages to each approach. The main problem with autocratic leadership is that it may lead to employee frustration and dissatisfaction. Laissez-faire management may give employees great satisfaction, but results might be slow and jobs may not be coordinated well. On the other hand, autocratic leadership may be effective. That is, it tends to get jobs done quickly and efficiently. A fine balance must be reached between the autocratic approach and the laissez-faire approach. There is no simple answer that applies to all companies. But the key to solving the problem is understanding the needs of employees. This means that the owner of a small business should devote some of his time and energy to employee problems. A manager who neglects this area is not likely to have an effective method of leadership, and the function of directing will be unsuccessful.

CONTROLLING

The owner of a small company can develop careful plans, organize his company effectively, and direct employees very well—and still be totally unsuccessful. This is because mistakes and problems are certain to develop, and unless the business is controlled effectively, the mistakes and problems may ruin the company. The managerial function of controlling refers to the measurement and correction of results in order to make sure that the objectives of the company are accomplished.

The control function presumes that plans have been developed. And if they have, actual results can then be compared to planned performance. For example, suppose you plan to have sales of $50,000 for the year. But if your sales are not very seasonal, and your company has sales of $10,000 in the first three months of the year, $12,000 in the next three months, and $8,000 in the following three months, you should not expect to reach your goal of $50,000 in sales. But you could not anticipate this problem unless you had definite plans and you had measured performance during the year. Notice that controlling always looks back at results— but not simply for record-keeping purposes. The real advantage in control is to discover problem areas so that corrective actions can be taken and the *future* direction of the company can be improved. Measuring past performance is of little value unless definite corrective action is taken.

The control function applies to all business firms, and it may apply at many different levels within a single company. The owner of the company will ordinarily be concerned with controlling the important operating results and basic problems of the company. At lower levels, supervisors may be involved in controlling the work of individual employees. In small companies the important areas of control are: (1) sales, (2) inventory, (3) credit, (4) expenses, and (5) quality of the product or service.

Controlling Sales.   To a careless businessman, the volume of sales may seem to be beyond control. But this should not be the case. A shrewd businessman sets up a detailed marketing program that may include several types of sales controls.

Sales quotas are frequently used as a sales control device. For example, you can tell each salesman how much you expect him to sell, and corrective action can be taken if a salesman fails to reach his quota. Usually sales quotas are broken down into long-run and short-run objectives. Then it is possible, to take corrective action before the problem becomes acute.

Sometimes it is helpful to analyze the volume of sales of each specific product. Your company may sell three products, X, Y, and Z. If you have forecasted the sales for each product, you may be able to find that total sales are less than expected but only because product Z was not sold as expected. This could lead you to improve the marketing for the product, or possibly discontinue it entirely and concentrate on products X and Y.

Inventory Control. The essential problem of inventory control is to have the correct quantity of goods at the right time in the right place. It is obvious that insufficient inventory can restrict sales and therefore profits. Customers are not likely to return to your company if they cannot find the goods they desire. But at the same time, there is considerable expense associated with inventory, and carrying too much inventory can hurt profits. Small businessmen often underestimate the cost of maintaining inventory. The cost of inventory may include the cost of:

1. Capital used to purchase inventory
2. Interest cost on money tied up in inventory. (The cost is explicit if money is borrowed to finance inventory. But there is an implicit cost that is real even if money is borrowed. An owner might use his own money to purchase inventory but he then loses the use of this money.)
3. Storage, insurance, and taxes
4. Depreciation and obsolescence
5. Losses caused by price changes

The problem of maintaining the proper amount of inventory is further complicated by the fact that often quantity discounts can be gained if large quantities of inventory are ordered. Because of the complexities involved in controlling inventory, large companies now commonly use computers to work out their inventory problems. Small companies normally must rely on simpler techniques.

One approach to the inventory problem is to determine the minimum amount of inventory that must be maintained at all times. Usually it depends on how long it takes to receive inventory after it is ordered, how serious an inventory shortage would be, and the stability of sales. Nevertheless, the owner of a small business should have a good idea of the minimum amount of inventory his company should carry.

Another helpful device for controlling inventory is the inventory turnover, computed by dividing sales by average inventory.[8] For example, if a store has an inventory of $10,000 on January 1 and $14,000 on December 31 and sales during the year amounted to $120,000, the inventory turnover would be 10 ($10,000 + $14,000 ÷ 2 = $12,000

---

[8] The ratio is sometimes computed in slightly different ways. Net sales (sales after returns, allowances, and discounts) may be used instead of sales, and cost of goods sold may be used instead of gross sales.

and $\$120,000 \div \$12,000 = 10$). The inventory turnover is a measure of how rapidly goods are being sold. If the turnover ratio is ten, it means the company sold ten times as much inventory as it had at any one time.

But an inventory turnover figure by itself is not very helpful. The figure is meaningful, however, when it is compared to previous inventory turnover figures and turnovers of similar companies. Suppose you notice that the turnover ratio has been declining. This usually implies that you have been more inclined to keep a full stock on hand. If so, your cost of carrying the increased inventory should be checked. Since inventory turnover ratios differ considerably among different types of companies, it is common to compare your ratios to other companies doing the same kind of business. Table 12–11 shows some average turnover rates. In looking at these figures, notice the great variation in the ratios.

Controlling Credit.   A small company uses credit in two ways; it can borrow funds, and it can make credit available to others (usually customers). Used in either way, credit must be controlled.

It is obvious that a small company should never borrow unless it is necessary. And it is important to obtain reasonable terms if a loan must

Table 12–11 Average Inventory Turnover Rates

Retail	
Department stores	5.4
Family clothing stores	3.9
Furniture stores	4.9
Gasoline service stations	12.7
Grocery stores	16.5
Jewelry stores	3.1
Shoe stores	3.4
Variety stores	4.3
Women's ready to wear stores	4.7
Wholesale	
Dairy products	29.2
Drugs	6.6
Electronic parts	4.1
Hardware	4.6
Paints and varnishes	6.4
Tires and tubes	5.3
Manufacturing and Construction	
Airplane parts	5.4
Farm machinery	3.7
Meat packing plants	30.0
Toys	5.4

Source: Dun and Bradstreet, *Key Business Ratios.* Used with permission.

be obtained. But what is not apparent to the owners of small businesses is an important concept called *financial leverage*. When a company borrows money and incurs the obligation to pay a certain fixed rate of interest, there is an important relationship between the rate of interest payable on the debt and the profit that is being earned by the company. The concept of financial leverage can best be understood by an example, so study Table 12–12 carefully.

Although Table 12–12 ignores the important effect of income taxes, it illustrates the principle of financial leverage. Notice that when a company has no debt, the rate of return it earns on its assets is the same as the rate of return available to the owner of the business. This is not the case when a company has debt. If a company pays 8 percent on its debts and earns 8 percent on its assets, the rate of return to the owner will also be 8 percent (as shown in Case B). But notice what happens when a company earns a higher rate on its assets than it pays. As shown in Case C of the table, a company that earns 12 percent and only pays 8

Table 12–12 Illustration of Financial Leverage

	With No Debt		With Debt (Assume Debt Costs 8%)
Total Assets	$10,000	Total Assets	$10,000
Total Debt	0	Total Debt	5,000
Net Worth	$10,000	Net Worth	$ 5,000

Case A. When Company Earns 4 Percent on Total Assets Before Interest:

	No Debt		With Debt
Earnings in Dollars	$400		$400
Interest Expense	0		$400
Rate of Return	4%		0%

Case B. When Company Earns 8 Percent on Total Assets Before Interest:

	No Debt		With Debt
Earnings in Dollars	$800		$800
Interest Expense	0		$400
Rate of Return	8%		8% $\left(\text{i.e. } \frac{\$400}{\$5,000}\right)$

Case C. When Company Earns 12 Percent on Total Assets Before Interest:

	No Debt		With Debt
Earnings in Dollars	$1,200		$1,200
Interest Expense	0		$ 400
Rate of Return	12%		16% $\left(\text{i.e. } \frac{\$800}{\$5,000}\right)$

percent actually makes a return of 16 percent to the owner (if debt equals one-half of the assets). This is because a company benefits when it can earn more than the debt costs. In other words, financial leverage can *magnify* profits. Of course, if a company borrows and incurs a fixed debt and then earns *less than* the interest rate on the debt, *losses* are magnified.

The concept of financial leverage indicates that a company should not borrow unless it is fairly certain that it can earn more than the interest rate it pays on the debt. But, on the other hand, if a company can earn a much higher rate than the rate it pays on borrowed funds, debt can be an effective way to increase earnings.

As the opposite side of the coin (making credit available to customers), credit control is extremely important for small businesses. If customer credit is not controlled properly, losses from bad debts can become excessive. Furthermore, credit control is important because excessive credit granted to customers can tie up too much working capital and prevent future sales to slow paying customers. These safeguards are not always fully appreciated by businessmen.

There are many problems involved in controlling customer credit, but a businessman should be particularly concerned with bad debts. These are normally controlled by using the bad debt ratio, which is simply the ratio of bad debts to total credit sales. A businessman who makes credit available to customers will almost always have some losses from bad debts. In fact, a businessman who tries to keep his bad debt ratio as low as possible might find that he is unduly restricting credit sales and hurting profits. Of course, a businessman should be concerned if his bad debt ratio is high and increasing. This can also be detrimental to profits.

Expense Control. In many cases the owner of a small business is anxious to "do things right" and therefore he spends more than is necessary to run his business. But unless expenses are controlled properly, a business is almost certain to fail.

Expense control is based on adequate accounting records. More specifically, the budget is the most widely used device for controlling expenses. We have seen that a budget has important uses as a planning device, but it is also used to control expenses. This is done by periodically comparing actual expenses to planned expenditures. When a businessman learns that his actual expenses are running ahead of his planned expenses, he should investigate and find out why the discrepancy exists.

To be most useful as an expense control device, a budget should be as detailed as possible. Usually, it helps for expenses to be divided into those that are controllable and those that are beyond the control of the businessman. Suppose, for example, that you start a business and rent office space. After the decision is made to rent the office and a fixed lease obligation is incurred, it makes little sense to worry about the monthly rent payment. But the expenses in running the office can be controlled, and if they are excessive they may be reduced.

Quality Control. The term "quality control" is often misunderstood by the owners of small businesses. It does not necessarily refer to "high" quality. Suppose you go into the business of making inexpensive watches. Should you try to make the best watch possible? Clearly not. You should, however, be vitally concerned with quality control. Quality control refers to the specifications set up by the company and the measures taken to assure that the product or service meets the designated specifications. A company, for example, can set up standards for the size, weight, color, strength, and many other aspects of its product. Products that do not meet the company's specifications can cause serious problems. If the product is inferior—compared to its specifications—customers may not return. But if a company consistently turns out a product that is better than its specifications, the results can be just as disastrous. Consider the case of an ice cream store that continually puts four ounces of ice cream in a 15-cent cone when the company can sell only three ounces for 15 cents and make a profit.

In performing the planning function, the owner of a small business should have established well-defined specifications for his product or service. And in the control function, a manager should design methods of controlling the quality of his production. Usually this means periodically checking to see that the product is within a certain range of its specifications.

THE SMALL BUSINESS ADMINISTRATION

It is evident now that owning and managing a small company involve a number of complex and difficult problems. Fortunately, not all of the problems must be handled entirely by the business owner. It is common —in fact, almost a necessity—to use the services of professionals such as attorneys, tax advisers, accountants, and others. In this connection the Small Business Administration provides some important services to businesses.

The Small Business Administration (S.B.A.) is a permanent body of the U.S. government that is designed to help small businesses. It does this in three principal ways: (1) advice and counseling services; (2) government contracts for the goods and services of small companies; and (3) loans to small businesses. The S.B.A. operates from its main office in Washington, D.C., but it has a large number of branch offices across the country.

The advice and counseling services of the S.B.A., according to many people, are the most important services of the S.B.A. The S.B.A. provides a great volume of printed literature that can be helpful to the owner of a small business. But the S.B.A. also provides direct advice and counseling services, and in some cases, will send a representative to work with your company for a while. Most of these services are either free or available at a nominal charge.

If the owner of a small business meets certain qualifications but cannot obtain funds from other lenders with reasonable terms, the S.B.A. will consider making financial assistance available. This is done either by a participation loan (in which the S.B.A. participates with private lenders) or by a direct loan. The S.B.A. prefers to make loans only to going concerns, but in some cases loans will be made or arranged to help get a company started. To qualify for a loan, a business must be "small" according to the S.B.A. definition and meet certain practical credit requirements.[9] The S.B.A. will not make loans or participate in loans to gambling and extremely speculative companies, to companies that can get funds from other sources at reasonable terms, and to companies that do not appear to have a good chance of success.

The terms of S.B.A. loans are quite favorable. Interest rates on S.B.A. loans cannot exceed 5½ percent, and the loan can be paid off over a period of time up to ten years (15 years on loans for construction purposes). The security for a S.B.A. loan may consist of mortgage on land, buildings or equipment, warehouse receipts, a mortgage on chattels (personal property), personal guarantees, or some combination of these.

The S.B.A. has helped thousands of small companies. But S.B.A. loans usually cannot provide much help to new companies that have a need for long-term funds. However, the S.B.A. supervises the Small Business Investment Company Act of 1958. This Act encourages privately owned and privately operated companies (known as Small Business Investment Companies or S.B.I.C.'s) to make long-term loans and supply equity capital to small firms. The encouragement to form the S.B.I.C. is derived mostly from the federal income tax advantages that are granted to these companies.

Suppose you wish to start a company but are ineligibile for a S.B.A. loan because you need funds for longer than ten years. You might be able to get help from the S.B.I.C. in the form of a long-term loan or an equity investment. An equity investment gives the S.B.I.C. a part ownership in the company. This is commonly done in one of three ways:

1. The S.B.I.C. can purchase company stock in the business.
2. The S.B.I.C. can make loans with warrants (which give the S.B.I.C. the right to purchase common stock in the company at a favorable price during a specified period of time).

---

[9] To be considered "small" by the S.B.A., a company must be independently owned and operated and not dominant in its field of operation. Furthermore, the S.B.A. sets up size classifications by considering the number of employees and sales volume. A manufacturer is classified as "small" if it has 250 or fewer employees and "large" if it has more than 1,000 employees, it may be considered small, depending on its industry classification. In wholesaling, a company is usually considered "small" if it has less than $5,000,000 in annual sales. A retailer or service company is normally classified as "small" if its annual sales amount to less than $1,000,000.

3. The S.B.I.C. can lend money to the business and receive convertible debentures. (This gives the S.B.I.C. the right to either accept repayment of the loan or convert the loan into common stock of the business.)

Most S.B.I.C.'s want an opportunity to share in the growth of the small companies they finance, but they are generally prohibited from acquiring a controlling interest in a small company. The businessman who owns a small company, therefore, need not worry that the S.B.I.C. will take over his company. At the same time, if the S.B.I.C. is getting a part ownership in the small company, the S.B.I.C. will be vitally concerned about the proper management of the small company. And for this reason, an S.B.I.C. frequently provides expert managerial services to the small companies they finance. Some S.B.I.C.'s restrict their loans to small companies that can provide excellent collateral, and these S.B.I.C.'s may not offer managerial assistance.

SUMMARY

Many young people become dissatisfied after working several years for a large company. In this situation, it is wise to consider the possible benefits of owning a business. Although the benefits can be great, a person should never embark upon a new business venture without first studying his personal qualifications and chance of success. If this is done carefully, many people will learn that they should not attempt to start their own business and will learn that business success is usually a difficult goal.

If a person decides to own his own business, he may be faced with the problem of choosing the appropriate field. This is an important decision because some fields are much better suited for small companies than others.

The most serious problem faced by many new entrepreneurs is the task of raising capital. After deciding how much capital is needed (which is itself an important decision), a person must raise the amount needed. Actually, there are a great number of possible sources of funds and the problem is often manageable if a systematic study of possible sources is made.

Another decision that merits careful attention is whether the company should be organized as a sole proprietorship, partnership, or corporation. Each form of organization has advantages and possible disadvantages.

The key problem in buying an existing business is placing a fair value on the company. Although this always involves some estimates, there are some principles that should be followed to arrive at a value. Probably the most common method of starting a new company in recent years has been to buy a franchise. These are now available for almost any type of business. The advantages provided by a franchise can be substantial, but a franchise should never be purchased until the franchise agreement has been studied carefully. Most companies that sell franchises are probably reputable, but there have been many many cases of outright swindle and poor business arrangements in recent years.

Much more is involved in managing a company than a person might imagine. Every manager must handle the basic management functions of planning, organizing, directing, and controlling the business. Some of those functions are more important to large companies, but still they are vital to companies of any size. The complex problems of managing a small business can often be alleviated by the services provided by the Small Business Administration.

Case Problems

1. Owning a small business appeals to Jerry Schuster. He worked himself through college and he has now had several years' experience selling paints and chemicals. Jerry knows the rates of failure for small companies are high, but he has decided to take his chances. However, in order to improve his chances of success, he wants to study the reasons small businesses fail and make sure that he has the necessary qualifications.
   (a) What are the major causes of small business failures?
   (b) What are the important qualifications a person should have before he starts a new company?

2. After carefully evaluating the pros and cons, Bart has decided to buy a small sporting goods store. His first problem is getting enough money to finance the purchase. Bart estimates that he will need $50,000 and this amount seems too high to raise. He has saved only $3,000 and his stocks are worth only $6,000. But Bart is determined, and he is not going to give up until he has exhausted every possible source of funds. His first step is to make a list of all possible sources. If you were going to help Bart, what are the sources you would include in the list?

3. Ted has been negotiating with Mrs. James to buy her jewelry store. The store was quite profitable when it was managed by Mr. James, but profits have been much lower since his death in 1970. Ted believes that he can buy the store and make the profit that would have been earned by Mr. James. The profits earned by the store are as follows:

1966	$18,000
1967	22,000
1968	20,000
1969	19,000
1970	21,000
1971	10,000
1972	12,000

   (a) How much should Ted be willing to pay for the store? (Assume that profits are capitalized at 20 percent.)

(b) What are the problems that are involved in estimating a purchase price by capitalizing profits?

4. Bob was frustrated by working for a large corporation so he saved several thousand dollars and bought a franchise. He worked hard and was reasonably successful from the very beginning. Bob had a good location and soon he found that his income was growing rapidly. Actually, however, Bob withdrew only a small salary from the business and used most of his profits to repay a bank loan he had obtained to buy the franchise. After four years Bob was looking forward to the day when the loan would be completely repaid and he could then start to plan his financial independence. One afternoon Bob received an interesting letter. The franchisor wanted to buy back the business from Bob. They offered a price that would have provided a nice profit for Bob, but he was not ready to sell the business. He, therefore, politely declined the offer. Over the next several months, the franchisor put increasing pressure on Bob to sell. Bob was not extremely worried until the vice president of the franchise told Bob that they were going to force him to sell. Bob checked his franchise contract and could not find any provision that would give the franchisor the right to buy his business. But when Bob talked with his attorney his attorney said that his contract was not "tight enough" to prevent the franchisor from taking over his business. Needless to say, this was terrible news for Bob. Explain how Bob might have prevented this problem from developing.

5. Dan Kiler and Frank Ramsey are partners in a small business. The company has been successful over the past few years. In fact, the problem now seems to be controlling the growth of the company. Sales have expanded and the need to finance the growth is becoming more and more apparent. Dan and Frank have not been withdrawing much from the company, but they both realize that the company needs additional funds if it is to continue to grow. Dan argues that the company should borrow a sizable amount of money, but Frank thinks the partnership should be incorporated and funds raised from new stockholders. The more the two partners have studied this question, the more they realize that the method used to finance the company will have a major influence on many important aspects of the company.
    (a) What are the advantages that could be given by Dan in favor of borrowing?
    (b) What reasons could Frank give as advantages of incorporating over borrowing?

6. Lloyd has developed a prosperous business. In fact, the business has expanded so much that he is thinking of incorporating. Although Lloyd is planning to talk with his attorney about whether he should incorporate, he wants to outline the advantages and disadvantages first.
    (a) If you were making a list of the possible advantages of a partnership over a sole proprietorship, what would you include?
    (b) What are the possible advantages of a corporation over a sole proprietorship?

7. Harry has operated his business on a profitable basis during the first two years of its operation, but he is beginning to worry. He has never kept very

accurate accounting records, and when his accountant was working out his income tax statement he suggested that Harry develop better financial planning techniques. Specifically, the accountant told Harry that he should prepare a cash budget and pro forma balance sheets and income statements. Harry is slightly confused because he doesn't understand the difference between a cash budget and a pro forma income statement. Could you explain the basic difference to Harry?

8. Although Bob had difficulty in getting his business started, he soon found himself in a pleasant situation—orders were coming in faster than he could fill them. Since Bob was earning a nice return (20 percent on the assets in his company) he was very concerned about the loss in sales he would have if he didn't expand his business. Bob had decided long ago that he would not incorporate or organize a partnership so long as he could operate as a sole proprietorship. He did not want to share the control of the business with anyone else. In fact, Bob had never even borrowed much for the business. Reluctantly, Bob talked with his banker about a loan. Bob was thinking of borrowing $10,000, but the banker suggested that he borrow $50,000 and take advantage of the increased demand for his product. The banker's basic argument was that Bob would have favorable financial leverage since the debt would cost only 10 percent. What is financial leverage? When is it favorable? If a company has favorable financial leverage, will profits double if earnings double? Explain.

9. The Small Business Administration has provided several major types of benefits to the owners of small businesses. What are the various types of services provided by the Small Business Administration?

Selected Readings

Anthony, Edward. *Choosing the Legal Structure for Your Firm.* Washington, D.C.: U.S. Government Printing Office.

Broom, H. N. and Longenecker, Justin G. *Small Business Management.* 2nd edition. Cincinnati: South-Western Publishing Company, 1966.

Changing Times, The Kiplinger Magazine:
    "Going Into Business: Gas Stations." February 1969, pp. 35–38.
    "How to Go About Buying a Business. February 1971, pp. 17–20.
    "Maybe You Need an Accountant." November 1967, pp. 45–47.
    "The Months Ahead: A Guide for Your Work and Personal Living." December 1966, pp. 3–6.
    "The New Look in Franchising." October 1967, pp. 17–20.
    "The Restaurant Business: What It's Really Like." March 1966, pp. 13–16.
    "So You'd Like to Go Into Business for Yourself." February 1970, pp. 43–46.
    "What It Takes to Succeed in a Franchise Business." May 1970, pp. 25–28.

Dias, Robert M. and Gurnick, Stanley I. *Franchising: The Investor's Com-*

plete Handbook, New York: Hastings House, 1969.

Faulke, R. A. *Practical Financial Statement Analysis.* 3rd edition. New York: McGraw-Hill Book Company.

Gardner, Fred V. *Profit Management and Control.* New York: McGraw-Hill Book Company.

Kohler, Eric L. *Accounting for Management.* Englewood Cliffs, N.J.: Prentice-Hall, Inc., 1965.

Kursh, Harry. *The Franchise Boom: How You Can Profit in It.* Englewood Cliffs, N.J.: Prentice-Hall, Inc., 1962.

Payne, Bruce. "How to Set Realistic Profit Goals." *Harvard Business Review,* September-October, 1958.

Prather, Charles L. *Financing Business Firms.* 3rd edition. Homewood, Illinois: Richard D. Irwin, Inc., 1966.

Robinson, Roland I. *Financing the Dynamic Small Firm.* Belmont, California: Wadsworth Publishing Company, Inc., 1966.

The Bank of America. *Sources of Small Business Capital and Credit.* San Francisco: Small Business Advisory Service (300 Montgomery, San Francisco).

Small Business Administration publications:

Management Aids:

How Trade Associations Help Small Business
How the Public Employment Service Helps Small Business
Getting Your Product on a Qualified Products List
How to Analyze Your Own Business
Know Your Patenting Procedures
Loan Sources in the Federal Government
Small Business Profits from Unpatentable Ideas
Protecting Your Records Against Disaster
Choosing the Legal Structure for Your Firm
Reducing the Risks in Product Development
Analyzing Your Cost of Marketing
Wishing Won't Get Profitable New Products
Steps in Incorporating a Business
Proving Fidelity Losses
Keeping Machines and Operators Productive
Publicize Your Company by Sharing Information
Designing Small Plants for Economy and Flexibility
The ABC's of Borrowing
Innovation: How Much is Enough?
Is Your Cash Supply Adequate?
Eliminating Waste in Small Plant R&D
Financial Audits: A Tool for Better Management
Planning and Controlling Production for Efficiency
Effective Industrial Advertising for Small Plants
Breaking the Barriers to Small Business Planning
Guidelines for Building a New Plant
Numerical Control for the Smaller Manufacturer
Expanding Sales Through Franchising
Preparing for New Management

Progressive Automation of Production
Matching the Applicant to the Job
Checklist for Developing a Training Program
Using Census Data in Small Plant Marketing
Developing a List of Prospects
Should You Make or Buy Components?
Measuring the Performance of Salesmen
Delegating Work and Responsibility
Profile Your Customers to Expand Industrial Sales
What Is the Best Selling Price?
Marketing Planning Guidelines
Setting Pay for Your Management Jobs
Tips on Selecting Salesmen
Pointers on Preparing an Employee Handbook
How to Find a Likely Successor
Expand Overseas Sales With Commerce Department Help
Is the Independent Sales Agent for You?
Locating or Relocating Your Business
Discover and Use Your Public Library
Are Your Products and Channels Producing Sales?
Pointers on Negotiating DOD Contracts
Pointers on Using Temporary-Help Services
Keep Pointed Toward Profit
Pointers on Scheduling Production
Technical Aids:
Principles of Plant Layout for Small Plants
Cash Values in Industrial Scrap
Reduce Waste—Increase Profit
Control of Expandable Tools—II
Surface Hardening Practices
Uses of Ceramic Coated Metals in Small Plants
Noise Reduction in the Small Shop
Cut Corners With Conveyors
Setting Up a Quality Control and Technical Development Laboratory
Keeping Shop Noise from Nearby Residences
Protective Coating for Steel Construction
Is Worker Fatigue Costing You Dollars?
Pointers on Dimensions and Tolerances
Pointers on In-Plant Trucking
Designing for Higher Profits
Tubular Riveting Uses in Small Plants
Are You Using Your Space Effectively?
Controlling Quality in Defense Production
Rented Tools Can Improve Efficiency
Electric Motor Maintenance for Small Plants
In-Plant Storage and Handling of Hazardous Materials
Inspection on Defense Contracts in Small Firms
Judging Your Electric Power Needs
PERT/CPM Management System for the Small Subcontractor

Value Analysis for Small Business
Small Plant Engineering Records Provide Evidence for Patents
Operations Research for Small Business
Welding and Flame-Cutting Processes and Practices
A Tested System for Achieving Quality Control
Using Adhesives in Small Plants
Small Marketers Aids:
How Distributive Education Helps Small Business
Are You Kidding Yourself about Your Profits?
Checklist for Going Into Business
Are Your Salespeople Missing Opportunities?
Checklist for Successful Retail Advertising
Pointers for Developing Your Top Assistant
Preventing Accidents in Small Stores
A Pricing Checklist for Managers
Finding and Hiring the Right Employees
Building Strong Relations With Your Bank
Building Repeat Retail Business
Stimulating Impulse Buying for Increased Sales
Controlling Cash in Small Retail and Service Firms
Interior Display: A Way to Increase Sales
Sales Potential and Market Shares
Quality and Taste as Sales Appeals
Pleasing Your Boss, The Customer
Are You Ready for Franchising?
How to Select a Resident Buying Office
Training the Technical Serviceman
Legal Services for Small Retail and Service Firms
Preventing Retail Theft
Building Good Customer Relations
Measuring the Results of Advertising
Controlling Inventory in Small Wholesale Firms
Stock Control for Small Stores
Knowing Your Image
Pointers on Display Lighting
Accounting Services for Small Service Firms
Six Methods for Success in a Small Store
Building Customer Confidence in Your Service Shop
Reducing Shoplifting Losses
Analyze Your Records to Reduce Costs
Retirement Plans for Self-Employed Owner-Managers
The Federal Wage-Hour Law in Small Firms
Can You Afford Delivery Service?
Preventing Burglary and Robbery Loss
Arbitration: Peace-Maker in Small Business
Hiring the Right Man
Outwitting Bad Check-Passers
Sweeping Profit Out the Back Door
Understanding Truth-in-Lending

Profit by Your Wholesalers' Services
Danger Signals in a Small Store
Steps in Meeting Your Tax Obligations
Factors in Considering a Shopping Center Location
Getting the Facts for Income Tax Reporting
Small Business Bibliographies:
Handicrafts and Home Businesses
Selling by Mail Order
Operating Costs and Ratios—Retail
Marketing Research Procedures
Retailing
Statistics and Maps for National Market Analysis
The Nursery Business
Recordkeeping Systems—Small Store and Service Trade
Store Location
Restaurants and Catering
Basic Library Reference Sources
Bakery Products
Advertising—Retail Store
Variety Stores
Laundry and Dry Cleaning
Training Retail Salespeople
Food Stores
National Mailing List Houses
Voluntary and Cooperative Food Chains
Retail Credit and Collections
Selling and Servicing Mechanical Refrigeration and Air Conditioning
Distribution Cost Analysis
Hardware Retailing
Jewelry Retailing
Buying for Retail Stores
Mobile Homes and Parks
Bookstores
Plumbing, Heating and Air Conditioning Job Shop
Job Printing Shop
Men's and Boys' Wear Stores
Woodworking Shops
Furniture Retailing
Trucking and Cartage
Store Arrangement and Display
Hobby Shops
Interior Decorating
Training Commercial Salesmen
Selling and Servicing Household Appliances Radio-TV
Painting and Wall Decorating
Sporting Goods
Footwear
Photographic Dealers and Studios
Real Estate Business

Discount Retailing
Machine Shop—Job Type
Automatic Merchandising
Sales Management for Manufacturers
Personnel Management
Retail Merchandising and Promotion
Retail Florist
Inventory Management
Pet Shops

Other:

SBA Business Loans
SBA: What It Is—What It Does
SBIC Financing for Small Business
Simplified Blanket Loan Guarantee Plan

The Franchise System of Distribution. Minneapolis, Minn.: Research Division, School of Business Administration, University of Minnesota, 1963.

U.S. Department of Commerce, *Franchise Company Data.* Washington, D.C.: U.S. Government Printing Office, 1965.

Villers, Raymond. "Profit Control." *Big Business Methods for the Small Business.* New York: Harper and Brothers.

CHAPTER THIRTEEN

SAVING FOR FINANCIAL EMERGENCIES

No one would quarrel with the idea that a person should regularly set aside a certain amount for savings. But most individuals, particularly young people, have a great deal of difficulty in actually following through with their savings plans.

The failure to build up a savings fund is a serious financial mistake. A person or family is certain to have financial emergencies and nonroutine expenditures from time to time, and the person who is not prepared financially can run into serious difficulties. Consider the case of the Bobbitts. They were struggling through college. Randy was a junior and his wife was working as a secretary. Their total net income was only barely enough to meet expenses and, like many young people, they had absolutely no savings. Randy's wife, Dottie, became pregnant unexpectedly and had to stop working. Randy believed he could work more hours at his part-time job and borrow enough to meet the crisis. Perhaps he could have, but complications developed from the baby's birth. Although the child was not critically ill, the doctors kept the baby in the hospital for about six weeks and ran a number of physical examinations and lab tests. The total cost was as follows:

Laboratory fees	$620
Hospital bills	990
Doctors fees	830
Loss of wife's income	1180

The total cost amounted to $3,620. Randy's only alternative was to drop out of school. He planned to return to college later but it took longer than he expected to pay off the bills and his financial obligations continued to grow. The result was that Randy became locked into a job that was unsatisfactory, and for many years he was unhappy and frustrated in his work.

Randy's problem was only one case, of course. And although the causes differ, similar financial problems happen to many people. These problems can be solved, or at least alleviated, by an effective savings plan. But what is an *effective* savings plan? Most people don't know how to plan savings effectively, they don't know how much they should save, and they are not very knowledgeable about the advantages and disadvantages of the various places savings can be kept. This chapter deals with these basic problems.

EFFECTIVE SAVINGS PLANS

Most people attempt to save by setting aside any surplus that remains after they pay their routine bills and meet their normal expenditures. These people do not have a very clear "plan." They simply intend to save what is not spent. One of the major problems with such a haphazard plan for saving is that most people receive more satisfaction from current consumption than they do by postponing their purchases. And this is what saving really is—a method of postponing expenditures. As a result, it is easy for "normal" expenditures to amount to 100 percent of your income. A person who intends to save the "surplus" from his income usually has no savings.

An effective savings plan is one that is a genuine *plan*. It is more than vague intentions or desires. Ideally, the plan is carefully thought out and expressed in writing.

MOTIVES FOR SAVING

The first step in planning for savings is to examine your reasons for saving. In other words, a person should have definite objectives. Savings can be used for a variety of purposes, as illustrated in Table 13–1. Table 13–1 shows that there is little difference in the savings objectives of those who save in banks and those who place their savings in savings and loan associations. Both groups seem to be motivated to save out of feelings of fear or insecurity. Although Table 13–1 gives ten different reasons for saving, most of the reasons can be placed into three major categories:

1. To meet unusual (nonroutine) expenses. Some expenditures do not fit easily into your income pattern. For example, a person may receive a paycheck twice a month but spend money for a vacation only once a year. It might be helpful, therefore, to save for a yearly vacation. Other unusual or sporadic expenses may include painting your house, paying large insurance premiums, buying household furniture and appliances, and buying a car.

Table 13–1 Reasons for Saving

	Percentage Distribution	
Purpose of Newest Account	Bank Savers	Savings and Loan Savers
Emergencies	37%	33%
Inner security	22	21
Education of children	20	19
Protection	16	17
Future investment	14	17
Old age retirement	11	16
Additional income	11	15
To pay cash	11	7
Vacations	10	8
Down payment on a house	3	2

Note: Percentages add up to more than 100 percent because savers could give more than one reason for saving.
Source: "Savings Survey," *Savings and Loan News*, Vol. XC1, No. 5, May 1970, p. 37. Reprinted with permission.

2. Investment reserves. A person must save before he can invest. Sometimes a person acquires a large sum of money that can be used for investments, but often it is necessary to build up a savings fund before a person can buy a house or common stocks. Aggressive investors might also want to transfer investments into savings when it appears that investment opportunities will be better later.
3. Emergency needs. Although a person should identify his reasons for saving as best he can, he should realize that unforeseen financial emergencies will still arise. Because financial emergencies can result from so many different sources, it is impossible to plan for every possible contingency. Even if a person carries adequate property insurance, liability insurance, and life insurance, financial emergencies will arise from time to time. Every person, therefore, should have an emergency fund to pay expenses that are not planned.

DETERMINING THE AMOUNT TO SAVE

The second major step in an effective savings plan is to determine how much should be saved. It is rather easy to determine how much should be saved for nonroutine expenses. For example, if you are saving to buy a car, you can estimate fairly closely how much you want to pay and whether or not it will be financed, and if so, how much must be saved for a down payment. The real problem is estimating the amount that should be kept in an emergency fund. Some financial authorities use a rule of thumb to determine the amount a person should maintain for this purpose. The usual rule is one month's gross income, but some authorities recommend at least one year's living expenses as the proper amount of the emergency fund.[1] This rule of thumb seems overly ambitious, especially for young people.

It is difficult to estimate the amount of money a person should keep in an emergency fund. A reasonable approach, however, requires a person to recognize several facts. First, a person should realize that savings can be held in many forms, and many people have "hidden" savings. For example, most types of life insurance policies contain a cash value. If a person has a life insurance policy with a cash value, he can obtain the cash value at any time by simply requesting his insurance company to pay it to him. Life insurance cash values make excellent emergency funds, but many people overlook these resources when they are thinking of their emergency fund. In addition to life insurance cash values, a person may have other liquid assets that should be recognized when estimating the need for emergency reserves.

The amount a person should maintain as an emergency reserve is greatly reduced if he carries adequate insurance. A person who carries adequate health insurance can get by with a smaller emergency fund than a person who has little or no health insurance. Adequate property and liability insurance also reduces the need for an emergency fund. Since insurance is a much more effective way to deal with financial emergencies that arise from poor health, property losses, and liability suits, a person should carry adequate insurance and not try to handle these problems with an emergency fund.

A person's need for an emergency fund is decreased if he can turn to other sources in times of financial crisis. Suppose, for example, that a young family is struggling through college but the husband's parents are wealthy. The young college student might reasonably assume that his parents would be happy to provide financial help if the young family ran into an emergency. Another source of funds that can be used in a financial emergency is credit. Some people have established their financial reputation and can borrow easily if a financial emergency arises. Before a person relies on this source, however, he should know that he can borrow without difficulty and that he can repay the amount borrowed without undue financial strain.

Despite all these problems, a person needs to determine how much he should set aside in savings. A dollar amount (or at least a range) should be determined.

Although it is not always wise to measure your success by other people, it might be helpful to know how much others are saving. It is

---

[1] Rex Wilder, *Family Finance* (New York: The Macmillan Company, 1967), p. 132.

not very helpful to know that the population as a whole saves 6 or 7 percent of their income, and it is not particularly beneficial to know that individuals in the United States save so many billion dollars. If any comparison is to be made, you should study the amounts saved by families in different income brackets, families of different ages, and families with different numbers of dependents. Table 13–2 provides this information.

According to Table 13–2, there is a wide variation among families in the amount they save. Sixty-five percent of the families with incomes of $15,000 or more have more than $2,000 in savings, but 92 percent of the families whose head is under twenty-five years of age have savings of less than $2,000. A majority of families whose head is under 25 have less than $200 in savings.

To determine how you compare with others, you should find the families in the table that are most similar to your own and see how your savings compare. If you are under age 25 and have about $200 saved, you are near the average of that group. But be careful in how you use Table 13–2. The table can be helpful, but the fact that you may have an average amount of savings does not mean you have enough savings. Most financial advisers believe that many families (particularly young families and families with low incomes) do not save enough.

After considering all these facts, a person should arrive at a specific dollar figure to represent the amount he should have available as an emergency fund. At a very minimum, every person should have at least several hundred dollars available to him as an emergency fund. The rule of thumb of one month's income might be appropriate for many individuals. As a person accumulates assets and becomes more sophisticated financially, he should acquire a better idea of the proper size for his emergency fund.

FORMALIZING A PROGRAM

The third major step in an effective savings plan is to set up a definite program for saving. This means a person should set aside money before he meets his normal expenditures. This decision is much more important than most people realize. Most people who try to save after they have met their expenditures do not save successfully. In setting up a definite program, a person should leave room for flexibility. In other words, if the savings program is not developing as planned, a person should re-examine his plans. Adjustments should be made from time to time because financial circumstances change.

SELECTING SAVINGS MEDIA

The fourth important step in an effective savings plan is to select the place where savings will be kept. A person can keep his savings in cash, checking accounts, savings accounts, credit unions, savings and

Table 13-2 Liquid Asset Holdings[a], Within Various Groups (percentage distribution of families)

	No Liquid Assets	$1 -99	$100 -199	$200 -499	$500 -999	$1,000 -1,999	$2,000 -4,999	$5,000 -9,999	$10,000 or more	Total
All families	19	9	6	12	13	11	13	8	9	100
Total family income										
Less than $3,000	48	7	3	8	10	7	7	5	5	100
$3,000-4,999	27	14	6	12	8	8	10	6	9	100
$5,000-7,499	19	13	10	15	12	9	10	6	6	100
$7,500-9,999	9	9	6	18	18	14	13	7	6	100
$10,000-14,999	4	6	6	14	15	14	19	11	11	100
$15,000 or more	1	3	2	6	8	15	20	17	28	100
Age of family head										
Under age 25	15	23	13	20	16	5	5	2	1	100
25-34	14	15	10	18	14	12	11	4	2	100
35-44	19	8	5	14	15	13	14	7	5	100
45-54	18	7	5	13	12	13	14	7	11	100
55-64	19	5	4	8	12	9	14	13	16	100
65-74	24	6	2	7	7	9	16	12	17	100
75 or older	25	4	3	5	11	12	10	13	17	100
Life cycle state of family head										
Under age 45										
Unmarried, no children	17	15	10	19	16	8	8	4	3	100
Married, no children	7	12	8	20	15	13	15	6	4	100
Married, youngest child under age 6	17	13	8	17	15	12	10	5	3	100
Married, youngest child age 6 or older	12	9	9	15	17	14	15	6	3	100
Age 45 or older										
Married, has children	18	8	7	14	13	12	14	6	8	100
Married, no children, head in labor force	12	3	4	11	10	10	17	16	17	100
Married, no children, head retired	19	6	3	5	8	9	15	13	22	100
Unmarried, no children, head in labor force	21	8	6	7	15	10	12	8	13	100
Unmarried, no children, head retired	35	3	1	7	7	12	10	10	15	100
Any age										
Unmarried, has children	40	20	3	8	9	7	6	4	3	100

[a] Liquid assets are the sum of amounts in checking accounts, savings accounts, and bonds.

Source: George Katona, et. al., *1968 Survey of Consumer Finances* (Ann Arbor: Survey Research Center, University of Michigan, 1969), pp. 114-115. Used with permission.

loan associations, life insurance policies, or in other media. In choosing among these, a person should seek a desirable combination of safety, liquidity, and yield. There is no single financial instrument or institution that offers the highest degree of safety, liquidity, and yield. Savings that are extremely safe usually do not provide a very high yield. Liquidity, also, is usually obtainable only with a sacrifice in yield. This means a person can only select an instrument or institution that best combines the degree of safety, liquidity, and yield that meets his objectives.

It is a serious mistake to assume that it makes no difference where you save. There are šome important differences among various savings media. And as a result, some are much better than others *for certain objectives.* Look at Table 13–3. It shows how people believe the different savings media should be used for certain purposes.

In Table 13–3, the most popular savings vehicle for each purpose is circled. Eighty-seven percent of the people believe a savings account is the best place to save for emergency purposes. A savings account is also the most popular method for objectives two, three, eight, and nine in the table. But most people think common stocks should be used for objectives four, five, and six. Series E bonds are believed to be the best savings vehicle for the purpose of accumulating funds to give to children or heirs.

The fact that the majority of people believe a certain savings vehicle is best for a certain objective doesn't necessarily mean that that vehicle is *actually* best for that objective. And, as an individual, your objectives are unique. You should use the savings medium that best meets your own objectives. You can do this only if you have an adequate understanding of each of the important savings media.

SAVINGS MEDIA

COMMERCIAL BANKS

Should you place your savings in a commercial bank? Many people do. In fact, in some areas commercial banks are the only practical outlet for savings. Still, a wise saver will be aware of the pros and cons of saving in a commercial bank.

Commercial banks are the oldest type of financial organization and they are essential to the operations of all types of businesses. Yet the basic nature of a commercial bank is often misunderstood. A commercial bank is a corporation, owned and controlled by stockholders, that may be chartered by state law as a state bank or by federal law as a national bank. A national bank is not one that does a national business; it is simply a bank that has been organized under federal laws. Although both national and state banks are closely supervised by the government, the bank is managed by stockholders with the ultimate purpose of making a profit.

Table 13-3 Savings Objectives and Media (in percent)

beyond reach of most people (handwritten)

	Pass-book Savings Account	Savings Certificate	Common Stocks	Mutual Funds	Series "E" Bonds	Real Estate	Corporate Bonds	Commercial Paper	Municipal Bonds	Federal Agency Obligations	Treasury Bills	Other Gov't Bonds
1. "Emergency" or "rainy day" funds	87	4	2	1	3	1	1	—	—	—	1	—
2. Funds you don't want to be tempted to spend	20	20	17	12	13	5	5	1	2	1	2	2
3. Funds for specific purpose (education, down payment on house)	41	17	10	11	11	2	3	—	1	1	3	1
4. To provide steady income	13	8	23	21	6	10	11	1	2	1	3	1
5. "Growth" money	12	7	36	21	7	11	5	—	1	1	1	1
6. Risk or speculative funds	5	1	67	7	—	12	2	1	1	—	1	—
7. Funds to give children or heirs in one's lifetime	15	7	21	14	22	8	7	—	1	1	1	2
8. Funds to be protected from loss	37	11	1	1	29	6	1	—	2	2	4	5
9. Uncommitted money	46	8	14	6	3	9	2	1	1	1	4	1

Source: "Savings Survey," *Savings and Loan News*, Vol. XCI, No. 5, May 1970, p. 38. Used with permission.

A commercial bank has two basic types of accounts: demand deposits (which are checking accounts) and time deposits (savings accounts). Although a person should have a comfortable margin in his checking account at all times, it is unwise to use checking accounts as a savings device because banks do not pay interest on demand deposits. In fact, there usually is a service charge on checking accounts. It is wise, therefore, to keep a minimum balance in your checking account and place excess funds in an account that pays interest. But your checking account must be adequate because you cannot write checks on time deposits.

Yield on Commercial Bank Time Deposits.   What rate of interest is earned on a commercial bank savings account? It depends on the bank. Some banks pay a higher rate of interest than others, and banks periodically change the interest rate they pay on savings accounts. The rate the bank pays depends partly on the supply and demand for funds. That is, a bank that needs funds will tend to pay a higher interest rate in order to attract savings accounts. But another major factor in determining the interest rate is Regulation Q of the Federal Reserve Board. This regulation specifies the maximum interest rate that most banks can pay on savings accounts. These maximum rates are changed from time to time, but as an example, in April of 1970, the maximum rates were those shown in Table 13–4.

The purpose of the interest rate ceilings is to prevent banks from paying such high rates that the banks will be forced to invest their funds in investments with excessive risk.[2] Although the limitations are intended to protect savers, the limitations mean savers can sometimes earn higher interest rates at other financial organizations. When other financial institutions are paying higher interest rates than the maximum rates permitted for commercial banks, banks must compete for savings accounts with prizes, extra services, and more convenience to depositors. Banks also try to attract savers by calculating interest on savings accounts in ways that will increase the rate of return the saver receives.

One study by the American Bankers Association showed that there are over 100 different methods of computing interest on savings accounts. Obviously it is impossible (and unnecessary) for a saver to know all the possible methods that might be used to calculate the interest rate he can obtain on a savings account. But every saver should be aware of the major factors that can cause the *true* rate of interest on his deposits to be different from the rate that is advertised by a bank.

One of the factors that determines the true rate of interest is the frequency of compounding. Traditionally, banks compound interest on

---

[2] An excellent treatment of this problem is found in Albert H. Cox, Jr., *Regulation of Interest Rates on Bank Deposits* (Ann Arbor, Michigan: Bureau of Business Research, 1966).

Table 13–4 Maximum Interest Rates Payable on Savings Deposits

Type of Deposit	Interest Rate
Savings deposits	4½%
Other time depostis:	
Multiple maturity:[1]	
30-89 days	4½
90 days - 1 year	5
1 year - 2 years	5½
2 years and over	5¾
Single maturity:	
Less than $100,000:	
30 days - 1 year	5
1 year - 2 years	5½
2 years and over	5¾
$100,000 and over:	
30-59 days	6¼
60-89 days	6½
90-179 days	6¾
180 days - 1 year	7
1 year or more	7½

[1] Multiple-maturity time deposits include deposits that are automatically renewable at maturity without action by the depositor and deposits that are payable after written notice of withdrawal.
Source: *Federal Reserve Bulletin* (Washington, D. C.: Board of Governors, Federal Reserve System), April 1970, p. A-11.

deposits every six months, but it can be compounded yearly, semi-annually, quarterly, monthly, or even daily. The more frequent the compounding, the higher the true rate of interest. An advertised rate of 4 percent compounded once each year is a lower rate than 4 percent compounded quarterly.

Banks, through their advertising, have made the frequency of compounding seem very important. But does it really make much difference to you if your interest is compounded monthly rather than daily? The truth is that it makes very little difference. This is shown in Table 13–5.

Table 13–5 is easy to use. To determine the dollars and cents importance of frequent compounding, just multiply the appropriate figure in the table by the amount in your account. For example, imagine that you had $100 in a savings account, and the bank advertises a 5 percent rate with daily compounding. This means you would earn $5.13 in interest over a year. But have you gained an advantage? Suppose the interest had been compounded every three months instead. Table 13–5 shows that you would have earned $5.09—or only four cents less. Even if you had $1,000 in your account the difference between daily compounding

Table 13–5   Effect of Frequent Compounding

Nominal Annual Rate	The True Annual Rate if Compounded				
	Semi-Annually	Quarterly	Monthly	Weekly	Daily
3.00	3.0225	3.0339	3.0415	3.0445	3.0453
3.25	3.2764	3.2898	3.2988	3.3023	3.3032
3.50	3.5306	3.5462	3.5566	3.5607	3.5617
3.75	3.7851	3.8030	3.8151	3.8197	3.8209
4.00	4.0400	4.0604	4.0741	4.0794	4.0808
4.25	4.2951	4.3182	4.3337	4.3397	4.3413
4.50	4.5506	4.5765	4.5939	4.6007	4.6024
4.75	4.8064	4.8352	4.8547	4.8623	4.8642
5.00	5.0625	5.0945	5.1161	5.1245	5.1267
5.25	5.3189	5.3542	5.3781	5.3874	5.3898
5.50	5.5756	5.6144	5.6407	5.6509	5.6536
5.75	5.8326	5.8751	5.9039	5.9151	5.9180
6.00	6.0900	6.1363	6.1677	6.1799	6.1831
6.25	6.3476	6.3980	6.4321	6.4454	6.4488
6.50	6.6056	6.6601	6.6971	6.7115	6.7152
6.75	6.8639	6.9227	6.9627	6.9783	6.9823
7.00	7.1225	7.1859	7.2290	7.2457	7.2500
7.25	7.3814	7.4495	7.4958	7.5138	7.5185
7.50	7.6406	7.7135	7.7632	7.7825	7.7875
7.75	7.9001	7.9781	8.0312	8.0519	8.0573
8.00	8.1600	8.2432	8.2999	8.3220	8.3277
8.25	8.4201	8.5087	8.5692	8.5927	8.5988
8.50	8.6806	8.7747	8.8390	8.8641	8.8706
8.75	8.9414	9.0413	9.1095	9.1362	9.1430
9.00	9.2025	9.3083	9.3806	9.4089	9.4162
9.25	9.4639	9.5758	9.6524	9.6823	9.6900
9.50	9.7256	9.8438	9.9247	9.9563	9.9645
9.75	9.9876	10.1123	10.1977	10.2310	10.2397
10.00	10.2500	10.3812	10.4713	10.5064	10.5155
11.00	11.3025	11.4621	11.5718	11.6148	11.6259
12.00	12.3600	12.5508	12.6825	12.7340	12.7474
13.00	13.4225	13.6475	13.8032	13.8643	13.8802
14.00	14.4900	14.7523	14.9342	15.0057	15.0242
15.00	15.5625	15.8650	16.0754	16.1583	16.1798

and semi-annual compounding is only $.64. The reason the frequency of compounding is not very important is that there is less to compound when interest is compounded often.

You should not worry much about the frequency of compounding interest on your savings account. It makes a slight difference in your true annual savings—but very little. Other factors have a much more important effect on the true rate of interest you receive.

Another important factor is the required length of time money must be on deposit in order to receive an interest payment. Some banks pay interest only on deposits that are maintained over the entire period for which interest is paid. Funds deposited after the beginning of the interest period or withdrawn before the end of the period may not earn any interest at all. On the other hand, some banks compute interest on deposits from the first day of the month even if the money is not deposited until the tenth or fifteenth day of the month.

The amount of money on which interest is calculated is very important. Some banks pay interest only on the lowest monthly balance (or the lowest balance over some other period). And the balance on which interest is figured might be determined by assuming withdrawals are from either the most recent deposits or the first deposits. A saver benefits from a method that assumes withdrawals are made against the most recent deposits. If the bank charges your withdrawals against your first deposits, you can lose interest on money that has been placed in the bank for a long time.

It should now be clear that the true rate of interest a saver earns may be very different from the rate advertised by a bank. In some cases, the true rate may actually be more than the advertised rate, but in many cases the real rate will be lower. Sometimes the true rate will be zero or close to zero. Therefore, if you are going to place your savings in a commercial bank, you should know how the bank will calculate the interest that will be credited to your account.

Liquidity of Commercial Bank Time Deposits. Ordinarily, a savings account can be converted into cash easily and quickly. Commercial bank savings accounts, therefore, receive a good grade for liquidity. Nevertheless, banks may legally postpone withdrawal from a savings account for 30 days. In other words, a bank can require 30 days notice before it has to honor a request for withdrawal. Under normal circumstances, however, a bank has an inflow of cash (from new deposits and collections of loans) and enough liquid assets to meet withdrawals from savings accounts with no problems. Even if a bank is having liquidity problems, it can borrow from a Federal Reserve Bank to meet demands for withdrawals. As a result, liquidity has not been a problem for savers who place their savings in commercial bank time deposits.

One of the relatively new types of accounts may be less liquid than other types of savings accounts. Certificates of deposits (commonly referred to as C.D.'s) may be either negotiable or nonnegotiable. If you purchase a negotiable C.D. and you wish to convert it into cash, it may be sold or assigned to a third party (someone other than the bank that issued it). These types of certificates, therefore, have good liquidity. Nonnegotiable C.D.'s, however, can present some liquidity problems. They can be cashed in, but at least 90 days interest must be forfeited and early redemption can take place only if the person who owns the certificate submits proof of hardship in writing to the bank. Many C.D. owners cannot understand why they cannot cash in their certificates prior to maturity without any trouble.[3]

Safety of Commercial Bank Time Deposits.   Since 1935 savers who deposited funds in commercial banks have seldom suffered a financial loss. This is because the Federal Deposit Insurance Corporation (commonly known as F.D.I.C.) insures the deposits of all banks that are members of the Federal Reserve System and other banks that want to be insured. If an insured bank is unable to meet its demands for withdrawals, the F.D.I.C. will pay insurance benefits to the bank to allow it to meet its obligations. It is the F.D.I.C., and not the federal government, that insures the accounts.

There is a $20,000 maximum insurance limit and this sometimes causes confusion as to how the F.D.I.C. insurance works. Suppose you inherit $60,000 from a distant relative. You probably would not have much trouble in finding uses for your new wealth, but suppose you decide to put the money in a savings account temporarily. Would your savings be adequately protected by F.D.I.C.? The $20,000 limit applies to a single depositor in a single bank. This limit applies regardless of the number of accounts you may have in your own name in any one bank. However, you may receive more than $20,000 of protection if you arrange the accounts properly. You may have an account in your own name, in your spouse's name, in a joint account, in accounts for your children, and accounts can be set up for you as a trustee, guardian, or administrator. Each of the accounts would be separately insured. Consequently, it is rather easy for most savers to be fully protected.

There is no direct cost to a saver for F.D.I.C. insurance. The premium is paid by the insured bank. Of course, the insurance premium is added to the cost of operating the bank, and the income available to bank stockholders and depositors may be reduced. In this sense, a saver may pay a small amount for the insurance coverage. But a person should always be sure his savings account is insured. This is usually not a problem since about 95 percent of all banks are protected by F.D.I.C. insurance.

Convenience.   Commercial banks have another characteristic that appeals to many savers. A commercial bank is normally a very *convenient* place to save. This is because they are numerous and located in almost every city of any size. Today there are more than 12,000 commercial

---

[3] The reason, of course, is that banks issue C.D.'s to be assured that the money will remain on deposit for a specified period of time. This enables the banks to invest in longer term, more profitable assets. See Donald L. Thomas, "The Savings Department," *The Banker's Handbook* edited by Willam H. Baughn and Charles E. Walker (Homewood, Illinois: Dow Jones-Irwin, Inc., 1966), p. 796.

banks in the United States. This means a person probably will not have to go far to do business with his bank.

Another reason why commercial banks are so convenient is that they offer a great many services. As a matter of fact, commercial banks are often called "department stores of finance" because they offer so many services. A typical bank makes several types of loans, rents safe deposit boxes to store valuables, provides investment advice and services, sells and redeems United States savings bonds, accepts checking accounts, provides trust services, and has systematic savings plans such as Christmas Clubs and Vacation Clubs. When a bank offers so many different services, it is convenient for a person to also save at the same institution.

MUTUAL SAVINGS BANKS

A commercial bank is organized and managed by stockholders who hope to make a profit. A mutual savings bank has no stockholders. It is owned by depositors and controlled by a board of trustees who have no direct financial interest in the organization and do not receive any income (or only a modest fee) from the bank. The original purpose of mutual savings banks was to promote thrift among poor people at the lowest possible cost. The cost of operating a mutual savings bank should be lower than the cost of operating a commercial bank because net earnings go to depositors rather than to stockholders. In keeping with their original purpose, savings banks accept only time deposits; they do not have checking accounts.

Yield on Savings in Mutual Banks. How does the investment return from savings in mutual savings banks compare to the yield on savings accounts in commercial banks? The average return paid by mutual savings banks is higher for two reasons. Since a mutual savings bank has no stockholders the entire investment return can be credited to depositors (after liabilities are adequately covered). None of the return has to be paid out as dividends to stockholders. A second reason for the higher yield is that mutual savings banks are not so restricted as commercial banks in their investments. Commercial bank investments are highly regulated and a large portion of their funds are in liquid, short-term assets. The investment of mutual savings banks are also highly regulated, but the government allows mutual banks to invest more in mortgages. Since mortgages are less liquid and longer term, they yield more than the short-term assets of commercial banks. This higher investment return is passed along to depositors in the form of higher returns to depositors. Table 13–6 shows the actual returns paid by mutual savings banks.

Liquidity of Savings in Mutual Banks. The liquidity characteristics of mutual banks are similar to those of commercial banks. As a practical

Table 13–6 Distribution of Mutual Savings Banks by Rates of Interest on Deposits (December 31, 1963)

Interest Rates	Number of Banks (in thousands)	Total Deposits (in thousands)	Percentage Distribution of Total Deposits
$4^7/_8$%	1	$ 49,682	.11%
$4^3/_4$	1	7,064	.02
$4^1/_2$	4	144,781	.33
$4^1/_4$	104	22,761,841	51.02
$4^1/_8$	6	622,898	1.40
4	345	19,098,045	42.82
$3^7/_8$	1	59,200	.13
$3^3/_4$	27	1,527,880	3.42
$3^1/_2$	14	258,525	.58
3	5	75,068	.17
$2^1/_2$	1	1,368	*
	509	$44,606,352	100.00%

*Less than .01 percent.
Source: National Association of Mutual Savings Banks.

matter, a depositor only has to present his passbook to request a withdrawal. Nevertheless, the liquidity of mutual savings banks is not quite so good as it is in commercial banks because mutual banks may require 60 to 90 days notice for withdrawals. The delay period is usually longer than it is for savings in commercial banks. Furthermore, the investments of mutual banks are not as liquid and the possibility of having liquidity problems may be slightly higher for mutual savings banks. We must conclude that a depositor has a high degree of liquidity in a mutual savings bank, but the liquidity rating would be a little below the liquidity rating of most commercial banks.

Safety of Savings in Mutual Banks.   Historically, the safety record of mutual savings banks is better than that of commercial banks and savings and loan associations. In the 1930's commercial banks and savings and loan associations had much greater difficulty than mutual savings banks.[4] Now insurance is available for mutual savings banks just as it is for commercial banks. In the event of a default by an insured bank, the F.D.I.C. would provide reimbursement for a depositor's loss up to $20,000. The trouble is that only about 65 percent of the mutual savings banks are insured by the F.D.I.C. If a bank is not insured, the depositor must rely upon competent bank management to protect his assets. Mutual

---

[4] National Association of Mutual Savings Banks, *Mutual Savings Banking: A Monograph Prepared for the Commission on Money and Credit* (Englewood Cliffs, N.J.: Prentice-Hall, Inc., 1962), p. 63.

banks are closely regulated by the government and most savings banks are carefully managed. Nevertheless, an uninsured bank does not possess the ultimate safety of an insured bank.

Convenience. Mutual banks do not offer the convenience and services of most commercial banks. They are found in only 18 states, and therefore it may be difficult to do business with them.[5] They offer many different types of savings accounts (such as Christmas Club accounts, Vacation Club accounts, and payroll deduction accounts), but usually they do not provide checking accounts, trust services, and many of the other services provided by commercial banks.

Mutual savings banks, however, offer one type of service that is not provided by most other financial institutions. In three states—Massachusetts, New York, and Connecticut—many of the banks sell savings bank life insurance. The basic purpose of this type of life insurance is to provide moderate amounts of insurance at low cost. The cost is low primarily because there are no sales commissions to be paid; the insurance is sold without agents "over the counter" at the banks.[6]

SAVINGS AND LOAN ASSOCIATIONS

Many consumers probably cannot distinguish very well between commercial banks and savings and loan associations. But there are some important differences, and a person who is not aware of these differences can run into serious financial problems.

Savings and loan associations are sometimes called "building and loan associations," "cooperative banks," or "homestead associations." In this chapter, the term "savings and loan association" will be used since this is their most common name.

In the past, savings and loan associations frequently used the word "shares" to describe their accounts, and this terminology created some confusion. If you place money in a savings and loan association, just what do you have? Are you a shareholder? a part-owner without shares? a member? or simply a depositor? By placing money in a savings and loan association, a person becomes a member of the association, with voting privileges, and a creditor of the institution to the extent of the amount he has deposited and earned on his deposit.[7]

---

[5] Mutual savings banks are located in Alaska, Connecticut, Delaware, Indiana, Maine, Maryland, Massachusetts, Minnesota, New Hampshire, New Jersey, New York, Ohio, Oregon, Pennsylvania, Rhode Island, Vermont, Washington and Wisconsin.

[6] While the cost of mutual savings bank life insurance is low, some people argue that a policyholder does not get the professional advice and service that he could if he purchased his insurance through a life insurance agent.

[7] William C. Prather, *Savings Accounts* (Chicago: The American Savings and Loan Institute Press, 1964), p. 59.

Approximately 93 percent of the savings and loan associations are organized as mutual companies; there is no capital stock and there are no stockholders.[8] These nonstock associations are organized with ownership and control in the hands of those who place their savings in the company. As a practical matter, however, most members of the association do not get actively involved in the management of the company. Most members assign their voting power to officers who are already managing the association.

There are many different types of accounts in a savings and loan association, but there are three basic types of accounts. The most common type of account is usually called a "savings account," but sometimes it is called a "regular account." This type of account is very similar to a savings account in a commercial bank. A passbook is issued to the saver and dividends are added at regular intervals. Just as there are many methods of computing interest on savings in a commercial bank or a mutual savings bank account, there are many methods of computing dividends on savings accounts in savings and loan associations. It is worth the time of a saver to familiarize himself with the method used to compute dividends on his account.

Many savings and loan associations have special plans that are designed to encourage systematic saving. These plans have a variety of names; they are sometimes called "bonus savings accounts," "installment savings accounts," or "serial savings accounts." Regardless of their name, these plans usually involve a definite plan to deposit a certain amount periodically (usually monthly) for a certain period of time. If the saver meets the requirements in the plan, an extra dividend is paid. The only penalty of not saving according to the schedule is the loss of the extra or "bonus" dividend.[9] In recent years, it has become popular to pay extra dividends in the form of merchandise (rather than cash) to savers who either open a savings account or meet the objectives of an installment savings plan.

The other basic type of account in a savings and loan association is the investment savings account. These accounts are designed for people who have already accumulated some savings or those who can save large amounts. With this type of account, a person buys certificates (usually in denominations of $100, $200, or $500) and the face amount of the certificate does not change. But the certificates can be cashed in and

---

[8] In 11 states (mostly in the western part of the United States) savings and loan associations may be established as stock companies. In such a company, the capital stock is not redeemable by the association. If a stockholder wishes to sell his stock, he must find a buyer other than the association.

[9] In the past, it was fairly common to impose a fine or penalty if the saver did not meet the requirements of the plan. Some savings and loan associations still use a penalty system, so a person should check the provision carefully if he uses some type of installment savings plan.

dividends will either be mailed to the certificate owner or accumulated in a separate account.

Notice that the terminology "investment savings account" is somewhat misleading. A person who has this type of account is not any more an "investor" than a person who has a regular savings or systematic savings account.

Now, having described briefly the basic characteristics of savings and loan associations, should a person use these associations as a place for his savings? The answer depends on a closer examination of the yield, safety, liquidity, and convenience of savings and loan shares.

Yield on Savings and Loan Accounts.   How does the dividend income on savings and loan shares compare to the interest income a person can earn in other savings institutions? The association invests the money received from members, and after paying operating expenses, the association's board of directors determines the rate that can be returned to members. Thus, the dividend income a member receives depends on the earnings of the association's investments. The earnings, in turn, depend primarily on the type of investments made by the savings and loan association.

Savings and loan associations were originally temporary groups of people who banded together to finance their homes. They reasoned this way: if each person saved enough to build his home, it might take 20 years or so to accumulate enough money. But if a group of people decided to save together, they could build a house each year. Those who were most eager to have a home could borrow from the group and those who were not as anxious to build a home could earn interest on their savings while they waited. Although there are more savers than borrowers, savings and loan associations to this day are still primarily specialists in home financing. This means that the great bulk of their investments is in the form of first mortgages on homes. Furthermore, it means that the dividend rate earned by members is tied closely to the rate of interest being earned on mortgages.

As a general rule, the dividend rate on savings and loan accounts is about 1 percent higher than the rate of interest paid by commercial banks on savings accounts, and about one-fourth to one-half of 1 percent higher than the rates paid by mutual savings banks. Look at Figure 13–1. It shows how the rates of return of savings and loan associations compare with mutual savings and commercial banks. The reason savings and loan associations pay a higher return is that they invest a higher percentage of their assets in mortgages, which normally pay a high return.

Liquidity of Savings and Loan Accounts.   The advantage of a higher dividend return is made possible by investments in home mortgages, which are not so liquid as many other investments. As a result, savings

Figure 13–1 Rates of Return Paid on Savings by Selected Types of Financial Institutions (1948–1968)

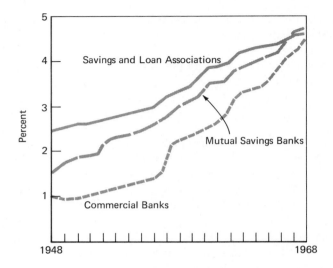

Source: National Association of Mutual Savings Banks, *National Fact Book: Mutual Savings Banking,* May, 1969, p. 28. Reprinted with permission.

and loan associations must pay special attention to their liquidity problems. If the association does not handle its liquidity problems carefully, an individual member could have trouble in withdrawing his savings from the association.[10]

A savings and loan association provides itself with liquidity in several ways. First, it is common for an association to hold at least 10 to 12 percent of its assets in cash or other assets that can be easily converted into cash at little or no loss in value.[11] Secondly, savings and loan associations are careful to establish borrowing privileges from other financial institutions. An association that is a member of the Federal Home Loan Bank System can borrow up to one-half of its total savings and investment accounts from the home bank if necessary to meet heavy withdrawals. As a final resort, a savings and loan association can sell its mortgages if there is an especially heavy outflow of funds.

All these sources of liquidity make it unlikely that a member will have trouble in withdrawing funds from his account. Nevertheless, a savings and loan association is *not* a demand deposit institution and does not

---

[10] Technically, a member does not withdraw funds. The association redeems or repurchases the member's shares.

[11] Savings and loan associations that are members of the Federal Home Loan Bank System are required to have liquid assets equal to at least 7 percent of their savings and investment accounts.

guarantee that funds can be withdrawn at any time. Unless there is an unusual financial emergency, however, savings and loan associations pay immediately when a member makes a request to withdraw his funds. If an association did not permit immediate withdrawal, members might be offended and more importantly, a wave of panic could set in and cause a deluge of withdrawals.

In the event of a heavy cash drain, a savings and loan association can legally require a 90-day written request for withdrawal. In an acute emergency, the association would not be forced to pay out the full amount of a savings or investment account to a member even at the end of the notice period. Each savings and loan association has withdrawal provisions that are designed to stretch out the payment of withdrawals so that withdrawals can be met with minimum difficulty.

Withdrawal procedures vary among associations. The specific withdrawal procedure depends on state law (if the association is chartered by a state) or on the Federal Home Loan Bank Board (if the association is a federally chartered association). During a financial crisis the following procedure might be used to systematize withdrawals. The XYZ Savings and Loan Association developed serious financial problems and invoked the notice requirement on withdrawals. This caused a panic among savers and a heavy demand to withdraw funds. As the Association received withdrawal requests, a number was given to each member. The individuals at the top of the list received their savings up to $1,000, but those who had more than $1,000 in their accounts had to be placed at the bottom of the list and wait until all those before them had received their money (up to $1,000). But the laws generally require an association to pay out only one-third of their available funds, so an individual might have to wait a long time before the association's income permitted his withdrawal request to be honored. A savings and loan association does not guarantee to honor withdrawal requests until it is financially capable.

All this means that a savings and loan association may delay repayments to savers by rotating their withdrawal requests. Complete repayment to an individual saver may be delayed almost indefinitely without the association being put into default.

Safety of Savings and Loan Accounts. How safe are funds in a savings and loan account? Can a person be assured that he can withdraw his savings? It depends on the specific savings and loan association. As a general rule, however, savings in a savings and loan association are very safe.

One of the important factors that determines the degree of safety is the type of investment made by the association. As we have seen, savings and loan associations put most of their funds in first mortgages on residential real estate. This type of investment carries a high degree of safety because the association can almost always sell a home for more than the debt if the home owner defaults on his mortgage.

Another reason for the excellent safety record of savings and loan associations is that the associations build up reserves in order to guard against financial problems. A young savings and loan association normally sets aside about one-fourth of its income (after operating expenses) in reserves. After the reserve amounts to about 10 percent of assets, the association usually stops accumulating a reserve, but at that point, the association has a sizable financial cushion.

Government supervision is another aid to safety. Most savings and loan associations are members of the Federal Home Loan Bank System, and this system provides liquidity and close supervision to savings and loan associations.

In the event of serious financial difficulties, a saver can be protected by insurance. The Federal Savings and Loan Insurance Corporation (F.S.L.I.C.) provides insurance to savings and loan associations that is essentially the same as the insurance provided to commercial banks by the Federal Deposit Insurance Corporation.[12] Accounts are insured up to $20,000 and the charge (one-half of 1 percent of total accounts) is paid by the association—not by individual savers. If there is a default, the insurance will either pay the amount holder or give him a new account in another insured savings and loan association.[13] The Federal Savings and Loan Insurance Corporation has never failed to pay all savers the total amount of their insured savings when an association has defaulted.

A person should not assume that all savings and loan associations are insured. In 1970, only about 75 percent of the savings and loan associations were insured. Insured accounts are probably about as safe as deposits in commercial banks and mutual savings banks, but the safety of uninsured associations can be questioned. An individual, therefore, should always check to make sure his account is insured, and if not, he should seriously consider placing his savings elsewhere.

CREDIT UNIONS

It might be surprising to you that credit unions are the most numerous and fastest growing of all savings institutions. Credit unions outnumber commercial banks by almost two to one, and there are about four credit unions for every savings and loan association.[14] But these figures can be

---

[12] There are some minor differences between the F.D.I.C. and the F.S.L.I.C. See, for example, Robert C. Earnest and John J. Andrews, "A Comparison of the Federal Deposit Insurance Corporation and the Federal Savings and Loan Insurance Corporation," *The Journal of Risk and Insurance,* Vol. XXIX, No. 1 (March 1962), p. 75.

[13] As indicated above, default does not necessarily occur when the association fails to meet a withdrawal request. Default is determined by the proper regulatory authority.

[14] At the end of 1968, there were 23,600 credit unions in the United States. See *International Credit Union Handbook* (CUNA International, Inc., 1969), p. 9.

misleading. Credit unions are usually small organizations and their total assets are not nearly so great as commercial banks, savings and loan associations, and some other financial institutions. Nevertheless, credit unions are attracting a larger proportion of consumer savings, and over 10 percent of the population is now saving in credit unions.[15] Perhaps you will someday consider placing your savings in a credit union if you are not already doing so.

A credit union is simply a group of people who save their money together and make loans to each other. They are organized and operated as a nonprofit association by people who work for the same employer, attend the same church, belong to the same fraternity, or belong to some other type of group. Most credit unions are set up to serve occupational groups because the credit union offers advantages to employers as well as employees.

Usually, but not always, a person becomes a member of a credit union in this way: an individual needs to borrow money and he is deciding where he should apply for a loan. A credit union will make loans only to members, but it is very easy to become a member of a credit union. A person only has to pay a small membership fee (perhaps one dollar) and buy at least one share in the association (which usually sells for five dollars or ten dollars each). Therefore, a person can apply for membership in the credit union, pay the small amount required, and obtain the loan he is seeking. As time passes, a new member learns more about the group and becomes involved in its operation (each member gets one vote regardless of the number of shares he holds). After the loan is paid off, the member can easily decide that the credit union might be a desirable outlet for his savings.

Technically, members do not make deposits; they purchase shares in the association. As a practical matter, however, a member saves in very much the same way that he could save with a bank or other financial institution.

Dividends on Credit Union Shares.   How attractive is the dividend rate that is paid to a person who saves in a credit union? The dividend rate that is paid by any credit union depends on several factors but the main factor is the investment return the credit union earns on its investments after paying for all costs of operating the association.

A credit union is normally a very economical operation. The association pays no federal income taxes because it is a nonprofit organization. Expenses for rent, salaries, and utilities may be very low because, in many cases, the group that holds the association together (the employer, church, etc.) donates the office space and other services. Thus, the total expenses of operating a credit union are low.

---

[15] *Ibid.*, p. 11.

This does not necessarily mean that the credit union's net investment return will be high. As indicated in Chapter Three, the maximum true annual rate of interest charged to borrowers is only about 12 percent. In other words, the benefits of economical operation can be passed along to borrowers (by a low borrowing cost) or passed to savers in the form of higher dividends. The truth is that most credit unions impose a reasonably low interest charge on borrowers, and as a result, the rate paid to savers is not particularly high.

Look at Table 13–7. It shows the dividend rate paid to credit union members in 1968. According to the table, only about one-fourth (26.69 percent) of the credit unions paid more than 5 percent in 1968. Most credit unions (29.36 percent) paid a dividend rate of only 5 percent to their savers. This is not a very attractive return considering the generally high interest rates that were prevailing in the economy at that time.

Liquidity of Credit Union Shares. When a member wishes to withdraw his savings from a credit union, his shares are repurchased. Shares cannot be sold to others. This means the credit union must have funds that can be used to purchase the members' shares. Normally this is no problem because credit unions hold a certain amount of their assets in cash and liquid investments to meet withdrawals. (They can also meet withdrawals from the cash that flows in from repayments on loans and new savings.)

Table 13–7 Dividends Reported by Credit Unions

Rate	Percentage of Credit Unions
3% or below	5.01
3.01% - 4.00%	14.00
4.01% - 4.49%	3.30
4.50%	15.47
4.51% - 4.99%	6.17
5%	29.36
5.01% - 5.50%	15.83
5.51% - 6.00%	10.44
6.01% and over	.42
	100.00

Source: CUNA International, Inc., *International Credit Union Yearbook*, 1969, p. 12. Used with permission of the Credit Union National Association.

Credit unions have the right to require members to give written notice to withdraw their savings, but like other financial institutions, this right is seldom exercised. To enforce the right would invite a heavy run on their assets. As a practical matter, therefore, liquidity is usually not a problem for a person who saves in a credit union.

Safety of Credit Unions. How safe are the funds placed in credit unions? Can a member be reasonably sure that he will be able to withdraw at least as much as he has put in? The answers to these questions depend on several important factors.

Although some credit unions are sizable, most are very small. About one-half of the credit unions in the United States have total assets of less than $100,000.[16] A small credit union, therefore, cannot afford to employ a large, full-time staff of officers to run the association. In many cases, the officers of the credit union are only part-time employees. They may be paid little or no salary. They may have little or no experience in the field of consumer finance. In this type of situation, the management ability of the officers may be questionable.

Another major problem with credit unions is that they generally are not able to diversify their investments very well. While credit unions have been making different types of investments in recent years, most of their assets are made up of loans to members. Since the credit union is usually made up of one organization, the association can get into financial difficulties if the group develops financial problems. As an example, consider a company credit union. If the company runs into financial problems, employees are likely to suffer. If so, they may be unable to meet their installment payments on their credit union loans.

Figure 13–2 can be helpful in estimating the chances of losing money in a credit union. As shown in Figure 13–2, a liquidation of a credit union does not necessarily mean savers will lose money. Indeed, only a small portion of the liquidations result in losses to savers. Still, in the period from 1958 to 1968, there were approximately 327 liquidations that resulted in losses.

But it is misleading to consider only the number of credit unions that involved losses. This is because most of the losses in credit unions are small. Examine the data in Table 13–8. Over half of all the credit union losses were less than $1,000. And only about 5 percent of the liquidated credit unions lost more than $10,000.

Credit unions have no insurance comparable to F.D.I.C. or F.S.L.I.C. insurance. Massachusetts and Rhode Island have insurance plans, but these cover only a small portion of all credit unions. There is also a program of stabilization funds that has been set up by CUNA International, Inc. The program is basically a method by which credit unions

---

[16] *Ibid.,* p. 15.

Figure 13-2 Liquidations of Federal Credit Unions, 1945–1968

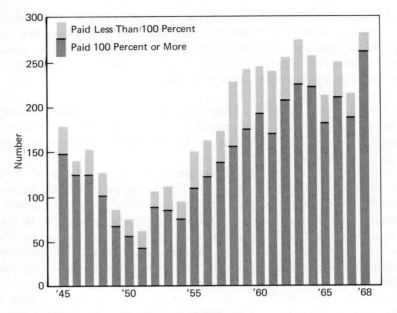

Source: United States Bureau of Federal Credit Unions.

Table 13-8 Distribution of Losses of Liquidated Federal Credit Unions, 1963–1967

$ 0 – 1,000		109	56.48%
1,001 – 2,000		24	12.43
2,001 – 3,000		12	6.22
3,001 – 4,000		10	5.18
4,001 – 5,000		7	3.63
5,001 – 6,000		6	3.11
6,001 – 7,000		5	2.59
7,001 – 8,000		6	3.11
8,001 – 9,000		1	0.52
9,001 – 10,000		3	1.55
10,001 – 20,000		5	2.59
20,001 – 30,000		2	1.03
30,001 – 40,000		1	0.52
40,001 – 50,000		1	0.52
50,001 – 60,000		–	–
60,001 – 70,000		–	–
70,001 – 80,000		–	–
80,001 – 90,000		–	–
90,001 – 100,000		–	–
100,001 – 110,000		–	–
110,001 – 120,000		1	0.52
Total		193	100.00%

Source: Walter Polner, "Losses in Federal Credit Unions," CUNA International, Inc. Unpublished research paper, Oct. 30, 1969. Reprinted with permission of the Credit Union National Association.

can provide financial help to each other, and there is evidence that the program has been fairly successful. One problem is that the program is voluntary, and as a result, not all credit unions participate. Numerous proposals have been made to establish some type of federal credit union insurance, but no such plan was in effect during 1970.

We must conclude that credit unions have had a reasonably good record of safety. Losses have been fairly frequent, but they have usually been small. Although stabilization funds have helped minimize financial problems, it appears that some credit unions may not offer the safety of most commercial banks and savings and loan associations until a more effective insurance plan is implemented.

UNITED STATES GOVERNMENT SAVINGS BONDS

At one time, U.S. government savings bonds were one of the most popular forms of savings. More than 60 percent of all families owned some savings bonds in 1946. Undoubtedly, the popularity of these bonds was largely a result of their appeal to patriotic motives. The U.S. government needed to borrow money to help finance its huge expenditures during World War II, and when a person buys a U.S. savings bond, he is, in effect, lending money to the U.S. government. After the war ended, however, patriotic motives for buying bonds were not nearly as important. The total amount of U.S. government savings bonds outstanding, therefore, has not increased significantly in recent years.[17] Still, more than one-fourth of the families in the United States own savings bonds,[18] and there are over $50 billion of savings bonds outstanding. Although these bonds are not so important as they have been in the past, they still must be included among the important forms of savings.

Since 1935 the government has issued ten different series of savings bonds, A, B, C, D, E, F, G, H, J and K. Now, however, most of these have been discontinued or replaced, and the only important savings bonds are Series E and H. Our discussion, therefore, will be limited to these bonds.

Corporate bonds and most government bonds can be sold to other individuals and institutions after they are issued. There is, in other words, a regular market for outstanding bonds. Series E and H bonds, however, are nonmarketable; they cannot be sold to others. They can be redeemed —a person can "cash in" his bond—but they cannot be sold in the way that stocks can be traded from one investor to another. Thus, there is no market for outstanding savings bonds; they are nonmarketable obligations of the U.S. government.

---

[17] The total amount of U.S. government savings bonds actually decreased in 1969.

[18] George Katona, William Dunkelberg, Jay Schmiedeskemp, and Frank Stafford, *1968 Survey of Consumer Finances* (Ann Arbor: Survey Research Center, University of Michigan, 1969), p. 111.

Another characteristic of U.S. savings bonds is that they are non-callable. Most corporate bonds are callable; that is, the issuing corporation can "call in" its bonds and force the bondholder to give up his investment. A person who buys a savings bond can hold his bond until maturity without worrying that the bond will be called. In fact, holders of savings bonds have the privilege of an optional extension period. Series E bonds issued after June 1, 1969 mature five years and ten months after they are issued. But they can be held after maturity into extended maturity periods and they will continue to increase in value. The same is true of Series H bonds. They mature ten years after they are issued, but they can be held longer and they will continue to pay interest.

In analyzing Series E and H bonds, it is important to realize that the government has made a number of changes in these bonds. The latest change (effective June 1, 1969) raised the interest rate so that savings bonds would be more competitive with other savings media. The interest rate was raised not only on newly issued bonds, but on outstanding savings bonds as well. A person does not need to redeem his old savings bonds to take advantage of the new, higher rate.

Series E Savings Bonds.   It is helpful to evaluate Series E bonds in the same way we evaluated other savings programs.

(1) Yield on Series E bonds.   When a person buys a Series E bond, he does not receive an interest income. Instead, the bond is bought at less than full face value and its redemption value increases over time. This is why Series E bonds are called "discount," "appreciation," or "accrual-type" securities. Table 13–9 shows how these bonds appreciate if they are held to maturity.

Look at Table 13–9. It shows that a Series E bond can be bought for $75. At maturity (five years and ten months after issue), the bond can be redeemed for $100. This increase of $25 over the period is equivalent

Table 13–9   Denomination and Issue Price of Series E Bonds (for bonds issued after June 1, 1969)

Issue Price	Denomination
$ 18.75	$ 25.00
37.50	50.00
56.25	75.00
75.00	100.00
150.00	200.00
375.00	500.00
750.00	1,000.00
7,500.00	10,000.00

to a 5 percent return. A person who saves with Series E bonds, however, does not have to hold the bond to maturity. What is the yield if the bond is redeemed before it matures? This is shown in Table 13–10. The table shows an important characteristic of Series E bonds. A person who buys a Series E bond (of any denomination) will receive a return of 5 percent if *he holds the bond to maturity.* But suppose you buy a $100 Series E bond and redeem it after three years. How much could you receive? According to Table 13–10, you would receive $85.56. Since you paid $75 for the bond, the difference of $10.56 ($85.00 − $75.00) is the investment return. This is shown in Table 13–10 as a return of 4.44 percent.

Notice that a person receives a higher percentage return the longer he holds the bond. For example, suppose you held the bond four years, rather than three years, before you redeemed it. Your return, according to Table 13–10, would be 4.64 percent. The annual percentage rate of return increases the longer the bond is held.[19] This provides a person with a strong incentive to hold the bond to maturity.

A person should be interested in the rate of return he will receive from the time he considers cashing in the bond to the end of the maturity period. Consider the case of a person who has held a Series E bond for three years and is considering cashing it in. If he cashes it in, he has earned a return of 4.44 percent. But if he holds it to maturity, the yield he will earn over the remaining period to maturity is 5.60 percent. This is shown in the far right column of Table 13–10. In the last six months before maturity, a person earns 6.15 percent on his savings.

The redemption values of Series E bonds, in other words, are staggered so that a person earns a lower rate in the beginning and a higher rate later. Nevertheless, the rate of return for the entire period is only 5 percent, which is not a very attractive return in the early 1970's when other safe investments are paying more. Our evaluation of the yield of Series E bonds, therefore, is that the return is low.

(2) *Liquidity of Series E bonds.* The liquidity of Series E bonds is excellent. Although these bonds cannot be redeemed in the first two months after they are purchased, they can be cashed in any time thereafter. And a person who redeems a Series E bond can always know in advance exactly how much he will receive when the bond is redeemed.

(3) *Safety of Series E bonds.* Since Series E bonds are obligations of the U.S. government, they are as safe as any investment. As a matter of fact, Series E bonds are safer than cash. If they are lost, stolen, or destroyed, they can be replaced by filing the proper forms. This is why it is a good idea to have a separate record of all Series E bonds that shows the serial number, amount, and issued dates of bonds you own.

---

[19] This is true up the maturity date. If the bond is held into an extended maturity period, the annual percentage rate of return is lower.

Table 13-10 Redemption Values and Investment Yields for United States Series E Savings Bonds (issued after June 1, 1969)

Issue price Denomination / Period After Issue Date	$18.75 25.00	$37.50 50.00	$56.25 75.00	$75.00 100.00	$150.00 200.00	$375.00 500.00	$750.00 1,000.00	$7,500 10,000	Approximate investment yield (2) On purchase price from issue date to beginning of each half-year period[1] *Percent*	Approximate investment yield (3) On current redemption value from beginning of each half-year period[1] to maturity *Percent*
	(1) Redemption values during each half-year period[1] (values increase on first day of period shown)									
First ½ year	$18.75	$37.50	$56.25	$75.00	$150.00	$375.00	$750.00	$7,500	0.00	5.00
½ to 1 year	19.05	38.10	57.15	76.20	152.40	381.00	762.00	7,620	3.20	5.17
1 to 1½ years	19.51	39.02	58.53	78.04	156.08	390.20	780.40	7,804	4.01	5.20
1½ to 2 years	19.95	39.90	59.85	79.80	159.60	399.00	798.00	7,980	4.18	5.29
2 to 2½ years	20.40	40.80	61.20	81.60	163.20	408.00	816.00	8,160	4.26	5.39
2½ to 3 years	20.88	41.76	62.64	83.52	167.04	417.60	835.20	8,352	4.35	5.49
3 to 3½ years	21.39	42.78	64.17	85.56	171.12	427.80	855.60	8,556	4.44	5.60
3½ to 4 years	21.93	43.86	65.79	87.72	175.44	438.60	877.20	8,772	4.53	5.71
4 to 4½ years	22.53	45.06	67.59	90.12	180.24	450.60	901.20	9,012	4.64	5.78
4½ to 5 years	23.16	46.32	69.48	92.64	185.28	463.20	926.40	9,264	4.75	5.85
5 to 5½ years	23.82	47.64	71.46	95.28	190.56	476.40	952.80	9,528	4.84	5.94
5½ years to 5 years and 10 months	24.51	49.02	73.53	98.04	196.08	490.20	980.40	9,804	4.93	6.15
Maturity Value (5 years and 10 months from issue date)	25.01	50.02	75.03	100.04	200.08	500.20	1,000.40	10,004	5.00	

[1] 4 month period in the case of the 5½ year to 5 year 10-month period.
Source: *Federal Register*, Vol. 35, No. 12, January 1970.

This bond record, of course, should be kept in a separate place from your bonds.

(4) *Convenience of Series E bonds.* The U.S. government has made Series E bonds one of the most convenient of all forms of savings. They can be purchased at most banks and many post offices. When they are bought, the purchaser does not pay any commission. And savings bonds will be held by the government for safekeeping. This service is provided at no cost. Furthermore, the bonds can be redeemed, without notice, at any institution that sells the bonds. Series E bonds are also flexible in the ways they can be registered. They can be registered in the name of one person, in the names of two persons as co-owners, or in the name of one person and a beneficiary. It is sometimes convenient to name a beneficiary who will assume ownership of the bond automatically if the registered owner dies. The registered owner has full control over the bond during his lifetime. He can redeem the bond, change the beneficiary, or take any other action on the bond without the beneficiary's consent.

Another convenient feature of Series E bonds is that the owner has flexibility for federal income tax treatment. The owner of the bond can choose to pay taxes on the increase in the redemption value each year, or he can wait until he redeems the bond and then pay taxes on the difference between the purchase price and the redemption value. The owner, therefore, can report the income in the manner that will minimize his income taxes.

Series E bonds cannot be used as collateral for a loan and they cannot be sold or given to another person. This detracts somewhat from an otherwise extremely convenient form of saving.

Series H Savings Bonds. These bonds are basically similar to Series E bonds, but they have some important differences.

(1) *Yield on Series H bonds.* Unlike Series E bonds, Series H bonds are sold at face value. The issue price, redemption value, and maturity value are identical. The investment return is obtained by an income that is paid to the bondholder. Checks are mailed every six months.

Still, the yield on Series H bonds is similar to that on Series E bonds because the yield to maturity is the same (5 percent on bonds issued since June 1, 1969) and the yield increases over time. This is illustrated in Table 13–11.

The increase in yield over time is provided in Series H bonds, not by larger checks each six months, but by a smaller check at the end of the first six months. Notice that in Table 13–11, a person who buys a $1,000 Series H bond will receive only $17.50 in the first six months (which is a return of only 3.5 percent), but he will receive a check for $25.50 every six months thereafter. To get the full 5 percent return, therefore, a person must hold the bond ten years. This is not an attractive return.

Table 13-11 Yields on Series H Savings Bonds (issued since June 1,1969)

Face value	Maturity value Redemption value [1] Issue price	$500 500 500	$1,000 1,000 1,000	$5,000 5,000 5,000	Approximate investment yield on face value	
Period of Time Bond Is Held After Issue Date		(1) Amounts of interest checks for each denomination			(2) From issue date to each interest payment due	(3) From each interest pay- ment date to maturity
					Percent	Percent
½ year		$ 8.75	$17.50	$ 87.50	3.50	5.10
1 year		12.75	25.50	127.50	4.29	5.10
1½ years		12.75	25.50	127.50	4.55	5.10
2 years		12.75	25.50	127.50	4.69	5.10
2½ years		12.75	25.50	127.50	4.76	5.10
3 years		12.75	25.50	127.50	4.82	5.10
3½ years		12.75	25.50	127.50	4.85	5.10
4 years		12.75	25.50	127.50	4.88	5.10
4½ years		12.75	25.50	127.50	4.90	5.10
5 years		12.75	25.50	127.50	4.92	5.10
5½ years		12.75	25.50	127.50	4.94	5.10
6 years		12.75	25.50	127.50	4.95	5.10
6½ years		12.75	25.50	127.50	4.96	5.10
7 years		12.75	25.50	127.50	4.97	5.10
7½ years		12.75	25.50	127.50	4.97	5.10
8 years		12.75	25.50	127.50	4.98	5.10
8½ years		12.75	25.50	127.50	4.99	5.10
9 years		12.75	25.50	127.50	4.99	5.10
9½ years		12.75	25.50	127.50	5.00	5.10
10 years (maturity)		12.75	25.50	127.50	5.00	——

[1] At all times, except that bond is not redeemable during first 6 months.
Source: *Federal Register*, Vol. 35, No. 14, January 1970.

(2) *Liquidity of Series H bonds.* These bonds can be redeemed any time after the first six months. Thus, their liquidity rating, is excellent.

(3) *Safety of Series H bonds.* The safety of Series H bonds is the same as all other government bonds. An investor can find no safer place for his savings.

(4) *Convenience of Series H bonds.* These bonds offer considerable convenience. They are as easily purchased, kept, and redeemed as Series E bonds. However, they are available only in three denominations ($500, $1,000, and $5,000), so they are not as convenient as Series E bonds for small investors. Also, the federal income tax liability cannot be postponed until redemption as it can with Series E bonds.

SAVING THROUGH LIFE INSURANCE

Despite the fact that many people do not look upon their life insurance policies as a savings plan, most life insurance policies contain an important savings element. Most policyholders who have *individual life* insurance (as opposed to group insurance) can surrender their policy for cash or obtain a policy loan after the policy has been in force for a certain period of time. Usually the cash value starts to build after the first or second year.

The advantages and disadvantages of life insurance as an investment are covered in Chapter Fifteen. At this point it is important only to recognize that life insurance policies provide an important outlet for the savings of millions of people. Figure 13–3 shows how the savings in life insurance compare to the other important savings vehicles.

Figure 13–3 Savings Held by Individuals in Selected Media

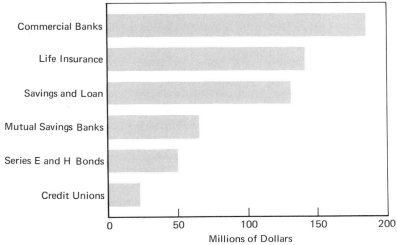

Source: National Association of Mutual Savings Banks, *National Fact Book: Mutual Savings Banking,* May, 1969, p. 36. Reprinted with permission.

Life insurance is the most important outlet for an individual's savings, with the exception of commercial banks. There is a greater amount of savings in life insurance policies than the total in mutual savings banks, Series E and H bonds, and credit unions.

SUMMARY

Few people manage to set up an effective savings plan. This is because they do not understand the importance of savings, they do not examine their reasons for savings, they are completely confused about how much they should save, and they are not aware of the advantages and disadvantages of the various savings media. This chapter points out the importance of savings. It emphasizes the fact that a person cannot establish an effective savings plan unless he attempts to understand why he is saving. Although it is difficult to determine how much a person should save, it is helpful to know how much others in similar circumstances set aside for this purpose.

Once a person has determined the amount he wishes to save, good financial management dictates that he investigate the differences among savings media—commercial banks, mutual banks, savings and loan associations, credit unions, and savings bonds. In selecting a savings media, a person should examine the safety, liquidity, yield and convenience of the financial institution he is considering.

Case Problems

1. Connie has taken a personal finance course in the community junior college and the instructor has emphasized that a person should be careful in selecting the financial institution where savings are kept. Connie learned that some banks pay a higher interest on savings accounts because they calculate interest more frequently than other banks. She has been telling Bob, her husband, that they should save in a certain bank because it pays 4½ percent, and the interest is compounded daily. Suppose Bob and Connie have $1,000 in savings for a full year. How much more would they earn if they save in Connie's favorite bank? (Use Table 13–5 in calculating your answer.)

2. Although Mike and Carol have been married only a short time and they have some financial pressures, they have decided to start a savings account. They can't save much, but they both believe it is important to establish the habit of regular savings. They talked about their savings plans and how much they would save, but they did not think much about where they would keep their savings. When Mike drove downtown to make their first deposit he parked in the block where he knew several banks were located. But as he walked down the street, he realized that there was a commercial bank on one corner and a savings and loan association directly across the

street. Does it make much difference to Mike where he takes his savings? Why? How should he decide between his two alternatives?

3. Ted has been arguing with Fred about the relative merits of commercial banks and savings and loan associations. Ted believes savings should be placed in a commercial bank but Fred thinks a savings and loan association is a better place to save.
   (a) If you were Ted, what arguments could you give to support your point of view?
   (b) If you were Fred, how could you argue in favor of savings and loan associations?

4. Jerry had worked in his new job for only about a week when his supervisor asked him if he wanted to join the company's credit union. Jerry didn't want to show that he did not know anything about credit unions, so he told his supervisor that he would think it over. That evening Jerry asked his wife, Pat, if she thought they should join the credit union. Pat had taken a course in personal finance, but she could not remember much about credit unions. So Pat suggested that Jerry call you, because you are now taking the course. If you received such a phone call, could you explain what a credit union is and how it operates?

5. John has just become an uncle for the first time. He has decided that he would like to give his new nephew a gift. He thinks it would be nice to give him a present that he could appreciate when he gets older. But still John cannot afford an expensive present. After thinking about his problem for a while, John has decided to buy a U.S. Government Savings Bond for his nephew. This seems to meet all his objectives very well. But when he asked for a bond at the bank, the teller asked John if he wanted a Series E or a Series H bond. John did not know how to answer, because he did not know the differences between the two types of bonds. If you were in John's position, could you describe the differences?

6. Fred believes that all commercial banks offer the same degree of safety. After all, Fred argues, they are all insured, and a person cannot lose so long as his account is insured by the federal government. There are at least three flaws in Fred's reasoning. What are they?

7. Bob and Faye agree that they should start a savings program. But in trying to determine how much they should save, they have run into some problems. Bob thinks they should save $200 and maintain this amount. His wife, Faye, believes they need to save more and continue a regular savings program. It would be helpful if Bob and Faye knew why they needed to save. If you were going to provide the three basic reasons for savings, what would you say?

Selected Readings

Brandeis, Louis D. *Other People's Money and How the Bankers Use It*. New York: Harper and Row, 1967.

Chandler, Lester V. *The Economics of Money and Banking*. 5th edition, New York: Harper and Row, 1969.

Changing Times, The Kiplinger Magazine:
"Maybe We Need 'Truth in Savings,' Too." February 1971, p. 7.
"Those No-Charge Checking Accounts." December 1970, p. 16.
"Ways to Make Your Savings Earn 7 Percent and Up." September 1970, p. 6.
"You Can Save in Spite of Yourself." October 1970, p. 40.
Dublin, Jack. *Credit Unions: Theory and Practice.* Detroit: Wayne State University, 1966.
Fischer, Gerald C. *American Banking Structure.* New York: Columbia University Press, 1968.
Savings and Loan Fact Book, United States Savings and Loan League. Published annually. A free copy can be obtained from the League at 111 East Wacker Drive, Chicago, Illinois.
Teck, Alan. *Mutual Savings Banks and Savings and Loan Associations.* New York: Columbia University Press, 1968.
Welfing, Weldon. *Mutual Savings Banks.* Cleveland: Case Western Reserve University Press, 1968.

CHAPTER FOURTEEN

PROTECTING YOUR ASSETS

The financial assets of most young persons are not great. But if you include *all* the assets you own, your assets probably add up to a surprisingly high figure. Even if you do not own any real estate, you probably own many different types of personal property. Actually, the most important asset most young people have is usually overlooked—future earning capacity. Your ability to earn an income is undoubtedly your greatest financial asset even though it will be converted into income as time passes. Over the years, the financial assets of most families tend to accumulate; a family that is reasonably successful financially will have a home, a substantial amount of personal property (such as household furniture, jewelry, and clothing), and one or more automobiles.

Any type of financial asset is subject to property and liability risks. In other words, property can be destroyed or damaged by any one of a large number of perils and future income can be imperiled by a liability judgment. How should a person handle these problems?

Should an individual purchase property insurance to protect himself against unforeseen losses? What about liability insurance? Is this type of coverage needed? If so, how much property and liability insurance should be carried? What type of policy should a person buy? What are the pitfalls that should be guarded against when a person buys property and liability insurance? These are important questions, questions that almost every person faces. This chapter, therefore, deals with these basic problems. It concentrates on insurance for the home and automobiles, because this insurance provides protection for the most valuable assets of most families.

HOMEOWNER'S POLICIES

Until recently, a home owner who wanted complete protection on the exposures arising from his home had to buy several separate policies. At a minimum, a home owner had to buy a fire insurance policy, a personal liability policy, a personal property floater, and theft insurance to get reasonably complete coverage. Today, almost all policies sold to home owners are the "Homeowner's Package Policy."

Separate policies are available for each of the coverages in the homeowner's contract. However, individuals who own their homes rarely purchase separate policies because a homeowner's policy costs only a little more than a separate fire insurance policy and most people realize that they need the other coverages provided in the homeowner's package. Therefore, you should not underestimate the importance of a homeowner's policy. Since it is a package contract that provides a number of coverages, it is one of the most important types of policies a person can buy. For many people, a homeowner's policy and automobile insurance provide all the personal insurance they need for their property and liability risks.

It is *not* the purpose of this chapter to describe the homeowner's policy in detail, but a brief description is necessary before a person can approach the basic decisions that arise when the policy is used.

TYPES OF COVERAGES IN A HOMEOWNER'S POLICY

There are seven possible coverages in a homeowner's policy. Coverage A is the basic coverage. It protects the dwelling. In addition, it provides coverage for building equipment, fixtures, and outdoor equipment. These include:

awnings	storm sashes
blinds	wire screens
screen doors	permanently installed air conditioning
shades	permanently installed heating equipment
storm doors	permanently installed lighting and plumbing equipment

Coverage B provides protection for private structures.[1] A detached garage, for instance, would be covered under Coverage B. The amount of insurance that applies to this coverage is 10 percent of the amount that applies to Coverage A.

Coverage C provides coverage for personal property owned, worn, or used by the named insured and members of his family of the same

---

[1] Structures used for mercantile, manufacturing, or farming purposes are not covered.

household.[2] This coverage, therefore, covers almost all the personal property usually found in a home. It has very few exclusions. Live animals, vehicles, and business property, however are not covered. In addition, there are some important limitations. The policy limits coverage on money to $100, on accounts, bills, deeds, and so forth to $500; on boats to $500; and on jewelry the theft limit is $1,000 for each article. The personal property coverage applies to property while it is located at the insured's home, but it also provides coverage when the property is away from the premises. Ten percent of the amount of the coverage on the personal property may be applied as additional insurance while the property is located anywhere in the world. Consider the example of a college student who is living away from home. Suppose a cigar burns a hole in a dress or sports coat? Would Coverage C in the parents' policy provide reimbursement for this loss? Yes, because a son or daughter at college is considered to be residing with the parents although they are not physically at home.

Coverage D is additional living expense and rental value coverage. If an insured peril damages the home and makes it untenable, the insured will be paid for the necessary and reasonable *increase* in expenses that are incurred while the home is being repaired. Suppose a family is forced to live in a motel and eat all meals in a restaurant for six weeks. Coverage D would pay the amount by which these expenses exceed normal living costs. It pays for the increase in costs for as long as it takes to repair or replace the damaged property or the time required for the family to become settled in permanent quarters. If all or part of the dwelling had been rented, Coverage D will also pay the insured for the loss in rents during the period the dwelling cannot be occupied.

Coverage E is comprehensive personal liability protection. This insurance covers the named insured and (if they are residents of the same household) his spouse, relatives, and any other person under the age of 21 who is in the care of the insured. It provides protection against several types of losses. The policy promises to pay all sums that the insured becomes legally obligated to pay as a result of bodily injury or property damage suits. Thus, if the son of the insured runs over a neighbor's foot with the lawnmower, the policy would pay the bodily injury award. The insurance company also agrees to pay expenses incurred by the insured for emergency first aid at the scene of the accident, to defend the insured and pay the costs of defense, and to pay the premiums on court bonds that might be required. These promises are commonly found in any type of liability policy.

---

[2] If the insured desires, Coverage C can be extended to cover the personal property of others while it is located on the insured's premises. (The reason this coverage is provided at the insured's option is that if there is a total loss there may not be a sufficient amount of insurance to cover someone else's property and provide full recovery for the policyholder as well.)

There are several important exclusions in the comprehensive personal liability protection. Liability that arises from business activities, automobiles, large boats and intentionally inflicted injuries are not covered.

Coverage F, medical payments insurance, is typically included with a liability policy, but it is actually a form of health insurance. It makes payments for injuries to persons other than the insured. The insured, and any person who lives in the same household, can never collect medical payments insurance benefits from a homeowner's policy. The coverage is designed to provide reimbursement for injuries sustained by others. Unlike liability coverages, medical payments insurance may be made even if the insured is not legally liable. If the insured's actions cause an injury, medical payments benefits can be paid even though the insured has not been negligent at all.

Coverage G is called physical damage to property. In a sense, it is similar to the medical payments coverage because it pays for the losses to people other than the insured without requiring negligence on the part of the insured. The difference is that Coverage G pays for the physical damage to property, rather than medical payments. Coverage G excludes cars, boats, and property owned or rented by the insured and residents in the same household. It is not an extremely important coverage—it pays a maximum benefit of $250. It is a convenient coverage, however, because it pays for losses to property that has been borrowed even if the insured has not been negligent.

MAJOR DECISIONS IN PURCHASING
A HOMEOWNER'S POLICY

As a practical matter, when a person buys a home he usually has little or no choice about whether he should buy a homeowner's policy. Practically all homes are financed. Very few people pay cash for a home. In this situation the mortgage holder will insist that the home owner protect the home with insurance. This is one way in which the mortgagee can protect his interest in the home.[3]

Although the lender can be protected in several ways, protection is usually handled as in the following example: suppose John borrows $17,000 and buys a $20,000 home. Since the lender needs to be protected so that a fire or some other peril does not destroy his security for the loan, any insurance proceeds will be payable to the lender. If an insured peril causes $10,000 damage, the mortgage will either be reduced $10,000 or the house can be repaired and John's mortgage will

---

[3] The mortgagee is primarily concerned that the home is protected against loss. He is not very interested in the insurance coverage on the contents, liability, medical payments and other coverages. A home buyer, therefore, could satisfy the mortgagee by buying property insurance on the home without buying a homeowner's policy. As indicated previously, this is rarely done.

remain unchanged. In this way, the lender is protected and John's mortgage can be reduced if the property is damaged.[4]

Even though home owners have little choice about buying insurance protection on a house, a buyer is faced with several important decisions or problems when he buys a homeowner's policy.

Selecting the Appropriate Form.   The first decision a person faces when he buys a homeowner's policy is the choice of the proper form. Five forms are available, and there are some important differences among the forms. The major differences are the perils covered and the cost of the insurance.

Homeowner's 1 is called the Standard Form. It insures the dwelling, private structures, and personal property against the following perils: fire, lightning, windstorm, hail, explosion, riot, civil commotion, aircraft, vehicles, smoke, vandalism and malicious mischief, and theft. Some of these perils are defined carefully in the policy, but surprisingly, some of the most important perils are not defined in the contract. This is because the meaning of these perils has been developed by court decisions over many years and the definition is found only in the common law. The word "fire" has come to mean combustion in which oxidation takes place so rapidly that a flame or glow is produced. Furthermore, a fire must be "hostile." A "hostile" or "unfriendly" fire is one that is outside its normal confines. It is in a place where it is not intended. This distinction is important because losses caused by friendly fires are not covered by insurance.

If damage or loss is caused by some event other than one of the named perils, the policy provides no coverage. Consider the problems of a person whose home is built on the side of a hill. If the earth beneath the house slides and the house collapses, a Homeowner's 1 policy would not provide any reimbursement. It is incorrect, then, to say that a Homeowner's 1 "insures a house." It is more correct to say that the house is insured *against certain perils.*[5]

It is important to realize that the face amount of the policy is *not* increased by covering a number of perils. For example, if a person has a $20,000 policy and his home is damaged to the extent of $5,000 by an explosion and $20,000 by a fire that starts from the explosion, the insured has suffered a total loss of $25,000. He can collect only $20,000, however, because the damage is really only one loss, and he can therefore be reimbursed for only *one* loss not to exceed $20,000.

---

[4] If the loss is more than the amount of the mortgage, the insurance proceeds can be used to pay off the mortgage and John would receive the proceeds in excess of the mortgage.

[5] Actually, a house is never insured. Legally speaking, a *person* is insured against loss to his house.

What happens to the face amount of the policy after a loss occurs? Does the loss reduce the face amount of the policy or does the face amount stay the same? At one time this was a problem for policyholders because the general rule was that each loss reduced the face amount of the policy. Modern policies contain a "loss clause," which states that the face amount of insurance is continued after a loss and no additional premium is payable.[6]

Homeowner's 1 (the Standard Form) provides additional living expense coverage, personal liability insurance, and all the other coverages previously described.

Form 2 is the Broad Form. It is practically the same as the Standard Form except that it adds a number of perils to the coverage. In addition to the perils covered in the Standard Form, the Broad Form also includes protection against most types of accidental losses to hot water heating systems, falling objects, collapse, water damage from heating and air conditioning systems or other appliances, glass breakage, freezing of plumbing, heating, and air conditioning systems, and most types of damage to appliances, fixtures, and wiring from electrical current. Again, adding these perils to the policy has no effect on the amount of insurance; the list of named perils is simply lengthened. Form 2 is the most popular of all home owner's forms.

Form 3, the Special Form, cannot be used by itself. It must be used with Form 4. The Special Form provides even broader coverage than the Broad Form. Rather than adding a specific number of additional perils, the Special Form provides "all-risk" protection to the dwelling. This is an important insurance concept. It protects against all sources of loss, except those that are specifically excluded. A "named peril" policy specifies the perils that are covered and does not protect against other sources of damage. An all-risk policy gives protection against all perils except those that are specifically excluded. Although the number of exclusions will be greater in an all-risk policy, the coverage will actually be much broader than in a named peril contract. The reason Form 3 must be used in conjunction with Form 4 is that Form 3 covers only the dwelling; it does not cover the contents.

Form 4 covers only contents, and is called the Residence Contents Broad Form. It provides named peril coverage on personal property. (The perils named are the same as those in Form 2.) Form 4 is used most often in two situations. If a person wants all-risk coverage on his home and named peril coverage on his personal property, he can buy Forms 3 and 4. Form 4 is also used by tenants. A person who rents an apartment, for example, does not need insurance on the building, but does need insurance protection on his personal property and liability coverage.

---

[6] It is possible that the policies of a few companies do not contain a loss clause. Obviously insurance buyers should avoid policies of this type.

Unfortunately for many young people, tenants are often subject to more liability than they realize. Suppose a young married couple rents an apartment, and an injury occurs in their living room? The general rule of law is that the tenant assumes the liability of the landlord. Furthermore, the terms of most leases make it quite clear that liability for injuries is transferred from the landlord to the tenant when the premises are rented or leased. Usually the courts will continue to hold the landlord responsible for injuries that occur in the hallways of an apartment building and other areas that are not rented to specific individuals. This means the tenants usually have a need for liability insurance.

Form 5, the Comprehensive Form, is the "deluxe" insurance package. It provides all-risk coverage on the building and on the personal property. All-risk coverage on personal property is very expensive, and this feature makes the premium high on Form 5.

Premiums for homeowner's policies depend a lot on geographical location, but Table 14–1 may be helpful in suggesting costs:

Table 14–1 Three-Year Prepaid Premiums for Homeowner's Policies

Amount of Insurance on Dwelling	Form 1	Form 2	Form 3	Form 4	Form 5
$15,000	$ 93	$111	$120	$ 79	$247
$30,000	$167	$200	$218	$133	$409

Form 5 is seldom used because of its high premiums. Likewise, Forms 3 and 4 are not used often together because the combined premium is high. Form 2 is by far the most popular. The reason the premium is high on Forms 3 and 5, however, is the all-risk feature. All-risk insurance is costly for the insurance company because the company has to pay more losses than the company on other forms. But from the buyer's point of view, this simply means the policyholders will suffer uninsured losses if they have the named peril forms. A logical question is why should a person protect himself against only certain, specified causes of loss? A loss is a loss, and the cause of the loss is of little importance to a policyholder.

DETERMINING THE AMOUNT OF INSURANCE TO BUY ON A HOME

You might think that it would be easy to determine how much insurance you should purchase. This is not the case. It is actually quite difficult to know how much homeowner's insurance is appropriate. If a person buys too little insurance, he will not be adequately protected. On the other hand; if he buys an excessive amount, he will pay an excessive premium and will not be able to collect the face amount anyway. Suppose a person buys a home for $15,000 and, to make sure he has adequate insurance, he buys a $20,000 policy. If the home is totally de-stroyed, how much will he collect? The answer is only $15,000 because a property insurance policy will not pay more than the "actual cash value" of the property at the time of the loss. This is called the "principle of indemnity," and is one of the foundations of insurance theory. According to the principle of indemnity, a policyholder should not be allowed to collect more than the actual cash value of the property at the time of the loss. In other words, a policyholder should not be permitted to benefit or profit from a loss. The term "actual cash value" is taken to mean the replacement cost of the property minus physical depreciation (or plus appreciation if the property has increased in value.)[7]

Suppose a young family buys a new home and pays $23,000 for it. If the lot on which the home is located is worth $2,000 and the founda-tion is worth $1,000, the amount of property that can be destroyed by fire (and practically any other peril) is only $20,000. How much in-surance should be bought?

The answer given by some insurance agents will be $16,000. Others will recommend $18,400. Confusion is caused by an important clause in the policy that is called the "replacement cost" provision.[8] Basically, this clause states that there will be no deduction for depreciation in the loss adjustment if the amount of insurance carried is 80 percent or more of the full replacement cost of the home. If the insured carries less than this amount of insurance, the insurance company will subtract the amount of depreciation from the replacement cost when the settlement is made. It is important, therefore, to carry at least 80 percent of the value of the house in order to avoid deductions for depreciation.

Some insurance agents, realizing that the replacement cost provision does not apply to the lot and foundation (which are generally regarded as indestructible) would recommend to the policyholder that he carry only $16,000 of insurance. This would be 80 percent of the value of the house, (80% × $20,000 = $16,000). Other insurance agents might sug-gest $18,400 as the proper amount of insurance since this would be 80 percent of the total property value (80% × $23,000 = $18,400).

If the policyholder carried only $16,000 of insurance, he would not have depreciation deducted from any loss settlement. This amount of insurance, however, could cause problems for two reasons:

1. The policyholder would be inadequately protected if the home is totally destroyed. The house is worth $20,000 and an insurance policy will never pay more than its face amount. The insured would collect

---

[7] Physical depreciation means true wear and tear and economic obsolescence. Accounting depreciation (the amount of depreciation carried on the books of a company) is influenced by tax laws and other factors and may not necessarily reflect true physical depreciation.

[8] This is *not* a coinsurance provision. Despite what many people believe, co-insurance applies only to commercial policies; it *does not* apply to homes.

only $16,000 for a loss that cost him $20,000. Of course most fire losses are small. There is little chance of a total loss. Nevertheless, if the policyholder cannot afford a $4,000 uninsured loss, he should carry insurance to the full value of his house.

2. The value of the house is likely to appreciate over time, so the amount of insurance may not be 80 percent of the value of the house at the time of the loss. Suppose the house (alone) has appreciated to $25,000 when there is a $1,000 loss. The insured would collect only $800. This is the proportion of the loss that the amount of insurance carried bears to the full replacement cost ($\frac{\$16,000}{\$20,000} \times \$1,000 = \$800$).

As a rule, then, a policyholder should carry an amount of insurance at least equal to the value of his house; in this case $20,000.

Since the value of a home changes, policyholders should make sure that the amount of insurance carried is appropriate. This can be done by periodically adjusting the amount of insurance or by adding the "inflation guard endorsement" to the policy. The endorsement is available from many companies, can be added for a small cost, and will automatically increase the amount of insurance 1 percent every three months.

So far, we have been considering only the amount of insurance to carry on the home. But as you know, a homeowner's policy is a package contract and provides coverage on the contents in the house, additional living expenses, personal liability, medical payments, and physical damage to property. How much insurance should be carried on these coverages? This is usually not a problem that most policyholders face because the policy limits for these coverages are either flat amounts or percentages of the amount of insurance on the house. Usually, the following amounts of insurance are automatically built into the home-owner's contract:

Coverage B—Private structures: 10 percent of Coverage A

Coverage C—Personal property: 50 percent of Coverage A
(10 percent applying off premises)

Coverage D—Additional living expense: 10 or 20 percent of Coverage A

Coverage E—Comprehensive personal liability: $25,000 per occurrence

Coverage F—Medical payments: $500 per person; $25,000 per accident

Coverage G—Physical damage to property: $250 per occurrence

Table 14–2 summarizes the principal features of the various home owner forms and shows how the amounts of coverage are related to the amount of insurance on the house.

Table 14–2 Homeowner's Policy Guide

	HO-1	HO-2	HO-3	HO-4	HO-5
Perils Covered (see key below)	perils 1-11	perils 1-18	perils 1-18 on personal property; all risks on buildings except those specifically excluded in policy	perils 1-18 except 11	all risks on buildings and personal property except those specifically excluded in policy
Standard Amount of Insurance on:					
House and attached structures	based on value of property; minimum, $800	based on value of property; minimum, $8,000	based on value of property; minimum, $8,000	used only for rented house and apartment and does not cover buildings	based on value of property; minimum, $15,000
Detached structures	10% of amount of insurance on house	10% of amount of insurance on house	10% of amount of insurance on house	no coverage	10% of amount of insurance on house
Trees, shrubs, plants	5% of insurance on house	5% of insurance on house	5% of insurance on house	10% of personal property amount	5% of insurance on house
Personal property on home premises	50% of insurance on house	50% of insurance on house	50% of insurance on house	based on value of property; minimum, $4,000	50% of insurance on house
Personal property away from premises	10% of insurance for personal property on premises	10% of insurance for personal property on premises	10% of insurance for personal property on premises	10% of insurance for personal property on premises	50% of insurance on house

Table 14-2 (continued)

	HO-1	HO-2	HO-3	HO-4	HO-5
Perils Covered (see key below)	perils 1-11	perils 1-18	perils 1-18 on personal property; all risks on buildings except those specifically excluded in policy	perils 1-18 except 11	all risks on buildings and personal property except those specifically excluded in policy
Standard Amount of Insurance on:					
Additional living expense	10% of insurance on house	20% of insurance on house	20% of insurance on house	20% of insurance on personal property	20% of insurance on house
Comprehensive personal liability	$25,000	$25,000	$25,000	$25,000	$25,000
Damage to property of others	$250	$250	$250	$250	$250
Medical payments	$500 per person up to $25,000 for all injured in same accident	$500 per person up to $25,000 for all injured in same accident	$500 per person up to $25,000 for all injured in same accident	$500 per person up to $25,000 for all injured in same accident	$500 per person up to $25,000 for all injured in same accident

Key to Perils Covered

1. fire, lightning
2. damage to property removed from premises endangered by fire
3. windstorm, hail
4. explosion
5. riots or civil commotion
6. damage by aircraft
7. damage by vehicles not owned and operated by people covered by policy
8. damage from smoke
9. vandalism, malicious mischief
10. theft
11. window breakage (including storm doors)
12. falling objects
13. weight of ice, snow, sleet
14. collapse of building or any part of building
15. bursting, cracking, burning or bulging of a steam or water heating system, or of appliances for heating water
16. leakage or overflow of water or steam from a plumbing, heating or air-conditioning system
17. freezing of plumbing, heating and air-conditioning systems and domestic appliances
18. injury to electrical appliances, devices, fixtures and wiring (excluding TV, radio tubes and resistors) from short circuits or other accidentally generated currents

Reprinted by permission from *Changing Times, The Kiplinger Magazine,* p. 17 (April 1969 issue). Copyright 1969 by the Kiplinger Washington Editors, Inc. 1729 H Street, N.W., Washington, D.C. 20006.

DETERMINING THE AMOUNT OF PROTECTION
ON PERSONAL PROPERTY

Although most policyholders automatically take the amount of insurance provided on personal property, many policyholders would be well advised to study this problem. The homeowner's policy puts a limit of $1,000 on the theft of jewelry and some other valuable property. It also provides a limit of $500 on boats.

If a person owns jewelry, furs, cameras, boats, and other articles that are more valuable than the limits provided in the homeowner's package, he should consider buying additional coverage for them. This is called "scheduling" personal items, and it can be done by buying a Personal Articles Floater. Although this is legally a separate contract, it can be attached to the homeowner's policy.

DETERMINING THE AMOUNT OF
PERSONAL LIABILITY PROTECTION

While the $25,000 liability coverage provided automatically in the homeowner's contract may seem sufficient, this may not be the case. It is well known that the courts have been increasing the amounts awarded in liability cases. Awards of several hundred thousand dollars are becoming more common.

When a person buys any type of liability insurance, he should realize that the amount of protection he needs should be determined by the amount of losses he can cause by his actions. But who knows how much loss he can cause? If an explosion occurs in a home and injures several guests, how much would a court award for the injuries? The answer is that no one knows. The best a wise insurance buyer can do is to be aware of the sizable liability awards that are being made and carry a large amount of liability insurance. This is not so expensive as it may seem because the cost of additional liability insurance is low. Figure 14–1 shows the cost of personal liability insurance.

Examine Figure 14–1 carefully. It illustrates a principle that is important to insurance buyers. Figure 14–1 shows that the three-year rate for $25,000 of liability protection is $.28. This means the cost is $7. (The rate is the cost per $1,000 of coverage; $25,000 of coverage at $.28 a thousand is $7.) The rate for $100,000 of insurance is only $.17 and the cost is $17. When a person buys $300,000 of insurance the rate is $.10 and the cost $30. If a person has $50,000 of coverage, he can double his protection for only $5. Since this is the three-year increase in cost, the annual cost for doubling his protection is only $1.67. The reason the insurance rate decreases as more insurance is bought is that smaller losses occur more frequently than large losses. An insurance company knows that it will have to pay many liability claims that are less than $25,000. Only a relatively few liability claims will be more than $100,000.

Figure 14–1   The Cost of Personal Liability Insurance

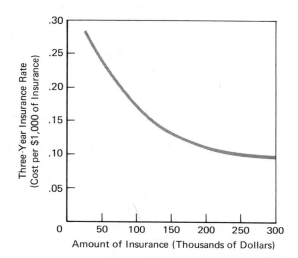

From the insurance buyer's point of view, however, he should protect himself against the large losses. Especially if higher insurance limits can be purchased with only a small increase in cost.

Young people often make a serious mistake when they buy liability insurance. They believe that a court will not impose a huge judgment because they are young and have few assets. Even if a huge judgment is awarded, young people often believe that bankruptcy would provide relief. This is poor reasoning because the size of the awards is determined (in theory, at least) by the amount of loss. Furthermore, while bankruptcy may excuse most debts, liability awards are often *not* excused by bankruptcy. And in many cases, the future income of a person may be attached. In such cases, it might take years for a young person with few assets to pay off a liability judgment.

DEDUCTIBLE CLAUSES

A provision that is found in many types of insurance policies, including homeowner's contracts, is the deductible provision.[9] These clauses are generally not liked by policyholders. In a sense, this is understandable because it means policyholders usually will not collect the full amount of their loss. Deductibles, however, serve a useful purpose and they would be received better if more policyholders understood why they are used.

A deductible clause states that the insurance company will pay a loss only when the loss is larger than a specified amount or percentage. The

---

[9] Deductibles apply only to property insurance, and not to liability coverages. In the new homeowner's policies, they apply to the property coverages, except the additional living expense protection.

simplest type of deductible is a "straight" or "flat" deductible. With this type, the insurance company simply pays the loss in excess of the deductible amount. Homeowner's policies have also used a "disappearing" deductible. With these clauses, the insurance company pays the full loss if it is larger than a certain amount. In the new homeowner's policies, a disappearing deductible works in this way:

Losses less than $50—the insurance company pays nothing
Losses between $50 and $500—the insurance company pays the
  loss minus $50
Loss more than $500—the insurance company pays the full loss

The new homeowner's policies offer deductible options of straight $100, $250, or $500 deductibles. Which should the insurance buyer choose?

The major purpose of a deductible is to eliminate small claims. When an insurance company does not have to pay small claims, it is possible to reduce the premium substantially. The premium saving is large because the cost of adjusting small claims (which is disproportionally high for small claims) is eliminated. Also, since most losses are small, the insurance company saves money on numerous claims. From the insurance buyer's point of view, a small loss may not be a burden and the premium saving may be worthwhile. As a general principle, therefore, insurance buyers should take the largest deductible that would not cause a financial problem for them. For example, a wealthy person might logically select a $500 deductible since a $500 uninsured loss would not cause financial problems. A young person, however, who does not have large financial resources could logically choose a $100 deductible.

AUTOMOBILE INSURANCE

It has been said that insurance policies are the "least read best sellers" in the country. This is perhaps more true of automobile insurance than of any other type of coverage. Almost everyone buys automobile insurance but very few people understand even the fundamentals about it. This is unfortunate because it is impossible to make intelligent buying decisions without some knowledge of automobile insurance.

UNDERSTANDING THE AUTOMOBILE INSURANCE POLICY

Perhaps the main reason people fail to understand the automobile policy is that it is truly a package contract. The automobile policy is actually a combination of coverages, and a policyholder selects the coverages he wants to purchase. There are usually nine separate coverages available: automobile liability insurance, medical payments, accidental death benefits, uninsured motorists protection, collision, comprehensive, personal effects, towing and labor, and transportation.

Automobile Liability Insurance. The basic agreement of the insurance company in the liability portion of the automobile policy is to pay for injuries or property damages for which the insured becomes legally liable. The coverage promises to pay "on behalf" of the insured. As in all liability policies, this coverage does not pay benefits directly to the insured. It pays others for the losses the insured inflicts upon them. Also, like other liability policies, the protection pays for the cost of legal defense for the insured, bond premiums, and first aid expenses.[10]

The coverage of persons and automobiles insured is much broader than most people realize. The liability portion of the policy covers the named insured (which includes his spouse if the spouse is a resident of the same household), residents of the same household, and *any person* who uses the automobile with the named insured's permission. If a father asks his son, or even a friend, to run an errand for him, the son or friend would be covered by the liability insurance. Suppose, however, that the friend then lets a girlfriend drive the car. The girlfriend would not be covered because she does not have the permission of the named insured to drive the car. This kind of situation is usually not a problem, however, because the girlfriend would probably be covered under her own insurance. The automobile provides protection when nonowned cars are driven, if the nonowned car is not used regularly. Furthermore, if an insured is using a car temporarily, he is covered. For example, if an insured borrows a car while his is being repaired, he is covered.

The medical payments coverage in the automobile policy, unlike the medical payments coverage in other liability contracts, gives protection to the insured. In most liability policies, medical payments coverage only protects persons other than the insured. In the automobile policy, however, it covers the insured, his family, and anyone else in his car. It even provides coverage for the insured and his household relatives while they are in nonowned cars, or even when struck by any car as a pedestrian.

The medical payments benefit pays for all reasonable and necessary medical expenses that are incurred within one year of the accident. It pays, for example, for surgical, dental, ambulance, hospital, nursing, and funeral expenses.

Another optional coverage in the automobile policy is accidental death benefits. This is a simple coverage. It pays the amount stipulated if the named insured (to include a spouse) is killed in an automobile accident. The accident can occur in any automobile, and coverage also applies if the insured is struck by a car. Death must occur within 90 days of the accident.

---

[10] The family automobile policy also pays the insured for his loss of earnings while attending hearings or trials. The maximum payment is $25 per day, with a total maximum of $500 for any occurrence.

Protection of the insured's car is provided by *physical damage* coverage. This protection should not be confused with property damage *liability,* which protects the insured when he has caused damage to the property of others. Physical damage insurance protects the care the insured is driving.

Collision insurance is one of the important physical damage coverages. It reimburses the insured for damage to the car he is driving when there is a collision with another car or object. The outstanding feature of collision insurance is that it uses a deductible. The insured has a choice of a $50, $100, $250, or even higher deductible amounts. As mentioned previously, the insured can save a substantial amount if he takes a higher deductible.

Comprehensive insurance is another physical damage coverage. It provides all-risk coverage to the insured's car. Therefore, all accidental losses are covered except those that are specifically excluded.[11] If a horse kicks the car and dents the fender, or if the car is accidentally sprayed by paint, the comprehensive coverage will reimburse the insured for the loss. Comprehensive insurance also gives protection (with a $100 maximum) for clothes and other personal effects that are damaged by fire and lightning while they are in the insured's car. If the insured's car is stolen, comprehensive insurance will also pay for transportation expenses (including a car rental) until the car is returned or the full loss is paid. The maximum benefit amount is limited, however, to $10 per day up to a maximum of $30Q or the value of the car.

One of the problems an insured often has is the distinction between a collision loss and a comprehensive loss. This distinction is sometimes important because a deductible applies to a collision loss, but a deductible is seldom applicable to comprehensive losses. Suppose the insured runs into a large dog and damages the front of his car. Is this a collision or comprehensive loss? The policy attempts to clarify this type of question by stating that damage by animals is included under comprehensive coverage. The policy also lists a number of perils that are not considered collision losses and are therefore covered under the comprehensive coverage.

Towing and labor costs may also be included in the automobile policy. This coverage pays for emergency road service, with a maximum payment of $25 for each accident.

IMPORTANT PURCHASE DECISIONS

Selecting the Coverages to Buy.   Should a person buy automobile liability insurance? Many people, perhaps most, believe they have no choice. A great many people think that automobile liability coverage is compulsory. This confusion is caused by the problem of the uninsured

---

[11] Collision is specifically excluded under the comprehensive coverage.

driver. Suppose you are driving down the street very carefully. A driver runs a stop sign and hits your car. Your car could be a total loss and you could suffer a serious disability. The total dollar amount of loss to you, considering the value of your car and hospital and medical bills, might be substantial. Since the other driver has been at fault, you naturally look to him for reimbursement, and if he has automobile liability insurance, his insurance company will pay you for your losses. But suppose he has no liability insurance. Without insurance, your chances of collecting much from him are small. This unfortunate situation, which is the problem of the uninsured driver, has become one of the serious problems in our automotive society.

Financial responsibility laws attempt to solve the problem of the uninsured driver. Although the laws differ slightly among the 47 states that have these laws, they are fairly uniform. A financial responsibility law requires a person who is involved in an accident to show that he was not to blame or show proof of financial responsibility. This proof can be a liability policy, a security bond, or a cash deposit. Most laws apply only if there has been bodily injury or $100 or more of property damage. A person who is unable to show he was not to blame and cannot prove financial responsibility will lose his driver's license (and maybe the registration on his car). Note that a financial responsibility law does not necessarily require a person to buy automobile liability insurance. The law only encourages people to buy liability protection. Still, because financial responsibility laws permit a choice, some people do not carry automobile liability insurance and the problem of the uninsured driver persists.

Compulsory automobile liability insurance is in effect in only three states (Massachusetts, New York, and North Carolina). In these states, all car owners are required to show ownership of a liability policy before license plates will be issued.[12] Compulsory insurance would seem to solve the problem of the uninsured driver but it does not. Not all drivers are insured because there are hit and run drivers, out-of-state drivers, drivers with lapsed insurance, and drivers with fraudulently registered cars.

An unsatisfied judgment fund is another possible solution to the uninsured driver problem. Five states (North Dakota, New Jersey, Maryland, New York, and Michigan) now have these plans. A fund is set up by a state for judgments arising from automobile accidents that cannot be collected by any other means. If a negligent driver has no liability insurance and cannot pay a judgment, the injured driver may collect from the fund. The negligent driver then loses his right to drive until he has reimbursed the fund for the amount paid on his behalf.

While the unsatisfied judgment fund helps to alleviate the situation, there are several problems. First, it is confusing to many drivers. The

---

[12] The laws also permit the filing of cash, bond, or collateral as an alternative to a liability policy. As·a practical matter, the only method used is a liability policy.

fund may be built up from charges to insurance companies, uninsured drivers, and insured drivers. (If a fee is collected from insured drivers as well as uninsured drivers, drivers without insurance usually pay more.) Confusion often results because uninsured drivers believe they have paid for insurance when they pay their assessment for the fund. Of course, this only increases the number of drivers without insurance. Another major criticism of the unsatisfied judgment fund approach is that it requires a person to exhaust all other means of collection before the fund will pay. This means an injured driver must sue, get a judgment, and then prove that the negligent driver cannot pay. This is time consuming and uncertain.

The uninsured motorist endorsement is another way to deal with the uninsured driver problem. This is an endorsement to the automobile liability policy which pays the insured driver when an uninsured, negligent driver causes injury. The endorsement applies only to bodily injury; it does not give protection for property damage. In other words, if there is a bodily injury claim, the insured driver's company will act as the insurance company for the negligent driver and pay for the legal liability that he would be obligated to pay. One of the main problems with the uninsured motorist endorsement is that it does not pay unless the other driver has been negligent.

With all these possible solutions to the problem of the uninsured driver, it is not surprising that people are confused about their automobile insurance purchase decisions. We may now conclude, however, that in practically every state a person is not legally required to buy automobile liability insurance. Nevertheless, as a practical matter, every person who drives a car should be protected by liability coverage. Without insurance a person exposes his assets and future income to severe losses. Furthermore, it makes good sense to purchase the uninsured motorist endorsement. It costs only about five dollars a year, and it assures a driver that he will not suffer financial losses from negligent, uninsured drivers.

It is also wise to purchase automobile medical payments coverage. The advantage of the medical payments insurance is that it pays without having to determine liability. Suppose someone runs into your car. Although you believe the other driver is at fault, he blames you for the accident. In such a case, both parties may sue. It might be years, however, before the liability is determined. The medical payments coverage pays promptly without raising the question of fault. The medical payments coverage also avoids embarrassing lawsuits. If a friend is injured in your car, he may be reluctant to sue you. If you have medical payments coverage, your friend can collect for his injuries without suing.

The cost of automobile medical payments coverage is low. It depends upon the basic premium for the bodily injury liability coverage and the limits of the medical payments insurance, but it usually costs between $5 and $20 per year.

There is little to recommend buying the accidental death benefit. The medical payments will pay for the cost of funeral expenses. Furthermore, life insurance policies and possibly health insurance coverages will also pay benefits if an insured is killed in an automobile accident.

Usually, a car owner has little or no choice as to whether or not he should buy physical damage coverage. This is because most cars are financed and lenders require sufficient physical damage insurance to be purchased to protect the value of the car. An insurance buyer should understand that the coverage the lender requires is physical damage protection on the car; they are not very interested in the more important liability protection.

To determine whether or not a person should buy comprehensive and collision insurance, only one question needs to be answered. Can the car owner afford to lose the value of the car if there is an accident? If a person buys a new car and pays $4,200 for it, the loss of the car is likely to be an important loss to him. If it is, he should have physical damage insurance. On the other hand, suppose a college student is driving an old car, worth only about $300. This may not be enough exposure to worry about. If a $300 loss would not be considered important, the student should not buy physical damage insurance.

The "large loss" principle should also be applied when the car owner selects the amount of the deductible. If the insured can afford a $250 loss without much financial strain, he should choose a $250 deductible rather than a $50 deductible, for example. If he selects a $50 deductible instead, he will be paying a higher premium to protect himself against a loss that is not important.

The "large loss" principle is also an argument against the towing and labor coverage. Why should a person select a $250 deductible on the collision coverage, for example, and purchase towing and labor benefits? On the one hand he is saying that he can afford a $250 loss, but the purchase of the towing benefit is in effect saying that he cannot afford a $25 loss.

Determining the Amount of Insurance to Buy.   How much automobile liability insurance should a person carry? Most people carry either "5, 10 and 5" or "10, 20 and 5." These are the insurance company's limits of liability, and they should be understood by every insurance buyer. "Five, 10 and 5" means the liability limits are $5,000 for each person who sustains a bodily injury, $10,000 for each accident involving bodily injury, and $5,000 for property damage liability. The first two figures refer to bodily injury liability, and the difference is that the first number applies on a "per person" basis and the second figure is the "per accident" limit. The third number is the property damage liability limit.

Suppose a person carries liability limits of $5,000/$10,000 bodily injury ($5,000 each person, and $10,000 each accident) and $5,000 property damage. He is careless and runs into a car and causes the following losses:

$4,000 bodily injury to Al
$5,000 bodily injury to Mary
$11,000 bodily injury to Dave
$3,000 bodily injury to Al's car

How much liability will the insurance company pay? The company will pay $7,000 to Al because both the bodily injury and property damage are within the limits. Mary's claim of $5,000 will also be paid. The company, however, will pay only $1,000 to Dave. This is because the aggregate bodily injury limit of $10,000 per accident will be exhausted when $4,000 has been paid to Al, $5,000 to Mary, and $1,000 to Dave. The insured will still owe $10,000 to Dave. If the insured had carried limits of "10, 20 and 5" his policy would have paid $7,000 to Al (for both bodily injury and property damage), $5,000 to Mary, and $11,000 to Dave. In this case, the policy limits would have been adequate to pay all the losses.

Because automobile liability judgments have become increasingly high, it is advisable to carry more than the standard limits. Many authorities believe the minimum bodily injury limit should be at least $50,000 per person and $100,000 per accident. The standard property damage liability limit of $5,000 is also considered inadequate by experts. Five thousand dollars is enough if the only damage is to an automobile, but suppose the insured runs into a store front? In some cases, the property damage is great. Consider the situation when a person drives into a gas pump at a filling station and the gas tank below the pump explodes.

Liability limits can be increased at less cost than might be expected. This is because the majority of cases can be settled within the standard limits; only a relatively few cases require more insurance. For example, liability limits can be doubled at less than twice the premium. And bodily injury limits of 100/300 cost only about 40 percent more than 10/20.

The usual limit for medical payments coverage is $500 per person. This limit is adequate for the majority of cases, and for more serious cases an injured person can sue and collect under the liability protection. Therefore, the argument for higher medical payments limits is not so strong as it is for higher liability limits. Nevertheless, because most medical payments benefits are small, an insurance company can afford to increase the limits without increasing the premium proportionately. For example, a person who pays $6 for $500 of medical payments coverage can usually get $5,000 of coverage for $13 or $14. This seems to be a small price for much higher limits.

The amount of physical damage insurance a person should purchase is never a problem. These coverages do not have a dollar limit. Instead, they are written on an "actual cash value" basis. If the insured damages his car, he is paid for the "actual cash value" of the loss rather than some stated amount.

Making Claims.   Many policyholders are confused when the question of making an insurance claim arises. Some people believe the best approach is to make as many claims as possible so that they can "recover" their insurance premium. Others think they should not submit claims unless absolutely necessary because their insurance might be cancelled and they may not be able to get new coverage.

Actually the question of whether or not a legitimate claim should be submitted should not arise very often. If the claim is large (important financially to the policyholder) it should be submitted. Even small claims should be made except in unusual circumstances. These circumstances can arise if the insurance company is likely to cancel the coverage and new protection would be difficult to buy. Questions of this type can usually be answered by your insurance agent. In any event, a policyholder who has sustained a loss should study the conditions in his policy that pertain to losses. Most insurance policies require a policyholder to notify the insurance company of a loss as soon as practicable. (Actually most policies require "immediate notice" but this means as soon as reasonably possible). If a policyholder fails to meet this condition, his insurance company may not pay any amount. The notice of loss is especially important if other people are directly involved. For example, suppose you are involved in an automobile accident and the driver of the other car shows absolutely no signs of being injured. If you fail to report the accident to your insurance company, the company may not come to your defense if the other driver later discovers that he has developed some type of injury.

FACTORS AFFECTING THE COST OF AUTOMOBILE INSURANCE

War is an unfortunate and regrettable part of our history. But it is a fact that each year there are more injuries in traffic accidents than casualties in World Wars I and II combined. In 1968, there were ten times more traffic injuries than war casualties in the previous nine years of the Vietnam war. The number of accidents and deaths caused by automobiles is truly staggering. To make matters worse, the economic loss from traffic accidents increases each year. Figure 14–2 shows this clearly.

When the number of automobile accidents increases, the cost of automobile insurance must increase. Table 14–3 shows how the average claim cost for liability insurance has changed since 1958.

The cost of automobile insurance concerns everyone. But it is a special problem for young drivers (generally those under age 25) because they are required to pay higher than average premiums for their insurance protection. And despite the fact that young drivers pay more, they often

Figure 14–2   Economic Losses from Traffic Accidents in the United States, 1945–1969

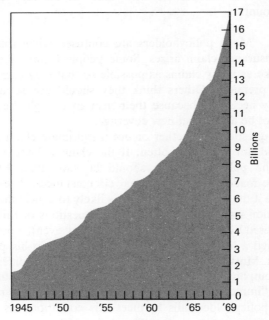

Source: Insurance Information Institute, *Insurance Facts,* 1970, p. 51.

Table 14–3   Countrywide* Average Paid Claims Costs** Liability Insurance, Private Passenger Cars

Year	Bodily Injury Average Paid Claim Cost	Property Damage Average Paid Claim Cost
1959	$1,031	$159
1960	1,070	167
1961	1,099	169
1962	1,113	176
1963	1,113	181
1964	1,129	189
1965	1,202	203
1966	1,296	221
1967	1,432	241
1968	1,550	267
1969	1,583	280

*Excluding Massachusetts which has different reporting methods.
**For all limits combined, and including all loss adjustment expenses.
Source: Insurance Information Institute, *Insurance Facts 1970*, p. 52. Used with permission of the Insurance Rating Board.

have more difficulty in getting insurance. Why? Is it fair to charge young drivers more for their car insurance? To answer these questions, it is necessary to understand the fundamentals of how automobile insurance rates are calculated.

When an insurance company determines the premiums it will charge, the first step is to decide which factors have an important effect on losses. Geographical location (i.e., territory), for example, is an important factor in automobile insurance. People who live in large cities have more accidents than those who live in rural areas. It is only fair, therefore, to charge those who live in cities more for automobile insurance.

Insurance companies have collected statistics that show the following factors also play an important part in accident losses:

1. Use of the automobile
2. Age, sex, and marital status of the driver
3. Driver training courses
4. Student grades
5. Driving records

The first factor, use of the car, is divided into pleasure use, business use, and farm use. Statistics have shown that cars used for personal pleasure are involved in fewer accidents than those that are used for business purposes. It is only fair, then, for automobile rates to be higher for cars used in business.

Insurance statistics also indicate that young drivers have more accidents than older drivers, and young unmarried males have more accidents than young women or young married men. Figure 14–3 shows how age is related to accidents.

Young drivers, especially unmarried men, are unhappy with their automobile insurance costs, but accident statistics indicate that they should pay more. Old men should pay higher premiums for life insurance (because the chances of loss are higher) and young men should pay higher automobile premiums for the same reason.

Intelligent students, however, argue that not *all* young drivers should be put in the same classification and charged high automobile insurance premiums. And there is some validity to this argument. Insurance companies therefore give young drivers discounts for driver training course, good grades, and driving records. Statistics have demonstrated that young drivers can become better automobile operators by taking approved driver training courses. Usually these courses involve about 30 hours of classroom work and six hours of driving. The discount is about 10 percent, so this factor alone can amount to a sizable saving for young drivers.

On the theory that good students use their cars less often than students with poor grades, insurance companies provide discounts for students with good grades. To qualify for this discount, a student must have a B

Figure 14–3   Accidents by Age of Drivers, 1969

Age Group	Number of Drivers	% of Total	Drivers in All Accidents	% of Total	Drivers in Fatal Accidents	% of Total
0-19	11,000,000	10.2	4,450,000	16.6	10,400	14.7
20-24	11,800,000	11.0	4,800,000	17.9	13,600	19.3
25-29	10,800,000	10.0	3,150,000	11.7	8,400	11.9
30-34	10,200,000	9.5	2,550,000	9.5	7,300	10.3
35-39	10,700,000	9.9	2,300,000	8.6	5,450	7.7
40-44	11,300,000	10.5	2,000,000	7.5	5,450	7.7
45-49	10,500,000	9.8	2,000,000	7.5	5,000	7.1
50-54	9,200,000	8.6	1,550,000	5.8	3,900	5.5
55-59	7,300,000	6.8	1,400,000	5.2	3,200	4.5
60-64	5,600,000	5.2	1,000,000	3.7	2,700	3.8
65-69	4,200,000	3.9	850,000	3.2	2,050	2.9
70-74	2,900,000	2.7	350,000	1.3	1,550	2.2
75 and over	2,000,000	1.9	400,000	1.5	1,700	2.4
Total	107,500,000	100.0%	26,800,000	100.0%	70,700	100.0%

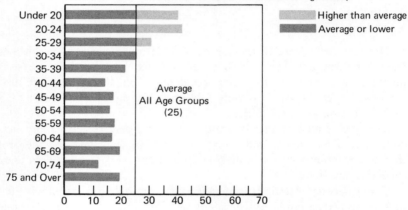

No. of Drivers in Accidents Per 100 Drivers in Each Age Group

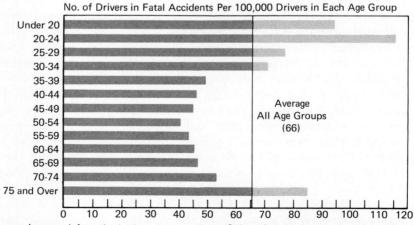

No. of Drivers in Fatal Accidents Per 100,000 Drivers in Each Age Group

Source: Insurance Information Institute, *Insurance Facts, 1970,* p. 50. Reprinted with permission of the National Safety Council.

average, be in the top 20 percent of his class, or on the honor roll or equivalent. The savings can be as much as 20 percent.

Safe driver rating plans provide discounts for drivers who demonstrate a good driving record. Points are assigned to accidents or traffic violations, and drivers who have few points receive a discount. This is another way young drivers can demonstrate that they deserve lower automobile rates.

Despite the fact that insurance companies charge higher rates for young drivers, insurance companies usually have poor experience with this business. In many cases the premiums collected from young drivers do not cover the insurance company's losses and expenses. As a result, insurance companies are not eager to write insurance on young drivers even if they collect higher premiums.

What happens to the driver who applies for insurance and is rejected? He can apply for insurance with other companies, but what happens if he is rejected time after time? Assigned-risk plans have been set up in every state to handle this kind of situation. Assigned-risk plans are not the same in all the states, but they generally follow the same pattern. A person who has been refused automobile insurance can apply to the assigned-risk plan and the manager of the plan will assign him to an insurance company. All insurance companies that do business in the state are obligated to take their share of risks that have been rejected.[13] Any driver can be refused coverage and forced to apply to the assigned-risk plan, but most plans are made up of young drivers, inexperienced drivers, very old drivers, and persons with poor accident records. Policyholders who are placed in the assigned-risk plan usually pay a higher rate than others. The extra charge may be as little as 10 percent, but some drivers pay as much as 200 percent or more than they would otherwise have to pay. The rate a person pays, however, is determined by the factors that contribute to losses. For example, it is very possible for an elderly man (say 75 years of age) to pay more than a 19 year old student. In other words, the plan does not charge everyone the same rate; the plan attempts to be fair.

Although a person who is forced into an assigned-risk plan is usually not happy with his higher rate, he should realize that insurance companies have not generally made any profit on assigned-risk plans. In fact, since 1938, losses have exceeded premiums by more than $150 million. This will require insurance companies to charge even higher rates in the future. The obvious solution for a young driver is to take every precaution and drive safely so that his insurance premiums will be as low as possible.

---

[13] Even in an assigned-risk plan certain individuals can be refused coverage. A company does not have to accept a person who can be shown to be involved in illegal activities. Habitual violators of the law need not be accepted. As a practical matter, however, almost anyone can get automobile insurance through an assigned-risk plan.

OTHER PROPERTY AND LIABILITY POLICIES

A typical individual's personal property and liability insurance needs are usually handled quite well by a homeowner's policy and an automobile insurance contract. Situations arise, however, where additional policies may be needed.

MOBILE HOMES AND FARMS

Individuals living in a mobile home or on a farm cannot use the homeowner's policy that we have discussed. But insurance companies sell policies that will serve these individuals' needs. These policies usually provide personal liability coverage, medical payments insurance, personal property insurance, and additional living expense protection as well as basic protection on the home.

RECREATIONAL VEHICLES

The sale of recreational vehicles such as motorcycles, boats, camping trailers, airplanes, and snowmobiles, really soared during the 1960's. And most of these vehicles were purchased by young people. If you own one or more of these vehicles and you are not extremely careful, you will run into some serious insurance problems.

Most of the insurance problems on recreational vehicles arise because there is confusion and misunderstanding about the coverage provided in a normal homeowner's automobile policy. Consider a camping trailer, for instance. Most homeowner's policies insure a camping trailer for theft up to a limit of $500. Some automobile policies provide liability for a trailer, and some policies may provide automatic but limited physical damage coverage for trailers if they are purchased during the policy period. However, some policies provide absolutely no coverage for a camping trailer. The situation with regard to boats, motorcycles, and other vehicles is similar.

To handle these problems correctly, you must first select the type of coverage you need, and then make sure you have adequate coverage. If the coverage is not provided in your existing policies, you should purchase a separate policy.

The owner of any type of recreational vehicle must protect himself with liability insurance. The possibility of having a sizable lawsuit is simply too serious to ignore. Physical damage insurance to cover the value of the unit might be needed, but only if the vehicle is valuable enough to insure. An old motorcycle worth only $100 probably should not be insured against physical damage, but a new motorcycle that costs $800 probably should be covered.

PROFESSIONAL MALPRACTICE INSURANCE

If you engage in professional activities or perform services that require special care and skill, you will be subject to special liability problems.

This is because it is relatively easy to obtain a judgment against a professional person because a professional is expected to use "special knowledge and skill common to the profession." The slightest failure to exercise extreme care is likely to result in a lawsuit, and quite possibly, a sizable judgment.

It is well known that doctors can be sued for malpractice, but just how many occupations have been classified as "professions" by the law? Although the following list is incomplete, courts have held in specific cases that these are professional servants: [14]

operator of a pool hall	journalist
private detective	landscape gardener
insurance agent	certified shorthand reporter
minister of the gospel	engineers, including:
operator of a school bus	surveyor, consulting
teacher of singing and music	engineer, civil engineer,
pharmacist	and industrial engineer
physician	lawyer
optometrist	dentist
architect	accountant
chemist	veterinarian
newspaper editor	

It is obvious from the above list that the professional malpractice problem can strike many individuals, and the size of these awards has been increasing rapidly in recent years.

Although professional malpractice insurance is carried by most doctors, many professionals do not protect themselves with proper liability coverage. For example, many attorneys, who should be more aware of the professional malpractice risk than almost any other profession, do not carry professional malpractice insurance. A recent study indicated that only 65 percent of the attorneys who are members of the bar in one large midwestern state carry professional liability insurance. [15]

The policies described previously in this chapter and practically all business liability policies exclude the professional liability exposure from their coverage. This means that a person who has any professional liability exposure at all should be sure to protect himself with a separate policy. Insurance companies sell separate professional liability policies for druggists, dentists, surgeons, insurance agents, and many other professions. While we do not need to describe the specific details of these

---

[14] C. Arthur Williams, Jr. and Richard M. Heins, *Risk Management and Insurance* (New York: McGraw-Hill Book Company, 1964), p. 147.

[15] Dick L. Rottman and Duke Nordlinger Stern, "Attorney's Malpractice Insurance" (unpublished study).

policies, it is interesting to know that an insurance company usually cannot settle a professional liability lawsuit without the consent of the policyholder. This is because these cases involve the professional reputation and livelihood of the policyholder.

CHOOSING AN INSURANCE COMPANY AND AN AGENT

A careful insurance buyer looks for three things when he purchases insurance:

1. A company that is financially strong and stable
2. Minimum cost
3. Good service

When a buyer makes comparisons on these factors, he should realize that they are interrelated. An insurance company that offers a lower premium than another may not provide very good service, or a company that has lower cost or better service may not be financially strong. A buyer, therefore, should check all three factors before he buys insurance.

FINANCIAL STRENGTH

A logical insurance buyer could raise the question, "Why do I need to check the financial strength of an insurance company—the insurance business is closely supervised and the government always protects policyholders?" It is true that the insurance industry is highly regulated. In fact, with the possible exception of banking, it may be the most closely regulated business. The government is extremely concerned with activities in the insurance industry. Why? Because there are reasons why insurance buyers should be protected more than buyers of other products and services. Most, but not all, insurance regulation is directed toward protecting insurance buyers.

Each state has a state insurance department or at least a governmental official who is responsible for protecting the interests of insurance consumers. In all states, the person with this responsibility has a large number of activities under his jurisdiction.

What Is Regulated?   The State Insurance Commissioner (or his equivalent) has a wide range of subjects under his jurisdiction. When insurance companies are organized, they must meet many detailed requirements before they can be licensed to do business in a state. Usually, the policies and the rates the companies will charge must be approved (either directly or indirectly) by the insurance commissioner. The sales methods of insurance companies are subject to close supervision. For example, it is illegal for insurance agents without a license from the state to sell insurance. The investments of insurance companies must be made in accordance with rather strict laws. Insurance companies' financial statements must be filed annually with the state, and companies are audited periodically by examiners in much the same way as banks.

The areas that are subject to regulation are almost unending. In fact, there is hardly anything an insurance company might do that is *not* regulated. This does not guarantee, however, that everything is so closely regulated that consumers are fully protected.

The Quality of State Supervision.   The present system of state regulation has been subject to periodic Congressional investigations and severe criticisms. The question asked is: are the states adequately protecting the insurance buying public?

A recent Congressional study has shown that some states apparently do a much better job than others. A few states have established excellent reputations in this regard, but others have demonstrated that they are doing practically nothing. In many states, the amount of money made available for regulation is so small that an adequate job seems impossible. Usually the State Insurance Commissioner is underpaid, and his department is understaffed and inadequately compensated. Too often, the position of State Insurance Commissioner is filled by a person who has little or no technical knowledge of insurance. Usually the position is a political appointment of the Governor, as a reward for faithful service, rather than a responsible position to be undertaken by a person who is competent in insurance affairs.

This regulatory environment means that an insurance buyer can only assume that almost all insurance company activities are subject to regulation, but the quality of the regulation is, at best, questionable. This means a person cannot assume that any insurance company that is permitted to do business in the state is financially secure. In the years 1953–57, 230 property and liability insurance companies has serious financial difficulties and had to become insolvent, merge with another company, dissolve, or have another insurance company take all its business.[16] In many of these cases, policyholders found that they had been paying premiums to insurance companies that could not pay their claims.

If a prospective policyholder cannot assume that the State Insurance Department will protect his interest, how can a buyer check the financial soundness of a company? There are two other approaches that can be used. The first is to check the financial rating of the insurance company. These are published by several companies and the ratings can be found in libraries, insurance offices, and state insurance departments. The most popular of these is provided by *Best's Reports*. This service gives two ratings to each insurance company, but the rating that is most important

---

[16] Herbert S. Denenberg, "Is A-Plus Really a Passing Grade?: Insurer Risk Capacity and Financial Ratings," *Journal of Risk and Insurance,* Vol. XXXIV, No. 3, September 1967, p. 379.

is the general policyholder's rating which reflects underwriting results, economy of management, adequacy of reserves, adequacy of policy-holder's surplus, and soundness of investments.

Table 14–4 shows the ratings, their meanings, and the percentage of property and liability companies with the various grades.

Table 14–4 General Policyholder Ratings Assigned by Best's Fire and Casualty Reports, 1969

Rating		Number of Companies	Percentage of Companies
A+ or A	(Excellent)	860	67.8
B+	(Very good)	71	5.7
B	(Good)	49	3.9
C+	(Fairly good)	19	1.5
C	(Fair)	13	1.1
Not Rated		254	20.0
Totals		1,266	100.0

Source: Herbert S. Denenberg, "Is A-Plus Really a Passing Grade?", *The Journal of Risk and Insurance,* Vol. XXXIV, No. 3, September 1967, p. 381. Reprinted with permission of the American Risk and Insurance Association.

Insurance companies that have low ratings or no ratings have been much more likely to become insolvent than companies with high ratings. Furthermore, companies usually do not get into financial difficulties overnight. It usually takes several years to develop serious financial problems, and in the process, the rating of the company usually declines. Policyholders can generally rely on the ratings given to the companies. If a person limits his choice of companies to those with "A+" or "A" ratings, he can still deal with about two-thirds of the companies.

The other approach, and the method that is most commonly used, is to rely upon the insurance agent to place the insurance with a good insurance company. This is sound advice if the insurance agent has the ability to evaluate insurance companies and the ability to place the insurance with a financially sound company. As pointed out below, not all insurance agents have such ability.

COST

How can an insurance buyer determine whether he is paying a reasonable price for insurance? This is an important question because the cost of insurance from some companies is much higher than it is from others.

Many people begin by deciding between stock companies and mutual companies. It is true that there are important differences between these two types of companies. A stock insurance company is organized and controlled by stockholders who receive profits (if any) from the operation. Mutual companies, on the other hand, have no stockholders. They are owned by policyholders. There is no "profit," but the difference between total income and total costs are returned to policyholders as a dividend. Many people argue that the cost of insurance from a mutual company should be lower. (There are no stockholders to receive part of the company's earnings.) Studies have shown, however, that the profits stockholders receive are only a small portion of the cost of insurance. Other factors have a much more important effect on the cost of insurance.

The factor that probably has the biggest impact on the cost of property and liability insurance is the marketing system the company uses. The traditional marketing approach is called the "American agency system." In this system, the agent is an independent contractor (not an employee of the insurance company); he represents a number of companies (typically five or six companies although some agents represent more companies); the agent is paid a commission, rather than a salary; and the agent has traditionally performed many administrative functions. In this marketing system the agent traditionally has sent premium notices, collected premiums, and generally kept all the insurance records.

The newer type of marketing system is called the "exclusive agency system." With this approach, the insurance agent is an employee; he represents only one company; he receives a salary, rather than a commission; and most administrative functions are handled by the company rather than the agent. The companies that use this system are able to handle administrative matters more economically than companies that use the other marketing system. The company can use modern electronic computers to send out premium notices and handle other functions. This means companies that use the "exclusive agency system" can usually provide insurance at a lower cost. An important question, then, is does the "exclusive agency system" of marketing tend to sacrifice *service* in return for lower cost?

SERVICE

Many people argue that a policyholder is apt to receive better service from a company that uses the "American agency system" than from an "exclusive agency system" company. The main reason for this claim is that an agent who represents a number of companies can shop around and place the coverage with a company that offers the best policy for the client's needs. An agent who represents only one company obviously cannot shop around; he must place the business with his own company and the coverage may not be well suited to the client. There is probably some truth in this argument. However, for most personal lines of insurance, the policies of different companies are very similar, so there may not be a great need to shop around.

The major factor that determines the quality of service a policyholder receives is the agent. Irrespective of the marketing system the company uses, the service a policyholder obtains usually depends on the agent. A good agent makes sure that his policyholder gets good service and a poor agent often will not. And there are substantial differences among agents.

A good insurance agent must have a thorough knowledge of the insurance business. Insurance is a highly technical, complex business. It normally requires at least several years of experience and education to become a competent insurance agent. A new agent is often unable to evaluate insurance companies, he has trouble in recommending proper amounts of insurance. As a result, an insurance buyer is usually well advised to deal only with experienced agents.

It is difficult for an insurance buyer to judge the professional competence of his agent. One very good indication of an agent's competence, however, is available. The Chartered Property and Casualty Underwriters (C.P.C.U.) designation is awarded to insurance agents who pass a series of five examinations. These examinations cover such topics as insurance contracts, insurance company operations, insurance and business law, accounting, finance, and economics. An insurance agent who passes all these examinations has demonstrated professional ambition and some degree of ability. Although it would be a mistake to deal *only* with C.P.C.U.'s, the designation is a helpful method of evaluating insurance agents.

SUMMARY

Most people can protect their personal assets with only two insurance contracts—a homeowner's pacakage and an automobile policy. A homeowner's insurance contract provides protection for the residence, personal property, and personal liability. When a person buys a homeowner's policy, he must be careful to select the appropriate form. Some forms provide much broader coverage than others, and some forms are designed for renters rather than home owners. Another important decision is the amount of insurance. If a person wants to be fully protected against real estate losses, he should be careful to have an amount of insurance equal to the value of the property that can be destroyed by an accidental peril. The proper amount of liability insurance is difficult to determine, but to be safe, a very high amount can be carried at only a small increase in cost.

Automobile insurance coverage is sometimes difficult to understand because the policy may actually provide as many as nine coverages. The liability coverages are most important, and coverage for the car itself may or may not be important, depending upon its value. Since the liability coverage is extremely important, a person should purchase high limits and also protect himself against uninsured drivers by adding the uninsured motorist endorsement to his policy. Young drivers have a legitimate concern about their automobile insurance rates, but insurance companies attempt to treat each group of policyholders fairly.

Choosing an insurance company and agent can be a difficult problem, but there are some precautions that can be taken. Insurance companies are graded by several rating agencies, and competent insurance agents have several distinguishing characteristics.

Case Problems

1. One of the basic problems a person faces when he buys a homeowner's policy is the selection of the appropriate form. This decision is important because the coverages and rates differ substantially.
   (a) Which form do you think a person should buy? Give your reasons.
   (b) Does a person who rents an apartment need a homeowner's policy? Explain why or why not.

2. Greg Steiner recently bought a home and paid $25,000 for it. Because he had accumulated some savings and wanted to reduce his monthly payment as much as possible, he made a $5,000 down payment. The real estate broker told Greg that he would have to buy a homeowner's policy before the lender would close the loan. Greg then called his insurance agent and asked for a policy. The insurance agent simply said, "Fine, how much insurance do you want on the house?" If you were in Greg's position, how much insurance would you purchase? Are the answers given by home buyers, lenders, and insurance agents always the same? Explain.

3. When Frank bought his new Corvette he was surprised to find out how much the insurance premium would be. His agent told him the liability coverage was more important than other coverages, so in order to save money, Frank bought only the liability protection. He bought limits of 10/20 and 5. Three months later Frank ran into Joe's car and caused considerable damage. The accident was clearly Frank's fault. The losses were:

Frank's car	$2300
Joe's car	1500
Frank's medical expenses	500
Joe's medical expenses	150

   How much will Frank's automobile insurance pay?

4. Tom was driving home from school and had stopped at a traffic light. While the light was still red, another car smashed into the rear of Tom's car. The accident caused $480 damage to Tom's car and $610 in medical expenses for Tom. Although the other driver was clearly at fault, Tom was upset when he found out that the negligent driver had absolutely no automobile insurance.
   (a) Will Tom's problems be solved by a financial responsibility law? Explain why or why not.

    (b) Will Tom's problems be solved if he has carried the uninsured motorist endorsement? Explain.

5. Dan was shocked when he found out how much his automobile insurance premium would be. He knew his premium would be high because he was young (20 years old), unmarried, and his car had a large engine in a small body. But he had no idea that his premium would be $465. After thinking about his problem, Dan has decided that his premium is not fair. He believes his premium is much too high. Can you explain why Dan's premium might be so high? Do you believe his premium is probably fair?

6. Would the following losses be covered by a home owner's policy? Explain why or why not.
    (a) An expensive watch is destroyed when it is thrown into a fireplace with some empty boxes and Christmas wrapping paper.
    (b) Cost to live in a motel and eat meals in a restaurant while fire damage to the home is being repaired.
    (c) Vandalism causes losses to the house and furniture while the family is on a short vacation.
    (d) Visitor slips on icy sidewalk and breaks his leg.

7. Jerry Walker is a young insurance agent who has all the major coverages on his car. Although Jerry normally parks his car in the garage, last night he parked it on the street. Unfortunately, the car was badly damaged during the night by a hit-and-run driver. Jerry is upset but his wife cannot understand why. "After all," she says, "the car is insured." Can you explain why Jerry is upset?

8. Mark always tries to buy his insurance from the company that offers the lowest premium.
    (a) What are the other factors Mark should take into account when he buys insurance?
    (b) What is the most important factor that determines whether a company will have a high or low cost?

Selected Readings

"Ahoy! Is That Boat Insured?" *Consumer Reports*, June 1969.

"Auto Insurance." *Consumer Reports*, June 1970.

Chambers, S. F. "What Do You Know About Yacht Insurance?" *Yachting*, March 1969.

Changing Times, The Kiplinger Magazine:
    "All In One Insurance for House Owners," April 1969.
    "Better Check That Property Insurance," September 1967.
    "If the House Catches Fire," February 1969.
    "Row Over No Fault Auto Insurance: Keeton-O'Connell System," May 1969.

Greene, Mark R. *Risk and Insurance*. Cincinnati: South-Western Publishing Co., 1968.

Gregg, D. L. "When Are You Wise Not to File an Auto Insurance Claim?" *Better Homes and Gardens*, March 1968.

Huebner, S. S., Black, Kenneth, and Cline, Robert. *Property and Liability Insurance.* New York: Appleton-Century-Crofts Inc., 1968.

Kulp, C. A. and Hall, John W. *Casualty Insurance.* New York: The Ronald Press Company, 1968.

Long, John D. and Gregg, Davis W. *Property and Liability Insurance Handbook.* Homewood, Illinois: Richard D. Irwin, Inc., 1965.

Magee, John H. and Bickelhaupt, David L. *General Insurance.* 8th edition. Homewood, Illinois: Richard D. Irwin, Inc., 1970.

Magee, John H. and Serbein, Oscar N. *Property and Liability Insurance.* 4th edition. Homewood, Illinois: Richard D. Irwin, Inc., 1967.

Michelbacher, G. F. and Roos, Nestor R. *Multiple Line Insurers.* New York: McGraw-Hill Book Company, 1970.

Mowbray, Albert H., Blanchard, Ralph H. and Williams, C. Arthur. *Insurance.* New York: McGraw-Hill Book Company, 1969.

"Progress Report on Auto Insurance." *Consumer Reports,* February 1969.

Rodda, William H. *Property and Liability Insurance.* Englewood Cliffs, N.J.: Prentice-Hall, Inc., 1966.

Werbel, Bernard G. *General Insurance Primer.* New York: Werbel Publishing Company, 1968.

CHAPTER FIFTEEN

PROTECTION AGAINST PREMATURE DEATH

One of the primary obstacles to meeting financial objectives is premature death. Life insurance is therefore an important purchase for anyone concerned about the financial security of his family. The question of life insurance raises several important problems. Should you buy life insurance? If so, how much insurance should you buy? What type of policy should be purchased? Which riders should be included in the policy? And after the contract is in force, how can the policy options be used most effectively? How does a person compare the policies and costs of various insurance companies? And how does a person select the agent and company with whom he wants to do business? These are the important, fundamental problems faced by every life insurance purchaser, and they are the questions that are considered in this chapter.

REASONS FOR BUYING LIFE INSURANCE

CLEANUP FUND

There are several valid reasons why a person may need to own life insurance. Life insurance provides a fund to meet the expenses that result from a person's death and to liquidate outstanding financial obligations. This fund is usually called a "cleanup" fund, but because this name is not very appealing, the fund has also been called the "last illness and expense fund," the "estate clearance fund," or some similar designation.

The cleanup fund provides money to pay such expenses as: (1) hospital, doctor's, and nurses' bills (these may be important because often a person incurs substantial expenses in a hospital before he dies), (2) burial expenses, which usually include funeral costs and a cemetery plot, (3) unpaid debts, including household bills, installment accounts and personal loans, and (4) expenses of estate administration. These may include such items as legal fees, court costs, and taxes. Even a person who has few assets probably will have some of these estate administration expenses. There will be more, of course, for a person with greater assets.

Some of the expenses that can be covered by a cleanup fund may be important to some people and completely unimportant to others. Consider the case of a college student, for example. A typical student would have expenses for funeral costs and may have an unpaid debt on his car. If so, this student may have a need for life insurance to cover these expenses. It is important to note that almost everyone has a need for a cleanup fund, and this need continues for as long as the person is alive.

FAMILY PROTECTION

The most important reason most people buy life insurance is to protect their families against financial loss. When the head of a family dies, his dependents suffer a loss that can be measured by the amount of earnings that would have been given to them if he had not died. Since most family heads devote a large portion of their income to their family, this loss of future income is substantial.

Consider the case of a young couple with two children—a daughter three years old and a son who is two. If the husband dies, the children will be deprived of the income they would have received until they are self-supporting. The widow is likely to have financial difficulties for the remainder of her life. Unless the wife has substantial wealth, there are usually only three ways she can alleviate her financial problems:
1. Social security (but even if her husband was covered by social security, the benefits are likely to be small)
2. Employment (but employment opportunities may be limited to a widow who has not been working)
3. Remarriage

The result is, in many cases, a financial struggle that puts serious problems and strains on the remaining family. Most men who establish a family assume voluntarily the financial responsibilities for the support of their wife and children. A person who wants to provide financial security for his family after his death needs life insurance.

INSURANCE ON WIVES AND CHILDREN

When the head of a family wishes to buy life insurance to protect his dependents, he buys life insurance on his own life. But is there a need to purchase life insurance on the life of the wife to protect the husband and children? And is there a need to insure the children's lives to protect the husband and wife?

What types of monetary loss would the family suffer if the wife dies? If the wife had been working, her death would cause a loss of income to the family. But even if she were not employed, a person would have to be hired to care for children, and the cost of hiring such a person would be an added expense. Also, income taxes would probably be higher because the husband could no longer take advantage of the extra exemption and the split income feature of the income tax law. And, of course, the death of a wife would incur expenses for her last illness and funeral. These are several possible reasons why a person might want to insure the life of his wife.[1]

Insurance on the lives of children usually cannot be justified as well as insurance on the life of a wife. There is always a need for a cleanup fund, of course, but this could justify only a small amount of life insurance. The reason usually given to justify life insurance on children is that it reduces the annual cost of the coverage. In other words, a $10,000 life insurance policy started at age ten, for example, might require an annual premium of $89.30; if the insurance is not taken until the person is 25 years old, the insurance would cost about $137.48 each year. The annual premium for an ordinary life policy stays the same after the policy is taken out, but the premium is higher the longer a person waits to start his insurance program. This is not a very valid argument for buying insurance at an early age. Even though the premium is lower when insurance is purchased at a younger age, the total premiums paid to the insurance company will be greater. This is only natural since insurance protection is purchased for more years when the coverage is purchased at a young age.

Very often the argument is made that insurance on the lives of children is justified if the purpose of the plan is to provide an educational fund. A father who has a young son, for example, can guarantee that funds will be available for his son's college education if he buys an endowment policy at age 18 on the life of his son. Suppose the father buys this type of policy for his son with a face amount of $5,000. When the son reaches age 18, the policy will "mature" and pay $5,000. If the father dies before his son reaches age 18, the policy will be kept in force until maturity without any premium payments after the father dies. This, then, is a very appealing policy to many young fathers. As long as the father continues to make premium payments if he is alive, the son can be guaranteed that he will have $5,000 for his college education. And if the father dies before his son reaches college age, the funds will still be provided.

A father's motive in such a case is admirable, but this method is dangerous. Unless there is already an adequate amount of life insurance on the life of the father, it is unwise to place insurance on a child's life. Of what benefit is a college educational fund if the father dies and the

---

[1] The loss of the marital deduction might be another reason for buying life insurance on the life of a wife. This subject is covered in Chapter Eighteen.

family does not have enough money while the children are young? A much better method of providing money for a child's education is to purchase insurance on the life of the father. Then, if the father dies, funds will be provided for college through the insurance proceeds. If, on the other hand, the father lives, he can provide money for college through other sources. The basic reason this is a more economical method of providing educational funds is that an endowment policy on the life of a child is very expensive. This means a father can probably afford only a small amount of insurance. But if he places a less expensive type of insurance on his own life, he can afford to purchase much more insurance.

We must conclude, therefore, that life insurance should not be placed on children's lives for educational purposes unless the father already has an adequate amount of insurance on his own life. This is, unfortunately, rarely the case.

PROTECTION OF INSURABILITY

Although some of the arguments in favor of placing life insurance on the lives of young people are not very valid, there is one extremely important reason why young people should consider buying life insurance. The problem is this: a young person ordinarily is healthy and would have no trouble buying life insurance. As a person gets older, however, health problems may develop. If a person develops a serious health problem, he may be unable to purchase life insurance. The life insurance company, in other words, may consider an unhealthy person to be uninsurable. Uninsurability, therefore, is a potential problem that becomes more and more likely as a person gets older.

Life insurance companies have developed several ways a person may handle the insurability problem. The most popular method is an option that permits a policyholder, at stated intervals, to purchase additional amounts of insurance without evidence of insurability. This option is given names (such as the "guaranteed purchase option" or the "guaranteed insurability option"), and the details of the plan differ among the various life insurance companies. In general, the option allows the policyholder to buy insurance up to a certain amount every three or five years until he reaches a certain age. The option protects the policyholder's insurability because the life insurance company cannot refuse to issue the additional policies if the insured applies, regardless of the policyholder's health.

For example, a person who is 20 years old could purchase a $10,000 life insurance policy and pay a small extra premium to add the guaranteed purchase option to the contract. Suppose the option allows the policyholder to buy additional insurance every five years until he is 45 years old. The policyholder could buy an additional $10,000 insurance when he is 25, 30, 35, 40, and 45 years of age. He would be able to purchase a total of $60,000 insurance even if he has developed a serious health problem and would not be considered insurable. When the specified purchase dates arrive, he may simply choose not to exercise his purchase option.

The important point to remember about the guaranteed purchase option is that it is one of the best ways a young person can guard against losing his insurability. The only way he can get the guaranteed purchase option, however, is to buy a policy with this option attached. This, then, is a very strong argument for a young person to buy life insurance.

SAVINGS

Another reason for buying life insurance is to accumulate savings. Most types of life insurance policies build up a cash value, which is (in some ways) similar to saving money in a bank. The cash value accumulated in a life insurance policy can be viewed as an emergency fund that can be used while the policyholder is still alive. The policyholder, however, can use the cash value for any purpose he desires.[2]

In summary, there are four basic needs for life insurance: (1) provision for a cleanup fund, (2) protection of the family, (3) preservation of a person's insurability, and (4) savings. Life insurance can also be used to provide funds for education, but life insurance for this purpose is not a basic need of most families. Some of these reasons are important to some people, but they may not be valid reasons for everyone.

DETERMINING THE AMOUNT OF LIFE INSURANCE TO BUY

After a person decides he needs life insurance, the immediate problem is how much life insurance should be purchased. It would be nice if there were an easy rule that would give an accurate answer to this important question, but unfortunately the problem is not that simple. There are several methods, however, that are used to determine how much life insurance a person should have.

THE HUMAN LIFE VALUE APPROACH

We have seen that the most important reason why people buy life insurance is to protect their families against financial losses. The earning power of a husband has a definite monetary value to his family, and in fact, the future earning ability of a person is almost always a family's most valuable asset.

The amount of the financial loss that a family suffers when the breadwinner dies may be estimated without much difficulty. Consider this example: Mr. A is 25 years old and has a wife and two children. He

---

[2] The savings feature of some life insurance policies is treated in more detail later in the chapter.

earns $6,000 a year now, but he expects his income to increase over the years. On the average, he expects his income to be $10,000 a year from now until he retires at age 65. How much is Mr. A worth financially to his family?

Are the future earnings of Mr. A worth $400,000 (that is, $10,000 a year for 40 years) to his family? There are two primary reasons why Mr. A is worth less than $400,000 to his family. First, Mr. A does not allocate his entire income to his family. He spends a portion of his income on taxes, life insurance premiums, and other self-maintenance expenses (such as personal clothing, transportation, and food). His family, therefore, actually receives only a portion of his net income. If Mr. A assumes that he spends $3,000 of his annual income on himself and devotes the remainder to his family, his family would suffer a financial loss of only $7,000 each year (on the average).

Mr. A is not worth $280,000 ($7,000 a year for 40 years) to his family, however, because there is a difference between $280,000 now and $7,000 a year for 40 years. The difference is caused by interest. In other words, it is better to have $280,000 in cash at the present time than $7,000 a year for 40 years because a person with $280,000 could earn interest on the money. How much money would a person have to have now to be equivalent to $7,000 a year for 40 years? If a person assumes 5 percent interest, reference to a present value table shows that $120,120 is needed to produce $7,000 a year for 40 years. In other words, if a person had $120,120 at the present time and could invest the money at 5 percent, he could pay $7,000 a year and his funds would be completely exhausted at the end of 40 years. At 5 percent, $7,000 a year for 40 years is equivalent to $120,120 now. Table 15–1 shows the present value of a stream of income for different periods of time at various rates of interest.

Table 15–1 Present Value of 1 Per Year

	Rate		
Years	**2½%**	**5%**	**8%**
1	.98	.95	.93
5	4.65	4.33	3.99
15	12.38	10.38	8.56
25	18.42	14.09	10.67
35	23.15	16.37	11.65
40	25.10	17.16	11.92
45	26.83	17.77	12.11
50	28.36	18.26	12.23

The present value of the income a person devotes to his family is often called that person's "human life value." When is a person's human life value at its peak? Look at Table 15–2 and compare the human life values of individuals at different ages with the same average annual earnings. At age 20, a person who expects to earn $10,000 is worth $118,472 to his family, but a person who is 30 years old earning the same amount is worth only $109,139. While it is true that many people will increase their annual earnings up to retirement, this only means they have a shorter period of earnings. The human life value concept is based on average earnings over a person's entire working life, and as a person grows older, he has a shorter period of income. Therefore, the human life value decreases for an individual over time. This means that the financial loss to a family is greatest at a time when a person is least able financially to purchase life insurance—that is, when he is young. The problem may not be so grave as it seems, however, because the human life value is not necessarily the amount of life insurance a person should own. Most young people who have worked a while are covered under social security, and group life insurance also provides protection for many employees. Part of the human life value, therefore, is protected in these ways.

Table 15–2 Human Life Value

Income	Age 20	Age 30	Age 40	Age 50
$ 5,000	$ 59,227	$ 54,561	$ 46,962	$ 34,597
7,500	88,850	81,850	70,450	51,900
10,000	118,472	109,139	93,938	69,193
15,000	177,700	163,700	140,900	103,800
20,000	236,947	218,261	187,862	138,397

Note: This table assumes two-thirds of the income is devoted to the family, an interest rate of 5 percent, and retirement at age 65.

The human life value is one way to measure the financial loss that will be involved if the head of a family dies, and as such it is a useful idea. However, as a practical matter, the concept is rather theoretical and requires several assumptions that may prove to be incorrect. The human life value concept, therefore, is only a guideline and it offers limited help in selecting the amount of insurance a person should buy.

THE NEEDS APPROACH

The needs approach is more practical, and therefore, a more commonly used method of determining the amount of life insurance a person should own. The needs approach asks the question, "How much money would be needed for various purposes if the head of the family dies?" Although families are different, there is a fairly common set of needs that may arise after death.

The needs approach to determining the amount of life insurance a person should own is made up of three basic steps: (1) determine the financial needs that would arise if the person died; (2) determine the financial resources that would be available at the present time to meet the needs that have been established (in this step it is important to recognize group life insurance and social security benefits); (3) subtract the present financial resources from the needs that have been established by the insured. The basic idea of the needs approach is simple, but when applied, a person must translate lump sum dollar amounts into income over a period of time. This is not easy for most laymen, but it is a simple problem for a competent life insurance agent.

The Cleanup Fund.   As we have seen, the cleanup fund is the first need for life insurance. The *amount* of this need, however, is hard to estimate because it is not the same for all people and changes from time to time.

If a person has adequate health insurance, the need for life insurance to pay last illness expenses may not be very important. Also, the amount of money needed to pay estate taxes and legal fees may not be very great if a person does not have substantial wealth. Burial expenses and unpaid debts will make up the bulk of the cleanup fund, and these can be estimated fairly accurately.

Dependency Period Income.   Another specific need for life insurance is a fund to provide an income to the family until the children, if any, are capable of supporting themselves. The purpose of this fund is to provide enough income to keep the family together so the widow can care for her children.

The amount of life insurance for this purpose depends on the amount of income desired and the time it will take for the children to become self-supporting. For example, a father with a 13-year-old son and a 9-year-old daughter and who assumes his children will be self-supporting at age 18, may want to provide income to both of them for five years and only his daughter for an additional four years.

If it is impossible to purchase enough insurance to replace fully the husband's income (which is normally the case), the husband will have to determine the reduced amount of income he wishes to provide. Most financial advisers agree that the family's income should not be reduced drastically. Therefore, if a substantial decrease in family income will be required, it may be better to reduce the income in steps in order to cushion the financial problems. Of course, if the wife is willing to work, the amount of income provided by life insurance can be reduced.

Life Income for the Widow.   Another specific need for life insurance is a fund to provide an income for the widow for the remainder of her life. To determine the amount of life insurance a person should buy, the question is asked, "Do you want to provide an income to your widow, and if so, in what amount?" Generally some amount is made available to the widow for the number of years equal to her life expectancy, starting at the end of the dependency period.[3] Since this is often a long period, the income a husband can provide is usually rather limited (because the premiums for an adequate amount of insurance may be more than the husband believes he can afford). Even though the income may be modest, it may be the difference between a reasonable standard of living and poverty.

Educational Funds.   If a father wants to use life insurance to assure that his children will be able to go to college, the problem is to decide how much the education will cost. This is very difficult to do because the cost of obtaining a college education has been increasing rapidly and the costs vary a great deal among students. The best a person is able to do is to decide whether room and board expenses will be incurred, whether he wants to assure his children an education at an expensive school and estimate the approximate fees that will be charged by the college at the time his children are prepared to start their higher education. This means the amount to be provided in a life insurance education fund is largely a guess, but a person can make better estimates if he investigates the probable expenses.

Mortgage Redemption Fund.   Many families have a sizable mortgage outstanding on their home when the father dies. And this, of course, might be a severe financial burden for a widow and children. If the husband wants his family to continue to occupy the home, he should determine the amount of the mortgage and purchase an appropriate amount of life insurance. Even though the mortgage is reduced as payments are made on the home, the amount needed for this purpose is easy to determine. Most mortgage companies provide forms that show the outstanding balance at any point in time.

Emergency Fund.   Since most families, particularly those without fathers, occasionally need funds for emergencies, an emergency fund might be provided by life insurance. The amount is almost a matter of pure judgment. It depends largely upon the policyholder's opinion of how well his wife will be able to manage her income after his death.

---

[3] In actual practice, the social security "blackout period" is usually recognized. This is the period from the youngest child's eighteenth birthday to the widow's age 60. During this period, social security benefits are discontinued.

In summary, the needs approach requires that a person determine how much is to be provided for specific purposes. Next, a person must determine how well his present resources (social security, life insurance, investments, etc.) will meet his needs. The final step is simply to fill the gap between his needs and present resources. Very often a person starts with generous amounts for his estimated needs and has to revise his figures downward when he learns how much life insurance will cost. The needs approach is a reasonable method, however, because it forces a person to examine his specific needs for life insurance and it requires a person to determine how well his present resources meet his needs.

THE MULTIPLE OF EARNINGS APPROACH

Some people argue that the human life value approach is too theoretical and the needs approach involves too many calculations. These people use a much simpler method, which can be called the multiple of earnings approach.

Using this approach, a person calculates the amount of life insurance he should own by simply multiplying his gross income by some multiple, such as two, three, or five. For example, suppose a person uses three as his multiple. If he earns $10,000 a year, his answer is $30,000. If he had used five as the multiple, he would decide to own $50,000 of insurance. Notice that this is equivalent to saying that the insured wants to continue his gross income to his family for five years after his death.

Despite the fact that many people use the multiple of earnings approach, there is little justification for it. The only advantage this method has is simplicity. It is very arbitrary and makes little sense. The needs approach is a much better method of determining the amount of life insurance a person should have, and it should be worked out by a competent life insurance agent.

TYPES OF LIFE INSURANCE POLICIES

One of the most important problems encountered by a life insurance purchaser is the type of policy he should buy. There are many types of policies, and they may have very different benefits and costs. The first step in selecting the appropriate policy, therefore, is to understand the types of policies that are available.

TERM INSURANCE POLICIES

Term insurance policies are the simplest of all life insurance contracts. With this type of policy the insurance company promises to pay the face amount of the contract if the insured dies during the period of protection, but if the insured survives the period of protection, the insurance company has absolutely no obligation. The period of protection may be as short as one year, but most term insurance contracts are for 5, 10, or

20 years. Long-term policies, in which protection is given to age 65, for example, are becoming increasingly popular.

Renewability.   What happens when a person buys a term insurance policy and later becomes uninsurable because of poor health, dangerous occupation, or some other reason? The policyholder would be extremely interested in buying another policy when his original contract expired, but unless the contract contains a renewability provision, the insurance company can refuse to renew the contract. The policyholder is then left without protection. This problem can be avoided by paying a little more and purchasing a term insurance policy with a renewable feature. The renewable provision allows the insured to renew the contract if he wishes, and the insurance company cannot require a medical examination or any other evidence of insurability. Even if the policyholder is on his deathbed, the insurance company has a contractual obligation to renew the policy. Thus, the renewable feature has the important function of protecting the insurability of the policyholder.

The renewable provision permits the policyholder to renew the policy for additional periods, usually of the same length of time as the original policy. For example, if a person buys a ten-year renewable term policy, he can replace the initial policy with another ten-year term policy.

Insurance companies are reluctant to renew term insurance policies at advanced ages because there is a strong tendency for healthy policyholders to drop their coverage and those in poor health to continue their protection. Healthy policyholders tend to drop their insurance because the premium increases with each renewal. The *scale* of renewal rates is guaranteed in the original contract and cannot be changed, but the renewal premium is based on the attained age of the insured at the time of renewal. For example, with a ten-year term policy purchased at age 20, the insured pays the same premium each year during his twenties, but if he renews for another ten years, his premium increases to the amount required at age 30. For this reason, renewal term insurance is sometimes said to have a "step rate premium." If healthy policyholders drop out of the plan and sick policyholders continue their insurance, the mortality rates may be higher than the insurance company anticipates. This is called adverse selection, and it is the reason life insurance companies limit the renewable feature. All companies will either limit the number of times the policy may be renewed or stipulate an age beyond which the policy cannot be renewed. Term policies are seldom renewable past age 60 or 65.

Convertibility.   Another important option that is available with term policies is the conversion feature. It is similar, in many respects, to the renewable clause.

The conversion privilege allows a policyholder to exchange his term policy for another plan of insurance without providing any evidence of insurability. The basic function of both the renewable feature and the conversion provision is the same—protection of the insured's insurability, The conversion feature is more effective, however, because it allows a policyholder to obtain permanent protection. That is, conversion permits a policyholder to change to another type of contract that provides protection for the entire life of the insured no matter how long he may live. The renewable feature, as we have seen, stops coverage at age 60 or 65.

A policyholder may use either the attained age method or the original age method to convert a term insurance policy. The simplest (and most common) method is to convert on an attained age basis. The premium rate and the policy form of the new contract will be the same as those being used by the insurance company at the date of the conversion. The original age method is retroactive; the premium rate and the policy form of the new policy will be those that were used when the policyholder obtained the original contract. With this method, the policyholder has the advantages of the lower premium (lower than the premium would be on an attained age basis) and possibly more favorable contract terms. However, the policyholder will be required to pay a lump sum to the insurance company to place the insurance company in the same position it would have been in if the new policy had been obtained originally. Usually the insured has to pay the difference in the premiums paid on the term policy and those that would have been paid on the new contract, plus interest on the difference. The policyholder's selection of the method of converting depends on several factors, but the health of the insured and the amount of the required payment for the original age conversion are always important.

Policyholders who are in poor health are more likely to convert and preserve their protection than those who are healthy. Therefore, insurance companies impose limitations on the conversion option to guard against adverse selection. Insurance companies usually require policyholders to make the decision to convert several years before the expiration of the policy period. For example, the option may be exercised during the first four years in a five-year policy, and the first 12 years in a 15-year policy.

WHOLE LIFE INSURANCE POLICIES

Whole life insurance, as the name implies, is a plan of insurance that is intended to provide protection for the entire life of the insured, no matter how long he lives. Unlike the temporary protection of term insurance, a whole life policy promises to pay the face amount when the insured dies and not *if* the insured dies within a certain period.

When a person buys a whole life policy, the annual premium he pays is determined by his present age and the premium remains the same each year. This is called the level premium concept, and although it is a simple idea, it is one of the most important concepts in life insurance. Figure 15–1 is an illustration of the level premium concept.

Figure 15–1   Illustration of the Level Premium Technique

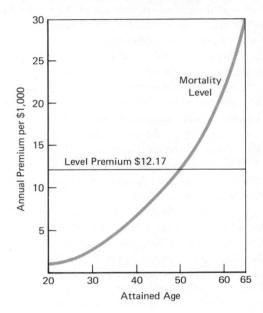

Figure 15–1 shows that the mortality rate increases rapidly as a person gets older, but the premium that is paid by a whole life policyholder remains level. At age 60, however, a policyholder who bought the policy at age 20 would still be paying $12.17 but the mortality rate is now higher. The effect of leveling the premiums is to require premium payments that are more than the amount needed for an insurance company to meet mortality costs in the early policy years, but the premiums in the later policy years will be insufficient to pay death claims. In Figure 15–1, the premium charged until about age 49 (the 29th policy year) is more than is needed for current mortality costs, but the premiums collected by the insurance company will not pay the death claims that arise. Policies issued at any age may be based on the level premium technique. Of course, policies issued at higher ages require higher level premiums, but in all cases the level premium is greater than the cost of mortality in the first *policy years.*

The "overcharge" in the level premium technique does not imply that policyholders are paying more than they should pay for their insurance. The "excessive" portion of the premiums in the early policy years creates assets that are used by an insurace company to provide benefits in the later policy years when the level premium is no longer sufficient to pay current mortality costs. In other words, insurance companies accumulate assets in the early policy years to meet liabilities from mortality claims that are more frequent in the late policy years. This is one of the major reasons why life insurance companies accumulate such a tremendous volume of assets. The assets, of course, are channeled into investments in order to earn an investment return that can be used to help meet death claims in the later policy years. And of course, the assets of life insurance companies are offset by liabilities of similar size.

From the point of view of a policyholder, the effect of the level premium concept has an important impact on the *structure* of an individual life insurance policy. A whole life policy is composed of two parts: the savings element and the protection element. The savings element arises because of the level premium technique.

Straight Life Policies. A straight life policy (frequently referred to as an ordinary life policy) provides protection for the insured's life and the premiums are calculated so that they are payable as long as the contract is in force. Figure 15–2 illustrates this type of policy. Notice that Figure 15–2 shows that a straight life policy is actually composed of a *decreasing* protection element and an increasing cash value. Where does the cash value come from? It is not an extra benefit that is added to a straight life policy. The cash value is a *result* of the level premium concept. When a policyholder pays level premiums over a long period of time, we have seen that this generates a huge volume of assets. These assets are allocated to individual policyholders in the form of a cash value. In other words, the cash value in a policy is a direct consequence of the level premium technique.

Limited-Payment Life Policies. Like all whole life plans, limited-payment policies provide protection for the insured's life, but the distinguishing characteristic of limited-payment contracts is the limited number of

Figure 15–2 Illustration of a Straight Life Policy (issued at age 20)

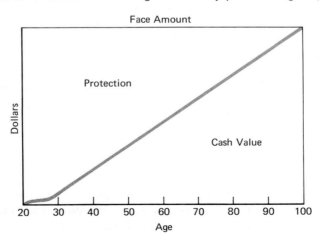

premiums that are required. The contract may require almost any number of payments, but premium payments over 10, 15, and 25 years are most popular. Another way of limiting the number of payments is to state the age to which premiums must be paid. Thus, a 20-year, limited-payment policy issued at age 45 would be identical to a life-paid-up at 65 contract. Ages 60 and 65 are the most common ages at which the premium payments are terminated. It should be apparent that the longer the premium paying period, the more closely it resembles a straight life policy.

Single Premium Policies.   A single premium policy provides lifetime protection that is purchased with only one premium. This type of contract may be regarded as an extreme form of limited-payment insurance.

ENDOWMENT CONTRACTS

An endowment policy is unique in that it agrees to pay the face amount of the contract if the insured dies within the period of protection *or survives* the policy period. Other types of contracts do not pay the full face amount if the insured lives, but an endowment policy *matures* at the end of the policy period and pays the face amount to the policyholder at that time. Endowment insurance, therefore, is used frequently when the policyholder wants to accumulate a principal sum for himself, and protection for beneficiaries is a secondary objective.

The policy period in an endowment contract may be almost any number of years. The period may be 10, 15, 20, 25, or more years, or the policy period may be arranged so that the policy will mature at a certain age. Endowments at age 60 and 65 are common. This means that endowment contracts do not provide protection for the entire life of the insured and should be regarded as temporary protection. Just as term policies may provide long-term protection and they are not regarded as permanent insurance, an endowment contract (even a long-term endowment) cannot be classified as permanent protection. After the policy matures, the insured no longer has insurance protection, although he will have accumulated a principal sum of money.

The premium-paying period usually, but not always, coincides with the policy period. A policy that matures at age 65 usually requires premiums to be paid until that age. But the limited-payment concept may be applied to whole life contracts. An endowment at age 65, for example, might require premium payments for only 20 years.

"SPECIAL" LIFE INSURANCE POLICIES

A great many life insurance companies sell policies that are said to be different, unique, or special in some way. In some cases, insurance agents represent their policies as the only ones of that type that are available.

These policies, because they are often given unusual names and may contain uncommon benefits, may present a considerable amount of confusion for an insurance buyer. In too many cases, it seems that life insurance companies purposely use unique terminology and benefit provisions in order to confuse the buyer and make it difficult to compare the policies and costs.

The Family Income Policy.   One of the most widely accepted special policies is the family income contract. This policy provides that income payments will be made to the beneficiary beginning at the death of the insured and continuing to the end of the specified period. The specified period is normally 20 years in length, but policies with periods of 10, 15, or 25 years are common. Usually, the monthly income is 1 percent of the face value of the policy, but other percentages are available from some companies. In addition to the income benefit, the policy provides that the face of the policy will be payable at the end of the specified period. Only the face amount of the policy is payable if the insured survives that specified period. Many companies have modified the provisions of the family income policy so that the face amount is payable upon the death of the insured, i.e., the beneficiary does not have to wait until the end of the specified period to receive the basic benefit.

A family income policy may appear complex at first glance, but it is actually a simple contract. It is simply a combination of decreasing term insurance and a basic policy, which is usually whole life. The basic policy makes the face amount payable at the end of the specified period, whether the insured dies during or after the period. The income payments are composed of the decreasing term proceeds and interest on the proceeds of the basic policy. Figure 15–3 is an illustration of such a policy.

Figure 15–3   Illustration of a Family Income Policy (issued at age 20)

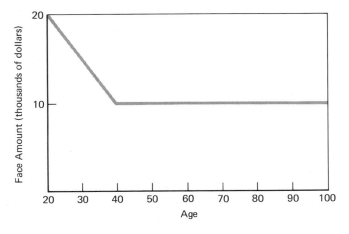

If a policyholder owned the contract illustrated in Figure 15–3 and died soon after the coverage became effective (at age 20), the most common form of the family income policy would pay the beneficiary $100 per month for 20 years and $10,000 when the insured would have been aged 45. If the insured dies at age 35, the beneficiary would receive $100 per month for 10 years and then the face amount would be payable. Only the face amount would be payable if the insured lived past age 45. If the policy makes the face amount payable upon the death of the insured (rather than at the end of the specified period) a larger amount of decreasing term insurance is required. The student should note that a decreasing term rider may be attached to a basic policy to achieve the same effect as a family income policy.

The premium for a family income policy remains level during the specified period but decreases to that amount required for the basic policy when the decreasing term insurance expires. However, premium payments for a decreasing term policy are usually stopped several years before the expiration of the coverage because of the small amounts of protection provided in the last years. Thus, the premiums for a family income policy usually decrease shortly before the term insurance is terminated.

Family Maintenance Policy.   The family maintenance policy is very similar to the family income contract. It is also a combination of term insurance and a basic policy. The family maintenance policy, however, uses level (rather than decreasing) term protection. The use of level term, of course, makes a substantial difference in the basic obligation of the insurance company. In addition to making the face amount payable at the end of the specified period (or at the death of the insured) the policy promises income payments for a period of time equivalent to the specified period. For example, if a 20-year period is specified and the insured dies 19 years after the policy is issued, income payments will be made for 20 years (and not only for the one year remaining in the period). The family maintenance policy is of more value to a policyholder than a family income policy because it makes income payments for the length of the specified period and not for the remaining length of time in the period. This greater benefit is available because the term insurance does not decrease. Figure 15–4 illustrates this type of policy.

Of course, the premium for a family maintenance policy is greater than the premium for a family income policy. Only the face amount of the policy is payable if the insured dies after the specified period, and the level term insurance protection has expired. Except for these differences the family income and family maintenance policies are identical. Since the premium decreases after (or shortly before) the period expires, the same effect can be obtained by obtaining a term insurance rider, and interest on the face supplements the income payments if the death proceeds are not payable until the end of the specified period.

Figure 15–4 Illustration of a Family Maintenance Policy (issued at age 20)

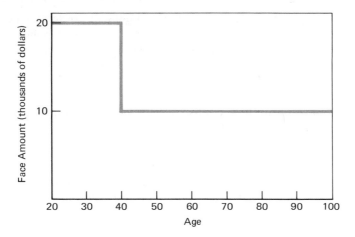

Multiple Protection Policy. Some policies agree to pay twice or three times the face amount if the insured dies within a stated period, but only the face amount is payable if the insured does not die within the period. These policies are only combinations of a basic policy and level term insurance. The similarity to a family maintenance policy should be obvious. The only differences between the two are: (1) a multiple protection policy provides an even multiple of the face amount whereas the total protection in a family maintenance policy would only be an even multiple of the face by coincidence, and (2) the family maintenance policy automatically provides income payments to the beneficiary without a specific election by the policyholder.

The Family Policy. An extremely popular policy is one that is usually called the "family policy" or "family plan." This policy provides insurance on all members of the family, with automatic coverage on children born or adopted after the policy is issued. The policy is sold in "units of coverage"—usually 5,1,1. This means the husband has $5,000 of insurance, and the wife and all the children have $1,000 of insurance for each unit purchased. If a husband bought five units, for example, he would have $25,000 of insurance and all the other family members would each be covered for $5,000. In many cases some type of guaranteed insurability option is provided with the insurance on the lives of the children when this policy is purchased.

Usually the coverage on the husband's life is straight life insurance; the protection on the wife may be whole life insurance, but often it is term insurance until the husband reaches age 65; the insurance on the children is almost always term insurance, usually to age 18, 21, or 25.

There are a great many other "special" policies. The most important types have been described, however, and it is possible for several conclusions to be drawn. A life insurance purchaser should recognize that all "special" policies are nothing more than combinations of term, whole life, or endowment insurance. There is no magic in special policies. Very often a person can achieve the same results by buying a straight life policy and also purchasing a term insurance policy.

INDUSTRIAL LIFE INSURANCE

Industrial life insurance is a misnomer; it is not anymore related to industry than other forms of insurance. Nevertheless, the name "industrial" has been continued for a long time.

Industrial insurance is characterized by:

1. Small face amounts. The face amount is usually $1,000 or less.
2. Frequent premium payments. Premiums are paid either on a weekly or monthly basis.
3. Personal collection of premiums. The insurance agent collects the premium at the policyholder's home or place of business.
4. Insurance is quoted in cents. In other words, the rate book shows the amount of insurance that can be purchased with weekly (or monthly) premiums of various amounts. For example, a 25-cent policy may buy $325 of insurance for a husband who is 30 years old.
5. Medical examinations are not usually required. This is not a unique characteristic of industrial insurance because most companies sell insurance in limited amounts without a medical examination. The company, however, will require evidence of insurability by questions on the application.

GROUP LIFE INSURANCE

Group life insurance, as the name implies, is issued on a group of people. In most cases, the group insured is a group of employees, but group insurance has also been issued to other groups such as clubs, associations, debtors, and labor unions. Although group insurance protects the members of the group, a master policy is issued to the employer and the employees receive certificates.

CHOOSING THE APPROPRIATE TYPE OF COVERAGE

How does a person decide which type or types of life insurance he should own? The decision with regard to industrial and group life insurance is usually easy. The decision to choose term, whole life, or endowment is fairly difficult.

INDUSTRIAL INSURANCE

Industrial insurance is an unwise purchase for those who can afford other types of coverage because industrial insurance is very expensive in relation to its benefits. In other words, the *rate* (that is, the cost per $1,000 of coverage) is high. Industrial insurance is expensive because it is subject to a high rate of mortality and expenses. The mortality rate is higher for people who buy industrial insurance because these people, as a group, generally work in more hazardous and less healthful occupations, follow poor diets, live in less sanitary environments, and receive inadequate medical attention. Life insurance companies have found the mortality rate among industrial policyholders to be higher than the mortality rate of other policyholders, and therefore, insurance companies use special mortality tables for industrial insurance. Expenses are higher on industrial insurance primarily due to the costs that are incurred in personally collecting premiums. For families who cannot pay the higher premiums that are charged for the other types of insurance, industrial insurance may be the only type of insurance that is financially feasible. However, persons who can afford larger amounts of insurance should never purchase industrial insurance.

GROUP INSURANCE

Group life insurance is almost always a wise purchase because the cost of the coverage to the individual is low. As a matter of fact, low cost is one of the outstanding characteristics of group life insurance.

Why is the cost of group insurance low? First, group insurance plans are either contributory or noncontributory. A contributory plan is one in which the employer and employee share the cost. A noncontributory plan is paid entirely by the employer. Therefore, an employee never pays the full cost of the coverage.

Another reason why the cost of group life insurance is low is that it uses economical methods. The life insurance company's selling expenses are lower because the commission rates paid to salesmen are lower than they would be on individual policies. The company's underwriting expenses are lower because they underwrite the group rather than the individual. This means there are no medical examinations for group life insurance. If the group is acceptable to the insurance company, individuals are covered without any evidence of insurability. Thus, group insurance makes insurance available to some people who otherwise would not be able to receive coverage.

Benefits are determined automatically in group insurance, according to earnings, position, length of service, or some combination of these. For example, a person's amount of group life insurance may be twice his annual salary. Or supervisors may get $5,000, assistant managers $7,500, and managers $10,000. In other words, the insurance company requires that the benefits in a group life insurance plan be determined automatically. An individual does not choose the amount of benefits he receives. Otherwise, unhealthy employees would tend to choose a high amount of insurance but healthy employees would tend to choose low face amounts. This feature of group insurance is the basis for the criticism that the amount of insurance available to individual employees is limited, sometimes to rather low amounts.

Another criticism of group life insurance is that it usually accumulates no cash values for employees. Most group life insurance is term insurance, which has no cash value. This means an employee will have protection while he is employed, but when he retires, his protection expires and he has no cash value to help finance his retirement.

Despite the criticisms made against group life insurance, an individual cannot find a better method of obtaining life insurance protection. A person should realize, however, that the amount of insurance he can obtain is limited and he probably will have no coverage after he retires.

THE DECISION AMONG TERM, WHOLE LIFE, AND ENDOWMENT POLICIES

The choice among term, whole life, and endowment insurance is difficult for most people. Nevertheless, this decision is crucial to the planning of an insurance program. Basically, the decision should be made by analyzing the following:

1. The length of time protection is needed
2. The length of time over which premiums should be paid
3. The attitude an individual holds toward the cash value element in most policies

In theory, a person should only have to make a decision on the basis of the first two factors. This is because the only differences among term, whole life, and endowment policies are the periods of protection and the premium-paying period. For example, suppose a person decides that he wants life insurance protection for the rest of his life (no matter how long he may live) and he wants to pay premiums for the remainder of his life. The only policy that will meet these requirements is a straight life policy. Or suppose he wants protection for his entire life but wants to pay premiums only until he is 65. This would indicate a limited payment policy—one that is paid up at age 65. As another example, suppose a person wants protection for only ten years. In this case, term insurance would be appropriate.

Figure 15–5 can be helpful in comparing the important differences among the various types of policies. The figure is useful because it shows the build-up of cash values in the various policies; the annual premium rates of the different contracts may be inferred from the figure. Consider first the whole life plans illustrated in the figure. In the straight life policy (AB), the limited-payment policies (AC and AD), and the single premium policy (FB), the basic promise of the insurer is exactly the same—to pay the face amount of the contract when the insured dies (or reaches age 100). Since the fundamental promise is the same in the three policies, the premiums paid by the policyholders must be mathematically equivalent to each other. In other words, the insurance company should

Figure 15–5   Comparison of Life Insurance Policies (issued at age 20)

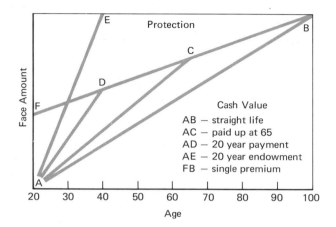

not prefer one premium-payment method over another. If policyholders receive the same basic promise from the insurer, it follows that the annual premium will be lower if the cost of the insurance is spread over a longer period. The annual premium for the straight life policy is the lowest of the three because the cost is paid over a longer period. The single premium contract has the highest annual premium because the premium paying period is the shortest.

Table 15–3 shows the annual premiums for the various types of policies. The table demonstrates the validity of the previous statement: the shorter the premium-paying period, the higher the annual premium for a given type of policy.

Table 15–3   Comparison of Premiums ($10,000 policy issued at age 20)

Type of Policy	Annual Premium
Straight Life	$113.30
Life Paid Up at Age 65	131.50
20-Year Payment	203.70
20-Year Endowment	436.80

The size of the annual premium has a significant effect upon the cash values of the policies. If the premium is paid over the entire life of the insured and therefore is relatively low, the "overcharge" that results from the level premium technique in the early policy years will clearly be less than if the premiums were higher. This explains why the cash values in a straight life policy are lower than those in other whole life contracts. Since the number of premiums is limited in a limited-payment policy they must be higher than the annual premiums required for a straight life policy. The higher premiums of the limited-payment contract necessarily will generate cash values that are higher than they would be in a straight life policy. Observe that the cash value of the limited-payment policy continues to increase after the premium paying period. This is because the insurance company will continue to earn interest on the savings element even after premiums are discontinued.

Line AE in Figure 15–5 illustrates the cash values of a 20-year endowment contract. Because the insurance company must pay the face amount of the policy to the policyholder when the contract matures, the cash values must accumulate to the face amount in 20 years. Of course, the portion of the figure that lies to the right of point E (age 40) does not pertain to the endowment policy because the policy will terminate at that time. Although the premium-paying period for the endowment policy is the same as that for the limited-payment contract, the premiums of the endowment must be higher because the cash value of the policy must equal the face amount of the policy at the end of the premium-paying period. As previously noted, this is not true for the limited-payment contract because interest will be earned after all premiums have been paid. Endowment contracts, then, place a heavy emphasis upon the savings element of the contract.

Analysis of the Savings Element. The decision to buy term, whole life, or endowment is complicated by the fact that the cash value in a policy might be viewed as a good investment by some people and a poor investment by others.

Since a life insurance policy that uses level premiums over a long period necessarily makes an investor of the policyholder, it is important to analyze the investment attributes of a life insurance policy. The characteristics most often considered are safety of principal, liquidity, and yield, but other factors may be important in particular cases.

(1) Safety of principal. An investor has a high degree of safety if the investor can be relatively certain that the principal sum he has invested will be returned to him (or his beneficiaries). An investment in life insurance certainly is extremely safe. In fact, historically, there has been no type of private financial institution or business organization that has equaled the solvency record of life insurance companies. One frequently quoted study found that policyholders lost less than one-tenth of 1 percent of their investment during the worst years of the Depression in the 1930's.[4]

---

[4] S. S. Huebner and David McCahan, *Life Insurance as an Investment* (New York: Appleton-Century-Crofts, Inc., 1933).

Three major reasons account for this remarkable safety record. First, the volume of assets in many companies is tremendous, by almost any standards, and therefore life insurers strive to obtain competent investment personnel. Many life insurance companies have large, well-equipped investment departments. Secondly, life insurance companies generally place their funds in rather conservative, safe investments. Table 15–4 shows the volume of assets held by insurance companies and the relative importance of each of the major types of investments.

Table 15–4 shows that the preponderance of life insurance company investments are in bonds and mortgages, and a relatively small portion in the form of more speculative assets. Of course the relative proportions of the investments change over time. At the end of World War II, U.S. government bonds accounted for almost one-half of the assets, but in recent years less than 5 percent of the funds are in this type of security.

Diversification is another major reason for the safety record of the industry. Several methods of diversification are possible and the insurance industry uses all of them. Life insurance companies place their funds into many types of industries. For example, investments are made in the railroad, chemical, automobile, agriculture, steel, and construction industries —to name only a few. Thus, an adverse experience in one particular industry will have only minor effects upon the entire investment portfolio. This is diversification by type of industry. Another method of diversification is obtained by spreading investments over a wide geographical territory. This restricts losses that might otherwise occur if one region of the country suffered an economic recession and investments were concentrated in that area. If investments in Canada are excluded, only a small proportion of life insurance company funds are allocated to foreign securities. Investments in countries other than Canada generally do not meet the high standard of safety required by the life insurance

Table 15–4 Assets of U.S. Life Insurance Companies

Type	Amount (000,000 omitted)	Percentage of Total
Bonds	$81,733	41.5
Mortgages	72,027	36.5
Stocks	13,707	7.0
Policy Loans	13,825	7.0
Real Estate	5,912	3.0
Miscellaneous	9,964	5.0

Source: Institute of Life Insurance, *Life Insurance Fact Book*, 1970, p. 70.

companies. Diversification of investments over time is also employed by life insurers. It is possible to diversify by both the time of purchase and the date of maturity. Securities are purchased so that the maturity dates will be spread over time. If maturities were not spread over time, insurance companies might obtain funds when investment conditions were unfavorable. Spreading the maturity dates increases the regularity of their income. Because of the persistent excess of current income over current disbursements, insurers are seldom forced to liquidate investments to meet obligations. Even during the depths of the Great Depression, few companies had cash needs that could not be satisfied by current premiums and interest income. This regularity enables insurance companies to take full advantage of the most favorable security prices. A final major method of diversification is diversification by size. If a policyholder has $10,000 invested in life insurance and the insurance company has 100,000 different investments, the policyholder has, in effect, ten cents invested in each of the investment accounts. Therefore, the sheer number of investments provides a spreading effect. With these major methods of diversification, a policyholder obtains a degree of diversification that is impossible for an individual investor to achieve.

(*2*) *Liquidity.*   Liquidity (the ability to quickly convert an investment into cash with little or no loss of principal) is an important consideration for an investor. A life insurance policyholder usually cannot receive so much from his policy as he has paid to the company. But this is because a portion of each premium goes into the protection element and therefore is not invested. Liquidity, of course, is only concerned with the investment characteristics of the savings element in a policy.

The cash surrender value (or cash value) of a policy is aptly named because a policyholder has a legal right to demand the savings element of his policy (subject to some conditions) and the insurance company must immediately pay this value to the policyholder. The cash surrender provision, then, is a major source of liquidity.[5]

Liquidity is also provided by the policy loan provision. This provision enables a policyholder to borrow an amount up to his cash value at any time by simply requesting a policy loan. The loan bears interest at the rate stipulated and guaranteed in the policy. Most of the large companies charge 5 percent and smaller companies usually charge about 6 percent. Since these are true annual rates of interest, the interest charge is quite reasonable.

A policy loan is a convenient source of funds because the loan can remain unpaid at the discretion of the policyholder. There is no repayment period, and an insurance company cannot force repayment. If the loan is outstanding when the insured dies or the policy is surrendered, the loan (with accrued interest, if any) is deducted from the amount payable. An

---

[5] The other options that provide liquidity are treated in the following pages.

important advantage of the policy loan provision is that it allows a policyholder to obtain part or all of his cash value and permits him to continue his insurance protection.

Only one factor detracts from the otherwise perfect liquidity of the life insurance investment. As a result of Depression experiences, life insurance companies include a *delay* clause in the policy. This provision gives the company the right to postpone the payment of the cash value (for policy loans or cash surrenders) for a period up to six months. The purpose of this clause is to forestall the possibility of excessive cash drains and forced liquidation on losses upon life insurers. The provision is mandatory in many states because it guards against losses that might otherwise be borne by policyholders who do not surrender their policies.

The delay clause cannot be regarded as a major obstruction to liquidity because in actual practice the number of companies that have exercised the provision has been extremely small. Because it would tend to encourage a "run" on cash values, insurers would invoke the clause only under the most trying financial circumstances.

(*3*) *Investment return.* One might think that the percentage rate of return that a policyholder obtains from his life insurance contract would be rather easy to determine. The truth is that it is extremely difficult to ascertain the rate of return a policyholder receives from a life insurance policy.

In calculating the investment return from life insurance, laymen frequently fail to make a distinction between the *minimum guaranteed* yield and the actual interest rate the policyholder obtains. When a life insurance company computes cash values for its policies, the companies assume a certain rate of interest will be earned, and these cash values are guaranteed to accumulate at the rate set forth in the contract. The entire financial resources of the company stand behind this guarantee. This implicitly guarantees the rate of interest used in the cash value calculation. The interest rate assumed in the calculation of cash values usually is rather conservative, since the company is committed to earn at least this rate over a long period of time. Most life insurance policies are participating, that is, they return dividends to policyholders. If the company earns a higher rate than it had assumed, the excess interest earnings may be returned to policyholders through dividends. Even though dividends are not guaranteed, the actual rate obtained by a policyholder usually is greater than the minimum rate assumed and guaranteed in cash value calculations.[6]

Another common error made by laymen in determining the investment return is the assumption that the entire premium is invested. A portion of

---

[6] For nonparticipating policies (i.e., those that do not pay dividends to policyowners) the interest assumption will not be as conservative and it may be very close to the actual rate the policyholder obtains.

each premium is used to pay current mortality costs and is not available for investment. That is, only the "overcharge" inherent in the level premium system goes into the savings element of a policy. A policy-holder, in other words, should regard the amount invested as the premium (less dividends, if any) minus the cost of insurance.

A theoretically correct approach to the yield calculation problem is not difficult to comprehend, but it requires laborious calculations (or the use of electronic computing equipment) to arrive at practical results. This approach involves the determination of the interest rate that would be necessary to compound the difference between the premium and the cost of insurance to an amount equal to the cash surrender value at the end of a certain period of time. Using this technique, an individual would have to select a time period over which the investment return is to be determined, a term insurance rate for each age, and the amount of protection required each year. The amount of protection needed each year would be the difference between the cash value and the face amount of the policy.

To determine the amount considered to be invested each year, the cost of insurance (the term insurance rate times the amount of protection required at each age) should be deducted from each annual premium (less the dividend, if any, paid at the end of the preceding year). The interest rate at which the remainder equals the cash value at the end of a certain time is the rate the policy owner has received.

Albert Linton, a noted actuary, calculated the yield that is attributed to straight life policies issued at various ages at the end of 20 years. These calculations show a return of 4.8 percent for policies issued at age 25.[7] Of course, a wide range of yields could be obtained, depending upon the assumptions employed in the calculation. The most important variables that influence the yield are the premium, cash values, dividends, the term insurance rate that is used to determine the cost of protection, and the time period over which the yield is measured. The assumptions employed by Linton, however, are considered fairly representative of the investment return that could be attributed to the policies of many life insurance companies during 1963. During the period of higher interest since that time, it would be reasonable to assume higher interest rates are actually being earned by policy owners.

The interest return on life insurance becomes more impressive when one realizes that the cash value accumulations in a life insurance policy are not currently taxable to a policyholder. This means a person in the 30 percent tax bracket would have to earn 6.86 percent on an investment that involves a current income tax liability in order to have a net return

---

[7] See Albert Linton, "Life Insurance as an Investment," in Davis W. Gregg, ed., *Life and Health Insurance Handbook,* 2nd edition (Homewood, Illinois: Richard D. Irwin, Inc., 1964), p. 242.

of 4.8 percent. In the 50 percent bracket, a taxable gross yield of 9.6 percent is equivalent to a net yield of 4.8 percent.

A more practical method of determining the investment return on a life insurance policy is to ascertain the net rate of interest actually earned by the company on its investments. This figure is usually easy to obtain, and if the company allocates operating expenses and claims equitably among policy owners, the interest rate should be reasonably close to the rate the policyholder will obtain. A small discrepancy between the published rate of return on invested funds and the rate a policyholder actually receives, however, may result from accounting practices, particularly those relating to the treatment of expenses and earnings on surplus. As an aggregate measure of investment yield performance, the net rate of interest earned on invested funds by all U.S. life insurance companies in 1968 was 4.95 percent.[8]

(*4*) *Convenience.* Some types of investments are much more convenient than others. The time, effort, and ability required to manage an investment should not be underestimated by the investor. Life insurance scores high on this criterion because practically all management problems are completely assumed by the insurer. The insurance company has a team of highly trained and educated investment analysts. Most companies are large enough to employ modern processing equipment to assist in the investment function. As a result, the policyholder receives competent investment management without devoting his time to investment problems. The investment is also convenient when the available denominations and durations are considered. A policyholder selects the amount he wishes to invest with very few restrictions and has complete flexibility. The time period of the investment has similar flexibility. The contract can be written for almost any length of time.

(*5*) *Tax treatment.* Generally speaking, life insurance receives favorable tax treatment. As previously mentioned, the accumulation of cash values in a life insurance contract is not currently taxable to a policyholder. And there is a strong likelihood that the benefits of the policy will never be taxable. Ordinarily the beneficiary does not incur an income tax liability when death proceeds are received. If a policyholder receives living benefits by surrendering the policy for cash (or by the maturity of an endowment) the benefits are taxable to the extent they exceed the aggregate premiums or other consideration paid. Even in this situation, however, the tax liability can be decreased or eliminated by using the optional methods of settlement in certain ways. (This point is discussed further in Chapter Eighteen.)

(*6*) *Price level changes.* This book has previously pointed out the importance of general inflation or deflation to a long-term investor. Since

---

[8] Institute of Life Insurance, *1969 Fact Book,* p. 59.

1939 inflation has been a serious problem for life insurance policyholders and there is considerable evidence that it will continue. Life insurance, because it provides fixed-dollar benefits, is injured by inflation and benefits from deflation. Thus, it seems logical to seek protection against both inflation (by investments that are likely to appreciate during periods of rising prices, such as growth stocks) and deflation (with investments, such as life insurance that provide more valuable benefits when prices decline). An investor's expectations about the level of future prices is not the only factor that should determine the proportion of fixed-dollar investments in his portfolio, however. Investors often want to start their investment program with extremely safe investments. After providing a solid foundation of safe investments, more speculative ventures may be appropriate. Generally, fixed-dollar investments have a higher degree of safety than other forms of investments. Consequently, most authorities believe that one of the important functions of life insurance is the establishment of a safe foundation of an investment portfolio.

(7) *Compulsion.*   Few individuals question the value of life insurance *protection,* i.e., the protection element in life insurance policies. There is a considerable body of opinion, however, that questions the attractiveness of the investment aspects of life insurance. This school of thought argues that many individuals would be better advised to buy "term and invest the difference" rather than build a savings program with cash value life insurance.

In evaluating this argument, an individual should consider all the previously mentioned investment criteria: safety, liquidity, yield, price level changes, convenience, and tax treatment. In addition, an important factor is the likelihood that the investment will be continued. Life insurance is semicompulsory in nature. That is, most policyholders are reluctant to give up their insurance investment because it takes something of value away from the beneficiary. A withdrawal from a bank account (or the termination of most other savings programs) may be easy to justify, but many policyholders are not prepared to deprive a beneficiary of life insurance protection. Consequently, after a life insurance policy has been in force for some time, there is a strong probability that the investment will be maintained until the investment objective is reached. Although the authors of this text believe some individuals might be able to equal or exceed the investment performance of life insurance companies through their own investments, many individuals may not have the discipline and perseverance required to do so over a long period of time.

UNDERSTANDING POLICY PROVISIONS AND
USING POLICY OPTIONS EFFECTIVELY

The important provisions in a life insurance policy may be divided into two categories: (1) nonoption clauses, which do not require the policyholder or beneficiaries to make decisions, and (2) the option clauses, which require decisions. A wise insurance buyer must understand the option clauses or he will not be able to use the options effectively. However, the nonoption clauses are also important because they describe the coverage.

NONOPTION CLAUSES

Grace Period.   A grace period is included in every life insurance policy. This is a period of time, of either one month or 31 days, that starts after the premium due date. During this period, late premiums may be paid without penalty. If a policyholder has a policy on which premiums are payable on the fifteenth of each month he can pay the premium due on June 15 before the fifteenth of July without any problems. The grace period is designed to avoid problems for policyholders who do not always pay their premiums on time.

Suicide Clause.   What happens when a policyholder commits suicide? Does the insurance company pay the policy proceeds to the beneficiary? The suicide clause, which is included in almost all policies, excludes death by suicide within two years (one year in some policies) after the policy is issued.[9] This is intended as an easy way for the insurance company to avoid paying when a person has purchased a policy with suicide in mind, yet it requires the insurance company to pay when suicide has not been planned for a long time. The basic assumption is that a person will not plan suicide far in advance and carry out his plans. If a person buys a policy and commits suicide during the suicide period, the insurance company's payment will be limited to a return of the premiums.

Aviation Clause.   Statistics have shown that persons who fly on regularly scheduled, commercial airlines are not subject to higher mortality rates. But persons who fly private aircraft pose an additional hazard for a life insurance company. The aviation clause, therefore, will either exclude death if it results from private aviation or will require an additional premium for coverage.

War Clause.   The war clause excludes death that results from war, or in some policies, death that occurs while the insured is in the military service. These clauses are used only when a war or military conflict is underway or appears likely, and after the conflict is over the clauses are usually cancelled. And of course, once the clause is cancelled, the insurance company cannot reinstate it. A war clause can never be added to a policy that has never had one.

---

[9] In Missouri, an insurance company must pay the full face amount of the policy whenever the insured commits suicide, unless the company can prove the insured contemplated suicide at the time he purchased the policy.

Incontestable Period.   One of the most valuable provision in a life insurance policy is the incontestable clause. Although the clauses used by the various insurance companies vary somewhat, the basic effect is to prevent a company from contesting the validity of the contract after it has been in force for a period of time—usually one or two years. This means the insurance company cannot deny liability after the contestable period has expired even if the policyholder has been guilty of misrepresentation, concealment, or fraud. The company can, of course, refuse to pay a claim if it contends that a valid contract is in force but it excludes the cause of death. For example, if a young man buys a policy with a war clause and is killed in combat four years later, the insurance company would return the premiums but would not have to pay the face amount of the policy. The incontestable clause would not require the insurance company to pay the full face amount.

The incontestable clause prevents the insurance company from using misrepresentation, concealment, or even fraud as a defense after the incontestable period has passed. For example, assume that a person learns that he is suffering from leukemia and probably will not live long. If he tells his insurance agent that he is healthy, has not been to a physician recently, and has no knowledge of poor health, he is guilty of misrepresentation, concealment, and possibly fraud but the insurance company will be required to pay the full face amount of the policy to the beneficiary if he dies after the contestable period.

The incontestable clause has great value to *every* policyholder—not only those who attempt to deceive an insurance company. Honest policyholders can be assured that their claim will not even be questioned if death happens after the contestable period.

Misstatement of Age Clause.   Occasionally, the age given for the insured is incorrect. This can happen by accident or be caused by vanity, and it may not be an attempt at fraud. The misstatement of age clause is designed to handle such situations in a convenient way. This clause states that the amount payable to the beneficiary will be adjusted to the amount that the premium actually paid would have purchased if the insured had correctly stated his age. For example, the insured may buy a $10,000 policy and give his age as 24 when, for insurance purposes, he is considered 25. (This can easily happen because insurance companies use a person's *nearest* birthday to determine his age for insurance purposes.) If the insured dies and the insurance company discovers the error, the amount payable will not be $10,000 but the amount the premium would have purchased at age 25.

OPTION CLAUSES

Beneficiary Clause.   One of the most important options given to a life insurance policyholder is the right to designate the beneficiary. This decision should be approached carefully because mistakes can upset the purposes of the entire insurance plan.

The first decision is to choose between a revocable and an irrevocable designation. Most designations are revocable. That is, the policyholder has the right to change the beneficiary and, perhaps more importantly, exercise policy rights. The consent of an irrevocable beneficiary is usually needed to exercise rights in the policy.

Another decision is the choice of secondary beneficiaries. The primary beneficiary has first claim to the policy proceeds, but if the primary beneficiary cannot receive the proceeds, they are paid to the secondary beneficiaries. A common situation is to name the wife as primary beneficiary and the children as secondary beneficiaries. As a practical matter, this arrangement may not be too harmful because the proceeds will almost always go to the wife. However, it may not be desirable if the husband and wife die in a common accident or if the wife dies first and the proceeds become payable to the children while they are still minors. Some states permit insurance companies to make payments to minors, but usually minors are not legally competent to make binding contracts on themselves. Insurance companies, therefore, are reluctant to make payments to minors. In most cases, it might be desirable to name the wife as primary beneficiary and a trustee as secondary beneficiary. The designation can be worded in such a way that proceeds payable to the trustee would be administered for the benefit of the children while they are minors.

Dividend Options.   A person may buy a participating policy (one that pays dividends to policyholders) or a nonparticipating policy (one that does not return dividends to policyholders). If a participating policy has been chosen, the policyholder must decide how he will take the dividends. There are four common options. Dividends may be taken in cash, used to reduce the next premium, used to purchase paid-up additional insurance, or accumulated at interest.

Taking the dividend in cash has little to recommend it. If this option is selected, the insurance company will send a check each year to the policyholder and normally the dividend will become larger as time passes. The annual dividend, however, is usually small (particularly in the early policy years) and the policyholder is likely to spend it impulsively.

Using the dividend to reduce the next premium may be an acceptable method of receiving dividends. This is a helpful option, especially if the premium seems to be a financial burden.

Accumulating dividends at interest is similar to depositing money in a savings account in a bank. If this option is chosen, the insurance company simply notifies the policyholder each year that dividends have been credited to his account and his total accumulated dividends (with interest) amount to so much. The interest rate at which dividends are guaranteed to increase is usually low, but each year the company actually credits the policyholder with the interest rate earned that year.[10] This option can produce a large fund if it is used for a long period of time. It is also a convenient method of accumulating funds for specific purposes. For example, if a person has included the guaranteed purchase option, it might be helpful to accumulate dividends at interest to pay for the first premium on a new policy when the purchase options are exercised.

The option that seems most appropriate for young policyholders who have a restricted insurance budget is the paid-up additions option. This option applies the yearly dividend to buy another insurance policy that is paid up. (No additional premium will ever be payable on the paid-up policy.) Of course, a dividend will purchase only a small policy, but if dividends are used in this way every year, the total amount of insurance can increase to a large amount. The paid-up policies are the same type as the original policy. If a person owns a straight life contract, for example, the paid-up additional policies will also be straight life policies. These paid-up policies will have cash values just as the original contract, and they may also pay dividends.

There are two main advantages of this option to a young policyholder. The insurance is purchased at "net" rates; that is, the insurance company does not load the premium for the paid-up policies for sales expenses. Thus, insurance obtained in this manner is economical. Secondly, most young policyholders need more insurance and this option permits them to gradually accumulate additional insurance. This insurance is added without evidence of insurability. The insurance company requires evidence of insurability when the *option* is selected, but evidence is not required each time insurance is purchased.

Nonforfeiture Options.   Another major decision faced by a life insurance policyholder is the method of taking the cash value of his policy. These options, sometimes called surrender options, are not available on policies that have no cash value and they are important only if the policyholder elects to terminate his policy.

The simplest method of surrendering a policy is to take cash. As explained earlier, a policyholder can surrender his contract at any time and receive its cash value.[11] Although this method is used often, other methods of taking the cash value are usually more appropriate.

If a person wants to discontinue premium payments but wants to continue his insurance protection, he may use the reduced paid-up insurance option. This option uses the cash value of the policy to

---

[10] To be more precise, the actual rate credited to the policyholders will be decided by the insurance company's board of directors. The rate will usually be close to the actual rate earned, but it is not necessarily the same.

[11] The policy may have no cash value in its first few years.

purchase a policy that is identical to his original contract, but the contract is paid up. If the policy is to be paid up, however, the face amount must be reduced. Every policy has a table that shows the amount of paid-up insurance that can be obtained as the years pass. A policy that has been converted to a reduced paid-up contract can later be surrendered for cash if the policyholder so desires.

Another nonforfeiture option is extended term insurance. This option converts the policy into a term insurance contract and continues the coverage for as long as possible. In effect, the cash value of the original policy is used to buy a paid-up term insurance policy. The face amount, however, is not decreased. Every life insurance policy with a cash value will have a table that shows the period of extended term insurance coverage that can be obtained by using this option. A person may buy a straight life policy at age 20, for example, and at age 30 use the cash value to buy term insurance for 23 years and 80 days.

The automatic premium loan provision is not actually a nonforfeiture option because the policy is not surrendered or converted, but it is similar to the nonforfeiture options. If a person chooses the automatic premium loan provision when he buys his policy and defaults, the premium will be automatically paid and charged against the cash value. From that date forward, the loan will be treated just as any policy loan. The effect of this provision is to keep the insurance in force automatically if premiums are missed, but of course, the loans will accumulate at interest and will be subtracted from the proceeds that later become payable. The automatic premium loan is usually a wise option for a policyholder. It does not require an additional premium, and it preserves a person's insurance protection in periods of financial stress.

Settlement Options. One of the most important decisions for a policyholder is selecting the method of paying the beneficiary. Most policyholders do not specify any method of payment, and as a result, the proceeds are usually taken in cash by the beneficiary. Studies have shown, however, that life insurance proceeds are not managed well by most beneficiaries. Too often the proceeds are taken in cash, and the widow spends the funds quickly. In these cases, the purposes of the insurance are not fulfilled.

Rather than taking the proceeds in cash, the policyholder may use the settlement options. These options can provide an income to the beneficiary in several forms. They can be arranged so that the beneficiary cannot change the form of payment, or they may be set up so the beneficiary has some flexibility in choosing the option.

(1) The interest option. This is the simplest and most flexible of all settlement options. It simply leaves the proceeds with the insurance company and the company pays interest (usually monthly) to the beneficiary. This option does not liquidate the proceeds and it must be

followed by a cash withdrawal or one of the other settlement options. With the interest option, the insurance company guarantees a minimum rate of interest and usually pays more (based on the actual rate earned by the company) once each year.

The interest option is useful when the proceeds are large enough to provide an adequate income for a widow. Used in this way, the full proceeds are preserved for the children. This option is also useful when a widow will have sufficient income for a certain period, but the proceeds will be more helpful later.

(2) *The fixed-period option.*   Under this arrangement, the proceeds are liquidated over the period chosen by the policyholder. For example, a policyholder who has an infant son may wish to guarantee that monthly benefits will be paid for 20 years (250 monthly payments). Forty-eight thousand dollars of life insurance proceeds would provide more than $200 each month because interest will be credited on the proceeds to the benefit of the policyholder. But it is easy to refer to a present value interest table and find the amount of monthly proceeds that can be paid from life insurance proceeds. Every life insurance policy contains a table that shows the monthly benefits that can be provided for various periods under the fixed period option.

The fixed-period option may be a logical choice if the policyholder wants to guarantee income over a certain period. The trouble is that the period over which a beneficiary needs income changes. As children get older, the period of benefits may become shorter.

(3) *The fixed-amount option.*   This is similar to the fixed-period option, but it has several advantages. The fixed-amount option pays the beneficiary a stipulated monthly income for as long as the proceeds (plus interest) will last. A $10,000 policy, for instance, will pay $100 a month for over ten years.

The main difference between the fixed-amount option and the fixed-period option is that the fixed-amount option provides a stipulated monthly income, regardless of other developments. Often, a $10,000 policy will pay more or less than $10,000. This is because policy loans are deducted from the proceeds, dividends may be accumulated or used to buy additional insurance, the policyholder's age may have been misstated, and other benefits may have been added. In other words, the amount payable when the policyholder dies is often not the same as the face amount of insurance. If the policyholder has selected the fixed-amount option and more than the face is payable, the amount of the monthly payments will not change but benefits will be payable over a longer period.

The fixed-amount option is also more flexible than the fixed-period option. The beneficiary may be given the right to change the amount of the monthly benefits under the fixed-amount option but this privilege is usually not available under the fixed-period option.

(4) The life-income option. These pay benefits as long as the beneficiary is alive. These can be provided with different types of guarantees, but the most popular is to provide benefits as long as the beneficiary is alive, but in no circumstances will benefits be paid in less than ten years. If a beneficiary uses the ten-year guaranteed life-income option, and dies two years after benefits begin, benefits will be continued for another eight years and paid to the secondary beneficiary. Other life-income options are available, but they are all variations of annuities and the subject of annuities is treated in Chapter Eighteen.

CHOOSING LIFE INSURANCE RIDERS

A life insurance buyer must decide if he is interested in only the basic life insurance policy or additional benefits that can be added by a rider. Additional benefits are available from all companies for an extra premium, but they may or may not be a wise purchase.

ACCIDENTAL DEATH BENEFITS

Many policyholders elect to have a double indemnity rider added to their policy. This provision adds an amount equal to the face of the policy to the proceeds if the policyholder dies in an accident. A $10,000 policy with this rider, for example, would pay $20,000 to the beneficiary if the policyholder is killed in an accident.[12]

The coverage is not nearly so broad as it might seem, however, because not all "accidental deaths" qualify for the double indemnity benefit. Often the coverage requires death to result from "accidental means." This terminology excludes those cases where the *result* could be regarded as an accident but the *cause* was not accidental. In other words, both the cause and the result must be accidental to collect under the normal double indemnity rider. Suppose a painter purposely attempts to jump from a ladder and falls to his death. The result was accidental, but the cause of the injury was not. The beneficiary, therefore, would collect only the basic face amount of the policy. The distinction between accidental means and accidental results is not always clearcut and has been a frequent source of litigation.

Another restriction on this coverage is that death must be caused entirely by external, violent, and accidental means. The purpose of this terminology is to exclude deaths from the double benefit if they result from disease. Consider the example of a person who has a heart attack and wrecks his car. If he is killed in the wreck, was the cause of death the heart attack or the wreck? Although it may be impossible to know

---

[12] In some riders, the additional payment is twice the face amount. This would provide a total death benefit of three times the face amount, so the provision is known as triple indemnity.

the true facts in a practical situation, the accidental death clause would provide payment only if an accident was the sole cause of death. The double indemnity rider also excludes deaths that result from suicide, violations of law, poison, inhalation of gas, and other causes such as war.

Is the double indemnity rider a wise purchase? Most authorities argue that it is not. They argue that the economic loss involved in the policy-holder's death is no higher when a person dies by accident. In fact, the economic loss to the family is usually less than it would be otherwise because usually there are no medical and hospital expenses. Furthermore, the double indemnity rider creates the illusion of doubling the amount of life insurance a person owns. The truth is that only about 6 percent of all deaths result from accidents[13] and even a smaller percentage of deaths are caused by accidents that would meet the requirements of the typical indemnity clause.

Despite these arguments, there is some economic justification for the double indemnity rider. First, the cost is low. Below the age of 30, the cost is usually about 85 cents for each $1,000 of insurance that is bought. One could argue that the cost is low because the insurance company knows the chances of paying this benefit are low. Nevertheless, the low cost enables many people to purchase the coverage. In addition, the chances of an accidental death are higher for young people than they are for older persons.

WAIVER OF PREMIUM

Perhaps the most common rider used with life insurance policies is the waiver of premium benefit. The typical waiver of premium rider keeps the policy in force when the policyholder is totally and permanently disabled and premiums are not paid. In other words, the rider does not require premiums to be paid when the policyholder is disabled. During the period when premiums are not paid, the policy continues to have the same cash values, death benefits, dividends and all the other benefits that it would have had if all premiums had been paid.

There is a waiting period of six months before the policyholder can terminate his premium payments. If the policyholder pays a premium during the first six months of his disability, he can get a refund of such premiums if his disability lasts for more than six months.

The cost of the waiver of premium benefit is low. At age 20, for example, the cost is about 25 cents for each $1,000 of life insurance. Since the cost is low and the rider assures that the life insurance plan will remain in effect regardless of the policyholder's health, the waiver of premium benefit is a worthwhile purchase.

---

[13] John G. Turnbull, C. Arthur Williams, Jr., and Earl F. Cheit, *Economic and Social Security,* 3rd edition, revised printing (New York: The Ronald Press Company, 1968), p. 57.

DISABILITY INCOME

The disability income rider provides a monthly income, usually of $5 or $10 for each $1,000 of face amount, if the policyholder becomes totally and permanently disabled. The waiting period is usually either four months or six months, and the coverage terminates if disability has not occurred before the policyholder reaches age 55 or 60. After disability income benefits begin, they are continued for as long as the policyholder remains disabled or reaches age 65, whichever comes sooner.

The disability income rider is not very popular. It is included on fewer than 5 percent of the life insurance policies being issued.[14] This is unfortunate, because many buyers should consider this coverage. Why should a person protect his human life value against death and not disability? A rational buyer should consider disability income insurance, and he should compare the benefits in life insurance riders to those available in health insurance policies.

COMPARING CONTRACTS AND COSTS

Most life insurance buyers are unable to make meaningful comparisons between life insurance policies. Some people assume that the policies of reputable companies are about the same and the costs are roughly equivalent. If this were true, a buyer could not be harmed much financially by selecting any policy. Unfortunately (or fortunately), there are important differences among the policies sold by life insurance companies and the differences in cost are great. A careful insurance buyer should, therefore, be aware of the important points to compare and know how to analyze the cost of insurance.

COMPARISON OF POLICIES

Life insurance policies are remarkably similar in their basic provisions. Virtually all policies will contain a grace period, misstatement of age clause, nonforfeiture options, settlement options, suicide clause, policy loan provision, and beneficiary designation. A knowledgeable buyer, therefore, cannot simply check to see that the contracts he is comparing each contain those basic provisions. A careful buyer, however, should compare contracts to see if the clauses are more liberal in one contract than another. For example, the incontestable period may be one year in one policy and two years in another. Differences may also exist in the suicide and grace periods.

A careful insurance buyer may discover a number of differences between one policy and another. If policies of reputable companies are being compared, however, the differences will usually be minor and not

---

[14] Dan McGill, *Life Insurance,* revised edition (Homewood, Illinois: Richard D. Irwin, Inc., 1967), p. 723.

especially important to the buyer. Nevertheless, there are at least five major points that should be compared any time policies are being analyzed.

(1) The cash value patterns differ considerably among policies—even when the policies are the same type. For example, Company A and Company B may each have straight life policies. Both may have cash values that start at the end of the second policy year and reach the face amount of the policy at age 100. The cash value of Company A's policy may increase rapidly, however, while the cash value in Company B's policy may increase slowly for a long period. Figure 15–6 illustrates this possibility.

Figure 15–6   Comparison of Cash Values

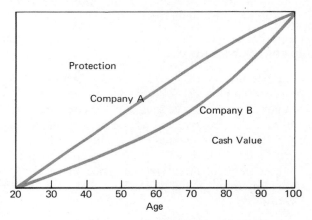

Unless there are some other offsetting differences, the policy of Company A is a more desirable contract than Company B's contract. The benefits in Company A's policy are the same as Company B's, but Company A's policy also provides a higher cash value.

When comparing decreasing term insurance policies, it is particularly important to notice how fast the face amount declines. In some policies, the face amount decreases more rapidly than it does in others. This may be true even if the policies start with the same face amount and decrease to zero over the same period.

(2) Another worthwhile point of comparison is the policy loan interest rate. Most large life insurance companies charge 5 percent interest, but most smaller companies charge 6 or even 6½ percent. This can be an important difference in cost.

(3) The exclusions in a life insurance policy are extremely important. Young buyers, more than others, should carefully compare the war and aviation clauses (if any) in the policies they are comparing.

(4) The amount of income provided by the various settlement options is another feature that should be checked. The tables in the policies might

show that one company provides only $6.30 for each $1,000 of proceeds under the life income option while another company guarantees $7.10. A difference of this amount might be considered sizable by the policy-holder.

(5) The wording of the disability benefits included in the various riders may differ considerably among companies. If a buyer is interested in these benefits, these clauses should be compared.

COMPARING COSTS

Comparing the costs of life insurance policies is a very difficult task. In fact, the best an intelligent buyer can do is to become aware of the major problems that are involved and become familiar with a simple method of comparing costs.

A buyer cannot simply compare the annual premiums of different policies. Even if the contracts are similar in duration, cash values, and other provisions, one or both of the policies may be participating. Suppose one company charges $120 a year for a nonparticipating straight life policy issued at age 20 and another company charges $135 for a participating policy that is otherwise comparable. Which contract is less expensive? If the company offering the participating policy pays a dividend of $15, the cost should be the same. A complication, however, is that the dividend will probably change over the years. It may be less than $15 in the early policy years and more than $15 later. Another complication is that dividends can never be guaranteed by life insurance companies. Dividend projections are used for "illustrative purposes," but these projections only indicate what will happen if conditions affecting the company's costs remain unchanged. A buyer is forced into using these dividend projections, but he should realize that they are subject to change.

The traditional method of comparing the cost of life insurance policies is called the "net cost" approach. Basically, this approach totals the premiums that would be paid over 20 years, subtracts the accumulated dividends and cash value, and divides the remainder by 20. This answer gives the average yearly net cost. This technique can be used for other periods, but it is customary to use 20 years for the comparison. Table 15–5 is an illustration of the net cost method.

The net cost method is subject to several criticisms, but it is a simple technique that has some meaning for insurance buyers. It is certainly better to use an oversimplified technique than to use none at all.

MINIMIZING THE COST OF LIFE INSURANCE

After a person decides to buy life insurance from a particular company, there are several ways he may reduce the cost of the insurance. One method of minimizing cost that is used often is to pay the premiums less frequently. Except for industrial insurance, life insurance premiums can

Table 15–5   Illustration of the Net Cost Method of Computing the Cost of Life Insurance ($10,000 policy issued at age 20)

Annual premium	$ 158.30
Total premiums paid over 20 years	3,166.00
Total estimated dividends	9,982.00
Guaranteed cash value (end of twentieth year)	21,260.00
Amount paid to insurance company	31,660.00
Amount available to policyholder	31,242.00
Difference	418.00
Average annual cost	20.90

be paid annually, semiannually, quarterly, or monthly. More frequent premium payments make the insurance more expensive because of higher administrative expenses incurred by the insurance company. In addition the insurance company loses interest on funds that could have been earned if the full year's premium had been paid in advance. Table 15–6 shows the cost of insurance with different premium intervals.

Table 15–6 shows that a person aged 20 who bought a $25,000 straight life policy would save $12.15 a year by paying for the insurance once a year rather than paying for it monthly. This can amount to a sizeable savings over the years. As a general rule, then, a person should pay premiums as infrequently as possible without upsetting his financial planning.

Sometimes a policyholder would like to take advantage of the lower cost when premiums are paid annually, but the annual premium might be difficult to pay. It is usually easier to pay for large expenditures in monthly installments. A convenient way to pay premiums on a monthly basis and still take advantage of the lower annual premium is to use the preauthorized check plan. This is a plan that has been developed only

Table 15–6   The Cost of Paying Premiums More Than Once a Year ($25,000 straight life policy issued at age 20)

Premium Basis	Premium	Total Yearly Payment	Excess Over Annual Basis
Annually	$284.25	$284.25	
Semiannually	143.80	287.60	$3.35
Quarterly	72.10	288.40	4.15
Monthly	24.70	296.40	12.15

in recent years by life insurance companies. With this plan, the policy-holder agrees to let the insurance company write a check each month against the policyholder's bank account for the amount of the premium. The effect is automatic premium paying. Most companies divide the annual premium by 12 and take this amount from the policyholder's account each month. The cost to the policyholder, therefore, is the same as it would be on an annual basis.[15]

Would it cost more for a policyholder to own five $5,000 life insurance policies or one $25,000 policy? It will almost always cost more to own five separate policies because life insurance companies give discounts for larger policies. Insurance companies do this in various ways. For example, a company might apply one rate to the first $5,000 of coverage, a lower rate to the next $5,000 of insurance, and so on. The rate decreases as more insurance is bought. Or the company may have a flat charge that is added to the insurance rate. If a company charges a certain rate and adds, say $8 for each policy, the $8 is equal to $4 per thousand on a $2,000 policy but it is equal to only $1 per thousand on an $8,000 policy. The effect is a lower rate when more insurance is bought. This is a good reason for insurance buyers to prefer one large policy rather than a number of small policies.

Another method of cutting down the cost of life insurance is to purchase "modified" life policies. This method is used most often by young policyholders. "Modified" policies have lower premiums during the first few years than they have thereafter. This can be done in two ways: first, the policy can actually be term insurance for a few years and then convert automatically into a permanent policy. The second approach is to redistribute premiums. In other words, the premium rates are calculated so that they increase after a few years (sometimes they increase in steps each year for several years). If the premiums are redistributed the premiums will be lower in the early policy years but later they will be higher than they would have been. Furthermore, the cash and other surrender values will be lower than normal in the years when the premium is low. Actually, a person does not save money by buying a modified policy; he simply pays less in at first and more later.

Another approach to saving money on life insurance involves "special" policies. When used in this context, the word "special" has a very definite meaning. A "special" policy is one that has lower premiums because the benefits are not so liberal as they are in other policies. For example, the cash values in a "special" policy may be lower. Although a buyer may be able to get a lower premium by buying a "special," he should realize that he may not be getting a bargain.

---

[15] Although insurance companies incur additional expenses with the preauthorized check plan, the companies usually do not collect more than the annual premium each year because they hope fewer policyholders will terminate their coverage.

A legitimate way for some people to save money on life insurance is to purchase a nonsmoker's policy. Some life insurance companies offer discounts to policyholders who have not smoked cigarettes, cigars, or pipes for a certain period of time and will agree not to smoke. The discount may be as high as 5 or 6 percent, so this type of policy may be worthwhile for a nonsmoker.

Many life insuarnce companies now sell life insurance to young people (particularly students) on some type of financing plan. With this approach, the buyer can use little or no money of his own for premiums for a year or two; he pays the premium by borrowing from the life insurance company. This method actually does not reduce the cost of insurance (because the insurance company naturally charges interest on borrowed funds), but it does permit some people to buy insurance when they otherwise would not be financially able.

SELECTING THE COMPANY AND THE AGENT

When a young person buys life insurance, he should have a sincere intention of keeping the insurance in force for a long time. Insurance serves its function best, and at the lowest cost, when it is maintained for many years. But in a long-range insurance program, a person will spend a large amount of money in the form of insurance premiums. This means an insurance buyer should regard insurance as a major expenditure and he should do business only with reputable companies.

CHOOSING THE COMPANY

We have already seen that there are important differences in the cost of insurance among life insurance companies and some differences in the policies they sell. These are two good reasons why a buyer should carefully select his life insurance company. But are all life insurance companies financially strong? Obviously a person should not pay premiums over a long period to a company that is not financially sound.

There are approximately 1,800 life insurance companies doing business in the United States today. Most of these companies are extremely secure, but it may be incorrect to assume that they are all financially sound. Since there are so many companies, a buyer cannot analyze all companies to determine which is the "best company." The best a careful buyer can hope to do is to study the two or three companies whose policies he is currently considering for purchase. The basic question, then, is how can a buyer tell the difference between a strong company and one that may not be so secure?

Some people assume that mutual life insurance companies are better than other types of companies. Other people believe stock life insurance companies are better. It is true that there are important differences between these two types of companies. A stock company is owned by stockholders, and the profit the company makes goes to stockholders rather than policyholders. As a general rule, stock companies issue nonparticipating policies, but many of them sell both participating and nonparticipating contracts. Stock companies are easier to organize than mutual companies, and as a result, most of the 1,400 life insurance companies started in the last 20 years are stock companies. As a result, stock companies are usually smaller than mutuals. Mutual life insurance companies, on the other hand, are owned by policyholders; there are no stockholders. In a legal sense, there are no profits. However, there usually is a "margin" between total costs and total income and this "margin" is returned to policyholders in the form of dividends.

The argument that a life insurance buyer should prefer a stock company over a mutual or vice versa makes little or no sense. There are good and bad companies of both types. A buyer should compare one company against another, and not one type against the other.

Probably the easiest method of checking on the financial standing and reputation of an insurance company is to go to a library and find published sources. Among the more popular sources are:

Best's Life Reports and *The Spectator Insurance Year Book.* These provide a historical background of most companies, the lines of insurance they write, the states in which they operate, and detailed financial data.[16]

Flitcraft and *Little Gem Life Chart.* They indicate the important policy provisions, the premiums and dividend rates, and the values used in settlement options.[17]

The Handy Guide. It reproduces an insurance contract for each company and shows premium information.[18]

Settlement Options. It describes in detail the settlement option practices of most companies.[19]

If it is inconvenient to find these materials in the library, you should not hesitate to ask an insurance agent for them. Reputable life insurance agents are pleased to provide unbiased information concerning their company.

SELECTING THE AGENT

There is an old adage in the life insurance business. It says, "Life insurance is not bought, it is sold." This is a way of saying that most people do not decide to purchase insurance and then find an insurance agent,

---

[16] *Best's Life Reports* (New York: Alfred M. Best Company, Inc., annual); *The Spectator Life Insurance Year Book* (Philadelphia: The Spectator Company, annual).

[17] *Flitcraft* (New York: Flitcraft, Inc., annual); *Little Gem Life Chart* (Cincinnati, Ohio: The National Underwriter Company, annual).

[18] *The Handy Guide* (Philadelphia: The Spectator Company, annual).

[19] *Settlement Options* (New York: Flitcraft, Inc., annual).

but usually an agent approaches a prospect and attempts to sell insurance to him. This may be correct, but how does a person know that the agent who has contacted him is professionally competent?

Life insurance agents come in all varieties. Some are extremely competent, highly educated, and motivated by a sincere desire to serve their clients in the best possible way. Other life insurance agents are poorly educated and almost totally incompetent. A poor agent is motivated by the desire to receive a commission (which usually amounts to 50–80 percent of the first year's premium and perhaps 5–10 percent of the premium for the next nine or ten years).

Unfortunately, most young insurance buyers come into contact with less professional life insurance agents. It is only natural for inexperienced agents to concentrate on young insurance buyers since smaller policies are easier to sell.

It is difficult for an intelligent buyer to recognize a competent agent. Almost all states require insurance agents to pass an examination before a license to sell will be granted, but in most states the license examination is too easy to be used as a guide to competence. There are, however, several ways a buyer can evaluate an insurance agent.

As a general rule, it is preferable to do business with an experienced agent. An agent who has had several years of experience is likely to know more about insurance than one who is just entering the life insurance business. An experienced agent is also more likely to be able to provide services after the policy is sold. Life insurance companies have had a great deal of difficulty in retaining agents. Very often an agent will sell insurance for only six months, one year, or so before he decides to change occupations. This means there is an excellent chance that an agent with little experience will not be able to provide services after the policy has been sold.

The education and knowledge an insurance agent has is more important than most buyers realize. A life insurance policy is a complicated contract and a wise purchase decision is based on a firm knowledge of economics, finance, and other subjects. A buyer can get some idea of the agent's knowledge by asking questions and observing how the agent responds. It is usually rather easy to determine whether the agent has a college education and if he has earned the C.L.U. (Chartered Life Underwriter) designation. The C.L.U. diploma is awarded only to the agents who meet the experience requirements and pass a series of ten examinations. These are college-level examinations that cover individual life and health insurance, life insurance law and company operations, social insurance and group insurance, pension planning, income, estate, and gift taxation, investments and family financial management, accounting and finance, economics, business insurance, and estate planning. An agent who passes these examinations is not necessarily an expert in all these fields, and all C.L.U.'s are not professionally competent. Nevertheless, a person has a better chance of finding a competent agent if he restricts his selection to only those who have earned the C.L.U. degree (or possibly to those who are in the process of obtaining the designation). Therefore, the C.L.U. degree is an excellent guideline for evaluating life insurance agents.

Perhaps the most important factor a buyer can attempt to judge is an agent's desire to serve the buyer's best interests. This is difficult to evaluate, but some indication can be obtained by learning something about the agent's reputation and observing how he handles your problems.

SUMMARY

Almost everyone owns some type of life insurance. But a person should never buy a life insurance policy until he has examined his reasons. Financial protection for a family, of course, is an important reason for buying life insurance, but savings is another important factor. Young people should also consider purchasing life insurance with a guaranteed purchase option so that they can protect their insurability.

The amount of life insurance a person should buy is a difficult decision. The human life value approach is helpful, but it is quite theoretical; the multiple of earnings approach does not provide a reasonable method; the needs approach is practical and reasonable, but it requires the services of a life insurance agent.

When a person selects the type of policy he wants, the decision should be based primarily on the length of time protection is needed and how the savings element is viewed. A person who views the savings element as a poor investment should purchase a term policy, but if the savings element is regarded as a favorable investment, policies that build a large cash value are appropriate. Life insurance cash values have many favorable investment characteristics, but nevertheless, they are subject to inflation.

Some clauses in a life insurance policy require no decisions from a policyholder, but they should be clearly understood. Other clauses require policyholders to make decisions. The most important of these clauses pertain to the beneficiary, dividend options, nonforfeiture options, and settlement options. Supplementary benefits (such as double indemnity, waiver of premium, and disability income) are usually worthwhile purchases.

Case Problems

1. Larry McLean has never thought much about life insurance. He is only 18, and he is not married. In fact, he plans to finish college before he

settles down to married life. But one of Larry's friends is now selling life insurance and he has asked if he could come to Larry's apartment this afternoon and talk to him about life insurance. Because he is a good friend, Larry said he would talk to him. However, Larry wishes he had told his friend that he is not interested in buying life insurance. Do you believe a person in Larry's position should buy life insurance? Your answer should include specific reasons why or why not.

2. One of the most difficult problems a person faces when he decides to buy life insurance is determining the amount of insurance he should buy. Bill Coe is now facing this decision. He has decided that he will buy some insurance, but he is undecided about how much he should buy. Bill's insurance agent has gathered some facts and had them analyzed by the insurance company's computer. This produced a figure of $235,000, which the agent called "the human life value." However, the agent has indicated that Bill should buy $100,000 of insurance based on his study of Bill's needs. A third figure, $50,000, was given by Bill's father. He arrived at this number by simply multiplying Bill's annual income by five. So Bill is now completely confused. He has three different answers, and they are very different. Which method do you think Bill should use to determine the amount of insurance he should buy? Your answers should give specific reasons.

3. John has decided to buy a life insurance policy but he is undecided about the type of policy he should buy. His insurance agent has recommended that he buy a straight life policy, but John knows that the premium would be lower on a term insurance contract. Furthermore, John believes that life insurance is a poor investment.
   (a) What are the advantages of term insurance over straight life insurance?
   (b) Is life insurance a good investment? Explain.

4. Even though Gary knows a little bit about life insurance, he cannot understand the policy his insurance agent is trying to sell him. The agent says it is simply a $10,000 straight life policy. But the agent has also said that Gary could buy the policy now, pay premiums until he is 65, and then stop paying premiums and receive monthly benefits for the rest of his life.
   (a) If Gary buys a nonparticipating policy, how can a straight life policy provide the benefits to Gary that have been described by his agent?
   (b) Could the benefits paid to Gary be larger if he buys a participating policy? Explain.

5. Barry Cartwright had just about decided to buy a life insurance policy from his insurance agent when another agent explained that he could provide the same policy to Barry at a lower cost. This interested Barry and so they decided to make a comparison of the two policies. They were both straight life policies in the amount of $15,000. The second agent quickly pointed out that his policy would cost less because the annual premium was $165 rather than $206, which was the annual premium on the other policy.

(a) Can Barry conclude that the cost of the second policy will be lower? Explain.

(b) Other than cost, what other factors should Barry study if he is going to make a careful comparison?

6. Tim has recently taken his first job after graduating from college. Although he remembers talking about fringe benefits when he interviewed for the job, he has not thought about group life insurance since that time. In filling out some forms for the personnel office, Tim came across an application for group life insurance. Since the plan was contributory, Tim would have to give his consent for his contribution to be deducted from his paycheck. Tim realizes that he needs more life insurance, but he is not sure of the advantages and disadvantages of group life insurance. What are the advantages and possible disadvantages of buying life insurance through a group plan rather than buying it through individual policies?

7. When Ted finished his physical examination, he was sure his doctor would tell him that he was in good health. Unfortunately, the news was tragic. The doctor told Ted that he had contracted a rare disease and probably would not recover. He gave Ted two or three years. After recovering from the shock, Ted started thinking about his life insurance. The idea occurred to him that only his family doctor knew of his problem and a routine medical examination would not reveal his disease. So he applied for a $50,000 life insurance policy. When he was asked by his agent if he had encountered any serious health problems in the past three years, Ted simply said no, and this answer was written on the application. The policy was issued, and Ted lived four years. After his death, but before the death proceeds were paid on the policy, the life insurance company investigated and learned all the facts. Will the life insurance company pay the death proceeds anyway? Is the pertinent policy provision important to honest policyholders? Explain.

8. When Larry Trane decided to buy a life insurance policy, his agent was eager to start filling out the application. Larry answered all the questions without much difficulty, but he didn't know how he should select a dividend option. His agent told him the choices, but left the decision to Larry.

(a) What are the common dividend options?

(b) Which option do you believe is usually the best for a young man? Explain.

9. Mony has been told that the only way to make money on life insurance is to die—and then you don't get the money anyway. This, of course, had the effect of dampening Mony's interest in life insurance. His insurance agent, however, has told him that life insurance companies actually pay more money to people who are alive than to beneficiaries in the form of death proceeds. What are the various types of benefits that are paid by life insurance companies other than death proceeds?

10. Explain carefully why the cash values are higher in a 20-year payment policy than in a straight life policy. (Assume the policies are both $10,000 contracts issued at the same age.)

11. Jim has had a life insurance policy for the past 12 years. Since he has a straight life policy, he knows it has a cash value and he can obtain a policy loan. Jim needs to borrow $1,000 and he is wondering if he should obtain a policy loan or arrange a loan at the bank.
    (a) What are the probable advantages of using a life insurance policy loan?
    (b) What are the possible advantages of borrowing from the bank?

Selected Readings

Belth, Joseph M. *The Retail Price Structure in American Life Insurance.* Bloomington: Bureau of Business Research, Indiana University, 1966.

Changing Times, The Kiplinger Magazine:
>"Borrowing on Your Life Insurance; Not Too Smart," April 1967, pp. 19–20.
>"Give Your Life Insurance This Checkup," June 1969, pp. 17–19.
>"How Should Your Life Insurance Pay Off?; Settlement Options," May 1970, pp. 41–42.
>"If You Quit Paying on Your Life Insurance," October 1969, p. 18.
>"Making a Living Selling Life Insurance," December 1969, pp. 15–17.
>"Optional Extras They Sell With Life Insurance," March 1968, pp. 43–45.
>"Picking the Beneficiary for Your Life Insurance," November 1967, pp. 11–13.
>"When Is Term Insurance the Best Buy?" March 1970, pp. 43–45.

Denenberg, Herbert S. *et. al. Risk and Insurance.* Englewood Cliffs, N.J.: Prentice-Hall, Inc., 1964.

Eilers, Robert D. and Crowe, Robert M. (eds.). *Group Insurance Handbook.* Homewood, Illinois: Richard D. Irwin, Inc., 1962.

Greene, Mark R. *Risk and Insurance.* 2nd edition. Cincinnati: South-Western Publishing Company.

Gregg, Davis W. *Group Life Insurance.* 3rd edition. Homewood, Illinois: Richard D. Irwin, Inc., 1962.

Gregg, Davis W. (ed.). *Life and Health Insurance Handbook.* Revised edition. Homewood, Illinois: Richard D. Irwin, Inc., 1964.

Greider, Janice E. and Beadles, William T. *Law and the Life Insurance Contract.* Revised edition. Homewood, Illinois: Richard D. Irwin, Inc., 1968.

Hammond, J. D. and Williams, Arthur L. *Essentials of Life Insurance.* Glenview, Illinois: Scott, Foresman and Company, 1968.

"How to Buy Life Insurance." *Consumer Reports,* January, February, March 1967.

"How to Choose Your Life Insurance Policy." *Successful Farming,* April 1969, pp. 72–73.

Huebner, S. S. and Black, Kenneth, Jr. *Life Insurance.* 7th edition. New York: Appleton-Century-Crofts, 1969.

Institute of Life Insurance. *Life Insurance Fact Book.* New York: Institute of Life Insurance. Published annually.

Institute of Life Insurance. *Your Life Insurance and How It Works.* New York: Institute of Life Insurance, 1965.

Kelsey, Wilfred R. and Daniels, Arthur C. *Handbook of Life Insurance.* 4th edition. New York: Institute of Life Insurance, 1969.

Krumme, R., "Should You Insure Your Wife and Children?" *Successful Farming,* June 1969, p. 46.

"Life Insurance." *Consumer Reports,* June 1967, pp. 312–316.

"Life Insurance: Selecting the Right Protection for a Family." *Good Housekeeping,* April 1967, pp. 202–203.

Lovelace, Griffin M. *Life and Life Insurance.* Hartford, Connecticut: Life Insurance Agency Management Association, 1962.

McGill, Dan M. *Life Insurance.* Revised edition. Homewood, Illinois: Richard D. Irwin, Inc., 1967.

Mehr, Robert. *Life Insurance Theory and Practice.* Austin, Texas: Business Publications, Inc., 1970.

Mowbray, Albert *et. al. Insurance.* 6th edition. New York: McGraw-Hill Book Company, 1969.

National Underwriter Company, *Tax Facts on Life Insurance.* Cincinnati, Ohio. Published annually.

Williams, C. Arthur, Jr. and Heins, Richard M. *Risk Management and Insurance.* New York: McGraw-Hill Book Company, 1964.

CHAPTER **SIXTEEN**

PROTECTION AGAINST DISABILITY

One of the primary obstacles to a person's financial security is the possibility of becoming disabled. When a person becomes disabled he usually incurs medical expenses. In addition, he may lose income while he cannot work. The total cost of these two losses can be very high. In severe cases, disability can completely destroy a person's chances of reaching his financial goals. Even minor disabilities, if they are frequent, can impose a substantial financial burden on a person.

An individual who plans his financial affairs carefully will be concerned about the possibility of becoming disabled and will adopt some method of paying for the cost of poor health. But does this mean a person should buy health insurance? If so, what kind of health insurance protection should a person buy? Do most people already have adequate health insurance from their employer or through the government? How can a person tell the difference between one health insurance policy and another? Should a person buy health insurance from an insurance company or from a Blue Cross-Blue Shield Association? These are the basic, important questions that are faced by every individual who makes careful financial plans. This chapter, therefore, deals with these questions.

THE COST OF DISABILITY

The total cost of poor health in the United States is estimated to be more than $66 billion—and the cost of poor health is increasing every year. In fact, the cost of medical care has been increasing much faster than the cost of other items in the Consumer Price Index. This is shown in Figure 16–1.

Because the cost of medical care has been rising so rapidly and U.S. families are demanding more and more medical services, the amount of

Figure 16–1 Increases in the Cost of Medical Care and Other Types of Expenditures Since 1957–59

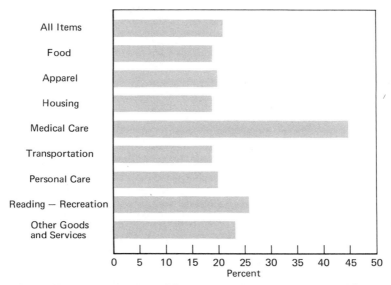

Source: Health Insurance Institute, *1969 Source Book of Health Insurance Data*, p. 50.

money spent on medical care increases. Not only has the amount of money spent on medical care increased, the *percentage* of total personal consumption expenditures has been rising. Examine Figure 16–2. It shows that U.S. families allocated 4.3 percent of their personal expenditure to medical care in 1948, but in 1968, medical care expenditures accounted for 7 percent of total personal expenditures. The only major products or services that take a larger portion of the family budget are food, housing, household operations, transportation, and clothing. More money is spent on medical care than for any one of the following items: recreation, tobacco, personal care, private education, religious and welfare activities, and foreign travel.

The average person spends about $200 each year for medical care. But averages are sometimes deceiving. The cost of medical care does not fall evenly on all persons. Many individuals spend little on medical care but some people are hit hard by a serious disability. This means the cost of medical care is largely unpredictable. An individual simply cannot have a very good idea of how much poor health will cost him. It is true that young people, in general, spend less on medical care than older people. But even young people also become sick, and accidents are actually more frequent among young people than they are among middle aged individuals.

Figure 16–2   Percentage of Total Personal Consumption Expenditures Spent on Medical Care

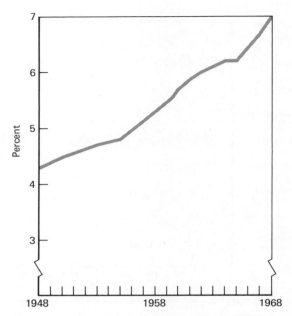

Source: Health Insurance Institute, *1969 Source Book of Health Insurance Data,* p. 49.

METHODS OF FINANCING DISABILITY LOSSES

How should a person pay for the cost of poor health? Basically, the cost can be paid by: (1) out-of-pocket expenditures, (2) private health insurance (including Blue Cross-Blue Shield and independent plans), (3) the government, or (4) by others. Figure 16–3 shows the importance of each of these methods of paying for the cost of disability between 1950 and 1967.

Figure 16–3 shows that the most popular method of paying for disability losses is out-of-pocket expenditures. In other words, most losses are paid by individuals without any form of government or private insurance. But Figure 16–3 also shows that more and more people are using government programs and health insurance to pay for the cost of disability. In 1950, only about 9 percent of the cost of poor health was paid through insurance, but in 1967 health insurance paid for about 22 percent of the cost. Apparently more people are realizing that the cost of poor health should be handled by insurance. This is logical because insurance is an excellent method of paying for losses that are largely unpredictable and can be financial catastrophes to most people who do not have large financial resources.

Figure 16–3 Methods of Financing Disability Losses

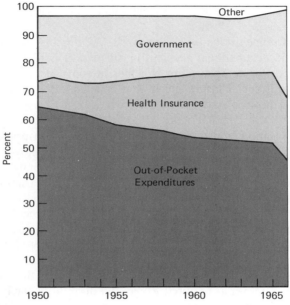

Source: Dorothy P. Rice and Barbara S. Cooper, "National Health
Expenditures, 1950-66," *Social Security Bulletin,* April 1968, p. 3.

GOVERNMENT PROGRAMS

There is not one, but several important government programs that
reimburse people for disability losses. These programs are important
because they provide a basic foundation of disability protection for many
people.

Public Assistance.   Every state (in cooperation with the federal government) provides public assistance benefits. These benefits are paid only
to persons who can demonstrate clearly that they are "needy." If a person
has an income above a certain level or if he has financial resources, he
cannot collect public assistance benefits. In a sense, public assistance is
a form of charity.

Although a person does not have to be disabled to collect public
assistance benefits, there are several programs that are directed specifically to the disabled. For example, all states have an "Aid to the
Blind" program. Also, there are "Aid to the Permanently and Totally
Disabled" and "Medical Assistance for the Aged." The programs for
those over age 65 are designed to pay benefits to those whose incomes or
financial resources are too high to qualify for benefits but who do not
have enough resources to pay for medical care costs.

Most families do not consider public assistance benefits as a part of their financial security program. These programs, at best, should be considered only as a last resort for serious financial emergencies.

Workmen's Compensation and Employer's Liability.   When a person is a victim of an occupational accident or sickness it is likely that he will receive workmen's compensation benefits. In some respects, workmen's compensation is social insurance, in that benefits are established by the government (through state laws) and coverage in many cases is compulsory. These are characteristics of social insurance plans. But workmen's compensation is also closely related to liability insurance. This is because workmen's compensation developed from employer's liability, and workmen's compensation insurance policies have many similarities to liability coverages. In another sense, workmen's compensation is health insurance. The benefits provided in workmen's compensation are basically health insurance benefits. Thus, even though workmen's compensation has characteristics of social insurance and liability insurance, it is basically health insurance and provides an important way of dealing with disability problems.

An important feature of workmen's compensation is that fault is not an issue. An employer is required to pay the disability benefit stipulated in the state law when an employee is injured regardless of who caused the accident. Suppose a young employee loses a hand when he carelessly operates a large saw. Even though the accident was caused by the employee's own negligence, the employer would be responsbile for paying the appropriate benefit. (Employers usually pay the benefits through insurance. In other words, employers buy a workmen's compensation policy that agrees to pay the benefits required by law.) The basic idea of workmen's compensation has been stated very well:

> The principle of liability without fault is quite simple. The employer is assessed the compensable costs of job-connected injuries to his employees not because he is responsible for them, not because he caused them, not because he was negligent, but simply because of social policy. The premise has been discarded that behind every disability there is a negligent party. Under modern industrial conditions the employment relationship itself is reason enough for assessing the employer to compensate his injured employees. Since the employment of labor involves the risk of disability, by social policy the employer must defray its costs.[1]

Another important feature of workmen's compensation is that benefits are prescribed by law and the plan is administered by a state board

---

[1] John G. Turnbull, C. Arthur Williams, Jr., and Earl F. Cheit, *Economic and Social Security,* 3rd edition, revised printing (New York: The Ronald Press Company, 1964) p. 314.

Table 16–1   "Small Shop" Workmen's Compensation Exclusions

Employees Exempted If They Have Fewer Employees Than:	States
2	Connecticut, Nevada, New Hampshire, Oklahoma
3	Arizona, Delaware, Florida, Kentucky, Ohio, Texas, Wisconsin
4	Colorado, Maine, Massachusetts, New Mexico, Rhode Island
5	Arkansas, Kansas, North Carolina, Tennessee
6	Vermont
7	Virginia
8	Alabama, Mississippi
10	Georgia
11	Missouri
15	South Carolina

Source: John G. Turnbull, C. Arthur Williams, Jr. and Earl F. Cheft, *Economic and Social Security*, 3rd edition, revised printing, p. 318. Copyright © 1968, The Ronald Press Company, New York. Reprinted with permission of the publisher.

or commission.[2] If there is a question or problem the state agency handles it, and contested cases can be appealed to the courts. By using a state administrative agency, injured employees can eliminate the uncertainty, delay, and expense of pursuing a case through the courts. In other words, one of the basic purposes of workmen's compensation is to provide prompt, reasonable benefits to injured employees.

(1) Coverage.   Contrary to what many believe, most employees are covered by state workmen's compensation laws. It is true that 12 states apply workmen's compensation laws only to hazardous industries, but in most states all occupations (or almost all) are covered. Still some employees are not covered because of exclusions in the state law. In many states, employers are not under workmen's compensation if they have fewer than a certain number of employees. This is called the "small shop" exclusion. Table 16–1 indicates those states in which the small shop exclusion applies.

In addition to the small shop type of exclusion, many states do not cover farm laborers, domestic servants, and public employees. In 12 states, workmen's compensation laws apply only to hazardous industries. Another type of exclusion is the provision for an "elective law." To be

---

[2] Workmen's compensation cases are administered by courts of law rather than an administrative agency in five states: Alabama, Louisiana, New Mexico, Tennessee, and Wyoming.

sure that their state workmen's compensation law would not be declared unconstitutional, some states made their laws elective rather than compulsory. In these states, an employer can decide that he does not want to come under the law.[3] The net result of all these exclusions is that only about 80 percent of the workers in the country are covered by workmen's compensation.

(2) *Eligibility requirements.* Workmen's compensation laws apply only if the injury occurs while an employee is involved at work. In fact, the disability must be "arising out of and in the course of" employment. If a worker is injured while he is on vacation, for example, he would not be entitled to collect workmen's compensation benefits. But what happens if an employee has a heart attack, or is disabled by a sunstroke, or hit by lightning? Are these cases "arising out of and in the course of" employment? Many of these cases are borderline, and there is no easy answer. A particular case must be judged by the state administrative agency.

Is an employee entitled to workmen's compensation benefits if he suffers from an occupational disease rather than an occupational injury? This has always been a problem in workmen's compensation. All states except Wyoming now provide occupational disease coverage, but in many states diseases are covered only by schedule. This means only the diseases listed in the state law are covered. If an employee has an occupational disease that is not scheduled, no workmen's compensation benefit will be paid to him.[4]

(3) *Benefits.* How much does an insured employee receive in workmen's compensation benefits? This depends on the type of benefits. Benefits are paid for permanent total disability, temporary total disability, disfigurement, death, medical expenses, and in some cases rehabilitation. Disability income benefits are shown in Table 16–2.

It is obvious from Table 16–2 that there is great variation among the states in the amount of workmen's compensation benefits. Furthermore, although most states specify two-thirds of a worker's income as the disability income benefit, all states place dollar limitations on the amount that will be paid. Limitations of $40–$50 a week are common. Consider what this means. If a worker is injured on the job and he has been earning $140 a week, and the maximum benefit is $50, the worker will receive only about 36 percent of his former income, not the two-thirds limit in the law. Because of the legal limits, few employees receive two-thirds of their previous income.

---

[3] If an employer decides not to be covered under workmen's compensation, he loses some of the important common law defenses in employee liability suits.

[4] There is great variation among the states in the number of occupational diseases they cover. One state covers 36 but at the other extreme, one state covers only two diseases.

Table 16–2 Disability Income Benefits Provided by Workmen's Compensation, by State*

State	Limitations on Permanent Total				Limitations on Temporary Total			
	Percent of Wages	Maximum Weekly Payment	Time Limit	Amount Limit	Percent of Wages	Maximum Weekly Payment	Time Limit	Amount Limit
Alabama	65	$ 50.00	550 weeks	$ 20,000	65	$ 50.00	300 weeks	$15,000
Alaska	65	82.55	life		65	127.00	disability	17,000
Arizona	65	150.00	life		65	150.00	433 weeks	65,000
Arkansas	65	49.00			65	49.00	450 weeks	19,500
California	65	52.50	life		$61\frac{3}{4}$	87.50	240 weeks	
Colorado	$66\frac{2}{3}$	59.50	life	18,623	$66\frac{2}{3}$	59.50	disability	18,623
Connecticut	$66\frac{2}{3}$	84.00	life		$66\frac{2}{3}$	84.00	disability	
Delaware	$66\frac{2}{3}$	75.00	life		$66\frac{2}{3}$	75.00	disability	
Dist. Col.	$66\frac{2}{3}$	70.00	life		$66\frac{2}{3}$	70.00	disability	24,000
Florida	60	56.00	life		60	56.00	350 weeks	
Georgia	60	50.00	400 weeks	18,000	60	50.00	400 weeks	18,000
Hawaii	$66\frac{2}{3}$	112.50	life	35,100	$66\frac{2}{3}$	112.50	disability	35,100
Idaho	60	43.00	life		60	43.00	disability	
Illinois		71.00	life			91.00	8 years	
Indiana	60	57.00	500 weeks	25,000	60	57.00	500 weeks	25,000
Iowa	$66\frac{2}{3}$	56.00	500 weeks		$66\frac{2}{3}$	61.00	300 weeks	
Kansas	60	56.00	415 weeks	23,240	60	56.00	415 weeks	23,240
Kentucky	$66\frac{2}{3}$	56.00	425 weeks	23,400	$66\frac{2}{3}$	56.00	425 weeks	23,400
Louisana	65	49.00	500 weeks	22,500	65	49.00	300 weeks	13,500
Maine	$66\frac{2}{3}$	73.00			$66\frac{2}{3}$	73.00		
Maryland	$66\frac{2}{3}$	85.00	life	45,000	$66\frac{2}{3}$	81.50	208 weeks	
Massachusetts	$66\frac{2}{3}$	70.00	disability		$66\frac{2}{3}$	70.00	disability	18,000
Michigan	$66\frac{2}{3}$	75.00	life		$66\frac{2}{3}$	75.00	disability	
Minnesota	$66\frac{2}{3}$	70.00	life		$66\frac{2}{3}$	70.00	350 weeks	21,000
Mississippi	$66\frac{2}{3}$	40.00	450 weeks	15,000	$66\frac{2}{3}$	40.00	450 weeks	15,000
Missouri	$66\frac{2}{3}$	58.00	300 weeks		$66\frac{2}{3}$	63.50	400 weeks	22,800
Montana	$66\frac{2}{3}$	60.00	500 weeks		$66\frac{2}{3}$	65.00	300 weeks	
Nebraska	$66\frac{2}{3}$	55.00	life		$66\frac{2}{3}$	55.00	300 weeks	16,500

Table 16-2 (continued)

State	Limitations on Permanent Total				Limitations on Temporary Total			
	Percent of Wages	Maximum Weekly Payment	Time Limit	Amount Limit	Percent of Wages	Maximum Weekly Payment	Time Limit	Amount Limit
Nevada	90	$ 66.46	life		90	$ 79.96	100 months	$ 29,250
New Hampshire	66 2/3	67.00	life		66 2/3	67.00		
New Jersey		91.00	450 weeks			91.00	300 weeks	
New Mexico	60	48.00	500 weeks	$24,000	60	48.00	500 weeks	24,000
New York	66 2/3	80.00	life		66 2/3	95.00	disability	
N. Carolina	60	50.00	400 weeks	18,000	60	50.00	400 weeks	18,000
N. Dakota	55	59.00	life		55	59.00	disability	
Ohio	66 2/3	56.00	life		66 2/3	56.00	disability	
Oklahoma	66 2/3	43.00	500 weeks	20,000	66 2/3	45.00	300 weeks	10,750
Oregon	55	62.50	life		90	80.00	disability	
Pennsylvania	66 2/3	60.00			66 2/3	60.00		
Rhode Island	66 2/3	70.33	life		66 2/3	70.33	disability	
S. Carolina	60	50.00	500 weeks	12,500	60	50.00	500 weeks	12,500
S. Dakota	55	50.00	life	78,000	55	50.00	312 weeks	15,600
Tennessee	65	47.00	550 weeks	18,800	65	47.00		
Texas	60	49.00	401 weeks	19,649	60	49.00	401 weeks	19,649
Utah	60	47.00	life	20,280	60	47.00	312 weeks	20,280
Vermont	66 2/3	61.00	330 weeks	20,130	66 2/3	61.00	330 weeks	20,130
Virginia	60	62.00	500 weeks	24,800	60	62.00	500 weeks	24,800
Washington		81.23	life			81.23	disability	
West Virginia	66 2/3	65.50	life		66 2/3	65.50	208 weeks	13,622
Wisconsin	70	79.00	life		70	79.00	disability	
Wyoming		34.61	life		66 2/3	63.46	disability	12,000

*The benefits of many states include technical exceptions and special limits. Furthermore, the reader is cautioned that state legislatures change the benefit levels periodically and it is impossible to assure that all figures will remain up to date.

Source: *Analysis of Workmen's Compensation Laws*, 1971 edition. (Washington, D.C.: U.S. Chamber of Commerce, 1971), pp. 22-23.

Workmen's compensation medical benefits are fairly liberal. Forty-four states put no limit on medical benefits.[5] Of the states that put limits on medical benefits, the typical limit is about $2,500.

Death benefits in workmen's compensation are often the same amount as the permanent total benefit, and limits are placed on the amount that will be paid. They range from $10,000 to $25,000.

(4) *Importance of workmen's compensation.* There is no doubt that workmen's compensation plans provide a needed source of income to many disabled people. It is important, however, to remember that workmen's compensation covers only *occupational* disabilities. In addition, even if a person is injured on the job he may not be covered under the state workmen's compensation law. And finally, even if a benefit is paid, the benefit will probably be only a small percentage of the injured worker's previous income. At best, workmen's compensation is only a partial solution to the disability problem.

Social Security.   Although the Social Security Act is best known for its retirement and survivor's benefits, the social security system contains very important disability provisions. There are three major types of disability benefits in our social security plan:

1. Disability freeze
2. Disability income payments
3. Medicare

A person must work in a covered employment before he will be eligible for any type of social security benefit.[6] Well over 90 percent of all employees are covered. Certain occupations, however, are excluded. Social security does not cover newsboys (under the age of 18), employees in family employment, nonprofit organizations, and government employees who are covered in other plans. Agricultural employees, clergymen, and the self-employed are covered under certain conditions.

The disability freeze benefit does not, itself, provide an income to a disabled person. This benefit is designed to protect a worker's retirement benefit if he is disabled. To qualify for retirement benefits a person must work in a covered employment for a certain period of time, and the amount of his retirement benefit is based on his average monthly earnings. Without the disability freeze benefit, a person who becomes disabled could lose his eligibility for retirement benefits or could have his retirement benefit decreased. The purpose of the disability freeze provision is to permit the retirement benefit to be calculated as if the person had never been disabled.

---

[5] About half the states limit medical expenses benefits for occupational diseases.

[6] Chapter Seventeen has a more complete description of certain aspects of the social security program.

The disability income benefit is paid to disabled workers who have worked in a covered employment and their dependents. It may also be paid to disabled dependents even if the person who has been covered is not disabled.[7] The amount of the benefit depends upon how much a person has earned in the past, but the basic disability benefit for a person who earns $650 a month is $218 a month.[8]

Medicare benefits are provided only to persons age 65 and over. They pay for hospital charges, doctor's fees, and other medical costs. The basic hospitalization benefit pays expenses for the period a person is in a hospital, up to 90 days. Eighty percent of doctor's fees are paid while a person is hospitalized.

How important are the social security disability benefits to a young person? There is no doubt that the disability freeze provision is valuable since it protects a disabled person's retirement benefit. And a disability income of several hundred dollars a month might be extremely helpful to a disabled person. But it is important to know that disability benefits are provided only to certain persons.

To collect disability benefits, a person must first be in a covered employment. This is usually not a problem, because most occupations are covered. But, in addition, a person must have worked a certain period of time. Specifically, a young person must have work in one-fourth of the calendar quarters since he was 21, and have at least 20 quarters of coverage during the last 40 quarters before he was disabled. This means a young person must have worked in covered employment at least five years before he will be eligible for disability benefits. Furthermore, the disability must be serious before a benefit will be paid. Benefits are not paid in the first six months of a disability and the disability must prevent the disabled person from engaging in "any substantial gainful activity." To make the eligibility for benefits even more restrictive, the disability must be expected to result in death, or continue for at least 12 months.

Medicare benefits are not very important to young people, since they are provided only to persons over age 65. These benefits, however, might be important to a young person if his or her parents are elderly.

As we have seen, government programs provide important disability benefits. But in most cases, a person will not have very complete health insurance protection from government programs. If a person wants fairly complete coverage, he must get protection from private sources.

INSURANCE COMPANIES

If a person wants more adequate health insurance protection than that provided by the government, he can buy a health insurance policy from

---

[7] Disability income benefits are now available to disabled widows and widowers between the ages of 50 and 62 if their former husband or wife was covered under social security.

[8] This benefit amount is presently scheduled to be increased.

a private health insurance company. Table 16–3 shows that only 42 companies in the United States write only health insurance, but many companies sell health insurance along with their other coverages.

Another feature of Table 16–3 that is important is the fact that a lot of health insurance is issued on a group basis. This is not surprising because group health insurance is an important fringe benefit that is provided by many employers.

BLUE CROSS-BLUE SHIELD ASSOCIATIONS

Blue Cross and Blue Shield Associations are not insurance companies, but these associations play an important role in providing protection against disability losses. Blue Cross plans provide hospital expense coverages and Blue Shield Associations provide coverage for physician's fees. Neither provide disability income benefits.

A Blue Cross Association is a voluntary nonprofit hospital expense prepayment plan that has received the approval of the American Hospital Association. There are about 80 such plans in the United States, and the details are different among the various plans.

One of the important characteristics of Blue Cross plans is that they usually provide benefits on a service basis. This means they do not provide coverage in terms of dollars, but in terms of service. In other words, an insurance policy might provide $25 a day for 120 days, but a comparable Blue Cross plan would provide hospital services for 120 days. Usually semiprivate rooms are provided, but if a Blue Cross member desires a private room he can pay the difference for the better room.

Blue Shield plans use the service basis for benefits, but many of them reimburse members for losses and the individuals pay the physician. Many Blue Shield plans state that if the member's income is less than a stated amount (say $4,000 for single members and $6,000 for family

Table 16–3 Number of Insurance Companies Writing Health Insurance (in 1966 by type of company and type of coverage)

Total Companies	Number of Companies
Life	706
Casualty	297
Monoline (offering health insurance only)	42
Number writing group insurance	703
Number writing individual insurance	942
Number writing both group and individual insurance	603
Number writing major medical expense policies	353
Number writing "substandard" policies	154
Number writing guaranteed renewable policies	438

Source: Health Insurance Institute, *Source Book of Health Insurance Data*, 1968, p. 51.

members) physicians who participate in the plan will accept the benefits in the plan as full payment for their services.

INDEPENDENT PLANS

Health protection is provided by independent plans that are neither insurance companies or Blue Cross-Blue Shield plans. These plans differ widely but they have several general characteristics.

First, many independent health care plans emphasize preventive medicine. Benefits such as annual examinations are common. Second, independent plans often provide services that are not provided in other plans. Dental care, eye care, and other routine expenditures are often covered. A third characteristic of independent health care plans is that many of them provide their own medical facilities and salaried staff. With an independent plan, a member simply goes to a medical center to receive medical attention, and most types of medical problems can be handled by the program. In terms of the number of people protected, independent plans are not nearly so important as insurance companies or Blue Cross-Blue Shield Associations.

TYPES OF HEALTH INSURANCE COVERAGES

One of the confusing features of health insurance policies is that several coverages are often combined together into one contract. It is helpful, however, to know that several types of coverages are available.

HOSPITALIZATION POLICIES

Hospitalization policies (often called hospital expense policies) are designed to reimburse a policyholder for hospital expenses; they do *not* pay doctor's fees. But a hospitalization policy usually covers room and board charges, laboratory fees, nursing care, use of the operating room, and certain supplies and medicines. Maternity benefits may or may not be covered. If maternity benefits are provided, they are not covered until the policy has been in force nine or ten months.

Medical expense policies sold by insurance companies usually state that the policyholder will be reimbursed for necessary hospital expenses up to a stated dollar amount, such as $25 or $30 a day. The policy then limits the number of days for which benefits will be paid. Many policies, for example, provide benefits up to 90 or 120 days.

Hospitalization contracts may be written on a family as well as an individual. If the coverage is provided to a family, children are usually covered from age two or three to a maximum age of 18 or 19. This means that students are often covered under their parents' medical expense policy while they are young, but later they must buy their own protection.

Figure 16–4 shows the importance of insurance policies, Blue Cross programs, and independent plans in providing medical expense coverage.

Figure 16–4   Number of Persons with Hospital Expense Protection

Insurance
Companies
100,298,000

Blue Cross
68,432,000

Independent
Plans
7,450,000

0   10   20   30   40   50   60   70   80   90   100
Number of Persons Protected (Millions)

Source: Health Insurance Institute, *1968 Source Book of Health Insurance Data,* p. 20.

SURGICAL EXPENSE POLICIES

Expenses for surgical operations are paid by the surgical expense coverage. This coverage sets forth a detailed allowance schedule that shows how much will be paid for various surgical procedures. An example of part of such a schedule is shown in Table 16–4.

Surgical expense coverages are usually included on an optional or compulsory basis as a part of hospitalization contract. In other words, a person who buys a hospital expense policy may have surgical benefits included automatically or he may have a choice, but rarely can a person buy surgical expense coverages by themselves. Figure 16–5 shows how surgical expense coverages are provided.

REGULAR MEDICAL POLICIES

Hospital expense coverage applies only to hospital expenses, and surgical expense insurance applies only to charges for surgery. Neither hospital

Figure 16–5   Number of Persons with Surgical Expense Protection

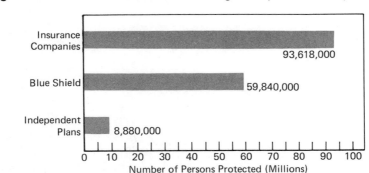

Insurance
Companies
93,618,000

Blue Shield
59,840,000

Independent
Plans
8,880,000

0   10   20   30   40   50   60   70   80   90   100
Number of Persons Protected (Millions)

Source: Health Insurance Institute, *1968 Source Book of Health Insurance Data,* p. 21.

Table 16–4   Example of Surgical Benefits

Operation	Maximum Benefit
Abdomen	
Appendectomy	$ 150.00
Gall bladder	200.00
Ulcer	125.00
Breast	
Excision of cyst	100.00
Complete mastectomy	212.50
Radial mastectomy	412.50
Digestive	
Total gastrectomy	675.00
Cholecystotomy	320.00
Exploratory laparotomy	260.00
Ear	
Myringotomy	20.00
Mastoidectomy, simple	320.00
Eye	
Sclerectomy for glaucoma	400.00
Fractures	
Nasal, closed reduction	50.00
Pelvis, open reduction	412.50
Femur, open reduction	500.00
Heart	
Repair aortic valve	1,000.00
Repair myocardial aneurysm	1,250.00
Excision intracardiac tumor	1,250.00
Maternity	
Cesarean section	320.00
Obstetrical dilation and currettage of uterus	100.00
Rectum	
Hemorrhoidectomy, external	130.00
Hemorrhoidectomy, internal and external	175.00
Fissurectomy and hemorrhoidectomy	175.00
Tumors	
Biopsy of skin	25.00
Malignant tumors of skin	87.50
Varicose Veins	
Infection treatment, one or both legs	62.50
Cutting operation, one or both legs	75.00

expense coverage nor surgical expense insurance covers doctor's fees (other than surgery). Regular medical coverage provides benefit payments for physicians' charges. Usually the benefit is expressed as so much (five dollars or eight dollars, for example) per visit. Most of the contracts pay these benefits if the doctor's visits are made in the hospital, the insured's home, or the doctor's office. Regular medical expense protection is usually included in a hospitalization policy.

MAJOR MEDICAL POLICIES

The type of health insurance coverage that has been gaining most in popularity in recent years is the contract known as major medical insurance. This coverage is designed to meet large medical expenses. Usually, a person would buy either major medical insurance or some combination of hospitalization, surgical, and regular medical expense insurance. In other words, if a person carries major medical coverage he usually would not carry the other coverages since the major medical policy covers hospital, surgical, and doctor's expenses.

Major medical coverages have four important characteristics. First, policies have high face amounts. Policies with $10,000, $15,000, and even $25,000 limits are common. Deductibles are another characteristic of major medical coverages. Most companies sell major medical policies with $100, $250, $500, and higher deductibles. This gives the policyholder a choice. Of course, the larger deductible selected by the policyholder, the lower the cost of the insurance. A third important characteristic of major medical policies is coinsurance.[9] This clause stipulates that the insurance company will pay only 75 or 80 percent of covered expenses after the deductible amount has been paid by the policyholder. The purpose of the coinsurance clause is to give the policyholder an incentive to keep expenses down. If the insurance company reimbursed the policyholder for 100 percent of his expenses he might be inclined to incur expenses that are not absolutely necessary. The coinsurance provision also has the effect of reducing premiums. The fourth characteristic of major medical coverages is broad protection with few "internal limits." In other words, the policy has few exclusions (most types of medical expenses are covered) and there are few (if any) limitations that apply to certain types of services. Other health insurance policies usually have separate limits for different types of expenses that are covered under the policies.

The following example will clarify the major medical coverage. Suppose Harry Smith is injured in an accident while he is on vacation in San Francisco. As a result of the accident, Harry loses $1,000 in income because he cannot work for ten weeks. In addition, he incurs $800 in doctor's bills and $1,200 in hospital expenses. If Harry has a major medical policy with a $250 deductible and an 80 percent coinsurance clause, how much will he collect? He will collect nothing for the lost income. Major medical policies cover medical expenses only. He will collect 80 percent of the hospital and doctor's fees, but only after the deductible has been paid by Harry. This means his collection will be $1,200. ($2,000 minus $500 times 80 percent). Without coverage the accident would have cost Harry $3,000.

---

[9] The student should realize that the word "coinsurance" does not mean the same thing it means when used in property insurance.

COMPREHENSIVE INSURANCE

The word "comprehensive" is one that is used in various ways in insurance. When it is used in medical expense insurance, however, it has a very definite meaning. In this context, comprehensive insurance is a combination of basic hospitalization and major medical insurance. The need for comprehensive insurance arises because some people believe the maximum benefit limits in hospitalization policies are too low, but they do not like the large deductible in major medical policies. A comprehensive policy, therefore, has a low deductible (of maybe $25 or $50) but very high limits.

OTHER EXPENSE COVERAGES

Many medical expense coverages exclude or limit the benefits for certain types of expenses. This is necessary because certain types of medical care involve special problems. Nervous or mental illness is a good example. Many policies do not cover mental illness (or cover it with low limits) because mental illness is poorly understood, insurance companies have trouble calculating rates, and the government has taken some responsibility in caring for the mentally ill. Special problems are also involved in expenses for nursing home care, prescription drugs, private duty nursing, vision and dental charges. As a result, only a relatively few people have coverage for these types of expenses. This is shown in Table 16–5.

If a policyholder wants coverage for these expenses, he should carefully check the provisions in the hospital, surgical, and regular medical policies. If these policies do not provide adequate coverage, he should consider the possibility of buying separate policies for such special coverages. More and more insurance companies have been making these policies available.[10]

DISABILITY INCOME

All the health policies previously described only cover medical expenses. Policies are also available that will provide an income to the policyholder when he is disabled. Disability income policies invariably have a waiting period, which means the policyholder does not collect for the first week, two weeks, or month of his disability. The length of the waiting period is chosen by the policyholder when he buys the policy. Waiting periods, since they are a form of deductible, are one way to cut down the amount of the insurance premium.

Suppose a person earns $150 a week. If he is disabled, the loss of income over a period of time may be substantial. Such a person could buy a policy that would replace a portion, say 80 percent, of his lost income. If he is disabled, he collects $120 a week. Notice that in this

---

[10] Some losses are not insurable under any policy. Injuries incurred in war and intentional injuries, for example, cannot be insured.

Table 16-5 Number of Persons with Health Insurance Coverage of Various Services

Type of Service	All Ages		Under Age 65		Aged 65 and Over	
	Number (In Thousands)	Percent of Population [1]	Number (In Thousands)	Percent of Population [1]	Number (In Thousands)	Percent of Population [1]
Hospital care	158,022	81.2	148,589	84.5	9,433	50.5
Surgery	144,715	74.4	137,448	78.1	7,267	38.9
In-hospital visits	116,462	59.9	110,754	63.0	5,708	30.6
X-ray and laboratory examinations[2]	93,459	48.0	89,750	51.0	3,709	19.9
Physicians' office and home visits	73,706	37.9	70,993	40.4	2,713	14.5
Dental care	4,227	2.2	4,143	2.4	84	.4
Prescribed drugs[2]	65,544	33.7	63,845	36.3	1,699	9.1
Private-duty nursing	68,722	35.3	66,632	37.9	2,090	11.2
Visiting nurse service	79,004	40.6	76,453	43.5	2,551	13.7
Nursing home care	17,814	9.2	14,999	8.5	2,815	15.1

[1] Civilian population.

[2] Out-of-hospital.

Source: Louis S. Reed, "Private Health Insurance: Coverage and Financial Experience 1940-66," *Social Security Bulletin,* November 1967, p. 4.

example, the person will not collect the full amount of his lost income. But a person who collects 80 percent of his income when he is not working is just about as well off financially as he would be working. This is because a disabled person does not pay certain expenses connected with work (such as transportation costs to work, taxes, and meals).

LIMITED POLICIES

Many health insurance policies have unusual exclusions, restrictions, or benefits. These limited policies often cover only disabilities that result from certain types of accidents (travel accident policies, for example) or they may cover only certain types of diseases. The "dread disease" policy, for example, may cover only polio, diphtheria, scarlet fever, leukemia, small pox, encephalitis, and spinal meningitis.

Most limited policies are not very popular, but accidental death and dismemberment policies seem to be growing in popularity. This is probably because their principal appeal is low cost and many of the travel accident policies are included in a group insurance plan.

IMPORTANT PURCHASE DECISIONS

SELECTING THE TYPE OF POLICY TO PURCHASE

When a person decides to buy health insurance protection, he has a wide range of choices. What type of policy should he buy? Should a person buy basic hospitalization, major medical, or comprehensive insurance? What about disability income? Is this more important or less important than expense coverage? Another decision may be involved with group versus individual insurance.

In evaluating the desirability of group health insurance, a person usually has no problem. Group insurance is almost always a bargain for an individual. If the plan is noncontributory (that is, the employer pays the full cost) the employee has no choice. If the plan is contributory (requires the employee to pay part of the cost), it is still usually a bargain because: (1) the employee is paying only *part* of the cost, and (2) group insurance can be sold at lower rates than individual insurance because the insurance company uses economical mass merchandising techniques with group insurance.

The decision to buy basic hospitalization, major medical, or comprehensive insurance is quite simple. A person should protect himself against the losses that are large enough to be important to him. This means a buyer should buy insurance protection for catastrophic losses and pay small, routine expenses himself. This is a strong argument in favor of major medical or comprehensive coverage.

Next, a person should decide how large a deductible he can afford. Consider the following example: Mr. A is 45 years old and earns $26,000 a year. Small losses are not important to him, and he decides that any loss less than $1,000 would not be a major problem. Mr. B, on the other hand, is a college student and is living on a small income. To him, a $50 loss would be a significant financial strain. Which type of policy should Mr. A and Mr. B buy? A major medical policy with a $1,000 deductible seems appropriate for Mr. A. He would be protected against large losses and could handle losses less than $1,000 himself, more economically than an insurance company. (Remember an insurance company must add in their expenses and profit when they calculate insurance rates.) Mr. B, however, must have a policy with a small deductible. This means he must choose between a basic hospitalization policy and a comprehensive contract. (He could choose a $50 deductible with either.) If he can pay the higher premium of the comprehensive policy, this would be preferable because he would be protected against large losses. If he decides that the premium is too expensive, he could choose the basic hospitalization protection.

Most people in the United States have health insurance. In fact, 85 percent of the population is protected by some form of health insurance coverage.[11] But relatively few individuals have any disability income insurance. The percentage of the population with disability income protection is only about 20 percent. Apparently most people either believe medical expense insurance is more important than disability income coverage or medical expense coverage is sold more effectively.

In any event, a person should recognize the importance of disability income insurance. When a person is disabled, the income loss can easily be more important than medical expenses. If a person incurs medical expenses he might be able to return to work and struggle along even with accumulating hospital and medical bills. But the effects of cutting off income cannot be postponed. Most families must have a regular inflow of cash to meet the necessities of life. Young families that operate on a tight cash flow should be particularly impressed with the importance of disability income insurance.

EVALUATING POLICY PROVISIONS

The policy provisions in health insurance contracts are not so uniform as they are in other types of policies. Some policies have much more liberal provisions than others. And too often, policyholders do not discover that they have carried restrictive protection until after they are disabled. When a person buys a health insurance policy, therefore, it is important to evaluate its provisions.

Persons Covered. A health insurance policy may cover only the applicant, but some policies provide coverage for dependents. Many group medical expense coverages provide protection for the family of the

---

[11] Health Insurance Institute, *1969 Source Book of Health Insurance Data*, p. 18.

employee. Loss of income policies, of course, are not provided to dependents. Working wives can buy disability income protection, but insurance companies are more cautious than they are when they sell insurance to husbands. This is because some working wives might be tempted to "retire" from their jobs if they can collect insurance benefits.

Before a person buys a health insurance policy he should check to determine if the policy covers his dependents. If it does, he should check further to determine if the coverage on his dependents is the same as the coverage on himself. Some policies give dependents' coverage, but the protection for dependents may be more limited.

Perils Covered.   Many health insurance policies provide coverage only if the policyholder is disabled by an accident. These *accident only* policies do not offer very broad protection because most people die from diseases rather than accidents. The limited coverage, however, is very popular because the premium is much lower if accidents are the only peril covered.

Broader policies cover illness as well as accidents. The cost of this broader coverage will be higher, but why should a person protect himself only against accidents? The loss is just as high (or higher) when a person is ill. Of course, even the broader policies will have exclusions, and these should be recognized before a person buys a policy. Common exclusions are losses caused by mental illness, tuberculosis, pregnancy, dental treatment, intentionally self-inflicted injuries, war, and losses under workmen's compensation laws. If a person wants to cover some of these perils, it may be necessary to buy separate policies.

Another type of exclusion that is extremely important is the exclusion of pre-existing conditions. Although these problems are handled in different ways, the most common approach is to exclude losses that result from health problems the policyholder had before he bought the policy. Suppose a person has an ulcer. If he buys a health insurance policy, the contract will probably exclude any losses that result from the ulcer. This is, incidentally, an important reason to buy health insurance when you are young. If you wait until you are older to purchase health insurance, it is very likely that health problems will develop and it may be difficult or impossible to get complete coverage. More and more insurance companies are selling policies that protect against preexisting conditions, but in these cases the premium might be quite expensive.

Definition of Disability.   In medical expense policies it is rather easy to determine when a person should be reimbursed for a loss. The only requirement is that hospital, surgical, or doctor's expenses have been incurred.[12] But when should a person qualify for loss of income benefits?

---

[12] Some policies provide reimbursement only when the insured has been treated by a licensed physician or is incurring expenses in a legitimate hospital.

This question is answered by the "definition of disability" given in the policy. Most policies have a fairly liberal definition for the first two or three years a person is disabled, but thereafter, the definition becomes more stringent. The typical definition is as follows:

> For the purpose of determining the commencement of total disability and thereafter for the first 36 months that the Monthly Income Benefit may be payable during any continuous period of such disability, total disability means only such complete incapacity of the Insured that he is unable to perform any of the duties of his occupation, and for the remainder of any such period of continuous disability, total disability means only such complete incapacity that the Insured is unable to perform the duties of any occupation.

Notice that the typical definition of disability changes from "his occupation" requirement to an "any occupation" standard. Consider an example of a college professor who loses his voice as the result of an accident. Since he would not be able to continue "his occupation" he would qualify for benefits. But later if he could work with a publisher in a position that did not require speaking, he would not be able to collect benefits.[13]

When a person buys a disability income contract, he should examine the definition of disability. Some policies have more stringent definitions than the typical provision described above.[14] Also, it is important to know how long a disability can last before the definition changes to an "any occupation" standard. Some policies change to the more stringent definition after two years, but others may change after three, four, or five years. Another reason for examining the definition of disability is that some policies provide partial disability benefits. These contracts pay a reduced income if a person can work but is not able to earn his normal income.

Supplementary Benefits. It is common for health insurance policies to have special, optional coverages. An accidental death benefit pays the lump sum death benefit stipulated in the policy if the insured is killed in an accident. Most people would probably be better off by buying life insurance. This is because life insurance provides protection when the insured dies from any cause with only a few exceptions.[15]

---

[13] Courts have generally interpreted "any occupation" to mean any occupation for which the insured is suited by education, training, and experience.

[14] For example, some policies have "house confinement" clauses. These provisions require a person to be unable to leave his home before disability income benefits will be paid.

[15] The possible exclusions in a life insurance policy were described in Chapter Fifteen.

A double indemnity benefit is also provided in many health insurance policies. There is an important difference between this benefit and the benefit by the same name in life insurance. In life insurance, a double indemnity provision pays the face amount of the policy when the insured is killed accidentally. Since health insurance policies often have an accidental death benefit, the double indemnity clause can only pay an additional amount if the insured is killed in *certain kinds of accidents*. In health insurance policies, the double indemnity benefit is usually payable only if the insured is killed:

1. While a passenger in public transportation
2. While a passenger in an elevator
3. By collapse or burning of a building
4. By explosion of a steam boiler
5. By a hurricane or tornado, or
6. By a bolt of lightning

Obviously, the double indemnity benefit is very limited and probably a poor purchase.

Another type of supplementary benefit that is found in many health insurance policies is a scehdule of specific dismemberment benefits. In some policies, the insured is given an option of continuing to receive disability income benefits or receive the specific dismemberment benefit. In other policies, the insured may collect both. Part of a specific dismemberment schedule is illustrated below:

Loss	*Benefit*
Life	The Principal Sum
Both hands or both feet or sight of both eyes	The Principal Sum
One hand and one foot	Three-fourths the Principal Sum
Sight of one eye and either one hand or one foot	Three-fourths the Principal Sum
One hand or one foot or sight of one eye	One-half the Principal Sum

Although insurance buyers may think it would be financially helpful to collect dismemberment benefits, it is more logical to provide benefits when there has been a financial loss (from any cause) and not restrict protection to certain events.

The waiver of premium benefit, which is the same as it is in life insurance, is a financially worthwhile benefit. It pays the premiums on the health insurance policy while the insured is disabled.

Change of Occupation Provision. The occupation of a policyholder is particularly important to a company that provides disability income benefits. Some occupations are much safer than others. What happens when a clerk buys a disability income policy and becomes a steeplejack? The change of occupation clause covers this situation. It states that the insured clerk will not collect greater benefits than the premiums he has paid will purchase for the more hazardous occupation. If the insured changes to a *less* hazardous occupation, the insurance company does not provide greater benefits (since this might cause some people to fake injuries), but the company agrees to return the difference in premiums between the two occupational classifications.

Deductibles. Most health insurance policies have a deductible of some type. In basic medical expense policies the insured may have to incur $25 or $50 in expenses before a policy will pay benefits, and the deductible may run as high as $500 or $1,000 in a major medical policy. In disability income policies, benefits are not paid for the waiting period, which is the first week, month, or six months after the disability has started. Since the logic of deductibles has been covered elsewhere in this book, little will be said here. Suffice it to state that a person should choose the largest deductible (or longest waiting period) that he can without causing a financial strain on himself if there is a loss.

Benefit Limits. One of the surprising facts about health insurance is that a large proportion of the population carries health insurance, but only a small portion of health losses are actually reimbursed. In many cases, a person has health insurance but he collects only a part of his loss when he is disabled. Why? Part of the answer is that most policies have some form of deductible and many policies have a coinsurance provision. But the policyholder should know that these provisions will keep him from collecting 100 percent of his loss. When a policyholder expects to collect more than he does collect, serious problems can arise. These problems arise frequently when the policy limits are inadequate.

Consider medical expense policies first. Suppose a person has a hospitalization policy that pays $18 a day for room and board in the hospital. If the actual hospital charges are $38 a day, the policyholder will lose $20 each day he remains in the hospital. If the surgical benefits are not so high as the actual charges of the surgeon, there will be an additional loss. The same is true for doctor's fees.

The aggregate limit is also important in severe cases. Some health insurance policies provide hospitalization for 60 days, but what happens if the person is disabled for a longer period of time? Of all disabled people, over 35 percent are disabled for more than 18 months.[16]

---

[16] O. D. Dickerson, *Health Insurance,* 3rd edition (Homewood, Illinois: Richard D. Irwin, Inc., 1968), p. 35.

It is very important, then, to examine the policy limits carefully before a medical expense policy is purchased. The potential policyholder should not only check the aggregate limit, but the internal limits as well.

When a person buys a disability income policy, the contract will provide benefits for only a maximum period of time. Policies may provide benefits for one year, three years, five years, or almost any period of time. Most policies give protection for a rather brief duration. Some policies, however, provide benefits for a long period, some even for a person's entire lifetime. The reason short benefit periods are popular is that the premium is lower. The cost of a long benefit period may seem high. In most cases, however, a person would be better off financially to take a longer waiting period in order to be able to afford a longer benefit period. This is because a person can usually manage without an income for a short period of time when he is disabled, but it may be difficult or impossible to have no income for a long time.

Cancellation and Renewability.   One of the most important provisions in a health insurance policy is the clause that deals with cancellation and renewability. There are at least five different types of provisions in common use.

Some health insurance policies are cancellable. These contracts can be terminated either by the policyholder or insurance company. If the policyholder cancels, the cancellation is effective immediately when the insurance company receives the notification, unless the insured has specified a later date. If the insurance company cancels, a minimum of five days notice is required.

Suppose Dick buys a cancellable medical expense policy. Six months later (during the policy period) he becomes seriously ill. Doctors discover that Dick is suffering from emphysema, a chronic lung disease. Dick's policy provides a maximum hospitalization benefit of 90 days, but after Dick has spent 23 days in the hospital his insurance company cancels his policy. What does this mean for Dick? An insurance company can never revoke its benefits, so Dick can continue to collect benefits for as long as he is in the hospital (up to 90 days) even if his policy has been cancelled. The real problem for Dick is getting a new policy. He might be able to get another policy, but even if he can, the chances are great that the new policy will exclude any chronic lung condition. Dick will then be unable to get health insurance coverage against his serious health problem.

Some health insurance policies are not cancellable, but they can be renewed only if the insurance company wants to renew them. These policies, called optionally renewable contracts, are only slightly better than a cancellable policy. The insurance company cannot cancel an optionally renewable policy, but they do not have to renew it. Since most health insurance policies are written for a period of one year, a policyholder is not very well protected. Suppose a person develops cancer. If he has an optionally renewable policy, his company will probably decline to renew his contract after the one year of protection expires.

A stronger guarantee is provided by a conditionally renewable policy. These contracts give the policyholder the right to continue his coverage (for a certain period of time or until the insured gets to a certain age) but the insurance company, under certain conditions, can refuse to renew the policy. Or, stated another way, the insurance company cannot use certain stipulated reasons to refuse the renewal. For example, the policy may state that poor health cannot be used as a reason to refuse renewal. If a person buys this type of policy and later becomes ill, he is assured that he will continue to have health insurance coverage against his illness.

A guaranteed renewable policy provides an even stronger assurance of continued protection. This kind of policy cannot be cancelled, and the insurance company must renew it at least until the insured reaches age 50.[17] Some guaranteed renewable policies are renewable for longer periods. An insurance company cannot change any provision in a guaranteed renewable policy while the contract is in force, except the company can change the premium *for classes of policyholders.* If a person's health deteriorates, his premium cannot be raised unless the insurance company decides to raise the rates for every other policyholder in his class. The insurance company will be reluctant to raise the premium for all policyholders in the class because healthy policyholders might be inclined to drop their coverage.

Noncancellable health insurance policies offer all the guarantees of a guaranteed renewable contract, but the insurance company cannot change the premium schedule at all. In other words, the insurance company cannot cancel the policy, the company must renew the policy at least until age 50,[18] and the insurance company cannot change *any* provision in the policy. If the policy has one rate, that rate will apply as long as the contract is in force. Some policies, however, have rate increases scheduled at various ages in the original policy. For example, the policy may state that the rate at ages 20–30 is so much, but a higher rate will apply between ages 30–50, and an even higher rate will apply at the older ages. Although the rate increases with age, the rates are guaranteed and cannot be changed even for classes of policyholders.

Examine Table 16–6. It shows the cost of different types of health insurance policies. How much would it cost a person aged 25 to buy a disability income policy that provides $200 a month? The answer (pro-

---

[17] Or, the policy must provide protection for at least 5 years if it is issued after age 49.

[18] The same time period described in the previous footnote applies to noncancellable policies.

vided by using Table 16–6) is $29 a year for a policy that is renewable at the option of the insurance company, and $51.20 a year for a noncancellable policy. The cost of the noncancellable policy is more than twice as high. Why should a person buy? It is very difficult to justify the purchase of a health insurance policy that does not have a relatively strong guarantee to continue coverage. If a person buys an optionally renewable policy, he is likely to be without coverage when it is most needed. Nevertheless, most people buy policies that are optionally renewable because the cost is lower.

Table 16–6   Cost of Disability Income Insurance Policies with Different Renewal Provisions

Type of Renewal Provision	Annual Premium (per $100 of Monthly Income)	
	Age 25	*Age 45*
Renewable at the option of the company	$14.50	$17.30
Guaranteed renewable	21.15	39.20
Noncancellable	25.60	48.12

SELECTING A HEALTH INSURER

Should a person buy health coverage from an insurance company, a Blue Cross-Blue Shield Association, or an independent plan? This question is answered, in part, by knowing the type of insurance a person wants to buy. Blue Cross-Blue Shield plans do not sell disability income insurance and they provide only a small amount of major medical (or comprehensive) coverage. As a practical matter, then, a person usually has a choice between insurance companies and Blue Cross-Blue Shield only when he is considering basic hospitalization (hospital expense, surgical expense, and regular medical) coverage.

Insurance agents usually argue that their plans are better than Blue Cross-Blue Shield coverages and Blue Cross-Blue Shield representatives contend that they have superior health plans. The basic arguments in favor of the Blue Cross-Blue Shield plans, which may or may not have much validity, are:

1. Nonprofit status. Most Blue Cross-Blue Shield organizations are legally nonprofit associations. This relieves them from paying certain taxes, or at least gives them tax advantages over insurance companies.
2. Service benefits. As indicated previously, Blue Cross-Blue Shield plans often provide benefits on a service basis. This is an advantage over typical insurance policies, because the benefit limits in insurance policies might not be adequate to pay hospital and physician's charges.

3. Contracts with physicians and hospitals. Blue Cross-Blue Shield representatives claim that they provide services at "wholesale rates." They make this claim because doctors and hospitals who participate in the plan often agree to provide their services at certain costs.
4. Community sponsorship. The objectives of Blue Cross-Blue Shield plan is to enable as many members in their programs as possible. They argue that the majority of the community is behind their plans.
5. Community rating. Traditionally, Blue Cross-Blue Shield plans have had few rating classifications. This means a family with many children may pay the same rate as a family with only a few children.

Insurance companies are quick to counter those arguments. According to insurance company employees:

1. Blue Cross-Blue Shield plans are not more "nonprofit" than mutual insurance companies. Even stock insurance companies, which are organized by stockholders to make a profit, argue that the profits are only a small proportion of total insurance costs.
2. Service benefits are sometimes provided by insurance companies. Furthermore, if the dollar limits are adequate in the insurance policy, there is no advantage of service benefits.
3. Contracts with physicians and hospitals may not be an advantage of Blue Cross-Blue Shield plans. In fact, they may encourage doctors to overutilize services.
4. Community sponsorship is a meaningless concept. Very few Blue Cross-Blue Shield plans have enrolled 50 percent of the population in their community in their plan.
5. Community rating may tend to produce lower rates for some members, but it also makes rates higher for others. If a Blue Cross-Blue Shield plan charges the same to a family of three as it charges to a family of ten, the small family probably can get lower rates from an insurance company.

The arguments between insurance companies and Blue Cross-Blue Shield plans undoubtedly will continue because it is probably impossible to determine which type is "better." There is great variation among health insurance policies; some are much better than others. The same is true of Blue Cross-Blue Shield plans. The only logical approach for an individual to follow is to compare the coverages and costs of one insurance policy to the coverages and costs of a specific Blue Cross-Blue Shield plan.

In considering the company from which to buy health insurance, most people overlook the fact that they can actually buy some of their health insurance protection through their life insurance policies. It should not be surprising to you that a great many life insurance companies sell health insurance. The waiver of premium, double indemnity, and disability income coverages sold with life insurance policies are actually forms of health insurance.

The disability income rider in life insurance policies, in fact, is a good way to buy health insurance. If you were to compare the disability income benefits in a typical health insurance policy to those that can be purchased with a life insurance policy, you would find that the life insurance approach has several advantages. A disability income rider on a life insurance policy is guaranteed renewable. Health insurance policies, we have seen, usually do not provide guaranteed renewable coverage. The benefits in a life insurance rider are payable for life (or either the policy will mature as an endowment if the insured becomes disabled). Benefits are seldom payable for life in health insurance policies. Another important advantage of life insurance disability income benefits is that the premiums tend to be lower than they would be for a health insurance policy with comparable benefits. This is because of the longer waiting period in the disability income rider and a smaller charge for expenses. (The expenses in the life insurance policy help cover some of the health insurance expenses.)

With all these advantages, it is unfortunate that so few people use the disability income provision on their life insurance policies. Disability income riders are sold with only about 4 percent of new life insurance policies.[19] Life insurance agents, it is said, are often reluctant to sell disability income benefits because they believe they may ruin the life insurance sale if they push the disability income provision. Perhaps more consumers will use their life insurance policies to get disability income protection as they become better educated.

SUMMARY

The costs of illness and disability are high and have been increasing rapidly. These costs are difficult to handle. They can be paid as an out-of-pocket expenditure, but this is a poor way to handle costs because disability and illness are so unpredictable for an individual. Some people may go years without a health problem, but others can be hit by a serious disability that costs many thousands of dollars.

The government provides several methods of helping people meet disability losses. Public assistance is important for poor people. Workmen's compensation is an important method of meeting disability losses, but only for those who are injured on their job. Social security also provides some important health insurance benefits. But most of the government programs provide low benefits and they do not cover all types of disabilities. More and more people, therefore, are buying health insurance protection from insurance companies, Blue Cross-Blue Shield Associations and independent health care plans.

When a person buys health protection, he should make sure he understands the basic types of policies. Then, after selecting the appropriate

---

[19] O. D. Dickerson, *Health Insurance,* p. 460.

form of coverage, a person should study the important provisions in his contract. Some health policies are much more liberal than others. It is especially important to analyze the provisions that determine how long the coverage can be continued. The decision to purchase coverage from an insurance company or a Blue Shield-Blue Cross Association is difficult, but every buyer should at least be aware of the basic issues involved.

Case Problems

1. Jim Sprayberry thinks social security is fine, but it is not too important to him. He realizes, of course, that social security provides some health insurance benefits, but Jim is young (only 18) and he believes he will not be eligible for benefits until he is much older. Jim understands that the health insurance benefits in social security are important to his father, who has been covered for about 30 years.
   (a) Jim has just started his first full-time job. Is he eligible for any type of health benefits under the social security system? Explain.
   (b) Suppose Jim is still a dependent of his father, would he then be eligible for other benefits? Explain.

2. Since Mike's employer does not provide group health insurance protection for his employees, Mike has decided that he should purchase some type of health insurance policy. Mike's agent has explained that he has a basic decision between a hospitalization policy and a major medical contract. But Mike is a little confused because the agent has said that both policies would cover about the same type of expenses.
   (a) How should Mike approach his decision between a basic hospitalization policy and a major medical contract?
   (b) If Mike's employer sets up a contributory group health insurance plan, should Mike participate in the plan?
   (c) Suppose Mike has no other coverage except a major medical policy, what is the next most important type of health insurance that Mike should consider?

3. Joe Dodd is a healthy young college student. In fact, during college Joe used to tell his friends that he "had never been sick a day in his life." And because Joe had such great faith in his health, he never purchased a health insurance policy. He even declined the group health insurance coverage he was offered because it was contributory and Joe didn't want to pay any health insurance premiums at all. When Joe was about 29 years old, he suddenly found out that he had developed high blood pressure. His doctor explained that the health problem was serious but he could probably expect a long life. It was amazing how interested Joe became in health insurance! He started talking to several insurance agents about a policy. But now Joe has been told that he can buy a health insurance policy but "there is a problem." If Joe can get the coverage, what do you think the problem might be?

4. When Bill bought life insurance, he decided to have "double indemnity" coverage on his policy. Now Bill is in the process of buying a health

insurance policy and the agent has asked him if he wants double indemnity coverage. How would you advise Bill on this question?

5. Frank has decided to buy a health insurance policy and he has narrowed down his decision to three policies. He has studied the policies carefully, and he is convinced that the coverages and provisions are very close. As a result, Frank has decided to compare their costs. The first policy, sold by Company A is optionally renewable and has a premium of $205 each year. The second policy, offered by Company B is guaranteed renewable and the annual premium is $350. The third is sold by Company C and noncancellable. It costs $385 a year.
   (a) Can Company A's policy be cancelled by the insurance company?
   (b) Which policy would you recommend for Frank?

6. Mary wants to buy Blue Cross-Blue Shield protection and her husband, Grant, wants to buy a policy from a health insurance company.
   (a) If you were supporting Mary's arguments, what are the points you would make?
   (b) If you were Grant, how would you argue with Mary?

7. Since Don works for a small company that does not have a group health insurance plan, he has decided that he should buy a health insurance policy himself. After talking with several insurance agents he has narrowed his decision down to two policies. They cover medical expenses and disability income, and the premiums are about the same. The problem for Don, therefore, is to decide which policy is more desirable. If you were to make a list of provisions that Don should check would you include?

8. Al and Betty Hoflander seldom have serious arguments. But still, sometimes small arguments develop into major problems. They have just about reached this stage in an argument they are having about their health insurance. Betty argues that all her friends believe Blue Cross-Blue Shield is better than other health insurance coverages, but Al thinks the insurance companies offer a better policy at lower rates. You have tried to stay out of the argument but now they ask you which is better. How would you answer?

Selected Readings

Avnet, Helen H. and Nikias, Mata K. *Insured Dental Care.* New York: Group Health Dental Insurance Inc., 1967.

Bartleson, Edwin L., *et. al. Health Insurance Provided Through Individual Policies.* Chicago: Society of Actuaries, 1968.

Blue Cross and Blue Shield Fact Book. Blue Cross Association and National Association of Blue Shield Plans, Chicago, Illinois. Published annually.

Changing Times, The Kiplinger Magazine:
   "How Would You Pay a $15,000 Hospital Bill?" August 1969, pp. 7–10.
   "Insurance That Pays You When You Can't Work." September 1970, pp. 31–33.
   "Time to Check Over Your Health Insurance." June 1970, pp. 15–18.

"What Kind of Health Insurance Should You Have?" May 1967, pp. 7–9.

Denenberg, Herbert S., *et. al. Risk and Insurance.* Englewood Cliffs, N.J.: Prentice-Hall, Inc., 1964.

Dickerson, O. D., *Health Insurance.* 3rd edition. Homewood, Illinois: Richard D. Irwin, Inc., 1968.

Eilers, Robert D. and Crowe, Robert M. (eds.). *Group Insurance Handbook.* Homewood, Illinois: Richard D. Irwin, Inc., 1965.

Faltermayer, E. K. "Better Care at Less Cost Without Miracles," *Fortune,* January 1970, pp. 80–83.

Follman, J. F., Jr. *Insurance Coverage for Mental Illness.* New York: American Management Association, 1970.

Greene, Mark R. *Risk and Insurance.* 2nd edition. Cincinnati: South-Western Publishing Company.

Gregg, Davis W. (ed.). *Life and Health Insurance Handbook.* Revised edition. Homewood, Illinois: Richard D. Irwin, Inc., 1964.

Harrison, B. P., "Health Insurance for Everyone." *Today's Health,* November 1968, p. 90.

"How to Buy Health Insurance." *Successful Farming,* December 24, 1970, March 1970.

Huebner, S. S. and Black, Kenneth, Jr. *Life Insurance.* 7th edition. New York: Appleton-Century-Crofts, 1969.

Kittner, D. R. "Changes In Health and Insurance Plans for Salaried Employees." *Monthly Labor Review,* February 1970, pp. 32–39.

Knox, G. M., "How to Deal with Your Biggest Health Costs." *Better Homes and Gardens,* September 1968, p. 44.

Mowbray, Albert, *et. al. Insurance.* 6th edition. New York: McGraw-Hill Book Company, 1969.

Williams, C. Arthur, Jr. and Heins, Richard M. *Risk Management and Insurance.* New York: McGraw-Hill Book Company, 1964.

CHAPTER **SEVENTEEN**

PROVIDING RETIREMENT INCOME

Young people are seldom interested in planning their retirement income. For a person who is 20 years old, the usual retirement age is 45 years away. Who can plan 45 years into the future? In 45 years a family may go through wars, economic depressions, inflation, deaths, divorces, disability, and other major problems. The typical young family has enough difficulty in obtaining current income, and income 45 years into the future usually does not seem very important.

THE IMPORTANCE OF PLANNING RETIREMENT INCOME

Although young people may not be very concerned about retirement income, a very important question is, "Why should a person—while he is still young—be interested in his financial security during retirement?" As a first step in answering this question, it is helpful to look at the income figures of persons who are now retired.

INCOME OF RETIRED PERSONS

How much income does a typical retired person have? Table 17–1 answers this question. Although people over age 65 have been improving their financial position, over one-half of the aged married couples have less than $3,000 annual income. Only 20 percent have incomes over $5,000, and the median income is only $2,875. Only 5 percent of the married couples have an income of over $10,000.

What does all this mean to a young person? It means this: although most young people probably believe they will never be forced into poverty, many young people will face a bare subsistence level of income after they retire unless they are much more successful than others have been in the past. How can a young person avoid the mistakes that others

614

Table 17–1   Income Status of Persons Over Age 65

Income	Percentage Distribution		
	Married Couples	*Nonmarried Men*	*Nonmarried Women*
Less than $1,000	5	32	49
$1,000–$1,999	24	37	34
$2,000–$2,999	25	16	10
$3,000–$3,999	16	6	3
$4,000–$4,999	11	3	1
$5,000–$5,999	15	6	3
$10,000 & over	5	1	*
Median income	$2,875	$1,365	$1,015

*Less than .5 percent

Source: John G. Turnbull, C. Arthur Williams, Jr. and Earl F. Cheit, *Economic and Social Security,* 3rd edition, revised printing, p. 73. Copyright © 1968, The Ronald Press Company, New York. Reprinted with permission of the publisher.

have made? What are the mistakes that other people have made to force them to such a low standard of living after they retire? Some people probably tried to plan their financial future but were set back by financial misfortunes. Others probably did not start to plan their financial security until it was too late.

THE IMPORTANCE OF EARLY PLANNING

When do people start thinking seriously about providing their retirement income? Young people are not interested but older people are vitally concerned. It is probably not until after children are raised and educated that most families start their planning. Suppose John becomes interested in retirement income when he is age 50. If John is going to retire at age 65, he has 15 years to accumulate a retirement fund. Suppose John decides that he would like to have $300 a month when he retires. How much would he have to set aside each year between the ages of 50 and 65 to have an income of $300 during retirement? If his savings are accumulated at 7 percent, John would need to save about $2,000 each year. For most people, it is impossible to save that much. This simply means John's retirement income will have to be lower. But what would have happened if he had started his retirement program earlier? If John had started at age 25, he could have met his objective of $300 a month after age 65 by setting aside only about $175 a year or only $14.58 a month!

The importance of starting a retirement program at an early age is understood by very few individuals. A person who plans his financial affairs carefully will be aware of the "magic of compound interest." When savings or investment are compounded over a long period of time, the total amount accumulated will be surprising. Look at Table 17–2 and see how much difference the time period makes.

Table 17–2   How Money Grows (at 7% compound interest)

Amount Saved Each Year	Number of Years			
	5 years	*10 years*	*20 years*	*45 years*
$ 50	$ 287.50	$ 690.80	$ 2,049.75	$ 14,287.45
100	575.00	1,781.60	4,099.50	28,574.90
200	1,150.00	3,563.20	8,199.00	57,149.80
500	2,875.00	8,908.00	20,497.50	142,874.50
1,000	5,750.00	17,816.00	40,995.00	285,749.00

Source: Computed from *Financial Compound Interest and Annuity Tables* (Financial Publishing Company, 1961), p. 706.

Table 17–2 shows that a person who can save $500 a year (at 7 percent) will have only about $20,000 at the end of 20 years. But invested over 45 years, $500 a year amounts to over $140,000. A person who can invest $1,000 a year for 45 years will end up with over a quarter of a million dollars! This is the "magic of compound interest," and it means that the person who starts to save at a young age has a tremendous advantage over the person who waits.

In summary, it is obvious that most retired people do not have adequate financial resources. Most people, however, could have financial security in the later years of their life if they had simply recognized the problem when they were young and started a retirement plan. Fortunately, there are many ways an individual can provide an income for himself during retirement.

SOURCES OF INCOME DURING RETIREMENT

As a first step in planning retirement income, it is helpful to be aware of the various methods of achieving financial security during retirement. Look at Figure 17–1. It shows the ways that are used to provide retirement income.

Figure 17–1 indicates that there are three major sources of retirement income: employment, social security (including other public benefits), and investment and rental income. Together, these three sources provide 77 percent of the income of people over age 65. None of the other types of retirement income have been very important in the past. This does not imply, however, that a person should not use the other sources of income for his own retirement security. For example, private pension plans and annuities are becoming more popular, and a wise person might use these to provide himself a retirement income.

Figure 17-1 Sources and Percents of Income for Persons Over Age 65 (including spouses)

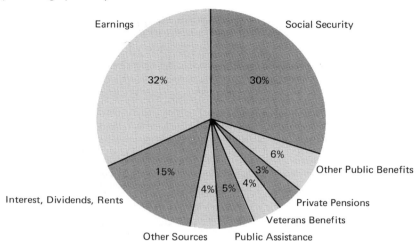

Source: Lenore A. Epstein, "Income of the Aged in 1962," *Social Security Bulletin,* Vol. XXIV, No. 1, (March, 1964), p. 4.

Which methods do you want to use to accumulate a retirement fund? You can answer this better if you know something about each approach.

EMPLOYMENT DURING RETIREMENT

The most important source of retirement income has been income from employment. However, there are several reasons why this is not a very satisfactory approach to retirement security. First, many people do not *want* to continue working after they reach age 65. Some people look forward to the day when they will not have to work.

Another reason why employment might not provide a retirement income to a person is that employment opportunities for those over age 65 are not very great—and they are decreasing. Look at Figure 17–2. It shows actual and projected rates of employment for people over age 65.

Many men who wanted to work after age 65 could do so in the past. In 1900, about 68 percent of the men over age 65 were employed. But in 1965, only about 28 percent were employed. In 1980, only about 22 percent will be working. The employment rate for women over 65 has not declined, but it has never been very high.

Why are fewer and fewer older people able to work? There are three basic explanations:

1. Economic and social changes. In the past, our society relied heavily on agriculture and families were more self-sufficient. Older persons

Figure 17–2   Percentage of Persons 65 Years and Over in the Labor Force
(projected to 1980)

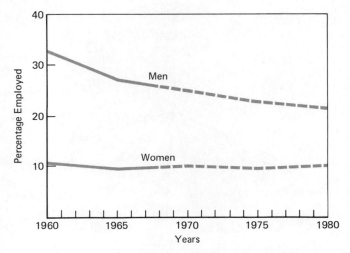

Source: *Manpower Report of the President* (Washington, D.C.: U.S. Government
Printing Office, 1968), p. 298.

usually lived with younger members of the family and helped with
household and farm chores. But with increasing urbanization, worker
mobility, and changing concepts of family responsibilities, older persons become less able to support themselves.
2. Compulsory retirement ages. Many companies now have compulsory
   retirement, usually at age 65. In these cases, a person has no choice.
   He must retire whether he has financial resources or not.
3. Poor health. Many elderly people would like to work but they cannot
   because of poor health. Almost 35 percent of the aged who do not
   work believe their health does not allow them to work.[1]

Another reason why it might be unwise to plan to work during retirement
is that most workers over age 65 cannot earn very much. This is shown
in Table 17–3.

The implications for young people are clear. Employment opportunities for the aged are low and declining and the earnings of those who do
work are low. A young person simply cannot plan to finance his retirement by continuing to work. Although a few people will be able to earn
a small income after they reach age 65, a person cannot safely make his
plans along these lines.

---

[1] Erdman Palmore, "Retirement Patterns Among Aged Men," *Social Security
Bulletin,* Vol. 27, No. 8 (August 1964), p. 6.

Table 17–3 Average Annual Earnings of Workers, Aged 65 and Over

Work Experience and Age	Average Earnings of Males	Average Earnings of Females
Full-time jobs		
65–72	$3,775	$2,132
73 and over	3,022	1,131
Part-time jobs		
65–72	969	652
73 and over	765	525
All workers		
65–72	2,835	1,410
73 and over	1,803	806

From Joseph A. Pechman, Henry J. Aaron, and Michael K. Tausig, *Social Security: Perspectives for Reform,* (Washington, D.C.: The Brookings Institution, 1968), p. 12. Reprinted with permission of the Brookings Institution.

RETIREMENT BENEFITS UNDER SOCIAL SECURITY

Most young people probably fail to appreciate the value of social security.[2] But the truth is that many families will collect more than $100,000 in social security benefits. These benefits, without doubt, will be an important part of the incomes of most young people when they retire. Since social security benefits will provide a basic foundation of financial security for many people, it is important to know something about the program.

QUALIFYING FOR BENEFITS

Not everyone is eligible for social security benefits. Basically, a person must earn a minimum income for a certain period of time in a "covered" occupation before he will be eligible for benefits. The first question then, is which occupations are covered?

Since well over 90 percent of the gainfully employed are covered, it is easier to know the occupations that are *not* covered than it is to learn which occupations are covered. The occupations that are specifically excluded are:

1. Newsboys under the age of 18
2. Domestic employees—such as students who work in fraternity or sorority houses

---

[2] The term "social security" is used here and throughout this book in its popular, narrow sense to mean only the O.A.S.D.H.I. program. It does not include such programs as unemployment compensation and public assistance.

3. Employees of nonprofit organizations—such as student nurses
4. Federal government employees. This group is excluded because they are covered under other retirement systems
5. Policemen, firemen, and railroad workers who are covered under other plans

Special eligibility requirements apply to certain occupations. Clergymen, for example, can apply for exemption from coverage. This is allowed because some clergymen are opposed to social security on the basis of their religious principles or conscience. Special rules also apply to agricultural employees. These rules are necessary because of the bookkeeping difficulties that are involved when a worker moves frequently from job to job. There is one occupational group with special eligibility rules that may be particularly important to young employees. Since 1966, a worker who earns $20 a month or more in the form of tips is covered under social security. Suppose Mary, who is helping her husband through school, is working in a restaurant. Is she covered by social security? If she receives more than $20 a month in tips, she is legally required to report those earnings and she will become covered under social security.

How long does a person have to work in a covered occupation to be eligible for benefits? To receive benefits for retirement, a person must have achieved "fully insured" status. This can be done in one of two ways:

1. If a person is credited with 40 quarters of coverage, he is fully insured. (A quarter is a three-month period.) A person who meets this requirement is fully insured *permanently,* even if he spends no more time in a covered employment.
2. If a person is credited with at least one-fourth of the quarters since 1950 or after the year in which he attains age 21, if later, until he reaches age 65 (age 62 for women), dies or becomes disabled. At least six quarters are required in any case.

Consider the case of Tom Smith. He worked as a newsboy when he was younger and he worked in a fraternity house during college. For three summers while he was attending college, Tom worked for a building contractor. He became 21 in January, 1970. If he goes to work in a covered occupation after graduating in June, 1971, how long must he work to achieve fully insured status? His work as a newspaper boy and in a fraternity house will not give him any social security credit. But he will receive credit for the three quarters he worked in the summer. After he has graduated and worked nine months, he will then have a total of six quarters and he will have more than one-fourth of the quarters since reaching age 21. Tom will be fully insured, then, nine months after receiving his degree.

TYPES OF BENEFITS

For purposes of retirement income planning, a person should recognize that there are four types of retirement benefits.

The basic retirement benefit is the income paid to a retired worker. If an individual has attained the age of 62 and is fully insured, he (or she) is entitled to a monthly income. This income is payable as long as the retired worker is alive.

A second type of benefit is the benefit paid to the wife of a retired worker. A wife is eligible for this benefit even if she has never worked. This benefit is payable because she is the wife of a worker who attained fully insured status in a covered occupation. The wife's benefit, however, is payable only if the wife is at least 62 years old or has a child of the retired worker under age 18 in her care.

The husband of a retired worker is also entitled to a retirement benefit. A husband's benefit is payable only if the insured is age 62 (or older), his wife was fully insured, and he was receiving at least one-half of his support from his wife at the time she became eligible for a benefit. This last requirement prevents most families from receiving a husband's benefit.

Children of a retired worker also receive a benefit. To be eligible, a child must be under the age of 18 (or under the age of 22 if attending an educational institution on a full-time basis), unmarried, and dependent upon the retired worker.

Notice that benefits will be stopped under certain conditions. Suppose a father retires at age 62 while his son is still in college. The son will receive a benefit (because his father is retired) but this benefit will stop when the son graduates (or drops out of school). A wife's benefit will also terminate if she divorces a retired worker. Changes in family status such as these can cause social security benefits to be terminated.

Another important reason why retirement benefits are terminated or reduced is the earnings test. A retired person can earn up to $1,680 a year with no reduction in benefits. But for earnings between $1,680 and $2,880, the benefit is reduced $1 for every $2 of earnings. And $17 benefits is lost for every $1 of earnings above $2,880.

For example, suppose a retired worker earns $4,000. If his retirement benefit was $200 a month before he started working, how much will he lose in social security benefits? He loses nothing for the first $1,680 of earnings. He loses one-half of his benefits between $1,680 and $2,880 (or $600) and he loses $920 for his earnings above $2,880. Therefore, his benefit will be reduced a total of $1,520. But notice this. If the worker does not work at all, he will receive $200 a month or $4,800 for the year. If he works and earns $4,000 he will receive a total income of $7,280 ($4,000 in earnings and $3,280 in benefits). The formula is set up so that a person will always make a larger total income if he works, even though his benefits will be reduced.

The earnings test applies only to retired workers under the age of 72. If a person over age 72 works, his earnings will never reduce his benefits. Also, it is important to know that the earnings test applies only to income received as wages and salary. It does not apply to other income such as investment, rental, or royalty income. One further important qualification should be noted. Retirement benefits are not reduced in any month if the retired worker earns less than $140 in that month. If the retired worker in the example above had earned $4,000 during the year, but had worked only ten months, his full benefit would have been payable for the two months he did not work.

AMOUNT OF BENEFITS

Just how much can a person receive as a retirement benefit under social security? The amount paid depends upon the person's "primary insurance amount," which, in turn, is based on the person's average monthly wage. The higher the average monthly wage, the higher the primary insurance amount and the retirement benefit. In other words, the retirement benefit is related to the amount of money a worker has earned; workers who have earned more will receive a larger retirement benefit. It is to a person's advantage, therefore, to have his average monthly wage as high as possible. To do this, the plan allows a person to drop out the five years of his lowest earnings. However, a person can include in his earnings only the amount from which social security taxes have been deducted. The following shows how the taxable wage base has been changed:

Before 1951	$3,000
1951–1954	3,600
1955–1958	4,200
1959–1965	4,800
1966–1967	6,600
1968–1971	7,800
1972 and after	9,000

In calculating a person's coverage monthly wage, it is important to determine the number of years that must be included in the computation. This number is five less than the number of years elapsing after 1950 (or after attainment of age 21, if later) up to the year the worker retires. For purposes of computing retirement benefits, this number cannot be less than five. The total earnings of the worker (including only the amount each year on which social security taxes have been paid) are then divided by the number of months that have elapsed during those years.

A simple example will clarify these rules. Bob was a fully insured worker when he retired in early 1970. Since 1951 he earned more each year than the taxable wage base. The number of years that must be counted for Bob is 15 (five years less than the number of years between 1950 and 1970). Bob's taxable earnings were as follows:

$7,800 each year for 1968–69	$15,600
$6,600 each year for 1967–66	13,200
$4,800 each year for 1965–59	25,000
$4,200 each year for 1958–55	9,200
Total Wage Credits	63,000

Bob's average monthly wage, therefore, would be $350 ($63,000 divided by 180—the number of months in the 15-year period). Bob's benefit, however, will not be $350. His average monthly wage will be used to determine his "primary insurance amount," which will be the same as his retirement benefit.

How much will Bob receive as a retirement benefit? Table 17–4 shows that an average monthly wage of $350 (average yearly earnings of $4,200) will produce a benefit (or primary insurance amount) of $177.70. (Note that the table shows yearly, rather than monthly earnings.) The table also shows that a person with an average monthly wage of $650 would receive a benefit of $275.80 a month.[3]

A person who receives the retired worker's benefit is entitled to 100 percent of the primary insurance amount. The wife or husband and children of a retired worker receive 50 percent of the worker's primary insurance amount. There are two important qualifications for these benefits. First, benefits are scaled down if they are taken when the retired worker, or husband or wife of a retired worker elect to receive benefits before age 65. The full benefit is payable at age 65, but reduced benefits can be started as early as age 62. Second, benefits are always subject to the overall family maximum. These are shown in Table 17–4.

FINANCING BENEFITS

Who pays the cost of our social security program? The answer is that employees and employers share equally in the cost. The employee pays a tax on the wages he receives, and the employer pays a tax on his payroll. Table 17–5 shows the tax rate.

The tax schedule shows that in 1972 employees pay 5.2 percent of the first $9,000 of their income, or $480.00. Notice that the table also shows that employees will be paying $544.50 in 1987. Being realistic, the tax will probably be higher because tax rates and the taxable wage base ($9,000 in 1971) will probably be increased. Young people are certain to pay a large amount of money into the social security plan over their working lives.

The employee's tax is withheld from his paycheck by his employer who sends the employee's tax and his own tax to the U.S. Director of Internal

---

[3] Most young men who graduate from college will earn enough to receive the maximum primary insurance amount. A complication, however, is that the benefits are liberalized frequently and only the amount on which social security taxes have been paid are used in the calculation.

Table 17-4 Social Security Benefits

Average Yearly Earnings After 1950	$923 or less	$1800	$3000	$4200	$5400	$6600	$7800
Retired worker—65 or older Disabled worker—under 65	$ 70.40	$111.90	$145.60	$177.70	$208.80	$240.30	$275.80
Wife 65 or older	35.20	56.00	72.80	88.90	104.40	120.20	137.90
Retired worker at 62	56.40	89.60	116.50	142.20	167.10	192.30	220.70
Wife at 62, no child	26.40	42.00	54.60	66.70	78.30	90.20	103.50
Widow at 60	61.10	80.10	104.20	127.20	149.40	171.90	197.30
Widow or widower at 62	70.40	92.40	120.20	146.70	172.30	198.30	227.60
Disabled widow at 50	42.80	56.10	72.90	89.00	104.50	120.30	138.00
Wife under 65 and one child	35.20	56.00	77.10	131.20	181.10	194.90	206.90
Widowed mother and one child	105.60	167.90	218.40	266.60	313.20	360.60	413.80
Widowed mother and two children	105.60	167.90	222.70	308.90	389.90	435.20	482.70
One child of retired or disabled worker	35.20	56.00	72.80	88.90	104.40	120.20	137.90
One surviving child	70.40	84.00	109.20	133.30	156.60	180.30	206.90
Maximum family payment	105.60	167.90	222.70	308.90	389.90	435.20	482.70

Table 17–5 Social Security Tax Rates

Calendar Year	Rate for Employees	Tax Rate for Self-Employed
1972	5.2%	7.5%
1973–1975	5.65	7.65
1976–1979	5.85	7.7
1980–1986	5.95	7.8
1987 and after	6.05	7.9

Revenue for his district. Every three months the employer files a tax return and a report that furnishes all the information about the employees covered, the wages paid to them, and their social security numbers. Although the employer sends in the information, the worker should periodically check his account. Keeping your account in order is important. Often, a person may work for several employers and the amount may be incorrect. Another way in which accounts are confused is marriage. When a woman marries, she should immediately (after the honeymoon) inform the Social Security Administration that her name has been changed. A new social security card should be requested whenever the old one has been lost, stolen, or destroyed. A worker can check his social security account by obtaining a wage credit inquiry card from the nearest field office of the Social Security Administration and mailing it to the Social Security Administration, Baltimore, Maryland 21203. If the records do not agree with his own, he should report the discrepency to the Administration. If there is a dispute, the worker is entitled to a hearing, an appeal from the hearing, and an eventual right to go to court.

THE VALUE OF SOCIAL SECURITY RETIREMENT BENEFITS

Undoubtedly, social security retirement benefits are important to many people. A monthly check of $218 (the maximum primary insurance amount) would be welcomed by almost everybody. There can be no question that social security provides great security for millions of families, but, viewed in another way, are social security benefits adequate? There can be no yes or no answer to this question. The benefits are probably adequate for some families and inadequate for others. However, it is important to notice that social security retirement benefits will always be a decrease in income for a retired worker. And for many families, the decrease in income will be substantial. The person who receives the maximum benefit will receive only about one-third of his previous income (if he earned the same amount as the maximum wage base). And for a person who earns more than the maximum wage base, the social security benefit will only be a small percentage of his average monthly earnings. Suppose, for example, that a person earned $16,000 a year. If he received $218 a month in benefits, his income would be only about 16 percent of his previous earnings.

Some people argue that there is no problem if income drops after retirement. They say a person usually has his home paid for, children are gone, and there are no taxes and other expenses connected with work. These arguments may not be entirely valid. Although some expenses decrease after retirement, others increase. Medical expenses, for example, are often a financial burden for retired people. In any case, social security benefits are a substantial decrease in income. These benefits can be regarded as providing an important foundation of financial security, but they cannot be considered adequate enough for most people to maintain their standard of living. If a person wants a comfortable retirement, he usually must be able to supplement his income from other sources.

PENSIONS

People who are retired at the present time receive only a small portion of their income from pension plans.[4] But most companies did not have pension plans in the past. Today approximately one-half of all employees in the United States are covered by a pension plan, and the number of plans is increasing every day.[5] This means pension plans are certain to be more important in the future.

A young person should not think an "old age pension" is a form of charity. There is nothing degrading or embarrassing about a pension benefit. And a pension plan is not a form of social security. A pension plan is simply a method an employer (or some organization) uses to provide an income to retired employees.

REASONS FOR PENSION PLANS

Why does a company provide a pension plan for its employees? There are probably several important reasons:

1. Productivity and improved employer-employee relationships. Employees are likely to be better satisfied with their jobs if they know their company is financing part of their retirement. As a result, employees will probably be more productive.
2. Union pressure. Since 1948, unions have had the legal authority to bargain with companies over pension plans. Unions, therefore, not

---

[4] Only 3 percent according to Figure 17–1.

[5] Dick L. Rottman, "Pension Plans for the Self-Employed," *Business and Government Review* (January/February 1970), p. 21.

only put pressure on companies to adopt a pension plan, they also bargain with companies for improved benefits.

3. Tax considerations. A pension plan that is "qualified" with the Internal Revenue Service (and most are) has important tax advantages. The contributions an employer makes to the plan are deductible from his income tax, the funds set aside for pension benefits accumulate tax free, and the contributions to the plan by the employer are not considered taxable income to the employee.

ELIGIBILITY FOR BENEFITS

Even if you work for a company that has a pension plan, you may not be included in it. In fact, most employees who are starting their first full-time job are not covered. A young employee, therefore, should check the eligibility provisions before he accepts his first job (or first few jobs).

Participation in the pension plan is usually limited to employees who satisfy one or more of these criteria: minimum age, minimum length of service, minimum earnings, type of remuneration (hourly wage or salary), and type of work. Many plans combine more than one of these requirements. For example, a plan may include only those employees over 30 years of age with at least five years of service. If you go to work for a company that has this requirement in its pension plan when you graduate at age 21, it would be nine years before you would be covered in the plan. In some cases, employees are never eligible to participate in the company pension plan. Obviously, participation in the pension plan is an important factor in planning retirement income.

TYPES OF BENEFITS

The basic benefit in a pension plan is, of course, the retirement benefit. This benefit is almost always payable as long as the retired person is alive. In fact, many plans provide retirement income as long as either the retired worker or his wife is alive.

Almost all pension plans establish a normal retirement age, which is usually age 65. A large number of plans, however, will allow early or late retirement. If early retirement benefits are available, the plan usually will provide a reduction in benefits. Late retirements normally do not increase benefits. A person who is planning to retire early (say at age 62) should be sure that his pension plan will provide a benefit and that the benefit will not be too small.

Another extremely important type of benefit, which is often overlooked by employees, is the benefit, if any, that is payable if the employee terminates his employment prior to retirement. Suppose Al graduates from college, works several years for a company, becomes eligible to participate in the company pension plan, and later decides to take another job. This is a very common situation. If Al has contributed $1,800 to the plan and his employer has contributed $3,600 to the pension plan on Al's behalf, what happens to this money? There is no question that Al will receive the $1,800 he has contributed to the plan (in one form or another), but his rights to the $3,600 contributed by the company depend on the vesting provisions in the plan. The term "vesting" refers to the rights the employee has in the *employer's* contributions, not his own contributions.

Vesting provisions differ greatly. Some plans provide full, immediate vesting. This means the employee is entitled to the employer's contributions whenever he leaves the company. Some plans provide no vesting. In these plans, an employee who leaves the company is not entitled to any of the money contributed by the employer on his behalf. Other plans provide gradual vesting. For example, a common provision is to have no vesting the first three years, and thereafter vesting will accumulate in 10 percent increments each year. With this arrangement, the employee is entitled to 10 percent in the fourth year, 20 percent in the fifth year, 30 percent in the sixth year, and so on. The benefits would not be 100 percent vested until after the thirteenth year. Notice that the vesting provisions may have an impact on an employee's decision to quit his job. Consider the case of Doug Trice. He graduated from college and became eligible to participate in his company's pension plan three years later. According to the vesting provisions in the plan, Doug's benefits are 50 percent vested now, but they will be 100 percent vested in two more years. Doug now earns $8,800 a year, but he has been offered a job with another company that pays $10,200 a year. This is a nice raise, but would Doug really be better off financially by taking the new job? It depends on the amount of money that Doug's employer has set aside for him. It is very possible that Doug should wait two years (until his pension benefit is fully vested) before he changes jobs. Young people should realize that the provisions in pension plans may be important to them long before they reach retirement age.

Death benefits are also common in pension plans. These can take several forms. The plan might provide death benefits if the employee dies before retirement, or if the employee dies after he retires. Some plans provide both types of death benefits.

Disability benefits are provided in a good pension plan. This is important because an employee needs to have his pension credits continue to accumulate even when he is disabled and not working.

AMOUNT OF BENEFITS

The amount of the retirement benefit is of utmost importance to an employee. It would be a serious mistake to assume that all plans provide about the same benefits. Some plans provide much greater benefits than others. The amount of the retirement benefit provided by a pension plan will be determined by a formula in the plan. Generally speaking, there are five basic types of retirement benefit formulas.

The simplest benefit formula is a flat amount. With this approach, all employees receive the same retirement benefit, regardless of how long they have worked for the company or how much they have earned.

A second approach is to provide a benefit that is a percentage of earnings. Rather than using actual earnings, many plans use earnings brackets, and benefits are expressed as a dollar amount per bracket of earnings. This is illustrated in Table 17–6. A percentage of earnings formula (or bracket) does not recognize the length of time an employee has worked. The plan, however, will normally require that an individual be employed for a minimum period to be eligible for benefits.

The third approach to a pension benefit is to provide a flat amount for each year of employment. The amount varies from plan to plan, but a benefit of two dollars or three dollars is common. If a plan provides a benefit of two dollars a month for each year of employment, an employee who worked 32 years would be entitled to a monthly pension benefit of $64.

A fourth approach, and the method that is perhaps most common, is to provide a pension benefit that reflects earnings and length of employment. This is often called a "percentage of earnings per year" formula. For example, suppose an employee earns $6,000 a year and the plan provides a 1 percent benefit. If he earned the same amount for 32 years, his benefit would be $192 (1 percent of $6,000 × 32).

Another approach is to provide a benefit that can be financed with the contributions that have been made. In other words, the pension plan does not guarantee any amount, but the benefit will be determined by how much has been accumulated. Some new plans provide benefits that are based on the accumulated value of a common stock portfolio or the cost of living. These plans are especially attractive during periods of inflation.

Table 17–6   Illustration of the Percentage of Earnings Pension Benefits (by brackets)

Monthly Earnings	Monthly Pension Benefits
$200–$280	$ 72
$281–$360	$ 96
$361–$440	$120
$441–$520	$144
$521–$600	$168
$601–$680	$192

FINANCING BENEFITS

Pension plans, like group insurance plans, can be contributory or non-contributory. If the employer pays the full cost, the benefits are likely to be lower than they would be in a contributory plan. As a result, an employee can seldom compare a contributory plan to a noncontributory plan very well. One thing is certain, however. An employee should be aware of the method used to finance the plan. A contributory plan can take a sizable deduction from an employee's paycheck. Some plans require 3, 4, or even 6 percent to be contributed to the plan by employees.

PENSION PLANS FOR THE SELF-EMPLOYED

Prior to 1962, a person who was self-employed was at a substantial disadvantage in providing retirement income for himself. The problem was this: a self-employed person had to earn an income, pay income taxes, invest the income, and pay income taxes on the investment earnings in order to build a retirement fund. If the same person worked for a corporation, the company could set aside money and earn an investment income without having the employee pay taxes. The 1962 Self-Employed Individual Tax Retirement Act (also known as the Keogh Act or HR-10) changed the tax law and provided a tax incentive for self-employed people to establish a retirement plan. Accountants, architects, dentists, doctors, farmers and other self-employed individuals now have tax advantages for pension plans that are similar to the advantages available to others.

A self-employed person can contribute 10 percent of his earned income (with a maximum annual contribution of $2,500) to his retirement plan and deduct his contribution from his taxable income. Furthermore, the income or capital gains on the invested funds will not be taxed until the funds are withdrawn. In other words, the retirement fund accumulates tax free. The money can be placed in mutual fund shares, annuities, U.S. Government Retirement Plan bonds, or placed in a trust. The most popular methods of funding these plans have been annuities and mutual funds.

There are, of course, some limitations on these plans. Probably the most stringent restriction is that all full-time employees must be included in the plan. If a self-employed dentist wants the tax advantages of the plan, he must provide pension benefits for all his full-time employees. Another restriction is that funds cannot be withdrawn before the self-employed person is age 59½. If funds are withdrawn prior to this age, tax penalties will be incurred.

How important are the tax advantages of the Self Employed Individual Tax Retirement Act? One way to answer this question is to find the investment yield that would be required on an investment outside the plan that would be equivalent to the tax sheltered investment yield on the plan. Comparisons of this type are provided in Table 17–7.

Table 17-7   Tax Advantages of the Self-Employed Individual Retirement Act

Investment Yield on Funds in the Plan	Years in Plan	Investment Yields on Funds Outside the Plan by Income Earned				
		$10,000	$18,000	$26,000	$34,000	$50,000
10%	40	13.4%	14.8%	16.8%	19.4%	25.0%
	34	13.5	15.1	17.3	20.0	26.2
	22	14.4	16.3	19.2	22.7	30.6
	16	15.4	17.7	21.3	25.6	35.7
	10	17.7	21.3	26.4	33.0	48.3
9%	40	12.1	13.4	15.4	17.7	23.1
	34	12.3	13.8	15.8	18.4	24.2
	22	13.2	15.0	17.7	21.1	28.7
	16	14.1	16.5	19.9	24.1	33.8
	10	16.5	19.9	24.9	31.4	46.4
8%	40	10.9	12.1	14.0	16.2	21.2
	34	11.2	12.5	14.4	16.9	22.3
	22	12.0	13.7	16.3	19.5	26.8
	16	13.0	15.2	18.4	22.5	32.0
	10	15.4	18.7	23.5	29.9	44.5
7%	97	9.7	10.8	12.5	14.6	19.3
	34	9.9	11.2	13.0	15.3	20.5
	22	10.8	12.5	14.8	17.9	24.9
	16	11.8	13.9	17.0	21.0	30.0
	10	14.1	17.4	22.1	28.3	42.6
6%	40	8.4	9.6	11.1	13.0	17.4
	34	8.7	9.8	11.6	13.7	18.5
	22	9.6	11.2	13.4	16.9	23.1
	16	10.5	12.7	15.6	19.4	28.2
	10	12.9	16.1	20.7	26.7	40.7
5%	40	7.3	8.3	9.7	11.4	15.6
	341	7.5	8.6	10.2	12.1	16.7
	22	8.4	9.8	12.0	14.5	21.2
	16	9.4	11.3	14.1	17.9	26.4
	10	11.7	14.8	19.3	25.1	28.7
4%	40	6.1	6.9	8.3	9.9	13.6
	34	6.3	7.3	8.8	10.6	14.8
	22	7.2	8.6	10.6	13.4	19.4
	16	8.2	10.0	12.8	16.3	24.5
	10	10.5	13.5	17.8	28.6	35.9

Source: Dick L. Rottman, "Pension Plans for the Self-Employed," *Business and Government Review,* Vol. XI, No. 1, January, February, 1970, p. 27. Used with permission.

For example use Table 17–7 to determine the tax advantage of an HR-10 Plan for an individual who earns $10,000 a year, has had a plan for ten years, and could earn 8 percent on his funds in a tax sheltered plan. The table, shows that such a person would have to earn 15.4 percent on a plan that does not have the tax advantages of an HR-10 Plan. This is almost twice as high a return. Furthermore, for a person who earns $50,000, the taxable yield that is equivalent to the 8 percent tax sheltered yield is 44.5 percent. Obviously the tax advantages of an HR-10 plan become more important as a person's income increases.

The implication of the table is that a person can accumulate a much larger retirement fund for himself if he uses an HR-10 plan and gets the same yield (before taxes) that he could earn in some other plan. Every self-employed person should at least consider the possibility of adopting an HR-10 plan. The disadvantages might outweigh the advantages, but the advantages can be very substantial.

Setting up a self-employed retirement plan is not difficult. Lawyers, accountants, insurance agents, and bankers are familiar with these plans and they will be happy to provide advice and guidance.

OTHER TYPES OF COMPANY RETIREMENT PLANS

Most retirement programs sponsored by employers are referred to as "pension plans," but there are several other types of plans that may be used to provide retirement income.

Profit-sharing plans, for example, are similar to pension programs. A profit-sharing plan is an agreement by which an employer agrees to allow employees to participate, according to a definite predetermined formula, in the profits of the company. Profits can be distributed annually or accumulated for a long period of time. If they are accumulated, they can be paid to the employee when he retires and the plan may meet the same basic objectives as a pension plan. However, there is a basic difference between a pension plan and a profit-sharing program. In a pension plan, the company agrees to provide a guaranteed amount of pension benefit or to contribute a definite amount each year. In a profit-sharing plan the employer does not make either of these guarantees. The employer simply agrees to make contributions to the plan if and when the company has profits. In a profitable year the company will make large contributions, but contributions will be low or nonexistent if profits are low or nonexistent. This means employees who participate in a profit-sharing retirement plan have no assurance of what their retirement benefits will be when they retire. The benefits can be larger or smaller than what they would have been under a pension plan.

Employee stock purchase programs can also be used to provide retirement income. Although these plans differ in several respects, they basically allow employees to accumulate common stock shares in the company. Often the plans permit employees to purchase the stock at a discount from its current market price. In some plans, the employer will make contributions to employees. If the plan is contributory, the investments being accumulated for an employee may be divided into two or more types of investments. For example, the fund may be split into a fixed-dollar investment such as government bonds and common stock of the employer.[6]

PROVIDING RETIREMENT INCOME THROUGH REAL ESTATE

A person who is not covered by social security or a company pension plan has a special need for other investments. And even a person who is covered by social security and a pension plan may want to supplement his income. For persons with these needs or desires, real estate may be an appropriate investment.

TYPES OF REAL ESTATE INVESTMENTS

A person can invest in real estate in a number of ways. The most common type of real estate investment, of course, is home ownership. As a matter of fact, the largest single investment of most families is their home. Chapter Five of this text treated home ownership primarily as an expense. But it can also be viewed as an investment. When a house is occupied by its owner, the owner receives, in effect, tax free income. The "income," however, is in the form of the use of the property rather than a money income. Since Chapter Five dealt with the subject of home ownership, the remainder of this section will deal with other types of real estate investments.

Rental units can be an effective way to provide a retirement income. A person can buy single-family dwellings, duplexes, apartment houses, or commercial buildings and use their income to provide a stream of income during retirement.

Real estate mortgages can also be purchased by individuals for investment purposes. This is, in a sense, an *indirect* investment in real estate. A mortgage is merely an investment in which real property is pledged as security for a loan. In other words, a mortgagee only lends money on real estate; he does not actually own the property. Mortgages are popular investments for banks, insurance companies, and other financial institutions, but they are not popular with individual investors. This is because they are not liquid, they require a large investment, and they are subject to the purchasing power risk.

Real estate trusts have been gaining in popularity since 1960. A real estate trust is much like a mutual fund. The trust sells shares to the public and invests the proceeds in real estate or real estate mortgages. Real estate trusts escape corporate income taxes on distributed earnings if they pay out at least 90 percent of their operating income in dividends. This is the same rule that is applied to mutual funds.

---

6 Plans that give certain executives or key employees the right to purchase the employer's common stock during a certain period of time at a stated price are usually called "stock option plans." These plans are designed to give executives an extra incentive to perform well and they can provide substantial profits to certain employees. These profits, however, are *not* a part of a formal retirement program.

The advantages to an investor of a real estate trust include diversification, possible protection against inflation, convenience, and management. The major disadvantages are that some of the trusts are quite speculative and current income is usually low.

ADVANTAGES OF INVESTING IN RENTAL UNITS

Many real estate investors get started almost by accident. This is what happened to Dick. When Dick started college, he had no idea that he wanted to become a real estate investor, but when he was married in his junior year and could not find a suitable apartment, he decided to purchase a small home. He had a little cash and the total house payment was less than (or at least no more than) it would cost him to rent. He intended to sell the house when he graduated but he was drafted immediately after getting out of school, so he decided to rent the house to a friend. Dick discovered that the house was a good investment. His total income from the property was greater than his total costs and he realized that the rental income would be a nice supplement to his income after the house was mortgage free. So Dick began buying houses to rent. Every time he accumulated enough for a down payment he bought a house. At the end of 14 years, Dick owned six houses; when he was 42 years old he had 12 homes. By this time the houses he had bought first were paid off and the income was almost completely free. A few years later, all the houses were free of debt and Dick had a monthly rental income of $1,680.

Not all real estate investors do as well as Dick, but the example can be used to point out the possible advantages of investing in real estate. First, real estate investments are particularly well suited for building up a source of income for later use. As a result, rental units can be used to provide a retirement income. A second advantage of real estate is that the investor may be protected from inflation risk. When the cost of owning real estate increases, the landlord may be able to raise his rent. A landlord may be able to increase his rental income even when costs have not increased. This can happen easily because the supply of land is fixed and the demand for real estate might increase substantially in certain locations. A third possible advantage of real estate investments is the federal income tax treatment. A landlord can often get enough income to cover all expenses including depreciation, and the property can be depreciated rapidly for income tax purposes. This decreases a person's income tax liability and provides funds that can be used to buy additional properties. In the event that the property is sold, the owner pays a tax on the gain, but the tax rates applied to capital gains are lower than those applied to ordinary income.

DISADVANTAGES OF INVESTING IN RENTAL UNITS

While the advantages of buying rental units may seem attractive, there are several possible disadvantages. A careful investor will, of course, weigh these against the benefits.

Appraisal.   Determining the value of real estate is a difficult task. Although many people probably think they can appraise property accurately, few buyers can claim true expertise. Yet the success of a real estate investment depends, to a large degree, upon the price paid for the property. It is easy for an inexperienced buyer to pay too much for real estate.

Need for Special Managerial Skill.   Another problem, which is closely associated with the problem of appraisal, is that a real estate investor must have managerial skill and knowledge of the real estate market. This means a person must watch the real estate market closely, know how to arrange favorable financing, and cope with the problems of collection, repairs, and general operation.

The Problem of Large Denomination.   Real estate purchases can only be made in certain amounts. If you want to buy a $20,000 house, you must have enough cash to finance the purchase. You cannot buy "ten shares" in the house or invest any amount you please. Furthermore, the purchase of real estate often requires several thousand dollars, or more, which rules out real estate as an investment for many people.

Tax Risks.   Property taxes can be raised and income tax laws are revised. Changes in either one of these taxes can affect a real estate investment. Hopefully, a real estate investor can pass these increased costs along to his tenants in the form of increased rent; but this cannot always be done.

Marketability.   Real estate is generally regarded as an investment with poor marketability. Of course, some property is more marketable than other property, but even desirable property may take several months or longer to sell at a fair price.

INVESTMENTS IN SECURITIES

Another method of providing retirement security is to use stocks, bonds, or mutual funds as a source of income. Many individuals have supplemented their retirement incomes in this way. There is no doubt that investments in stocks, bonds, and mutual funds can be used to accumulate a retirement fund. But how can these investments be used during retirement? A very common approach is to change from growth investments to income securities when a person nears retirement. This approach has some merit, particularly for those who have accumulated a large sum.

Invested at 8 percent, a principal sum of $100,000 will return $8,000 a year or $667 a month. Another possible advantage of this approach is that it preserves the principal. In other words, when the investor dies, the investments will continue to provide an income for someone. If a person wants to leave some assets to his children, for example, this method of providing a retirement income might be appropriate.

The main problem with retiring on investment income is that the invested funds may not provide an adequate income. If a person accumulates investments worth $40,000 and earns a return of 8 percent, his income will be only $3,200 a year or $267 a month. And there is no assurance that a person will be able to earn 8 percent on his investments when he retires. Interest rates have been high in recent years but interest rates have been cyclical in the past. Suppose you accumulate $40,000 but can only receive a 4½ percent return. Your monthly income then would only be $150. (See Chapters Eight and Nine for a discussion of growth rates.)

Another possible problem with retiring on an investment income only is that this technique does not liquidate the principal. If a person has no heirs or does not desire to have his estate left to his children, he could have enjoyed a large retirement income if he had liquidated the principal.

An approach that can be used to obtain a larger retirement income is to liquidate part of the principal each year. In other words, a person can receive current income in the form of interest, dividends, or both and sell some of his investments each year. This technique is used in the "withdrawal plans" of many mutual funds. With a withdrawal plan, the mutual fund owner simply indicates the amount of money he wishes to receive each month or quarter. The fund will continue to give the share owner credit for capital appreciation and dividends, but the monthly payments, of course, will be subtracted from the share owner's account. Mutual fund withdrawal plans are very flexible. The share owner can periodically change the amount he chooses. Most mutual funds make withdrawal privileges available only to accounts larger than $10,000 and the usual minimum monthly payment is $50.

Despite the fact that mutual fund withdrawal plans are popular with many investors, most plans that involve liquidating the principal have a serious drawback. The problem is that a person never knows how much he can safely withdraw each year. Suppose a person accumulates $40,000 by retirement and needs at least $400 a month. If he earns a return of 6 percent, the income will amount to only $200 a month. Therefore he will have to liquidate $2,400 of his principal in the first year to get the other $200 a month. In the second year he will have only $37,600 invested because he has withdrawn $2,400. This means he will only earn $2,256 and he will be forced to liquidate more the second year. Each year the interest will decrease and this will require a larger amount of principal to be taken. After a few years, the principal will be diminishing rapidly, and if the investor continues to take $400 a month (in interest and principal), the total fund will soon be exhausted. What happens if the investor lives longer than the fund lasts? There is a distinct possibility that an individual who withdraws principal to increase his income will outlive his income and lose his financial security. This is an unhappy situation for a person who had saved over the years in order to build up a retirement fund.

ANNUITIES

Another method of providing retirement income is to purchase an annuity. Annuities have not been popular in the past, but there are strong signs that they will be more popular in the future.

THE ANNUITY PRINCIPLE

To understand annuities, it is necessary to understand the "annuity principle." This is the principle that is used to liquidate a sum of money, and it has important practical implications.

Suppose a person saves $40,000 to finance his retirement. He has decided that he needs at least $3,600 a year in addition to his social security benefits. He can earn $3,600 a year on his savings, but as we have seen, it is dangerous to start liquidating an accumulated fund. It seems as though the individual cannot meet his objective. But what could be done if a large number of individuals who are the same age each put $40,000 into a fund, and they liquidated the fund according to *average* life expectancy? If this were done, some individuals would die earlier than expected and others would outlive their life expectancy. But if the fund were liquidated according to average life expectancy, the fund could provide an income to each person as long as he lived. This is the annuity principle. A life insurance company can predict mortality rates for a group of lives very accurately, and if it accepts money from a large number of annuitants, the company can liquidate the principal and guarantee income to everyone.

What are the important advantages of the annuity principle? Basically, it offers two advantages over most other investments during retirement. First, a person is guaranteed an income for the rest of his life; he cannot outlive his income. If a person starts receiving annuity benefits and lives to be 109 years old, the payments will continue because others will have died. The second advantage of an annuity income is that it is larger than the income from interest alone. A person who has accumulated $40,000 could receive about $3,600 a year from an annuity. This is a return of 9 percent. Why is the annuity benefit larger than those from most other investments? The answer is that each annuity benefit payment is composed of interest earnings (since the insurance company invests the money collected from annuities) and a partial liquidation of principal. Remember that an annuity liquidates a sum of money for a group of individuals.

TIME WHEN BENEFITS START

Annuities are either *immediate* or *deferred*. An immediate annuity is one that starts benefit payments without a long delay.[7] When a person pays a lump sum to an insurance company and starts to receive benefits the next month, the annuity is immediate. Immediate annuities are sometimes purchased by a person who has accumulated a retirement fund in real estate, stocks, bonds, or mutual funds. For example, a person can purchase common stocks, and at age 65, sell the stocks and use the proceeds to buy an immediate annuity.

Life insurance policies are another popular way to purchase an immediate annuity. One of the important settlement options included in a life insurance policy is the "life income option." This is, in effect, nothing more than an immediate annuity. When an insured dies, the proceeds can be taken in the form of a guaranteed life income through this option. Most life insurance companies will also pay life insurance cash values in the form of a life income. If this is done, a living policyholder can use the life income option as an immediate annuity.

An immediate annuity is an unwise purchase for a young person. This is because a young person has a long life expectancy and very little of the principal can be liquidated. The annuity benefit, therefore, is only slightly higher than the interest that could be earned by investing the money instead. Why put money into an annuity (which is a nonliquid asset because it cannot be exchanged for cash) at a young age when the income is not much greater than interest?

A deferred annuity can be a wise purchase for a young person. Benefits under this type of annuity do not begin until a later date. For example, a person who is 25 could purchase a deferred annuity that would not start benefit payments until age 65 or some other age designated by the annuitant.

METHODS OF PAYING FOR ANNUITIES

Annuities can be purchased with single premiums or periodic payments. An immediate annuity must be purchased with a lump sum payment. An insurance company will not start benefits while the annuity is still being purchased. A deferred annuity could be purchased with a single premium, but most deferred annuities are purchased with monthly or annual payments. For example, a person aged 25 could agree to pay an insurance

---

[7] To be more accurate, an immediate annuity starts benefit payments *one payment interval* after the annuity is purchased. If you buy an immediate annuity that provides a monthly income, the first payment is received one month after the annuity is bought. Or, if the annuity provides quarterly benefits, the first benefit will begin three months after purchasing the annuity.

company $100 a year until he reaches retirement age, and then the company would start benefit payments to him.

NUMBER OF LIVES COVERED

An annuity may cover one person, but annuities that cover two lives are common. Rarely are more than two persons covered by an annuity (except in pension plans).

A joint-and-survivor annuity covers two lives, usually a husband and wife. It guarantees an income as long as one person is alive. In other words, benefit payments stop only after the death of the last life covered. This type of contract is ideal for a retired husband and wife because it decreases the need for life insurance. If an annuity covers only the life of the husband, benefit payments would stop when he died, leaving the widow with no income. In such a case, life insurance would have to be carried on the husband's life to provide guaranteed income to his widow. With a joint-and-survivor annuity, benefits will be continued after the husband dies.

Because a joint-and-survivor annuity covers two lives, it is the most expensive of all annuities. The cost of the annuity can be reduced by decreasing the benefit payment after the first annuitant dies. A joint-and-two-thirds annuity, for example, provides only two-thirds as much income after the first death. To reduce the cost even more, some annuities decrease the benefits to one-half of their previous level. These contracts are appropriately called "joint-and-one-half" annuities. A reduction in income makes some sense because one person does not require as much income as two.

REFUND FEATURES

What happens when a person buys an immediate annuity and dies a short time later? An individual can accumulate a retirement fund in common stocks, for example, and at age 65 pay $50,000 for an immediate annuity. If he receives three monthly benefit payments that total only $1,200, what happens to the other $48,800 (that is $50,000 − $1,200)? Or, what happens if a young man buys a deferred annuity and makes payments to the insurance company and dies before he receives any benefits? The answer to these important questions depend on the type of refund feature that is included in the annuity contract.

Refund features may pertain to the period when benefits are being paid to the annuitant, which is the *liquidation* period, or to the period before benefits are started, which is the *accumulation* period. All annuities have a liquidation period (if the annuitant lives long enough) but immediate annuities do not have an accumulation period.

During the accumulation period, almost all annuities provide a refund if the annuitant dies. Suppose Jerry Rosen, aged 25, buys a deferred annuity and pays $100 a year but dies when he is 58 years old—before the liquidation period has started. His beneficiary (who has been designated by Jerry) will receive a refund. Usually the amount of the refund is the total amount paid in by the annuitant. In Jerry's case, the beneficiary would receive $3,400. Some contracts stipulate that the beneficiary will receive the total amount paid in, plus interest, minus a charge for the insurance company's administrative services. Theoretically, an annuity could provide absolutely no refund if the annuitant died during the liquidation period. These contracts would not be popular with individuals and therefore are not sold.

Pure Annuities.   A pure annuity (sometimes called a "regular" or "straight life" annuity) provides no refund if the annuitant dies during the liquidation period. Benefit payments stop when the annuitant dies during the liquidation period, even if the annuitant dies after receiving only one check from the insurance company. This type of annuity protects only the annuitant; it provides no benefits to beneficiaries.

Life Annuity with Installments Certain.   Many people object to a pure annuity. They do not like to take the chance that they might pay a large amount to the insurance company and collect little in return. Refund features, therefore, are common.

The most popular type of refund feature is the kind that guarantees benefits for a certain minimum length of time. If the contract promises benefits for at least five years, it is known as a "life annuity with five years certain"; if it guarantees benefits for at least ten years, it is called a "life annuity with ten years certain," and so on. The ten-year guarantee is the most widely used.

A life annuity with ten years certain does not mean the contract will pay benefits for ten years. It is important to realize that the ten-year period is the *minimum* length of time benefits will be paid. If the annuitant lives more than ten years after benefits are started, he will continue to receive benefits. In fact, the annuitant will receive benefits as long as he is alive. The refund feature provides protection only if the annuitant dies during the first ten years of the liquidation period. If an annuitant dies three years after benefits are started, benefit payments will be continued to his beneficiary for the next seven years (the remainder of the guaranteed period).

Installment Refund Annuities.   An installment refund annuity promises that if the annuitant dies before he has received monthly benefit payments equal to the purchase price of the annuity, the benefits will be continued to the beneficiary until the full cost has been recovered. As an example of this type of refund feature, suppose an annuitant pays $30,000 for an annuity and receives $12,000 in benefits before he dies. The installment refund annuity would continue benefits to his beneficiary until another $18,000 had been paid. Of course, benefits are continued as long as the annuitant is alive, even though the purchase price may have been recovered.

Cash Refund Annuities. This type of annuity promises that when the annuitant dies, the insurance company will pay to the beneficiary the difference, if any, between the purchase price of the annuity and the total benefits already paid. Unlike the installment refund annuity, a cash refund contract returns the unpaid benefits in cash, i.e., in one lump sum. Under both types of annuities, the purchaser or beneficiary will receive at least the amount paid for the annuity.

If you are wondering how an insurance company can sell an annuity and guarantee the purchaser that the total purchase price will be paid out in benefits (and possibly more if the annuitant lives a long time), the answer is simple. The insurance company earns interest on the funds. The company does not guarantee to return the purchase price *plus interest,* but simply the amount paid for the annuity. The interest the company earns goes to pay benefits for those who outlive the guaranteed period, to pay the insurance company's expenses, and perhaps contribute to the profits (or surplus) of the insurance company.

CHOOSING THE APPROPRIATE REFUND FEATURE

Which type of refund guarantee should an annuitant prefer? There is no doubt that a "life income with ten years certain" is a stronger guarantee than a pure annuity, an installment refund contract has a better guarantee than a "life income with ten years certain," and a cash refund annuity has the strongest guarantee of all. If all the annuities cost the same, then, a person would certainly select a cash refund annuity. The problem is that annuities with stronger guarantees cost more. Or, stated another way, for every $1,000 paid to an insurance company, the annuities with stronger refund provisions will provide a smaller monthly income to the annuitant. Table 17–8 shows this clearly.

A person can select the most appropriate refund feature only by knowing the cost of the various annuities, his financial situation, and his desire to leave money to others. Consider the case of Mary Hays. She is 64 years old and retiring as a school teacher this year. Since Mary never married and has no close relatives, she has no great desire to leave money to others after her death. Mary is worried about her retirement income. She has figured that she needs to add at least $355 each month to her social security retirement benefits, but she has saved only $50,000. Refer to Table 17–8 and recommend the type of annuity that would be most appropriate for Mary. A pure annuity (i.e., no period certain) seems to be a perfect choice. It is the only annuity that will meet her objectives. The lack of a refund feature is not a problem because Mary does not need to pay for the refund provision.

Table 17–8   Annuity Rates (monthly income per $1,000 of accumulations)

Payee's Age		Type of Annuity					
Male	Female	No Period Certain	Five Year Certain	Ten Year Certain	Twenty Year Certain	Install-ment Refund	Joint and Two-Thirds*
40	44	$4.49	$4.49	$4.48	$4.45	$4.45	--
45	49	4.84	4.84	4.82	4.72	4.75	--
50	54	5.30	5.28	5.24	5.05	5.12	$4.71
55	59	5.91	5.88	5.78	5.41	5.60	5.12
60	64	6.73	6.65	6.44	5.78	6.21	5.64
65	69	7.84	7.67	7.24	6.12	7.00	6.36

*With female age five years less than males'.
Source: Large life insurance company, July 1970.

But what about Bob Bray? He is retiring on a comfortable income and has six children, two of whom are still in college. He would like to assure himself an income for the rest of his life, but he wants to leave his children something if he should die soon. Bob can afford to buy a more expensive annuity. He should purchase a "life income with ten years certain" or even an annuity with a stronger guarantee.

One word of caution. An annuity is always a poor purchase for a person who is not in good health. An insurance company may require a physical examination for a life insurance policy, but it never requires medical examinations of annuitants. The person who benefits most from an annuity is one who buys the annuity and lives a long time, and the person who benefits least from an annuity is one who dies soon after buying it. It is wise, therefore, for a prospective annuitant to have his own doctor give him a complete physical examination before buying an annuity.

VARIABLE ANNUITIES

Annuities sold by insurance companies in the past have not been very popular, since annuities are susceptible to inflation risk. In other words, annuitants have received a fixed-income for life. If a person buys an annuity that provided $200 a month, he will receive exactly $200 each month. And of course, with continued inflation, the $200 a month becomes less and less valuable. In other words, the income buys fewer and fewer goods and services. The variable annuity was developed to meet this kind of problem.

The Variable Annuity Idea.   A variable annuity attempts to solve the problem of inflation by providing benefits that fluctuate in dollar amounts according to the value of an accumulated fund of common stocks. In other words, a variable annuity contract does not promise to pay so many dollars of benefits each month; it promises to pay the value of so many "units" each month, and since the value of the "units" changes, the monthly benefit will change. If the value of the common stock fund increases, the annuitant will receive a larger check. If it decreases, the monthly benefit check will be smaller.

Most variable annuities are deferred annuities and operate in the following manner: suppose you are 25 years old and agree to pay $25 a month to an insurance company for a variable annuity. The insurance company will first make a deduction from your monthly payment to cover expenses, and the remainder of your money will flow into the insurance company's portfolio of common stocks. The funds provided by all variable annuity buyers will be pooled together, but these investments will be kept separate from the funds provided by others.

During the accumulation period your payments will buy *accumulation* units. The number of accumulation units credited to your account will depend on the price of the units when you make your payment. If $2 is deducted for expenses from your first monthly payment of $25 and the price of an accumulation unit is then $11.50, you will receive credit for two accumulation units ($25 − $2 = $23 and $23 ÷ $11.50 = 2 units). If the value of the accumulation units decreases in the next month, your $23 *net* payment will buy more than two units. Suppose it buys 2.5 units in the second month. You will then have a total of 4.5 units in your account (two units bought the first month and 2.5 purchased in the second month). Of course, if the value of the accumulation units increases, your monthly payment will buy fewer accumulation units, but the total number of units accumulated in your account will increase.

During the accumulation period the value of the common stock investments will probably fluctuate. This will change the value of each accumulation unit, but the number of accumulation units in your account will always increase with each premium payment.

When you decide to retire, your accumulation units will be exchanged for *annuity units*. The number of annuity units you receive will depend on mortality and investment experience, but the important point to remember is that once you retire, the number of annuity units does not change. Suppose you become entitled to receive the value of 100 annuity units each month. The variable annuity contract will promise to pay you the value of 100 annuity units, but the company does not make any dollar guarantees. If the value of the portfolio increases, the annuity units will increase in value and your monthly benefit check will increase even though you still receive only the value of 100 units. When the portfolio decreases in value, your 100 units will be worth less and your monthly check will be smaller.

The basic idea of a variable annuity is that a person's income will not be eroded by inflation if benefits are increased when the cost of living increases. But notice that variable annuity benefits are *not* tied directly to the cost of living. Variable annuity benefits are tied directly to the value of a common stock portfolio. This means there must be a positive correlation between stock prices and consumer prices. If stock prices go up when consumer prices are rising, the variable annuity should provide a good hedge against inflation. The critical question, then, is do common stock prices and consumer prices move together? The answer is given in Figure 17–3.

Figure 17–3   Consumer Prices and Stock Prices, 1900–1967

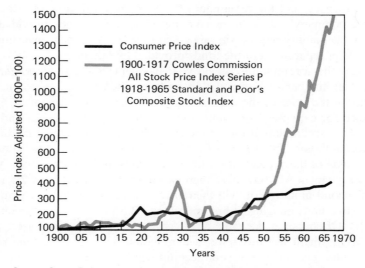

Source: George E. Johnson and Donald S. Grubbs, *The Variable Annuity* (Indianapolis: Research & Review Service of America, Inc., 1968), p. 144. Reproduced through special arrangement with Research & Review Service of America, Inc.

There have been periods in the past when the stock market decreased when consumer prices have increased. This means variable annuity benefits can go down even when consumer prices are rising. But, in general, stock prices have tended to go up during times of inflation. In fact, Figure 17–3 shows that stock prices have gone up much faster than consumer prices since 1950. If this continues, variable annuity owners will be more than protected by inflation—their real income will actually increase.

Experience of Variable Annuity Plans.   The variable annuity sounds fine in theory, but how well has it performed in actual practice? The oldest variable annuity plan is the College Retirement Equities Fund (C.R.E.F.) established in 1952. Figure 17–4 shows the performance of this plan.

Figure 17–4 Value of the C.R.E.F. Accumulation Unit (1952–1970*)

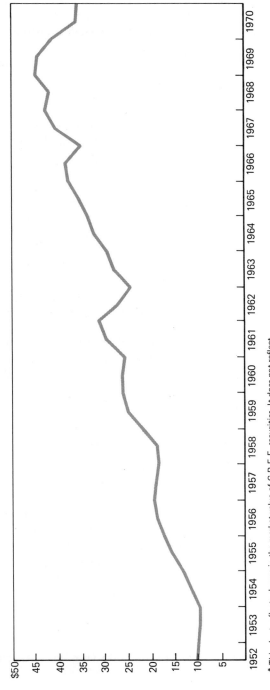

* This chart reflects change in the market value of C.R.E.F. securities. It does not reflect portfolio income, which is reinvested and apportioned to participants.

Source: Teachers Insurance and Annuity Association, *TIAA-CREF Annual Report, 1970,* p. 8. Reprinted with permission.

The variable annuity experience of C.R.E.F. has been very favorable. Accumulation units were valued at $10 in 1952, but by the end of 1970 they were worth more than $39. It is true that annuity values have declined in some years, but they would have never declined more than three consecutive years. Over the long term, C.R.E.F. annuitants have had their benefits increased more than the Consumer Price Index has increased.

It is hard to judge the results of other variable annuity plans because most of them are very new. Variable annuities have become available to the general public only in the last few years.[8] But insurance agents are now promoting them aggressively, and they are being sold on both a group and individual basis.

Comparison of Mutual Funds and Variable Annuities.   A variable annuity is, in several respects, very similar to a mutual fund. Both invest in common stocks, both achieve a high degree of diversification for the investor, and both can use the dollar averaging principle. In fact, some people have said that a variable annuity is nothing more than a special *type* of mutual fund. If this is the case, should a person prefer one over the other? Which would you prefer?

A person could logically prefer a mutual fund or a variable annuity if he expected the investment performance of one to be better than the other. Advocates of mutual funds argue that the investment performance of mutual funds will be superior to that of variable annuities. But those who favor variable annuities believe that the investment performance of variable annuities will be at least as good as, or even better, than that of mutual funds.

Do variable annuity plans or mutual funds have characteristics that would appear to give one an investment advantage over the other? No. Both are investing in common stocks with approximately the same objectives and equally competent investment officers. Although *some* mutual funds undoubtedly will outperform *some* variable annuities, some variable annuity plans will perform better than some mutual funds. There is no reason to believe one *group* will outperform the other. Investment performance, therefore, is *not* a factor a person should consider in his choice between a mutual fund and a variable annuity.

What about expenses? Does it cost more to buy a mutual fund or a variable annuity? When the expenses are compared carefully, they appear to be about the same.[9] A buyer, therefore, cannot find a reason for preferring one over the other on this basis.

---

[8] C.R.E.F. is a retirement plan for college teachers only.

[9] No load mutual funds have lower costs to the buyer than variable annuities or other mutual funds.

A valid difference between a mutual fund and a variable annuity is the annuity principle. A person cannot outlive the income provided by a variable annuity, but upon his death (and the end of guaranteed benefits, if any) the contract has no value. A mutual fund cannot be liquidated without taking the chance that the fund will be depleted before the investor dies. The annuity principle, therefore, is a strong argument in favor of a variable annuity *for purposes of providing a retirement income.*

This argument does not imply that a person should always prefer a variable annuity to a mutual fund. In fact, a person in some circumstances could logically prefer a mutual fund because:

1. He may be in poor health. As indicated previously, an annuity is a poor purchase for a person in poor health.
2. He may want to leave some money to his heirs. A variable annuity will liquidate a person's investments. If you want to leave an estate, you should not buy an annuity.
3. A mutual fund share owner has more flexibility than a variable annuity owner. A variable annuity owner has an income tax problem if he discontinues the plan prior to retirement. He will be taxed on the gain, at ordinary income rates, in the year he stops payments and takes cash out of the plan. If a mutual fund had been purchased instead, the income tax liability would have been spread over the years.

In short, a person can make a wise decision between a mutual fund and a variable annuity only if he knows the differences between the two and he recognizes his financial objectives.

The Future of Variable Annuities.   In 1956, only four insurance companies were selling variable annuities. The period from 1956–1964 was a time of major problems with variable annuities, and few companies tried to sell in this market. But some of the problems have been solved, and a larger and larger number of companies are selling variable annuities.

The recent growth of variable annuities is shown in Figure 17–5. In studying this figure, it is important to notice that it is scaled on semilogarithmic graph paper. This means that equal distances on the vertical scale represent not equal *amounts* of change but equal *percentage* changes. A semilogarithmic scale is more appropriate for showing rates of growth than the most customary arithmetic chart. Figure 17–5, therefore, is not very helpful in studying the size of the various financial institutions (notice that variable annuity data are shown in millions of dollars and the other data are shown in billions of dollars), but the steepness of the lines in the figure illustrates *rates* of growth.

Notice that life insurance assets and savings in savings and loan associations and savings banks have grown at about the same rate. (These three lines in Figure 17–5 are almost parallel.) The steeper slope depict-

Figure 17–5   Recent Growth of Variable Annuities and Other Investment
Media

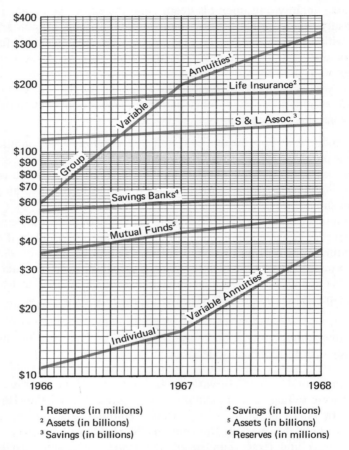

¹ Reserves (in millions)   ⁴ Savings (in billions)
² Assets (in billions)   ⁵ Assets (in billions)
³ Savings (in billions)   ⁶ Reserves (in millions)

Sources: Institute of Life Insurance (Private Correspondence); Investment
Company Institute, *Mutual Fund Fact Book, 1969,* p. 16; *Federal Reserve
Bulletin,* January, 1970, p. A37, 38, and 47.

ing mutual fund growth shows that mutual funds have grown faster
than life insurance assets, savings in savings and loan associations, and
savings in mutual savings banks. This is not surprising because the rapid
rate of growth in mutual funds is well known. But compare the growth
rates of mutual funds and variable annuities. Figure 17–5 shows that
variable annuities (both group and individual) have a much higher rate
of growth than mutual funds. Reserves for group variable annuities increased more than five times in these three years.

Another interesting comparison is the growth rate of group variable
annuities versus that for individual variable annuities. For the three-
year period covered by the figure, group annuities have grown faster.

From 1967 to 1968, however, individual variable annuities grew faster than group variable annuities.

One could argue that Figure 17–5 is misleading because it is easier to achieve a high rate of growth from a smaller base. That is, variable annuities are in their infancy and it may be easier for them to grow faster than the other huge financial institutions. This argument may have some validity. However, it may be significant that since 1945 (when mutual funds were beginning to gain in popularity) there has never been a three-year period when their growth rate even approached the recent growth rate of variable annuities.

One conclusion is inescapable: variable annuities are destined to become an extremely important financial vehicle for millions of individuals. Perhaps you will someday consider a variable annuity in your own financial plans.

SUMMARY

The importance of planning retirement income is seldom recognized by young people. But it is usually impossible to accumulate a retirement fund if a person waits too long. Studies have shown that few people in the past have been able to provide themselves with much income in their retirement.

Some people plan to work after they reach the normal retirement age. This approach has a number of disadvantages, and should be used only as a last resort. Our social security system provides important retirement benefits, but the amount of the benefits is limited. For a person who has earned a reasonably good income, the social security benefit may be only a small fraction of his previous income. Pension plans have not provided an important source of retirement income in the past, but they are becoming more important. A person who is covered by a pension plan should attempt to understand the basic provisions of his plan and approximately how much income it will provide during retirement. Investments in real estate and common stocks are used by some individuals to provide a retirement income. These approaches involve several possible advantages and disadvantages. Annuities have seldom been used because they have been subject to losses from inflation. Variable annuities, however, offer some of the advantages of common stocks and still have the advantages of an annuity. They have shown rapid growth and undoubtedly will be more popular in the future.

The only logical way a person can approach the problem of providing himself with a retirement income is to study the various investment media. In other words, a person should be aware of the advantages and disadvantages of each approach. Then he can plan his retirement sensibly.

Case Problems

1. Many strange things go through an expectant father's mind when he is in a hospital waiting room. Jeff has been waiting for his first child six hours now, and he is starting to think about the things he will hope to teach his son. And this reminds him of a conversation he had with his father only last week. Jeff's father had been trying to tell Jeff that he should start a savings program at an early age in order to accumulate a sizable fund for retirement. But Jeff is only 20 years old, and he cannot get very excited about saving for his retirement. Jeff's father has recommended that Jeff save $15 a week during 50 weeks in each year. This seems like a lot of money to Jeff, but more importantly, he cannot understand why he should not wait until he is about age 45 to start his savings for retirement. If he saves until age 65, he will still have 20 years to build up a retirement fund. How much difference would it make if Jeff waited until age 45 to start his retirement fund? Note: Use Table 17–2 (which assumes 7 percent interest) to make actual calculations.

2. After working for a large company for eight years, Harry is considering changing jobs. He believes his opportunities for advancement are about the same with either company, but his present position pays about $1,000 less than the new job he has been offered. Harry's decision to change employers was almost final when one of his friends told him that he should consider the vesting provisions in the pension plan. This was a factor that Harry had completely overlooked in his decision. Harry has asked you to explain what is meant by "vesting" and how the vesting provisions could influence his decision. How would you respond?

3. Tom is a young dentist who has been thinking about his investment program. He has a savings account, life insurance, stocks, mutual funds, and a little real estate. He has not been worrying as much about the amount of money he has been accumulating, but he has been thinking about the way he has been selecting his investments. Specifically, he has heard about the HR-10 plan and he wonders if he should be using it himself.
   (a) What is the advantage of an HR-10 plan?
   (b) Why don't all self-employed individuals use the plan?

4. Hugh has been investing money in a mutual fund for the past several years. He has other investments for certain purposes, but he plans to use the mutual funds for his retirement. A friend told Hugh that he was doing the same thing, but he was buying a variable annuity instead of a mutual fund. Hugh had never heard of a variable annuity, but he has never liked annuities very much and he doubted if he could be interested in a variable annuity. However, his friend said that a variable annuity was nothing more than a type of mutual fund and Hugh should consider the advantages and disadvantages. What are the similarities, and differences between mutual funds and variable annuities?

5. Art simply cannot get excited about building a retirement fund. First of all, Art is only 20 years old now and he realizes he may not even be alive 45 years from now. Secondly, Art believes he would just keep working if

he had to after age 65. Criticize Art's plans. Be as specific as possible with your criticisms.

6. Dick has decided that he would like to retire at an early age—maybe 45 or 50. He realizes this will be tough, but he enjoys the challenge of successful investing and his desire for early retirement is strong. Dick has decided that the best approach for him is to invest in apartment units. He started with duplexes, but now he owns several four-plexes. He is thinking of selling some of these and buying a large apartment house.
   (a) What are the major advantages of building up a retirement fund with rental apartments over most other types of investments?
   (b) What are the usual disadvantages of using apartments to build up a retirement fund?

7. Jerry Hall's father is approaching retirement age. He has accumulated $100,000 and he is covered by social security, so Jerry and his Dad have believed there is no serious problem. But one night they were talking and the question came up "exactly how should Jerry's father use the $100,000?" Jerry's father has come to the conclusion that he will need $11,800 each year. His social security benefits will amount to $200 a month. Therefore, he must use his accumulated sum of $100,000 to provide $9,400 each year. Jerry thinks his dad should put the money in a mutual fund and withdraw $9,400 each year. His father, however, is not convinced that he should do this.
   (a) What is the major disadvantage of Jerry's idea?
   (b) Use Table 17–8 and determine if Jerry's father can meet his objective with an annuity.

Selected Readings

Bailey, J., Jr. "Answers to Your Questions About Social Security and Medicare." *Successful Farming,* January 1969, pp. 72–73.

Board of Trustees of the Federal Old-Age and Survivors Insurance and Disability Insurance Trust Funds. *Federal Old Age and Survivors Insurance and Disability Insurance Trust Funds.* Washington, D.C.: U.S. Government Printing Office. Published annually.

Campbell, Paul A. *The Variable Annuity.* Hartford, Connecticut: Connecticut General Life Insurance Co., 1969.

Denenberg, Herbert S. and Ferrari, Robert J. *Life Insurance and/or Mutual Funds.* New York: Pagent Press, 1967.

"Find Out What Your Social Security Will Pay." *Changing Times, The Kiplinger Magazine,* March 1969, pp. 47–48.

"For Women: Advice on Social Security." *Changing Times, The Kiplinger Magazine,* November 1969, pp. 37–38.

Holzman, Robert S. *Guide to Pension and Profit-Sharing Plans.* Lynbrook, New York: Farnsworth Publishing Co., Inc. 1969.

Ivry, David, Johnson, Harry M., and Ackerman, Lawrence, J. *Fundamentals of the Federal Old-Age, Survivors, and Disability Insurance System and the*

Medicare Program, Revised edition. Bryn Mawr, Pa.: The American College of Life Underwriters, 1968.

Johnson, George E. and Grubbs, Donald S. *The Variable Annuity.* 2nd edition. Indianapolis: The Research and Review Service of America, 1970.

Katona, George. *Private Pensions and Individual Savings.* Ann Arbor: Institute for Social Research, University of Michigan, 1965.

McGill, Dan M. *Fundamentals of Private Pensions.* Homewood, Illinois: Richard D. Irwin, Inc., 1964.

Melone, Joseph J. and Allen, Everett T. *Pension Planning.* Homewood, Illinois: Richard D. Irwin, Inc., 1966.

Myers, R. J. "Social Security at the Crossroads." *Reader's Digest,* April 1970, pp. 81–85.

————. *Social Insurance and Allied Government Programs.* Homewood, Illinois, Richard D. Irwin, Inc., 1965.

Sorb, Jozetta H. *Portable Pensions.* Ithaca, N.Y.: School of Industrial and Labor Relations, Cornell University, 1969.

Turnbull, John G. *The Changing Faces of Economic Insecurity.* Minneapolis: University of Minnesota Press, 1966.

Turnbull, John G., Williams, C. Arthur, Jr., and Cheit, Earl F. *Economic and Social Security.* 3rd edition. New York: Ronald Press Co., 1968.

Wood, Glenn L., *Variable Annuities.* Bryn Mawr, Pa.: The American College of Life Underwriters, 1969.

———— and Lee, Finley. *An Analysis of Variable Annuities: Concepts, Contracts, Problems and Opportunities.* Bryn Mawr, Pa.: The American College of Life Underwriters, 1971.

CHAPTER **EIGHTEEN**

THE IMPORTANCE OF ESTATE PLANNING

Estate planning is one of the most complex and most misunderstood areas in personal financial management. It is also one of the most interesting. Broadly defined, estate planning is concerned with all the financial decisions that are involved in acquiring, using, accumulating, and transferring property—including financial assets such as savings accounts, stocks, bonds, and insurance policies. This means that all previous chapters have really been estate planning topics, and that you have already learned a great deal about estate planning. But a broad concept of estate planning is not very useful, and it can be misleading. The more popular (and more useful) concept of estate planning is that it consists of the financial decisions that should be involved in transferring ownership or use of property. Viewed in this way, estate planning is concerned with wills, trusts, and taxes.

At this point you might believe that estate planning is something for someone else, but not for you. You may feel this way because there are several common misconceptions about estate planning. It is commonly believed that:

1. Estate planning pertains only to wealthy people.
2. Estate planning is not important for a person who does not plan to transfer his property to someone else.
3. Estate planning applies only after death.

Since these fallacies can lead to serious mistakes, let's consider each. First, estate planning should not be limited to the wealthy. Do you have an estate? Of course you do. Your estate consists of all the property you own. Do you have a car or a house? Do you own some furniture? What

This chapter was written by Duke Nordlinger Stern, a member of the Missouri Bar, who dedicates the chapter to SAGS and Nordcroft.

about financial assets? If you have a savings account (or even a checking account) you own property. And if you own any property, you have an estate. It is true that mistakes in estate planning may cost wealthy people a lot of money, but estate-planning errors can be just as damaging to a person of modest resources. Suppose a person has $10,000,000 and loses $100,000, and a person with $10,000 loses $1,000 through poor estate planning. Which person has lost more? In a relative sense, the wealthy individual has lost only 1 percent of his wealth but the other person has lost 10 percent of his assets. Estate planning, therefore, can be as important (or even more important) to a person without a large estate. Furthermore, estate planning should be important to anyone who believes his estate will increase in the future.

The idea that estate planning is not important unless a person plans to transfer his assets to someone else is also a serious misconception. In the first place, *everyone* transfers his property when he dies, if not sooner. It is often advantageous to transfer property before death. As you will soon learn, a person can actually give property to someone and receive valuable financial benefits.

Thirdly, estate planning is not limited to those who have died or may be near death. In fact, often it is too late to plan an estate for a person who is near death. Estate planning is most useful when begun early, and a young person is in an ideal position to plan his estate. Moreover, a young person should realize that the estate plans (or lack of plans) of *others* may have an important effect on his own financial planning.

The basic purpose of estate planning is to set up an orderly and efficient plan of transferring property. This plan should reflect an individual's personal intentions and minimize waste in costs and taxes. Since everyone should have an estate plan, estate planning is a problem about which everyone should be concerned. It should not be considered important only for wealthy or old people.

This chapter is not designed to make you a professional estate planner. You should acquire a basic understanding of the estate planning process and the fundamentals that are involved in setting up an orderly and efficient estate plan. Perhaps the most important objective of this chapter is to develop an appreciation of the importance of estate planning.

In almost all cases, an estate plan must be custom-made for each individual. People differ so much in their financial circumstances, family relationships, financial objectives, and temperaments that each plan must be unique. But even though estate plans of individuals differ greatly, the *process* by which plans are developed is fairly standardized. For purposes of analysis, it is helpful to break down the estate planning process into six steps.

The first step in developing an effective estate plan is to gather facts. Although it is impossible to list all the facts that might be needed, nonetheless, as a general rule, the more facts that are available, the better the estate plan. But at a minimum, facts must be obtained for financial objectives, current estate plans, property owned, and family relationships.

The second step in estate planning is an evaluation of possible problems and costs. Estimates should be made for such items as estate taxes, attorney's fees, probate costs, and many other factors that can cause estate shrinkage. This is an important step because unless potential problems are recognized and evaluated an estate plan cannot safeguard a person's assets.

Designing the estate plan is the next step. This is where an estate planner uses his creative imagination and ability to meet a person's objectives. A plan is designed to move assets in the proper direction at the right time with a minimum of cost. To do this, an estate planner calls on his knowledge of wills, trusts, and taxes.

The fourth step in the estate-planning process is to test the plan. The purpose at this stage is to find out what would happen under various circumstances. In other words, the question is asked, "Would the objectives of the estate owner be met efficiently if this happened, or this, or this?" Changes that are usually considered are death, remarriage, changes in income, and changes in family situations.

The next step is to put the plan into operation. This is done by developing and executing the necessary legal documents. For example, if the plan calls for the establishment of a certain type of trust, a trust agreement must be drafted and implemented. Wills may have to be rewritten, gifts may have to be arranged, life insurance might need to be purchased, and investments may have to be started or stopped.

Finally, every estate plan must be periodically reviewed. No matter how careful an estate planner has been and how flexible the plan, some changes cannot be anticipated. Laws change, tax rates are changed, investments become more or less attractive, and family relationships change. Estate plans simply become out of date and they must be revised.

A person should have a general understanding of the estate-planning process so that he can see that his plans are soundly developed. But this raises an important question: who should be the estate planner? Is the estate planner the person who owns the estate, his accountant, investment adviser, life underwriter, attorney, or trust officer? The answer is that a professional in each of these fields might be needed. In a large estate, the estate-planning process requires a team of advisers and the services of many professionals may be needed. But how does a person with a small estate develop a plan? As a practical matter, most people with small estates become involved in their estate planning problems through a life underwriter. A competent life insurance salesman attempts to set up a comprehensive estate plan and does not simply sell a policy to meet a single financial need. But a life underwriter is prohibited by law from engaging in the practice of law. The services of an attorney, therefore, are always required in developing and implementing an estate plan. If, after studying the remainder of this chapter, you decide to start your own estate plan, you could contact an attorney, life underwriter, accountant, trust officer, or investment adviser or any competent person in one of these fields who can at least provide enough advice to initiate your plan.

WILLS

Before one can understand the benefits of a will it is important to understand what would happen to your estate if there were no will. For example, if you still are not convinced of the advantages of estate planning, and if you die tomorrow, what would happen to your property?

DEATH WITHOUT A VALID WILL—INTESTACY

If you die without having made a valid will you are said to die intestate. Your property is disposed of not by your act or according to your intent, but by operation of law. The applicable laws are known as the law of descent for real property and the law of distribution for personal property. These statutes are enacted by each state. There is no single intestate descent and distribution statute, but rather a variety of them all differing to one degree or another.

Consider a typical example. Assume that David Isle dies in his early thirties without a valid will. Besides Jackie, his wife (spouse), and his two children, Davey and Susan (issues), he is survived by his parents, two brothers (one of whom is a half-brother), two aunts and an uncle. One of his two children is adopted. His estate consists of a house valued at $20,000, a piece of land in a subdivision, worth $3,000, $7,000 of furniture in the house, 100 shares of XYZ Corporation stock with a market value of $2,000, $1,500 in a savings account, $250 in a checking account, a car worth $3,000, $500 in personal effects (including a $100 gold watch), and a $20,000 life insurance policy. He has a $15,000 mortgage on the house, a $2,000 mortgage on the land, a loan outstanding of $2,000 which is secured by the car, $100 still owed on the dishwasher, and a personal loan of $100. When David died his funeral and last expenses were $600.

Two questions must be answered: what is the estate and to whom does it go if no will has been made? The answers to these questions vary somewhat because the laws governing the passing of real and personal property are subject to the particular statutes of the state having jurisdiction over the estate. Generalizations are only helpful to see how a statute may operate, but it is imperative to consult an attorney to determine the exact terms of descent and distribution in any specific case.

Allowances.   Most states have what is known as homestead exemptions and family allowances. The former term refers to an amount of real property specified by statute that is set aside for the head of the family (either before or after death) that passes to his family without being liable to the claims of the creditors of his estate. In some states the homestead exemption also applies to personal property. The family allowance, an amount of property set aside by statute in addition to the homestead exemption, is available for the use of the deceased's family for their support while his estate is being settled.

Allowances vary a great deal by state. For example, in one state the widow or surviving minor children are entitled to an amount equal to one year's maintenance as a family allowance. This same state allows a homestead exemption of $7,500 or one half of the estate, whichever is less. Another state only allows a family allowance of $500 and even this is subject to funeral expenses of up to $200.

Disbursement.   Most of the states' statutes governing such matters distinguish between real and personal property, although many states have the same rules for both. As noted earlier, real property refers to land. In the Isles' case, land would certainly include the subdivision lot. Furthermore, since real property includes all items permanently attached to land, such as a building, David's house is also real property. Permanent additions to a dwelling are also considered real property and are called fixtures. These would include a central air-conditioner and storm windows. However, a window air-conditioner or removable screens are not permanently attached to real property and are treated according to the law of personal property.

To determine the passing of the real property, you must first determine the type of ownership prior to David's death. If the real property were owned by David and Jackie together (as joint tenants or tenants by the entirety), then by operation of law at his death, Jackie would become the sole owner of the property. These forms of ownership do not require a will, since the surviving owner takes the property. Joint ownership takes the property out of the intestate descent statute, and serves as one way to avoid intestacy problems. However, it may not be the family's desire to leave all the real property to the spouse. For example, there are tax advantages to using transfer by will or trust compared to transfer according to the laws that automatically apply when anyone dies without a will.

If David and Jackie had held the real property as tenants-in-common when David died, Jackie would continue to own her half as a tenant-in-common. David's half of his property would transfer according to the particular state statute, and the new tenant would be a tenant-in-common with Jackie. In general, David's half would be divided among Jackie, Davey and Susan. Jackie would get one-third and the children would get two thirds, which in our example would be one-third each. As to the total real property, Jackie would own one-half by operation of law as a surviving tenant-in-common, plus one-third of one-half, by virtue of the descent statute; she would then own a total of two-thirds. Davey and Susan would each take one-third of one-half or one-sixth each, for a total of one-third. Jackie, Davey and Susan would be tenants-in-common in proportion to their respective shares.

If David were the sole owner of the real property the entire amount of real estate would have descended just as his one-half portion would if he were a tenant-in-common with Jackie. Jackie, Davey and Susan would then be tenants-in-common, each holding a one-third interest.

A Typical Statute. The District of Columbia Intestacy Statute affords an example of what happens if you die without a will. In the District of Columbia, descent and distribution are treated the same; therefore there is no distinction between real and personal property. In our example, David left a wife and two children. But suppose both parents, had been in the same accident, and Jackie had died before David, or she could have survived, but they had no children. In still another alternative, David could die without ever being married. The following description illustrates what would happen under these various alternative situations in the District of Columbia.

1. If there are children and grandchildren, the surviving spouse takes one-third and the children and a child of a deceased child take two-thirds. (They take *per stirpes* and not *per capita* so that if two children survive and the deceased child had two children, these grandchildren would take an equal portion of their parents share. Each would take one-half of one-third, or one-sixth. *Per capita* descent or distribution means the estate is divided by the number of surviving children and grandchildren and here each would receive one-fourth.) It is common for the statutes in other states to give one-half to the surviving spouse and one-half to the surviving child, if only one child, and one-third to the surviving spouse with the remaining two-thirds to the surviving children if more than one child survives.
2. If there are no children or grandchildren, the surviving spouse takes one-half and the decedent's father and mother take one-half.
3. If there is no father or mother, the surviving spouse takes one-half, and the decedent's brothers and sisters or their descendant's take one-half.
4. If there are no children, grandchildren, father, mother, brothers, sisters or descendants of brothers and sisters, the surviving spouse takes all of the real and personal property.
5. If there is no spouse, children, grandchildren, father, mother, brothers, sisters or descendants of brothers and sisters, all collateral (nonlineal descendants) of equal degree take *per capita*.
6. If there are no collaterals, the grandparents, or such of them as survive take *per capita*.

7. If none of the above, spouse, descendants, or relations, survive, then all real and personal property escheats (passes) to the District of Columbia for the benefit of the poor.
8. The District of Columbia makes no distinction among children of whole and half-blood; children born after the death of the decedent; children born out of wedlock but acknowledged by the decedent as his child and the decedent subsequently marries the child's other parent; and adopted children.

A Typical Family. In our illustration, David's house and land would pass to his heirs, subject to their respective mortgages, according to the Intestacy Statute. The car and dishwasher would also pass subject to their liens. To satisfy these liens (the personal loans and last expenses) there is $1,750 in cash in the savings and checking accounts. To make up the balance, 53 shares of the XYZ stock would have to be sold. (It is assumed that any homestead exemption and family allowance were deducted before determining David's estate.)

The total value of the personal property in the estate would be $940 worth of XYZ stock, $10 left after the sale of the stock, $500 in personal effects, the $3,000 car and the $7,000 worth of furniture. According to the law governing the transfer of personal property without a will, this $11,450 would be divided equally among Jackie and the two children. The life insurance policy would be paid to the named beneficiary and would not be included in the personal property of the estate (unless the estate were designated as the beneficiary). Although $11,450 can be divided three ways, it is another matter to divide cars and furniture into thirds. Since we are dealing with a family, it is probable they will keep all the property together to preserve the family unit, or at least decide among themselves who will get what specific article. It is possible, however, that one or more members will not go along with such a plan, and the assets may have to be sold to satisfy those shares. Estate sales are forced sales with no time to wait for the best offer. They rarely bring as much as the market value of the assets, and if David's entire personal estate were sold at auction, it is conceivable that the proceeds would be closer to $5,000 than to $11,450. In effect, David did not satisfy his responsibilities very well. In all probability, he really wanted Jackie to receive all the property so she could maintain the family at a higher income level for a longer period of time. Furthermore, the lack of an estate plan might force valuable assets to be sold to meet expenses. In essence, David wasted his assets.

This discussion of intestate descent and distribution should illustrate one crucial point: the person who dies without leaving a valid will has little or no control over the distribution of his estate. Property could end up in the hands of those for whom it was not intended. After years of building an estate, that estate is left to the mercy of a statute. Therefore, no intelligent estate planner should die without a will.

DEATH WITH A WILL

A will is a written instrument in the form prescribed by law by which the maker of a will (the testator) disposes of property. The right to distribute property by will is created by law, and each state has its own statutes concerning wills. A will takes effect only upon the death of the testator, and therefore, it may be revoked at any time before his death.

What can a will do for you? Most importantly, a will determines your beneficiaries. You can dispose of your property as you wish and are not bound by the state laws of descent and distribution. Through a will you can make certain that particular items of your property will be given to specific persons. Quite often you will want loyal friends or distant relatives to receive property at your death. Without a will, this is impossible. If you own a going business, a will can be used to preserve the existence of the firm. Unless you make gifts to charities and other institutions during your lifetime, there is no way to accomplish these gifts after your death without a will. Furthermore, wills provide the means to appoint personal representatives for your estate, and to allow them to serve without a bond. Guardians of your choice for your minor children can only be appointed with a will. In addition, skillful use of wills may result in a possible savings in income taxes, inheritance taxes, and estate taxes. Figure 18–1 may be very helpful to you as it provides rather simple definitions of various terms used in wills. In constructing any will, however, you just must use an attorney.

Requirements for a Valid Will.   In order to make a valid will, a person must be of legal age and have testamentary capacity. In every state, an adult—a person 21 years of age or older—is of legal age to make a valid will. However, many states allow testators to be younger and still make a valid will depending upon the circumstances. Those states which have lower legal ages may distinguish between men and women testators, married, and unmarried testators and wills which dispose of real or personal property.

In addition to being of legal age, a testator must have testamentary capacity, which, in turn, is measured by several elements:

1. Does the testator understand that he is making a will? The testator need not comprehend all the legal innuendos, nor does he have to be learned in the law. It is sufficient that he realize the instrument is for disposing of his property upon his death.
2. Does the testator understand what property will be disposed of by his will? If he is fully aware of which of his holdings will be disposed of by the will this requirement has been met.
3. Does the testator understand which persons normally will expect to receive property under his will? He does not have to leave something for every descendant or relative, provided the will and the circum-

Figure 18–1 Vocabulary of Wills

Administrator or Administratrix (Female). The probate court appointed representative of your estate.

Beneficiary. A legatee, one who receives property under a will.

Bequest. A gift or legacy of personal property by will.

Codicil. A testamentary instrument which modifies or adds to a will.

Devise. A gift of real property by will.

Estate. Your interest in real and personal property.

Executor or Executrix (Female). The person named by you in your will to be the representative to your estate.

Fiduciary. One who acts for another and has the duty to act with the highest degree of care and good faith. Your executor or administrator is a fiduciary.

Intestate. To die without a valid will.

Issue. Children.

Legacy. A disposition of personal property by will.

Legatee. A person who receives property under a will.

Per capita. A gift to a class of beneficiaries who share equally in the gift.

Per stirpes. A gift to a class determined by lineal (from a line) descent, for example, father to son. Members of this may share per capita as to the gift, but the amount that is divided is the same as their lineal ancestor would have received.

Probate. Matters under the jurisdiction of probate courts, including the administering of all estates.

Spouse. A husband or wife.

Testamentary. Any instrument, including a will and codicil, which is only effective after death.

Testate. To die with a valid will.

Testator or Testatrix (Female). The maker of a will.

Will. An instrument drafted to determine the distribution and disposition of property after death.

---

stances under which it was made show he had the soundness of mind to meet this test.

4. Does the testator understand how the instrument will operate to dispose of his property? If he intends to have certain property go to a relative for their life and then to someone else, and the words give an absolute title to the relative instead, testamentary capacity may be lacking.

With only these two requirements, several valid wills may be made, and an understanding of them will help the estate planner avoid making an invalid will and ending up in intestacy.

Types of Wills. There are many types of wills. Each has its place, but you should be wary of those that will not accomplish your goals. Although various complications may be included for specific purposes, your goals may well be achieved best with a relatively simple will.

(1) Attested will. This is the most common form of will. It is in writing, handwritten or typewritten, signed by the testator or by someone for him and acknowledged by him. His signature must be witnessed by two or more adults at the time of execution.

(2) Holographic will. This type of will is written entirely in the handwriting of the testator but is not witnessed. Although the holographic will is valid in some states, it is invalid in the majority of jurisdictions and should be avoided.

(3) Nuncupative will. This is an oral will and is, for the most part, invalid. Some states allow oral wills in the case of a member of the armed forces in active service, and during a last illness. There are usually strict requirements for validity of such wills such as a certain number of credible witnesses. They, in turn, must write down the substance of the oral will within a certain period of time. Unless an emergency exists, the use of an oral will is not a good tool in estate planning.

(4) Conditional will. This form of will meets all the requirements of a valid will, but the validity does not become effective until the occurence of some condition. The condition, such as the birth of a child, must be perfectly clear in the wording of the instrument. The condition must be fulfilled before the will becomes operative. To avoid intestacy courts often distinguish between a condition and an inducement. For example, a will might only be effective if the maker returns from a trip; that would be an inducement to write the will, rather than a condition. If the words are interpreted as an inducement, the will is operative immediately upon execution. To avoid the possibility of intestacy, however, conditions as to execution have no place in a will.

(5) Joint will. This is an attested will which is executed by two or more persons. Many times a husband and wife will make a joint will to avoid the time and cost involved with separate instruments. However, if either estate is large or there is the likelihood of changing circumstances, a joint will may be more difficult to change than a separate will. Furthermore, as each testator to a joint will dies, the will must be probated.

(6) Mutual will. These are separate wills executed by different persons but having reciprocal provisions. In most situations mutual wills are unilaterally revocable by one testator without consent of the other. This feature is a strong argument against having mutual wills.

Contents of Wills. The beginning of the will sets the stage for the document as well as providing certain important information. For example, refer to Figure 18–2 (on pages 664–665). First, the maker of the will (the testator) gives his name and domicile. Next, he states that he has the required testamentary intent, and that he is of legal age to make a will. Finally, he expressly revokes all previously made wills and codicils (additions to a previous will), so that there will be no conflict in terms.

(1) Debts. In the first paragraph of his will, the maker directs that his debts and last expenses be paid. Actually, these debts must be satisfied prior to the distribution of property under the will even if this paragraph was not included. This provision can be useful, however, if the testator wants these expenses to be limited in amount (such as the funeral cost), or wants to show what provisions he has previously made for payment.

(2) Gifts or legacies. There are four types of legacies: (1) specific, (2) general, (3) demonstrative, and (4) residuary. A specific legacy is a gift of property which can be identified and distinguished from the rest of the property in the testator's estate. This gift can only be satisfied by the delivery of that specific property. For example, assume a testator has two watches, one gold and one silver. If he wills his gold one to his son but later sells it, the gift to the son fails; the son cannot receive the silver watch by virtue of this legacy. A general legacy is one payable out of the general estate, such as a gift of $100 to Jim. This is a gift not of specific property, but of a specified amount of property. Usually courts interpret any legacy as being general rather than specific when there is any doubt. Such interpretation is intended to avoid the failure of gifts, and to carry out the testator's true intent. A demonstrative legacy is a gift of a specified amount of property to be paid from a specific source. If the source is insufficient to provide the amount, then the gift can be satisfied out of the general estate. If there is a provision to the contrary, then the gift is a specific legacy and the beneficiary is limited to the amount available from the specified property. A gift of the residue of the estate includes all property remaining after the payment of debts and satisfaction of prior legacies.

If a particular beneficiary dies before the testator, and if that beneficiary is survived by issue, they will inherit unless a will shows a contrary intent of the beneficiary. If there is no issue, then this gift would go back into the residue of the estate. When the residuary legatee dies before the testator, then this part of the estate passes as if the testator had died leaving no will.

(3) Devises. Gifts of real property under a will are known as devices. These gifts follow the same rules as apply to specific, general and residuary legacies.

(4) Executor. The executor is the person (or persons), individual, bank or trust company, who is named by the maker of a will to settle his estate and distribute the property in accordance with his will. The probate court actually appoints the executor (or co-executors), and certainly attempts to follow the nomination of the testator. If the testator is unqualified, incompetent, unwilling to serve, or fails to nominate an executor, then the probate court will appoint an administrator to serve in this capacity. However, a testator is more likely to have his intentions fulfilled by a person of his own choosing. For this reason, he should nominate two or more persons, co-executors who have the capacity to serve and are willing to undertake this responsibility. A clause in the will

Figure 18–2   Illustrative Last Will and Testament

Introduction

I, David V. Isle, of Columbia, Boone County, Missouri, of sound mind and disposing memory and more than eighteen years of age, do hereby make, publish and declare this as my Last Will and Testament, and do hereby revoke all Wills and Codicils at anytime heretofore made by me.

Debts

FIRST: I direct that all my lawful debts and expenses of my last illness añd funeral expenses be paid by my Executor hereinafter named as soon after my decease as conveniently may be. I direct that I be buried on my farm, Kent Bunk Port, located in Boone County, Missouri.

Specific Legacy

SECOND: I give and bequeath my gold watch to my son, Davey T. Isle, if he survives me.

General Legacy

THIRD: I give and bequeath the sum of Five Hundred Dollars, ($500.00) to my daughter, Susan A. Isle, if she survives me, with the hope that she use it for her wedding. (It is not mandatory that this money be used for her marriage.)

Demonstrative Legacy

FOURTH: I give and bequeath the sum of Five Hundred Dollars ($500.00) to each of my two children, Susan A. Isle and Davey T. Isle, if they survive me, to be paid out of and to be charged upon the One Hundred (100) shares of XYZ Corporation owned by me and standing in my name, but if these shares are insufficient then out of my general estate.

Specific Devise

FIFTH: I give, devise and bequeath my home, and the real estate on which it is located, known as Kent Bunk Port, Boone County, Missouri, and all policies of fire, property damage and other insurance on or in connection with the use thereof to my wife, Jackie M. Isle, free and clear of any encumbrances which may exist at my death, if she survives me.

Residuary Legacy

SIXTH: I give, devise and bequeath all the rest and residue of my estate of every kind and description, real, personal and mixed, wheresoever situated, now owned by me, or that which may be hereafter acquired by me, to my wife, Jackie M. Isle, absolutely and in fee simple, if she survives me; if not, then to my children and adopted children in equal shares, the issue or adopted child of any such children or adopted children who may be living at my death to take by right of representation the share to which the parent would have been entitled to as if living.

---

usually provides for the executor's bond and his powers. Since the executor (or the administrator) is a fiduciary who owes the highest degree of loyalty to the estate, the court usually wants some form of guarantee or bond that he will perform satisfactorily. Some states allow an executor

Figure 18–2   (continued)

Guardian

SEVENTH: I appoint my wife, Jackie M. Isle, Guardian of the person and, if one is required, Guardian of the property of each minor child of mine. If she shall fail to qualify or cease to act as such Guardian, I appoint, Ward A. Keeper of Columbia Missouri, in her place.

Executor

EIGHTH: I appoint the Ever Safe Bank and Trust Company, a state banking association now located in Columbia, Missouri, its successor or successors by any merger, conversion or consolidation, Executor of this my Last Will and Testament.

I appoint my wife, Jackie M. Isle, as Co-Executor of this my Last Will and Testament. If my said wife shall fail to qualify or decline or cease to act as Co-Executor hereunder, it shall not be necessary to appoint a substitute or successor in her place, but in such event the Ever Safe Bank and Trust Company shall act as sole Executor hereunder.

Bond

NINTH: I direct that no guardian or executor shall be required to give any bond in any jurisdiction and that if, notwithstanding this direction, any bond is required by any law, statute or rule of court, no sureties be required thereon.

Closing

IN WITNESS WHEREOF, I have subscribed my name to this my Last Will and Testament, consisting of two (2) typewritten pages, this included, on the margin of each of which, except the one where my signature appears, I have placed my initials for purposes of identification this 14th day of April, A. D. 1942.

David V. Isle
Testator

Attestation

On the day and year last above written, the foregoing instrument, consisting of two (2) typewritten pages, including the page on which this attestation clause appears, was signed, published and declared as and for his Last Will and Testament by the Testator, David V. Isle, in the presence of us, and thereupon we, at his request, and in his presence, and in the presence of each other have hereunto subscribed our names as witnesses this 14th day of April, A. D. 1942.

Mickey Q. Nordcroft, residing at 1607 Sylvan Lane
Lucy I. Prep, residing at 14 Heart Court
K. C. Guy, residing at 22 Players Avenue

---

to serve without a bond if the testator so desires; other states permit the testator to relieve the executor from giving a surety bond to satisfy the performance of his duties. By state statute, the executor has certain powers which govern his actions in the settlement of an estate. Frequently, however, an executor will need additional powers to carry out a testator's particular intentions. These powers should be specifically granted to him.

(5) *Closing.* After the testator has accomplished all that he had set out to do he must close the will by signing his name with the date to show that this is the last will and some indication that all the pages form the whole will. This protection is accomplished by stating the number of pages in the instrument on the page where the signature appears, and by initialing all the other pages.

(6) *Attestation.* Most states require that two or three persons witness the testator executing his will. He should sign in their presence and they should sign as witnesses in his and each other's presence.

Often it is desirable to include a common disaster clause in a will. There may be no children; or if there are, they too could die in the same disaster as their parents. As a result, all of the husband's estate could pass (by virtue of the law of descent and distribution) to the wife's family, if it can be shown that she survived him by even a short time. To prevent this occurrence, a common disaster clause can be incorporated into the will. This clause provides that the beneficiary must survive the testator by a certain length of time before the beneficiary's heirs would take the property. The average period of time provided is 60 days. Occasionally, the clause includes death from causes other than common disasters.

No one should adopt as his own the will used in the illustration. Doing so might well be the equivalent of a decision to die without a will. Any will improperly executed is invalid, and there is no universal statute of wills. Only by carefully following the laws of the appropriate state, can there be any certain validity of the instrument. The state in which the will is probated determines the validity of the will. The state in which the testator is domiciled determines where probate will take place. In our mobile society, there is no guarantee that the state where you execute the instrument will be the state that probates the will. Furthermore, some states have greater requirements for valid execution than do others. Even though you conform to the law of the state where you make your will, it is wise to include any additional requirements for execution that may be part of another state's statute. If you move to another state, it is wise to be certain your will is still valid.

Modifying a Will. Since a will is only effective as of the day the testator dies, he can alter or revoke the instrument as he desires until that time. In addition, there are circumstances that occasionally arise which may be viewed by the law as altering or changing the testator's will. In some states, if the testator marries subsequent to the execution of his will, the courts will treat the will as revoked unless provisions had been made for his bride-to-be. Furthermore, in some states the birth of a child after the death of the testator will alter the will to include a share for the child.

The testator may revoke his will in several ways. He may make a later will which expressly revokes all previous wills or one which is completely inconsistent with the former will; he may also revoke his will by intentionally and actually destroying the will, for example, by cutting off his signature or he may add a codicil which expressly revokes a previous will. A codicil is an addendum to a will which can add to, qualify or revoke the will. For example, refer to Figure 18–3. The codicil refers to a previous will and updates the date of the will to the date of the codicil. Consequently, a codicil must conform to the same formalities as a will. This instrument provides a simple and inexpensive method for a testator to keep his will current with his changing circumstances.

Choosing an Executor.   Your executor, or executrix, may be a person, a bank or trust company, although some states require that the executor be a resident of that state. Before deciding who your executor should be, consider what his duties will be.

1. He locates and reads your will and codicils.
2. He safeguards and manages your assets.
3. He probates your will.
4. He gathers your estate property and has any necessary appraisals made.
5. He settles claims, debts and taxes.
6. He makes an accounting to the probate court and distributes your net estate.

Your executor should not only be someone who is familiar with your wishes, but also someone who will be able to manage your property in accordance with the law. If your estate is uncomplicated, perhaps with the bulk of the property being life insurance that will be paid directly to

Figure 18–3   An Example of a Codicil

I, David V. Isle of Columbia, Boone County, Missouri, do hereby declare this present writing to be a first codicil to my Last Will and Testament, bearing the date of the 14th day of April, 1942. All provisions of said will not affected by this instrument are expressly ratified.

Whereas I desire to supplement the provisions made for my son, Davey T. Isle of Boone County, Missouri, in said Last Will and Testament, I do hereby give and bequeath to him the sum of One Thousand Dollars ($1,000.00) if he survives me, with the hope he will use it for continuing his graduate studies.

IN WITNESS WHEREOF, I have hereunto set my hand and seal this 20th day of March, 1970.

David V. Isle

(Attestation clause which includes statement of legal age, testamentary disposition and witnesses).

your wife as beneficiary, another relative should be satisfactory in this role. However, if your estate is composed of considerable investments or other financial assets, you should consider choosing a professional in this area.

For his services, your executor is entitled to a fee. If he retains an attorney to assist him, an additional fee would be paid out of your estate. Often, these fees are based on the property that flows through the estate. If life insurance proceeds are paid to a beneficiary, rather than your estate, it would not be included; similarly, any unsold real estate would not pass through your estate. Therefore, they are not considered in determining an executor's or an attorney's fee. In a typical state, the minimum fees for the executor are expressed as a percentage of personal property. For example, consider the following:

First $5,000	5%
Next $20,000	4
Next $75,000	3
Next $300,000	2¾
Next $600,000	2½
On all over $1,000,000	2

The basis for the fee in David Isle's estate (assuming his house is not sold), therefore, would be the furniture worth $7,000, the $2,000 stocks, his $1,500 savings, the $250 in his checking account, personal effects of $500 and the car worth $3,000, for a total of $14,250. After deducting debts and expenses of $2,800, the base would be $11,450. The minimum fee for David's executor would be $508. This fee can be increased by the probate court if the executor performs extraordinary or unusual services.

Avoiding Probate.   Unless your property or estate has been transferred before your death, such as by gift or trust, or unless your property is held in joint tenancy, your estate will probably have to pass through the probate court in the state of your residence. There is a cost for probating an estate. However, these costs are minor when weighed against the benefits to the estate that the probate court can provide. The probate court validates your will and oversees the disposition and distribution of your estate. Through this process the rights of your heirs are protected and there is assurance of an orderly transfer of your estate in accordance with your will or the laws of descent and distribution. Your estate is further protected as the court provides for the collection of debts owed to you, and protects the rights of your creditors by making sure your debts are paid.

The probate court formally appoints your executor, and if you die without a will or the executor named in your will cannot or will not serve, the court appoints an administrator to perform these duties. In addition, the probate court establishes title to your real estate, and guarantees the collection of all taxes. A widow is often the victim of swindlers; therefore, a crucial function of the probate court is to protect her. The court makes every effort to be certain she is aware of her rights.

The following list explains the steps in probating a will:

1. Delivery of your will to the probate court by the person or bank that has custody of it.
2. Application for letters testamentary (authority to act as executor) by the person you named as your executor.
3. Proof of your will and admission of it to probate. This is done by the witnesses to your will testifying under oath in court that they saw you sign the will and witnessed it at your request and in your presence.
4. Issuance of your executor's letters testamentary and notice of his appointment published in a local newspaper. This notice is to your creditors and gives them a time limit to file their claims or lose their right to do so.
5. Your executor has your assets appraised and files this along with an inventory with the probate court.
6. Your executor makes certain that all valid claims against your estate are paid and files reports of these settlements with the probate court.
7. A semi-annual settlement and accounting is filed by your executor. A final settlement and accounting is filed.
8. Final distribution of your estate by your executor in accordance with the terms of your will.

Protecting Your Will. In the beginning of the discussion on wills, it was pointed out that there is no uniform law in this area; each state has its own statute. The law on this subject is basically similar, but important differences exist in the disbursement of personal and real property, number of witnesses required to the will, and nonresident executors. To safeguard against your will being held invalid, and to protect against your executor being disqualified or your property not being distributed in accordance with your wishes, your will should be drawn so that it complies with the law in other states. Your personal property will be distributed according to the law of the state in which you reside, but the passing of your real property follows the laws of the state where it is located. However, if your will complies with the laws of that state, it will govern how the real property passes. Do not take chances; always review your will periodically and review it immediately when you move to a new state.

The testator's wife, his attorney, and his prospective executor should know where all his important papers are kept, including his will. All documents which are irreplacable should be kept in a safe deposit box. All important papers which are in the home should be stored in one location. There also should be an inventory of the safe deposit box kept at home. The following illustrates by location some of your most important papers:

At Home	*Safe-Deposit Box*
1. Small amounts of cash	1. Legal documents: wills, codicils, all insurance policies, certificates of title, notes and other instruments of indebtedness, deeds and other real estate instruments
2. Locations of safe deposit box and keys	
3. Check book and current statements	
4. Savings account passbooks or statements	2. Large amounts of cash and all securities
5. List of all credit card numbers	3. Copies of income tax returns and checking account statements for the past three years, plus important paid bills and social security number
6. Inventory of safe deposit box	
	4. Instructions and directions for business
	5. Instructions for funeral and burial
	6. The names and addresses of attorney, accountant, insurance and investment advisors

THE USE OF CO-OWNERSHIP

In addition to property passing to heirs under a will or by intestacy statute, property can be transferred automatically at death if it is held in certain types of co-ownership. The three main forms of co-ownership are tenancy in common, joint tenancy and tenancy by the entireties. These forms apply to both personal and real property. Any co-owner owns an undivided interest in the entire property. The crucial difference among these forms is the effect of the death of a co-owner.

In the case of a tenancy in common in their personal property between two people, say Jackie and David, if David dies Jackie retains one-half interest and this is not subject to probate. David's half is probated and passes to his heirs by the directions in his will or by the law of distribution. If there was no will, Jackie would have her original one-half interest plus one-third of one-half through distribution for a total of two-thirds. While tenancy in common can be useful when used in conjunction with other estate-planning tools, in David's situation one-half of the property would be probated and all of the property would not go to Jackie in the absence of a will.

Joint tenancy and tenancy by entireties both have the characteristic of the right of survivorship. When one tenant dies his interest automatically passes to the remaining owners without going through probate. Initially this would seem attractive, but the tax loss involved quickly outweighs the advantages. For computation of the estate tax base the entire property is used unless Jackie could prove she contributed to its purchase. In addition, when she dies the entire property is again taxable to her estate. In essence joint tenancy can be more costly than the expense of probate.

Joint tenancy or tenancy by entireties can also leave property in the hands of inexperienced management. If all the property went to an emotionally depressed heir it might be quickly dissipated. Furthermore, joint tenancy can cut off other heirs. However, joint tenancy or tenancy by entireties may be necessary in mortgaging property. These types of co-ownership should never be used exclusively in estate planning.

The basic difference between joint tenancy and tenancy by entireties (husband and wife) is that in the former a co-owner can dispose of his interest thereby creating a tenancy in common between the new owner and former co-owner. Any benefit from automatic title passage would then be lost. Furthermore, any joint tenant can force a partition (physical division) of the property among his co-owners and even force a sale if partition is not economically feasible. Any estate-planning advantages would then be gone.

ESTATE, GIFT, AND INHERITANCE TAXES

Estate planning would be greatly simplified if there were no tax consequences of transferring property. Unfortunately, taxes can extract a heavy toll when property is transferred. But the amount a person pays in estate, gift, and inheritance taxes depends—to a great extent—on the amount of planning he has done. A person who makes careful plans can greatly reduce his estate, gift, and inheritance tax burden; a person who ignores these taxes can easily have his entire estate destroyed to pay taxes.

THE FEDERAL ESTATE TAX

The most important tax that is involved in transferring property is the federal estate tax. This is not an inheritance tax. An inheritance tax is a tax on the right to *receive* property, but an estate tax is a tax on the right to transfer an estate at death. Also, inheritance taxes are levied by state governments, but estate taxes are generally imposed by the federal government.[1]

---

[1] A few states levy an estate tax, but these are not nearly so important as the federal estate tax.

The primary purpose of the estate tax is to raise revenue for the government. But it has the effect of redistributing income. The tax takes money from sizable estates and distributes funds to everyone (through government services). The net result, therefore, is to promote equality in incomes and wealth. But from the point of view of an individual, the estate tax is a major cause of estate shrinkage. The effect can be disastrous to an estate, particularly when an estate is passed through several people, and the tax is levied at each death. This is a common situation. For example, Mr. A is married to Mrs. B and they have a child, C. Normally, the estate will pass from Mr. A to Mrs. B and then to C. Without careful estate planning, the estate tax will be levied on the estate when Mr. A dies and when Mrs. B dies. Even if Mr. A had a sizable estate, C may not receive much unless Mr. A develops his estate plans carefully.

COMPUTING THE ESTATE TAX

Although a person does not need to understand all the details that may be involved in computing the federal estate tax, he should have a basic understanding of how the tax is calculated. If a person has this basic knowledge, he will then be in a much better position to minimize his taxes.

Property Included in the Estate.   The starting point for the calculation of the estate tax is the determination of the property that will be included in your estate. This is known as your gross estate. In general, all property (whether it is real or personal, tangible or intangible) is included in your estate. This means that a person's gross estate consists of his home, furniture, clothing, cash, bank accounts, stocks, bonds, automobiles, and almost any other type of property he may own.

Most people realize that federal income taxes are not normally payable on life insurance death proceeds and life insurance proceeds normally pass outside a person's will. Undoubtedly these facts lead many people to believe that life insurance proceeds are exempt from the federal estate tax. This is not true. If the proceeds are payable to the estate or if a person has any "incidents of ownership" in a life insurance policy on his own life, the proceeds will be included in his gross estate. "Incidents of ownership" are rights such as the power to change the beneficiary, assign the policy, borrow on the insurance, or exercise any other contract right. Furthermore, if a person owns a life insurance policy on the life of someone else, the cash value of the policy will be included in the estate of the policyholder when he dies.[2] Since many people have a fairly large

---

[2] Actually, the cash value is not included. The value that is included is either the replacement cost or terminal reserve of the policy. For our purposes, these values are always close to the cash value.

amount of life insurance relative to their other assets, their estates are much larger than they realize.

Another misconception that many people have about estate taxes is that estate taxes do not apply to jointly owned property. For example, suppose a husband and wife own their home jointly and they have a joint bank account. If the husband dies, will any or all of this property be included in his estate? The answer is that property owned jointly (either as joint tenants or tenants by the entireties) is included in a person's gross estate when he dies. And, as a general rule, the entire value of the property will be included in the estate. Actually, however, only a portion of the value will be included if it can be proven that the deceased contributed only a portion of the purchase price of the property. If it can be shown, for example, that a husband only paid half of the purchase price of the property, only one-half of the value of the property would be included in his estate.

Property placed in a trust is includable in a person's estate if he reserves the right to use or receive income from the trust property or reserves the right to revoke or change the terms of the trust. Therefore, all property placed into a revocable trust is included in a person's gross estate. Property to be used in testamentary trust, of course, is also included. The only way a person can minimize estate taxes by using trusts is to set up an absolutely irrevocable living trust and not receive any financial benefit from it.

It is even possible for property that has been given away to be included in a person's gross estate if these gifts are made "in contemplation of death." Suppose a person realizes that he does not have long to live and his estate taxes are expected to be high. Why, then, can't he give some or all of his property to his wife or children (who will receive the property anyway) and thereby remove the property from his estate? There is nothing to prevent such gifts but the law provides that the value of gifts made within three years of a person's death are presumed to be gifts in contemplation of death, and they will be included in his estate for purposes of computing the estate tax. However, the law only presumes that these gifts are made in contemplation of death to avoid estate taxes. If it can be proven that the deceased had a motive other than avoiding estate taxes, the value of the gifts will *not* be included in his estate—even if they were made shortly before death.

Valuation of Property. Having determined what real and personal property and interests must be included in the gross estate, the next step is to ascertain the corresponding fair market value. This is an extremely difficult process. Since this value is the price that a willing seller will offer to a willing buyer or the price at which a comparable item will be sold for in the open market, it is clear that the figure is most often open to debate.

The date on which the value is determined is the date the owner dies, or if his executor or administrator elects, one year after the date of death. This option is very beneficial to the estate because if there is a decrease in the value of the property during the year after death a lower valuation and federal estate tax will result from electing the later date. If the property appreciates in value, the actual date of death can be chosen and the estate tax will not reflect this increase.

To see how complex the valuation process is an example of determining the fair market value of real estate is useful. This figure is arrived at only after considering many factors. What are comparable houses and lots selling for in the same community? Are many houses sold at this price and how quickly are they sold? What is the appraised value by qualified real estate experts? What value was accepted by the probate court for determining the state taxes? If the real estate is sold within one year after the owner's death the selling price will be the fair market value if the sale is on the valuation date. If the sale occurs on another day during this period the selling price will still control unless there has been a substantial increase or decrease in value after the sale and before the valuation date. However, in all cases the valuation by the Commissioner of Internal Revenue will be the deciding factor unless the estate proves a different value.

Assuming that stocks are owned in corporations listed on a stock exchange the fair market value is the average of the lowest and highest selling price on the valuation date. If there were no sales on the valuation date then the value is determined by prorating the averages from the sales reasonably nearest before and after the valuation date.

It might be helpful to examine the case of Mr. Drill. His gross estate could be computed as follows:

Property Owned by Mr. Drill		*Property Owned Jointly with Mrs. Drill*	
Cash	$ 1,000	Checking account	$ 3,000
Stocks	110,000	Savings account	2,000
Personal property	24,000	U.S. savings bonds	2,000
Life insurance policies:		Real estate	38,000

Insured	*Beneficiary*	
Mr. Drill	Mrs. Drill	$60,000
Mrs. Drill	Mr. Drill	10,000

Mr. Drill's gross estate amounts to $250,000. Notice that all the jointly owned property is included in his estate (apparently he paid the full purchase price of this property). Even though Mrs. Drill is the beneficiary of a $60,000 policy, the proceeds will be included in Mr. Drill's estate because he is the owner of the policy. The policy on Mrs. Drill's life is also included because Mr. Drill is the owner. The $10,000, however, is only the cash value of that policy.

Deductions and the Specific Exemption. After the gross estate has been determined the next step is to reduce the gross estate for allowable deductions. Funeral expenses, claims against the estate, probate expenses and other costs of estate administration, and uninsured casualty losses that occur during the settlement of the estate may be deducted. Claims against the estate may be particularly important because they might include unpaid household bills, unpaid notes for cars, an unpaid mortgage on a home, and accrued property and income taxes. The *adjusted gross estate* is determined by subtracting all deductions from the gross estate.

Mr. Drill's adjusted gross estate could be calculated as follows:

Gross Estate		$250,000
Deductions:		
Cost of estate administration	$ 7,000	
Current bills	1,000	
Unpaid loan on stocks	5,000	
Unpaid notes on car	3,000	
Unpaid mortgage on home	28,000	
Funeral expenses	4,000	
Unpaid property and income taxes	2,000	
Total Deductions		50,000
Adjusted Gross Estate		$200,000

Charitable bequests can be deducted from the gross estate. It is important, for reasons that will be clear later, that this deduction is separated from other deductions and taken only *after* the adjusted gross estate is calculated. Every person is then permitted a $60,000 specific exemption. Deducting this exemption and any charitable bequest from the adjusted gross estate gives the taxable estate. In Mr. Drill's case, since he made no charitable bequests, his taxable estate is $140,000 ($200,000 minus $60,000). By looking at Table 18–1 you can easily compute the tax that is payable by Mr. Drill's estate. The estate tax is $20,700 plus 30 percent of the excess over $100,000, so the tax on a taxable estate of $140,000 is $32,700. Observe that Mr. Drill is in the 30 percent estate tax bracket, but the tax rates are progressive. Large estates may pay up to 77 percent in estate taxes.

Credit for State Death Taxes. All states, with the exception of Nevada, impose some type of death tax. These taxes are either inheritance taxes, estate taxes, or both. The tax is usually a progressive tax based on the value of the property transferred and on the relationship between the deceased and the person who receives the property. Although it is dangerous to make generalizations about state death taxes because they differ

Table 18–1 Table for Computation of Federal Estate Tax

(A) Taxable Estate Equalling	(B) Taxable Estate Not Exceeding	Tax on Amount in Column (A)	Rate of Tax on Excess Over Amount in Column (A)
—	$ 5,000	—	3%
$ 5,000	10,000	$ 150	7
10,000	20,000	500	11
20,000	30,000	1,000	14
30,000	40,000	3,000	18
40,000	50,000	4,800	22
50,000	60,000	7,000	25
60,000	100,000	9,500	28
100,000	200,000	20,700	30
200,000	250,000	50,700	30
250,000	400,000	65,700	32
400,000	500,000	113,700	32
500,000	600,000	145,700	35
600,000	750,000	180,700	35
750,000	800,000	233,200	37
800,000	1,000,000	251,700	37
1,000,000	1,250,000	325,700	39
1,250,000	1,500,000	423,200	42
1,500,000	2,000,000	528,200	45
2,000,000	2,500,000	753,200	49
2,500,000	3,000,000	998,200	53
3,000,000	3,500,000	1,263,200	56
3,500,000	4,000,000	1,543,200	59
4,000,000	5,000,000	1,838,200	63
5,000,000	6,000,000	2,468,200	67
6,000,000	7,000,000	3,138,200	70
7,000,000	8,000,000	3,838,200	73
8,000,000	9,000,000	4,568,200	76
9,000,000	10,000,000	5,328,200	76
10,000,000	—	6,088,200	77

Source: Internal Tax Service tax tables.

considerably among the states, Table 18–2 might be helpful in seeing how a "typical" state death tax works.

State death taxes are important for two reasons: first, they must be paid. Even though the tax rates are lower than the rates for the federal estate tax, a person can incur a sizable tax liability. Secondly, the federal estate tax law permits a person to take a credit against his federal estate tax for amounts paid for state death taxes. In other words, a person can deduct state death taxes from his federal estate tax liability. The credit, however, is limited. The state death tax credit is either the actual amount paid or the amount computed by using the tax table in the law (Table 18–3), whichever is less. Notice that the allowable credit is not very high

Table 18-2 An Illustration of State Death Taxes

Value of Inheritance		Class A;B (Spouses, parents, children, adopted children, grandchildren; United States)		Class C (Brothers, sisters, or direct lineal descendent of a brother or sister)		Class D (Uncle or aunt, or direct lineal descendent of an aunt or uncle)		Class E (All Others)	
		Tax on Col (1)	Rate on Excess	Tax on Col (1)	Rate on Excess	Tax on Col (1)	Rate on Excess	Tax on Col (1)	Rate on Excess
(1)	(2)	(3)	(4)	(5)	(6)	(7)	(8)	(9)	(10)
$ 500 —	$ 1,000	$ 0	0%	$ 0	0%	$ 0	0%	$ 0	5%
1,000 —	10,000	0	0	0	0	0	4	25	5
10,000 —	25,000	0	0	0	3	360	5	475	6
25,000 —	50,000	0	1	450	4	1,110	6	1,375	8
50,000 —	100,000	250	2	1,450	5	2,610	7	3,375	10
100,000 —	200,000	1,250	3	3,950	6	6,110	10	8,375	12
200,000 —	500,000	4,250	4	9,950	7	16,110	10	20,375	12
500,000 —	750,000	16,250	5	30,950	8	46,110	12	56,375	15
750,000 —	1,000,000	28,750	5	50,950	9	76,110	12	93,875	15
1,000,000 —	—	41,250	6	73,450	10	106,110	15	131,250	20

Source: These data were computed using the laws reproduced in *Vernon's Civil Statutes of the State of Texas Annotated, Taxation General* (St. Paul, Minn.: West Publishing Co., 1969), Vol. 20A, pp. 572-581.

Table 18–3   Credit for State Death Taxes

(A)	(B)	For Total Maximum Credit	
Taxable Estate Equalling	Taxable Estate Not Exceeding	Credit on Amount in Column (A)	Rate of Credit on Excess Over Amount in Column (A)
—	$ 40,000	—	—
$ 40,000	90,000	—	.8%
90,000	140,000	$ 400	1.6
140,000	240,000	1,200	2.4
240,000	440,000	3,600	3.2
440,000	640,000	10,000	4.0
640,000	840,000	13,000	4.8
840,000	1,040,000	27,000	5.6
1,040,000	1,540,000	38,800	6.4
1,540,000	2,040,000	70,800	7.2
2,040,000	2,540,000	106,800	8.0
2,540,000	3,040,000	146,800	8.8
3,040,000	3,540,000	190,800	9.6
3,540,000	4,040,000	238,800	10.4
4,040,000	5,040,000	290,800	11.2
5,040,000	6,040,000	402,800	12.0
6,040,000	7,040,000	522,800	12.8
7,040,000	8,040,000	650,800	13.6
8,040,000	9,040,000	786,800	14.4
9,040,000	10,040,000	930,800	15.2
10,040,000	—	1,082,800	16.0

Source: Internal Revenue Service tax tables.

for small estates, but the credit can be important for people who have a large estate.

With one or two simplifying assumptions, we can follow Mr. Drill's case. Let's assume that his taxable estate is the same amount for both federal and state death tax purposes. This would probably not be true since the rules for calculating state death taxes are usually different than those used for federal estate taxes. For example, as a general principle, most states do not tax life insurance proceeds if they are paid to a beneficiary other than the estate. Also, let us assume that the state death tax rates shown in Table 18–2 apply to Mr. Drill. If Mr. Drill's taxable estate is $140,000 (as determined previously) for state tax purposes and he leaves his entire estate to Class A beneficiaries (as shown in Table 18–2) the tax would be $5,150.

Now, by referring to Table 18–3, you can see that the maximum credit that would be given to Mr. Drill's estate would be $1,200. Previously we determined that his federal estate tax would be $32,700. With the credit, his tax is $31,500. Therefore, the total death taxes payable on Mr. Drill's estate would be $31,500 (federal state taxes) and $5,150 (state death taxes), or a total of $36,650. This is over 18 percent of the amount actually transferred (the adjusted gross estate).

MINIMIZING ESTATE TAXES

There are several methods by which you can minimize the federal estate tax and have a larger estate to pass on to your beneficiaries. These include the marital deduction, gifts and trusts. Other estate-planning tools such as co-ownership can have an adverse effect on lessening the tax burden. These methods are not exclusive of each other and you should try to find the best combination in order to minimize the federal estate tax and accomplish your other estate planning goals.

Using the Marital Deduction. For the purpose of determining property ownership, states can either follow common law or community property rules. Under community property rules, half the family property belongs to the husband and half belongs to the wife. In these states, only one-half of the total value of the property is included in the gross estate. However, in common law states a husband owns individually what he acquired and the same is true for his wife. Therefore at the husband's death his gross estate would usually be greater than if he had lived in a community property state since he normally owned more property. As a result, there would be greater federal estate tax and more shrinkage.

To correct this inequity the Internal Revenue Code contains a marital deduction provision for estate, gift and income taxes. The effect is that if certain qualifications are met, up to 50 percent of the property left by a husband or wife to the surviving spouse is not included in calculating the taxable estate. As a result the federal estate tax can be mitigated substantially.

The marital deduction is limited to the amount a person leaves to his or her spouse, up to a maximum of one-half the adjusted gross estate. Suppose a person has an adjusted gross estate of $200,000 (as in the case of Mr. Drill). If he leaves his wife $50,000, that would be the amount of the deduction. If he leaves his wife his entire estate, the deduction would be $100,000 because it cannot exceed one-half of the adjusted gross estate. In order for property to qualify for the marital deduction, the property must be given to the spouse outright. That is, the property cannot be given with conditions or be given only for a limited period of time.

The use of the marital deduction can have a substantial effect on a person's federal estate tax. This is illustrated in Table 18–4. For example, Mr. Drill's taxable estate is $140,000. He would have a federal tax liability of $32,700 (not considering credits for state taxes). But if he

Table 18–4 Importance of the Marital Deduction

Adjusted Gross Estate	Taxable Estate	Tax on Estate Without the Marital Deduction	Tax on Estate With Maximum Marital Deduction
$ 70,000	$ 10,000	$ 500	—
80,000	20,000	1,600	—
130,000	50,000	7,000	—
160,000	100,000	20,700	$ 1,600
200,000	140,000	32,700	4,800
260,000	200,000	50,700	12,300
310,000	250,000	65,700	19,300
460,000	400,000	113,700	41,700
560,000	500,000	145,700	56,700
1,060,000	1,000,000	325,700	136,100
5,060,000	5,000,000	2,468,200	983,500
10,060,000	10,000,000	6,088,200	2,449,300

used the marital deduction, his tax would be only $4,800. His taxes would be reduced $27,900![3]

Despite the fact that a person can realize substantial savings by using the marital deduction, its use is not necessarily always desirable. The basic question that must be raised is, "Does the person really want to leave half his net assets to his wife?" Often a person will want to consider the needs of his children, and possibly the needs of his grandchildren. Sometimes it may be desirable to leave money or other assets to a wife but safeguard the assets against unwise spending. This can be done, but it might sacrifice the marital deduction.

Making Gifts.   Many people try to understand gifts and gift taxes without seeing the relationship between them and the federal estate tax. But a person cannot understand gift taxes very well unless he realizes that gift taxes arise *because of* the federal estate tax.

Imagine a person who has a large estate and is concerned about federal estate taxes. In his will he has left his entire estate to his wife and two children. Could such a person give his estate (or part of it) to his wife and children while he is alive and therefore avoid the estate tax? We know that gifts made in contemplation of death will be included in a person's estate, but what about other gifts? The answer is that estate taxes can be avoided or reduced by making gifts. But the federal government has provided a *partial* roadblock to this approach of avoiding estate taxes by imposing a gift tax. A gift tax is paid—not by the recipient of a

---

[3] Keep in mind that a person could leave his wife some part or all of his estate and still not have it qualify for the marital deduction. This could happen if he left his estate to his wife but made the wife's interest conditional.

gift as many people think—but by the person who makes the gift, i.e., the donor. And the major purpose of the gift tax is to prevent people from avoiding all taxes on the transfer of their estate.

Now the question should occur to you, "If estate taxes must be paid at a person's death a gift tax on property must be paid before his death, how does he save money by making gifts?" The answer is that the rates and rules for gift taxes are different than those for estate taxes.

Every person is entitled to a lifetime gift tax exemption of $30,000. This means that a husband and wife together can give, at any time during their lives, $60,000 and not pay any gift tax. In addition, every person has a $3,000 annual exclusion. This exclusion applies to each recipient. In other words, a person can give up to $3,000 each year to as many people as he wants, and never incur a gift tax. The law grants this annual exclusion so that people can make small gifts (such as Christmas presents) without worrying about the gift tax.

To illustrate the gift tax rules, suppose a husband and wife start transferring their estate to their two children. The parents can give $72,000 tax free in one year. This would use up the lifetime exemptions of both parents ($60,000) and the $6,000 annual exclusion for each recipient. (The annual exclusion is $3,000 for one person, but a husband and wife together can give $6,000 each year to each recipient). In a following year the parents could give only $12,000 to the children without incurring a tax liability because they have already used up their lifetime exemptions. But suppose they gave the children $22,000. This would exceed their combined annual exclusion by $10,000. Therefore, *each* parent would have to pay a gift tax on a $5,000 gift. By referring to Table 18–5, you will see that each parent would owe $112.50.

There are three reasons why gifts may reduce the estate tax. First, the gift tax rates (shown in Table 18–5), are lower than the federal estate tax rates (illustrated in Table 18–1). In fact, the gift tax rates are exactly three-fourths of the estate tax rates. Secondly, the lifetime exemption and annual exclusions reduce the effective gift tax rates. Thirdly, property given away from an estate is removed from taxation at the top of the estate tax bracket and placed in the bottom of the gift tax table where rates are lower. The net result is that a person can normally save a considerable amount in estate taxes by making gifts.

A person who attempts to use gifts as a method of reducing his estate tax liability should make sure that the property he transfers will be considered legally as gifts. There are two important legal requirements for a gift. Since a gift is unsupported by consideration (that is, the recipient gives nothing in return), the gift must actually be made to constitute a true gift. A promise to make a gift in the future is not effective. This does not necessarily mean that *actual* physical delivery must be made. *Constructive* delivery may be sufficient. In these cases, the donor gives some representation of the property to the recipient to signify the

Table 18–5 Gift Tax Rate Table

| Taxable Gifts[1] | | | | Of Excess |
From	To	Tax =	+ %	Over
—	$ 5,000	$ 0	2¼%	—
$ 5,000	10,000	112.50	5¼	$ 5,000
10,000	20,000	375	8¼	10,000
20,000	30,000	1,200	10½	20,000
30,000	40,000	2,250	13½	30,000
40,000	50,000	3,600	16½	40,000
50,000	60,000	5,250	18¾	50,000
60,000	100,000	7,125	21	60,000
100,000	250,000	15,525	22½	100,000
250,000	500,000	49,275	24	250,000
500,000	750,000	109,275	26¼	500,000
750,000	1,000,000	174,900	27¾	750,000
1,000,000	1,250,000	244,275	29¼	1,000,000
1,250,000	1,500,000	317,400	31½	1,250,000
1,500,000	2,000,000	396,150	33¼	1,500,000
2,000,000	2,500,000	564,900	36¾	2,000,000
2,500,000	3,000,000	748,650	39¾	2,500,000
3,000,000	3,500,000	947,400	42	3,000,000
3,500,000	4,000,000	1,157,400	44¼	3,500,000
4,000,000	5,000,000	1,378,650	47¼	4,000,000
5,000,000	6,000,000	1,851,150	50¼	5,000,000
6,000,000	7,000,000	2,353,650	52½	6,000,000
7,000,000	8,000,000	2,878,650	54¾	7,000,000
8,000,000	10,000,000	3,426,150	57	8,000,000
10,000,000	—	4,566,150	57¾	10,000,000

[1]After deducting exemption of $30,000, and after taking annual exclusions for individual donees ($5,000 through 1938; $4,000 after 1938 and through 1942; and $3,000 after 1942). The annual exclusions do not apply to gifts of future interests. Neither do they apply to gifts in trust made after 1938 but before 1943.

Note: "Taxable gifts" in the table are determined by deducting the $30,000 specific exemption (allowed only once, but cumulative until used up) and by deducting an annual exclusion of $3,000 per donee of gifts of present interests.

Source: Internal Revenue Service tax tables.

transfer. For example, if you want to give a book to a friend but the book is not in your possession, a letter to him telling of the gift would be a constructive delivery. A gift can also be made by giving property to someone to deliver to the recipient.

The second important legal requirement for a gift is intent. The donor must have the intent to make a gift. To determine the donor's intent the courts will look at the circumstances surrounding the transfer. If the delivery is merely to allow the recipient to have the use of the property with the giver to regain possession at a later date there is no valid gift. It is not imperative that the donor of a valid gift relinquish all rights; it is only necessary that he intends to make a gift and for title to the property to pass to the donee. Therefore, one can give a savings account with the condition that the donor receive the income from it and still have an effective gift.

Potential tax advantages are not the only reasons why gifts play an important role in estate planning. Another benefit of transferring property by gift is that it immediately transfers legal title. If you desire someone to have some portion of your property you can avoid the delays encountered in passing title necessitated by the probating of your estate after your death. Furthermore, you may not have a will, or your will or the section of it applicable to this property may be declared invalid. If this happens, an unintended heir may end up with that property.

Gifts, however, are not always useful in a particular estate plan. If you are conserving your assets for future growth, giving them away at this stage is usually out of the question. Furthermore, since a gift is an irrevocable passage of title you must absolutely give up control and enjoyment of the property. Gifts should be made only after all the advantages and disadvantages are given careful consideration.

TRUSTS

Trusts, either in addition to or in conjunction with wills, are an extremely useful tool in estate planning. Most people believe that trusts are very complicated, but this is not really true. Part of the problem is simply terminology. As shown in Figure 18–5 (on the next page), the legal terminology that is used with trusts can be confusing. But while it can be helpful to know some of the terms in Figure 18–5, we are not concerned with terminology for its own sake.

Basically, a trust is simply an arrangement by which one person (or organization) holds property for the benefit of another person. The person who sets up the trusts is the settlor or grantor. And a trustee is the person or organization that holds the property for the benefit of the beneficiary. A trust must have property of some type (or must be expected to have property), otherwise, it is a "dry" trust and invalid. Figure 18–4 below is a simple graphic illustration of a trust.

Figure 18–4   Illustration of an Income Trust

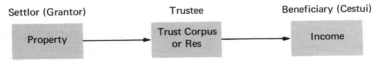

Settlor (Grantor)	Trustee	Beneficiary (Cestui)
Property	Trust Corpus or Res	Income

THE TRUSTEE

One of the first problems encountered by a person who sets up a trust is to select a trustee. The trustee may be an individual or a corporate entity. The main advantage of an individual trustee is that the grantor may be

Figure 18–5   Vocabulary of Trusts

Beneficiary. The person for whom a trust was created and who receives the benefits from a trust.

Cestui. The beneficiary of a trust.

Charitable trust. A trust in which a legal charity is the beneficiary.

Corpus. The real and personal property in a trust.

Employee trust. A trust in which an employee is the beneficiary such as a pension trust.

Fiduciary relationship. A relationship between persons based on trust and confidence. A fiduciary, such as a trustee, owes a duty of utmost good faith.

Insurance trust. A trust whose corpus is either life insurance contracts, life insurance proceeds, or both.

Inter Vivos trust. A trust that is created during the lifetime of the settlor.

Life in being. A beneficiary living at the time a trust is created.

Living trust. An intervivos trust.

Power of appointment. The power given by the settlor of a trust to the income beneficiary whereby the income beneficiary can determine who is to receive the corpus at his death.

Res. The corpus of the trust.

Settlor. The person who creates the trust and transfers his property to the trustee.

Testamentary trust. A trust created at a person's death under the terms of his will.

Trustee. An individual or corporate body, such as a bank, who administers a trust for the benefit of the beneficiary.

Vested. Giving the rights of absolute ownership, although enjoyment may be postponed.

---

able to select a person who is familiar with a unique problem he might have. The argument against an individual trustee is that the death or disability of the trustee could create some problems. This is not a problem with corporate trustees since they have perpetual life, and therefore more people are using trust companies and trust departments in commercial banks.

The trustee should be chosen with care because the trustee normally has a large number of duties. He may have duties to the grantor of the trust and duties to third parties (such as creditors), but the most important duties are obligations to the beneficiary or beneficiaries of the trust. These duties may be modified by the terms of the trust, but in general, a trustee has the following duties to a beneficiary:

1. Administer the trust until relieved of his obligations.
2. Serve the interests of beneficiaries with loyalty.
3. Not to delegate duties that reasonably expected to be performed by the trustee.
4. Keep and render accurate accounts.
5. Furnish information.

6. Exercise reasonable care and skill.
7. Take and keep control of the trust property.
8. Preserve the trust property.
9. Enforce claims for the trust.
10. Defend actions against the trust.
11. Keep trust property separate from other property.
12. Use bank accounts prudently.
13. Make the trust property productive.
14. Pay income to beneficiary if available and authorized by the trust terms.
15. Deal impartially with beneficiaries.

One of the important questions that naturally arises is the degree of authority that should be given to a trustee. Should a trustee have the power to select investments for the trust? In the absence of specific authorization, trustees are limited in the investments they can make for a trust. Some states follow the "prudent man" rule, which means the trustee is expected to exercise sound judgment and reasonable care. Other states use the "legal list" approach and limit a trustee's investments to those on the list approved by the state. In either case, a trustee will be inclined to follow extremely conservative investment policies unless the trust agreement gives considerable freedom and flexibility to the trustee. Therefore, if good investment performance is desired, a trustee should be given discretionary powers to make investments as his judgment dictates.

RIGHTS OF BENEFICIARIES

The person who sets up a trust can give the beneficiaries as much, or as little, interest in the trust property as he desires. At one extreme, he may provide that the beneficiary can receive only the income on the trust property for a certain period of time. On the other hand, the grantor can give the beneficiary an absolute right to withdraw any or all of the trust property at any time. Depending on the purpose of the trust, it may be desirable to give the beneficiary substantial freedom.

Sometimes it is desirable to give beneficiaries *powers of appointment*. These are rights to designate, within the limits set by the grantor, the people who shall receive property. Consider this example: a father may set up a trust for the benefit of his son, and give the son the right to dispose of the property. If he wishes, the father may stipulate that the son can transfer the property only after certain events have taken place or after a certain length of time has passed. The important point, for our purposes, is that a trust is an extremely flexible arrangement. A grantor can give rights in the trust property almost any way he desires.

THE DURATION OF A TRUST

Subject to some limitations, a grantor can use his own judgment in establishing the duration of a trust. He can set the trust up for a duration of one year, five years, ten years, for his lifetime, or for almost any reasonable length of time. The law, however, has recognized that it is not desirable to have trusts run for too long a period of time. One of the important reasons for the restrictions on the duration of trusts is that even a modest amount of property can accumulate into a large fortune if it is allowed to accumulate over several generations.

Limits on the duration of trusts are based on two common law rules. One is known as the "rule against perpetuities" and the other is the "rule against accumulations." The rule against perpetuities states that trust property must be given absolutely ("vested") within the lifetime of the beneficiaries living when the trust was created or within 21 years after the last of the named beneficiaries dies. If a trust does not meet this requirement, at the time the trust is created, the trust will fail altogether or at least be partially invalid. In most states the rule against accumulation follows the same pattern. That is, a trust can accumulate only as long as the time allowed for trust property to be taken from the trust.

Both of these rules are extremely complex and have tested the skills of many experts. Furthermore, the rules stated above are the *common law rules*. They have been changed by statute in so many states that a person who sets up a trust must have his attorney check the duration that is permitted in the appropriate state.

USES OF TRUSTS

If a person wanted to make a list of all the possible, specific advantages that might be gained by a trust, the list would indeed be long. Trusts can be used to meet a great number of specific objectives. But it is helpful to classify the uses of trust into two categories: estate management benefits and tax advantages.

Estate Management.   Very often a person has confidence in his own ability to manage his estate while he is alive, but he is concerned about how well the estate will be managed after his death. This concern can arise from a number of reasons. Widows may not have the ability or time to manage property. Heirs may be physically or mentally incompetent. Young heirs may not be mature enough to handle assets, or they may have a very limited experience in managing financial affairs. In cases of this type, it may be advantageous to establish a *testamentary* trust. This is a trust that is created in a will and does not become effective until the grantor dies. Its main advantage, when used for estate management purposes, is that it permits the grantor to manage his own property but provides effective management after his death through a trustee.

A living trust (often called an *inter vivos* trust) can also provide estate management benefits. This type of trust is created and made effective while the grantor is still alive. The grantor can name himself as the beneficiary of the trust, he can designate other beneficiaries, or he may include himself as one of the trust beneficiaries. You might ask, "Why would a person establish a trust with himself as the beneficiary?" This might be done because the grantor wants to let someone else (the trustee) assume the burden of managing his property. A person who wants to free himself of estate management during retirement, for example, might establish this type of trust. Or a person may want to safeguard himself against poor business judgment or carelessness. In some cases a grantor could set up a living trust and name himself as the beneficiary so that he could build up an independent estate. If this is the reason, a person might place only a small amount of assets into the trust and add to them over the years.

One of the main advantages of a living trust (when used for estate management purposes) is that it gives the grantor a chance to evaluate the performance of the trustee. This is an important consideration because many trusts of this type are designed to continue after the grantor dies. In this type of arrangement it is easy (but not always desirable) to have life insurance proceeds placed into the trust when the grantor dies.

Tax Advantages. To understand how a trust might be used to save income taxes, it is important to realize that trust income might be taxed to the grantor, beneficiary, or the trust itself. Although the trust itself is not a person (it is an artificial legal entity similar to a corporation in this regard) it may be taxed in much the same way as an individual is taxed. A trust has its own tax bracket, deductions, and exemptions that are similar to those provided to individuals. A grantor can decide how he would like to have trust income taxed and then set up the trust agreement accordingly. As a general rule, if trust income is paid out to a beneficiary, the beneficiary pays the income tax. And if the trustee must accumulate the trust income, the income tax is paid by the trust. However, if the grantor is not careful, he might find himself with the income tax liability.

The opportunity to minimize income taxes arises because income is shifted from one person who is in a high tax bracket to a trust or beneficiary who is in a lower income tax bracket. A father, for example, who is in the 50 percent tax bracket might be able to establish a trust for the benefit of his son and have either the trust itself or the son pay the income taxes on the trust income. The son, particularly if he is young, will probably be in a much lower income tax bracket than his father. If so, the difference in the tax treatment can provide a substantial reduction in income taxes.

Not all types of trusts have the effect of shifting the income tax liability. In general, a trust that can be altered, modified, or revoked by the grantor will not transfer the tax liability. This type of trust (known as a revocable trust), cannot provide income tax advantages. But if a grantor establishes an irrevocable trust, he may be able to shift the income tax liability. In fact, if a trust is set up to last more than 10 years (or for the lifetime of the beneficiary, whichever is less) the grantor can often transfer the income tax liability from himself to the trust or the beneficiary and not give up his property forever. This leads many people to establish a trust to last for 10 years and one day. They get the income tax advantage and also receive their property back from the trust after a certain period of time.

Testamentary trusts as well as living trusts can be used for income tax savings. The basic principle is the same—income might be shifted from high tax brackets to lower tax brackets. If several beneficiaries are involved a trustee can be given the power to "sprinkle" income to them according to his own discretion. Tax advantages can be one of the important factors the trustee takes into account when he allocates the trust income.

It is extremely important to realize that we have been talking about the possibility of saving federal *income* taxes. Trusts can also be used to minimize *estate* taxes.

Using Trusts.   Many people who are concerned with estate taxes use trusts to minimize these taxes. But not all trusts are effective for this purpose. A revocable living trust and a testamentary trust will not reduce the grantor's estate taxes at all. In either case the trust property is under the control of the grantor up until his death, and therefore the trust property will be included in his estate.

If a person sets up an irrevocable trust, the property in the trust will normally not be included in his estate when he dies. This is because a person who establishes an irrevocable trust has, in effect, given the trust property away. In fact, setting up this type of trust is legally considered as a gift, and a gift tax may be payable. Even if an irrevocable trust is established, there is a possibility that the trust property will be included in the grantor's estate. This danger can arise easily if there is a possibility that the trust property will return to the grantor before he dies. For example, suppose a person establishes a trust for his wife, and for his daughter if his wife dies. But what happens if both die? Usually the grantor would want the trust property returned to him. If this possibility exists, some or all of the trust property may be included and taxed in the grantor's estate.

As mentioned above, if a person establishes a testamentary trust, the property in the trust will be included in his estate when he dies. The trust, therefore, does not reduce the tax burden on his estate at all. Still, testamentary trusts can help solve a common estate tax problem. A person who has not considered the tax consequences of the estate tax laws is often inclined to leave his entire estate to his wife and have her leave her estate to the children when she dies. This can invite a serious estate shrinkage problem. The husband might die and his estate would be taxed, and then the same estate could be taxed in the wife's estate when she dies. In these circumstances the children may get only a small fraction of the original estate.

The problem of having the entire estate taxed in the wife's estate can be avoided by leaving the wife only part of the estate and establishing a trust for the benefit of the children. The property left in trust for the children would not be taxed in the wife's estate at her death. If the wife needs as much income as possible, she can be given limited rights to the *income* on the property in trust for the children without having the trust property taxed in her estate.

SUMMARY

In the field of estate planning, your will is the most important first step. There are two crucial points about writing a will that you must consider. First, if you do not write a will, your estate may well be distributed in ways that you would find thoroughly unacceptable. Second, if you do not write a will, you could lose the majority of your estate through taxes. Many people have some hesitancy about writing a will. However, because they find the thougths of misusing or losing their estates even more distasteful, some do go ahead and write their wills despite the unpleasantness they may feel in so doing. You should take the attitude that writing a will is a means of solving very real problems that your family must one day face, and indeed, might face imminently through some unfortunate accident. The satisfaction that can be achieved through any successful problem-solving effort should more than compensate for the dissatisfaction of considering your eventual death. In all probability, you will not want your estate distributed according to the provisions of your state's statutes. Furthermore, you will surely want to lose as little as possible of your estate to taxes.

In the process of writing a will, you should consider the advantages and disadvantages of the various statutory provisions whereby you may reduce your income and estate taxes. You can avoid some estate problems through co-ownership. You may wish to place some of your estate in trusts for various members of your family or for charitable purposes. In so doing you can conserve what you leave your heirs by minimizing taxes. You may wish to reduce your estate taxes by giving some of your estate to those members of your family who would ultimately inherit your estate anyway. Keep in mind the advantages of gifts over testimentary bequests. Once you become aware of these alternatives and your own goals, you can periodically modify your estate plan in response to changing personal or economic conditions. However, you should begin your estate plan today.

Case Problems

1. David's brother, Otis, had a safe deposit box at the Guardian National Bank. Upon his death the box was opened and inside there was an envelope containing a gold watch. Written across the front of the envelope was "This watch is for my brother, David." Who will receive the watch?

2. Jackie and Irving are joint tenants in a parcel of land near Meg Harbor. She sells her interest in the land to Nordcroft Farms. Later Irving dies and Nordcroft Farms claims the entire property. Is their claim valid?

3. David created a trust for the benefit of Davey with the Speculative Trust Company to serve as trustee. The purpose of the trust was to provide for Davey's education. To increase the assets in the trust the trustee invested the corpus in shares of Eureka Gold Mine Fields Ltd. The Fields failed and the corpus was lost. Does Davey have any recourse?

4. Harry Duff created a trust with the corpus consisting of urban life insurance policies on his life. Upon his death the Internal Revenue Service claimed the proceeds from the policies were part of Harry's estate for computation of the estate tax. His executor disagreed claiming the policies were gifts to the trust. Who is correct?

5. Sunny Right wrote the following words on a piece of paper, "I give all my property, real and personal, wherever located, to the Pennsylvania S.P.C.A." He then gathered three witnesses, dated and signed the instrument in their presence, and each witness in turn signed it in his presence and in the presence of each other. Should this instrument be admitted to probate as Sunny's will?

6. Tom Wilson died intestate and was survived by his brother and his only heir at law. The previous year his other brother had died and this brother's child claims a share of Tom's estate. Is this claim valid?

7. Robert Temple had made and executed a valid will just prior to his marriage to Margaret. In his will he devised one-half of his property to her and the remaining half to his close friend, Jim Tate. Robert, by then the father of one son, died ten years later and Margaret claims the will invalid and the entire estate belongs to her. Is her claim correct?

8. In his will Barry Buster left a particular rare book in his library to his friend Peter. Barry died in a fire that also destroyed his house and the book. He carried dwelling and contents insurance which paid Barry's estate for the loss. Can Peter recover an amount equal to the value of the book?

Selected Readings

The American College of Life Underwriters. *Readings for Estate Planning—1*. Bryn Mawr, Pa.: The American College of Life Underwriters, 1969.

Bowe, W. J., *Estate Planning and Taxation—Chartered Life Underwriter*

Edition. 2nd edition. Buffalo, N.Y.: Dennis and Company, Inc., 1965.

Commerce Clearing House. *Federal Estate and Gift Taxes Explained.* Chicago: Commerce Clearing House, Inc., 1963.

Leach, W. Barton, and Logan, James K. *Future Interests and Estate Planning.* New York: The Foundation Press, 1961.

Loring, Augustus Peabody. *A Trustee's Handbook.* Farr Revision. Boston: Little, Brown and Co., 1962.

Michaelson, Arthur M. *Income Taxation of Estates and Trusts.* New York: Practicing Law Institute, 1961.

The Research and Review Service of America. *Fundamentals of Federal Income, Estate and Gift Taxes.* 15th edition. Indianapolis: The Research and Review Service of America, Inc., 1969.

Wormser, Rene A. *The Planning and Administration of Estates.* New York: Practicing Law Institute, 1961.

INDEX

Acceleration clause, mortgage, 137
Accountants, 178, 656
Accumulation plans. *See* Periodic investment plans
Adjusted gross estate, 675
Adjusted gross income, 152–53
  averaging, 176
Administrator, estate, 663, 664, 668, 674
Aggressive portfolio management, 268, 271–72, 286, 293–303
  dollar cost averaging, 276
  and financial risk, 295–97
  and inflation risk, 299–301
  and interest-rate risk, 301–3
  and market risk, 297–98
Alcoa, 313, 324
Alimony payments, taxability, 170
American agency system, 527
American Express, 61
American Hospital Association, 593
American Stock Exchange (Amex), 232, 236–37, 249
American Tobacco, 324
Annuities, 630, 637–49
  annuity principle, 637–38
  deferred, 638, 639, 643
  immediate, 638
  joint, 639
  refunds, 639–42
  selection, 641
  variable, 355, 356–57, 642–49
Apartments, 113
  cooperative, 128–29
  See also Condominiums
Appraisal, real estate, 116–18, 635
Appreciation:
  earnings, 320, 326, 331–34, 335, 340, 342
  mutual funds, 384–85
  real estate, 254
  stocks, 224, 274, 275, 277–79, 280, 281–82, 302, 358
Assessment, property tax, 109–10

Assets, 92–93
  and borrowing, 52
  earning power, 28–29, 92, 536, 538
  education, 16, 40–41
  market price, 29–30
  taxability, 171
Assigned-risk plans, automobile insurance, 521
Audits, tax returns, 173, 178
Automatic reinvestment plans, 375, 376, 405
Automobile insurance, 17, 25, 167, 510–21
  adequate, 515–17
  assigned-risk plans, 521
  compulsory, 513
  cost, 517–21
  coverages, 510–15
  liability, 511, 516
  uninsured drivers, 512–14

Bailment lease, 62
Balanced funds, 358–59, 360, 378, 385, 388, 392, 394
Balance sheet, 92–94
  pro forma, 439–41
Bank credit, restrictions on, 29–30
Bankruptcy, personal, 79, 80, 509
Bear markets, 275, 296, 297, 298–99, 300, 301, 359, 364, 394
Best's Reports:
  Fire & Casualty, 525
  Life, 575
Bethlehem Steel, 313
Blue Cross-Blue Shield Associations, 593–94, 608–9
Bonds. *See* Corporate bonds; Savings bonds
Bonuses, 95
Book value, stock, 221
Borrowing, 38, 44–45, 52–70, 78–79, 259–60, 448–50

costs of, 65–69
excessive, 50–51
on life insurance, 65, 133, 423, 493–94, 556
purposes, 46–47
Brokerage firms. *See* Stock brokers
Budgets, 40–41, 80, 85, 91
cash, 439, 450
components, 94–97
monthly detailed, 86–89, 91, 93, 94
monthly summary, 89–92, 93
Building and loan associations. *See* Savings and loan associations
Bull markets, 296, 298, 302, 359, 394
Business expenses, taxability, 167, 174
Business failures, 411–13
Business ownership, 409–53
acquisition, 430–32
forms of, 423–30
risk, 411–13, 430, 433
See also Franchising
Buy-and-sell agreement, 423

Capital:
raising, 9, 417, 420, 426
requirements, 313
Capital gains, 164, 171–72, 173, 177, 224–25, 230, 254–55, 280, 281, 634
mutual funds, 363, 375, 376, 380, 384, 389
unrealized, 363, 380
Capitalization rate, 323, 326–28, 331, 431–32
Career:
function of interests, 187–93
future demand, 197–203
as a goal, 4, 183–84
occupational groups, 196–97
salaries, 208–9
Career Guidance Index, 207
Career Index, 207
Carrying charges, 60, 67–68
Carte Blanche, 61
Cash buying, 45
Cash ratio, 336–37

Cash value, life insurance, 465, 552, 553, 554, 556–58, 559, 565, 674
patterns, 570–71
Certificates of deposit, 473–74
Charge accounts:
revolving, 59–60
30-day, 59
Charities:
bequests to, 675
contributions to, 162–64
Chartered Life Underwriters (C.L.U.), 576–77
Chartered Property and Casualty Underwriters (C.P.C.U.), 528
Chattel mortgages, 61–62
Checking accounts, 53, 84–86, 470
stubs as records, 85–86
Child care expenses, 534
taxability, 170
Child support payments, taxability, 170–71
Closed-end investment companies, 355, 356
Closing costs:
home purchase, 105
real estate, 258
Clothing expenditures, 97
Codicils, 662
Collectable items as investment, 26
College Retirement Equities Fund (C.R.E.F.), 644–46
Commercial banks, 468–75
borrowing from, 52–54, 133, 422
convenience, 474
liquidity, 473–74
safety, 474
trust funds, 357
yield, 470–73
Commercial Credit Corporation, 55
Commercial property, as investment, 253
Common stock, 29, 280, 359, 362, 381, 468
financial risk, 288–89
and inflation, 227, 283
interest-rate risk, 34, 301
shareholder liability, 222–23
Community property, 158, 679

Competition, 312–16
Competitive nature, 76
Completion insurance, mutual funds, 373, 404, 405
Compounding interest, 470–72, 616
Comprehensive health insurance, 598, 600–601, 608
Compulsive buying, 81
Conditional sales contracts, 63–65
  acceleration clause, 63
  add-on clause, 64
  balloon contracts, 64
  and defective goods, 64–65
Condominiums, 127–28, 129
Conservative stocks, 242, 271, 339–40
Consumer credit, 47
Consumer credit companies, 54–58, 64
Consumer needs manipulated, 82
Consumption patterns, 43–44, 46, 76, 78–79, 81, 83, 87, 94, 226
  and goals, 5, 42
Conversion privileges, life insurance, 542–43
Cooperative apartments, 128–29
  and taxes, 165
Cooperative banks. *See* Savings and loan associations
Corporate bonds, 29, 220, 334–35
  and interest-rate risk, 33
Corporate earnings, 295, 298, 322, 324, 329, 335
  appreciation, 320, 326, 331–34, 335, 340, 342
  depressed, 295–96, 298
  estimated, 331, 333, 341
  retained, 281
Counselor's Guide to Occupational and Other Manpower Information, 207
Counselor's Information Service, 208
Credit:
  control of, 448–50, customer, 450
  and home ownership, 103
  purposes, 46–47
  trade, 422
Credit cards, 60–61
Credit unions, 58, 65, 482–87

liquidity, 484–85
  safety, 485–87
  yield, 483–84
CUNA International, Inc., 485
Current ratio, 336, 340
Customer relations, 309–10
Cyclical stocks, 276, 295

Debt, 44, 45, 92, 532
  bad debt ratio, 450
Deductible clauses:
  automobile insurance, 509–10, 512
  health insurance, 597, 600–601
Deductions, tax, 159–67, 177, 255–56
  estate tax, 675, 679, 680
  itemized, 160–67, 177
  standard, 160, 177
Deed, 133
Defensive portfolio management, 268, 270–72, 287–93
  dollar cost averaging, 275–76, 289, 291
  and financial risk, 288–90
  inflation risk, 291–92
  interest-rate risk, 292–93
  market risk, 292–93
Deferred annuities, 638, 639, 643
Delegation of authority, 444
Demand deposits, 53, 470. *See also* Checking accounts
Dependents, 153–54
Depreciation:
  home, 110, 113
  real estate, 255
Dictionary of Occupational Titles, The, 207
Differential Aptitude Tests (D.A.T.), 192
Diners Club, 61
Disability:
  costs of, 582–83
  defined, 602–3
  income insurance, 569, 571, 592, 593, 598–600, 601, 603, 607, 608, 628
  risk of, 21–22
Discipline and financial success, 11
Discretionary income, 51

Disposable income, 9
Dissatisfaction, and planning, 3, 10
Diversification, portfolio:
 financial risk, 289
 inflation, 292
 interest-rate risk, 293
 market risk, 273–74, 290
 mutual funds, 362, 364, 365, 382
 safety of principal, 279, 555–56
Diversified companies, 274, 278, 289, 290
Dividends:
 corporate policy and, 282
 life insurance, 557, 563–64
 mutual fund, 363, 375, 376, 380, 389, 404, 405
 stock, 151, 221, 222, 223–24, 226, 243, 328
 taxability, 151, 224, 230
Dollar cost averaging, 274–76, 289, 291
 and mutual funds, 362, 364–65
Double indemnity provisions:
 health insurance, 604
 life insurance, 567–68
Dow-Jones Industrial Average, 324–25, 366, 383
Down payments:
 home, 105, 119–21
 real estate, 258
Driver training courses, 519
Dual funds, 375

Earned income, 37, 79
Earnings. *See* Corporate earnings; Earned income
Eastman Kodak, 324, 383
Education:
 and career, 210–13, 414
 deductability of cost, 169–70
 and income, 9, 15, 211
 saving for, 4, 534, 540
Emergency funds, 17–18, 70, 80–81, 464–65, 540
Emotion and financial planning, 10–11, 80, 81–82, 219, 267, 286
Endowment policies, 546, 552, 554
Escalator clause, mortgage, 138–39

Estate planning, 653–56, 659
 intestacy, 656–59
 tax consequences, 671–83
 trusts, 673, 686–87
 wills, 660–70
Estate tax, 671–81, 688–89
 adjusted gross estate, 675
 deductions, 675, 679–80
 gross estate, 672, 679
Evaluation:
 mutual funds, 388–97
 portfolio, 272, 293
Exclusive agency system, 527
Executors, 663–66, 667, 668, 674
 bond for, 664–65
Exemptions:
 gift taxes, 681
 income taxes, 153–54
Expenditures:
 controlled, 2, 9, 37, 41, 82–97
 estimated, 86, 88, 95
 flow of, 77–79
 planned, 75–84
 uncontrolled, 79–82
Expensiveness, stock, 320–29, 337
 defined, 321

Family:
 as a goal, 4–5
 insurance for, 533–35, 547–49, 594
Family income policies, 547–48
Family maintenance policies, 548
Family policies, 549
Federal Deposit Insurance Corporation (F.D.I.C.), 288, 474, 476
Federal Home Loan Bank Board, 481
Federal Home Loan Bank System, 480, 482
Federal Housing Administration (F.H.A.), 134–35
Federal Reserve Board, 470
Federal Reserve System, 301–2
Federal Savings and Loan Insurance Corporation, 58, 288, 482
F.H.A. loans, 109, 134–35

Finance companies. *See* Consumer credit companies
Financial management, aspects of, 2, 219
Financial ratios, 419–21
Financial records, 84–85
balance sheet, 92–94
budgets, 85–92
check stubs, 85–86
tax purposes, 174–75, 178
Financial risk, 28–29, 258, 272, 291
and aggressive policy, 295–97
and defensive policy, 288–90
Financial security, 81–82, 103, 618, 619
as a goal, 6–7, 82, 267, 614–15
and occupation, 185–86
Fixed asset capital, 419
Fixed-dollar securities, 282–83, 288, 290, 291, 292
life insurance as, 559–60
Flitcraft, 575
Food and sundry expenditures, 95–96
Forbes, 367, 370
Fund ratings, 394–95
Forecasting:
market prices, 302
sales, 419–20, 430
Franchise Journal, 434
Franchising, 433–37
Front-end load funds, 371–73, 374, 404, 405

Gifts, 681–83, 688
taxes on, 150, 671, 679, 680–83, 688
General Electric, 324
General Motors, 313, 433
General Motors Acceptance Corporation, 55
Goals, 77, 79, 82, 267
investment, 272, 276–86, 384–88, 394, 397
saving, 463
setting, 3–7
small business, 438
See also Priorities

Go-go funds, 375
Goodwill, 432
Government bonds. *See* Savings bonds
Government health programs:
public assistance, 585
social security, 21, 533, 538, 591–92, 619–26, 637
workmen's compensation, 586–91
Government regulation, 316
insurance industry, 524–25
mutual funds, 381–83
small business, 425
stock trading, 240–41
zoning, 252–53
Gross estate, 672, 679
Gross income, 150, 152
Gross national product and corporate growth, 331
Group insurance plans:
health, 161, 600
life, 178, 538, 550, 551–52
Growth funds, 359, 364, 378, 385, 388, 389–91, 393, 394, 405
Growth stocks, 29, 223, 242, 271, 272, 287, 293, 295, 297, 299–300, 302, 331–32, 334, 335, 40–42
Gulf Oil, 315

Handy Guide, The, 575
Health insurance, 22, 465, 500, 539, 582, 584
Blue Cross-Blue Shield, 593–94, 608–9
cancellability, 606
costs, 607
coverage, 601–2
deductible clauses, 597, 600–601, 605
government, 584–92
group, 161, 600
private companies, 592–93, 608–9
selection, 600–610
types, 594–600
Hedge funds, 374
Home ownership:
costs, 104–11

reasons for, 101–4
rental compared, 111–15
See also Condominiums; Cooperative apartments; Homeowner's insurance; Mobile homes
Homeowner's insurance, 25, 109, 498–510
   adequacy of, 503–9
   coverages, 498–500
   forms of, 501–3
   liability, 499, 508
Home purchase:
   closing costs, 105
   contract, 131
   down payment, 105, 119–21
   and income, 125–27
   insurance, 108–9
   mortgage factor, 57, 107–8
Homestead associations. *See* Savings and loan associations
Homestead exemptions, 656–57, 659
Hospitalization policies, 594, 596, 600–601, 605
Household Finance Corporation, 55
Housing:
   apartments, 113, 128–29
   condominiums, 127–28, 129
   as an expenditure, 96
   mobile homes, 129–31
   tax on sale, 172–73
   utilities, 96
   See also Home ownership; Home purchase
HR–10 plans, 630–32
Human life value, life insurance, 536–38, 541

I.B.M., 313, 318
Immediate annuities, 638
Income, 94–95, 410
   current, 38, 280–81, 359, 375
   defined, 37
   flow of, 39, 44–45, 78
   future, 38, 44, 45, 46, 91, 95
   and home ownership, 125–27
   investment, 280–81, 384, 388
   management, 2, 8–9, 37–70
   planning, 39–45, 76

real, 40
from real estate, 253–54, 633–34
retirement, 616–49
taxable, 149–52, 156
Income tax, 147–79, 281, 377, 425–26, 427, 429, 483, 534, 558–59, 627, 634, 672, 679, 687, 688
   exemptions, 153–54
   and home ownership, 111, 120
   rates, 156–59
   taxable income, 149–52, 224, 230
Incorporation, 423, 428–29
   liability, 428
Indebtedness, corporate, 334–35, 338, 340
Industrial life insurance, 550–51
Inflation, 282–84, 285, 332, 357, 559–60, 642
   risk of, 30–33, 226–27, 283, 287, 292–93, 299–301
Inheritance tax, 150, 671, 672, 676, 678–79
Installment buying, 46–47, 54–56, 61–65
   costs of, 53–54
   and tax liability, 165
   See also Charge accounts
Institutional investors, 277
   insurance companies, 555
Insurance, 81
   automobile, 17, 167, 510–21
   cost of, 526–27, 571–74, 607
   deductible clauses, 509–10, 512, 597, 600–601
   health, 22, 465, 500, 539, 582, 584–610
   homeowner's, 25, 109, 498–510
   liability, 23–25
   life, 18–20, 30, 532–77, 603, 609–10, 638
   medical, 17, 595–96, 605
   mortgage redemption, 109, 540
   professional, 25, 522–24
   selection, 524–28, 550–60, 600–610
   title, 105–7
Insurance agents, 527–28, 575–77
Insurance companies, 524–27, 574–75

investments by, 555
mutual, 527, 574–75
stock, 527, 574–75
Insurance programs, 18–26
Interest equalization clause, mortgage, 139
Interest rates:
compounded, 470–72, 616
computation, 67–68
installment loans, 53–54, 57, 67
mortgages, 107–8, 120–23, 135, 136, 138–39
risk, 33–34, 287, 292–93, 301–3
S.B.A. loans, 452
true rates, 470–73, 484, 556
See also Yield
Inter-industry competition, 313–14
Internal Revenue Service. *See* United States Internal Revenue Service
International competition, 314–15
International Harvester Corp., 324
Intestacy, 656–59
allowances, 656–57, 659
homestead exemptions, 656–57, 659
statute, 658–59
Intra-industry competition, 313
Inventory control, 447–48
Investment Advisers Act of 1940, 240
Investment clubs, 308
Investment Company Act of 1940, 240, 382
Investment portfolio, 26–34, 229–32, 244, 267
aggressive, 269
building, 268–86
defensive, 269
diversified, 29, 34, 225, 273–74, 279, 289, 290, 292, 293
evaluation of, 272
management, 286–303
modification, 27–28, 227–28, 231, 269
Investments:
defined, 219–20
fixed-dollar, 282, 288, 290, 291, 292, 559–60
real estate, 251–62

securities, 221–51
Irrevocable trusts, 673, 687, 688

Job Guide for Young Workers, 207
Job satisfaction, 186
Joint annuities, 639
Joint stock companies, 430
Joint tenants, 657, 670–71, 673

Keogh Act. *See* Self-Employed Individual Tax Retirement Act
Keogh Plan, 404

Labor-management relations, 310–11
Land, as investment, 252
Landlord's lien, 115
Leases, 114–15
on land, 252
Leverage, 259–60, 449–50
Liability:
partnership, 428
proprietor, 426
shareholder, 222–23, 261, 428
tenant's, 503
Liability insurance, 23–25, 465, 522
See also Automobile insurance; Homeowner's insurance
Life insurance, 18–21, 603, 609–10, 638–39, 655
adequacy, 19–20, 536–41
borrowing on, 65, 133, 423, 493–94, 556
cash value, 465, 552, 553, 554, 556–58, 559, 565, 570–71, 674
costs, 571–74
group, 178, 538, 550, 551–52
and inflation, 32
market risk, 30
non-option clauses, 561–62
option clauses, 562–67
riders, 548, 567–71, 610
savings bank, 477
selection, 550–60
types, 541–50
Limited partnership, 427–28
Limited-payment life insurance, 545–46

Limit orders, 247
Line and staff organization, 442–43
Line organization, 442
Linton, Albert, 558
Liquidity, 279–80, 335, 336–38, 342
    cash ratio, 336–37
    commercial banks, 473–74
    credit unions, 484–85
    current ratio, 336
    life insurance, 556–57
    mutual savings banks, 475–76
    real estate, 635
    savings and loan associations, 479–81
    savings bonds, 489, 493
    See also Redemption privileges
Little Gem Life Chart, 575
Load funds, 368–69, 405
Loans:
    single payment, 65
    sources, 52–58, 422–23
    See also Mortgages
Loan sharks, 57
Longevity, risk, 20–21
Losses, tax consequences, 165–67

Maintenance, home, 110
Major medical policies, 597, 600–601, 605, 608
Malpractice insurance. *See* Professional insurance
Management:
    corporate, 308–12, 318, 341
    small business, 413, 437–51
Margin accounts, 244
Marketability. *See* Liquidity
Market orders, 247
Market risk, 29–30, 259, 272
    and aggressive policy, 297–98
    and defensive policy, 290–91
    and portfolio diversification, 273–74
Market value:
    real estate, 256
    real value compared, 326
    stocks, 221, 222, 225, 326
Mechanics' liens, 132
Medical expenses, 532, 626
    taxability, 160–62

Medical insurance, 17, 595–96, 605
    medical payments, 500, 511, 514, 516
    See also Health insurance
Medicare benefits, 592
Mobile homes, 129–31
    insurance for, 522
Mobil Oil, 315
Monetary policy, 301
Monopoly, 316, 317, 318
Morbidity risk. *See* Disability
Mortality risk, 18–20. *See also* Life insurance
Mortgages:
    amortization, 103
    debts, 47
    F.H.A., 109
    and inflation, 32
    interest-rate risk, 34
    interest rates, 107–8, 120–23, 135, 136, 138–39
    points, 121–22
    provisions, 137–39
    redemption insurance, 109, 540
    savings and loan associations, 57
    selection of lender, 133–34
    and taxes, 165
    See also Open-end mortgages; Package mortgages; Second mortgages
Moving expenses, 107
    tax deduction for, 168–69
Municipal bond funds, 374–75
Mutual funds, 355, 356, 358–405, 630, 636
    balanced, 358–59, 360, 374, 378, 385, 388, 392, 394
    completion insurance, 373, 404, 405
    convenience, 365–66
    evaluated, 388–97
    front-end load, 371–73, 374, 404, 405
    growth, 359, 364, 374, 378, 385, 388, 389–91, 393, 394, 405
    load, 368–69, 405
    no-load, 367, 369–71, 374, 397
    objectives, 384–88, 394, 397
    regulated, 381–83

special features, 374–81, 397–405
specialty, 359, 374
variable annuities compared, 646–49
Mutual insurance companies, 527, 574–75
Mutual savings banks:
convenience, 477
liquidity, 475–76
safety, 476–77
yield, 475

National Association of Security Dealers (N.A.S.D.), 241
Negligence, and liability, 25, 586
Net worth, 92
New York Stock Exchange (N.Y.S.E.), 232, 233–36, 245, 249, 277
No-load mutual funds, 367, 369–71, 374, 397

Occupational Index, 208
Occupational Outlook Handbook, 207
Odd lot trading, 235
Open-end mortgages, 138
Outgo, 37
Over-the-counter (O.T.C.) market, 232, 237–42, 249
stock liquidity, 280

Package mortgages, 139
Partnerships, 427–28
liability, 428
Patents, 316, 317, 318
Pension plans, 21
Keogh Plan, 404
self-employed persons, 630–32
vesting provisions, 628
Periodic investment plans, 375, 376–77, 404, 405
Personal property:
distribution of, 656–57
insurance for, 498–99, 508
Personal satisfaction. *See* Satisfaction
Planning, 2–8, 219
expenditures, 75–84
income, 39–45, 76

for retirement, 614–16
small business, 437–41
Plans, personal financial:
example, 14–34
purposes, 7–10
savings, 463–68
Points, mortgage, 121–22, 258
Polaroid Corporation, 318
Portfolio approach, 270
aggressive, 268, 271–72, 293–303
defensive, 268, 270–72, 287–93
See also Investment portfolio
Preferred stock, 29, 280, 359
and interest-rate risk, 34
maturity prices, 283
Prepayment privilege, mortgage, 137–38
Price-earnings multiple. *See* Price-earnings ratio
Price-earnings ratio, 29, 222, 290, 295, 302, 320, 322–28, 331, 333, 340, 350, 354
Price levels, 30–32, 559
depressed, 295–97, 301
forecasting, 302
stocks, 274, 275, 277–79, 280, 281–82, 283, 290–91, 300, 302, 324
Priorities, financial, 79, 83, 94
Prizes, taxability, 151
Probate court, 663, 668–69
Problem solving, and financial management, 2, 9–10
Product differentiation, 316
Professional assistance, 139–41
career counselling, 190
state planning, 655–56
fund management, 355, 360, 362, 363–64, 366, 374, 384, 405
investing, 277, 307
small business, 423, 451–53
taxes, 178–79
Professional insurance, 25, 522–24
Profitability, stocks, 329–31, 337
Profits:
corporate, 299–300, 313, 314
and employee morale, 310
small business, 410, 425
Profit-sharing plans, 426, 632

Progress:
  and career, 186
  as a goal, 5–6
Promotional expense capital, 419
Property:
  joint-ownership, 158, 657, 670–71,
    673, 674, 679
  risk to, 22–23, 497
Property insurance, 465. *See also*
    Homeowner's insurance
Property taxes:
  assessment, 109–10
  deduction for, 255–56
Public assistance benefits, 585
Purchasing power risk. *See* Inflation

Quality controls, 451
Quitclaim deed, 133

Real estate:
  appraisal, 116–18, 635
  inflation risk, 254
  interest-rate risk, 34
  as investment, 26, 220, 251–62,
    633–34
  investment trusts, 261
  limitations, 257–60
  management, 260
  types, 252–53
Real estate brokers, 140–41, 261–62
Real estate investment trust, 261,
    355, 357, 633
Real income, 30, 40
Real property, homestead exemption,
    656–57, 659
Recessions, 298, 301
Records. *See* Financial records
Recreational vehicles, insurance for,
    522
Redemption privileges, mutual fund,
    376, 380–81
Refinancing, 125
Renewal options:
  health insurance, 606–8, 610
  leases, 114
  life insurance, 535, 542
Rental, apartment:

home ownership compared, 111–
    15
  leases, 114–15
  tenant's insurance, 502–3
Repayment of loans, 44
  as savings, 69–70
Residential property, as investment,
    252
Retained earnings, 281
Retirement, 20
  adequacy of income, 21, 32, 284,
    357, 591, 592, 614, 627
  employment during, 617–18
  financing, 616–49
  as a goal, 4
  pensions, 626–32
  real estate, 633–34
  social security benefits, 619–26
Return on investment, 269, 272, 298,
    323, 362–63, 389
  and risk, 27
Revocable trusts, 673, 687, 688
Revolving charge accounts, 59–60
Rexall Drugs, 433
Riders, life insurance, 548, 567–71,
    610
Risk:
  disability, 21–22
  education as, 16
  excessive longevity, 20–21
  financial, 28–29, 258, 272, 288–
    90, 291, 295–97
  inflation, 30–33, 226–27, 254, 283,
    287, 291–92, 299–301
  interest-rate, 33–34, 287, 292–93
  liability, 23–26
  market, 29–30, 259, 272, 290–91,
    297–98
  mortality, 18–20
  property, 22–23
  and return, 27
Royal Dutch Shell, 315

Safety of principal, 277–79, 282,
    283, 293, 335
  commercial banks, 338, 384, 388,
    394, 474
  credit unions, 485–87

life insurance, 554
mutual savings banks, 476–77
savings and loan associations, 481–82
savings bonds, 489, 493
Sales:
 controlling, 446–47
 forecasting, 419–20, 430
 plans, 438–39
Satisfaction, as a goal, 6
Saving, 17, 95, 465–66
 and borrowing, 69–70
 and emotion, 11, 80
 function of income, 9, 38, 42, 78, 80
 and home ownership, 103
 through life insurance, 536, 554
Savings accounts, 17, 53, 70, 362, 468, 470, 478
 and expenditure control, 83
 financial risk, 288
 and inflation, 32, 283
 market risk, 30
 yield, 470–73
Savings and loan associations, 477–82
 and borrowing, 57–58, 133
 liquidity, 479–81
 safety, 481–82
 yield, 479
Savings bank life insurance, 477
Savings bonds, 17, 29, 220, 468, 487–93
 convenience, 491, 493
 financial risk, 288–89
 and inflation, 32, 282–83
 interest-rate risk, 33, 301
 liquidity, 489, 493
 safety, 489, 493
 Series E, 487, 488–91
 Series H, 487, 491–93
 trading, 238
 yield, 488–89, 491
Savings-investment plans, 42–43, 79
Savings plans, 463–68
S.B.A. loans, 452
Sears Roebuck Acceptance Corporation, 55

Second mortgages, 136–37
Securities, 26, 221–51
 fixed-dollar, 282–83, 288, 290, 291, 292
 listed, 232, 233
 and retirement income, 635–37
 unlisted, 232
Securities Act Amendment (1964), 240
Securities Act of 1933, 240, 381, 382
Securities and Exchange Commission (S.E.C.), 234, 240, 241, 277, 372, 382
Securities Exchange Act of 1934, 234, 240, 381–82
Security. *See* Financial security
Self-Employed Individual Tax Retirement Act (1962), 630–32
Service to others:
 via career, 194–95
 as a goal, 4
 tax liability, 164
Settlement Options, 575
Shakespeare, William, 45
Short-term notes, market risk, 30
Small business:
 capital needs, 417–19
 forms of, 423–30
 management, 413, 437–51
 organization, 441–45
 risk of failure, 411–13, 430, 433
 starting, 432–33
 See also Franchising
Small Business Administration (S.B.A.), 451–53
Small Business Investment Company Act of 1958, 452
Social security, 21, 533, 538, 591–92
 elegibility, 619–20
 Medicare, 592
 retirement benefits, 619–26, 637
Social Security Administration, 625
Sole proprietorships, 423, 425–26
 liability, 426
Specialty funds, 359
Spectator Insurance Year Book, The, 575

Speculative stocks, 29, 225, 230, 242, 271, 272, 273, 343–44
Staffing, small business, 444–45
Standard & Poor's:
    Company Reports, 351–54
    Stock Guide, 347–49, 354
Standard Oil (Calif.), 315, 324
Standard Oil (N.J.), 315
Stock brokers, 241–51, 277, 340, 368–69, 373, 382, 388
    accounts with, 244, 247
Stock exchanges, 232–37
Stockholders:
    liability of, 222–23, 261
    management attitude to, 311–12
Stock insurance companies, 527, 574–75
Stocks:
    certificates, 243
    defined, 221–23
    expensiveness, 320, 321–29, 337
    new issues, 247–49
    price-listings, 245–46
    profitability, 320, 329–31, 337
    trading, 229, 235, 238, 241–51, 298
Stocks on the Big Board (N.Y.S.E.), 347, 350–51, 354
Straight life insurance, 545, 552
Strong Vocationaal Interest Blank (S.V.I.B.), 190
Supply, control over, 316–17
Supreme Court. See United States Supreme Court
Surgical expense policies, 595

Taxes:
    estate, 671–81, 688–89
    gift, 150, 671, 679, 680–83, 688
    income, 111, 120, 147–79, 281, 377, 425–26, 427, 429, 483, 534, 558–59, 627, 673, 679, 687, 688
    inheritance, 150, 671, 672, 676, 678–79
    property, 109–10
    and real estate, 254–56, 634
Tenants by entirety, 657, 670–71, 673

Tenants in common, 657, 670
Tenant's insurance, 502–3
Term life insurance, 541–43, 552, 565
Testamentary trusts, 673, 688
Tests:
    aptitude, 192
    interest, 190
Texaco, 315
Time deposits, 53, 470, 475. *See also* Savings accounts
Title insurance, 105–7
Torrens system, 107
Transportation expenditures, 96–97
    tax liability, 162
Treasury Department. *See* United States Treasury Department
Trustees, 683–85
Trusts, 430, 673, 683–89
    commercial bank, 357
    irrevocable, 673, 687, 688
    real estate investment, 261, 355, 357, 633
    revocable, 673, 687, 688
    tax consequences, 687–88
    testamentary, 673, 688
    trustees, 683–85
Truth-in-lending regulation, 68

Unawareness, and financial planning, 10, 267
Underwriters:
    mutual funds, 368
    stock, 247, 250
Unemployment, 16–17, 195–96
    education as insurance against, 16, 212–13
Uninsurability, 535, 536
Uninsured motorists, 512–14
Uniqueness, corporate, 316–19
United States Bureau of Employment Security, 208
United States Civil Service Commission, 208
United States Department of Labor, 210
United States Internal Revenue Service, 173, 174, 178, 623, 627
United States Supreme Court, 148

United States Tax Court, 174
United States Treasury Department, 154
U. S. Steel, 313

V.A. loans, 135–36, 138
Value determination:
    estate, 673–74
    home, 117–18
    real estate, 256
    small business, 431
Variable annuities, 355, 356–57
    mutual funds compared, 646–49
Veterans Administration (V.A.), 136

Wall Street Journal, 147
Warranty deed, 133
Weisenberger Services' *Investment Companies,* 367, 370, 388
Westinghouse Electric, 324
Whole life insurance, 543–46, 554
    limited-payment, 545–46, 552, 554
    straight life, 545, 552
Wills:
    codicils, 662, 666–67
    executors, 663–66, 667, 668, 674

intestacy, 656–59
legacies, 663
probating, 669
types, 662
validity of, 660–61
Withdrawal plans, mutual funds, 375, 379–80, 397, 404, 405, 636
Within-group conversion, mutual fund, 375, 376–79, 404
Women, career opportunities, 203–6
Working capital, 417, 419, 422, 450
Workmen's compensation, 586–92
    exclusions, 587–88

Xerox Corporation, 313, 318

Yield:
    commercial banks, 470–73
    credit unions, 483–84
    dividends, 224, 328, 330, 340
    life insurance, 537, 557–59, 570
    mutual savings banks, 475
    savings and loan associations, 479
    savings bonds, 488–89

Zoning regulations, 252–53